THE INSIDERS' GUIDE

TO

Maine's
SOUTHERN COAST

by
Giselle A. Auger
and
Meadow Rue Merrill

Insiders' Publishing Inc.

The Insiders' Guide®
An imprint of Falcon® Publishing Inc.
A Landmark Communications Company
P.O. Box 1718
Helena, MT 59624
(800) 582-2665
www.insiders.com

Co-published and marketed by:
Coastal Journal and
The Portland Newspapers
P.O. Box 705
Bath, ME 04530
(207) 443-6241

Sales and Marketing: Falcon Publishing, Inc.
P.O. Box 1718
Helena, MT 59624
(800) 582-2665
www.falcon.com

Advertising: Coastal Journal
Executive Publisher: John S. Brill
Sales Representatives:
Linda Horstmann
Larry Koch
Deb Nelson
(207) 443-6241

•

SECOND EDITION
1st printing

•

©1999 by Coastal Journal and The Portland Newspapers

•

Cover photos (clockwise from top left): Summer color in Maine (Merry Farnum);
Fun at the beach (Merry Farnum); Portland Headlight (Convention and Visitor's
Bureau of Greater Portland).
Spine photo: A Maine dining tradition (Merry Farnum).
Facing page photo: Portland Headlight (Convention and Visitor's Bureau of Greater Portland).

•

Printed in the United States of America

•

Publications from *The Insiders' Guide®* series are available at special discounts for bulk
purchases for sales promotions, premiums or fundraisings. Special editions, including personalized covers, can be created in large quantities for special needs.
For more information, please contact Falcon Publishing.

ISBN 1-57380-115-1

Preface

Welcome to Southern Maine! Welcome to small towns and pleasant cities, rocky vistas and smooth white beaches. Welcome to our wealth of natural beauty — fabulous coastline, scenic hills and hundreds of sparking blue lakes. Welcome to the state that is home to moose and bear, porcupines, red squirrels and deer, not to mention the Maine coon cat and the famous Maine lobster.

One of the most wonderful things you'll discover about the state is that the people who live here love it. Whether they're true Mainers, born and bred here with generations of Mainers before them, or transplants who came for a vacation and decided to stay, the people of Maine tend to live here because they've made a conscious choice to live here. Once you've become acquainted with us, you'll understand why.

Maine is famous for the independent, hardy nature of its people and the contrasting beauty and harshness of its environment. Visit in spring and you'll encounter the notorious "mud season," when the earth thaws and the snow melts with water seeping and running everywhere, turning the many dirt roads throughout the state to mud. Yet this season is glorious in its own way, as days grow longer, the air gets warmer and the trees seem to burst out with leaves overnight.

Spring arrives in Maine with less of a gentle progression from winter than in other New England states. Sometimes it seems that winter runs straight into summer, with temperatures in the 40s in May and the 70s in June. Regardless, whenever and however it comes, spring brings a rhapsody of scent and color to warm the senses. You'll find lilacs of astonishing size in colors from white and pink to the deepest of purples, alongside fountains of forsythia, bright azaleas and hillsides covered with daffodils, lupines and dandelions. In the evenings, the cool air drifting in through the bedroom window brings with it the unforgettable perfume of Southern Maine in bloom.

Come see us during summer, and many of the homes you pass will be proudly displaying the American flag. Hanging baskets, window boxes and tubs filled with petunias, impatiens, begonias and geraniums adorn houses of all description, and flower beds bloom with roses and snapdragons, marigolds and mums. Summer is a busy time for Southern Mainers. Many people depend on the few short months of summer for their income for the entire year. Others are merely overjoyed by the warmth of the season; they're ready to take advantage of good weather to get out and play!

Since many of the people who live in Maine have an affinity for nature and outdoor pursuits, it isn't surprising that they seem to take advantage of every nice day (and many that aren't so nice) to get out to the woods, rivers and sea. Hiking, swimming, canoeing, boating, fishing, biking and strolling are some of the activities that get the natives, as well as the tourists, out on the road. To help you enjoy these pursuits while you visit, we've included some of the best places for outdoor fun in Southern Maine in our Parks and Recreation chapter.

There's something special about fall in Maine. Perhaps it's the crisp air, the delicate scent of apples or the sight of ranks of bright orange pumpkins that have been harvested from our fields. Or maybe it's the joy of discovering yourself alone on a wide expanse of beach with just the sea, the sky and the fresh salt air for company. It's no secret that autumn in New England provides a uniquely dramatic spectacle of nature. Brilliant reds, oranges and yellows flame against the deep green of fir trees. Tourists, nicknamed "leaf peepers" by locals, take to our roads, filling hotels, motels and bed and breakfasts so recently emptied of summer visitors.

In the fall you'll also find Mainers getting ready for winter — bringing in the harvest, replacing screens with storm windows, storing patio furniture, raking leaves, wrapping burlap around bushes and generally making sure everything is ship-shape for the coming cold. Outdoor enthusiasts take advantage of this season to enjoy mosquito-free hikes and bike rides.

Once the days draw short and the first snow falls, the people of Maine start thinking about skiing, ice fishing, snowboarding and ice skating. Farms that offer hayrides in other seasons now offer romantic sleigh rides through the snow while the "snowbirds" (people who winter in Florida and other southern destinations) head south. Year-round residents revel in the smaller population, returning to roads they'd avoided in summer and fall.

We don't get many tourists along the Southern Coast in winter, though the Christmas Prelude in Kennebunk, Christmas by the Sea in Ogunquit and the Victorian Christmas events in Portland are gaining in popularity yearly (see our Annual Events and Festivals chapter). Maine ski resorts at Pleasant Mountain in Bridgton, Sunday River in Bethel and Sugarloaf and Saddleback Mountains near Rangely have also been gaining in popularity, and you'll find a steady stream of out-of-state cars with ski racks heading north throughout the winter.

Whatever the reason, whatever the season, there is magic in Maine.

To help you best enjoy the attractions of our state in general and the Southern Coast in particular, regardless of the time of your visit, we've included specific chapters on Annual Events, Spectator Sports, Parks and Recreation, Attractions, Kidstuff, Beaches and Shopping. You'll also find chapters on Hotels and Motels, Bed and Breakfast Inns, Campgrounds, Restaurants and Nightlife. For those of you who visit and think you might like to stay, there are also chapters on Education and Child Care, Real Estate and Neighborhoods, Worship and Retirement to help you gain an understanding of the society you'll experience in Southern Maine.

We're a state of pathfinders and individuals. Among those who have blazed trails of international repute are Admiral Robert E. Peary, the first person to reach the North Pole, and Margaret Chase Smith, the first woman to be elected to the U.S. Senate, famous for standing up against Sen. Joseph McCarthy in the 1950s. Other famous Mainers include L.L. Bean, who created a boot and hence founded a legend in retailing, and author Stephen King, the world-renowned master of horror.

Yet it isn't only the famous who retain the spirit of individuality that marks Maine. We're a state filled with people who have been drawn to Maine because they feel more free to be themselves here than anywhere else. They are people who are willing to perhaps earn a bit less so that they can enjoy a less dense population and tremendous natural beauty.

We want you to feel like you belong here. To that end we've tried to incorporate fun facts about our state as well as all the information you'll need to choose where to go, what to see, where to stay and where to eat. Each chapter includes Insiders' Tips to help you feel like one of us as quickly as possible. Each restaurant, hotel and motel that we've included has been personally visited by one of us or recommended by a trusted friend or associate. As we researched the book, we asked storekeepers, restaurateurs and anyone else who would give us a moment where they've stayed, visited or dined, and what they would recommend.

The result is what you will find in the following pages. To get a better handle on how the book is organized and what has been included, check out the first chapter on How To Use This Book.

Happy reading. We hope you enjoy your visit as a Southern Maine Insider.

About the Authors

Giselle A. Auger

Giselle A. Auger loves Maine. She loves her husband, family, friends and pets, but Maine holds a special place in her heart. From the moment she witnessed the wonder of the northern lights in the Western Maine Mountains in 1994, Giselle knew she was home to stay.

As a child Giselle wrote plays and stories and was editor of her Senior Year High School Yearbook. She majored in independent studies in political communications at the University of Massachusetts at Amherst to receive her Bachelor's degree in 1986, then went on to complete her master's degree in international relations at the University of Lancaster in England in 1988.

Since then she has worked as a journalist, editor and marketing consultant. In Maine she has written for *The Lewiston Sun-Journal, The Scarborough Leader, The Biddeford-Saco Courier, The Old Orchard Beachcomber,* and *The York County Coast Star.*

Elsewhere, Giselle has written for the *Woonsocket Call* and for a business publication in England. In addition to freelance writing, Giselle is the Communications Manager for Kennebec Girl Scout Council, Inc. which provides Girl Scouting to nearly 11,000 girls and 3,000 adult volunteers in an area that encompasses half the state of Maine.

Meadow Rue Merrill

As a child Meadow Rue Merrill liked to write stories for friends and relatives, and she read them to whoever would listen. The hobby turned into a profession and her audience grew soon after she graduated from Gordon College in Wenham, Massachusetts, and took a job as a reporter at *The Times Record*, a daily newspaper in Brunswick, Maine.

During her two years covering everything from schools and city government to local scandals and merriment, Meadow won two writing awards from the Maine Press Association including a first place in feature writing. Although she loved the paper, she left in early 1997 when she and her husband, Dana, had their first child, Judah Eli.

Now a freelance writer, Meadow frequently contributes to *The Boston Sunday Globe*. Her work has also appeared in *Down East*, the *Portland Press Herald* and *Family Circle*. She lives in Bath with her family and does what writing she can in between changing diapers and pushing a baby carriage down the city's tree-lined streets. Although her childhood was spent running around barefoot on a farm in Elmira, Oregon, Meadow has grown to love Maine, where she moved with her mother and brother when she was 10.

Some of her fondest youthful memories here are of scampering over the rocks on the beach by her grandmother's house in Cape Neddick and of catching sea creatures and building forts of driftwood and broken lobster traps that washed up on shore. Meadow enjoys Maine's spectacular outdoors, and in addition to hiking along the state's coasts and up its mountains, she has spent a year living in Darwin, Australia, and several months in Jerusalem. And, yes, she still reads her stories to anyone who will listen.

Acknowledgments

Giselle A. Auger

Writing a travel book of this magnitude is not the work of only the authors. It involves the cumulative effort of hundreds — all of you who provide services to tourists and the communities covered in this guide. To all of you who offer clean rooms, amusing attractions, good food, excellent educational opportunities and social, religious or business services — thank you. You are all a part of what makes Southern Maine a wonderful place to live, work and visit.

Thanks in particular go to those who have graciously answered my dozens of questions: real estate agents, librarians, recreation department staff, police department members and town clerks. Also helpful with all sorts of answers were school superintendents and principals, religious leaders, shop owners, restaurateurs and all the wonderful people at the chambers of commerce from Kittery to Greater Portland.

To my husband, Andrew Bloss, and my family — Mom, Denise, brother Joe, and sisters, Monique and Nicole — I send my greatest love. Without your support, your hugs and understanding, this project would have been much more difficult. I also thank the friends and relatives who visited while I revised material for this second edition for their tolerance — Angela Burke, Jo and John Bloss, Ruth-Ann Stevens, Richard Bloss and Jacqui, Pauline Latour and Michele Coffey.

Thanks also to Beth Storie of Insiders' Publishing for choosing my resume from among the many, to Meadow for being the best co-author possible, and to Dave McCarter at Insiders' Publishing for patiently answering all my questions and sending me the occasional encouraging note.

Meadow Rue Merrill

Such a large project as this book is never undertaken alone, and I have many to thank for their encouragement, direction, help and humor.

Thank you to my husband, Dana Merrill, for encouraging me to give up a steady paycheck to pursue my dream of writing from home (and thank you, Dana, for working overtime so I could). Thank you to my wise and wonderful mother, Lucy Lincoln, for clipping the help wanted ad out of the newspaper so that I could apply for (and then get) the job of writing this book. Thank you to my son, Judah Eli, for letting me bundle you up in the car and drive you all over the coast checking out bed and breakfast inns, hotels and restaurants (mostly without protest).

Thanks to my mom-in-law, Pat, for helping out with Judah so I could actually write; and to Beth Storie, Dave McCarter and Carol Millner for all their kindness and help. You are truly good people and have my sincere thanks and best wishes. Thank you Giselle for giving this your all and to John Harrington for pulling this together on such short notice.

To all the informative and enthusiastic people at the local chambers of commerce, visitors bureaus, town offices and state offices, thank you for great tips. Thank you to the reference librarians at the Patten Free Library in Bath for digging up obscure books to help me on my hunt. To my many teachers at *The Times Record* and Gordon College, thank you — you inspire me. And to the One who created the spectacular beauty of this rugged state — thank you.

Table Of Contents

Directory of Maps

Maine's Southern Coast Region

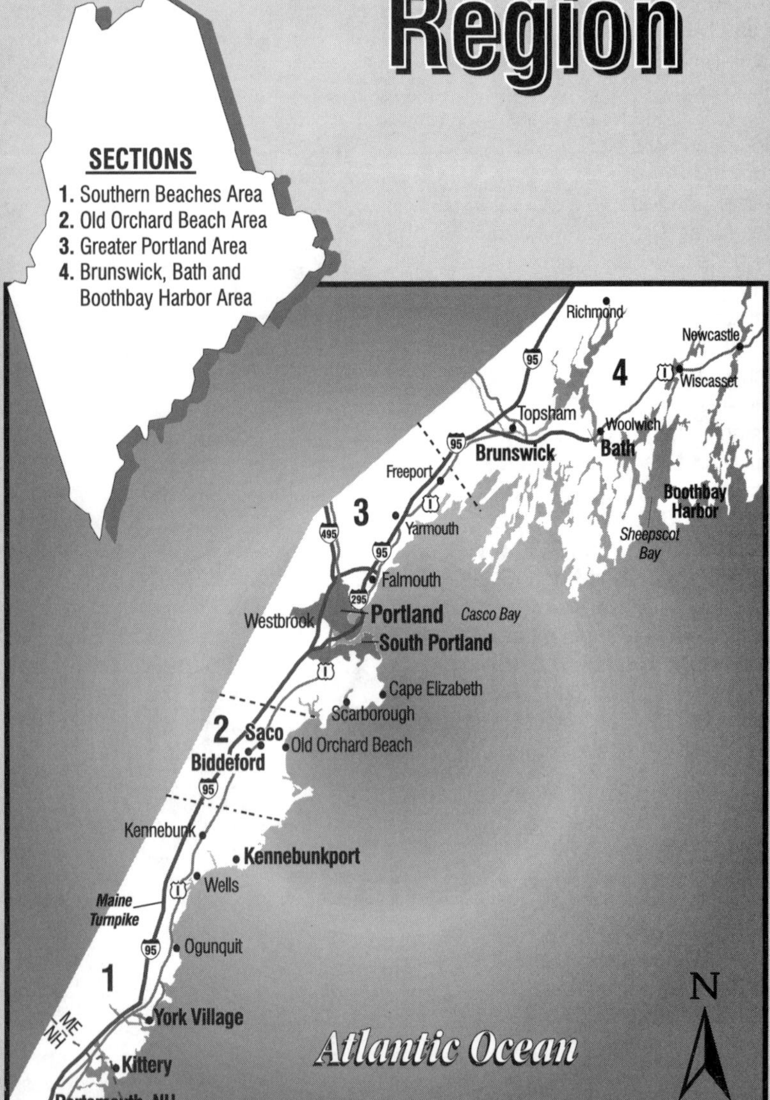

Richmond

Newcastle

4

95

Wiscasset

Topsham

Woolwich

Brunswick   Bath

Freeport

Boothbay
Harbor

3

Yarmouth

Sheepscot
Bay

495

95

Falmouth

295

Portland   *Casco Bay*

Westbrook

South Portland

1

Cape Elizabeth

Scarborough

2 Saco

Old Orchard Beach

Biddeford

95

Kennebunk

Kennebunkport

Wells

*Maine
Turnpike*

95   Ogunquit

1

York Village

ME
NH

Kittery

Portsmouth, NH

95   1

N

Atlantic Ocean

Southern Beaches Area

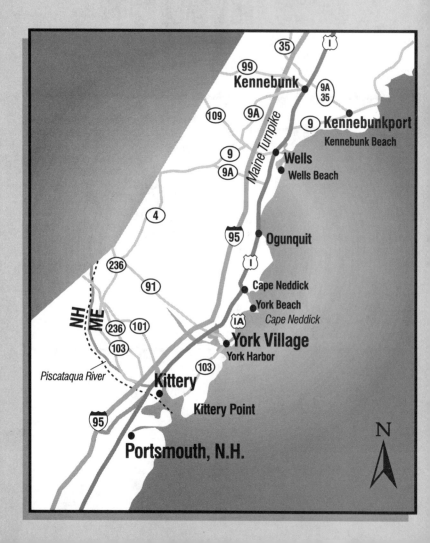

Old Orchard Beach Area

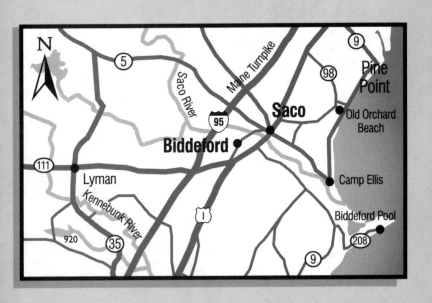

Greater Portland Area

Brunswick, Bath & Boothbay Harbor Area

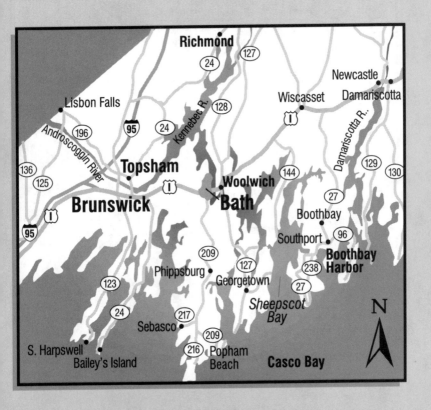

Downtown Portland

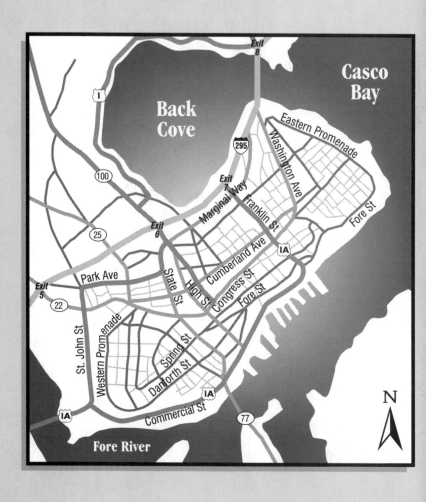

We've divided our guide into four main geographic areas: the Southern Beaches Area, the Old Orchard Beach Area, the Greater Portland Area, and the Brunswick, Bath and Boothbay Harbor Area.

How to Use This Book

If you've ever traveled on the East Coast of the United States, you've probably encountered Interstate 95. This impressive highway spans the length of the Eastern Seaboard from Houlton, Maine on the Canadian border to Miami in south Florida, and it plays a major geographical role in the organization of this guide.

The coverage area for our book runs from Kittery, at the southern tip of Maine, to Boothbay Harbor along the coastal (eastern) side of Interstate 95, then along the coastal side of U.S. Highway 1, or Route 1, which is how most Mainers will refer to it. We use the two names interchangeably in the text of our guide, but for consistency we will always call the road U.S. Highway 1 in address listings. It's an area we are calling Maine's Southern Coast. Some people may argue that Boothbay is actually in the mid-coast area, but if you look at a map you'll see why we consider it part of Southern Maine — it falls in the southern third of the state.

We've divided our guide into four main geographic areas: the Southern Beaches Area, the Old Orchard Beach Area, the Greater Portland Area, and the Brunswick, Bath and Boothbay Harbor Area. Throughout the book, you'll see chapters with listings divided into these areas, which run from south to north along Interstate 95 to Brunswick, then along Route 1 to Boothbay.

The Southern Beaches Area includes the towns of Kittery, York (with York Village, York Harbor, York Beach and Cape Neddick), Ogunquit, Wells, Kennebunk and Kennebunkport (including Cape Porpoise and Goose Rocks Beach).

The Old Orchard Beach Area incorporates the cities of Biddeford and Saco and the town of Old Orchard Beach.

The Greater Portland Area covers Scarborough, Cape Elizabeth, South Portland, Portland, Falmouth, Yarmouth and Freeport.

The Brunswick, Bath and Boothbay Harbor Area covers these towns as well as Wiscasset, Harpswell, Phippsburg, Woolwich, Georgetown and Edgecomb.

At times you'll also notice listings for attractions in towns adjacent to those in our coverage area, ones we feel are worth a short drive. We've also included a chapter on Daytrips and Weekend Getaways to help with your exploration of not-too-distant destinations such as Boston and Portsmouth, New Hampshire.

To better orient yourself, you may want to read through both the Area Overviews chapter and the Neighborhoods and Real Estate chapter. You may also want to read the Getting Here, Getting Around chapter, which outlines the area's main highways and byways and includes information on airports, buses, taxis and trolleys.

To get a grasp on the history that has helped shape the state and Southern Coast area, take a spin through the History chapter. To learn more about the wildlife, sea life and flora you'll find as you explore our parks, nature preserves and beaches, make sure you read through Maine's Natural World.

Our Parks and Recreation chapter will help you find the best places to experience firsthand our truly great outdoors. In this chapter we have departed from the usual geographic divisions and organized the chapter by activity. We've included parks and nature preserves, biking, boating, ballooning, canoeing, fishing, golfing, skating and more in this chapter. Beneath each activity heading you'll find entries listed in the usual geographic format from south to north. You won't find beaches in this chapter — they have one all their own.

In The Arts we have once again divided the chapter by type of activity, then by geography. Here you'll find information on Museums and Galleries, Literary Arts (including writing groups and Maine authors) and Performing Arts, which are broken down into dance, music and theater. The end of the chapter includes listings for venues.

A travel guide wouldn't be a travel guide if it didn't include Restaurants and Accommodations. Restaurants have a large chapter all to themselves, but we have organized accommodations into four different chapters. When looking for a place to stay, you should read through our separate chapters on Hotels and Motels, Bed & Breakfasts and Inns, Campgrounds and Summer Rentals. Within these chapters we have either listed a price-code key, or we have included information on what to expect to pay within the individual write-ups. Keep in mind when noting the prices that the "shoulder seasons" on either side of July and August, as well as the off-season, usually bring significantly lower prices. In prime "leaf peeping" time in October rates may go up again, but you'll still pay less than in summer.

In addition to the information listed in Parks and Recreation and our chapter on The Arts, we have included a chapter on Nightlife and others on Attractions and Kidstuff. There is even a separate chapter highlighting our Annual Events and Festivals. In Attractions we've included categories such as Historic Houses and Forts, Lighthouses, Cruises and Islands, Amusement Parks, Breweries and another that we've dubbed "Odds and Ends" to catch all the nifty stuff that didn't fit snugly into the other categories.

Kidstuff is a chapter filled with attractions aimed at or likely to be of interest to children. Here we've organized the chapter into three main categories: Kids in Motion, Things in Motion and Minds in Motion. You'll find listings organized geographically from south to north. Kids in Motion includes listings for attractions where kids can move around; Things in Motion includes activities where kids take part on something that moves, from boats to amusement rides; and Minds in Motion includes attractions such as museums and children's theater productions. Many of the activities are great for adults too, so look into them even if you're not travelling with kids.

The Annual Events and Festivals chapter is organized by calendar month from January to December. Items are listed chronologically, then by geography. In other words, if an activity takes place in Kennebunk in early June and another takes place in Brunswick in early June, the Kennebunk listing will come first.

What about shopping, you ask? We've included a hefty chapter outlining the best places to look for antiques, books, crafts and more. There's also info on the major shopping malls and plazas and a special section called "Shopping the Maine Streets." In this chapter you'll also read details on the outlet shopping areas (primarily in Kittery and Freeport) and information on Specialty Foods shopping and Farmers' Markets.

We hope that whatever you're looking for — be it a traditional tourist attraction or a quiet walk in the woods — the *Insiders' Guide® to Maine's Southern Coast* helps you find it. Remember, however, that our guide is not meant to be a complete, exhaustive listing of all there is to do in our area; that could fill several books. If we've skipped over one of your favorite shops, restaurants or attractions or if you've found any of our information to be in error, we invite you to drop us a line, either in the mail or via our website (www.insiders.com). Each year the guide will be updated with each entry verified for factual information and quality. You can write to us at:

The Insiders' Guide® to Maine's Southern Coast, P.O. Box 1718, Helena, MT 59624

We look forward to hearing from you!

Photo: Merry Farnum

During any season, the beaches along Maine's Southern Coast beckon visitors.

Portland, surrounded by water on three sides, helps keep the state economy afloat as Maine's major commercial center.

Area Overviews

So you've decided to visit the Southern Coast of Maine. Good decision! Let us encourage you to begin your visit here, in this chapter, even before you pack the car or hop on the plane. If you're already in the area, take a spin through the next few pages prior to making your next important vacation decision. Our Southern Coast is loaded with interesting places to visit or live, and we want to give you an Insiders' tour before you buy your first lobster lollipop or Maine magnet.

This chapter is meant to give you a broad overview of the towns in each of our geographic areas and what they have to offer. That way you can better plan your vacation, and when you get home you won't be saying, "Oh, I wish we had known about…" For more detailed information on the best places to tour, eat, sleep, shop and so forth, you'll need to refer to those specific chapters. This, however, will serve as an appetizer — both to whet your appetite and to let you know a feast of fun waits just behind the kitchen door.

Life along Maine's Southern Coast

Remember high school? Well, your English teacher would have flunked our Southern Coast. It's a mixed metaphor. On one hand, it's teeming strip malls full of the latest fashions, accessories, technologies and home furnishings, where traffic creeps through the center of town and throngs of shoppers push their way between cars to get from one store to the next. On the other, it's a deserted beach surrounded by swaying pines and the endless sea with seagulls surfing on the wind overhead. The Southern Coast is tight-knit towns and villages built by the same families that still live there — the Morses and Soules and Baileys — where fishermen rise before dawn to haul traps and tie up at sunset to

take their seats on the town boards of government. It's exclusive summer resorts and three-story summer "cottages" on the ocean where people come to entertain and be entertained. And it's also the largest city in the state, Portland, surrounded by water on three sides as it keeps the state economy afloat as Maine's major commercial center. Portland draws business people from around the country and people seeking cultural refinement — theater, art, the ballet and symphony — and a way to support their families on a good wage.

Our Southern Coast is all these things. It is the flirtatious belle at the masquerade ball with a different mask in hand for each suitor. This is the reason we love it. Although neither of us was born here, we decided to stay because of the coast's many offerings and their proximity to each other. From the southernmost point of the state to the tip of the Boothbay Harbor peninsula — the coverage area of our guide — it is a little less than a three-hour drive. Many of our towns have fewer than 2,000 people and don't even have centers to mark them (although most do have a little town hall hidden back in the woods somewhere). Then there are the towns such as York and Old Orchard Beach that seem to disappear altogether once the souvenir shops and arcades close after summer and all the tourists head home.

Tourism is one of the state's largest industries. Fishing is another. As you drive down our back roads, you'll see stacks of lobster crates piled high on more than one lawn. These are not ornaments or a new concept in fencing — they're business tools. Some people place signs in their front lawns advertising "fresh shrimp" or "fresh lobster" for sale. Much of the financial strength along our Southern Coast comes from out of state and goes south when the summer ends, but the real wealth here in Maine is in its people. We know one woman who dresses like she couldn't afford her next meal but lives in her town's most luxurious house. She just doesn't feel like buying the clothes to prove it. That's part of Maine sensibility. The native residents come from a people who generations ago decided to dig in and live in a land that the first English colonists called "uninhabitable" because of the fiercely cold winter that buried their fort with snow. They are the people who will finish shoveling their driveway then help you shovel yours. They are also protective of what belongs to them and to their neighbors. So when you tread, tread lightly. And when you openly admire what it is we have here, expect an appreciative, "Ayuh," and a smile.

Chambers of Commerce on the Southern Coast

Kittery-Eliot Chamber of Commerce, (207) 439-7545

York Chamber of Commerce, (207) 363-4422

Wells Chamber of Commerce, (207) 646-2451

Kennebunk-Kennebunkport Chamber of Commerce, (207) 967-0857

Kennebunk Bureau of Tourism, (207) 967-8600

Biddeford-Saco Chamber of Commerce, (207) 282-1567

Chamber of Commerce of Old Orchard Beach, (207) 934-2500

Chamber of Commerce of the Greater Portland Region, (207) 772-2811

Portland's Downtown District, (207) 772-6828

Yarmouth Chamber of Commerce, (207) 846-3984

Chamber of Commerce Bath-Brunswick Region, (207) 725-8797 (Brunswick), (207) 443-9751 (Bath)

Boothbay Harbor Region Chamber of Commerce, (207) 633-2353

Southern Beaches Area

If you're venturing into Maine by car from the south, your first view of the state will probably be from the center of the arching, green Piscataqua Bridge that spans the river of the same name. The river flows between Maine and New Hampshire, separating the two states. For many of us who live here (and others who visit regularly), the bridge lifts our hearts; it can even cause us to press a little harder on the gas pedal to speed our way into the state we love best.

Just across the bridge you'll find Kittery, which has a population of around 9,300. Famous since the late 1980s for the outlet stores located on a mile-long stretch of U.S. Highway 1 entering town (remember, the locals know it as Route 1), Kittery is also noteworthy for the beauty of the Piscataqua River and seafront. It assumes an important role in Maine history — Kittery is the oldest incorporated community in the state. The town celebrated its 351st birthday in 1998. While the outlet mall area (see our Shopping chapter) is certainly a central component of the town's economy, the Portsmouth Naval Shipyard on Seavey Island plays an even bigger role. Once supplying jobs for close to 25,000 people during World War II, the shipyard is still one of the largest employers for both York County and the New Hampshire seacoast with approximately 4,000 employees.

York, the next town you'll encounter heading north, is comprised of four distinct areas: York Village, York Harbor, York Beach and Cape Neddick. The second-oldest community in Maine, York has a fine history museum (see our Attractions chapter), attractive riverfront and seafront and a small harbor where the York River flows into the sea. Two popular beaches, descriptively called Long Sands and Short Sands (see our Beaches chapter), are found in York, and it is the home of one of the most photographed lighthouses in the United States, familiarly referred to as "The Nubble" at Cape Neddick (see Attractions).

About a mile north of the lighthouse, you can enjoy the Victorian charm of York Beach village, which features a number of eateries and an enjoyable Main Street area (see our Shopping chapter). The population of the town

Photo: Merry Farnum

In Casco Bay, the views are spectacular from both the city and the water.

is around 14,000, but unlike Kittery, which has far fewer places to stay, York's population swells to around 40,000 in summer. With those kinds of numbers it isn't difficult to see that tourism forms the backbone of this community's economy.

Continuing north on Route 1 you'll come to the towns of Ogunquit and Wells. Until 1980 Ogunquit was part of Wells, and the towns still share a school district. Ogunquit boasts a delightful Main Street area and a picturesque fishing village-turned-shopping area in Perkins Cove. A marvelous walking path called the Marginal Way leads from Main Street to the Cove, where you will find a small harbor with boats bobbing at rest and a white painted drawbridge designed strictly for pedestrian traffic (see our Kidstuff chapter).

Ogunquit is famous not only for its beauty but also for the artists who have been attracted to it through the years. At the turn of the century, painter Charles Woodbury instituted the

Ogunquit art colony by offering painting classes. By the 1920s to late 1940s, the town's status as an art destination was firmly established, having attracted artists such as Marsden Hartley.

Today Ogunquit is still a mecca for artists, and you'll find a wealth of galleries throughout the town. You'll also find a number of tourists. Like York, the population of this town booms in summer, but in significantly lower numbers. Off-season, the population of Ogunquit lands somewhere around 1,000.

What Wells may lack in charm it makes up for in natural beauty. If you take the time to wander off U.S. 1, you'll enjoy the "woodsy" atmosphere normally associated with the northern part of Maine. Along the seafront you can enjoy a long, sandy beach backed by a tidal river and frequented by seabirds. Or if you prefer, you can take a self-guided walk through either Laudholm Farm and the Wells Reserve or the Rachel Carson Nature

Preserve, both of which are found here (see our Parks and Recreation chapter). Lovers of old, rare and secondhand books will also love Wells. If you begin at Annie's Book Stop (see our Shopping chapter), the staff can give you a map of town highlighting the secondhand and rare book dealers.

Kennebunk and Kennebunkport are next as you journey north. Entering Kennebunk on Route 1, you'll see a Main Street that has retained much of its early 20th-century character (see Shopping). Stop in at the highly respected Brick Store Museum (see Attractions), which houses art and artifacts detailing the Kennebunks' past. As you head down Maine Highway 35 (Summer Street) from Main Street, look for the magnificent architecture for which the Kennebunks are noted, including the much-photographed, Federal-style "Wedding Cake House," which is a private residence.

Unlike neighboring seacoast towns, many of the businesses in the Kennebunks stay open year round. In summer you can enjoy the towns' beaches (see our Beaches chapter for details), but all seasons offer fun in the form of romantic getaways at area bed and breakfast inns, shopping on Main Street or in Dock Square (see Shopping) and gastronomic delights in fine restaurants. In fact, the Christmas Prelude, held in early December, is so popular that sidewalks are filled with happy people strolling, shopping and enjoying the old-world charm of a Maine winter (see our Annual Events and Festivals chapter).

The off-season population of the towns is about 8,000 for Kennebunk and 3,000 for Kennebunkport. In summer, of course, the numbers are significantly higher. Among the famous names who have lived or vacationed in the Kennebunks are former President George Bush, who retains a summer home on Walker's Point; author Booth Tarkington, creator of the children's classic Penrod; and

author Kenneth Roberts, whose historical novels were so popular they led the folks in North Kennebunk to change the town name back to Arundel (see our chapter on The Arts).

Old Orchard Beach Area

The three towns that make up this area could not be more diverse. Biddeford, Saco and Old Orchard Beach have individual characters that make it impossible to mistake one for the other. From enormous red brick mill buildings in the city center to stretches of peaceful beaches along the coast, Biddeford maintains a strong sense of identity and civic pride. It's the only city in this area that has a theater (see The Arts), and is noteworthy for the successful launch of a local newspaper a decade ago (see our Media chapter).

The population of Biddeford doesn't vary much by season, hovering around 21,000 year round. It's worth noting that Biddeford's strong French-Canadian heritage has led the city to create one of the largest French-Canadian festivals in the United States, La Kermesse, held at the end of June each year (see our Annual Events and Festivals chapter). Biddeford is also home to the University of New England, which specializes in medical pursuits (see our Education and Child Care chapter), and to the East Point Bird Sanctuary in Biddeford Pool, which is recognized as one of the best birding spots in New England.

Biddeford Pool, so called to distinguish it from the city proper, is one of the most beautiful communities in Southern Maine. Located south of Biddeford center off Maine Highway 9, you'll find a large tidal pool, a number of sandy beaches (see our Beaches chapter) and lovely, quiet, tree-lined streets perfect for bicycling or strolling.

Like similar cities throughout New England that were bustling, important mill towns at the

---

INSIDERS' TIP

Almost one quarter of Mainers live in the Greater Portland area, which has a population of 230,000.

Bath Iron Works Continues Full Speed Ahead

Drive from Bath to Woolwich over the arching Carlton Bridge and along the banks of the Kennebec River below you will see a jumble of ships, buildings and docks. These make up one of the greatest naval shipyards in the world, the Bath Iron Works.

Ships have been built in Bath since the days of Maine's earliest settlers, who supported their families and built the community by felling trees from the nearby forests and building massive wooden ships along the riverfront. The first large ships built in Bath were constructed during the 1740s when the town  was still part of nearby Georgetown. At one time the Kennebec cradled more shipyards than any other river in North America. Today the Iron Works dominates Bath's riverfront and employs 7,500 men and women. They design, cut and weld steel into massive fighting ships.

In 1864, Civil War veteran Thomas Hyde hired seven employees and began the iron foundry that would one day grow into the shipyard. Hyde was known to his workers as "the General." Although he came from a prominent Bath family, Hyde, who was barely out of his teens, donned work clothes and toiled alongside his employees. He invested everything he had into the small business that made ship hatches and plates and even took a second job as Bath's inspector of customs to help support his wife and six children.

Six years after taking over the foundry, Hyde had doubled the number of employees, expanded the product line and turned it into the nation's leading manufacturer of deck machinery. A decade later the business was still growing, this time under the name Bath Iron Works.

The days of steam and steel eventually put an end to wooden shipbuilding, but BIW hung on, eventually building destroyers to fight in World War I. Shortly after the war, however, the yard was dismantled. There just wasn't a need for more ships. It wouldn't build another destroyer for 14 years. For a while the yard was used as a paper

— continued on next page

Today Bath Iron Works handles only military contracts.

manufacturing plant, then in 1928 former BIW manager Pete Newell brought a group of investors together to buy the yard. Instead of military vessels, which weren't in demand, Newell set out to build yachts, such as the 343-foot Corsair, which was the largest yacht ever constructed in America when it was finished for J.P. Morgan in 1929. It's likely that no one has ever built a larger vessel of this design. The yard also fashioned small fishing trawlers, which were later used as mine sweepers during World War II, and Coast Guard cutters, which were used to reinforce Prohibition.

In 1931, the yard aimed at the Navy market and won its first destroyer contract since reopening; it was commissioned to build the Dewey. The subsequent buildup leading to World War II put BIW back in business big time - shipyard employment skyrocketed to 12,000, and the yard built an average of two ships a month, a record unparalleled in the history of world shipbuilding.

Today the shipyard relies solely on military contracts. It has plants in Bath, Brunswick and Portland, and when its employees go to work, they pass beneath gates that feature a quote bearing testimony to the shipyard's history: "Through these gates pass the best shipbuilders in the world." The shipyard is open occasionally for tours, and several times a year BIW opens its gates to the public for scheduled ship launchings and christenings. For more information, contact Bath Iron Works at (207) 442-4143.

turn of the century, the era after World War II brought a decline in Biddeford's fortunes, as mill owners headed south for warmer climates and cheaper labor. Today the city's future appears brighter. In 1997 the city received an economic boost when J.J. Nissen relocated its Portland bread factory to Biddeford, and there is a great deal of building going on near the Biddeford exit (Exit 4) of the Maine Turnpike. Since 1995 Wal-Mart, Shaw's Supermarket, a gas station, VIP Auto Parts and Staples office products have all opened branches in this area. Southern Maine Medical Center, the area's local hospital, sits within a stone's throw of the Biddeford exit (see our Healthcare chapter).

The city of Saco lies just across the Saco River from Biddeford. Whether you're looking for a town with a quaint Main Street and stately homes, one with long stretches of sandy white beach, or one with great amusement parks, Saco can fill the bill. Home to the Funtown/ Splashtown USA and Aquaboggan amusement parks (see our Attractions chapter), Ferry Beach State Park and about 4 miles of great beach (see Beaches), Saco also boasts a great Main Street shopping area and beautiful homes along tree-shaded avenues.

Originally called Pepperellboro, Saco has an off-season population of around 15,000. It's home to Thornton Academy, which serves as the city's high school (see Education and Child Care). Tourism is the major industry for Saco as visitors, attracted to the city's amusements and beaches, ante up by eating in local restaurants and staying in the city's hotels, motels and bed and breakfast inns. Like most towns along the coast, fishing is also an important industry, but the local economy also includes a number of banks and financial institutions and some working farms. The city is also home to the York Institute Museum, whose collection traces the history of Southern Maine (see Attractions).

North of Saco and east of Route 1 is Old Orchard Beach. Famous as a resort destination that rivaled Newport, Rhode Island, at the turn of the century, Old Orchard Beach (population about 7,500) retains much of its Victorian seaside charm. You'll find an amusement pier jutting out to the Atlantic, the Palace Playland amusement park along the seafront (see our Attractions chapter) and fast-food vendors selling summer fare such as fried dough, hot dogs, cotton candy and pretzels along with pizza and fried clams. The beach is wide, sandy and somewhat crowded in summer unless you walk a few hundred yards from the pier, but Old Orchard Beach is a happy, fun place beloved by families who return year after year.

A number of annual events such as Beach Fest and Fourth of July Fireworks take place every summer (see our Annual Events and Festivals chapter), and the only nightclubs in the area operating in-season are in this town (see our Nightlife chapter). Shopping in Old Orchard Beach is nothing to write home about, but there's an extensive selection of T-shirts, swimwear, beach accessories and souvenirs to be found along Old Orchard Street, which serves as the town's Main Street.

Greater Portland Area

Scarborough marks the division not only between geographic regions in this book but also between counties. York County is to the south; Scarborough, the rest of Greater Portland and areas to the west as far as Bridgton comprise Cumberland County. The abundance of natural beauty in this town is a mixed blessing. Scarborough enjoys fabulous beaches (see our Beaches chapter), the largest salt marsh in the state (see our Parks and Recreation chapter) and acres and acres of woodlands and fields. In the '90s its beauty and proximity to Portland brought rampant growth and the problems that come with it, particularly the strain placed on the local school system to accommodate a rapid influx of school-age children. At present the population is about 14,000, but Scarborough is continuing to grow.

Fields, farms and woodlands define Scarborough, and the beauty of its coastline remains unchanged. Farming is still a viable industry here, though in recent years the town has also enjoyed considerable business development along Maine Highway 9 (Payne Road), near the Maine Mall in South Portland. Other small plazas and malls have sprung up along Route 1, particularly between Oak Hill and the South Portland line.

Cape Elizabeth is blessed with a number of state parks, a scenic rocky coastline, lovely stretches of beach and one of the most fa-mous lighthouses in the world — the Portland Head Light (see our Attractions chapter). Located near Portland but off the main traffic arteries of Route 1 and the Maine Turnpike, Cape Elizabeth has escaped the development and commercialism generally associated with those stretches of highway. The best way to access Cape Elizabeth is from Maine Highway 77 off Black Point Road in Scarborough, or along Shore Road from South Portland.

In Cape Elizabeth (population about 9,000), things appear much as they would have looked at the turn of the century. Graceful houses that were built originally as summer cottages line Shore Road. Though the town maintains an aura of exclusivity, it is not just for the wealthy. You'll find modest housing and friendly neighborhoods here as well.

South Portland is known for its shopping areas. Offerings include the Maine Mall and a number of smaller plazas and malls nearby. Located on the western edge of town about a mile from the Portland Jetport, the Maine Mall and its neighboring retail areas comprise the bulk of South Portland's industry (see our Shopping chapter). Southern Maine Technical College and a number of marinas that house both pleasure and fishing boats (see the Boating section of our Parks and Recreation chapter) are also on that side of town. The city is one of the few places in Southern Maine with a municipal pool, and it also features a number of golf courses (see Parks and Recreation) and a small community beach. South Portland's population is about 23,000, which remains fairly steady despite the number of hotels and motels that draw guests year round.

With a population of 65,000, Portland is large enough to be called a city and small enough for residents to recognize some of the faces they pass on the sidewalk. Driving into or past Portland, a number of modern, high-rise office buildings mask the old skyline. Hiding amidst them are rows of old brick buildings along the waterfront forming the Old Port.

INSIDERS' TIP

July tends to be Maine's hottest month, with an average high of 80 degrees. January is the coldest with an average low of 12 degrees, although temperatures often soar into the 30s.

You'll have to drive into town to appreciate them.

The Old Port is known for intimate shops with everything from apparel and fine china to children's toys and antiques and rare books (see our Shopping chapter). A few blocks down Congress Street is the Arts District, home to the Portland Ballet Company, the Maine College of Art and the Portland Museum of Art (see our chapter on The Arts). With the Portland Sea Dogs baseball team and Portland Pirates hockey, Portland is also the sports capital of the Southern Coast (see our Spectator Sports chapter). If you'd rather get out and play rather than watch, the city has a handful of small parks, some with harbor views, nearly all with a choice of basketball, tennis or winter ice skating (see our Parks and Recreation chapter). The Cumberland County Civic Center is one of the largest venues in the state — a great place to catch a concert or show.

Within Portland's 26 square miles are quiet residential neighborhoods, condominiums on the water and an array of apartments. American poet Henry Wadsworth Longfellow was born and raised here, and his house (along with many other historic homes in the city) is still open for tours (see our Attractions chapter).

Portland's economy is very diverse with financial, legal, accounting, insurance and manufacturing concerns making up 30 percent of gross regional production. B&M Baked Beans are made in a large factory on the outskirts of the city, and the Sappi paper factory employs a large number of people in nearby Westbrook (in case you were wondering what that smell was as you drove up I-95 . . . Take heart though — it doesn't permeate Portland). Maine Medical Center, the third-largest employer in the state, brings with it some of the most advanced medical services north of Boston (see our Healthcare chapter). On the harbor, Bath Iron Works employs people at its drydock (see this chapter's Close-up). Another growing component of Portland's economy is tourism. Many larger cruise ships including the Queen Elizabeth II dock here. One of the newest attractions is the $6 million Portland Public Market, which opened its doors in October 1998. The glass and timber building off Congress Street is full of fresh produce, piping hot breads and pies, fresh roasted coffee beans, specialty smoked meets and more. For more on this see the Up-close box in our Shopping chapter.

Just up Route 1 is Falmouth, a wealthy hub with 8,300 people, where space in both waterfront neighborhoods and rural wooded areas is in high demand. It's the home of the Maine Audubon Society and the state-owned Baxter School for the Deaf (see our Education and Child Care chapter). Most people in Falmouth work in Portland, though the town does have an outdoor shopping center, restaurants and businesses along Route 1. Cumberland (population 5,860) is sandwiched between Falmouth and Yarmouth, but most of its neighborhoods are inland.

Yarmouth itself is a town that's similar in population and disposition to Falmouth. Main Street has a handful of fun shops to scout through and a scenic park on the Royal River. It also has a well-known July clam festival (see Annual Events and Festivals), and Yarmouth Academy, one of the state's leading prep schools (see Education and Child Care). Most Yarmouth residents head to work in Portland. However, the quaint Main Street shops provide jobs for many locals.

Freeport, the next town north along the U.S. 1 corridor, is a fun shopping experience that has become one of the largest tourist attractions in the state. More than 3.5 million people visit downtown Freeport each year — many of them on their way to L.L. Bean, the largest retail store for outdoor clothing and equipment in the state, and one of the largest in the world. The enormous, three-story store is open 24 hours a day, 365 days a year and dominates the town's downtown area. Freeport (population 7,100) has side-street neighborhoods and a village center, where historic homes and buildings have been con-

The first chartered city in the United States was York, chartered in 1641.

Portland Head Light is the most photographed lighthouse in the world.

verted into outlet stores. (See our Shopping chapter for much more on the retail options in Freeport.) Wolfe Neck Woods State Park and the Haraseeket Inn, one of the most acclaimed restaurants in the state (see Restaurants), are also here.

Brunswick, Bath and Boothbay Harbor Area

The largest town in our guide's northernmost area is Brunswick, which has 21,000 people spread across its rural countryside. The downtown area is a terrific place to shop. Not only does the town have the widest main street in the state (it's actually called Maine Street), it also has plenty of stores, from resale shops that specialize in children's items to craft guilds and more restaurants with more cuisine choices than just about any other town on the Southern Coast.

Brunswick is also home to Bowdoin College (see our Education and Child Care chapter), which has graduated famed American personalities such as the aforementioned Longfellow and our own Civil War hero, Gen. Joshua Chamberlain. One of the oldest colleges in the country, Bowdoin was founded in 1794 and has a student population of about 1,500. The liberal arts school plays a prominent role in the community's economy. Harriet Beecher Stowe wrote Uncle Tom's Cabin just a couple of blocks away from the school. (For information on the home of Chamberlain, which is open to the public, see our Attractions chapter.) Brunswick is just off Route 1 and is connected to the nearby peninsula of Harpswell, a quaint fishing village with beautiful ocean views and darling bed and breakfast inns (see our Bed and Breakfasts and Inns chapter).

Farther up Route 1 is West Bath, a small community on the New Meadows River. Then comes Bath, a city of 10,000 best known for Bath Iron Works. It's the state's largest employer, with about 7,500 workers construct-

ing ships for the U.S. Navy. Bath's shipbuilding history goes back to the 1700s, and BIW is the longest operating shipyard in the country. It is also home to the Maine Maritime Museum, where you can get an up-close look at how the old, tall-masted wooden ships were made (see our Attractions chapter). Bath's downtown area has a wide variety of shops and some fine restaurants.

Driving south from Bath on Maine Highway 209 brings you to Phippsburg, a peninsula at the meeting of the Kennebec River and the Atlantic Ocean. At the point of Phippsburg is the old Civil War bunker Fort Popham and 3 miles of sandy beach at Popham Beach State Park (see our Beaches chapter). Farther north along Route 1 is the community of Woolwich (population 2,570) and to the east are the neighboring towns of Arrowsic and Georgetown. Both are small, with most residents working in Bath, Brunswick or Wiscasset. The peninsula of Georgetown is known for the Georgetown Pottery kiln and Reid State Park (see Beaches).

Wiscasset, the next town on Route 1, claims to be the prettiest village in Maine. With church steeples pointing heavenward and quaint shops along the Sheepscot River, it's not hard to see why. Wiscasset is home to Sarah's, one of the most popular family restaurants in our area (see Restaurants), and a Main Street lined with beautiful Victorian and Federal-period houses. It is also chock-full of antique stores (see our Shopping chapter). Wiscasset is a little larger than the communities to the south, with a population just topping 3,000.

Pass over the bridge across the Sheepscot to Edgecomb, and when you turn south onto Maine Highway 27 toward Boothbay Harbor, keep an eye out for Edgecomb Potters (it's more of a pottery and art museum than a kiln) on the left side of the road. Downtown Boothbay Harbor is teeming with galleries, souvenir shops, antique stores, hotels and restaurants. It is also the busiest harbor north of Boston, and there are plenty of boat rides to take you out on the water (see Attractions). Nearby are Southport Island and East Boothbay, two small communities that share schools with the other towns along the peninsula. Boothbay Harbor is home to the Maine Resources Aquarium (see Kidstuff) and some lovely seaside and in-town inns such as the Newagen Inn and the Greenleaf Inn (see our Bed and Breakfasts and Inns chapter). While the summertime population of the town makes it bulge at the seams, Boothbay Harbor only has about 2,500 year-round residents.

With 75 flights arriving daily, Portland International Jetport is becoming a more important player in transportation to and from Maine.

Getting Here, Getting Around

Southern Maine isn't as inaccessible as you might think. In fact, it's not that far off the beaten path at all. By car, Kittery is about 90 minutes north of Boston; a journey to Portland adds another 45 minutes, and Brunswick tacks on 30 minutes more. To get to Damariscotta, just outside our coverage area, takes about another 45 minutes from Brunswick. Buses run from Boston's South Station and Logan International Airport to Portland many times a day, and a couple of times a day to Brunswick and Bath. You can also fly into Portland Jetport or Bangor International Airport, or sail your boat up the coast to one of our many marinas (see our Parks and Recreation chapter).

To get off the main thoroughfares and explore backroads and byways, you'll need a car or a bicycle and lots of energy. For those who've traveled to Maine by air or bus but would like to do some more personal exploring, we've included rental car companies. You'll also find information on local bus lines and taxi and trolley services that can help you get around. Since there are few listings in most of this chapter's categories, we've departed from the usual geographical subdivisions in this chapter, instead organizing information by type of transportation, then arranging listings from south to north.

By Car

Highways and Byways

Throughout this guide you'll see references to Interstate 95 (which is also known

here as the Maine Turnpike) and to U.S. Highway 1 (which we use interchangeably with "Route 1"). These two roadways run parallel to one another from Kittery to Brunswick. There I-95 continues north to Bangor, and Route 1 veers to the east along the coast toward Bar Harbor. You should note that a slightly confusing aspect of the Maine Turnpike is that at Exit 9 (Falmouth, Freeport), I-95 branches off while the Turnpike continues as I-495 north through Lewiston and Auburn until merging once again with I-95 just south of Augusta.

Accessing the Southern Coast

From I-95 or Route 1 you can access all of the towns in the Southern Beaches and Old Orchard Beach areas. Exits on I-95 are well-posted with signs to Kittery, York, Wells and Ogunquit (Exit 2), the Kennebunks (Exit 3), Biddeford (Exit 4), and Saco and Old Orchard Beach (Exit 5). Scarborough can be reached from Exit 6 off the Maine Turnpike or by traveling north along Route 1. You can also get to Scarborough via Interstate 295, discussed below. The Maine Mall area of South Portland can be accessed off Exit 7 of the Maine Turnpike. From this exit you will also find signs leading to Portland Jetport, which is about five minutes from the exit.

Cape Elizabeth is not readily accessible by either the Maine Turnpike or Route 1. To get there you'll need to take Black Point Road (Maine Highway 207) from Route 1 at Oak Hill in Scarborough and head east toward Prout's Neck. From there, take a left onto Maine Highway 77, which leads to Cape Elizabeth. Alternately, you can pick up Maine 77 in Portland by crossing the Casco Bay Bridge into South Portland and then into Cape Elizabeth.

Portland and Points North

Another confusing aspect to our road system is that from I-95 you can access Portland directly only via Exit 8. To get to intown Portland, you should take Exit 6A onto I-295, which will bring you into the city. You can choose from exits that lead to the waterfront, Congress Street (Maine Highway 22), Forest Avenue (Maine Highway 9), Franklin Street or Washington Avenue (Maine Highway 26), depending on where you want to go.

I-295 is also noteworthy because it provides an alternate route to Brunswick. Instead of carrying on up I-95, you can take Exit 6A onto I-295. This route will save you some mileage, but depending on the traffic heading through Portland, may not save you any time. You should also note that the (enforced!) speed limit on I-295 is 65 mph and drops to 50 mph in places.

North of Portland I-295 merges back into I-95 as it heads towards the next popular tourist destination: Freeport. You'll find three different exits leading into this shopping mecca — Exits 19, 20 and 21 — all of which connect to U.S. Highway 1. If you're approaching Freeport from the south, Exit 19 is your best bet. From here, as you head north along Route 1 you'll see a large visitor information center on the left. The center has restrooms and plenty of information on much of what there is to do in the region. Arriving from the north, you'll want to take Exit 21 into Freeport and head south along Route 1.

Route 1, also known as Main Street here, heads straight through the center of Freeport.

As you drive into town you'll find outlet malls and plenty of other shops (see our Shopping chapter). The L.L. Bean Retail Store is also on Route 1 in the center of town; it's on the left if you are driving north along Route 1. From the town center, side streets will take you to plenty more shops.

Getting to Brunswick, Bath and Boothbay Harbor

Continuing north on I-95 to Brunswick, Exit 22 will get you back to Route 1 and will lead you into the downtown shopping district. If you want to see the sights in Brunswick, continue along Pleasant Street (it's one-way) until its T-intersection with Maine Street, where most of the shops are. If you take a right at the intersection of Pleasant and Maine streets, you will see signs for Maine Highway 123, which leads out to the Harpswell peninsula.

If you are headed to Bath or Boothbay Harbor, you have two alternatives. You can take Exit 22 to Brunswick and continue north along Route 1, or for less congestion you can stay on I-95 until you reach "The Coastal Connector" by taking Exit 24 in Topsham, just a few miles farther from Brunswick and its often crowded commute. To bypass Brunswick, take Exit 24 and turn right onto Maine Highway 196 east. Go past the Topsham Fair Mall and straight through each set of traffic lights, following the highway until it merges with Route 1 just north of the busiest section of Brunswick. (Note: Taking the bypass is definitely the best way to travel during summer *unless* Brunswick is your destination).

North of Brunswick, Bath is the next major

INSIDERS' TIP

Portland's Downtown Guides are available to serve you. You'll spot them by their broad brimmed hats and purple shirts. Guides carry maps of the area to help you find what you're looking for. They also carry cellular phones they can use to track down the answers to your questions. Downtown Guides patrol Portland's Downtown District daily from the end of May to the beginning of September from 11:30 AM to 8 PM.

Horse-drawn carriages are a unique way to see Portland during festivals.

community along U.S. Highway 1. If you want to see the sights, stay in the right lane and follow the signs for "Historic Bath," which will lead you down a hill and beneath an overpass into the center of town. Numerous signs will direct you to various destinations. If you're headed out to the Phippsburg peninsula, you'll also want to get off in Bath, but follow the signs for "High Street, Route 209." Maine Highway 209 south will take you through Bath to the peninsula.

If you're headed to Wiscasset or Boothbay Harbor, continue north along Route 1, which will take you on the overpass above Bath and across the Kennebec River. Expect traffic delays and possibly road detours as you cross the river. In spring 1998, the Maine Department of Transportation began a two- to three-year construction project to build a new bridge over the river. When the bridge is completed it should alleviate the severe traffic conges-

tion created when the state's largest employer — Bath Iron Works — changes shifts at 3:30 PM each weekday.

After you cross the bridge, you'll have the option of driving to the islands of Arrowsic and Georgetown by following Maine Highway 127 south. Continuing north along Route 1 will bring you to the center of Wiscasset (about 20 minutes north of Bath), home of one of the worst summertime traffic bottlenecks around. Just after you pass through Wiscasset and over the Sheepscot River, you'll see signs directing you to Maine Highway 27 south to Boothbay Harbor. Maine 27 will take you all the way down the peninsula and into the center of town.

Maine Transpass

The Maine Transpass system was instituted in October 1997. It is meant to be a revolutionary method of toll collecting, improving traffic flow and reducing the number of employees necessary to operate the Maine Turnpike. Unfortunately, many people who live in the Transpass area (and probably all of our visitors) haven't a clue what the system is all about. To find out, read on.

When you enter Maine on Interstate 95, you don't pay a toll until you reach York. At that point the road becomes a turnpike, and you must fork out $1.50. When you exit the turnpike at Exit 6A or Exit 9, you have to pay another 50¢. Also, as you head south on the turnpike you will pay 50¢ as you enter and another $1.50 as you exit.

Locals and commuters who have purchased a "transponder" (a little gadget that sits on your dashboard and beeps as you pass through the toll area) do not have to stop at the toll but are supposed to slow down and drive through the "Transpass Only" lanes.

Since the system is still in its infancy, there are a lot of bugs to work out, so be patient, drive carefully and slow down at exits!

Rental Cars

Most of the car rental companies on Maine's Southern Coast are found at Portland Jetport. However, you'll find a few rental outlets in the Southern Beaches and Old Orchard Beach areas.

If you're visiting Kittery, you might want to try Budget Rent A Car, 445 U.S. Highway 1 Bypass, Portsmouth, New Hampshire, (603) 433-1177. In Kennebunk, U-Save Auto Rental, (207) 985-9885, is on Alewife Road, and in Saco, Enterprise Rent-A-Car, (207) 284-2004, has a location at 890 Portland Road (U.S. Highway 1).

For rentals in Portland, Avis, (207) 874-7500, (800) 831-2847; Budget, (207) 772-6789; and Hertz, (800) 654-3131, are all at the Portland Jetport. Just 100 yards away from the Jetport at 1000 Westbrook Street is Thrifty, (207) 772-4628, which offers airport valet parking. In Brunswick you'll find Enterprise at 173 Pleasant Street (U.S. Highway 1), (207) 725-1344. In Woolwich, just beyond Bath along Route 1 north, there's U-Save Auto Rental, (207) 442-7733, (800) 798-7733, where we have gone several times when our car was on the fritz.

Taxi Service

Here on the Southern Coast of Maine, we probably have fewer taxi companies between Kittery and Boothbay than there are in the city of Boston alone. Still, there are a few vendors who are more than happy to take you where you need to go. Some taxis even offer sightseeing tours and special rates for longer journeys. Before embarking on a taxi ride, however, you should call ahead to find out how much it will cost — it might be more than you'd expect. For instance, a journey from Saco to Kennebunk (a 13-mile ride that usually takes about 20 minutes) can cost about $20, so beware.

For taxi service in the Southern Beaches Area, try Kittery Kab, (207) 439-5689; York Taxi, (207) 363-7007; Mom's Taxi in York Beach, (207) 363-5525; Brewster's Taxi & Travel Service in Ogunquit, (207) 646-2141; or John's Coastal Taxi in Kennebunk, (207) 985-6291.

In the Old Orchard Beach Area, taxi service is offered by Alternative Taxi Network in Saco, (207) 284-0269; John's Taxi, (207) 284-7511, and Twin City Taxi, (207) 284-7911, in Biddeford; and Old Orchard Beach Taxi at (207) 934-7706.

Around the Greater Portland Area, taxi service is available from a number of companies including Kangaroo Taxi Service of Scarborough, (207) 883-2366; Big John's Taxi

INSIDERS' TIP

Be aware that when it snows in Maine, many towns and cities impose community-wide parking bans. This means if you park along streets or in public parking lots, your vehicle will be towed. Parking bans are announced on the evening news and typically are in effect from 11 PM until 7 AM the next day, giving plows a chance to clear the streets.

in South Portland, (207) 828-4047; Old Port Taxi, (207) 874-7872, and Freeport Taxi, (207) 865-9494. You can also get service to Logan Airport in Boston from Mermaid Transportation (207) 772-2509 and Airport Limo & Taxi in Portland, (207) 773-3433. Cost for a one-way ticket from Mermaid Transportation was $35 in 1998. A limo will cost you around $110 one way.

In the Brunswick, Bath and Boothbay Harbor Area, Brunswick Taxi, 729-3688, serves the Brunswick-Topsham-Bath triangle. Drew's Taxi, 443-9166, can get you around the triangle and also makes airport runs. Boothbay Harbor Taxi, 633-6001, offers transportation along the Boothbay peninsula.

By Air

Logan International Airport
U.S. Hwy. 1A, Boston, Mass.
• **(617) 568-5600**

Most visitors traveling by air to Maine will probably land at Boston's Logan International Airport, which serves most airlines. The phone number listed is for the airport's administrative offices, so you'll need to contact your travel agent or favorite airline directly for specific flight information. During the next few years the airport will be undergoing a $1 billion modernization project dubbed "Logan 2000." Throughout the project parking will be significantly reduced, though an additional 3,150 parking spaces will ultimately be added in a new west garage — increasing total parking capacity by about a third.

Logan Airport has five terminals labeled A through E. All international departures (except Virgin Airways) and most international arrivals use Terminal E. You'll find automated concierges in Terminal A and car rental booths in the lower level of all terminals except Terminal D. The chapel is on the arrivals level of Terminal C.

Duty-free shops are between the baggage lockers and the elevator on the departures level of Terminal E, in the lobby of Terminal C near the nurseries and infant changing rooms, and on both sides of Terminal B. You can get ground transportation information from booths on the lower levels of terminals A, C, and E,

or make hotel reservations from the Reservation Phone Boards in the lower levels of Terminal A, Terminal B, orTerminal C, and in the hotel reservations area in the lower level of Terminal E.

Other services available include a lost-and-found area, the state police on the lower level of Terminal D and near Terminal E, and a medical station adjacent to the state police. Mailboxes are in the lobby of Terminal C and on the lower levels of all terminals except Terminal D. There's a stamp machine adjacent to the mailbox in Terminal E.

Cost for long-term parking is $20 for the first day, $15 for each additional day and $70 per week. There are short-term parking lots throughout the airport that cost about $2 per hour. Follow directions on signs for the one nearest your terminal.

Portland International Jetport
1001 Westbrook St., Portland
• **(207) 775-5809**

It has yet to make an international name for itself, but Portland International Jetport is becoming a bigger and better player in transportation to and from Maine. With 75 flights arriving daily, the Jetport attracts a growing number of tourists and business travelers. The cost of flying to Maine is on the decline, and the cost of commuter flights and direct jet flights here are beginning to come in line with those at larger airports such as Logan.

The Portland airport handles an average of 36 jet arrivals and departures daily and offers direct jet service to Albany, New York; Bangor, Maine; Chicago; Cincinnati; Manchester, New Hampshire; Newark, New Jersey; Philadelphia; Pittsburgh; and Washington. It also offers commuter flights to a number of destinations, includingHartford, Connecticut, Boston, New York and Washington. It's not nearly as crowded as larger airports, but the Jetport does offer a small newsstand, gift store and a full-service restaurant, The Shipyard.

Nearby are a half-dozen car rental companies (see our Rental Car listings in this chapter's "By Car" section) as well as properties of many major hotel chains (see our Hotels and Motels chapter). A variety of cabs and limousines and the Portland public bus system also serve the airport. Best of all, the Jetport is just 10 to 15 minutes from Portland's downtown area, and you get great views of the city and harbor as you come in for a landing.

The easiest way to get to the Jetport is to take Exit 7 off I-95 and follow the signs to the airport. From I-295 you would take the Congress Street exit. The Jetport has three parking lots designated for short-term parking at $1 per half-hour and long-term parking for one day or longer. If you leave your car in the short-term parking lot for a day or more it will cost you $15 each day. In the long-term parking lot the rate drops to $7 a day, and in the satellite lot, which is a little farther away, a day will cost you $5.50, with a weekly maximum of $27.50. Parking is on a first-come, first-served basis, and you should allow extra time to find a parking space during the Thanksgiving and Christmas holidays and during school vacation in February. If the lot you want to access is full, an attendant will direct you to alternative parking options where you can catch a shuttle bus from a nearby hotel or use the nearby Thrifty Rental Car lot. For more parking information, call (207) 772-7028.

Airfields

Wiscasset Airport
Chewonki Neck Rd., Wiscasset
• **(207) 882-9401**

This is about the only public, paved airstrip along the coast north of Portland. Pilots can fly in any time day or night and use one of the available tie-downs. The airport office is open weekdays from 8 AM to 5 PM and until 8 PM during the summer. Fuel, however, is available 24 hours by charge card. The airstrip has two cars available for rent and offers scenic flights of the area and flight lessons. A maintenance person is available on weekdays. The airport has one 340-foot runway.

By Bus

Interstate Bus Lines

Concord Trailways
100 Sewell St., Portland
• **(207) 828-1151, (800) 639-3317**

You can take Concord Trailways to Boston from Bath, Brunswick and Portland, year round. In-season (Memorial Day to Labor Day) you can also pick it up in Biddeford, Kennebunkport, Ogunquit and Portsmouth, New Hampshire.

At the time of this writing, buses were departing Portland nine times a day, but only twice a day from Bath and Brunswick. A same-day round-trip ticket from Portland was $23 in 1998. A regular round-trip ticket was $28, and a one-way ticket was $16. From Bath, tickets were $21 one way and $39 round trip; from Brunswick they were $20 and $37. A round-trip ticket to Logan International Airport in Boston is $32 from Portland; it's $19 one way.

You'll find the bus stop in Bath in front of Mail It 4 U at 9 Coastal Plaza. In Brunswick the stop is at the Brunswick Clipper Mart at 162 Pleasant Street.

Greyhound/Vermont Transit Lines
950 Congress St., Portland
• **(207) 772-6587, (800) 537-3330**

Vermont Transit is the area's Greyhound link. There is no actual Greyhound service in the Southern Maine region. Vermont Transit buses depart Portland for Boston seven times daily, with an extra service on Friday, Saturday and Sunday. Once in Boston, the entire Greyhound network is accessible. Cost for a same-day round-trip ticket in 1998 was $18. A regular round-trip ticket was $23, and a one-way ticket was $13.

INSIDERS' TIP

Schedule travel through Bath and Brunswick to avoid the weekday departure of Bath Iron Works employees at 3:30 PM. Use bad timing, and you will find yourself in a traffic jam. The bottleneck usually subsides between 4 and 4:30 PM.

Local Bus Lines

Shuttle Bus
**Alfred Road Business Park, Alfred Rd.,
Biddeford • (207) 282-5408**

Shuttle Bus operates two buses continuously throughout the day in the local area — Biddeford, Saco and Old Orchard Beach. It also runs six trips to Portland Monday through Friday, four trips on Saturday and two trips on Sunday. Pick-up and drop-off points are throughout Biddeford, Saco and Old Orchard Beach, either at stops with bus shelters or spots where you find a white "Shuttle Bus" sign with green lettering. Buses to Portland will stop at the Maine Mall and travel up Congress Street to Monument Square — you can pick up the Shuttle Bus at Metro stops along this route in Portland.

Cost for a local fare is $1, and children younger than 5 ride free with an adult. Fares to Portland are $3 each way, or $2 each way if you pick up the bus along Route 1 in Scarborough. Those age 62 or older can ride to Portland for half-price on Tuesdays. In addition, you can purchase a $25 local pass that gives you 50 local rides. For $24 you can get a 10-ride pass to Portland from the Biddeford area, or for $16 you can get a 10-ride pass that allows you to travel from Scarborough to either Portland or the

Biddeford area. Outside the local area, Shuttle Bus stops are marked by green and white stripes on telephone poles.

South Portland Bus Service
**42 O'Neill St., South Portland
• (207) 767-5556**

The South Portland Bus Service provides transportation throughout South Portland, to the Maine Mall area and to downtown Portland. Bus stops are marked with blue and white South Portland Bus Service signs. A regular fare is $1; the price for those age 65 or older and the disabled is 50¢, and children younger than 5 ride free with a paying adult. There is no bus service on Sunday.

Greater Portland Metro
114 Valley St., Portland • (207) 774-0351

Metro bus stops are located throughout Portland and extend to Portland Jetport, the Maine Mall area in South Portland and to Exit 8 of the Maine Turnpike in Portland. The bus stops are clearly marked with Metro Bus Stop signs and/or poles marked with an orange band.

Cost for a regular fare is $1; for riders age 65 or older and people with disabilities, the fare is 50 cents. Children younger than 5 ride free when accompanied by an adult, but there is a two-child limit for each paying adult. You can purchase a 10-ride pass for $9 or monthly

Photo: Merry Farnum

Shopping in Maine can be a "berry" tasty experience.

passes for $30. Passes are available at a variety of locations including Portland City Hall (Room 102) at 389 Congress Street, and at Westbrook City Hall at 790 Main Street, Westbrook. Free transfer passes are issued to facilitate continuous travel on the Metro between points not served by one direct route. These transfers are valid only on the day of issue. There is no bus service on Sunday.

By Trolley

During the summer season, many of the towns in the Southern Beaches Area offer open-sided trolley services. Fares are usually around $1, and trolley stops are generally marked by signs, shelters or benches.

In York, trolleys link York Village, York Harbor, York Beach and Cape Neddick from June through Labor Day from 10 AM to 8 PM. A similar service is offered in Ogunquit and Wells along U.S. Highway 1, to the beaches and into Perkins Cove. In the Kennebunks, the Intown Trolley Company offers narrated sightseeing tours for $6 per day, which also allow you to shuttle from Dock Square to Kennebunk beach. You can pick up maps for these trolley services from the various chambers of commerce.

INSIDERS' TIP

For scheduled trips to the Portland International Jetport, call Mid-Coast Limo at (800) 937-2424. You'll get direct door-to-door service from the Bath-Brunswick area, and you won't have to worry about leaving your car at the airport. Reservations are required.

In Boothbay Harbor, two trolleys run through the downtown shopping area, to the Small Mall and out to the aquarium from Memorial Day to Labor Day. One is run by Captain Fish's, the other by The Rocktide. Each trolley is free, runs on a half-hour schedule and can be picked up at numerous locations. Some stops are marked with signs, and all are located on downtown walking-tour maps that are available at the chamber of commerce. Call the chamber at (207) 633-2353 for more information. The trolleys typically run from 9 AM to 5 PM.

The health of the Maine economy has always been tied to nature.

History

Maine is a frontier state. It has always been so. You won't find a history filled with cowboys, wagon trains and gunslingers here, but you will find a past populated by an independent people — pioneers and entrepreneurs who built towns and cities and founded businesses so they could live life the way they felt it should be lived. As we near the 21st century, people are moving to Maine from across the United States in search of "the good life," while others leave here to seek their fortunes.

The "good life" in Maine has not always been easy to come by. Economic prosperity has come and gone like the tides of the sea to which the state is so inexorably linked. From fur trading in the 1600s to shipbuilding, lumber, textiles and ice in the 1800s and paper and tourism in the 1900s, the industries that have helped shape the state of Maine have all been bound to its natural resources.

The Ice Age and Early Humans

Looking back through history, you'll find the key to Maine's geography and resources in the last ice age. About 15,000 years ago the glaciers that covered the state began to recede, leaving deep river valleys, sandy coastline, barren rock, lakes and offshore islands that had once been high points in the land.

About 3,500 years later, around 11,500 years ago, the first humans appeared in Maine. From archaeological digs in Oxford and Piscataquis counties (north and west of Portland), it has been determined that these people, called Paleo Indians, had encampments in Maine, hunted caribou and used flaked tools and weapons.

Five thousand years ago the Paleo Indians disappeared, to be replaced by the people of the Archaic period. At that time, pine forests had begun to supplant the less densely treed areas of willows and poplars, so the deer hunting was not as good. As a result, the people of the Archaic period looked more to the rivers and lakes for sustenance, fishing for salmon, shad and trout. These people also disappeared and were followed by the Red Paint People, so named because of the quantity of red ochre found in their sophisticated burial sites.

Some argue that these weren't a "people" but merely a burial cult. Regardless of whether they were a people or a cult, archaeological sites east of the Kennebec River indicate that they were seafaring Mainers who ate swordfish and traveled as far north as central Labrador and northern Newfoundland. It's estimated that the Red Paint People arrived in the area around 4,500 years ago.

By around 1800 B.C., the Red Paint People were gone, replaced by the Susquehanna culture that reached as far south as Pennsylvania. Known for their fine stone implements and sculpted stone bowls, the Susquehanna inhabitants were followed by the Ceramic Age, so called for the advent of clay pottery. In Maine, the most intriguing archaeological find from the Ceramic Age was made in 1956 at Naskeag Point in the town of Brooklin, located on a peninsula just south of Mount Desert Island. There, among the more than 30,000 items found was a small piece of silver eventually identified as a Norse coin from the reign of King Olav Kyrre (1066-1093).

So did the Vikings come as far south as Maine? No one knows, and the debate has raged on for decades.

The Vinland of the Norse sagas was discovered in 1961 in northern Newfoundland, but there is little evidence, other than the coin, that Vikings came to Maine. How then did the coin get here? It is argued that the coin could have been traded from village to village; in Europe, similar trade carried objects such as amber and ivory from northern Europe to the south of France.

The Europeans Arrive

Though forays had been made into Maine in the 1500s by the Spanish, French and English, serious exploration with an intent to colonize didn't begin until the turn of the century. The first decade of the 1600s saw a number of ventures by Europeans into the bays and rivers of Maine. As early as 1602 the Concord, commanded by Capt. Bartholomew Gosnold, sighted land at Cape Porpoise and explored the New England coast as far south as Martha's Vineyard. In 1603 Martin Pring sailed into Saco Bay and up the Saco River. He was followed in 1605 by explorer Sieur de Monts and his cartographer, Samuel de Champlain, who settled on an island in the St. Croix River and explored Mount Desert Island and the coast as far south as Cape Cod.

Among the early explorers, Capt. John Waymouth, who visited Monhegan Island and the mainland in 1605, is the most famous — or notorious. At the time of his departure for England, Waymouth, with the help of a crewman, kidnapped five Indians, four of whom were native and one who was visiting. The visiting Indian's name was Tisquantum, but you may know him as Squanto, later a friend and interpreter for the Pilgrims. Why would Waymouth do such a thing? He wanted to know what economic opportunities there were in Maine, and he believed that once the Indians could speak English, they would give him the information — and they did! Three of the Indians, including Squanto, stayed with Sir Ferdinando Gorges while in England, and the other two stayed with Sir John Popham. All

eventually returned to America, Squanto departing with Capt. John Smith in 1614.

The First Colony

In August 1607, more than a decade before the Mayflower landed at Plymouth, Massachusetts, the Gift of God, under the captaincy of George Popham, and the Mary and John, skippered by Raleigh Gilbert, sailed into the mouth of the Kennebec River. There, 120 sailors and settlers, all men, began a colony close to what is now Phippsburg. These men also began the history of shipbuilding in Maine.

Though more than half the colonists left in December 1607, those who stayed raised a fort and built the Virginia, a 30-ton pinnace that later carried supplies to the colony established at Jamestown, Virginia. Despite their accomplishments, the colonists did not stay in Maine. Leadership of the colony had passed to Gilbert on the death of Popham, and when Gilbert was called home on the death of his brother, the colonists departed with him.

Just the Beginning

The Popham Colony was just the beginning of colonization in Maine. Because of disputes between the French, the British and subgroups of the British (such as the London Corporation and the Plymouth Corporation) as to who had the right to Maine, settlement was not always straightforward. Title and ownership of large parcels of Southern Maine claimed by the British changed hands depending on who was held in favor in England.

INSIDERS' TIP

For more information on the history of Maine, pick up one or more of the following excellent books: *Maine: A Narrative History,* by Neil Rolde (1990, Harpswell Press); *River of Fortune: Where Maine Tides and Money Flowed,* by Bill Caldwell (1983, Guy Gannett Publishing Co.); *Maine: A History,* by Louise C. Hatch (1919, 1973, New Hampshire Publishing Co.); and *Coastal Maine: A Maritime History,* by Roger F. Duncan (1992, W.W. Norton & Co.).

Photo: Merry Farnum

This statue of Henry Wadsworth Longfellow sits in the heart of Portland.

French and British skirmishes continued along the north and northeastern boundaries of Maine well into the 1700s, until the secession of Canada by the Treaty of Paris in 1763. Still, people came.

In 1616, for instance, Richard Vines was sent by Sir Ferdinando Gorges to establish a site for a colony. Vines spent the winter of 1616-17 at the mouth of the Saco River in what is now Biddeford Pool. He returned in 1623 with John Oldham to found a colony. In 1630 they received title from the Plymouth Council to a tract of land on the south side of the river that included 4 miles of shore and extended 8 miles inland. On the north side of the river, Thomas Lewis and Richard Bonython received title to a similar-sized parcel of land — the area we know today as Camp Ellis in Saco.

In 1623, Christopher Levett received 6,000 acres from Sir Ferdinando near what is now Portland harbor. He settled 10 men at the site, but the colony soon disappeared. At about this time Sir Ferdinando also established the first chartered city in the New World at the site where there had been a small settlement called Agamenticus. The city, named Gorgeana, is known today as York. North along the coast, in Falmouth, George Cleeve settled on the Spurwink River in 1630.

In other parts of Maine, colonization was taking place in New Harbor, along the St.

George's River, at Sheepscot, in Waldo, on Damariscove Island (off Boothbay Harbor) and at Castine, which commanded a strategic location for access to the Penobscot River. Colonists were also heading up the Kennebec River, settling on the banks and islands as far inland as what is now Augusta.

Massachusetts Imposes Its Rule

Before the century was half over, the Puritans of Massachusetts Bay decided they needed to establish themselves as the authority over Maine. Why did they feel they had the right to do this? Well, the Puritan leaders interpreted their charter, which granted them territory up to 3 miles north of the Merrimack River, to mean 3 miles north of the source of the river rather than the mouth of the river. Thus, they felt entitled to territory as far north as New Found Lake, just west of Lake Winnipesaukee in New Hampshire, and then east in a straight line to Casco Bay, which incorporated all of what is today's York County, Maine. Interpreting the charter to the mouth of river would have allowed them territory only as far as the current Massachusetts/New Hampshire border at Newburyport, Massachusetts.

Beginning in Kittery on November 15, 1652,

court was convened, and the inhabitants of the town were summoned to attend and swear acknowledgment that they were subject to the government of Massachusetts. After four days of heated debate and threats from Massachusetts, 41 Kittery inhabitants signed papers acknowledging they were subject to the jurisdiction of Massachusetts and became the first chartered town in the Province of Maine. The court then moved on to Gorgeana, which became the second town in Maine, but under the new name of York. Onward up the coast the court moved, to Cape Porpoise, Kennebunk, Wells and Saco, establishing Massachusetts as the sovereign of Maine.

By 1677 Massachusetts had a clear title to the Province of Maine as far north as the Kennebec, but by 1691 there were only four surviving towns left — Wells, York, Appeldore and Kittery. The rest had been ravaged by both Indians and war with the French.

Maine Takes Shape

If the 1600s were a century of colonization and land-grant disputes, with France, England and various other entities rushing to stake a claim in the New World, the 1700s saw a mustering of arms by both the French and English to fight for the territory they had claimed. In addition, the Native Americans launched attacks against the European powers who had decimated their villages with disease and taken their land. Still, this was a century of growth for Maine.

From the ashes of the 1600s sprang a group of settlements determined to survive. Though war followed war, the population of Maine increased steadily through the 1700s, and towns were established along lines we recognize today. In part, the wars themselves helped provide fresh settlers; soldiers came to fight and decided to stay when they saw the opportunities the new land had to offer. In

some cases, towns were formed as the government set aside land for the veterans of the various wars. Buxton, Gorham, Bethel and Raymond are just a few of the towns formed this way. Other towns were formed by splitting up larger towns. The towns of Berwick and Eliot were split from Kittery, and from Berwick came South Berwick and North Berwick. Still other towns, such as Brunswick and Topsham, were formed in previously settled areas.

Roads were built, settlements founded, ferry routes established, and the tide of colonists moved from the coast up the rivers. Maine was taking shape, yet it would have to do more fighting — first for its independence from the British; second for its independence from Massachusetts — before it could take its place as the 23rd state of the Union.

The Colonists at War

King Phillip's War in 1675 marked the end of acute danger from Indians in southern New England, but it was just the beginning of the bloodiest century of Indian Wars in Maine. King Phillip's War, which claimed 260 whites and 3,000 Indians, was led by Metacom, called "King Phillip," the son of the Pilgrim's friend, Massassoit. This war ended in 1678 with the signing of a peace treaty at Casco, but attacks by other Indian groups continued. The most infamous was launched against York in 1692. It is referred to today as the Candlemas Massacre, though there were also major battles at Black Point in Scarborough and other sites throughout the state. To the northeast, the English fought against the French, who were allied with the Indians. For decades, war followed war, with little gained by either side. In 1713, as the result of the Treaty of Utrecht, which signaled the end of Queen Anne's War, the French lost Acadia. Then in 1745 the French were defeated at Louisbourg on Cape

INSIDERS' TIP

Did you know that Maine was admitted as a state as part of the Missouri Compromise? Secretary of State Henry Clay proposed as part of his plan that Maine be admitted as a state along with Missouri — Maine would be a free state and Missouri would be a slave state, thereby keeping the number of free and slave states equal.

Breton, Nova Scotia. The French agreed to accept the return of this fort from the British in exchange for Madras, India — an exchange that angered the English colonists who had been led by William Pepperrell of Kittery.

This wasn't the first move by the British that angered the colonists. Like their counterparts in Massachusetts, the colonists of Maine had begun to resent the high-handed sovereignty of the Crown.

The American Revolution

It's ironic that the wars fought by the British against the French and Indians to establish their claim to Maine resulted in the ultimate loss of this land. English settlers fighting a common foe obtained an identity separate from that of their homeland. Though Maine's colonists fought on the side of the British Crown, they fought for land they considered their own, quite separate from England — they were becoming Americans.

The Battle of Louisbourg was the worst of English misdemeanors as far as the colonists were concerned. There they had fought valiantly and successfully only to have their victory thrown away for a city on the other side of the world. For decades the colonists had been learning to fight for themselves, defending their settlements from the Indians, often at a high cost of lives and property. Thus, with the threat from France ended, the colonists began to feel they had little use for the British. They resented the high-handed manner in which the Crown commandeered all the best mastmaking trees in Maine — any trees with trunks 24 feet or larger in circumference were used for British vessels. The colonists also were concerned with the actions of Parliament, which they felt sought to usurp their liberties. Of particular concern was England's power of taxation. As part of Massachusetts, Maine was a leader in the revolutionary movement. When the first Massachusetts Provincial Congress was called at Salem in October 1774, the three existing counties of Maine — Cumberland, York and Lincoln — sent representatives. Other early revolutionary events that took place in Maine included a "tea party" in York, where 150 pounds of tea were seized by town meeting, and the taking of the ship Margaretta in Machias.

Of the war's early incidents, the burning of Falmouth, which we know today as Portland, ranks among the most famous. Captain Mowatt of the ship Canceau, a man who was captured on Munjoy Hill in May 1775 only to subsequently escape, returned to Falmouth to seek his revenge in October. With most of the men of the town off fighting elsewhere, the people of Falmouth could do little to defend themselves — Mowatt barraged India Street and the waterfront with more than 64 naval guns. When the firestorm ended, more than 130 buildings were destroyed, including the library, town hall and the Anglican St. Paul's church, but no one was killed.

Statehood and Prosperity

The next century in the settlement of Maine brought tremendous change. Maine had always had a wealth of natural resources (beaver fur, timber and fish), yet the monetary rewards had always been reserved for those who laid claim to the land — first the English, then Massachusetts. The 19th century saw the continuing growth of shipbuilding, textile mills and the short-lived but very profitable ice industry, all of which served to provide Maine with the greatest economic boom it has ever seen.

Since early colonization, politics had been central in the shaping of the state, and the 1800s were no different. There were those who favored remaining a part of Massachusetts and those who did not, depending on which situation they felt would be the most provident. Later there were arguments regarding the site of the state capitol. Some favored Portland, which was the largest city; others favored Augusta for its more central location; and still others favored Wiscassett, Hallowell and Bangor.

The political changes in Maine at the turn of the century were due in part to an enormous population growth. It is estimated that before 1770 Maine had a population of around 10,000; by 1820 there were nearly 300,000 people living in the state. Many of these new settlers were small landowners and favored power for the people; the wealthier landown-

Photo: Pauline Dimino

The Lobsterman statue in Portland pays tribute to the
area's relationship with the famous crustacean.

ers, some of whom owned entire counties, preferred an elitist society.

In the early 1800s there were two main political parties — the Jeffersonian Party (known as the Democrat-Republicans) and the Federalists, who supported James Madison and Alexander Hamilton. The Jeffersonians opposed major landowners and supported the rights of squatters, while the Federalists were more elitist. Interestingly, however, it was a group of Federalists who called the first meeting to discuss state separation. Held in September 1785, the meeting attracted 30 men, among them Stephen Longfellow, father to the famous poet, Henry Wadsworth Longfellow. The men accepted an invitation to attend a convention in Boston, where they tendered a list of local grievances that included the location of the Supreme Court and clerk's office in Boston, the pricing of lumber to the detriment of Maine, and a lack of representation for Maine towns with fewer than 150 residents.

From this start, the separatist movement was launched. Through the last years of the 18th century and into the second decade of the 19th century, debate raged between those who favored statehood and those who did not. For the most part, the Federalists favored remaining with Massachusetts, and the Democrat-Republicans favored a separate state.

The final separatist move was launched in Saco in 1816. Following a special town meeting where 220 voted for separation and only seven voted against, Massachusetts decreed that all towns in Maine would hold a vote on the first Monday in September. Tallying the votes from that Monday became a convoluted affair. When the votes had been counted, 11,927 were for separation and 10,539 were against it, but there were not enough votes for the necessary five-to-four majority. As a result, an intricate scheme of tallying votes by delegates was proposed — the end result was that 103 delegates favored separation with 84 delegates opposed. The five-to-four majority was reached, but this was not the end of the voting. A constitutional convention was held in Portland in 1819, and a final vote was taken. On March 15, 1820, Maine was admitted as the 23rd state.

Maine had only a few decades to enjoy statehood before plunging into war once again. Admitted to the Union as a "free state," Maine took part in the Civil War between North and South over the issue of slavery. Of all the men and regiments from Maine that took part, the most famous by far are Gen. Joshua L. Chamberlain and the 20th Maine.

Though Maine regiments took part in many noteworthy battles — Bull Run, Antietam and Appomattox to name a few — it was Gettysburg and the defense of Little Round Top for which the state is remembered. At that battle, Chamberlain and the 20th Maine held the far left of the Yankee line between Big Round Top and Little Round Top along Cemetery Ridge. A mile away, the Confederate troops were arrayed along Seminary Ridge. Brilliant regimental maneuvering by Chamberlain and a brave charge by his outnumbered men prevented the Confederates from outflanking the northern troops and changed the tide of the war.

Chamberlain and the 20th Maine are also remembered for their role at Appomattox Court House, where Confederate Gen. Robert E. Lee surrendered. At the time of surrender, two of Lee's flags of truce came into Chamberlain's lines, and Union Gen. Ulysses S. Grant gave

the man from Maine the honor of accepting the Confederate surrender.

Cities and Industry

Certain areas in Maine saw greater growth than others, and by the 1830s population centers were large enough to be chartered as cities. Portland began the trend in 1832 and was followed by Bangor (1834), Bath (1848) and Augusta (1849). South of Portland, Biddeford was chartered in 1855, Saco in 1867 and South Portland in 1895.

Cities usually grow where there is industry, and from industry develops infrastructure. Among the more famous industries that helped shape Maine were timber, shipbuilding, paper and the textile mills of Biddeford and Saco, Lewiston, Augusta and Waterville. As for infrastructure, there was the arrival of the railroads and the beginning of Central Maine Power Company (CMP).

Bath Iron Works

Bath Iron Works was founded on the banks of the Kennebec River in the late 1860s as the Bath Iron Foundry by a local boy turned war hero, Thomas Worcester Hyde. Within a few years of establishing his business, Hyde invented and patented the famous Hyde windlass, which became standard equipment for raising anchors on ships. He soon had 25 men on his payroll making brass and iron castings for the shipping industry. In 1884 Hyde incorporated Bath Iron Works (BIW) Ltd., with him and his wife as sole owners.

The company continued to grow, expanding to include the former Goss Marine Iron Works on the Kennebec and winning large military contracts. In December 1891, BIW launched its first Navy vessel — the beginning of a century-long relationship. By 1917, when the wife and heirs of Hyde's son, John, sold his stock in BIW, the shares were worth $3

INSIDERS' TIP

William Phips (1650-1695), born on the banks of the Kennebec near Woolwich, became the first knight born in America. King James II knighted Phips for finding close to a million dollars worth of treasure in the Bahamas.

million and close to 2,000 Mainers were employed at good wages.

A few years later, however, employment was down to a third of what it had been, and in October 1925, BIW was put up for public auction. Ultimately, BIW was saved by William S. Newell, who led the company to new heights, building glamorous yachts for the wealthy in the 1930s and powerful destroyers for the Navy in World War II. BIW was sold in 1995 to defense giant General Dynamics and has expanded to include an enormous dry dock on the Portland waterfront for the repair, modernization and overhaul of very big ships. It is currently engaged in a $200 million expansion. (For much more on BIW, see the Close-up in our Area Overviews chapter.)

Land, Lumber and Paper

By the time Maine became a state, there were still large portions of public land available — approximately 11 million acres in total. Within the next 15 years, the state sold 1 million of these acres for about 40 cents an acre. As the lumber trade continued to grow, so did land speculation. Bangor, located to the north on the Penobscot River so that it was nearest to the timber land, benefited greatly from the speculation. So many people rushed to the city seeking land that there were no hotel rooms available, and men rented out their beds during the day. Parcels of land would be sold several times in a day, beginning in cents and ending in dollars. Like all good things, the land speculating boom eventually ended, but its end in 1837 was just the beginning of the lumber boom that would sweep the state for half a century.

Bangor was ideally suited for the lumber industry. On the Penobscot, which leads to the sea, and south of the valuable pine forests with rivers to carry the logs to the sawmills, Bangor was geographically perfect. By 1850

an estimated 8,600 men and 6,700 oxen and horses were working in the lumber trade. During the boom years between 1832 and 1888, Bangor shipped more than 9 billion feet of lumber worldwide.

From lumber and the completion of the Bangor and Aroostook's railroad branch came the paper industry and the formation of the Great Northern Paper Company in 1899 in Millinocket. Within a year of its founding, 2,000 people had settled in the area. Until that time smaller paper mills such as the Rumford Falls Paper Company had been the norm. The Great Northern Paper Company was the first of the major paper industries that continue to operate to this day. It's an industry that employs thousands of Maine workers in the north woods and at mills in towns such as Westbrook, Rumford and Millinocket.

Textiles

Biddeford and Saco are unique among the cities and towns along the southernmost coast of Maine. Here, on islands in the Saco River that separates the two towns, you'll find acres of red brick mill buildings rising dramatically toward the sky. Today some of these buildings have been converted to condominiums and small businesses, and you'll even find the Biddeford-Saco Chamber of Commerce in one of them. Yet just 50 to 100 years ago, these mills housed booming industries employing thousands of farm girls and immigrants.

In 1825, the Boston-owned Saco Manufacturing Company built a cotton mill that was 210 feet long and seven stories high on Cutt's Island, which is today known as Factory Island. This building, made of wood, was big enough to hold 12,000 spindles and employ 500, but by 1829 the building had burned down and 700 people had left town. Within three years the remains of the mill had been sold to a group of 18 Boston men who formed the

INSIDERS' TIP

Those who know something about shipbuilding may know that Norway pines were considered the best trees for the masts of ships. What you may not know is that these trees were named not for the country, but for the town of Norway, Maine, which had a tremendous wealth of these grand white conifers.

Photo: Convention and Visitor's Bureau Greater Portland

Victoria Mansion is New England's foremost house museum of the Victorian era.

York Manufacturing Company and rebuilt the mill, this time with fire-resistant brick. By July 1832 the mill was turning out products and making a profit, and in less than a decade 200 men and 1,000 women and girls were employed in three mills, machine shops, a counting house and a dye house.

Like Bangor, which became a city because of timber, Saco and Biddeford became cities because of cotton. Between 1830 and 1860, Saco's population doubled and Biddeford's population quadrupled, and their importance lasted to the end of World War II. Then, in the 1950s, the textile industry throughout New England began to head south to warmer climates and cheaper labor. The grand brick buildings fell into disrepair until their rebirth as condos, boutiques and office space in the '80s.

Kennebec Ice

The 1800s saw the growth not only of industries that have lasted to this day, but also of others that were unique to a short period in history. One such industry was that of ice harvesting along the Kennebec River from 1860 to 1900.

Until 1860 most ice was harvested from the Hudson River in New York state. From there it was shipped down the East Coast, to Europe and as far away as India. That year, however, the ice crop failed on the Hudson, and James L. Cheeseman came to the Kennebec to harvest 30,000 tons of ice. Before the end of the decade, Cheeseman had sold out to another New York firm, the Knickerbocker Ice Company, and he used the profits to build a dozen ice houses along the Kennebec at Pittston. Each ice house was 700 feet long. Combined, they could store a total of 70,000 tons of ice. More out-of-state companies followed Cheeseman and Knickerbocker, and by the height of the ice rush there were as many as 60 ice companies along the Kennebec. These companies employed thousands of Mainers and new immigrants to build the ice houses, cut the ice, board the workers and make the sawdust that was used to insulate the "crop."

By 1886 the ice crop from the Kennebec topped the million-ton mark, and it stayed there for a decade. But the end came quickly. It was hastened by the monopolistic activities of a local Bath entrepreneur, Charles W. Morse, who bought up the smaller ice companies and merged with Knickerbocker. The ice industry ground to a halt with the advent of the electric refrigerator at the turn of the century.

20th-century Maine

Like the rest of the United States, Maine saw its young men fight and die in World War I, heard arguments rage over the question of Prohibition, watched many of its industries wither in the Depression, and enjoyed the resurgence of many of these same industries through the years during World War II. Following that war, many of its major textile and shoe mills moved South, and many of its young people headed to the South and West, seeking more profitable employment than they could find at home.

Still, Maine is holding its own. It has always suffered from de-population, whether from Indian wars in the 1600s and 1700s or from its lumbermen heading west. Yet it has always attracted new blood — people looking for a fresh start and people attracted by low population, smaller, friendlier cities, acres of forest and miles of beautiful coast.

Industry in 20th-century Maine is not unlike that of its earlier centuries, if somewhat reduced in volume. We still have shipbuilders and sailors, fishermen and lobstermen, paper mills, lumber and textiles. In addition, the 20th century brought a new industry to Maine — tourism.

Tourism

By the turn of the century, the word regarding Maine's beautiful Southern Coast and of Mount Desert Island to the northeast had begun to spread through the ranks of the wealthy from Boston to New York. These exclusive visitors came to enjoy the beauty and amusements to be found at resorts at York Harbor and Bar Harbor, but they were soon followed by throngs of common folk, anxious to share in the delights of Maine's coast. Among the foremost of the destinations sought by visitors, then as now, were York Beach, Ogunquit and Old Orchard Beach.

Casinos and dance halls, amusement parks and arcades, restaurants and grand hotels sprang up, seemingly overnight. Though many of these structures were lost to fire during the heyday between the 1880s and 1920s, new ones have been joined by hundreds of smaller places to stay and play. Today tourism is one of Maine's most important industries. In fact, so many tourists enter the state between June and August that a referendum to increase the width of the Maine Turnpike from two to three lanes on each side between York and Portland was passed in November 1997.

Influential Mainers

The years since World War II have seen not only a resurgent boom in tourism in Maine but also the rise of several political figures who have proven memorable on a national scale.

INSIDERS' TIP

Maine shipbuilding has been famous worldwide for centuries. Some of the most memorable ships launched from the state include the largest four-masted ship, the *Bath*; the first five-masted ship, the *Governor Ames*, built in Waldoboro; the first six-masted ship, the *George W. Wells*, built in Camden; the first seagoing barge ordered by the Pennsylvania Railroad; J.P. Morgan's famous yacht, the *Corsair*; the first and only ramming ship ordered by the Navy, the USS *Katahdin*; and the racing yacht *Ranger*, which won the America's Cup in the 1930s.

Two of the most famous personalities to emerge from Maine in the postwar era were Margaret Chase Smith and Edmund S. Muskie.

Margaret Chase Smith, a Republican, was the first woman elected to Congress. In 1948 she ran for the Senate against three men and won with more votes than her three opponents combined. In 1950 she delivered her "Declaration of Conscience" speech that helped reverse the tide of the Communist witch-hunt activities of Sen. Joseph McCarthy. Smith was also the first woman to make a serious bid for the presidency. In 1964 she ran in Republican primaries in New Hampshire, Illinois and Oregon, but lost the nomination to Barry Goldwater. She died in 1995.

Edmund S. Muskie died in 1996 at age 81. He is famous as one of only five Democrats elected governor from the Civil War to 1954, and for running for the vice presidential nomination on a ticket with Hubert Humphrey in 1972. (George McGovern of South Dakota eventually won the nomination.) As governor (Muskie was elected in 1955, but resigned in 1958 to take a U.S. Senate seat), Muskie established the Department of Economic Development, obtained the classification of Maine rivers and actively promoted clean air and clean water. He was also instrumental in the imposition of four-year terms for governors. Muskie was Secretary of State under President Carter during the Iran hostage crisis.

Other notable Maine personalities include James B. Longley and Angus King. In 1974, Longley made history as the first Independent to be elected governor. Today, King, the second elected Independent governor, holds the state's highest office.

You may also recognize the names of George Mitchell and William Cohen. A former Senate majority leader, Mitchell has been making news since the start of President Clinton's second term in 1997, when he was sent to Ireland to help negotiate peace. Cohen is presently Secretary of Defense.

Preserving Maine's Wealth

The health of the Maine economy has always been tied to nature. As the 20th century draws to a close, Mainers realize they must take action to preserve their wealth for the future. Oil spills, over-fishing and over-harvesting of lumber are some of the issues faced by Maine today.

In late September 1996, Casco Bay was polluted by thousands of gallons oil that poured into the bay when the tanker Julie N. hit one of the pilings of the since-dismantled Million Dollar Bridge. (The Casco Bay Bridge replaced it in August 1997.) The spill was cleaned up quickly, but the dangers such ac-

Photo: Giselle A. Auger

War monuments can be found in public squares and parks in most towns and cities in Maine. This Civil War monument is in York Village.

cidents pose to the fish and natural beauty of Maine were brought dramatically to the fore.

Within two weeks of the oil spill, Maine suffered another natural disaster. Close to 20 inches of rain fell within 48 hours in the Greater Portland and Old Orchard Beach areas. The resulting floods wiped out large sections of the Maine Turnpike, U.S. Highway 1 and dozens of smaller roads as tiny, usually unnoticed streams swelled, undermining the gravel and subsoil supporting the thoroughfares. Portland, surrounded by river, ocean and bay, nearly became an island as access roads disintegrated. The morning after the flooding, 18-wheelers lined the Maine Turnpike from Exit 6 (Scarborough), where the road had collapsed,

INSIDERS' TIP

Did you know that Abraham Lincoln's first vice president came from Maine? His name was Hannibal Hamlin, and he lived on Paris Hill in South Paris. The house he lived in is privately owned today, but it's worth a peek if you're in the area to check out the commanding views across the hills and plains of Oxford County to the White Mountains. You'll find South Paris west on Maine Highway 26, about an hour from Portland. To get to Route 26, take Washington Avenue from Portland or get off at Exit 11 of the Maine Turnpike at Gray/New Gloucester.

to the New Hampshire border. Out of the aftermath arose one good point — the remaining oil that had lined the banks of the Spurwink River and parts of Casco Bay was gone, effectively flushed out to sea by the flood.

More recently, in the elections of November 1997, voters rejected the so-called "Compact for Maine Forests." The compact, which was supported by Governor King and the paper companies, was developed as an alternative to another conservation measure brought forward by the Green Party, led by Jonathan Carter.

In the elections of 1996, voters were asked to choose from three options regarding policies for managing Maine's north woods. The first was brought forward by the Green Party, the second was the Compact for Maine Forests, and the third option argued that the north woods be left as they were. The option that was chosen at this election would then be brought to voters for confirmation in November 1997. The compact won a thin victory in 1996, but in 1997, when voters were asked to support the compact, they did not. Why? Because many voters — those who had supported the Green Party's measure in 1996, as well as others — felt the compact wasn't sufficient to preserve the natural resources of the north woods. If voted in, they felt, no new or stronger measures would be accepted for decades.

As we enter the last year of the 1990s, Maine wrestles with the issue of overfishing. Large portions of fishing grounds to the south, along the coast of Massachusetts and Rhode Island, have been closed, and Maine now has to consider which areas it, too, should close to ensure the future of cod fishing in the state. Also at issue is the pollution of inland rivers and lakes with mercury, the result of dioxins rained on Maine from industries in states to the west.

Yet Maine remains a beautiful state filled with people who fish its waters and harvest its timbers, writers and artists and small business people. It is a state with an independent nature and a strength and will of iron. There is little doubt, as we enter the 21st century, that the current batch of issues will be dealt with as all previous obstacles to life in Maine have been dealt with — they will be overcome. The state, whose essence is embodied by its symbol of a tall, singular white pine, will endure and prosper.

Some travelers are a bit timid about staying in another person's home, but you can make your reservations at any one of these establishments with confidence.

Bed & Breakfasts and Inns

The smell of fresh-baked muffins wafting upstairs, the sound of the surf breaking outside your window, the buffed shine of antiques that have been in a family for generations, conversations with newly made friends around a crackling fire — these are the sensations and experiences offered by many of our bed and breakfasts and inns.

These places tend to be less formal and more friendly than larger hotels, although some of our inns have as many as 35 rooms. Often you'll find family members in the kitchen, family pouring the coffee, family doing the laundry and making up beds. The food is home-cooked and so are the stories your hosts will be happy to share with you about the house or inn you're visiting.

We like to think of such accommodations as miniature museums of real Maine — they show our history, our heritage, our family tree, so we've included plenty for you to choose from. You'll find sea captain's houses, turn-of-the-century inns, old railroad stops and island inns — some with original furnishings and family mementos intact. Some travelers are a bit timid about staying in another person's home, but you can make your reservations at any one of these establishments with confidence. We've checked them all out for you, and we liked what we saw.

Another great thing about bed and breakfasts is that they tend to be less expensive than hotels, and (obviously) breakfast is included in the room rate — that includes everything from Maine blueberry pancakes and crab quiche to piping hot coffee and fresh fruit. Some inns also have complimentary breakfasts; where applicable, we've included

that information in our listings. As with just about everything in Vacationland (the motto on our license plates), you'll almost always pay more during peak season. For some bed and breakfasts and inns, peak season runs from mid-June, when things begin to heat up, all the way until the end of October, when the leaves have changed colors and dropped off the trees.

Pricing Code

Our price chart reflects the cost of overnight accommodations for two people and gives an indication of what you should expect to pay during peak season. Bed and Breakfasts almost always offer a range of rates as rooms tend to differ considerably in size and facilities (whether they have private bathrooms, for instance). Inns sometimes have less expensive rooms (under the eaves, for instance) and/or more expensive rooms (with a view of the ocean, perhaps). When there is an extra charge for a third person to stay in the room with you, we've pointed that out. Here's how we break it down:

$	$80 and lower
$$	$81 to $120
$$$	$121 to $160
$$$$	$161 and higher

We've organized the information in this chapter using our four main geographic headers and combined the write-ups for inns with those for bed and breakfasts, listing them from south to north. As you read through, there are a couple of guidelines you should note.

You should assume an establishment is entirely nonsmoking, unless we say smoking rooms are available. If pets are allowed, we'll point that out, and children are welcome unless we say otherwise. Many bed and breakfasts offer a choice of rooms with or without private baths. We'll let you know when there's a choice (shared baths are typically less expensive). If there's no mention of bathroom set-ups, assume the establishment offers private baths. Also, you can count on a place being open year round unless we give you the dates when it opens and closes. Have fun!

Southern Beaches Area

Enchanted Nights Bed & Breakfast
$ • 29 Wentworth St. (Maine Hwy. 103),
Kittery • (207) 439-1489

You won't be able to resist the whimsical charm of this Princess Anne-style Gothic Victorian. The exterior, painted in cheerful, bright colors, and the interior, decorated in colorful country-French and Victorian style, welcome you. A symphony of lace and flowers, gilded frames and rich colors fills the house along with comfortable quilts and cushions. Each room has been lovingly decorated to make guests feel pampered and (if so inclined) romantic!

You can choose from seven rooms, some with large whirlpool baths. One of the most popular choices is the Turret Room. Though small, this exquisite room has a 13-foot pointed ceiling, French wrought-iron bed, a settee and a bathroom, which is divided from the turret by lace curtains. Another popular choice is the Cottage Room, which features a private entrance and two rooms with a country-French, hand carved oak double bed and a wrought-iron double bed with tub and shower. In the Victorian and the Princess rooms you'll find claw-foot tubs where you can relax in your bath amid the elegant furnishings of your room.

Enchanted Nights is open year round and accepts pets, with restrictions; call for more details. Breakfast is served in the ornate morning rooms and consists of tasty cuisine with a vegetarian-bent, served on antique floral china. If you opt to eat elsewhere, there is a $12 reduction in room price.

Candleshop Inn
$ • 44 Freeman St.,
York Beach • (207) 363-4087

Parents with children younger than 12 will want to check out this inn. It not only accepts them, it welcomes them! Rather than being stuck in an ordinary motel, you'll be able to enjoy the old-fashioned charm of lavender and old lace as well as wonderful ocean views at this Victorian guest house. Children younger than 12 are charged $5 per night if they stay in the same room as their parents. There is no charge for infants, and the inn carries cribs and other baby paraphernalia to make your stay more enjoyable. In fact, they'll even arrange babysitting for you so you can go out for a dinner without worrying about what to do with the children.

Though the inn is definitely "child-friendly," people without kids will enjoy it too. Owners Stan and Genie Jennings say many people feel like they've been visiting with friends or relatives within a few minutes of arriving, and people return year after year for summer reunions. The Candleshop Inn has 10 guest rooms. There are no rooms with private baths. It's open from the end of June to early September.

Cape Neddick House
$$, no credit cards • 1300 U.S. Hwy. 1,
Cape Neddick • (207) 363-4499

Perhaps you've dreamed of having an aunt and uncle living in a wonderful village near the sea in Maine. Or maybe you've just dreamed about getting away from it all, returning to the way life used to be in the country. Whichever or whatever your dream, you're sure to feel your dream's come true at the Cape Neddick House. This Victorian farmhouse, built in 1885, has connected outbuildings and a slate roof and has been in the Goodwin family since its construc-

INSIDERS' TIP

Bed & breakfasts and inns are subject to Maine's 7 percent Lodging Tax.

tion. Today, Dianne and John Goodwin invite you to share the beauty of their home and grounds, just a mile from the renowned coast and beaches of Maine.

Five bedrooms, each appealingly unique and filled with antiques, wait for you. Named for New England states, you can choose from the Vermont room, with a country atmosphere and oak bedstead; the New Hampshire room, which overlooks 10 acres of woodlands; or the spacious Maine room, with lovely watercolor wallpaper and two double beds. Bird lovers will get a kick out of the Connecticut room, which features birdcages, birdhouses and a wallpaper border of songbirds. If you're on a romantic weekend or simply want to treat yourself to gracious Victorian elegance, ask for the Massachusetts-Rhode Island suite. Here you'll find a high-backed bed, marble-topped toilet, a working fireplace and an adjacent sitting room. All rooms have private baths.

Breakfasts at the Cape Neddick House are a joy. Fill up on fresh fruit, cinnamon popovers with wild raspberry jam, blueberry cheese torte, strawberry scones and ham and apple biscuits, garnished with fresh flowers and absolutely delicious! Depending on when you visit, you may also enjoy spending time with the Goodwins on the deck or sitting before a roaring fire in the living room. The Cape Neddick House welcomes children aged 6 and older. Specialties of the house include a six-course, woodstove-cooked dinner, perfect for couples or entertaining corporate clients. The inn also offers cooking classes. Call for more information on these specialties.

York Harbor Inn
$$$ • U.S. Hwy. 1A, York Harbor
• (207) 363-5119, (800) 343-3869

A fascinating history lies at the core of the York Harbor Inn, giving it a truly unique character. The oldest part of the inn dates to around 1637, making it one of the oldest structures in Maine. Known as the Loft Room and located at the center of the inn, where it is used as a guest lounge, this room was once a

sail loft on the Isles of Shoals. In the early 1800s the residents of the Isles, 10 miles off the coast, dismantled their homes and transported them to Stage Neck at the mouth of the harbor. It was probably at that time that the sail loft was transported to York Harbor.

In the late 1800s, the inn was known as the Hillcroft Inn, and it served the needs of visitors who flocked to Southern Maine, making the area a rival to Bar Harbor to the north and Newport, Rhode Island. At the turn of the century, the inn launched the Reading Room social club, which met here from 1897 to 1910. The club is still in existence today.

More recently, the inn has seen the completion of a large renovation project. All 33 rooms have been redecorated or totally renovated. Paint, wallpaper and window treatments have been updated, and new furniture has been purchased, including 18 lovely four-poster beds. The York Harbor Inn features a choice of dining experiences, from its renowned dining room, to the Cellar Pub Grill, which offers a casual menu. Off-season, you'll need to call ahead to verify days and hours of dinner service. Your room rate at the inn includes a continental breakfast featuring homemade pastries and muffins, breads, bagels and the usual accompaniments. Complimentary Poland Spring Water and soft drinks are included.

Hartwell House
$$$$ • 118 Shore Rd., Ogunquit
• (207) 646-7210

In a town filled with Victorian architecture, the Hartwell House stands out with its somewhat Mediterranean facade. Painted white, with a series of arched windows along its front, and topped by low white balconies, it's a graceful building overlooking verdant lawns and gardens. Inside you'll find a warm, elegant country atmosphere with wide, knotty pine floorboards and distinctive period furnishings. Each of the inn's 16 rooms is carefully decorated with antiques and offers gleaming floors, attractive paints and wallpapers and lovely bed coverings. Some also feature canopied four-poster beds, and most rooms include French doors leading to terraces or private balconies. Nine of the inn's rooms are in the main house; four rooms and three suites are in a second building across the street.

A gourmet breakfast and afternoon tea are served daily, and in the off-season the inn offers "Inn-House" dining weekend packages where you receive one night's accommodation, breakfast, tea and a seven-course dinner for two. These packages are exceedingly popular and sell out up to six months in advance, so act quickly. Other getaway packages are offered throughout the year. An added bonus for guests who like to golf: The inn holds a membership for guests at the private Cape Neddick Country Club. Children ages 10 and older are welcome at the Hartwell House. Those between 10 and 14 must share a room with an adult.

www.insiders.com

See this and many other **Insiders' Guide** destinations online.

Visit us today!

schemes are featured: One room has a burgundy, green and gold theme; another is done in blue, yellow and white; two others have a violet and ivy theme and a floral theme. Bed styles range from wrought-iron to four-posters. We must warn you, however, that the rooms are redecorated yearly so you can't really know what to expect until you get there! If you need to sleep three to a room, ask for the Anna-Marie or the Victoria-Ruth rooms, which have both a queen and a twin bed.

Celebrating a special occasion? Ask for the Judy-Lind. It's on the ground floor, overlooks the Atlantic at one end of the large, wraparound porch and has its own private entrance. Children aged 15 and older are welcome at Rockmere Lodge.

Rockmere Lodge
$$$ • 40 Stearns Rd., Ogunquit
• (207) 646-2985

Not only is this lodge located in the delightful town of Ogunquit, it also sits on the Marginal Way — which means commanding views of the Atlantic and shops and restaurants within a stone's throw in Perkins Cove and the town center. White wicker furniture invites rest on the expansive porch, but you might prefer gazing at the view from the third-floor observation room. For those who like to be outside but have an aversion to bugs, there's a lovely screened gazebo in the garden.

Rockmere Lodge was built in 1899 as the warm-weather getaway for the Stearns family, and it is constructed in the traditional shingle style of such early summer homes. Lovely flower gardens with fountains and statuary will enchant you, and you'll have a choice of eight beautifully appointed rooms. Various color

The Nellie Littlefield House
$$$$ • 9 Shore Rd., Ogunquit
• (207) 646-1692

The Nellie Littlefield House stands out as one of the beautiful properties at the upper portion of Shore Road, where it intersects with Route 1. A white picket fence, hanging sign and the charming elegance of its curving tower make it an attractive component of this lovely town. Built in 1889 by J.H. Littlefield for his wife, Nellie, it has been a welcome destination for travelers since its construction.

Eight rooms are available, all of which are tastefully decorated, some with antiques and period furniture. Four rooms have private decks and ocean views. All rooms feature queen-size beds. Amenities include free in-room movies and an extensive breakfast, which includes one hot dish each day (such as eggs or pancakes), juice, cereal, muffins and breads. The Nellie Littlefield House does not offer accommodations for children.

INSIDERS' TIP

Unless you know exactly which room you want to stay in, arrive at your destination early, around noon, and see whether you can choose among the different rooms.

Relax and enjoy Maine's serenity from an Adirondack chair.

Sundial Inn
$$$ • 211 Beach St., Kennebunkport
• (207) 967-3850

The Sundial Inn has greeted guests since 1891. This gay yellow inn has an expansive porch overlooking Kennebunk Beach. Owners Larry and Pat Kenny have meticulously decorated the interior in the Victorian style. You'll love the antique charm and ambiance of rooms featuring Victorian furnishings and designer linens. Completely smoke-free, all 34 rooms at the Sundial have private baths, and your stay includes a hearty continental breakfast in the dining room overlooking the sea.

About 1.5 miles from Dock Square in Kennebunkport, the Sundial Inn is perfectly located for a peaceful seaside vacation away from the hustle and bustle, but it's still close enough that you can enjoy the amenities of town when you feel so inclined. In addition to providing the perfect weekend getaway location, the Sundial offers off-season packages. It is open year-round.

The Kennebunk Inn
$$ • 45 Main St. (U.S. Hwy. 1),
Kennebunk • (207) 985-3351

This is the kind of inn you'll want to explore, with interesting hallways and staircases leading to who knows where. With maroon carpets and some rooms with exposed beams, it isn't hard to imagine travelers stopping to rest here in the early 1800s. The front part of the inn was built in 1799, and the barn was added in the early 1800s. Later, a middle section was constructed to connect the two, resulting in the configuration John and Kristen Martin own and operate today.

Amenities in the 28 rooms and suites vary. Rooms in the front section of the inn, overlooking Main Street, have exposed beams and a rustic feel. These rooms do not have telephones or televisions, but there's an adjacent porch that provides a great vantage point for watching parades or merely relaxing as the world goes by. Other rooms have painted furniture or high-posted dark furniture, with wallpapers ranging from a cheerful yellow floral to blue floral to darker, more old-fashioned looking florals. All rooms are individually decorated, and all are charming. Two-room suites are available for business travelers or families who need a bit more space. Families will enjoy a two-bedroom suite that features a separate bathroom with a claw-foot tub.

Continental breakfast is included in the room

rate and served in the dining room. You may also want to try dinner at the inn — the menu changes every two or three weeks. For those who want to have a drink before dinner, try the inn's pub, which opens at 4 PM daily.

The Kennebunkport Inn
$$$ • Dock Sq., Kennebunkport
• (207) 967-2621

Set in the heart of picturesque Dock Square, the Kennebunkport Inn has everything you could wish for — old world charm and modern comfort. Thirty-four rooms are available, featuring period furnishings and private baths. Comprised of an elegant 19th-century mansion and the attached River House, which dates from the 1930s, the inn has a small but charming hexagonal-shaped swimming pool, a restaurant where you can enjoy fine dining and a piano-bar pub where you can relax with a drink before dinner. Rooms are elegantly appointed with warm, floral wallpaper and gleaming furniture.

The Kennebunkport Inn's dining room operates from mid-May through late October. Breakfast is not included in your room rate. The inn welcomes children; cost for more than two occupants per room is $12 per extra person.

The White Barn Inn
$$$$ • Beach St. (Maine Hwy. 35), Kennebunkport • (207) 967-2321

In the 1800s, weary travelers looked forward to a warm welcome at the old Boothbay boarding house, where they knew they would receive comfortable lodging and excellent meals. Today the White Barn Inn continues this tradition, though on a much more luxurious scale. The guest rooms and suites have been meticulously decorated in delicate and dramatic floral wallpapers and fabrics, with four-poster beds and other period furnishings. "Fireplace pool house" rooms feature whirlpools and fireplaces, while the Carriage House junior suites provide fireplaces, whirlpools and king-size, four-poster beds.

Whichever type of accommodation you choose, you're sure to enjoy the subtle touches of the inn — the abundance of fresh flowers, the thick robes and elegant toiletries and having your bed turned down in the evening. There's also a heated outdoor pool. The White Barn Inn is a perfect place for a romantic getaway, honeymoon or special occasion, but you can make any weekend extra special with a visit. The inn offers a variety of off-season getaway packages that include accommodations, dinner and breakfast. Those who opt to stay elsewhere should consider having dinner at the White Barn Inn. Its restaurant is one of the few five-star establishments in all of New England. Though on the expensive side, it will leave you with a memory to savor.

Old Orchard Beach Area

Bowers Mansion Inn
$, no credit cards • 408 Main St., Saco
• (207) 284-1734

Join Cherie and James Pace in their marvelous Victorian bed and breakfast inn on Saco's Main Street. Built around 1885 by town Mayor Roscoe Bowers, the inn is constructed in the Stick Gothic style, which combines English Gothic and Swiss Chalet styles for a unique look. The exterior is painted in a rose and white color scheme, and the interior has been lovingly restored to turn-of-the-century elegance.

Three rooms and a suite are available at the Bowers Mansion Inn. Named for previous occupants of the house, you'll find the George R. Love Suite, with a king-size bed, private bath and adjoining sitting room with TV and fireplace; the Mary Sawyer Room, with twin beds and a private bath with claw-foot tub; and the Alyse Mackena and Roscoe Bower rooms. The Alyse Mackena room has twin poster beds and a shared bath; the Roscoe Bower has a queen-size canopy bed and private bath.

Children aged 12 and older are welcome at the inn. Breakfast is served in the Sun Room overlooking the gardens and always consists of three courses. Special dietary needs can be accommodated with advance notice.

Cristina's Bed & Breakfast
$ • 36 Main Ave., Camp Ellis, Saco
• (207) 282-7483

This charming purple trimmed bed and breakfast overlooks Camp Ellis beach. When we visited there was a gray cat snoozing on the wicker porch furniture and another skulking about the flower beds. The garden is lovely — you can see the sand dunes and hear the sea as it rushes against the beach at high tide as you swing in a large string hammock or have lunch at the picnic table. The house celebrated its 100th birthday in 1998 and is one of the oldest in Camp Ellis. A tri-gabled, gothic Victorian farmhouse, Cristina's features three double rooms and one single. Two of the double rooms and the single share a bath while the third double has a private bath.

Your stay at Cristina's includes a healthy continental breakfast of granola, fresh fruit salad, muffins with fresh Maine blueberries, fresh squeezed orange juice and a selection of coffees and teas. In addition, Cristina's features a private outdoor hot and cold shower where guests can slough off the salt and sand after a day at the beach. Cristina's is open year-round.

Crown 'N' Anchor Inn
$$ • 121 North St., Saco
• (207) 282-3829

Timeless elegance awaits at this inn, located in the Thatcher-Goodale House, which is listed on the National Register of Historic Places in the State of Maine. Built in 1827-28 by George Thatcher Jr., this marvelous Greek Revival bed and breakfast features six individually decorated rooms on two floors with private facilities and a bountiful country breakfast. Antique lovers will adore the double parlors with twin mirrors and the period furnishings found throughout.

You'll want to bring your camera for a photo of the exterior of the building, which has four stately columns, a number of chimneys and green shutters to set off its crisp white paint. The inn sits on a slight diagonal to the road, and you might pass it without recognizing it, so look carefully. Often you

can spot it by the white tent set up on the grounds for wedding receptions. The inn does not accept children younger than 12. Breakfast is included in the room rate.

The Atlantic Birches Inn
$ • 20 Portland Ave. (Maine Hwy. 98),
Old Orchard Beach • (207) 934-5295

Couples and families will enjoy the charm of this turn-of-the-century Victorian, with its wraparound porch and rooms that have been lovingly decorated. You can choose a room with pale yellow and green decor, one with pale lavender walls and a brass bed or one with a semicircle of windows and a four-poster bed. There are many other options to choose from among the inn's 10 rooms, which are located in the main house and the cottage guest house next door.

In addition to the large continental breakfast served in the formal dining room, you'll enjoy amenities such as an in-ground pool, badminton and croquet on the lawn. Old Orchard Beach pier and the attractions near it are only a five-minute stroll away.

The Webfoot Inn
$ • 2 Temple Ave., Ocean Park,
Old Orchard Beach • (207) 934-5328

For all of you who would love to just get away from it all with no telephones and no television, the Webfoot is your place. This large seaside inn sits right on the beach in the peaceful community of Ocean Park. There are rocking chairs on the porch, picnic tables by the dunes and a large, welcoming common room where guests often gather for impromptu parties.

Jay and Ron Farris have run the inn since the late 1970s, but it was an inn long before that. Word has it that it was built in the 1890s by a man from Oregon; he is said to have named it Webfoot because that's a nickname for people from his home state. In any case, the cottage became an inn at the turn of the century and has remained one ever since. You can choose from 23 rooms — some have private baths, some have only private toilets and share a bath or shower. All oceanfront rooms have private baths.

Continental breakfast is included in the room rate, but it offers more than just toast and coffee. Muffins and fruit are always on the menu, and sometimes you'll find a homemade bread pudding or other delicious treat. Children are welcome at the Webfoot.

Greater Portland Area

The Breakers
$$, no credit cards • 2 Bay View Ave., Higgins Beach, Scarborough
• (207) 883-4820

You can't get much closer to the sea than this. Located in the quiet seaside community of Higgins Beach, The Breakers features 15 rooms in a white house on the beach. No houses stand between the inn and the beach, but you do have to cross the road and go down a few steps to stick your toes in the sand.

All rooms have private bath facilities, some with showers only and others with tub and shower. In spring and fall the inn is run as a bed and breakfast. During summer, however, room rates include breakfast and dinner. You'll enjoy fresh food prepared from scratch and a dinner menu that changes daily. When we visited, lemon meringue pies were in the making, and they looked wonderful.

Operated by Rodney Laughton, The Breakers has been run by the Laughton family since 1956. Children are accepted at the inn. Rodney asks that you call to discuss the number of children and their ages — that will help determine the rate. The Breakers is open from April through October. It is a non-smoking facility.

The Holiday House Inn & Motel
$$ • 106 E. Grand Ave., Scarborough
• (207) 883-4417

You can't beat the view from this inn — most of the rooms overlook the sea. Owned by the Boutet family since 1964, it's no wonder the Holiday House is a well-loved vacation destination for generations of families who return year after year.

Each of the eight rooms in the inn is named for a different holiday, and each has its own charm. Our favorite, the Easter Room, has a curving window overlooking the sea. All guests enjoy the use of a parlor area and receive continental breakfast in the dining room. The inn was renovated for the 1996 season. It does not accommodate children, though kids are very welcome in the adjacent motel (see our Hotels and Motels chapter). The Holiday House Inn & Motel is open from mid-May to mid-October.

The Higgins Beach Inn
$, no credit cards • 34 Ocean Ave., Higgins Beach, Scarborough
• (207) 883-6684

You'll feel as if you've stepped back in time as you enter the Higgins Beach Inn. Built in 1897 in Colonial Revival style, the white, three-story inn is less than a five-minute walk to the sandy curve of Higgins Beach. The inn was originally the home of Mr. and Mrs. Edward Samuel Higgins. Not long after moving into the house, they added 24 rooms, a kitchen and an office, and it became the Higgins Inn.

Today the inn is operated by Bob Westburg and Diane Garofalo, but it retains the character of yesteryear. When you stay at the Higgins Beach Inn, you give yourself permission to relax. Oriental-style carpets greet you in the entrance lobby area, where an enormous old cash register sits on the counter and old-time signs hang on the wall behind. Rooms glow with the warmth of old wood and old-fashioned summer charm, and you won't find televisions or telephones in them.

A light, sunny dining room with French doors and cozy sitting rooms branch off from the hall. Breakfast is served from 7:30 to 11 AM in the dining room or on the front porch. Of the Higgins Beach Inn's 24 rooms, 14 have private baths and 10 have shared baths. It is open from the middle of May to the middle of October.

INSIDERS' TIP

If you want to make dinner reservations for a particular night you'll be in town, many bed and breakfast owners will be happy to do the dialing for you before your arrival.

Andrews Lodging Bed & Breakfast
$$-$$$ • 417 Auburn St., Portland
• (207) 797-9157

A traditional bed and breakfast since 1992, this 250-year-old home has been extensively modernized for year-round comfort. You'll find antique furniture, including bowl and pitcher sets, along with wonderful old family photographs and historical postcards and pictures of Portland in each room.

Guests can choose from rooms with either a queen-size bed or two twin beds (which come with snuggly down comforters just waiting for you to dive under) and shared or private baths. All the bathrooms are modern with full tubs and showers. We recommend you check out the three-room suite, which has a queen-size bed, private sitting room, bath, Jacuzzi and skylights. It goes for $155 per night on a weekend during peak season.

Upstairs you'll enjoy the complete guest kitchen, sitting room with television and library with plenty of books to browse through. Downstairs is a solarium with board games, foosball and a water garden, and a formal living room where guests can tickle the ivories of an 1860s grand piano or, on cold days, cozy up to a crackling fire in the hearth.

Each morning, innkeepers Douglas and Elizabeth Andrews serve steaming coffee along with a full breakfast of sweet breads, egg and meat dishes and fresh fruit and juice. When you're done, take time to explore outside the inn, where you'll find a thriving apple orchard, all kinds of berry bushes, a perennial garden full of birds and trees, and a water garden complete with fish. In winter you can skate on the backyard ice rink, then come inside and sit by the warm fire. This bed and breakfast is set back in the charming outskirts of the city, but it's just a 10-minute drive to downtown Portland.

Inn on Carleton Bed and Breakfast
$$$ • 46 Carleton St., Portland
• (207) 775-1910, (800) 639-1779

On a quiet, tree-lined street in Portland's historic western promenade, this restored 1869 Victorian home makes for a pleasant haven after a full day spent exploring the city's shops and museums just a short walk away. Step through the arched double doors of the inn's entryway, and you'll find yourself in the front hall, where an elegant stairway climbs up to seven guest rooms, each furnished with antiques.

Four rooms have private baths, and almost all have marble-topped washstands. One has a shared bath and twin bed and goes for $65 a night. Also, there are two adjoining rooms that can be made into a suite. Guests can relax in a common parlor, and in the morning all will enjoy a breakfast with such treats as homemade muffins, cinnamon rolls, blueberry pancakes, eggs or waffles. The inn welcomes children ages 9 and older, although there is an additional charge of $15 a night for an extra person in the room. Pets are not welcome, but guests with allergies may want to know the inn does have its own felines, Tigger and Smokey. It is run by owners Sue and Phil Cox.

Quaker Tavern Farm B&B
$ • 377 Gray Rd. (Maine Hwy. 26),
Falmouth • (207) 797-5540

This Federal house was made into a tavern in the early 1820s by the Quaker family that owned it. Inside you'll notice the original tavern keeper's closet in the parlor and working fireplaces throughout the entire house. There are four guest rooms, each with a fireplace and either an antique, four-poster double bed (one room also has a trundle bed) or two vintage twin beds. Most have shared baths.

In the morning, you'll know you're off to a good start after eating a full "holistic" breakfast. A favorite is crustless broccoli quiche, with cut and prepared fresh fruit and a tray of assorted breads. Your hostess, the former president of the Falmouth Historical Society, is still working on researching the history of the house, but she'll be happy to share what she knows with you. Outside, there's plenty of room to roam on 13 private acres way out in the country. The house is off Maine 26, also known as Gray Road, and it doesn't have a sign out front, so watch the street numbers.

Chebeague Orchard Inn
$$ • RR1, Box 453,Chebeague Island
• (207) 846-9488

Part of the allure of staying at the

Chebeague Orchard Inn is the 15-minute mail boat ride that takes you to Chebeague Island where the old-fashioned bed and breakfast is located. We took the Chebeague Transportation boat, (207) 846-3700, from the landing on Cousins Island, which is just off Yarmouth. You could catch the Casco Bay Lines ferry, (207) 774-7871, from Portland, which takes about 70 minutes. Either way, you'll get a chance to chat with some of the people who live on the island and draw in a deep breath of salty air as you leave the mainland behind.

The bed and breakfast is about a mile away from the boat landing, and on arrival you'll be met by inn owners Vickie and Neil Taliento. The Greek Revival-style home is set on 3 acres of woods and orchards with a sprawling field of organically grown flowers and vegetables stretching down to the sea. Inside there are five bedrooms, each of which is named for a historic island family; the Talientos have also selected a memento from each historic family to grace the room named for them. The Hamilton Room, for example, is named for the family that settled the island, and a model ship built by a member of the family sits on a bedroom bureau.

Several rooms have water views, and all bring back memories of a simpler country life with homey quilts, fresh flowers (in season), painted wood floors and several claw-footed tubs. Families will enjoy the option of a two-room suite with a double bed in one room and two twin beds in an adjoining room. Downstairs is a spacious living room with an exposed-beam ceiling and a large brick hearth. Nearby is the breakfast room, where you'll be served a complimentary meal flavored with certified organic vegetables from the Taliento's garden. Afterward, rent a couple of bikes from the inn and take a scenic ride down quiet roads to some of the island's beaches. There's plenty of room to explore on the 4.5-mile-long island (see our Attractions chapter).

Captain Briggs House
$$ • 8 Maple Ave., Freeport
• (207) 865-1868, (800) 217-2477
From the moment we saw it, we loved this quaint, Federal house set back on a dead-end street just a short walk from L.L. Bean

and the surrounding outlet stores (see our Shopping chapter). The flavor is European-country, and inside you'll find original hardwood floors dating to when the house was built more than 140 years ago. Downstairs there's a cozy sitting room where you'll find plenty of books and games, a television and VCR, and there's a dining room where you'll enjoy a full breakfast complete with home-made breads and muffins, fresh fruit, a choice of hot and cold beverages and, frequently, pancakes or french toast.

Children ages 6 and older are welcome, and the six cheerful guest rooms come with a choice of beds in all sizes. Each room has white lace curtains to let in plenty of sunlight, and each has a private bath. Several rooms also have telephones. Outside is a well-groomed lawn with flower gardens and shade trees, and chairs are set out for you to soak it all in. If you're thinking this sounds an awful lot like a B&B known as the Bayberry Inn, this used to be it. Lee Frank, the owner, decided to change the name because so many guests wanted to know the history of the house. Well, in the 1880s it was owned by shipbuilder Captain Briggs, so there you have it.

Harraseeket Inn
$$$$ • 162 Main St., Freeport
• (207) 865-9377, (800) 342-6423
You'll enjoy the luxury of this sprawling 84-room inn in downtown Freeport just steps away from the town's many outlet stores and L.L. Bean (see our Shopping chapter). From the moment the door is opened and you step inside, you're surrounded by elegance and luxury. The spacious downstairs drawing room — where in the afternoon you may enjoy a complimentary fine tea of pastries, fruit and finger sandwiches — has a baby grand piano, a large stone hearth surrounded by mahogany paneling brought over from England and plenty of fine furnishings. The day we visited there was a crackling fire going, and cheerful little groups of guests had gathered to enjoy the warmth and fellowship.

Nearby is The Maine Dining Room, set with intimate tables and fine china. In the morning you will enjoy a full breakfast, which is included in the room rate. The Broad Arrow Tavern, with a pub-like atmosphere, is just outside (see more on these in our Restaurants chapter). In a new section of the inn, you'll find an indoor swimming pool surrounded by sky lights and floor-to-wall windows with views of the outside gardens.

There are 26 types of rooms to choose from, and each has a private bath (some with one- and two-person Jacuzzis) and many have fireplaces, poster beds and antique-style furnishings. Families can choose between adjoining rooms or rooms with pull-out couches, and several handicapped-accessible rooms with roll-in showers are also available. All furnishings are of the finest quality. If you want to save money and still enjoy all the amenities the inn has to offer, ask for the one guest room under the eaves — it's quite a bit less expensive. There is an additional charge of $20 for an extra person age-10 or older.

The inn is set on 5 acres near Casco Bay. It's actually two period buildings (from 1798 and 1850) and an addition completed in 1997. Owned by the Gray family, it has been operating as an inn since 1984 and has earned the reputation as one of the best places in the country (some have argued in the world) to stay and dine. One of our favorite features is the backyard garden with beautifully landscaped stone walls and millstones set in unsuspecting places.

Holbrook Inn Bed & Breakfast
$$ • 7 Holbrook St., Freeport
• (207) 865-6693, (888) 865-6693
This tall white 1870s Victorian with pale-green shutters has been added on to over the years, making a sprawling bed and breakfast with plenty of space for guests and owners Sue and Marc Trottier. Just a block from downtown shops, the inn is close enough to access Freeport's outlets and far enough off Main Street to offer a little seclusion. The inn features three recently renovated rooms with private bathrooms and a choice of rooms with fireplaces and a Jacuzzi. One room has vivid rose wallpaper and an antique poster bed. It adjoins a common sitting room with wing backed chairs and can be made into a three room suite with the bedroom on the other side. The cost for four people to rent all three rooms is $150 per night. Upstairs in what used to be the carriage house is the third guest room, with a lofted, beamed ceiling, pine furniture and plenty of privacy. Two rooms have television, and the inn has central air-conditioning. There is a charge of $20 for each additional child sharing a room with parents. In the morning your hosts will prepare a full, country breakfast of assorted dishes such as cinnamon french toast, blueberry coffee cake, egg dishes, yogurt, and hot and cold drinks.

Nicholson Inn
$$ • 25 Main St., Freeport
•(207) 865-6404
If you've come to shop at Freeport's famous outlets (see our Shopping chapter), this inn takes the cake for convenience. Separated from the town's bustling sidewalk by a white picket fence and flower garden, the quaint inn is smack in the middle of downtown. Take a break from shopping, and put your feet up on the front porch and watch the tourists stroll by for an afternoon of promising entertainment. If you want a break from all the hustle and bustle, there's a finely appointed living room where you can select a book or tune into the television. Across the rose-papered hallway is a grand, sunlit dinning room where you will be sure to wake up to a full breakfast of fresh fruit, omelets, toast, sausage, home-baked muffins and beverages. The Federal-period house with traditional black shutters has just three guest rooms, each with its own tiled bathroom. The furnishings are inviting. One room has rich blue wallpaper and white eyelet curtains fluttering in the windows. A white lace quilt covers the brass bed. Rooms are nicely appointed with antiques and are large, clean and uncluttered.

INSIDERS' TIP

If the bed and breakfast you call is booked, ask the owner to refer you to a place they'd recommend. Most B&B owners know each other well and would willingly select another well-run house for you to stay at.

The Kendall Tavern Bed & Breakfast
$$ • 213 Main St., Freeport
• (207) 865-1338, (800) 341-9572

The color of this sunny yellow house with the white front porch is what first attracted us to it, and what we found inside cheered us up even more: glass-domed plates piled with chewy, chocolate chip cookies, and melt-in-your-mouth brownies set out in the kitchen. In the morning, the dining room's several small tables host a full country breakfast with home-baked sweet breads. Down the hall are two sitting rooms, one with a television and VCR and an array of classic movies on video. The other parlor has a fireplace, piano and plenty of books and magazines to read through. Another flavorful accent: You'll find colorful candy bowls dotting the house.

The 1800s New England farmhouse first lodged guests unofficially, when travelers journeyed up the coast and stayed the night, bringing news from faraway places. Now guests come from equally distant locales, but they stay in charming guest rooms with private baths and enjoy full use of the indoor hot tub downstairs. Five rooms accommodate two people; two other rooms are larger. All have plush carpeting, poster beds and colorful quilts.

The bed and breakfast is set on 3½ acres on Kendall Corner, about a 10-minute walk from the downtown stores. Children ages 8 and older are welcome.

White Cedar Inn
$$ • 178 Main St., Freeport
• (207) 865-9099, (800) 853-1269

Innkeepers Carla and Phil Kerber will welcome you to their historic home, which once belonged to Arctic explorer Donald B. MacMillan. MacMillan was also the designer and captain of the schooner Bowdoin, which is now the official sailing vessel of the state of Maine. The Victorian inn has seven air-conditioned bedrooms — two are on the first floor, and one has its own outside entrance. All rooms have private baths and country furnishings, and four have two beds. Only one room has a television, and there are no phones in the rooms, but there is a portable phone that may be taken into any room.

Downstairs there is a comfortable living room with a television, reading materials, comfortable furniture and a computer outlet for guests' use. In the morning, you'll enjoy a hearty, home-cooked breakfast in the sun room, and in the afternoon, come in from a long day of shopping to an afternoon tea with baked goods and refreshments. The atmosphere is friendly and relaxed, and the inn is just a couple of minutes from Freeport's outlets and L.L. Bean. Children must be 12 or older to stay.

Brunswick, Bath and Boothbay Harbor Area

Brunswick B&B
$$ • 165 Park Row, Brunswick
• (207) 729-4914

This completely restored, 30-room 1800s Greek Revival home has eight spacious guest rooms with private baths (a few of which are in the hall adjacent to the rooms). You couldn't ask for more charm. Each room is graciously furnished with antique beds and sitting areas, and in the bathrooms you'll find terry-cloth bathrobes. Beautifully stitched handmade quilts, some of which were made by innkeeper Mercie Normand, adorn the walls throughout the inn.

Children older than 5 are welcome; on the third floor are two suites, each with a king-size bed and two twin beds and a sitting area. Another room has two twin beds, and others have a single queen, king or double bed. There is also a garden cottage with a queen-sized bed, sitting area, full kitchen and loft with two twin beds. The cottage usually rents for $450 per week (see more under Summer Rentals). In the morning Mercie and Steve Normand prepare breakfast in the downstairs dining room where guests can enjoy hot entrees such as blueberry-cornmeal pancakes and other scrumptious fare. The large living room overlooks the town green and has a fireplace and comfortable chairs and sofas. On warm days, the wraparound porch is a favorite place to relax amidst hanging flower pots and a blooming front yard. When you feel like heading out, Bowdoin College is just two blocks away (see our Education and Child Care chapter for more on Bowdoin), and the downtown shopping district along Maine Street is about a five-minute walk. The bed and breakfast is closed for the month of January.

The Captain Daniel Stone Inn
$$$ • 10 Water St., Brunswick
• (207) 725-9898, (800) 267-0525

Elegantly restored and carefully expanded, this Federal-style home was built in 1819 for Capt. Daniel Stone and his family. The original house sits on a hill, with a large adjacent addition featuring a spacious welcoming area and spiral staircase. The Federal-era furnishings are in keeping with the original house, and you'll get to choose between standard rooms, rooms with whirlpool tubs (for not much more money) and both small and large suites.

There are 34 rooms in all, each with a TV and VCR. The suites, which run from $160 to $200 a night, have bedrooms set off with glass French doors and spacious sitting rooms with pull-out couches. Handicapped-accessible rooms are available. The room rate includes a large continental breakfast of sweet breads, cereals, juice and coffee. The award-winning Narcissa Stone Restaurant and lounge is open for both lunch and dinner (see our Restaurants chapter). Guests also get to use the facilities at health club with an indoor pool and tennis courts located about a five-minute drive away.

The Country Inn
$$ • Maine Hwy.1, Brunswick
• (207) 729-1359

While some people may prefer country inns that have been completely renovated and papered with designer names to look "country," this inn is for people looking for the real thing. With no fancy prints or papers, this beautiful old country farmhouse is much the way it must have looked 100-years ago: wrap around porch with tablecloths blowing in the wind, all

wood floors, antique beds and dressers in each room and not much more, claw footed tub to share, tall grasses, gardens, pantry cupboards and a post-and-beam barn.

The barn is where you're likely to find innkeepers Don and Katherine Day and their young daughter. They move their beds out there in the summer so they can let out their own rooms. There are just three rooms, which share two bathrooms, and Katherine is completing separate guest rooms to suit young children — complete with dolls and pink curtains and teddy bears and trucks.

Flowers bloom everywhere, indoors and out, and the whole house is open to guests who can select herbs for a relaxing bath, or relax on the plush living room couch and watch T.V. (okay, the T.V. probably wasn't here 100 years ago). Spend the evening exploring the 14 surrounding acres of woods and fields on foot or mountain bike, and help yourself to some lemonade or tea on your return. In the morning you can relax on the porch and enjoy a full country breakfast of delectables such as organic roasted potatoes, crustless quiche, fruit salad and breads. Don just happens to be the head chef at the Freeport's acclaimed Jameson Tavern (see Restaurants), and while Katherine does the cooking here, she says Don taught her everything she knows. The inn is open from the end of May until Veterans Day.

Harpswell Inn B&B
$$ • 141 Lookout Point Rd., South Harpswell
• (207) 833-5509, (800) 843-5509

We were so glad we found this elegantly restored inn on a quiet street overlooking Middle Bay, and we think you will be too. The large white house was built in 1760 and originally served as the cookhouse for the Lookout Point Shipyard, which used to be just down the way. The original dinner bell, used to call shipbuilders in for a hot meal, still remains atop the inn's high roof.

INSIDERS' TIP

Plan a mini-vacation with stops along the entire Southern Coast by booking a couple of nights at a bed and breakfast or inn in each of our geographic areas. That way, you'll spend less time driving and get to know more historic houses and haunts.

Inside you'll fine a spacious, antique-filled living room built around a huge stone fireplace. Fine details and hand-painted walls make each of the inn's 11 rooms and three suites well worth exploring. One room has an entire wall of windows looking toward the bay, another has a hand-painted antique headboard, others have claw-foot tubs, and all have beautiful window treatments and furnishings. We found each room delightfully different — especially the Texas Room, where towels are hung on steer horns.

The suites are spacious and perfectly pampering. One, the Captain's Quarters, is set apart from the main house with its own deck and comes with a completely furnished modern kitchen, breakfast nook, whirlpool tub, queen-size poster bed, gas fireplace and an open living room with water views, and it's just $165. If our price-code average puts the regular rooms here out of your budget, don't despair. You can stay in a smaller room with a shared bath for just $64 a night. Also, if the idea of three stories of living space intimidates you, there are rooms on the first floor. Children older than 10 are welcome.

Outside, a sprawling lawn with gardens, chairs and intimate benches faces the bay; there's plenty of room to roam, and a dock goes down to the water. Downtown Brunswick and Bath are both about a 20-minute drive away, but with all the peace and quiet out here, we don't think you'll mind. We almost forgot breakfast, but you won't want to. Innkeepers Susan and Bill Menz will treat you to a home-cooked spread with favorites such as maple-orange French toast, blueberry-stuffed French toast or Texas pecan waffles. We told you this place was a find!

Tower Hill Bed and Breakfast
$$ • Harpswell Island Road, Harpswell • (207) 833-2311, (888) 833-2311

This 1790 house holds lots of history and oceanfront comfort for travelers. Around the turn of the century, James Seymour, an assistant to Thomas Edison, lived here. The atmosphere is casually elegant. The house is on a saltwater marsh across the street from the ocean and has 22 acres, much of which is landscaped with gardens fit for roaming. The property does extend all the way to the sea and a small, private beach on which swim-

ming is possible. About a 15-minute drive from Brunswick's downtown, the grounds are a great place to relax, explore and watch birds.

Tower Hill has four two-room suites, the largest of which lets for $135 per night. The Fan Room, however, with just one double bed, goes for just $65 a night. Children older than 10 are welcome, and one suite has a day bed in the sitting room. Two suites face the ocean and one looks out over the tall marsh grass. Two rooms have private baths and two share one bath. And you'll get to choose between two old-fashioned, claw footed tubs, if you wish. The rooms are beautifully appointed with antiques collected from Asia, Europe and America, and all have sitting areas. The Iris Suite is named for owner Susan Whiteside's favorite flower and is filled with colors and images of the iris.

A full breakfast is served on china with sterling silver flatware, and Whiteside says that it is an event for which some guests linger until noon sharing in lively conversation with she and her husband, Bill, a retired professor at nearby Bowdoin College. A favorite dish is homemade pancakes topped with seasonal fresh fruit. Other specialties are fresh-baked breads, quiches and a three-cheese omelet flavored with herbs cut from the gardens. A fax and modem are available, and spayed or neutered mature pets are allowed by prior approval, although there is an additional charge. However, if your furry friend doesn't get along with the owners' dog, yours will have to make its home in your vehicle.

The Captain's Watch B&B
$$-$$$ • 2476 Cundy's Harbor Rd., Brunswick • (207) 725-0979

Built during the Civil War, this elegant oceanfront house is perched on a bluff overlooking a small working harbor where you'll see fishing boats going out or coming in after a long day's work. First operated as the Union Hotel in 1862, the property survives as the state's oldest-known coastal hotel structure. History buffs will enjoy an array of photos and stories from the days when visitors arrived by schooner, steamer or stage, and anyone looking for a relaxing and comfortable getaway will enjoy the quaint village atmosphere.

There is a wide variety of rooms to choose from, but our favorite is the two-room suite over-

looking lush woods behind the house. The bedroom has rich wood paneling, a king bed and a twin bed, and the adjoining living room has a working fireplace, upright piano, couch, several chairs, a television and VCR (most of the other rooms don't have TVs) and plenty of privacy. This suite is a favorite with honeymooners and families traveling with children.

The common guest living room is nearby. It has a fireplace as well as several reading chairs and a couch. Across the hallway is the formal dining room, decked out in warm peach. There's a second, smaller bedroom on the first floor, and upstairs are several more rooms, each with their own character and fine, comfortable furniture — one even has its own dressing room. Each room has a queen- or king-size bed and a private bathroom. Two rooms share access to the octagonal cupola crowning the house's roof; from there you'll get a stunning panoramic view of the Atlantic and its islands and bays (it's also a great place to perch in a chair and escape).

In the morning, breakfast is prepared in the sunny kitchen, where guests gather around and get tips on the best places to eat and visit. You'll savor the gourmet omelets, cinnamon-raisin French toast and sour cream blueberry pancakes — all favorites of guests who have visited before. Prior arrangement is necessary for children to stay (in the suite only), and during the peak season a two-night minimum may be required. One additional bonus: Hosts Donna and Ken offer coastal sail charters and give discounts to their guests. While you can book your reservation at the Captain's Watch by credit card, payment must be made with personal check, travelers' checks or cash.

The Driftwood Inn
$ • P.O. Box 16, Bailey Island
• (207) 833-5461

The oldest inn on Bailey Island, The Driftwood has been in operation for more than 75 years and lays claim to some of the most beautiful ocean views we've ever seen. The shingled, gambrel-roofed cottages with large porches are set on jagged rocks overlooking Casco Bay. No traffic here — the only noise is the surf pounding against the shore. And the only sight is the beautiful Atlantic spreading

to the horizon with an occasional sailboat gilding by far out at sea.

Each cottage houses a handful of rustic guest rooms with either twin or full-size beds, wood-sided walls and either wash basins or private baths. You'll find a cozy, camp-like sitting room in each cottage, furnished with an older television, piano, throw rugs and older couches. Some also have fireplaces. But with views like these, who wants to sit inside? We recommend one of the wooden rocking chairs out on the porch, just out of reach of the crashing waves. Private housekeeping cottages are also available, and breakfast and dinner, which can be included in your room rate for an additional charge, are served in a large wooden hall facing the ocean. The dining room, which serves a full breakfast for $5 per person, is open from June until Labor Day, and the inn is open from May 20 through October 15. Check out the saltwater swimming pool (fed by the bay), or just sit on the lawn soaking in the sunshine and the views. While this historic inn is a wonderful place for children to experience the real Maine, we do have one word of caution for parents: You'll need to keep a close eye on children because the rocks are treacherous and not always guarded by rails.

The Log Cabin Lodging & Fine Food
$$$ • Maine Hwy.24, Bailey Island
• (207) 833-5546

The eight rooms at this lodge each have sunset views of Casco Bay and the White Mountains and outdoor decks to enjoy them. Individually decorated from log cabin to country to flowing florals, the rooms offer a variety of sleeping arrangements including one suite with two sleeping quarters with a double bed each. All have well-stocked refrigerators and coffee makers, and several have kitchenettes and Jacuzzis. The Mount Washington Suite is a favorite for its cathedral ceilings, king bed, leather sofa, top-of-the-line entertainment center and (who could forget) hot tub on a private deck.

The Log Cabin, which has been honored for its gracious accommodations and excellent food, is a family run business owned by Susan and Neil Favreau. In the morning they offer a complimentary early continental breakfast with fresh pastries, fruit and juices, coffee and tea as well as a full sit down affair with entrees such as sizzling ham and eggs, Belgian waffles and pancakes. This is one place you won't leave hungry, although we think you will want to make a reservation for dinner (see our restaurants chapter). Enjoy the beautiful vistas, lounge beside the in-ground pool, explore the peninsula then relax — that's what this place is all about.

Benjamin F. Packard House
$ • 45 Pearl St., Bath
• (207) 443-6069, (800) 516-4578

Once owned by prominent Bath shipbuilder Benjamin Packard, this gracious 1790 Georgian-style house now welcomes visitors with three spacious guest rooms, each with a private bath. One reason we like this inn so much is the intimacy that comes with only having three guest rooms; others are the many remnants of the Packard family — such as the silverware in the dining room, a graduation diploma of a daughter in a bedroom — displayed throughout the house.

When you walk up the granite steps into the front hallway, you'll see the elegant dining room with its crystal chandelier to your right and a sitting room with a marble-encased fireplace to your left. There's also a less formal living room with a huge hearth and plenty of reading material. Upstairs,' nicely appointed rooms feature a king, queen or two twin-size beds. The suite, which is in the same price range, has a separate sitting room with a comfortable loveseat that opens into a bed.

In the morning, hosts Debby and Bill Hayden will wake you up with the aroma of a full breakfast — sometimes it includes oatmeal-buttermilk pancakes, a favorite. The Packard House is in a quiet neighborhood in the city's Historic District and is just a 10- to 15-minute walk to the downtown shops and restaurants. Children older than 12 are welcome, but there is an additional charge

of $15 for a third person in the suite. A two-night minimum is required on Friday and Saturday nights during peak season.

Fairhaven Inn
$$ • N. Bath Rd., Bath
• (207) 443-4391

Set back in the countryside on a hill overlooking the Kennebec River, this gray, shingled 1790 Colonial home has plenty of charm and plenty of history. You'll be drawn in from the moment you walk up the stone pathway through the front door and smell the aroma of fresh-baked bread lingering in the halls. Innkeepers Susie and Dave Reed bought the inn in 1995 after selling their pastry shop in Washington D.C., so there's no doubt you'll get a scrumptious breakfast here (we're told a favorite is strawberry-and-banana-stuffed French toast).

Downstairs is a wood-floored dining room set with three small tables and plenty of chairs. Just across the hall is the spacious Tavern Room, where guests can enjoy games or television or just lounge on one of the couches. Outside, where several lawn chairs and tables are set up, is a small stone patio overlooking a lush field and the meandering Whiskeag Creek.

Back inside and up the staircase you'll find hand-picked, antique furnishings in the inn's eight guest rooms, each with different flowered wallpaper and quilts that will make you want to dive right into bed. One room has two twin beds, another has a double bed and a twin-size sleigh bed in an adjoining nook, and the rest have larger beds. All but two guest rooms have private baths.

When you're ready to explore, head outdoors to roam the 16 acres of woods and fields. If you're really adventurous, ask about the inn's truly unique fall and winter packages that allow you to stay the night and take courses in everything from wreath-making to baking gingerbread houses. A special shopping package and a Thanksgiving package

---

INSIDERS' TIP

One bed and breakfast owner confided in us that this is the business of bargaining. If you're traveling off season and the house you want to stay at has a couple of extra rooms to fill, some proprietors will let you dicker on the price of your stay.

(they'll cook up your family's favorite recipes for this one) are also available.

The Galen C. Moses House
$ • 1009 Washington St., Bath
• (207) 442-8771

Built in 1874, this historic bed and breakfast is filled with charm and elegance. It's also hard to miss. The Italianate house is painted rose with teal and pink accents, and in the summer it is surrounded by lush gardens, including charming window boxes and two trees shaped like giant pineapples. Inside you'll find rooms detailed with original frieze work, intricate wood paneling, Italian-tiled fireplaces and stained glass windows.

In the summer an assortment of wines and iced-tea is served on the small outdoor porch. In winter, you'll find sherry and hot tea set beside the fireplace in the Library, a small room filled with books and a wood-canopied window seat. Other rooms on the first floor are a sitting room with a TV, twin parlors with cozy period chairs and a formal dinning room where breakfast includes fresh fruit and specialties such as Belgian waffles, lemon-chiffon pancakes and baked French toast. Interior decorations in the house and in its four guest bedrooms are in keeping with the rich colors — plum, wine, gold, deep green and pink — of the era in which it was built. The furnishings are family heirlooms and treasured antiques. One bedroom has a white-finish brass bed with a wicker sitting area near a bay window, another has two twin beds. All have private bathrooms, and Jim Haught and Larry Kieft, who own the inn, are working to restore the original sink fixtures in the bedrooms themselves.

The inn has plenty of history — including the private movie theater in the attic — which reportedly played "blue movies" to men stationed at the nearby naval air station during World War II. Children 13 and older are allowed, but smoking is not.

The Inn at Bath
$$-$$$ • 969 Washington St., Bath
• (207) 443-4294

This exquisite 1810 Greek Revival home in the heart of Bath's Historic District is the work of Nick Bayard, who left Wall Street to move to Maine and restore and manage this inn in the late 1980s. From the moment you walk through the front door of the traditionally painted white house with black trim, you'll be immersed in color.

The glowing peach dining room was painted to match Bayard's family china, which is displayed in an alcove. The second dining room is a striking lemon with streaks of red. Comfortable adjoining parlors each have their own fireplace.

Upstairs, the bedrooms are a palette of colors — from elegant wallpapers to stark white walls and elegant furnishings such as canopied four-poster beds. Downstairs, you'll find several more guest rooms, all with inviting hues and some with old brick fireplaces and wood beams. Many rooms offer plush daybeds, and two even have hot tubs within the arc of the fire's glow (expect to pay nearly double the listed rate for the hot-tub rooms). Each room has a private bathroom and air conditioning. And if you need a little more space to sprawl, a couple of rooms join together to form a suite. The first-floor Garden Room has beamed ceilings, wide pine floors and a fireplace, and it is fully handicapped-accessible. Rooms have king- or queen-size beds.

In the morning, wake up to a complimentary breakfast served in the dining room, then stroll downtown and explore Bath's many shops and restaurants — they're all a 10-minute walk away. When you're done, head back to the inn for a relaxing cup of tea or coffee in the afternoon. Children older than 6 are welcome, as are well-behaved pets. A fax machine and laundry facilities are available.

Stonehouse Manor
$$$, no credit cards • Maine Hwy. 209, Popham Beach, Phippsburg
• (207) 389-1141

After living in this spacious house with her family for six years, owner Jane Dennis decided to share it with others by turning it into a bed and breakfast. From the moment you step through the giant wooden door into the mahogany-paneled entryway, you'll want to thank her. Jane has done a magnificent job restoring this stone and wood manor to its prime.

There's plenty of space to roam downstairs, with an elegant dining room, a sitting room with a baby grand piano, a small library where guests can use the phone and a glass-enclosed porch. The woodwork throughout the house brings a rich flavor to every room. The four spacious bedrooms on the second floor of the house each have their own bathrooms, and two have hot tubs. All are meticulously appointed with fine furniture and lacy curtains. The rooms have either a queen-size bed or two doubles, and the Carriage House Suite, which is in a separate building, has a private deck and kitchen, a double bed in the bedroom and a full-size sleeper sofa, couches and dining room table in the sitting area.

The room names — Beach Tree, Lake View, Garden — speak of relaxation, and that's just what you'll find here. The house is part of a historic estate on 8 acres complete with groomed lawns, gardens, a swing set and an orchard, all on the shore of Silver Lake, less than a mile from sandy Popham Beach. Gaze out at the shimmering lake as you drift to sleep, or peer toward the slice of sea on the horizon.

In the morning, you'll wake to a full breakfast cooked and served by Jane. On the day we visited, guests had just finished a breakfast of crab omelets, blueberry pancakes, muffins, juice, coffee and fruit. There is a two-night minimum stay on weekends and holidays, and the Carriage House usually rents for a week at a time. Children are welcome, and a crib is available. There is an additional charge of $25 for an extra person in a room. However, children younger than 2 stay free, and the charge for an additional person younger than 10 is just $15.

The 1774 Inn at Phippsburg
$$ • 44 Parker Head Rd.,
Phippsburg Center • (207) 389-1774

This pre-Revolutionary War estate still has heavy window shutters with peepholes and strong bars to defend its occupants against Indian raids in an era long past. It also has high ceilings, five fireplaces, paneled wainscoting, ceiling moldings and wide pine floors. Still need other reasons we love it so much? How about its location in a quiet, picturesque village and its wide lawn rolling all the way down to the wide Kennebec River.

Each of the four guest rooms is furnished with antique beds, chests and highboys and either Colonial Williamsburg patterns, Laura Ashley chintz or Ralph Lauren country florals. Two have queen-size beds, and two have double beds. Most rooms are large and include sitting areas and private baths, and one also has a fireplace. Another has river views.

In the morning you'll wake to coffee or tea served outside your bedroom door. When you're done, head downstairs to home-baked muffins and breads, fresh fruit and other delectables such as Maine blueberry pancakes and fresh bacon or sausage. In the afternoon you'll find the pantry stocked with home-baked goodies and refreshing drinks. Children older than 12 are welcome.

Outside there's plenty to do. A Congregational church built in 1802 is just a short walk away, and you can swim, canoe or fish in nearby Center Pond, a favorite community water hole. The sandy shores of Popham Beach are about a 10-minute drive away. You'll enjoy all this, plus the house's wonderful history. It was built by Isaac Packard for prosperous lumber and commerce trader James McCobb. From 1782 to 1842, Mark Hill, the first U.S. Congressman from Maine, lived here, and Charles Minott, the state's best-known shipbuilder, later bought the house.

Popham Beach Bed & Breakfast
$$$ • 4 Ocean View Ln., Popham Beach,
Phippsburg
• (207) 389-2409

You can't sleep much closer to the beach than this. Walk out the door of this 1883 Coast Guard station, and you'll find yourself on the stretching sandy shore of Popham Beach (see our Beaches chapter). The red-roofed building was constructed as a U.S. Lifesaving Station to save stranded mariners from the tide, wind and fog and to watch over the mouth of the nearby Kennebec River. It actively housed Coasties until it was decommissioned in 1971.

Now you can sleep in the officers' quarters or the men's bunk room and eat in the elegant dining room where the mess hall used to be. The daring can climb up two steep staircases to the portico on top of the roof and view the surrounding sea. The guest rooms are tastefully decorated with airy window treatments and cozy chairs, and they afford both comfort and style. Among them are The Library Room, which has a queen-size bed and a large bay window overlooking the beach, and The Captain's Quarters, a second-floor suite with beach views. The Garden View Room, which is smaller and has a shared bath, lets for nearly half the cost of the larger rooms but is furnished just as nicely. All the other rooms have private baths, and most have water views.

You won't find televisions in the rooms, but don't worry — with views like these, you won't need them. You will find a large common room overlooking the ocean. In the morning, enjoy breakfast served by innkeeper Peggy Johannessen. This bed and breakfast is open May through October. A two-night minimum stay is required during peak season.

The Grey Havens Inn
$$-$$$$ • Sequinland Rd., Georgetown • (207) 371-2616

This old-fashioned inn on a grassy hill above the ocean has some of the best Maine views you'll find — inside and out. Relax on the wide, wraparound porch and take in the flower gardens, the salty sea breeze and the unobstructed view of the ocean, a forested peninsula and an uninhabited island. Unlike many other waterfront properties, the scenery here is not marred by development.

The gray-shingled, turreted inn was built in 1904 for summer travelers pining for a summer of refined but rustic living... where they could roam the rough shoreline or stroll through dense woods and still have a relaxing hearth to warm them up at the end of the day. Today's visitors can still do the same. Inside, the common lounge is a picture of relaxation and old-time elegance. Persian carpets, sea captain's chests and antique chairs and couches rest around an enormous rock fireplace. In one corner is a wicker bar; in another is a bookshelf with reading material. A historic, 12-foot picture window looks out over the ocean; when the inn was built, the window was the largest piece of glass in Maine!

The inn is known as the last classic, shingle-style hotel in the state. Each room is individually decorated with the guest's ultimate comfort in mind — from down quilts to canvas tote bags stocked with beach supplies to binoculars on several bureaus. Our personal pick is the suite, which has a two-person wooden swing suspended from the ceiling of the bedroom facing a private balcony and the sea. Several rooms have hand-painted walls, assorted flower-print wallpapers, airy lace curtains, fresh flowers and claw-foot tubs. Each has a private bathroom. Nearly all the rooms have water views, and four turret rooms have 180-degree views of the ocean.

Outside, Adirondack chairs are set about the lawn near a shaded swing set for children (only the most well-behaved are allowed at the inn). The inn has its own dock, from which fishing is allowed, and deepwater anchorage for guests' boats. When the inn was built by Walter Reid, the same man who donated the land for Reid State Park just a hop, skip and jump away (see more on this in our Parks and Recreation chapter), it was named the "Seguinland." But when the Hardcastle family bought it three generations ago, they renamed it Grey Havens in reminiscence of the fantasy embarkation point at the end of the earth, written of by J.R.R. Tolkien.

The same family runs the inn today. Bill Eberhart, who married the original owner's daughter, runs the kitchen, preparing a complimentary breakfast of muffins, coffee cakes, fruit, cereal, juices, coffee and tea. Breakfast is served in an intimate dining room overlooking the water (hardly any space here doesn't) or on the porch as guests prefer. Visitors are welcome from April through December, and a two-night minimum stay is required on weekends.

Snow Squall Bed & Breakfast
$$ • U.S. Hwy. 1, Wiscasset • (207) 882-6892, (800) 775-7245

Named after a Maine clipper ship, the Snow Squall is an early 1850s house and barn that have been completely restored as a residence for the innkeeper's family and spacious rooms for guests. There are rooms to accommodate large families or couples traveling together, with four single guest rooms and three two-bedroom suites, which range from $125 to $195 per night. Each room has a choice of queen- or king-size beds and is charmingly named after a clipper ship built in Maine. All have private baths, and two rooms have fireplaces.

Steve and Anne Kornacki bought the bed and breakfast in June 1998 so they could run a home business and leave the hustle and bustle of Massachusetts behind. Each room is decorated with fine furniture and bright, airy bed spreads and curtains. The suites are either adjoining rooms or two-storied with private entrances. Whichever room you choose, you'll enjoy relaxing on the large porch overlooking the back yard and gazebo or sitting in front of the fireplace in the comfortable library. In the morning you'll be called from slumber by the aroma of fresh-baked breads and gourmet coffee, while the Kornacki's prepare a spread of pancakes, breakfast meats and fruits.

Cod Cove Farm Bed and Breakfast
$$ • 117 Boothbay Rd., Edgecomb • (207) 882-4299

This classic 1840s cape with its rambling red barn sits on a hill overlooking a pond, the Sheepscot River and the steeples of Wiscasset. Inside you'll find a traditional parlor accented with flowers and lace and antique furnishings surrounding a baby grand piano. Nearby is a simply furnished dining room with custom-built cabinetry and a library, which has a television for guests enjoyment (there aren't any TVs in the rooms).

Upstairs, however, the furnishings are anything but traditional. The four imaginative guest rooms are unlike any we've seen before, and whichever one you choose, the experience is sure to delight you. Innkeepers Don and Charlene Schuman picked a theme for each room and developed it with both taste and comfort in mind. The Moon and Stars Room has hand-stenciled glittering white stars around the room's border with a golden verse of poetry flowing on one wall. Anything but childish, the room has an heirloom-quality queen-size birch and bent-twig canopy bed made of intertwined branches arching toward the ceiling. The attached private bathroom has a sunset painted over the tops of pine trees.

Next door is the Adirondack Room, which Charlene stenciled with a long birch branch strung with a vine of feathers and leather medicine pouches. The Schuman's chose the theme because Don's family has had a camp in the Adirondacks for three generations. Here pictures on the wall reflect the wilderness, and you'll find more bent-twig furniture. This room has a private sink but shares a bathroom with the Scottish Room across the hall. Charlene's family is the Scots, and that room is full of her heritage, from her family kilt which serves as a window treatment to the many plaids and Scotty dogs highlighting the room. The Scottish room has two twin beds and its own sink, made of an antique cabinet.

The largest room in the bed and breakfast is the Cod Cove, with a large picture window looking toward the pond and flowing flowery drapes. Many-colored flowering vine stencils that match the drapes play in corners of the room. The hand-painted, king-size bed is a work of art portraying ships sailing along a wooded river. Charlene pins her artistry on her "funky sense of humor." But funky or not, we think she holds her own against world-class decorators. Her flair touches each room with style and whimsy without falling prey to excess.

The bed and breakfast has central air-conditioning, and children older than 12 are welcome. In the morning you can look forward to Adirondack flapjacks, Scottish scones, fresh fruit and yogurt and more of the Schuman's imaginings. The bed and breakfast is closed from Thanksgiving through New Year's Day. Just so you don't have a hard time getting here, "Boothbay Road" is just a fancy name for Maine Hwy. 27.

1830 — Admiral's Quarters Inn
$$$ • 71 Commercial St., Boothbay Harbor • (207) 633-2474

Set on a flowering lawn overlooking the harbor, this white, hip-roofed house has six guest rooms, most of which are two-room suites and all of which have their own bathrooms. The house dates back to the early 1800s, but the inn was only recently established by hosts Les and Deb Hallstrom. They have decorated each room with flowing drapes and antique and wicker furniture, making each room fresh and refreshing. Each has a king, queen or twin beds, color televisions, telephones, and several have couches or daybeds for additional guests, although children must be older than 12. All rooms also have private entrances and balconies.

Downstairs guests can watch the harbor and Commercial Street shoppers from a large solarium with a wood stove, comfortable furniture, games and puzzles. There's also an outside deck. At daybreak, you'll be greeted by the sun shimmering across the calm harbor and a hearty breakfast home-cooked by the Hailstorms. In the afternoon, stop back at the inn for refreshing beverages and treats.

Albonegon Inn
$$ • Capitol Island • (207) 633-2521

This 120-year-old inn, which boasts of being "determinedly old-fashioned," is perched on the edge of the rocks just above the crashing Atlantic with spectacular views of a nearby island from its double-decker outdoor balconies. To get here you'll drive over a wooden bridge so narrow you might wonder whether it's a footbridge and pass summer cottages lining the ocean road to the inn's front door. Inside you'll find a huge stone fireplace surrounded by all variety of couches and sitting chairs. And just above the water, the many-windowed dining room set with intimate tables overlooks the ocean.

Upstairs are 11 rooms, all with water views and cottage-style furniture (we were told it's a lot like staying overnight at your grandmother's house). Most have wash basins in the rooms and a shared bath, although rooms with private baths are available. In the morning you'll enjoy fresh-baked blueberry muffins, cinnamon coffee cakes and whole wheat breads, along with your coffee.

The inn is open from Memorial Day weekend until Columbus Day, and when we say open, we mean open. This place is so old fashioned, there aren't any locks on the outside door. One word of advice: Make your reservations well in advance.

Captain Sawyer's Place
$ • 55 Commercial St., Boothbay Harbor • (207) 633-2290

Insiders know this rambling yellow house with green trim is one of the best downtown deals overlooking the waterfront — unless you plan on sleeping under the stars, that is. Each room in the historic sea captain's home is simply furnished with a sitting area, bed and its own bathroom. Colorful quilts and decorations brighten the rooms, and many have views of the harbor just across the street. The Captain's Suite has its own private deck, and for all to enjoy there is a large wraparound porch with sitting chairs facing the water. On the first floor of the inn is a homey living room for guests to share with the Upham family, which runs the inn.

A continental breakfast with coffee cake, quiche, cereal, juice, coffee and tea is included in the price of a room, and downtown shops and restaurants beckon just outside. Children older than 12 are welcome, and there is a $10 charge for an additional person in a room.

Ocean Point Inn
$$-$$$ • Shore Rd., East Boothbay • (207) 633-4200, (800) 552-5554

Right on the edge of Linekin Bay, this inn is a combination of adorable white cottages, a modern lodge and the white, gabled inn itself offering a whole range of choices to guests. You'll get to choose from modern two-bedroom suites with separate living rooms and kitchens to old-fashioned guest rooms with poster beds and country-style decor. The Hatchard House is the oldest building on the property, dating back to 1856, and it used to be a farmhouse. Now guests can enjoy the seven bedrooms housed in it.

All rooms at the inn have private baths, and cribs and rollaway beds are available for $5 and $10 respectively. Many have been recently renovated in the country style to include painted wall paneling, country borders and new carpet. The main inn has seen some change as well with the addition of a spacious library-game room complete with plenty of books, at least one checker board, and comfortable sofas and chairs. On the first floor of the inn, a large dining room with a full bar overlooks the ocean. Off season, a continental breakfast of bagels, muffins, cereal, juice, coffee and tea is included in the room rate, and during the main season, a full breakfast is available for additional cost. The inn's restaurant is also a popular place to come for dinner.

Besides the food, the people we talked to said the main reason they come is for the great ocean views and the seclusion. The only thing separating the inn from the sea is a narrow road and a walkway lined with Adirondack chairs overlooking the water.

Elsewhere on the property is a duck pond and the largest heated outdoor pool in the area. There is plenty of lawn space for energetic children, and a community pier is just next door. If you want to rent a cottage or apartment by the week, expect to pay about $939 to $1,000 during peak season. Also, if you call, ask about Ocean Point's many package deals including boating trips.

Five Gables Inn
$$-$$$ • Murray Hill Rd., East Boothbay • (207) 633-4551, (800) 451-5048

Set on a hillside overlooking picturesque Linekin Bay, this 125-year-old country inn is the only remaining summer hotel in the Boothbays. In its early years guests arrived by steamboat, hauling their trunks up the hill to its wraparound porch. Now they drive past beautiful summer homes, down a secluded dead-end street and park in its landscaped parking lot.

Inside, chamber pots have been replaced with private bathrooms, but besides such modern luxuries, not much else has changed. Each of the inn's 15 cozy guest rooms overlooks the bay and is individually decorated with elegant furnishings such as pencil-post beds and wing-backed chairs. Five have private fireplaces, including the deluxe room with a king-size bed. In the morning you are likely to find your host Mike Kennedy in an apron conversing with guests about the best places to explore the Maine coast. He and his wife, De, are the geniuses behind the complimentary breakfast buffet of fresh-baked muffins, breakfast meats, egg dishes and fruits invitingly displayed on a groaning board set with fresh flowers. In the afternoon, you'll enjoy their spread of homemade pastries and refreshing beverages.

It is the atmosphere and attention to detail that make the inn such a charming retreat. You'll find carefully groomed gardens (complete with a five-gabled birdhouse), antique mugs of fresh flowers arranged on each of the indoor and outdoor tables and a five-day weather forecast framed on the front desk. On chilly days the Kennedys light a crackling fire in the fireplace of the inn's common room, which is a favorite gathering place, and on a rainy day, check out the books and games in the adjoining parlor. But on a sunny morning, most people take to the porch, which has comfortable chairs and a hammock.

Just across the street you can swim in the bay, and two moorings are available for guests by arrangement.

Children must be older than 12 to stay at the inn, which is open mid-May through the end of October.

Greenleaf Inn
$$ • 91 Commercial St., Boothbay Harbor • (207) 633-7346

The first invitation you might receive to stay at the Greenleaf Inn is the broad front porch set about with wicker furniture facing the distant harbor down the road a bit. Take up the tempting first offer and you'll find yourself in the welcoming hallway of the expanded and updated cape which has a small dinning area, a large sitting room and library built around a stone fireplace and five bedrooms with full baths and queen-sized beds. Three of the rooms also have day beds, and all have televisions and VCRs.

The decor is fine country, and all rooms in the inn have water views. The downstairs common area is a real treasure, and many have enjoyed warmth and fellowship around the fireplace. Lingering over a full breakfast of baked French toast, gingerbread, breakfast meats, fruit and the inn's own coffee while enjoying the sunrise over the water is an honored tradition. Pick up the binoculars on the dinning room window sill and see what sea life you might spot splashing in the harbor. For afternoon refreshment, the common fridge is stocked with fruit juices and sodas. Owner Jeff Teel, a former accountant, took over the inn in 1998 and has made many appealing changes. The rate includes a full breakfast, and children older than 12 are welcome to stay with their families.

Lobsterman's Inn
$ • Rt. 96, East Boothbay • (207) 633-5481

Although our rate chart begins at $80 per night, the rates at this old-fashioned rooming house actually begin at only $45. Set back from the water with views of Lobsterman's Wharf, a favorite place to eat (see more on this in our Restaurants chapter), we think this is one of the best deals around for people traveling on a limited budget. The rooms are neat and simply furnished, and although the beds looked a little squishy, several rooms have great water views. Our pick for cuteness, although it doesn't overlook the water, is No. 9, a good-sized blue room with twin beds, a checkered sitting chair and table with two chairs. All the rooms have cottage-style furniture. And in the common corridors you'll find coffee pots and sitting chairs on each floor.

The inn is open from Mother's Day weekend through Columbus Day.

The Atlantic Ark Inn
$$ • 64 Atlantic Ave., Boothbay Harbor • (207) 633-5690

Located just across the harbor's historic footbridge, The Atlantic Ark Inn is a charming get-away filled with fresh flowers, the salty sea air and period antiques. Owner Donna Piggot has tastefully furnished each of the inn's seven guest rooms with mahogany poster beds, floor-length drapes and paintings, and each has a private bath. Most rooms offer harbor views, and some have terraces. A special treat is the third-floor suite, which has cathedral ceilings and a panoramic view of the harbor. It also has oak floors, 17 windows, its own balcony and french glass doors opening to a beautiful Jacuzzi for two. In the morning you'll be treated to a full breakfast made with fresh, natural, ingredients. The kitchen is kosher, and from it come delectables such as home-baked breads, vegetarian quiches, fresh fruit and gourmet coffee. When you're ready to go out and enjoy the day, a stroll across the footbridge will bring you to downtown shops.

The Lawnmeer Inn
$$ • P.O. Box 505, West Boothbay Harbor • (207) 633-2544, (800) 633-7645

The oldest operating inn in the region, the Lawnmeer is a graceful old lady trimmed in yellow with flowers streaming from her hair. It is set on a sprawling lawn on Southport Island facing the rocky cove where boats bob on the shimmering water and gulls pick at seaweed among the rocks. The white-clapboard, yellow-shuttered main building has a wraparound porch and warm guest rooms with hand-stenciled walls and individually picked furnishings. Teddy bears will meet you

at every turn, propped up on beds and tucked in baskets. Downstairs is an intimate parlor with wing-backed chairs and a fireplace to cozy up to on chilly evenings. You'll also find two dining rooms, one of which has a fireplace and a wall of windows looking out toward the water (see more on this in our Restaurants chapter).

Just next door the lodge has plenty more comfortable rooms with simple, hotel-style furniture and more of the same great views. In either building, you'll have a choice of twin, queen or king-size beds, and some rooms have balconies and private entrances. A cottage is also available. The only air conditioning you'll get — or need, probably — is a cool ocean breeze. And if you want a television, plan to reserve one of the suites. Outside Adirondack chairs are scattered across the lawn, and there is a boat dock from which you may launch your canoe or kayak. Extra people are $25 per night; children younger than 5 stay free. One small pet per room is accepted as space is available for $25 per stay. There are also discounts for stays of seven or more days. The inn is open from May through mid-October.

Newagen Seaside Inn
$$$ • Maine Hwy. 27, Southport Island • (207) 633-5242, (800) 654-5242

This sprawling, old-fashioned inn is set on 85 acres at the tip of Southport Island facing the open ocean. What more do we need to say? The two-story building reflects a simple elegance of days gone by with its narrow corridors and simple furnishings. You'll find 17 standard guest rooms, three one-bedroom suites and six rooms with private decks. All come with private baths, and most have dramatic views of the sea, the surrounding islands and nearby lighthouses. The understated furnishings only serve to magnify the glorious views.

Downstairs, in the Great Room, you'll find stuffed chairs and couches arranged for intimate conversations around the large stone fireplace. Tucked away in one corner is an upright piano. Another corner shelters a small library of books and board games. Just around the corner is a full bar with windows facing the ocean. There you will find a collection of chairs and tables spread with the inn's trademark green and white checkered clothes. The dining room, just across the hallway from the bar, is a local's favorite for its fabulous cuisine and casual atmosphere. You'll get to enjoy it every morning when you wake up to a complimentary breakfast buffet. of sausage, bacon, eggs, waffles, fruit and hot and cold beverages.

Outside, gravel walkways lined with beds of flowers lead down to the rocky waterfront. On your way you'll wind by a horseshoe pit, shuffle board, heated swimming pool, gazebo and a saltwater pool where you can swim with guppies and seaweed without the threat of waves. There's also a mile of rock-bound shore to walk along, rowboats to take out, nature trails to wander, tidal pools in which to forage for sea creatures and two all-weather tennis courts. Well-supervised children are welcome.

Spruce Point Inn
$$$$ (includes breakfast and dinner)
(50 Grand View Ave., Boothbay Harbor
• (207) 633-4152, (800) 553-0289

Where to begin? This sprawling resort overlooks the rocky shoreline of a secluded point on outer Boothbay Harbor. The old-fashioned inn, modern suites and cottages are pictures of both grace and comfort, and if you can't relax here, well, we recommend therapy. Up the stone walk and through the front doors of the inn you'll find a spacious welcoming room adjoining a parlor complete with fireplace. Nearby is the inn's elegant dining room, which is divided into a room for casual attire and a room for jackets only (see more on this under Restaurants). The tables are set with maroon linens and crystal, and nearby there's a separate bar where you' can enjoy nightly entertainment.

Most of the resort's accommodations are based on the Modified American Plan where both a huge breakfast buffet and a four-course dinner are included in the cost of your room during peak season from July through Labor Day weekend. Rates drop to about $110-$215 during the off-seasons and do not include meals. Also, some cottages and ocean-side condominiums have their own kitchens, and guests can opt to subtract the cost of meals in their lodging fee even during the months when its not an option for others.

Upstairs in the main inn, the rooms are decorated in designer fabrics and include intimate sitting areas. The Captain's Quarters is a room with two huge picture windows with both harbor and ocean views. The management is spending millions to completely redecorate the rooms and to build new lodges, a conference facility and other amenities. A short walk outside the main inn will take you to the newly built Evergreen Suite: pure luxury. Within its oversized rooms, most of which have ocean views, you' can bask in luxury with whirlpool tubs surrounded by Italian porcelain, separate walk-in showers, private porches, glass-door fireplaces, 27-inch televisions and a king or two queen beds. The rooms also have overstuffed furniture, and those with king-size beds have sofa beds. A second lodge with similar rooms has just been built nearby.

The large, white-clapboard cottages are some of the nicest you might expect to find along the Maine coastline, with two or more bedrooms, separate living rooms, kitchens and rolled-stone fireplaces. Recently, the average price (including restaurant dining) was $500 per night. As part of ongoing renovations, the cottages have been completely restored to their heyday with 1950s motifs, vintage accents and antiques. The Oceanhouse Condominiums have two or three bedrooms with full kitchens, dining areas, living rooms with cathedral ceiling, private porches, fireplaces (some have the fireplace in the master bedroom) and washers and dryers. In 1997 the price per night for those was $355 for a two-bedroom and $517 for a three-bedroom.

Spruce Point is great for an overnight getaway but even better if you have time to spend several days and enjoy all the amenities. There's a heated spa, massage services, a brand-new playground, salt-water pool at the ocean's edge, a solar-heated freshwater pool, championship clay tennis courts, weekly boat cruises, outdoor lobster bakes and a bus service to town. The inn also offers many choices for vacation packages, so ask about them when you make your reservation.

You'll find rooms with beach views, coastal views and distant views of the sea, as well as others that overlook lush gardens or woodlands.

Hotels and Motels

Whether you're looking for a seaside resort or merely somewhere to rest your head at night, our Southern Coast has accommodations to meet your needs. We have everything from grand hotels dating to the turn of the century to ultra-modern resort facilities to small motels just off the beach with two beds and a shower and not a lot more. You'll find rooms with beach views, coastal views and distant views of the sea as well as others that overlook lush gardens or woodland. With hundreds of hotels and motels from Kittery to Boothbay it was hard to decide which ones to include, but we picked our favorites and included some great values (that might overlook the parking lot) as well.

In this chapter you'll find hotels and motels and some places that call themselves inns, but these are accommodations that we felt lacked the history and character of a truly "old inn." To find listings for those, check out our Bed & Breakfasts and Inns chapter. Similarly, if you're looking for a campground, cottage or summer rental, look up our Campgrounds and our Summer Rentals chapters.

Unless stated otherwise, accommodations in this chapter have both smoking and non-smoking rooms. Public common areas are generally nonsmoking. Again, unless we say otherwise, rooms include television, telephone and a private bath or shower. Rates are based on double occupancy. Where stated, rates include breakfast or breakfast and dinner. We have noted where pets are allowed and if a facility is not accessible to the handicapped.

When reading this chapter, don't forget that the price codes are based on in-season rates; that's basically July and August. Rates at the beginning and end of the season tend to be lower — in early June and mid-September you'll often find rates dropping by a third to half of in-season costs. Note that in some of the more seasonal, tourist-driven locations, some properties may close in the off-season.

Price Code

Please note that we have chosen the code that best represents the majority of rooms in a given establishment. Many places will have rooms that fall into lower or higher key categories. Rates do not include add-on extras such as room service or premium cable channels.

$	$80 and lower
$$	$81 to $120
$$$	$121 to $160
$$$$	$161 and higher

Southern Beaches Area

Days Inn
$ • U.S. Hwy. 1 bypass, Kittery
• (207) 439-5555

While the exterior of this hotel is uninspiring, the interior is welcoming. The lobby smells clean and fresh and the lighting is pleasant. You'll find 108 rooms that are basic but nice and an indoor heated pool. The lounge is open Monday through Saturday evenings and in-season the Fife & Drum Restaurant, on the premises, serves dinner. You can get breakfast at the restaurant year-round for under $5.

Business travelers will be happy to note that there are four meeting rooms available. In addition, the hotel offers a variety of packages and promotions throughout the year, so call ahead to see if one is being offered when you intend to travel.

Country View Motel & Guesthouse
$ • 1521 U.S. Hwy. 1, Cape Neddick, York
• (207) 363-7160, (800) 258-6598

Though located on busy Route 1, the Country View does indeed have a country view.

There are no buildings across the street from it, but rather a lovely open field with tall grasses backed by trees. A variety of room types are available — from standard rooms with two double beds to rooms with one king-sized bed and a sitting area with game table. Superior rooms have either two doubles or a queen-sized bed and also include a microwave and refrigerator. In the studio apartment you'll find a queen bed, sleeper sofa and fully equipped kitchen. If you need more room, opt for the two-bedroom apartment. Country View also has a guesthouse with six rooms, each with private bath. Guests selecting this accommodation get continental breakfast. Pets are accepted in the motel but not in the guesthouse. (A $10 fee is charged for pets.) There is no charge for children younger than 12 sharing a room with their parents; older children and adults are charged $10.

Anchorage Motor Inn
$$$ • Long Sands Rd., York Beach • (207) 363-5112

Located directly across from Long Sands beach, the Anchorage Motor Inn features two outdoor pools, an indoor pool, free parking on the day of check-out if you want to enjoy the beach and tastefully decorated rooms. Rooms are located in two buildings: the main building, which was renovated in 1994, and the Atrium, which was built in 1992. You can choose from rooms with two double beds, a queen-sized bed, two queen-sized beds or a king-sized bed, or from one of five efficiency suites. All rooms come equipped with refrigerators.

According to the management the Anchorage has the most courteous staff in Southern Maine and a housekeeping staff that is "second-to-none." Furnishings and carpet are upgraded on a regular basis and the grounds are beautifully maintained. If you like, you can enjoy dining at the Sun & Surf restaurant located across street (see our Restaurants chapter), which shares the same owners as the Anchorage Motor Inn. The Inn is open year-round.

Long Beach Motor Inn
$$$ • U.S. Hwy. 1A, Long Sands, York Beach • (207) 363-5481

Along a strip of motel after motel, the Long Beach Motor Inn stands out with the brilliance of its flowers and lush greenery. Set sideways to the road, the motel extends back into green lawns with lovingly landscaped picnic, badminton and shuffleboard areas and a private swimming pool. Unlike other motels where the pool is set along the road so everyone and anyone can see you, the Grossman family decided it would be much nicer to place the pool in the back. Dwarf apple and pear trees are just a couple of the plants you'll find in the landscape around the pool, along with white Adirondack chairs and a swing.

A bird preserve is part of the grounds. This unusual piece of wilderness is close to the beach, which is just across the street. The Grossmans built the motel 20 years ago and say guests have been returning since day one. All 32 rooms are efficiency units complete with a table and chairs in the kitchen area. Oceanfront windows were placed in the sides of the rooms facing the sea in 1998, and all rooms are renovated yearly.

Stage Neck Inn
$$$$ • Stage Neck Rd., York Harbor • (207) 363-3850, (800) 222-3238

When the settlers living on the Isles of Shoals, 10 miles off the coast, packed up and moved their homes to York Harbor, they landed at Stage Neck, at the mouth of the York River where it meets the sea. Today the Stage Neck Inn sits on this point of land with the river at its back, the ocean at its front, and harbor beach to one side.

In addition to large, comfortable rooms decorated in the Queen Anne style, you can indulge yourself with time in the Jacuzzi after a swim in the indoor pool or with fine dining in the elegant dining room. A masseuse is available by appointment, and there is an exercise room on the premises. All rooms at the Stage Neck have water views and have two double beds or one queen- or king-sized bed. The

entire inn is nonsmoking. Children aged 6 to 12 are charged an extra $5 each while those older than 13 are charged $10. Children younger than 6 are free, but there is a $10 charge for cribs. A rollaway bed for an extra person is $15.

The Cutty Sark Motel & Victorian Cottage
$$ • 58 Long Beach Ave., York Beach • (207) 363-5131, (800) 543-5131

Many motels feature some rooms with ocean views, but all of the rooms at the Cutty Sark feature ocean views! Located at the northern end of Long Sands beach, on the corner, the Cutty Sark has beautiful green lawns edging down toward the sea with picturesque tables covered with cheerful umbrellas.

The motel is owned and operated by the Hughes family. Continental breakfast is included in the room rate. Children older than 5 and adults are charged $15 for extra occupancy.

The Rockaway Hotel
$$$ • Main St., York Beach • (207) 363-8470, (207) 363-2080

The Rockaway Hotel was originally a rooming house above a general store for summer visitors. Built in the Tudor-revival style, the building, known as Hawkes Pharmacy, has been fully restored and now offers luxury suites with modern comforts. You'll love the unique and charming facade of the hotel with its shops on the lower level.

Entrance to the hotel is from the door located at the middle of the row. Two types of accommodations are offered. Choose from a two-bedroom suite that sleeps six or a loft suite that sleeps four. Weekly rental rates are also available. Extra adults and children old enough to sleep in beds are charged approximately $25. Smoking is not permitted in any part of the Rockaway, which is not handicapped-accessible.

Betty Doon Motor Hotel
$$ • 5 Beach St., Ogunquit • (207) 646-2469

If you like to be at the center of things, you'll love the Betty Doon. Located a few steps off Route 1 at the center of the Main Street area and just 100 yards from the beach, the Betty Doon puts you in the middle of a great area for shopping, restaurants and entertainment. In fact, the motel has shops along Beach Street on the ground floor.

Rooms at the Betty Doon are clean and pleasant, some with neutral paint and others with knotty-pine paneling. Most rooms have an outside deck or sitting area and the two-bedroom penthouse features a full kitchen and large deck overlooking the village. The Betty Doon is open from early May to early October.

Operators are available to take reservations beginning in March.

The Cliff House on Bald Head Cliff
$$$$ • Shore Rd. (3 miles from town center), Ogunquit • (207) 361-1000

In 1997 the Cliff House celebrated its 125th year in operation. Run by the fourth generation of Weare Family innkeepers, the Cliff House retains the hospitality of a small inn, though it offers much more. Located on 70 acres of land overlooking a dramatic, rocky stretch of coast, the Cliff House offers all the amenities you would expect from a well-established resort: two swimming pools (one indoor and one out), a whirlpool, sauna, exercise room, tennis courts, walking paths and a game room.

Each of the 150 or so guest rooms features an ocean-view balcony and spacious accommodations. A charge of $15 per day is added for extra occupants older than 3 and for corner rooms. For those who like to take mini-vacations, the Cliff House offers several accommodation and dinner theme packages, from the Chocolate Lovers Weekend and the Beer Tasting Weekend to New Year and Easter packages.

While staying at the Cliff House don't miss their excellent dinners. The dining room faces the sea, but it'll be the food, not the view, that captures your heart.

The Footbridge Motel
$$ • 320 U.S. Hwy. 1, Ogunquit • (207) 646-2796

Named for the footbridge that leads to Footbridge Beach, just a three-minute walk away (see our Beaches chapter), this motel has 19 clean rooms with one queen or two double beds, refrigerators and coffee makers. Other amenities include a heated pool, barbecue facilities and pretty sitting areas amid flowered landscaping. Additional room guests are charged $10 each; children younger than 12 are charged $5.

The Sparhawk Oceanfront Resort
$$$ • Shore Rd., Ogunquit • (207) 646-5562

Spacious grounds and a spectacular view make the Sparhawk a popular destination for visitors to Southern Maine. In addition to large rooms that have been tastefully decorated, you can enjoy the heated swimming pool from June 15 to September 15, get in a game of tennis or shuffleboard or challenge some friends to croquet.

Complimentary breakfast is served in the Sparhawk Hall, and the staff at the resort are always happy to assist guests with planning side trips or dinner or theater reservations. Accommodation choices at the Sparhawk include oceanfront motel units or oceanfront suites and apartments with limited ocean view. The Sparhawk apartment familiarly known as the Little White House is at street level with a fireplace, living room, two bathrooms, two bedrooms and a private deck. The Little White House is extremely popular: Reservations for it are made more than a year in advance, but you can always try!

From July 5 to August 16 a one-week minimum stay is required in all accommodations. In-season extra occupants are charged $15, off-season the charge is $10.

Garrison Suites Motel & Cottages
$$ • 1099 U.S. Hwy. 1 (Post Rd.), Wells • (207) 646-3497, (800) 646-3497

Blue skies reflecting off a tidal marsh and Wells beach in the distance — what more could you want for a view? At Garrison Suites you get the view plus a pool, shuffleboard and badminton facilities and a choice of motel rooms, suites or efficiency cottages. All rooms have cherry, high-posted bed frames and are clean and pleasantly decorated with pictures of sea scenes on the walls. If you opt for a suite you'll find a pull-down double bed, a sofa bed and a separate bedroom as well as a kitchen area with dishwasher, microwave, coffee maker and other conveniences. Cottage kitchens are similarly equipped.

INSIDERS' TIP

Regulars who summer along Maine's Southern Beaches know it's wise to make reservations a year in advance whenever possible.

The Colony Hotel: Not Just Grand, But Green

Picture yourself sitting on a wide veranda overlooking the ocean, sipping a cocktail or a cup of tea as the sweet scent of old roses drifts toward you on the breeze. Imagine the opulence of a bygone era as you enjoy the timeless elegance of The Colony Hotel

in Kennebunkport - among the most graceful of the "Grand Old Hotels" built in the early 20th century. Now imagine this grand hotel as a leader in the "green hotel" movement. It seems difficult to merge the two images, doesn't it? Perhaps that's because opulence has al-

ways been considered somewhat synonymous with wastefulness. Yet at The Colony, Maine's only "green" hotel, environmental responsibility is key.

How did it happen? In 1989, owner Jestena Boughton, daughter of the Boughtons who have owned and operated the hotel since 1948, began an incremental program of environmental responsibility at the family's two hotels. The second hotel, also called The Colony, is in Delray Beach, Florida, and operates during the months when the Kennebunkport hotel is closed - October to May. As an internationally recognized landscape architect and CEO of Boughton Family Hotels, Jestena felt it was important to implement green programs at her hotels.

In 1995, The Colony Hotel became a charter member of the Green Hotel Association. Founded in 1993 in Houston, the association aims to provide environmental information and "green" suggestions to hotels. At present there are approximately 150 member properties in the association - 75 percent are in America, 20 percent in the Caribbean and 5 percent scattered worldwide. Members are issued the association's booklet of guidelines and ideas for creating a green hotel, but there is no requirement for joining other than a commitment by management.

According to Janet Byrd, director of marketing and environmental programs, The Colony's programs were very low-key at first, taking place in the infrastructure of the hotel - things that were not easily visible to visitors. Today, guests clearly know about the hotel staff's green ways of thinking, and they readily participate. There are no televisions in the Main House guest rooms, smoking is prohibited throughout the hotel, recycling bins are scattered on the premises, and there are water-saving devices in toilets and showers. In addition, guests are issued a paper stating the hotel's green policy. To

— continued on next page

Photo: The Colony Hotel

The Colony Hotel in Kennebunkport is one of only 150 "green" hotels in the world.

reduce energy, water and detergent use, guests are given the option of not having their sheets and towels changed daily.

"We became entirely nonsmoking in 1995, and there was a little resistance at first, but now even the smokers like it - they like the fresh, clean smell when they come back to their rooms," says Byrd.

Other visible signs of the environmental program are the non-chlorinated, heated saltwater pool, occasionally brown lawns and the plenitude of birds and other wildlife on the hotel's 11-acre grounds.

"Like Jestena says, 'Brown is beautiful,'" Byrd said, explaining that the grass, except for the putting green, is never watered. A firm believer in sustainable design, Jestena has structured the gardens at the hotel to incorporate indigenous plant communities, thereby encouraging native ecosystem development, food and shelter for wildlife and eliminating the need for excessive watering, fertilizing and pest control. In keeping with its environmental focus, the hotel does not use chemicals and weed-whacking tools but instead has extra gardeners to deal with weeding. As for fertilizer, only the putting green is catered to, and it doesn't get anything chemical - only Milorganite, which is made from the sewage sludge from the City of Milwaukee! As a result, plants either thrive or they die, yet most seem quite happy. Those old roses described above were planted by Jestena's grandmother more than 40 years ago, and they are doing just fine, rioting over the trellises on the ocean side of the hotel.

In 1997 the hotel received the Environmental Protection Agency designation as a Backyard Wildlife Habitat. According to Byrd, the hotel was aiming for a Backyard Bird Habitat distinction but received the more difficult Wildlife designation. The classification was based on the number and variety of bird and wildlife sightings and habitats on the premises and the quality of the food, shelter and places available to raise young wildlife. There are bird feeders and birdbaths throughout the grounds, and bird- and animal-sighting lists are posted on the "Eco-Tip Board" (along with other environmental notices and information), adjacent to the gift shop in the lobby. The gift shop stocks only Maine-made products.

For the 1997 season, The Colony expanded its environmental program by hiring a staff naturalist who provided Saturday morning tours and education sessions on ecology, tide pools and other environmental issues. Each year the staff strives to expand the scope of its green scene. Presently, the hotel is implementing a program to replace incandescent lighting with low-energy-use florescent and halogen lights. In addition, each season 20 guest rooms are renovated. Instead of using fiberglass insulation in the walls, the staff uses cellulose, 80 percent of which is made up of post-consumer recycled newspaper. Carpets are removed and not replaced since they were often made using chemicals. Instead, natural hardwood floors are waxed until they glow.

Behind the scenes, the hotel uses both sides of paper for photocopying, purchases recycled paper products and recycles as much as possible. All new machinery bought for the hotel is, if possible, Energy Star Compliant (meaning it was designed to significantly reduce the amount of energy needed to operate it), and a Green Meetings Guide has been developed for those interested in holding business meetings and retreats at the hotel.

In a time of increased affluence and spending, it is refreshing to see an establishment that caters primarily to the wealthy echelons of society taking a stand on environmental issues and working to ensure a safe and beautiful future. Here is the hotel's pledge, as written in its Environmental Responsibility Program literature:

"We acknowledge our interdependence with all living things and we operate with the belief that ecological, economic and cultural sustainability require equity and balance among all parties. The Colony Hotel is making great strides toward incorporating this philosophy into all of its phases of business. We are committed to protecting our environment and helping to ensure a future for all living things."

LAFAYETTE'S
OCEANFRONT RESORT AT WELLS BEACH
"Where memories that last a lifetime are made"

ON THE OCEAN • OPEN YEAR 'ROUND

LAFAYETTE'S OCEANFRONT RESORT offers oceanfront lodging on one of Maine's finest beaches. Accommodations feature color cable T.V., refrigerators and an indoor swimming pool and spa for your year 'round enjoyment. The Ledgeview Inn has a guest elevator and telephones have been added to all of our guest rooms. Fine food is available next door at the Forbes Restaurant and Take Out (in season) and the shops of One Casino Square are nearby for your after-beach browsing.

LAFAYETTE'S OCEANFRONT RESORT AT WELLS BEACH

Driftwinds - Wells Beach Motor Inn - Beach Front Lodge - Ledgeview Motor Inn

P.O. BOX 6391 • WELLS BEACH, ME 04090 • 207/646-2831

Weekly rental rates for cottages in 1998 were $600 to $725 for two bedrooms and a maximum of four occupants. There is a $10 charge for extra occupants. Children are not charged if they stay in the same room as their parents.

Lafayette's Oceanfront Resort at Wells Beach
$$ • 393 Mile Rd., Wells • (207) 646-2831

Relax and unwind at one of Wells' oldest oceanfront resorts. Nearly all of the 128 rooms have ocean views or are right on the sand. You'll love the large, comfortable rooms, which have been designed to showcase the views. Oceanfront rooms have sliding glass doors onto patios so that you can step from your room onto the beach.

Founded by the Forbes family 75 years ago, the Lafayette's Oceanfront Resort at Wells Beach has grown to incorporate five separate buildings, but it has retained its romantic seaside charm. It is no wonder that year after year families return to the resort — those who came as children now bringing their grandchildren.

The Lafayette Oceanfront Resort is one of the few accommodations in the Southern Beaches area that features an indoor heated pool and hot tub. Refrigerators and telephones are supplied in every room. The resort is open year round.

USA Inn
$ • 1017 U.S. Hwy. 1 (Post Rd.), Wells • (207) 646-9313, (800) 783-8258

You'll find this motel at the corner of Route 1 and Mile Road in Wells, just a mile from the beach. The 42 rooms feature two double beds and a microwave. Free continental breakfast is included in the room rate. At this motel, rates are based on single or double occupancy and the use of one bed. Use of the second bed or extra occupants is $10, and children younger than 12 are $5.

Econo Lodge
$$ • 55 U.S. Hwy. 1 (York St.), Kennebunk • (207) 985-6100, (800) 336-5634

The Econo Lodge stands out on this portion of Route 1 with its immaculately trimmed lawn, fresh white-painted trim and floral land-

INSIDERS' TIP

Even if you can't afford to stay by the ocean or in a Jacuzzi suite for your entire vacation, treat yourself to one or two nights of luxury, and save money by staying in a less-expensive room for the remainder of your vacation.

scaping around the outdoor pool. The 46 rooms are equally pleasant, with two double beds or a king-sized bed and in-room amenities such as a hairdryer, coffee maker, iron and ironing board. Some rooms also have small refrigerators. Room rate includes a deluxe continental breakfast.

Seaside Motor Inn & Cottages
$$$$ • Beach St., Gooch's Beach, Kennebunkport • (207) 967-4461

A private beach and 20 acres of grounds await you at the Seaside Motor Inn, which is open year round. Run by Michael and Sandra Severance, the motel has been run by the Gooch-Severance family for 12 generations. Rooms feature two queen-sized beds, refrigerator, teleport for modems and a private deck or patio. In addition to the Motor Inn, and the 1756 Inn, ten cottages are available with one, two or four bedrooms (see our Summer Rentals chapter for information on these cottages).

The Colony Hotel
$$$$, includes dinner and breakfast • Ocean Ave. and King's Hwy., Kennebunkport • (207) 967-3331, (800) 552-2363

In the tradition of "Grand Old Hotels," The Colony ranks among the finest (see the Closeup in this chapter). Perched majestically atop a slight rise, overlooking the sea, this graceful white painted building would make a perfect backdrop for a painting of women wearing gauzy dresses and summer hats and carrying sun umbrellas. Hotel amenities include a heated saltwater swimming pool, private beach, organic gardens and a putting green. A gracious dining room and intimate pub are also on premises, and guests are encouraged to spend time on the wide porch overlooking the sea and in the lounge and library.

In the tradition of sociable summer visits, guest rooms do not have televisions, but there is a television room on the main floor. The Colony is an entirely smoke-free establishment. Cost for additional occupants is $25. Pets are welcome for an additional charge of $25. The nightly rate includes breakfast and dinner.

Old Orchard Beach Area

D'Allaire's Motel & Cottages
$ • 528 U.S. Hwy. 1 S. (Elm St.), Biddeford • (207) 284-4100

A fun, kind of kitsch statue of a cheerfully plump man holding his hand up displaying a large golf ball stands before the entrance to D'Allaire's, illustrating that the motel features a miniature golf course. There's also an old-fashioned wagon with a mannequin driver in the driveway. All in all, it's difficult to miss.

The motel features eight motel rooms and 12 cottages. The cottages and some rooms in the motel have efficiency kitchens. Amenities at D'Allaire's include the miniature golf course ($2 for children younger than 12, $3 for adults), a large heated pool, game room, laundry facilities, shuffleboard, horseshoes and a billiard room as well as a covered barbecue area. There is no extra charge for children sharing a room with their parents. Extra adults are $5.

Eastview Motel
$ • U.S. Hwy. 1 (Jct. of Maine Hwy. 98), Saco • (207) 282-2362

Backed by woods and located on Route 1 at the intersection with Maine Highway 98 (Cascade Road) this 22-room motel features an immaculate exterior, pool and complimentary coffee from the reception area. Rooms have one or two double beds or a queen-sized bed and a sleeper sofa. The Eastview Motel has been run by Bob and Pat Dube since 1986. It is open from the middle of May to the middle of October.

INSIDERS' TIP

If you need a child-care provider to watch the kids while you take off for a night on the town, some hotels have lists of sitters. If not, check in with the local YMCA. They often know of babysitters who have taken safety courses.

The Classic Motel
$ • 21 Ocean Park Rd., Saco
• (207) 282-5569, (800) 290-3909

A couple of minutes drive from Exit 5 of the Maine Turnpike, close to the junction of Ocean Park Road and Route 1, The Classic Motel has 19 units and features an indoor heated pool and complimentary beach parking. Rooms have either queen- or full-sized beds and kitchenettes with microwaves. The motel is open year round. Group rates are available.

Billowhouse Oceanfront Motel and Guesthouse
$$ • 1 Temple Ave.,
Ocean Park, Old Orchard Beach
• (207) 934-2333

Cheerfully painted in yellow and white, this Victorian-style bed and breakfast and motel sits at the edge of the dunes overlooking 7 miles of sandy beach. In-season, it's just a minute's walk to the old-fashioned soda fountain in Ocean Park's square where you can try the famous Raspberry Lime Rickeys, a hot dog or hamburger or ice cream.

Motel rooms at the Billowhouse feature kitchenettes and one double and one single bed, two doubles or a double and two singles. Guesthouse rooms also have a variety of bed arrangements. Continental breakfast is available for two people in rooms without kitchens. Smoking is not allowed at the Billowhouse,

though you may smoke on the decks and at the outside tables. Studio rooms will sleep up to four people at no extra charge. Guesthouse rooms are limited to two occupants.

Crest Motel
$$ • 35 E. Grand Ave., Old Orchard Beach
• (207) 934-4060, (800) 909-4060

Situated on the beach, this motel has clean, comfortable rooms facing either the pool or the sea. All rooms feature refrigerators and microwaves, and there's a picnic area with barbecue facilities available for guest use. Children will enjoy the play area and the entire family will appreciate the motel's proximity to Old Orchard Beach's pier and other amusements.

There's no extra charge for children aged 15 or younger. Older additional occupants are charged $10, and there's a charge of $5 per day for cots and playpens. Discounted weekly rates are available.

Kebek Motel 3
$$ • 53 W. Grand Ave.,
Old Orchard Beach • (207) 934-5253

The exterior of this motel is always neatly painted. Don't be surprised if this popular accommodation is sporting a No Vacancy sign. All rooms are efficiencies and are kept scrupulously clean. Those with ocean views will cost you a bit more than those that don't. Thirty-five rooms available; for most of the season the motel requires a three-night minimum stay.

Run by the Beaulieu family since 1988, the motel doesn't have a pool but it doesn't need one — the beach is less than a minute's walk away! After a day of sun and surf, if you decide you'd rather barbecue than cook at a stove, head on over to the pleasant barbecue area available for guests. Discounted weekly rates are available. There is no additional charge for children aged 15 or less; older additional occupants will be charged $10.

Sea Drift Motel
$$ • 126 E. Grand Ave.,
Old Orchard Beach • (207) 934-2641

This motel has come a long way since it was purchased by the Mokarzel family in 1968. It has undergone extensive renovations and added second-floor rooms with private balconies and kitchen areas. The family provides courtesy, cleanliness and comfort. A heated pool and complimentary coffee are available to all guests.

During the off-season this 32-room motel will accept small dogs. Additional guests older than 6 will be charged $10. The Sea Drift is open from mid-May to mid-October.

Aquarius Motel
$ • 5 Brown St., Old Orchard Beach
• (207) 934-2626

You get more than just a room on the beach when you sign in at the Aquarius Motel. Owners Wes and Barbara Carter do their utmost to make sure guests have a wonderful time by providing lots of local and historical information at the front desk and in the rooms. During the time they're open (from the first weekend in April to the last weekend in October), there is always someone on duty at the Aquarius — you'll never find a "Back in an Hour" sign here!

The Carters have operated the Aquarius since 1985, and they find that two-thirds of their guests are repeat customers who have had a wonderful time in previous years. Barbara takes lots of pictures throughout the summer, and proudly displays a collage of happy faces on the wall in the office. She often sends photos to guests to remind them what a wonderful time they had.

The Aquarius has 16 rooms, some with kitchenettes and some without. You can choose a room for two people with one double bed, or a larger room that can accommodate from two to six.

The Old Colonial
$$ • 61 W. Grand Ave.,
Old Orchard Beach • (207) 934-9862

For the 1997 season, the rooms at the Old Colonial were completely remodeled, leaving 1970s decor behind for a fresh, clean look. Carpets, fabrics and furniture have been replaced. Now these rooms are some of the nicest in town. Five types of rooms are available, including oceanfront deluxe rooms that feature kitchens, microwaves, a large-screen TV, a VCR and a private oceanfront balcony. The Old Colonial has a heated pool and provides movie, beach chair, umbrella and boogie board rentals in the office.

There is no additional charge for children younger than six years old. Older children are charged $5 and adults are $15. Cost for a cot is $5 and a crib is $4. Before June 20 and after Labor Day there is no charge for children, regardless of age.

Greater Portland Area

Blackpoint Inn Resort
$$$$, includes dinner and breakfast
• Prouts Neck, Scarborough • (207) 883-4126

It is no wonder that Winslow Homer called Prouts Neck home for many years. Deep blue and turquoise water, bobbing sailboats and white-sand beaches stretching along the shore in every direction make this part of Maine one of the most beautiful. Pine studded islands lay offshore, beach roses line the roads in summer, and velvety lawns lean towards the sea. This is where you'll find the Blackpoint Inn Resort.

For more than a century guests at the Inn have gained entrance to an exclusive summer community. Public on-street parking is not allowed at Prouts Neck. As a result the roads are uncluttered and the beaches quiet. If you prefer swimming in a pool, the Inn has both indoor and outdoor heated facilities. You'll love the breathtaking views from the outdoor pool, which is situated at the end of a flower-lined flagstone path at the edge of a cliff overlooking the sea. When you tire of swimming you can enjoy a drink under the blue-and-white-striped umbrella-topped patio tables around the pool. In addition, you'll find tennis courts, and you are in proximity to a number of golf courses. You can also enjoy the scenic cliff walk past Winslow Homer's studio, or try sailing, fishing or biking.

In keeping with the inn's understated elegance, its 80 guest rooms are tastefully decorated with views over the sea or the beautifully manicured gardens. As a special touch, evening turn-down service is provided. Peak-season rates include dinner and breakfast. The elegant dining room overlooks both rose gardens and the sea, and you will find the menu changing daily (though Maine lobster is always available). A variety of weekend packages are offered; rates vary depending on which month you visit, May and November being the least expensive and July and August the most expensive. Cost for an extra person in a room during peak season is $75, which includes breakfast and dinner. In May and November, that cost drops to $20 and does not include meals. If children are old enough to eat in the dining room, they will be charged the extra person rate.

The Holiday House Inn & Motel
$$ • 106 E. Grand Ave., Scarborough
• (207) 883-4417

You'll love the oceanfront location of this motel and inn. Family owned since 1964, the inn features eight rooms with private baths while the motel offers 16 units with two double beds, bath and dressing area and a communal kitchen to prepare and eat meals. Guests of the inn receive continental breakfast in the seaside dining room and use of the guest

lounge (see our Bed & Breakfasts and Inns chapter).

The best amenity of this motel is the Atlantic Ocean. You'll enjoy walking the flower-fringed path to 7 miles of beach or sitting under umbrellas on the oceanfront patio, listening to the soothing sound of the surf. The Holiday House is open from mid-May to mid-October.

The Lighthouse Inn at Pine Point
$$ • Pine Point Beach, Scarborough
• (207) 883-3213, (800) 780-3213

You won't find many amenities at the Lighthouse Inn because you don't need them! Located on the beach at Pine Point, the Inn has 22 units featuring two double beds with full baths and a dressing area. Peter, Cathy and Nick Truman have operated the Inn since 1985, though the inn itself was established in 1959. From the inn you can walk along 7 miles of sandy beach or explore Scarborough Marsh, which borders Pine Point. If you tire of the quiet, you can take a short drive into Old Orchard Beach and enjoy the amusement arcades and the activity the town offers in summer. In the off-season (May, part of June, September and October), the inn offers Danishes and coffee to guests. It's open from the middle of May to the middle of October.

The Pride Motel and Cottages
$ • 677 U.S. Hwy. 1 S.,
Scarborough
• (207) 883-4816, (800) 424-3350

On Route 1, south of Dunstan Corner, the Pride Motel and Cottages are painted dark red with white trim and have pretty baskets of flowers hanging from the porches. The Motel is set sideways to the road and has a country atmosphere despite its location on the highway. Grass and old trees frame the site, which

---

INSIDERS' TIP

If Fido or Fifi isn't allowed to stay at your hotel, check your pup into a doggie hotel (otherwise known as a kennel) and take him or her for romps during the day. This way your dog will still get your company as well as plenty of exercise, and you'll know it's being well cared for. Ask your desk clerk or concierge about reputable nearby kennels, or check out our vet listings in the Healthcare chapter.

features 17 rooms distributed among a motel and cottages.

The O'Reilly family has operated the Pride Motel since 1967. Today, Patrick and Sue O'Reilly welcome guests to their motel, which features amenities such as a heated outdoor pool, available from June to the beginning of September, a recreation room with a pool table, and laundry facilities. Cottages also feature efficiency kitchens but have no telephones. Pets are accepted for an additional charge of $5. Room sizes vary, some accommodating no more than two people and others accommodating as many as six. Each additional person will be charged $5. The motel is open from April to November.

Inn by the Sea
$$$$ • 40 Bowery Beach Rd., Cape Elizabeth • (207) 799-3134

In classic seaside resort style, the Inn by the Sea has sweeping green lawns, manicured flower beds and wonderful views of the Atlantic. In addition you'll find a private boardwalk entrance to Crescent Beach State Park with its salt marsh and curving stretch of sand. Forty-three one- and two-bedroom suites are available either in the main house or as cottage suites away from the main house. As a guest in the main house, you'll find rooms furnished in Chippendale cherry furniture, featuring kitchens and VCRs. You can opt for the loft suite that has two levels with an ocean view balcony on the first level or a garden suite that's on one level but features individual porches complete with rocking chair. Cottage suites have two bedrooms, with the same amenities as main house suites, and are furnished in classic summer style with light pine and wicker.

You can enjoy playing shuffleboard and tennis or merely sitting in the English gazebo, listening to the sea.

Fine dining is available from the Audubon Room restaurant, which features fresh Maine seafood and regional cuisine. There is no extra charge for children or additional occupants at the Inn by the Sea. Furthermore, you'll find a warm welcome for pets here: They're referred to as "little people with fur coats." Special beds and bowls are available for your fur-coated friends.

Best Western Merry Manor Inn
$$ • 700 Main St. (U.S. Hwy. 1), South Portland • (207) 774-6151

Just off Interstate 295, this hotel is a few minutes drive from the Maine Mall area, downtown Portland and the airport. Manager Greg Goforth ensures that the hotel is continuously renovated. One hundred and fifty-one rooms are available — 75 percent of them are non-smoking. Rooms have two double, two queen-sized, or one king-sized bed. This Best Western features an outdoor heated pool; the fenced-in patio area with umbrellas, tables and chairs and is adjacent to Governor's Restaurant where you can enjoy great homestyle food and famous desserts at reasonable prices. Laundry and meeting facilities are also available.

Pet owners will be happy to note that the Best Western accepts pets at no extra charge. There's a wooded area behind the hotel for exercising pets. Books, magazines and Maine-made products are available in the comfortable sitting area of the lobby. There is no additional charge for children younger than 12. Everyone else is charged $5.

Econo Lodge
$$ • 738 Main St., South Portland • (207) 774-5891

The Econo Lodge is off I-295 next to Governor's Restaurant. It features a small, pleasant lobby, meeting room and outdoor pool. You'll find bright, clean rooms that were renovated in 1997. Rates vary depending not only on season but also on which day of the week you wish to stay. There is no additional charge for children 13 or younger. Those older than 13 are charged $10.

Hampton Inn
**$$ • 171 Philbrook Ave.,
South Portland**
• **(207) 773-4400, (800) 426-7866**

Set amid tall pines with lovely flower beds, picnic tables and a rustic wooden swing on the grounds, you'd never guess the Hampton Inn was across the road from the Maine Mall, two minutes from Exit 7 of the Maine Turnpike. The inn's lobby is inviting, with comfortable tables and chairs where you can enjoy an extensive free continental breakfast buffet, sit and write a letter or go over paperwork while enjoying a cup of coffee or tea (available throughout the day). If you prefer to sit outside, there's a sunny courtyard behind the lobby.

The hotel's 118 rooms are decorated in deep jade and purple colors, giving them a rich, warm ambiance. Amenities include free local phone calls and free in-room movies shown on the 25-inch televisions. Each room has dataports, iron and ironing board. Rooms have either one king-sized bed or two doubles. There is no charge for children 18 or younger and a Lifestyle 50 program is available for people older than 50 (single rates are charged regardless of number of room occupants). There is a $10 fee for rollaway cots; cribs are free.

Holiday Inn by the Bay
$$$ • 88 Spring St., Portland
• **(207) 775-2311, (800) 345-5050**

With views of Portland, Casco Bay and Portland Harbor, this modern, 11-story hotel has 239 guest rooms, a large indoor pool, fitness center, saunas, restaurant, lounge and free parking for registered guests. In the busy entry room you'll find mahogany tables, comfortable couches and wing-backed chairs surrounded by carpets and wallcoverings in relaxing greens and maroons.

Upstairs you'll have your choice of guest rooms from a standard with queen-sized bed or two double beds. More expensive rooms have a king-sized bed, and an executive room has a king-sized bed, pull-out couch and widescreen television. There is also a Presidential suite with a kitchenette, three bedrooms and a parlor and a Governor's Suite with two-bedrooms and a parlor. Some rooms have a view

of the harbor. Certain room rates also include a buffet breakfast served in the downstairs dining room.

When you're ready to hit the town, the waterfront is just a few blocks away, and the shopping district is about a 10-minute walk into town. The hotel also has a shuttle to transport passengers to the Portland Jetport.

DoubleTree Hotel
$$$$ • 1230 Congress St., Portland
• **(207) 774-5611, (800) 989-3856**

Formerly a Ramada Inn, this hotel became the first DoubleTree Hotel in the state in August 1997. We like it, because upon arrival, you're greeted with fresh-baked chocolate-chip cookies! The hotel has 149 guest rooms with either two double beds or one king-sized bed, desks, data ports, voice mail, speaker phones, irons and ironing boards, hairdryers and coffee makers. For roughly $239 during peak season, suites are also available. The room rate includes a complimentary morning newspaper and plenty of free parking. For an additional charge there's a breakfast buffet in the morning. Lunch and dinner are served in the dining room.

If you're ready for a little R 'n' R, try the indoor heated pool, fitness room and Jacuzzi. Nonsmoking and handicapped-accessible rooms are available. The hotel provides complimentary shuttle service to downtown shops, the Maine Mall, and the Portland International Jetport.

Embassy Suites
$$$$ • 1050 Westbrook St., Portland
• **(207) 775-2200, (800) EMBASSY**

Each of this hotel's 119 suites consists of a bedroom with one king- or queen-sized bed or two double beds and a separate living room with a pull-out sofa and desk. The rooms also have a galley that comes with a wet bar, microwave, refrigerator and coffee maker. In addition there are two-bedroom suites. Rooms also have data ports and voice mail.

The room rate includes a complimentary full American breakfast buffet each morning at Cafe Stroudwater (see Restaurants) and access to the indoor pool, whirlpool, sauna and fitness center. The hotel also provides a complimentary morning newspaper, guest laundry, valet, business and room services and wheel chair accommodations. Children younger than 18 stay free in the same room with their parents.

Portland Regency Hotel
$$$$ • 20 Milk St., Portland
• (207) 774-4200, (800) 727-3436

Luxury abounds in this historic hotel housed in a 19th century, brick and pink-granite armory in the heart of the Old Port. There are 95 gorgeously appointed guest rooms with poster beds, highboys, floor-to-ceiling drapes, cozy sitting corners and gilt mirrors of the Queen Anne style. A standard room has two double beds or one queen, and suites have a king-sized bed with a larger sitting area. Guests can also take advantage of a weight room, cardiovascular center, Jacuzzi, sauna, steam room, tanning booths and various aerobic and body-sculpting classes.

The four-star Armory restaurant downstairs (see our Restaurants chapter) is elegant — intimate tables and fresh flowers. For less formal occasions, there's The Armory lounge, serving up cocktails, light fare and room service. For formal or business occasions, the hotel has conference rooms for groups of six to 200. When you're ready to hit the town, all you'll have to do is walk out the front door (which is always attended by doorpersons, we might add). The waterfront is just two blocks away, and shopping is just around the corner.

Radisson Eastland Hotel Portland
$$$ • 157 High St., Portland
• (207) 775-5411, (800) 333-3333

From the moment you step under the red awnings and into the grand welcome area of this historic hotel, you'll be immersed in charm and elegance. A crystal chandelier drips from the ceiling; brass sconces cling to the walls. Comfy lounge chairs are tucked away in corners, and the entry room basks in soothing pink hues.

Standard rooms are simply furnished with either one queen or two double beds, sitting chairs and end tables. Much of the charm here comes from the harbor views (should you select a room with one). For a little more money, you can reserve a luxury suite, equipped with a king-sized bed, pull-out sofa, large sitting

area and floor-to-ceiling windows with city views. The brick, high-rise hotel was built in 1927 and is located in the heart of downtown, within walking distance of the Old Port and Arts District. The hotel also has a fitness center, a restaurant, cafe, lounge, 5,000-square-foot ballroom, and conference rooms to accommodate as many as 750 people.

Brookside Motel
$$ • U.S. Route 1, Yarmouth
• (207) 846-5512

Tucked behind a grove of birch trees, this small motel is a refreshing place to pull off the road and relax. With just 12 rooms, the one-story motel is very low-profile, and one might not spot it all except for the antique carriage house complete with carriages that instantly draws the attention of the curious. The motel is nicely decorated with flower boxes, and a small porch area. Inside, the rooms have gingham curtains, flowered bed spreads with two queen-sized beds and small bathrooms. Flowers bloom in back of the hotel, filling the windows with blooms of yellow. The motel is operated by owners Mary Ellen and Jim Hesselbacher.

Casco Bay Inn
$ • U.S. Route 1, Freeport • (207) 865-4925

This dark brown motel with batten-board siding is edged with spruce green trim and dotted with flower boxes, giving it a charming, country flavor. There are 30 rooms, many of which are brand new and have new carpeting and furniture. All rooms are non-smoking and have two queen-size beds. One handicapped-accessible room is available, and dark green (plastic) Adarondack chairs are set about the property for guests' enjoyment. There are also a handful of toddler toys including a kiddy pool, sandbox and slide. The motel is set directly on the side of busy Route 1, but that also makes it a short drive to downtown outlet stores.

Down-East Village
$ • 705 U.S. Route One, Yarmouth
• (207) 846-5161, (800)STAY-DEV

This 31 unit motel is conveniently located off Route 1 near the bank of Yarmouth's Royall River. The Ferrell family founded the motel in

1950 and hosts Ed and Sue Ferrell continue to operate it today. The motel includes an executive conference suite, private dinning facilities and a popular family-style restaurant, the Down-East Village Restaurant, where you can get a tasty breakfast, lunch and dinner. Just a 10-minute from downtown Freeport and only 15-minutes from Portland's Old Port, the motel offers standard accommodations for a reasonable price.

Freeport Inn & Cafe
$$ • 335 U.S. Hwy. 1, Freeport
• (207) 865-3106, (800) 998-2583

Set on a hill overlooking 25 acres of wind-swept lawns and a tidal river, the Freeport Inn has 80 rooms with private baths and air-conditioning. Each is tastefully decorated with cheerful, country wallpaper and has either two double beds or a queen bed, comfy chairs, bedside tables, televisions and voice mail. For $10 extra, deluxe rooms come with a refrigerator, hairdryer, coffee maker and a river view. Outside you might enjoy strolling about the property, swimming in the pool, paddling a canoe in the river or watching your children as they romp in the play area.

Dining is as easy as a stepping inside one of the inn's two restaurants, the Cafe and the Muddy Rudder (see our Restaurants chapter), where you'll get home-style meals and fresh-baked deserts, breads and nightly entertainment served up until midnight. The inn is just several minutes' drive from the nearby shops, and pets are allowed in a handful of rooms on the first floor.

Coastline Inn
$$ • 209 U.S. Hwy. 1, Freeport
• (207) 865-3777, (800) 470-9494

This modern motel, made up of newly built gray buildings with white trimmed porches, has a pleasant atmosphere and tidy, tastefully decorated bedrooms with two double beds or one queen-sized bed, air conditioning, a desk and sitting area. It's just off Route 1, a short drive from the shopping district and L.L. Bean. There is also one suite, which comes with a king-sized bed, a living room and kitchen. Room rates include a complimentary continental breakfast and free incoming faxes.

Brunswick, Bath and Boothbay Harbor Area

Comfort Inn
$ • 199 Pleasant St.,
Brunswick • (207) 729-1129

This newly built, country-style hotel has 80 rooms, with either two double beds or one king-sized bed, and is conveniently located off U.S. 1 within a minute's drive of all the downtown shops and restaurants. Inside the rooms you'll find brass headboards, bedside tables and comfortable wing-backed chairs. Each room comes with free HBO, CNN and ESPN, and you can start the day with a complimentary continental breakfast.

The Parkwood Inn
$$ • P.O. Box 92, Maine Hwy. 24,
Brunswick • (207) 725-5251, (800) 349-7181

The large red awning and the marble and mahogany entryway at Parkwood tells you you've come to a place that puts quality first. This newly completed two-story hotel is furnished with poster beds, desks, wing-backed chairs and brass fixtures. You can choose from standard rooms with two queen-sized beds or rooms with one king-sized bed and a jetted bathtub. King-size suites, with a separate living room, pull-out couch, gas stove, wet bar, refrigerator, large-screen TV and jetted tub are also available. All the rooms are large, and even the standard comes with a built in hair dryer, coffee machine, ironing board and iron.

Downstairs you'll find a cozy fireplace and dining room on the Parkwood Grille where all guests can enjoy a complimentary deluxe con-

---

INSIDERS' TIP

Maine is a popular getaway spot for three-day holiday weekends. You should be aware that many hotels and motels will charge in-season rates on these weekends regardless of the time of year.

tinental breakfast. You'll also get a free copy of *USA Today.* Brunswick's Maine Street, which has great shops, restaurants and plenty of places for browsing away an afternoon, is a couple of miles from here (see our Shopping chapter).

Bailey Island Motel
$$ • Maine Hwy. 24,
Bailey Island • (207) 833-2886

This place is so cute, it could almost pass as an inn. Directly across from the world's only cribstone bridge (see more on this under Attractions), this small, two-story motel has rooms with two double beds, bedside tables and wicker chairs. One efficiency unit has a queen-size bed and kitchen. The upper rooms on the motel have a shared balcony overlooking the bridge, and outside the motel is a beautiful lawn nestled against the ocean.

In the morning you'll be greeted with fresh-baked muffins, coffee and juice, all included in the room rate. Downtown Brunswick is about a 15-minute drive away, but out here on the peninsula, you can enjoy all the ocean has to offer from great seafood to beach combing. The owner, Ralph Black, is a lifelong resident of the area and will be happy to get you started in the right direction.

Sebasco Harbor Resort
$$$$ (breakfast and dinner included)
• Maine Hwy. 217, Sebasco Estates
• (207) 389-1161,(800) 225-3819

Set on a secluded cove of Casco Bay, this is one of the areas only resorts and it has more than 600 acres of fields, pond and woods overlooking the ocean. One of the first amenities you'll see as you approach the resort is its nine-hole golf course, which is open to guests and the community. The shingled Maine Inn rises behind the course and houses the majority of the resort's guests. Others choose to stay in one of 22 different cottages or in the Lighthouse, which is built right at the water's edge.

In the last year extensive renovations have been done to rooms in The Lighthouse and the Maine Inn as well as other buildings on the property. Guest rooms now have new sets of contemporary furniture and matching floral drapes and bedspreads. Rooms in the Lighthouse are spacious and include a sitting area. Almost any combination of accommodations is available from a single King-size bed to two twin beds to separate adjoining rooms in one of the cottages.

The Maine Inn boasts beautiful views of a large pond, which is home to many birds, and has a screened in porch with rocking chairs. There is also a common room with wicker couches and more water views. Some rooms in the Maine Inn have balconies. The Lighthouse is shaped like its name sake, and has deluxe accommodations. Cottages range from the one-bedroom Honeymoon cottage, which has a jacuzzi and king-bed, to Shoreledges, which has six bedrooms, six bathrooms, a fireplace, kitchenette and two decks.

The resort was purchased in May 1997 by Bob Smith, who has been in the hospitality industry for more than 20 years. Prior to Smith's arrival the resort had more of a lodge style with few luxuries. It now has a fully equipped health club with a beautician and three massage therapists, a brand new cedar playground with tented platforms and two slides, televisions in most rooms and a "village green" with a gazebo and gardens — it used to be a parking lot. A new restaurant has been added down at the waterfront. On the first floor is the Pilot House with wooden cafe tables, an elaborate wooden bar and a rock wall surrounding a fountain. The Pilot House serves up snacks and drinks in a pub-like atmosphere and provides live entertainment. Upstairs is fine din-

INSIDERS' TIP

Maine's magnificent display of autumn foliage brings a huge number of tourists to the state in early October. If you're planning to visit during the three-day Columbus Day weekend (the second weekend in October), make sure you make reservations. Since many hotels and motels and most campgrounds are closed for the season, those that are open fill up quickly.

ning at The Ledges, an airy dining room with stunning views of the harbor and a five-course dinner menu that changes nightly. Reservations are required at The Ledges, and jackets are strongly recommended.

Also available at the resort are boat trips on The Ruth, a full children's program with arts and crafts, swimming and recreational activities, one-on-one babysitting for infants and toddlers, a salt-water swimming pool, bowling alley, canoes, tennis, shuffle board, a youth game room and shuttle buses to nearby beaches and outlet shopping in Freeport.

For those who don't wish to pay for the Modified American Meal Plan, bed and breakfast rates are available. Children 10 and younger stay and eat free, and there is a cost of $45 per day for guests 11 and older. Guest golf greens fees are $12 a day and $60 for a seven-day pass, and tennis fees are $6 per court per hour.

Wiscasset Motor Lodge
$ • 596 Bath Road, Wiscasset
• (207) 882-7137, (800) 732-8168

A handful of tan, woodsy cottages tucked back from the road behind and cluster of trees and a lodge-style motel and front office with a newly constructed cathedral ceiling will meet you at this tastefully decorated motor lodge beside Route 1 (in town it is it known as Bath Road). Many of the rooms have been recently renovated to include beamed, lofted ceilings, pine paneled walls, full bathrooms and private porches facing the woods. Flower gardens and tall pines surround the lodge, and there are several nice grassy areas for children to play.

One-bedroom and one-room cottages have their own entrances but do not have cooking areas. Lodge owners Bill and Nancy Gillies live in a house attached to the front office, so they are at hand to meet guests needs. Room rates start at just $39.50, and the lodge is open from early April through late fall. From July through Labor Day a complimentary breakfast is served in the Hearth Room. There are 30 units all-together and smoking is allowed in some rooms.

Boat enthusiasts will enjoy looking at two ship models of the Hesper and Luther Little, which used to rest in the Sheepscot River harbor until the summer of 1998, when the rotting

schooners were torn down. The ship models are to scale and are built of wood from their namesakes. They sit in the lodge entryway.

Edgecomb Inn
$$ • 306 Eddy Rd., Edgecomb
• (207) 882-6343, (800) 437-5503

This inn and its separate motor lodge are perched above the bank of the tidal Sheepscot River where you'll be able to watch fishing boats sail by from your bedroom window. The inn is a large barn-style building with individually decorated and hand-stenciled rooms. The flavor is modern and hotel-like, but the rooms maintain the feel of a more intimate environment. We especially like the plants and flowers, painted and stenciled in unsuspecting places. Each room has a private bathroom

A bit closer to the water is the motor lodge, which has large one- and two-room suites with complete kitchens. Some have a sitting room with fold-out couches and a dining table and two full-sized beds in the adjoining bedroom. Suites come with either a shared balcony or a small patio leading down to a wide lawn along the river. You'll also find a handful of pleasant, white-clapboard one and two room cottages tucked away in the woods. For a little daytime entertainment, try the tennis court or follow the walking trail to nearby Fort Edgecomb (see our Attractions chapter).

All of the accommodations include a complimentary breakfast of muffins, coffee and juice in a small dining area at the inn. At the adjoining Muddy Rudder restaurant (see the Freeport listings in our Restaurants chapter), you'll enjoy fine dining and nightly entertainment on the patio. Downtown Wiscasset is about a half-mile walk across the bridge. Complete meeting and banquet facilities are also available, and pets are allowed.

Cod Cove Inn
$$ • P.O. Box 36,
Junction of Maine Hwy. 1 and Maine Hwy. 27, Edgecomb
• (207) 882-9586, (800) 882-9586

Conveniently located on a hill high above Route 1 with distant views of the Sheepscot River and Wiscasset village, this elegant motel has 30 rooms that are tastefully and comfortably decorated with floral wallpapers, reproduction antique furniture and wing-backed chairs. Each has a private balcony or patio and can sleep up to four people. Several rooms have miniature glass-fronted stoves, and a suite has Oriental carpets, a fireplace, sunken Jacuzzi and wet bar. There is a small exercise room, and outside there's a large, heated swimming pool, hot tub and flower garden with gazebo. The motel is open from April through November. Room rates include an expanded continental breakfast of fruit, cereal, english muffins, bagels and coffee in the first-floor dining room. The inn also rents out a full-sized salt-box house on the property. The one-bedroom house sleeps seven and includes a lofts, living room with fireplace and post-and-beam construction. It is available year-round by the week for $1,000.

Sunset Vista Cottages
$ • 39 Sunset Vista, Edgecomb • (207) 882-8032

We weren't really sure where to include these four 1960s cottages set on a huge lawn with distant views of the Sheepscott River and the village of Wiscasset, but they are among the best-priced cottages you'll find. The feel and smell is of a true Maine camp. Each cottage has a compact kitchen, dining area, two bedrooms, screened porch, bathroom with shower and a picnic table. The furnishings are from yesteryear but are in good condition, as the cabins were unused for quite some time. You'll find brightly painted rooms of yellow, peach and blue to brighten the atmosphere on even the foggiest days. And the furniture is just as vivid, with a bright red chair in one cottage set off by equally colorful and mismatched pieces.

The truly humorous and lively colors are one reason we like these cabins so much; the other reason is the privacy. Separated from the main road by a wide expanse of trees, the units are just next door to a large farmhouse owned, like the cabins, by the Chadbourne family. The units are surrounded by a lush field and plenty of Maine foliage that you can explore by following a well-groomed trail all the way to the water's edge — a good 15-minute hike away. Closer to the cabins, you'll find badminton and volleyball nets as well as a variety of other lawn games. Children and pets are welcome, and your cabin comes with a clothesline and porch chairs for a true Maine vacation. Sunset Vista is located just off Maine Hwy. 27.

Hillside Acres Cabins & Motels
$ • P.O. Box 300, Adams Pond Rd., Boothbay • (207) 633-3411

One and two bedroom cottages and motel rooms are available on this nicely kept property, which is largely made up of a sweeping lawn set back from the road by a row of trees and an in-ground swimming pool. We think this is a great place for kids, because you'll get extra privacy in one of the quaint white cabins, and young people will have plenty or grassy space to run free. The cabins are appointed with nice pine furniture and decorated with hand-sewn quilts on the walls, and pets are allowed.

Hillside Acres also has two motel units (where pets are not allowed). Both are almost completely brand new from the carpeting to the furniture. These have pull-out couches, large kitchens and country curtains in the windows. The motel units and cabins can be rented daily or weekly, and a breakfast of muffins and coffee is included in the room rate from July through Labor Day.

White Anchor Motel
$ • Maine Hwy. 27, Boothbay • (207) 633-3788

These gray, shingled motel units are just off the main road to town, but some are set back from the road. What we really like about them was that they offered a clean, comfortable place to stay within a few minutes drive to town — for a bargain price. The motel has 29 rooms in two buildings, and the owners live on the same property in a quaint gray house surrounded by flower gardens. (There's also a tackle shop on site for sport fishermen!) The rooms are plain, but nice, with either one queen bed or two double beds, a television and small table and chairs. Ruffled curtains hang in the windows, and out back some rooms have small private porches facing the woods behind the motel. Muffins and coffee are served in the morning to get you off to a good start, and the Boothbay Rail Museum is just across the street (see Kidstuff).

Brown's Wharf
$$$ • 121 Atlantic Ave., Boothbay Harbor
• (207) 633-5440, (800) 334-8110

The first things that struck us when we pulled up to this L-shaped, three-story motel were the window boxes overflowing with vines and flowers from every level. Each room has a deck (although they're not private) directly overlooking the bustling harbor where anglers unload their catch and boaters tie up at the docks. From one side of the motel, you can actually see lobsters scurrying beneath the pilings.

The rooms are simply furnished with traditional poster beds and side chairs and have sliding-glass doors leading to the balconies. You'll get to choose from two full-size beds or a queen or king. For $30 more, one efficiency unit with a small kitchen is available, and suites are $50 extra. Near the main entry of the motel are Brown's Wharf Restaurant (see our Restaurants chapter) and the Old Salt Shed lounge, a 200-year-old post-and-beam shed where cod were salted down before being shipped to England. Now built into the motel complex, it is one of the oldest buildings in the harbor.

The motel itself used to be the site of Brown Brothers' wholesale fish, lobster and sardine factory during the early 1940s. The Brown family still runs it today. For information buffs, this motel was a favorite of the late newsman Charles Kuralt, who once said he felt like part of the family here. The charge for an additional person in a room is $10.

Ocean Gate
$$$ • Maine Hwy. 27, Southport Island
• (207) 633-3321, (800) 221-5924

Once you drive through the stone-pillared entryway down the thickly wooded dirt road, you'll leave all the hustle and bustle of the modern world behind. With nine guest houses tucked into the trees facing the water, Ocean Gate has soothing accommodations and surroundings. From your guest room or cottage, you'll awaken to the scent of white birches, spruce and pine and the gentle breeze of the sea. Put your feet up on your private deck and watch the boats bob by.

The snug rooms are tastefully decorated with modern wood furniture and fixtures. All rooms have private baths, and some have air conditioning. In the morning, indulge in a complimentary breakfast buffet or relax and enjoy fresh-brewed coffee in your room. Non-smoking rooms are available, and some room rates include refrigerators. The property also has a number of cottages, suites and efficiencies with two bedrooms. Some have sunken living rooms, kitchens, fireplaces and porches. Cribs can be rented for an additional charge. For recreation you can choose between a walk around the resort's 85 acres, a swim in the heated pool, a game of tennis or a row in one of the boats. Fishing is plentiful off the resort dock (although you'll need to bring your own pole and tackle). There are also play areas for children, a fitness center, a hot tub, and more. In the evening your way will be lighted by wrought-iron lanterns hanging from the trees. For large gatherings, Ocean Gate also puts on full-course lobster bakes for family and class reunions of 20 or more people.

Fisherman's Wharf Inn
$$ • 22 Commercial St., Boothbay Harbor
• (207) 633-5090, (800) 628-6872

This medium-sized hotel and restaurant built on piers above the harbor is an old-time family favorite. Return visitors come for the laid-back environment and simple furnishings but most of all for the beautiful harbor views. Each of the hotel's 54-guest rooms has a picture window overlooking the harbor, and many have private balconies. The furniture is a little outdated, but comfortable, and the hotel is constantly making improvements. Rooms have queen-sized beds and sitting chairs, and there is a three-room suite with water views on all sides.

From the outside the hotel may not attract much attention, but the main building boasts a popular restaurant, lounge, outdoor dinning area and adjoining dock. A continental breakfast is included in the room rate. Open from late May through late October, the wharf is

located within a five-minutes walk from downtown shops, eliminating the need to pay for downtown parking.

Leeward Village Motel & Cottages
$ • Route 96 East, Boothbay
• (207) 633-3681, (888) 817-9907

For families on budget vacations, this is an unpretentious place on Linekan Bay, about a five-minute drive from the downtown shopping area. The rustic red cottages have real camp furniture and compact kitchenettes, while rooms in the motel have standard motel furniture. All rooms have water views, and two are completely handicapped accessible. Picnic tables and outdoor grills abound, and there are family games set up on the sprawling lawn. Fishing is available off the Village's pier, and dogs are sometimes allowed with advanced notice. Weather permitting the village is open from May 15 to October 15.

The Howard House Motel Bed & Breakfast
$ • 347 Townsend Ave., Boothbay Harbor
• (207) 633-3933

Rock ledges, tall trees, green lawns and winding paths of flower beds surround this quaint, family-run gambrel-roof house and motel. The main house and office is in one building, and the two-story motel unit is in back. A hammock invites guests to take a breather in between checking in and unpacking. The motel rooms are large and have floor-to-ceiling windows, beamed, cathedral ceilings, private balconies overlooking the motel's 20 private acres and other nice touches such as solid wood counters surrounding the bathroom sinks. The rooms are quiet and clean.

In the morning a buffet breakfast of homemade scones, egg casseroles, fruit salad, yogurt and cereals is included in the room rate (which is how the motel got a bed and breakfast name). There is a $15 charge for an extra person on a rollaway bed and 10-percent discounts for stays of two or more nights.

Rocktide Inn
$$$ • 35 Atlantic Ave., Boothbay Harbor
• (207) 633-4455, (800) 762-8433

On the east side of Boothbay Harbor, this hotel has four buildings with 98 comfortably furnished rooms, many of which have recently been refurbished. Some rooms have private balconies directly over the water, while others are set back from the shore by a parking lot and have shared outdoor decks. Most rooms have two double beds and a small sitting area. The furnishings are modern. With so much to do, you won't want to stay in your room for long.

The Rocktide has the only indoor swimming pool along the harbor. It also has a cocktail lounge and restaurant with water views. A full buffet breakfast is included in the room rate. When you've filled up and are ready to move out, take the hotel trolley downtown (it runs from mid-June through Labor Day) or walk across the harbor's famous footbridge, which will take you directly downtown. The cost for an additional child in the room ranges from $10 to $16 a day; children younger than 5 stay free.

Tugboat Inn
$$-$$$ • 80 Commercial St., Boothbay Harbor
• (207) 633-4434, (800) 248-2628

This recently remodeled modern hotel is built directly over the harbor, with up-close views of fishing and cruising vessels at their moorings. It features tastefully furnished rooms with king- or queen-size beds, air conditioning and some private balconies. Non-smoking rooms are available. There are several other guest buildings on site that also have accommodations and water views. These are just beside the main tugboat building, and they offer balconies. For boaters, slips and moorings are available for both short- and long-term stays. Next to the hotel is the tugboat-shaped restaurant and the marina lounge. The downtown shopping area is just one block away. The inn recently underwent a $2.5 million renovation of the entire facility. Ask about the various packages, which include a two- or three-night stay, breakfast and dinner and various entertainment. The hotel is open from April through November.

There aren't as many cottages, condos, apartments and houses to rent as there are grains of sand on the beach, but sometimes it seems that way.

Summer Rentals

Remember childhood vacations when the family would pile into the station wagon and head north? You'd stay in little cabins in the woods with the scent of balsam redolent in the air and clear sparkling water a few steps away, and you'd spend the cool evenings playing games on a linoleum-covered table. The sheets were always slightly damp, and the mattresses always sagged a bit in the middle, but you slept more soundly than ever again in your life. You were in Maine.

Today the Maine summer rental scene needs to cater to different vacation needs. Not everyone wants the rustic approach. Some want fancy bathrooms with spa tubs, shiny tile and sophisticated equipment, and that's OK, too. You'll find everything here from mansions to beautiful houses and condos with fireplaces and decks overlooking the sea to little studio cottages built in the 1940s and '50s. Prices vary depending on proximity to the water and amenities, but there are rentals to meet every pocketbook.

In this chapter we've listed a variety of rental opportunities, from cottages to condos as well as some agencies that handle summer properties. The listings are organized using our four main geographic areas — towns are listed from south to north, and companies within towns are in alphabetical order.

You can also find summer rentals in the classified section of Down East Magazine, the Portland Press Herald, the Maine Sunday Telegram and other local newspapers (see our Media chapter). The Yellow Pages of the local telephone book and the local chambers of commerce are also good resources to help you find what you need.

Using a Real Estate Agent

From the air, the coast of Southern Maine from Kittery to South Portland stretches like a wide white ribbon. There is sand as far as you can see. There aren't as many cottages, condos, apartments and houses to rent as there are grains of sand on the beach, but sometimes it seems that way. Oceanfront and near-ocean property is valuable in the summer. With the price they can get on the market, it's little wonder that people move away from these properties to rent them, or buy them specifically to stay in for a week and rent out the rest of the time.

While some owners handle their own rentals, many use real estate agencies to manage these properties. If you're looking for a rental, you might want to consider calling one of these agencies. Most will be happy to send you a catalog illustrating their various properties to give you a better idea of what you're renting.

General Information

Most weekly rentals run from Saturday to Saturday with check-in around 2 PM and check-out between 10 AM and noon. For the most part, weekly rentals do not provide bed linens, towels or paper products (i.e., toilet paper, paper towels and trash can liners). Some have telephones that will allow you to call only locally, while others allow you to call long distance. Some properties allow pets, and some don't. Some are nonsmoking, and others are not. Policies vary quite a bit, so you'll need to find out exactly what's included and allowed in your rental when you make your reservations. In very general terms, a weekly, in-season rental can cost anywhere from $500 to $2,000.

Keep in mind when taking a weekly rental that you're not staying in a hotel. You are expected to leave the premises clean when you depart. If you don't want to be bothered with cleaning during the week, your rental agency can probably provide cleaning for a fee. Maintenance is provided by the property owners, managers or agency, and there is usually someone on call 24 hours a day in the summer. If you have any questions about what your responsibilities are with regard to the property, ask when you make your reservations.

Rental Listings

Southern Beaches Area

From Kittery to Kennebunk there are a dozen beaches and probably 100 times that many places to stay. We've selected a variety of places you might want to try, some near the beach, others farther away; some that allow pets, and some that don't; some at the low end of the price scale, and others at the high end.

Crowe's Cottages
Long Beach Rd., York Beach • (207) 363-3524
This quiet colony of seven small cottages lies between Long Sands Beach and Short Sands Beach, within easy walking distance of downtown York Beach. The cottages are two-story clapboard and have been updated regularly. Each cottage has two bedrooms, a large combined living room and kitchen area and a bathroom with shower. The cottages come equipped with all the basics you'll need for light housekeeping, but you need to bring your own bed linen and towels. Ron and

Priscilla Crowe particularly welcome families. In 1998, rates for four people in a two-bedroom unit were $425 a week.

Kingsbury Cottage Luxury Rental Condominiums
Harmon Park, York Harbor
• **(207) 363-5688**
Kingsbury Cottage is a large Colonial Revival house in historic York Harbor. One of the original annexes to the famous Emerson Hotel, Kingsbury Cottage has been tastefully divided into three exceptional rental condominiums. You'll see fireplaces and charming Victorian architectural detail throughout the building, which is listed on the National Register of Historic Places. Glowing hardwood floors, carefully painted woodwork and appropriate furnishings will make you feel at home in any of the three units. You'll enjoy the walk to York Harbor through a neighborhood filled with period homes and pleasant gardens. Weekly rates for July and August 1998 were $1,150 for a two-bedroom unit and $750 for a one-bedroom unit. Call for off-season rates.

Rundlett Cottage Rentals
9 Kendall Rd., York Beach
• **(207) 363-3078**
Six properties with the enticing names of Robin's Nest, Hilltop, Windswept, Maine Stay, The Barn and Kendall House are available to rent from Verna and Henry Rundlett. All these houses have charming exteriors, and most have porches to sit on as the sky turns to sunset. The number of bedrooms varies depending on the property (Rundlett's largest place would sleep eight or nine people), but they all have ocean views and are located a lazy stroll away from Short Sands Beach, gift shops, restaurants and Nubble Lighthouse (see our Attractions chapter). Intended to be "homes away from home," the properties come completely furnished with central heat and fireplaces. Weekly summer rates range

Children and adults delight in pressing the bell to activate
this pedestrian drawbridge in Perkins Cove, Ogunquit.

from $500 to $1,300. Winter rates drop to $500 to around $700 (plus utilities) per month.

Seaside Vacation Rentals
65 Main St., U.S. Hwy. 1, York Beach
• (207) 363-1825

Annette Regan and daughter Maureen Regan launched Seaside Vacation Rentals in 1984. From managing a few rentals, the company has grown to handle 365 properties in York and Ogunquit. All types of properties are available for rent through the Regans. Apartments, condominiums, cottages, houses and even a mansion are part of the portfolio. Rates begin at $350 for a very cozy, one-bedroom cottage that's not on the ocean and go up to $3,500 a week for Greystone Mansion on the point in Cape Neddick.

On average a two-bedroom property near the ocean will run you between $650 and $750 per week. Oceanfront property rentals begin at about $1,000 per week. Off-season weekly rates are available for September, early October and late June, and winter rates are available for September through June. The Regans guarantee cleanliness on all of their properties, and they have a handyman on call 24 hours a day to help with emergencies. Properties begin booking up in January, Feb-

ruary and March, and many people reserve the next year's rental at the end of their current vacation.

Waverly Cottages
York Beach • (207) 363-5275

Since 1983, Mike and Janice Roberge have welcomed families to Waverly Cottages. The three cottages are set amid trees in a quiet residential area just a short walk from Short Sands Beach or town. Each cottage includes such amenities as individually controlled heating, an electric stove and refrigerator, shower, dishes, silverware and cooking utensils. The Roberges furnish two blankets and pillows for each bed, but you will need to bring your own sheets, pillowcases and towels. A picnic table and grill are also provided. Rental rates depend on the size of cottage. In summer 1998, the weekly rate for the two-bedroom cottages was $550; the three-bedroom was $750.

Garnsey Brothers Rentals and Real Estate
510 Webhannet Rd., Wells
• (207) 646-3091

Garnsey Brothers is the exclusive rental agency for a number of condominium complexes in Wells. They also have apartments, houses and cottages available to meet your rental needs. Most condos have a two-night minimum stay requirement (at anywhere from $100 to $200 per night), but they will occasionally be able to get you in for just one night. Choose from condos in a variety of settings including Harborside Motor Inn, located on the tidal river; East Winds, a block from the beach; Point East Resort, which abuts the salt marsh and has wonderful views; Ocean Dunes, which is beachfront at Moody Beach (one-week minimum stay); Bellevue by the Sea; Wellington Manor, on U.S. Highway 1 with an indoor pool; and Coastal Cottages and Efficiencies, on Atlantic Avenue across from Wells Beach. A week at an oceanfront condo runs between $700 and $1,500. Oceanfront houses require a two-week minimum stay and run about $1,800 per week. Security deposits on houses vary between $50 and $250.

Seaside Cottages
276 Atlantic Ave., Wells
• (207) 646-3351

If you like to be near the water, you'll like it here. The cottages are about 150 feet from the beach, separated from it by a small street and one row of houses. Behind the cottages you'll find the harbor, where many people like to pull out a rod and reel and fish. There isn't much of a yard with these cottages, and there aren't any trees in the area, but the units are clean and there are a few tables with umbrellas and chairs set out for guests to enjoy. Rates vary from $385 per week for a unit that sleeps two to $530 and $630 for units that sleep four and six, respectively. Lower rates are available in the off-season.

Adams Agency
84 Main St., Kennebunk • (207) 985-4841

Drake's Island is one of the best-kept secrets in Maine. A strictly residential island between Wells Harbor and Laudholm Farm Estuary, the island has no commercial development and is reached by a small bridge that crosses the tidal river. At low tide you can walk across on the mud. If this is where you'd like to vacation, Adams Agency is the place to call. They specialize in Drake's Island property and will help you find the right rental. Rental properties on the island are single-family homes; there are no condominiums here. Weekly rentals begin around $800 and top out at about twice that. If you rent here, you'll have access to private tennis courts and a community center. Pets are allowed in some properties but require a substantial security deposit.

Cabot Cove Cottages
Maine St., Kennebunkport
• (207) 967-5424, (800) 962-5424

White wicker furniture awaits you in these charming cottages placed at the edge of a tidal cove. One- and two-bedroom units are available, and all have kitchenettes. Other amenities include a dock with a rowboat and canoe for guests to use, badminton, volleyball, croquet and a jungle gym for the kids. Daily, weekly and monthly rates are available. Prices in 1998 ranged from $85 to $110 daily and $535 to $640 weekly off-season, and $110 to $145 daily and $700 to $850 weekly in July and August. Pets are welcome here.

Wild Wood Cottages
Wildes District Rd., Kennebunkport
• (207) 967-3377

You can get away for a night, a weekend or a week at Wild Wood Cottages, located a short drive from either the Colony Beach or Goose Rocks Beach and the picturesque fishing village of Cape Porpoise. Two each of two types of units — chalets and cottages — are available. Chalets have open floor plans with lofts that are furnished with two single beds and reached by a ladder. There's also a

---

INSIDERS' TIP

If you want to ensure a comfortable stay and make your cottage feel like home, you might want to bring your own pillow.

futon-bed arrangement in the main living area, and a kitchenette. Cottages have more privacy, with two bedrooms and a kitchenette. Picnic tables and grills are provided with all units. At Wild Wood, cottages come with everything you need including bed linen. All you need to bring are your beach chairs and towels. Both types of units rented for $70 a night or $450 per week in 1998. Pets are allowed but require a one-night security deposit.

Old Orchard Beach Area

Old Orchard Beach was once the place to see and be seen in the summer. Its long sandy beach, its pier jutting into the sea and the Palace Playland amusement park (see our Attractions chapter) along the beachfront continue to make it a popular summer destination for families. Biddeford doesn't have much in the way of summer rentals, though you might find something at Biddeford Pool through a rental agency. Saco, with Ferry Beach State Park, miles of sandy beach adjoining Old Orchard Beach and Camp Ellis, is also a popular summer rental area.

Brookside Inn
Ocean Park Rd., Saco • (207) 284-4191

Before the spur of Interstate 195 was built to take people from Interstate 95 (Maine Turnpike) to Old Orchard Beach, the main road off U.S. Highway 1 was Ocean Park Road. More of a motel-type facility with individual cottages instead of attached rooms, the Brookside Inn is nestled between Ocean Park Road and I-195. You can hear traffic from the Ocean Park Road in front of the cottages, but trees muffle the sounds from the Interstate. While these cottages aren't on the beach, there is a pool and playground. Rentals are offered on a nightly basis, but you can rent one for as long as you like. In summer 1998, a two-bed cottage without a kitchen was $45 per night. A larger cottage with two bedrooms and a kitchenette was $95 per night.

Exit 5 Motel & Cottages
18 Ocean Park Rd., Saco • (207) 284-4727

Just around the corner from the busy commercial strip of U.S. Highway 1 and the on-ramp to Interstate 195, you'll find this throwback to the 1950s. Painted white with raspberry trim, the complex is comprised of a neat little motel and a cluster of individual cottages on pleasantly maintained grounds. There are lots of flowers and trees here, and extensive amenities including an indoor pool, sauna, spa, pool table, shuffleboard and volleyball. The rate for a cottage with a kitchenette and separate bedroom with two double beds is $95 per night during the summer season. A unit without a kitchenette will run you $75, and rooms in the motel are $80. All units have air conditioning, color television and cable. A three-night minimum stay is required for the cottages.

Vacationland Motor Court
U.S. Hwy. 1, Saco • (207) 284-6643

In true 1950s style, this wide semicircle of about 20 white, painted cottages sits with an in-ground pool at its center on a grassy, tree-backed hill. You'll enjoy the quiet evenings here as kids play on the extensive lawns after a day at the beaches or nearby attractions. Rates differ depending on which week and month you want to visit and whether you want a cottage with a kitchenette or just a refrigerator. A two-room cottage that sleeps four with a kitchenette will cost you $450 per week in the middle of August and around $350 in June. Though the cottages are usually rented on a weekly basis, you may be able to rent one for a single night or weekend at $70 per midsummer night. Vacationland Motor Court closes for the season at the end of the first weekend in September.

Patry Family Realty
133 Saco Ave., Old Orchard Beach • (207) 934-4432

Patry Family Realty was launched in December 1985. Through a strong belief in service and integrity and a can-do attitude toward the real estate business, this father and son team (Dan Sr. and Dan Jr.) has built a solid reputation in the area. Dan Sr. was president of the Old Orchard Little League for four years and served on the town's planning and budget committee; both he and Dan Jr. keep an active interest in town events. The company provides both summer and long-term rental services.

Seashore Realty
4 Fourth Ave., Old Orchard Beach
• (207) 934-4391

Seashore Realty is a full-service property management agency that has been serving the Old Orchard Beach community for 30 years. Owned by Gerry and Georgette Proulx, the agency has three of its own rental properties, the Seashore Guest House, Chez Gerard Tourist Home and the Seashore Motor Lodge, and manages an extensive number of other properties. Apartments, condominiums, houses and cottages, motels and rooms are available through Seashore. Rates range from $350 to $1,300 per week depending on amenities. Call for a catalog of available properties for rent.

White Lamb Cottages
3 Odessa Ave., Old Orchard Beach
• (207) 934-2231

These cottages are as cute as cute can be! You'll just love the 10 little white cottages with peachy-orange trim, surrounded by white picket fences. Located amid a pine grove just two houses from the beach, they provide an ideal summer beach vacation. Though built in the 1940s, the cottages have been regularly updated. You can choose from studio-type cottages with open layouts or cottages with separate bedrooms and living rooms. Units have either a queen-size bed and a full-size futon bed or two twin beds and a full-size futon bed. Amenities include a large outdoor Jacuzzi (shared by all units) and access to the outdoor

heated pool at the Edgewater Hotel less than a half-mile away. Picnic tables are shared by the cottages, but you must bring your own hibachi for outside grilling. Weekly rates in July and August are between $675 and $750, but they drop to $325 to $450 in September.

Wight Realty
125 W. Grand Ave., Old Orchard Beach
• (207) 934-1603

This well-established local agency handles both sales and rentals. They can find you a summer rental in condominiums, houses, cottages or apartments. From properties nestled under the trees in Ocean Park to old summer houses with large porches along West Grand Avenue, they will search to meet your needs. As usual, weekly rates vary a great deal — from $450 to close to $2,000. Call for information on what's available.

Greater Portland Area

Portland itself has a very limited number of houses that are rented on a short-term basis, and those that are available are mostly handled by real estate management agencies, some of which we've listed here. On the Portland waterfront, however, there are a few condos available for three months or longer. And there are luxurious townhouses on the island resort of Diamond Cove.

Some of the rural towns in the Greater Portland area, such as Freeport, have cottages available both on the water and in the woods. Most are advertised individually by the people who own them, and the best way to find out about them is by calling the area chambers of commerce or scouting them out in a local newspaper.

Curry Agency
362 Pine Point Rd., Scarborough
• (207) 883-6444

You'll love Pine Point, with its views of the ocean and Scarborough Marsh and sandbars to walk on at low tide. The Currys, a husband and wife team of brokers, will help you find exactly the right property to make the most of your summer vacation. In business since 1969, the Currys know most of the properties in the area and have sold and rented out many of them through the years. Weekly rentals will cost from $475 for a basic two-bedroom with not much of a view to $1,700 or $1,800 for a large oceanfront home with three to four bedrooms. Some of the properties allow pets; only one is completely nonsmoking.

Gaspar Real Estate
19 Greenwood Ave., Scarborough
• (207) 883-2526

Mary Defusco is the person to speak to if you're looking for summer rentals at pretty Higgins Beach. She has a wide selection of properties with varying rates and is sure to have something to pique your interest. Two-, three- and four-bedroom properties are available, ranging from $600 to $1,300 per week. Mary starts taking reservations in March; give her a call for a complete list of properties.

Diamond Cove
Great Diamond Island, Portland
• (207) 766-5804

You'll find what you need for a great vacation at this 193-acre resort community of luxury and deluxe three-bedroom townhouses and year-round homes. A secluded island of woods and beaches, Diamond Cove is a 20-minute ferry ride from Portland. In addition to great accommodations, you'll find a private restaurant, tennis courts, five beaches, a general store and a heated pool. Some of the homes date back to the 1800s.

Townhouses rent for a seven-night minimum. In 1998 a deluxe townhouse with one bathroom and a deck rented for $1,250 a week, and a luxury townhouse with two-and-a-half bathrooms (including a master bath with a Jacuzzi) and several covered porches rented for $1,470. The rental season runs July through September. If you can't bear to leave, you can buy one of the resort's private homes.

Port Island Realty
14 Welch St., Peaks Island • (207) 766-5966

Looking for a small cabin or fine home on an island that's far enough from civilization to relax but close enough to a city to enjoy cultural entertainment and shopping? This real estate company will be happy to set you up on one of the Casco Bay Islands. The majority of its summer rentals are on Peaks Island, which is 1 mile wide and 2 miles long. Although 1,000 hardy inhabitants do live here year round, the number swells to 4,000 during the summer. Being 3 miles away from the mainland and taking a 15-minute ferry ride to get here will keep you feeling comfortably isolated. This is the closest Maine comes to Martha's Vineyard, without being so exclusive. Rentals start at about $600 and climb to $3,000 per week in the summer. A lower-range rental could get you a summer cottage with two to four bedrooms away from the water, while a house in the upper range would include more bedrooms and would most likely be on the water. Some of the more expensive places come with luxury kitchens and baths. The ferry ride to your summer home will cost you about $5 round trip.

Visitors Information Center
305 Commercial St., Portland
• (207) 772-5800

For a wide variety of information on agencies that handle summer rentals in the Greater Portland area or for a copy of the Maine Guide to Camp and Cottage Rentals, call the Visitors Information Center. It doesn't list individual cottage or condo rentals, but it does have specialists who can point you in the right direction. The camp and cottage rental guide, published by the Maine Publicity Bureau, is a 50-page picture catalog of various homes and cottages for rent from Kittery north.

The Rental Guide
P.O. Box 9739, Portland 04104
• (207) 878-3857

Get a free, black-and-white picture brochure featuring long- and short-term rentals in the Greater Portland area by calling for a copy of this referral guide. The monthly magazine highlights apartments, condos and houses, with photos and write-ups on their amenities. There's a classified ad section in the back that deals with seasonal rentals, and you can call for a more complete listing.

Go sailing on Maine's pristine waters.

Freeport Merchants Association
16 Mill St., Freeport • (207) 865-1212

Locals with private cabins for rent often list them with this chamber of commerce. Call and they will mail a current list to you. While there aren't many cabins available here, there's one tucked away in the backwoods for about $350 a week and a couple on the water. One property even has its own waterfall! Expect to pay a bit more for those by the water.

Brunswick, Bath and Boothbay Harbor Area

You'll find hundreds of little cabins and cottages and some fantastic grand homes scattered across this section of Maine. With so many peninsulas here, there's plenty of coastline, and people have taken advantage of it, building beautiful summer and year-round homes along the coves, inlets and harbors of the region. You'll enjoy spectacular water views and many rural settings, but have no doubt, you'll end up paying for them too.

For this area we have written up property management agencies that oversee summer rentals, and we've also included private owners who have more than one property for rent. You won't find much in the way of condos in Brunswick or Bath, but there are a few on the water in Boothbay Harbor. Again, the chambers of commerce and local newspapers as well as *Down East* magazine (see our Media chapter) are good ways to find individuals who have single houses or cabins for rent.

Chamber of Commerce, Bath-Brunswick Region
59 Pleasant St., Brunswick
• (207) 725-8797
45 Front St., Bath
• (207) 443-9751

This chamber has information on a couple of privately owned cottages. One is a four-season home in West Bath on a rural, wooded lot with views of the New Meadows River. The living room features a 28-foot ceiling, a large stone fireplace and a wall of glass facing the river. Another is on Atkins Bay, a tidal inlet in

Phippsburg, and includes a suspended glass circular fireplace. That rents for $600 a week. A third cottage you can find information on through this agency is The Cottage at Five Islands, a two-bedroom cabin with vaulted ceilings in Georgetown that rents for $800 a week during peak season.

Harpswell Property Management
Maine Hwy. 24, Bailey Island
• **(207) 883-7795**

A division of Rob Williams Real Estate, this company specializes in summer rentals on the Harpswell mainland (the town is made up of a large peninsula and two islands). The cottages and houses they oversee range in price from $475 for a cottage without water views to $2,200 for an upscale house on the shore. The business has been operating for five years. All but one of the properties they work with require that you bring your own linens.

Sea Escape Cottages
Maine Hwy. 24, Bailey Island
• **(207) 833-5531**

Overlooking Casco Bay, these four matching cottages are set back on a spacious lawn that slopes down to the water. Rates include linens, bedding, one towel change per week, complete kitchen equipment, a TV, wall-to-wall carpeting, a private porch and one or two bedrooms. The surrounding grounds have a playground, game room and bicycles. From the last week of June through the first week of September, rates range from $595 to $750 per week. During May, early June, September and October, rates drop. The cabins are owned by Donna and Les McNelly, who also offer fishing trips and two-hour sunset, island and seal watch cruises on their outboard motor boat. The cost for these trips is from $25 to $225 per person depending on what you want to do and how long you want to stay on the water. Cottage guests receive 25 percent off cruise prices.

Spinney's Guest House, Efficiencies and Housekeeping Cottages
Maine Hwy. 209, Phippsburg
• **(207) 389-2052**

If you're looking for a comfortable but not too frilly or expensive room, cottage or one-room apartment on the water, this is a good place to check in. Jack and Fay Hart are the owners of this long-standing complex, just a few steps away from the sandy shore of Popham Beach and a few minutes walk from Fort Popham, a Civil War fort (see our Attractions chapter). If you want to get to know your neighbors, try the guest house, which has four individual rooms sharing a single bathroom. In the morning, come downstairs to enjoy the comfy screened-in porch and free coffee. The cost for a guest room with breakfast is $64 a night. For more privacy try one of the cottages or apartments, which rent for $550 per week. The cottages have two bedrooms and a combined living room/dining room. The apartment is a single room with enough space for two people. You'll need your own linens for both.

T. Percy Cottages
Various locations, Phippsburg
• **(207) 389-2639**
(nights and weekends)

Tom Percy owns these five cottages, all within a couple miles of Popham Beach. In 1998 they ranged in price from $500 to $600 a week for a place with between two and four bedrooms. One, a cute bungalow with a covered deck, overlooks the mouth of the Kennebec River, another is on a freshwater lake, and three others are in the woods overlooking a bay. All are fully equipped except for linens. To get one for a week or for the summer, you'll have to reserve early (by March at the very latest) because many regulars come back year after year. The cottages are available from June through October and in the fall on a weekend-only basis.

INSIDERS' TIP

Keep in mind that the last two weeks in July and the first two weeks in August are the most popular vacation weeks. Properties are booked as much as a year in advance during this time.

Son Rae Coastal Cottages
Various locations, Georgetown
• (207) 371-2813

Relax in one of three newly built cottages furnished with antiques and set on 9 acres of woods snuggled up to Gott's Cove and a freshwater pond. The cottages are available for $500 a week, and are furnished with toasters, coffee makers, microwave ovens and televisions, but you will need to bring your own linens. The cottages comfortably sleep six, and each has a private master bedroom. Off the beaten path, they are also within walking distance of Five Islands Dock — you can watch fishermen haul in their catch, and a small restaurant, The Love Nest, will cook it up for you fresh! Son Rae Fishing Charters will even arrange a private fishing trip if you want to give it a try. Well-behaved pets are allowed in one of the cottages.

Three Cottages at Five Islands
Maine Hwy. 127, Georgetown
• (207) 371-2442

These roomy and comfortably rustic cottages offer views of a nearby wharf, where anglers and lobstermen haul in their catch.

The units are set just above the water, with small lawns at the water's edge. The furniture and furnishings are reminiscent of the 1970s, but the view outside can't be beat. Sit on the screened porch of one and enjoy the panoramic view of the islands and Hendrick's Head Lighthouse. You'll get a real feel for one of Maine's prettiest fishing villages, all for between $500 and $800 a week. Rent a cabin for three months (June through August) for $7,000, or come in the fall for just $250 a week per couple.

Cottage Connection of Maine
Maine Hwy. 27, Boothbay Harbor
• (207) 633-6545

Need a cook, cleaning person, firewood, linens, crib or babysitter during your vacation? How about a summer cottage or house? This agency handles it all. It even has an on-staff travel agent to handle your flight, car rental and itinerary if you want. Based in Boothbay Harbor, Cottage Connection handles more than 200 private rental listings from Boothbay Harbor all the way to Bath and the peninsulas. For $500 to $4,000 a week you can get cottages, condos, cabins and

INSIDERS' TIP

Short-term rentals are charged 7 percent Maine state tax.

castles. The $5,000 price tag would buy a week in an island home with water on three sides and your own dock and mooring. No matter what property you choose, the company's inspectors will go through it before you arrive to make sure everything is in working order, and its cleaning people will sweep the way for your arrival. Most of the dwellings listed with the agency are private homes that people rent out for part or all of the summer season. Those looking to spend a little less might also try this agency as it lists everything from rustic cabins on up.

Lewis & Pottle Realty
1 Townsend Ave., Boothbay Harbor
• (207) 633-6911

This real estate company handles many long-term summer rentals in the Boothbay Harbor area, from $2,500 to $4,000 a month for a two-bedroom condo with views of and access to the water, to a little less for some houses and cottages away from the water. (For more information on the company, see our Neighborhoods and Real Estate chapter.) If you want to pay less, come during the winter or spring when the same condos will rent for $550 a month.

From campgrounds nestled against the ocean to those tucked back in the woods, we have plenty to choose from when picking a spot to get back to nature.

Campgrounds

Pack up your sleeping bag and kerosene lamp, think up some great ghost stories to share around the fire and don't forget the marshmallows — we're taking you camping.

From campgrounds flush against the ocean to those tucked back in the woods to the ones in lush fields, the Southern Coast of Maine has plenty to choose from when picking a place to get back to nature. We've included a wide selection of camping spots, from rustic ones (without flush toilets) to places that are fully developed with paved roads, swimming pools and even miniature golf courses. With so much forest, so many tidal rivers and so many miles of coastline, there is a gamut of getaway sites. We've taken a sampling of the ones we like most and have listed them under our four main geographic headers.

Unless we say otherwise, you can assume pets are allowed. However, most places require that they be on a leash at all times. Also, the prices we list are based on having one tent or camper on a site during peak season, which generally runs from mid-June through the end of August. Be sure to note the opening and closing dates of campgrounds — most are not open year-round, though a few do take winter camping.

Southern Beaches Area

Burnette's Trailer and Tent Area
21 Railroad Ave., York Beach
• **(207) 363-4756**

If you want to camp near the beach, this is certainly a nice place to consider. Less than a five-minute walk from Short Sands beach, this camping area has trailer sites with electric, water, sewer and cable TV hookups and tent sites. Most of the 186 sites are on a wide, grassy expanse, though there are some sites shaded by trees. You can buy propane and ice on site, and there is also a coin-operated laundry room. In addition, two recently updated utility buildings contain coin-operated showers. Because of Burnette's proximity to the beach, be prepared for the campground to be pretty crowded.

Rates in 1998 for up to three people were $26 for a trailer with all hookups and $20 per tent. An extra person was $3 as was a guest pass; overnight guests were $5. Burnette's does not accept credit cards. Reservations for particular sites are accepted for visits of a week or more. If you intend to stay less than a week, sites will be filled on a first-come, first-served basis. Burnette's is open from May until October.

Camp Eaton
Long Sands Beach, York Harbor
• **(207) 363-3424**

Once you see Camp Eaton you'll understand why visitors come back year after year. Located on 35 acres with woods, fields and a lily pond, this campground is only 300 yards from the beach! This well-planned campground has been run by the Wagner family since 1923; today, Peter and Kathy Wagner are proud to be the fourth-generation owners. The grounds incorporate 200 seasonal RV sites and 50 wooded tent sites. There are also short-term RV sites.

Kids will love the playground areas, one of which is sized for toddlers, and you'll enjoy watching them climb and swing on the wooden equipment set on sand. Camp Eaton also has pay phones, a dumping station and a recycling program. You can buy firewood and ice on site. For your convenience, there are four well-lit, clean utility buildings that house flush toilets and free hot showers. Water, sewer and electrical hookups are available at the all-season and short-term RV sites. Electricity is offered at the tent sites.

Cost to camp in 1998 was $34 for full hookups, $30 for two-way hookups and $27 for no utilities, based on two people per site. Children older than 6 are charged $3 per day, and extra adults older than 18 are $5 per day. The campground is open from May 1 to October 1.

Dixon's Campground
1740 U.S. Hwy. 1, Cape Neddick, York
• **(207) 363-2131**

Though located in York, this campground is the closest to Ogunquit and offers a free shuttle to Ogunquit beach in-season. Whether you prefer an open, grassy camp site or a more secluded, tree-shaded site, you'll find it at Dixon's, which has 100 sites on 40 acres.

This campground caters to tents and small RVs (there's a 30 foot limit) and has a store where you can purchase ice, groceries, supplies and daily newspapers. Each of the four wooded and open areas of the campground has its own restroom building with metered showers. Children will enjoy the playground area while the whole family will love sitting around a cheerful campfire in the designated area in the evenings.

Cost per campsite for two people with either one tent and a car or an RV (remember the size restriction) was $24 in 1998. Each additional adult was $7.50, and each child younger than 16 was $3. There are additional fees for extra cars and equipment, electric and water hookups and a dumping station. A visitor's pass was $3 per day, $7.50 for overnight. The campground is open from late May to mid-September. Dixon's does not accept pets.

Pinederosa Camping Area
128 North Village Rd., Wells • (207) 646-2492

Why choose between starry nights under the pines or sunny summer days on the beach? You can do both at Pinederosa. Just 2 miles from the beach, the campground has plenty of tall pines for campers to nestle under. Established in 1976 by the Stevens family, the Pinederosa features about 150 sites, both wooded and open. Though there are facilities for smaller RVs, this campground caters mainly to tenters and pop-ups. Water, electric and sewer hookups are available, as is transportation to the beach in-season. At Pinederosa you'll enjoy amenities such as a swimming pool, hot showers and fitness club privileges. All sites have picnic tables and fireplaces.

Cost for camping in 1998 was $23.50 for a full hookup, $22.50 for water and electric hookup and $18.50 for no utilities. Rates are based on two occupants per site. Additional campers ages 12 or younger are charged $1; those older than 12 are $4.

Kennebunkport Camping
Old Cape Rd., Kennebunkport
• **(207) 967-2732**

Tenters will appreciate this campground. It caters mainly to people with tents and pop-up campers, though there are some sites for RVs up to 40 feet long. As a tenter you can choose from 25 tent sites set amid tall trees with golden sunlight filtering gently through the branches. Each site comes equipped with a picnic table and fireplace, and you can purchase firewood, ice, soft drinks and snacks from the camp store. For those of you with RVs, you'll find two daily sites with full hookups and 26 with water and electric hookups. Two restroom facilities are convenient to all sites, though only one has hot showers, which you may use at no extra charge.

Cost per tent site for a family of four was $15 in 1998, a site with water and electricity was $18, and full hookups were $21. Additional people were $2; there is a six-person maximum per site. Since opening in 1986, Kennebunkport Camping has been owned and operated by the Roberge family. The campground is open from May 15 to October 15, and pets are permitted.

Mousam River Campground
Alfred Rd., West Kennebunk • (207) 985-2507

This is an RV only park. Unlike parks that have been developed to the extent that you can get lost wandering roads lined by row after row of RVs, this campground is quiet and nicely laid out. Its main roads are paved so you don't have to hear the sound of gravel kicking up when your neighbors come home at night, and there are plenty of trees to provide screening and a great deep-woods feeling. While the property does extend to the Mousam River, it has not yet been developed that far.

You can choose from wooded sites or sites in a grassy field — all sites have three-way hookups. In addition, there's a pool and a camp store where you can pick up ice, firewood and other necessities. The campground offers parking passes to its guests for $1; these will allow you to park in permit parking areas at Kennebunk beaches, which are about 6 miles away. The cost per site for two adults in 1998 was $22 for vehicles up to 35 feet. For those over 35 feet the cost is $25. Pets are permitted.

Old Orchard Beach Area

Cascadia Park Camping
911 U.S. Hwy. 1 (Portland Rd.), Saco
• (207) 282-1666

This may be the place for those looking for a quiet camping area with very little in the way of distractions. Located off U.S. 1 North, just before the intersection with Maine Highway 98, the campground has 94 deeply wooded sites that offer three-way hookups and plenty of branch-filtered sunlight. According to the Fitanides family, which has owned the park since 1965, Cascadia appeals to an older crowd because of the limited amount of kid-type amusements. Cost to camp in 1998 was $22.95 for a full hookup and $18 for no hookups. Pets are not allowed in tents. The campground is open a bit later than most, from May 1 to November 1, and is located about two-and-a-half miles from the beach.

Acorn Village
42 Walnut St., Old Orchard Beach
• (207) 934-4154

The owners of this camping area call it a "village" because it accommodates people in tents, pop-ups and RVs up to 32 feet, and also rents cottages to those who prefer not to rough it. Amenities include a fireplace and picnic table at every site, a pool and a small play area for kids.

The biggest draw however, is its proxim-

ity to the beach. If you don't want to take the five- to 10-minute stroll, you can take the trolley (see our Getting There, Getting Around chapter) that stops at the campground in summer. Located on a low-traffic street off busy E. Grand Avenue, Acorn Village provides a kind of "safari" camping experience where you set up camp around a wide, grassy circle backed by trees. Full hookups are available, but there are only four RV sites for daily rentals; call ahead and make reservations.

Cost to camp in 1998 was $19 with no hookups and $26 with full hookups. Cottages sleep from two to six people and range from $230 to $495 per week. The units are rather Spartan (there's no phone or TV), but they do have tables and chairs and private baths. The campground is open from late May to the first weekend in September.

Paradise Park Resort Campground
Adelaide Rd., Old Orchard Beach
• (207) 934-4633

What a gem! You might not expect to find this great campground at the end of quiet, residential Adelaide Road. Look for Adelaide Road across the street from St. Margaret's church at the corner of Old Orchard Street and Saco Avenue. The Saco & Biddeford Savings Institution sits on the corner. Follow the road until it ends, and you're there.

Spring-fed Milliken Pond is the highlight to this campground, which has about 200 sites. You can swim and fish in the pond, rent paddleboats ($5 per hour) or merely enjoy the view. Sites 92, 101 and 102 look particularly nice, nestled under the trees by the shore of the pond, though there are dozens of good spots to choose from. Deeply wooded sites predominate, and they are nicely spaced. In addition to paddleboat rental, you can play horseshoes, shuffleboard, basketball and volleyball, take a dip in the pool or relax in the

---

INSIDERS' TIP

If you're thinking about camping in Maine, you should check out *The Maine Campground Owners Association's Camping Guide,* which is published yearly. It has charts detailing the facilities and amenities of member campgrounds across the state and includes maps and interesting camping-related articles. To request a copy, call (207) 782-5874.

Farm stands and farmers' markets display ranks of bright orange pumpkins from September through the end of October.

hot tub. All sites have fireplaces, picnic tables and access to the two restroom facilities with hot showers.

Cost to camp in 1998 was $27 for three-way hookups, $24 for two-way hookups and $19.50 for no services. Waterfront sites cost an additional $3. All types of camping vehicles can be facilitated. The park is owned by the Halle family. Pets are permitted, but groups of single campers are not — this is a family- and couples-only campground. It is open from May 1 to October 15.

Powder Horn Family Camping
Maine Hwy. 98 (Cascade Rd.), Old Orchard Beach • (207) 934-4733, (800) 934-7038

Like Wild Acres (see subsequent listing), which is also owned by the Ahern family, Powder Horn has trolley service to the beach in-season, a camp store and modern, spotless restrooms with hot showers. In addition, you'll find two pools plus one for children, a mini-golf course, volleyball, shuffleboard, basket-ball and two Jacuzzis. The Old Orchard Beach

Country Club's 18-hole golf course is across the street.

As for campsites, they've got 450 of them, both grassy and shaded, that will accommodate all types of campers. Three-way, two-way and no-utility sites are available. Cost for camping in 1998 was $33 for a full hookup, $29 for two-way hookups and $24 for no utilities. The campground is open from late May to early September.

Wild Acres Family Camping Resort
179 Saco Ave., Old Orchard Beach • (207) 934-2535

If the laughter and splashing coming from the pool area are anything to go by, people have a wonderful time at Wild Acres. One of two campgrounds owned by the Ahern family (along with Powder Horn), Wild Acres has 500 to 600 campsites, some seasonal (whereby owners leave their campers at the site year round but only use them in-season), some with three-way hookups, some with two-way hookups and some with no utilities. It is

INSIDERS' TIP

It's a good idea to bring a waterproof jacket with you so that you can enjoy yourself regardless of the weather.

managed by Rick Ahern's daughter, Tammy Rullo, who personally ensures the cleanliness of the park; it's no wonder the place is spotless!

Miniature golf, horseshoes, volleyball, tennis, basketball and shuffleboard are just some of the activities available. You can also enjoy a game of pool or a board game in the adult recreation hall, while the youngsters will love their own recreation hall with video games, billiards and arcade games. If none of that grabs you, take a swim in one of three pools, relax in one of five Jacuzzis or grab your fishing pole and go fishing in the campground's well-stocked pond.

Wild Acres features special theme weekends in-season. Take part in a spooky summer Halloween hayride while the kids have a wonderful time dressing up or enjoy a Thanksgiving or Christmas theme, minus the snow. Restrooms with hot showers are conveniently located throughout the grounds, and as of 1998, Wild Acres boasted the closest seasonal sites to the beach, with access a mere two-tenths of a mile away. If you forget any necessities, you can probably find them in the camp store, or you can take the trolley into town in-season (see our Getting There, Getting Around chapter).

Cost for camping in 1998 was $33 for full hookups, $29 for partial hookups and $24 for no utilities. Site fees are for two people per day; extra adults and children older than 3 are $3 each. Pets are permitted, but single campers are not at this family- and couples-only campground. Wild Acres is open from late May to early September.

Greater Portland Area

Bayley's Campground
Maine Hwy. 9, Scarborough • (207) 883-6043

This is the only campground in the area that features professional entertainment regularly during summer. Shows featuring comedians and musical groups usually take place at Bayley's outdoor theater on Wednesday and Saturday evenings in-season. Other featured activities at Bayley's are their famous Pool Pole Plunge (similar to a log-roll contest), fireworks at Old Orchard Beach and bingo. A full schedule of events is planned throughout the day all summer long, from fishing derbies to relay races and parent-child Olympics. Bayley's Five-Star counselors supervise all scheduled activities.

If you'd rather do your own thing, enjoy the use of pools and Jacuzzis, play a round of miniature golf, go fishing or pedal a paddleboat. You'll also find horseshoes, volleyball, basketball, a recreation hall and game room and a large camp store on the premises. Bayley's even features a distinctive double-decker red bus that will take you to the beach if you're in the mood to enjoy sun, sand and sea.

Bayley's has more than 400 sites to meet every camper's needs. There are meadow sites with lush green grass and a sprinkle of trees for shading, pull-through sites under the pines for those who prefer not to turn their RVs around in tight spaces, and lots of open and shaded spots around the three ponds for those who like a water view. The campground is open from May 1 to mid-October. Cost to camp in 1998, based on two people was $38 to $42 for electricity, sewer, water and cable TV; $35 to $37 for electricity, water and cable TV; and $32 for no utilities. Rental trailers are also available at a rate of $795 per week for four people.

Wild Duck Campground
39 Dunstan Landing, Scarborough
• (207) 883-4432

Located in the heart of Scarborough Marsh with both a wild duck pond and a river, Wild Duck campground is an ideal location for bird watching or merely relaxing. With 70 sites, clean restrooms, free hot showers and laundry facilities, this small campground accepts RVs, tents and conversion vans. In 1997 a special area overlooking the marsh was set aside for conversion vans, and this has proved very popular. If you have one of these vans, ask for sites 34, 35 or 36 — they look wonderful.

You'll find electric, water and sewer hookups, a dump station, ice and firewood on the premises. For recreation you can rent canoes for $6 an hour, fish in the saltwater river or go bird watching. Sandy beaches are a five-minute drive away. Pets are allowed in the RV area if they are on leashes and supervised at all times. Pets are not allowed in the tent area, and children are not allowed to walk dogs. Cost to camp in 1998 was $19.95 for a full hookup and $17 for no utilities. The campground is open from mid-May to Columbus Day (mid-October).

Winslow Memorial Park
Staples Point Road, South Freeport
• (207) 865-4198

This town-owned campground is situated on a beautiful grassy point jutting out into Casco Bay. Its 100 sites offer a choice of woods or fields, and 23 sites are directly on the water (you'll have to reserve early for one of those). Each site has a picnic table and fire ring, and full bathrooms with hot showers are available. The camp is a great place for children, and has a large playground on the grass as well as a terrific beach where swimming is recommended at high tide (at low tide you'll lose your feet in the mud). The cost for camping is regularly $17 and jumps to $19 for water views. Leashed dogs are allowed, and the campground is open from Memorial Day through the last week in September.

The Desert of Maine
95 Desert Rd., Freeport • (207) 865-6962

Stay at this campground, and you will be just across from one of Maine's most unusual natural phenomena — a huge desert surrounded by pine trees. (See more on this attraction in our Kidstuff chapter.) Water and electric hookups are available at camper trailer sites, while rustic tent sites offer neither. Most tent sites are wooded, with moderate seclusion, and RV sites are either at the entryway to the woods or spread out in a more open grassy field with a handful of oak trees. The camp also has a large above ground-pool surrounded by a large deck.

During peak season the cost is $25 per night for trailers and sites with water and electric and $19 for tent sites within walking distance of public water and bath-houses. The campground has a total of 44 sites, open May 4 through October 15, and it also has a dump station, store, laundry, coin-operated showers and tents you can rent by the night. A free walking pass for the desert and a half-price discount for a narrated bus tour come with your stay. The campground also has shuttle bus service to Freeport center. Dogs are allowed, but check with the camp before coming to make sure they fit its criteria.

Florida Lake Campground
82 Maine Hwy. 125, Freeport
• (207) 865-4874

At this wooded campground on the banks of a 30-acre, artificial lake with a clay bottom, there's plenty to do including fishing, swimming and boating. A flat-bottomed boat is available for those wishing to paddle around — rental cost is $2 an hour or $10 a day. You'll find a total of 40 campsites for either tents or camper trailers. The trailer sites have both water and electric hookups, and there is a dump station on site. For those who prefer the confines of a swimming pool to a large lake, the campground also has one of those. The cost for a campsite with water and electric hook-ups is $16, and it is $14 without. Florida Lake does not accept credit cards. The family-owned campground is open from May 15 to October 15.

Flying Point Campground
10 Lower Flying Point Rd., Freeport
• (207) 865-4569

With Casco Bay on one side of this small peninsula and Maquoit Bay on the other, this 38-site campground is about as close as a camper can get to the water. The day we visited, most sites were taken by RVs, though there were a few spots for tents tucked back

---

INSIDERS' TIP

When you're packing your camp gear, don't forget a large pot to boil lobsters and clams and skewers for shrimp-kabobs. A metal grill to lay over the fireplace may also come in handy, just in case your site doesn't have one.

in the trees. The campground mostly consists of fields, so there isn't much privacy outside your camper. However, the water views are truly unsurpassed. Flying Point has fishing, boating, canoeing, ocean swimming and lawn games for recreation.

Camper sites come with water and electric hookups, and there is a dump station and restrooms with hot showers and flush toilets. The campground is open May 1 through October 15, and the cost of camping is $15 for tents and $20 for RVs. If you pay by credit card, expect to pay $2 more.

Recompense Shore Campsites
8 Burnett Rd., Freeport • (207) 865-9307

Set in thickly forested woods at the end of a long dirt road that ends up on Wolfe Neck Point, this campground offers plenty of seclusion. Many of the 107 sites are set back in the woods, others open up to a large meadow, and some overlook the ocean. One of our picks is site 76, which is in a grassy clearing near the water and within hollering distance of a small playground.

The bathrooms are rustic, though both water and electric hookups are available for camper trailers. The campground also has ocean swimming, boating, fishing and a dump station and store. It is open from Memorial Day through Columbus Day. Cost for camping runs from $15 to $22 depending on how large the site is and whether it is near the water. Flush toilets and regular showers, which cost $1 each, are also available.

Brunswick, Bath and Boothbay Harbor Area

Thomas Point Beach & Campground
29 Meadow Rd., Brunswick • (207) 725-6009

Set to the side of the 80-acre Thomas Point Beach park, these tent and camper trailer sites are spread out between woods and fields.

Water is available at stations along the camp road, and electric hookups are available on site for $21 a night Regular sites without electricity are $17 a night. Swimming is available at the park's sandy beach within walking distance of the campground, and there are large fields, picnic groves and a good-sized playground to work out all those kinks from the car ride. The campground also has a dump station, store, laundry, recreation hall, hot showers and flush toilets. There are boating and fishing opportunities and even an ice cream parlor.

Orr's Island Campground
RR 1, Box 650, Orr's Island • (207) 833-5595

Open from Memorial Day weekend through September 15, this family-owned campground is set on a 42-acre point of land reaching into Casco Bay and is surrounded by a half-mile of beach with a pebbly cove for swimming. The campground has 70 sites, and both water and electric hookups are available. Cost ranges from $17 for a wooded site with no hookups to $28 for a site with hookups and an ocean view. You'll be able to spend leisurely days berry-picking, fishing, playing field games or boating (canoe rentals are available). The campground has a bathhouse with hot water and flush toilets.

Meadowbrook Camping Area
33 Meadowbrook Rd.,
Phippsburg • (207) 443-4967

Set on a wooded ledge above Brighams Cove, this campground has more than 100 sites. RV haulers will find plenty of spots with water and electric hookups, and some semi-secluded sites are surrounded by grass. The tent sites are a little more rustic, and many have rocky terrain. The day we visited, camper trailers largely outnumbered tents, but that left scores of vacant tent sites, affording the people who were there more privacy.

The campground is open from May 1 to Oct. 1 and has a store with a tank where you can pick out fresh lobsters and clams. There is a heated swimming pool, recreation hall, all

INSIDERS' TIP

A campsite on the ocean with a nice breeze or in an open field is likely to attract fewer mosquitoes than one in the woods.

Our lighthouses are seamlessly integrated into the landscape.

kinds of outdoor games, miniature golf, bathrooms with showers and a laundry facility. The cost is $16 for tent sites and $20 to $24 for trailers. Some people like it so much they decide to stay for the whole season, and special rates are available; just ask about them.

Hermit Island Campground
6 Hermit Island Rd, Phippsburg
• (207) 443-2101

Located on a 255-acre island with whispering sea grass, sand dunes, knobby birch groves and the surrounding sea, this campground has 275 secluded tent sites, many with panoramic ocean views, for $25 to $35.75 per night. When you're staying here, it's hard to go wrong. The sandy road that winds through the campground is great for biking or hiking, and in the morning you'll wake up to the sound of surf. Spend the day searching for sea creatures among the rocks, or bask on one of the campground's private, white sandy beaches.

The campground also has bathrooms with showers, a general store, recreation hall, swimming, boating and fishing. The only people we think this campground would disappoint are those driving RVs, because there aren't any sites

for them here. (Pop-ups and truck campers, however, are welcome.) The campground is open Memorial Day through Columbus Day. You'll find Hermit Island Road and the camp entrance at the end of Maine Hwy. 216.

Camp Seguin
HC 33 Box 287, Seguin Land Rd.,
Georgetown • (207) 371-2777

Adjacent to Reid State Park (see our Recreation chapter), this campground has tent and RV sites along the rocky coast and scattered through the dense woods. The cost is $28 for sites along the ocean and $23 for wooded sites, although it is less expensive from Memorial Day weekend through September 15.Water and electricity are available on nine of its 31 sites. Most tent sites come with wooden platforms to keep occupants high and dry.

The campground also has a playground and recreation hall, coin-operated showers with flush toilets, a camp store, basketball court and dump station. Motor homes must be 30 feet or shorter to stay here; trailers can be up to 23 feet long. Fishing is available at the campground, and swimming is possible at a sandy beach at Reid State Park, although it does cost to get in. Admission is $2.50 for adults and 50¢ for children ages 5 to 11.

Chewonki Campgrounds
P.O. Box 261, Chewonki Neck Rd.,
Wiscasset • (207) 882-7426

Set on a large grassy hill overlooking a tidal inlet, this campground has wooded and field sites (both with plenty of grass) for both camper trailers and tents. The campground is tucked back off the main road and offers seclusion to its guests. Our favorite tent sites are 10A, 10B and 10C, which offer amazing views of the river and surrounding marsh and are set off the camp road in a large field with plenty of privacy — it's like having an entire field to yourself.

INSIDERS' TIP

Hermit Island is so named because a sheep farmer used to live there in total seclusion. Whenever anyone came knocking on his door, he would bar it shut - even if it was the town butcher, who came to buy meat. The butcher claimed he had to hide in the bushes and pounce on the poor man before he could do any business.

The camp has a store, dump, sewer, water and electricity. For fun there is a recreation hall, swimming, fishing, boating, an in-ground pool, swing set and a hole or two for golf. The campground has 48 sites that are open from May 15 through mid October. The cost ranges from $18 to $28.

Little Ponderosa
RR 1 Box 915, Maine Hwy. 27, Boothbay • (207) 633-2700

You'll find a mix of wooded RV and tent sites tucked beneath swaying Maine pines at this campground, which has been run by the same family for more than three decades. Each site has a circular stone fireplace, water and electric hookups, and partial privacy from the surrounding tents and campers. For a water view, ask for a spot overlooking the lush tidal inlet surrounding the campground (but be aware more mosquitoes may find you). The view is spectacular, and if you're quiet you might spy a blue heron looking for its lunch.

To catch your own lunch, go fishing. Or for a day on the water, take out a boat. If you need more to do, there's swimming, volley-ball, basketball, miniature golf, a recreation hall and playground as well as other activities right on the grounds. When it's time to clean up, haul your grungies to the on-site laundry. On Saturday evenings during July and August, the camp has gospel music concerts at its pavilion called The Corral. The rectangular building has a dirt floor, a roof and screened-in walls to keep the bugs at bay. On Friday nights there are family movies. Get up early Sunday morning and head down to the chapel for a mini church service. The campground has 130 sites and is open Memorial Day through October 15. The cost of an overnight stay ranges from $17 to $23.

Gray Homestead Ocean Front Camping
Box 334, Maine Hwy. 238, Southport Island • (207) 633-4612

Camper and tent sites are interspersed throughout the woods at this family campground run by Suzanne and Stephen Gray. A handful of the wooded sites (17A through 17D and 18) overlook the ocean, and several open trailer sites are directly on the ocean.

One trailer site (lettered OE) is so close you'll be on the beach when you step out your front door!

The campground has 40 sites, a cottage and two recently built apartments in a house dating back to 1812. Each site has water and electricity, and the apartments (which rent by the week and sleep up to five people) are modern, with a bedroom, kitchen and living room. Those go for $525 a week (see Summer Rentals). If you want fresh seafood to roast over your campfire at night, just call down to the homestead and Suzanne or Stephen will order it for you. There is also swimming, boating and fishing and a swing set. The cost to camp is $17 to $24 per night, and the Grays don't take credit cards. The campground is open from May through Columbus Day weekend

Shore Hills Campground
RR 1 Box 448, Maine Hwy. 27, Boothbay • (207) 633-4782

This sprawling campground claims to have some of the cleanest bathrooms in the country. It also has more than 150 sites — many are nestled back in the woods; some are in an open field. The majority of the people who stay here are retirees, and most drive their RVs here; there are, however, a few small sites designated for tents only. A tidal inlet surrounds the campground, and several sites have great water views. If you're tenting, scout out the ones along the road marked "George's Hide-A-Way." Our favorites were sites 11 and 57 because they had more privacy and more space than others. For trailers (or if you don't mind tenting among trailers), pick any of the sites numbered in the 60s. We don't think you'll be disappointed.

The campground is well-developed with paved roads, water, electricity, a sewer, dump station, store, laundry, recreation hall and cable TV (the cost for cable is $1 per night; you supply the TV). Bring along some change for the showers, which accept dimes and quarters in exchange for hot water. After you're dried off, there are plenty of ways to get wet again, from swimming to boating (canoe rentals are free) to fishing. The campground is open from April 15 through Columbus Day, and the cost ranges from $14 to $22.

Even the most elegant restaurants offer fine dining at very reasonable prices. . . . No matter what your budget, there's just no excuse to stay in.

Restaurants

Whether you're in the mood for a romantic dinner at a restaurant with harbor views and moonlight or a quick meal at a bustling brewpub where the wait staff knows the regulars by name, we've got what you're looking for on Maine's Southern Coast. We've even got lobster shacks where you can select your seafood before you eat it. Best of all, we've got it all for a bargain price. Even the most elegant restaurants offer fine dining at very reasonable prices. So no matter what your budget, there's just no excuse to stay in.

We've filled this chapter with everything from diners and hot-dog stands to the finest inns and five-star restaurants. No matter which end of the spectrum you choose, you're likely to be dressed appropriately for both. Only a small number of establishments require dinner jackets, and we let you know which ones do. The owners of most upscale restaurants say they serve quite a number of diners who come in after an all-day sail or a long day at the beach, so they are very accommodating. At the same time, you are likely to find that locals do dress up when they go out for special occasions. So you should also feel comfortable if you want to primp a little. Pretty much anything goes.

The chapter is organized by our four main geographic areas from south to north up the coast. That's because we locals stick pretty close to home when going out to eat. The next colony of restaurants might be a half-hour drive away. But there's usually a good variety of places to eat, no matter which town you're in. For example, Brunswick, a town of just 20,000 people, has authentic Indian, Chinese, German, Greek, Italian and American restaurants within a couple of hundred yards of each other. Just about any restaurant you select — everything from Caribbean to Cajun — will have a good variety of fresh seafood on the menu.

Because many of the restaurants cater mainly to tourists, a large number close for the winter, especially in Old Orchard Beach and Boothbay Harbor. We give as much detail as possible on when they are likely to be open or closed. Times can change, however, and some restaurants aren't specific, so we recommend calling ahead. Also, unless otherwise noted, assume that smoking is allowed in at least some area of the listed restaurants and that credit cards are accepted.

And one last word of caution: Don't read this chapter on an empty stomach. . . . We can just about guarantee you'll be going crazy for a taste of our food by the end of it.

Price Code

We've priced the standard entrees offered at the restaurants included in this chapter and labeled each eatery with a dollar-sign code to denotes prices. The key represents what you would expect to pay for two entrees, excluding appetizers, drinks, dessert and gratuity. However, you could pay more or less, depending on your taste buds. Again, unless otherwise noted, all restaurants listed accept major credit cards.

$	$15 and less
$$	$16 to $30
$$$	$31 to $45
$$$$	$45 and more

Southern Beaches Area

Cap'n Simeon's Galley
$ • Maine Hwy. 103, Kittery Point
• (207) 439-3655

Located behind Frisbee's Supermarket (see the Specialty Foods section of our Shopping chapter) on picturesque Route 103, Cap'n Simeon's offers lunch and dinner daily in-season and brunch on Sunday. Off-season, beginning after Columbus Day (the second Mon-

Photo: Merry Farnum

Maine is famous for its delectable lobsters.

day in October) the restaurant is closed on Tuesdays.

The building that houses Cap'n Simeon's was the original Frisbee's. In the early 1900s the new store building was constructed, and today you can enjoy marvelous views of Pepperell Cove while dining here. According to the management, the most popular item on the menu is fresh, flaky broiled haddock; other favorites include native scallops and steamed lobster. Cap'n Simeon's offers take-out service and occasionally features entertainment in the lounge on weekends.

The Mrs. & Me Restaurant
$ • U.S. Hwy. 1, Kittery • (207) 439-2291

Good plain food and a good plain atmosphere prevail in this restaurant. You'll sit on red vinyl chairs at tables that have been scrubbed clean and retain no sticky residue from the hundreds of maple syrup-drenched breakfasts that have been served on them. Open until around 8 PM in-season, The Mrs. & Me serves breakfast, lunch and dinner.

The menus aren't extensive, but you'll find Maine staples like clam chowder, fresh lobster or crabmeat rolls and a native fried clam roll as well as tuna sandwiches, hamburgers and fish and chips. Homestyle plates — like "Grandma's Baked Beans & Dogs & Cornbread & Coleslaw" — are available, plus fried haddock, shrimp, scallops and clams.

For dessert you may want to try their homemade ice cream; it's made with 16 percent butterfat and prime ingredients. A couple of good examples are the maple walnut ice cream, made with real Grade B Maine maple syrup and California walnuts, and the Coffee

Kahlua Brownie ice cream, made with brownies and fresh-brewed coffee made on the premises.

Warren's Lobster House
$$ • U.S. Hwy. 1, Kittery • (207) 439-1630

Warren's is at the base of the drawbridge that connects Portsmouth, New Hampshire, to Kittery. From the Kittery outlet area, head south on U.S. 1 (NOT the Route 1 Bypass) toward Portsmouth, and you'll see Warren's nestled to the left at the base of the bridge over the Piscataqua River. There's a big sign to help you out — there's a lobster on it and an arrow pointing left that says "Warren's."

Built on pilings above the Piscataqua, Warren's got its start in 1940. It specializes in lobster and seafood, but you can get a variety of steaks and chicken dishes. While most Maine restaurants serve some form of lobster, not many offer lobster thermidor, lobster scampi or a "Pile of Claws." Other lobster dishes at Warren's include lobster alfredo, tail and claws, and baked stuffed lobster tails. The restaurant is also well-known for its salad bar, large enough to be a meal in itself for most people.

The lunch menu offers less lobster variety, but you can always get baked, stuffed or boiled lobster or a lobster roll. For those who prefer something other than seafood, Warren's offers a selection of sandwiches, appetizers and lunch entrees.

A unique feature at Warren's is 150 feet of free dockage on the Piscataqua for those patrons arriving by boat. There's also a gift shop and a full-service bakery on the premises. Warren's is open daily for lunch and dinner. Full bar service is available.

Cafe Shelton
$$ • Ocean Ave., York Beach
• (207) 363-0708

Cafe Shelton is in one of two surviving pre-1910 hotels in York Beach. Originally called the Yorkshire Hotel in the 1890s, then the Kearsage Hotel, the building is known today as Shelton's and features the restaurant, shops and apartments. A white fence adorned with flower boxes separates the outside patio area of the cafe from the sidewalk. We enjoyed sitting on the patio not only for the view, but also because we were able to tie our dog to the outside of the fence so she could sit on the sidewalk and be with us while we ate.

Both the food and the service at Shelton's are good. For those of you who like club sandwiches, we recommend you try the one served here — surely this is what a club is meant to be! Cafe Shelton is open for lunch and dinner daily. Full bar service is available.

Cape Neddick Lobster Pound Harborside Restaurant
$$ • Shore Rd., Cape Neddick
• (207) 363-5471

You'll find the Cape Neddick Lobster Pound perched on the banks of the Cape Neddick River on Shore Road between York Beach and Ogunquit. While best known for its lobsters and steamed clams, "The Pound" serves a wide selection of fresh seafood, steak and chicken dishes. You may want to try a baked salmon filet, the harborside curry or the vegetable stir-fry. For those of you with a heartier appetite, go for the filet mignon and lobster or the bouillabaisse. A choice of candlelit dining rooms or an outside roof deck is available. The restaurant is open daily for lunch and dinner, and live entertainment is offered every Monday night in-season (see our Nightlife chapter).

Fazio's Italian Restaurant
$$ • 38 Woodbridge Rd., York
• (207) 363-7019

At Fazio's you'll learn that "Italian food" doesn't just mean tomato sauce! Renowned for its use of fresh ingredients, Fazio's pasta is made from scratch, as are the soups and sauces. Ingredients are chemical-free with no additives, and the chef can prepare some

INSIDERS' TIP

If you're eating out on a weekend, make dinner reservations early. We once spent an entire summer evening trying to find a restaurant with a wait of less than 30 minutes.

dishes without salt or butter on request. In addition to traditional favorites like meat lasagna and eggplant parmesan, Fazio's also offers a variety of interesting appetizers, including Pasta Chips 'n' Dip (made from fresh pasta triangles that are spiced, deep-fried and served with spinach parmesan dip) and caponata, a unique Italian eggplant spread served with garlic bread.

Dinner entrees include a number of chicken and veal dishes as well as calamari and other seafood offerings. The restaurant's most popular signature item is Bistecca, which features a tenderloin steak served as part of a different recipe each day. Fazio's features a banquet room that accommodates up to 150 people. The restaurant is open for dinner daily. Full bar service is available.

For those who prefer lighter fare, there's Fazio's pizzeria, Lastalla, (207) 363-1718, adjacent to the restaurant. In addition to the regular toppings, Lastalla offers asparagus, artichoke hearts, sun-dried tomatoes and Fontina cheese. Eight-inch Lastalla pizzas are available on Fazio's dinner menu, but in the pizzeria you can choose from an 8-, 12- or 16-inch pie. Lastalla is open for lunch and dinner daily.

Foodee's
$ • 449 U.S. Hwy. 1, York
• (207) 351-3378

For those of you who thought pizza came in two types of crust — thin and deep pan — Foodee's will be a pleasant surprise. Here you can choose from original, Chicago deep pan, Bavarian six-grain, San Francisco sourdough and whole-wheat crusts. Toppings are equally unique; there are more than 40 to choose from including fresh shrimp, sliced almonds and artichokes as well as the more common pepperoni, sausage, green pepper and onion.

You can eat in, take out or ask for a "Take 'N' Bake" pizza to take home and bake when it's time for dinner. Good news for parents: With an adult dine-in order, kids receive a drink and a free slice of cheese or pepperoni pizza. Foodee's is part of a franchise with a number of branches in New Hampshire and one each in Massachusetts, New Jersey and Vermont. This is the only Foodee's in Maine and is totally smoke-free.

Frankie & Johnny's Natural Foods
$$, no credit cards
• 1594 U.S. Hwy 1, Cape Neddick
• (207) 363-1909

Of all the interesting choices on the menu, ostrich surely takes the cake! You can choose to have it grilled or ash-blackened. Other specialties include ginger-marinated black beans with spicy coconut curry sauce and citrus sautéed julienne vegetables; and the lobster mushroom pasta, which features chunks of lightly smoked fresh Maine lobster meat sautéed with wild mushroom duxelle, tossed with hand-cut pasta noodles and topped with tarragon shallot butter.

Frankie & Johnny's also has its own style of pizza called a Crustoli. Toppings include spicy shrimp, arugula and salmon, and the pies come in 10- and 14-inch sizes. The restaurant is closed Tuesdays in-season, and it is open Thursday through Sunday off-season. Weekend reservations are recommended. Frankie & Johnny's doesn't have bar service, but you're invited to bring your own spirits.

Harbor Porches
$$$$ • Stage Neck Inn, 22 Stage Neck Rd., York Harbor
• (207) 363-3850, (800) 222-3238

Harbor Porches offers fine dining in one of southern Maine's most spectacular oceanfront settings. The restaurant is perched high above the ocean on a craggy peninsula "where the river meets the sea" at the Stage Neck Inn at York Harbor.

INSIDERS' TIP

It's OK to wear the plastic bib you get when you order boiled lobster. You won't look out of the ordinary; even the locals put them on.

The dinner menu changes weekly and focuses on fresh seafood and shellfish yet includes creative preparation of poultry, pork and beef. Lovers of lobster shouldn't miss the house specialty — succulent seafood baked stuffed lobster.

Down East magazine has said of the Stage Neck Inn's two restaurants (see Sandpiper Grille, below) that "dining is either casual or formal but the fare is consistently excellent — among the best in southern Maine."

Sandpiper Bar & Grille
$$ • Stage Neck Inn, 22 Stage Neck Rd., York Harbor • (207) 363-3850, (800) 222-3238

This intimate beachside restaurant housed within the Stage Neck Inn offers a diverse menu served continuously from Noon to 9 PM (10 PM on Friday and Saturday). The restaurant features a mahogany piano bar with live entertainment on the weekends, and a semi-enclosed seasonal outdoor terrace.

Specialties include Maine clam chowder, Caesar salad served traditionally or with your choice of chilled Maine shrimp, grilled chicken or grilled jumbo shrimp. Other selections include the petit filet mignon sandwich and blackened Maine crabcakes. An extensive wine list is available. For information on the Stage Neck Inn see our chapter on Hotels.

Sun and Surf
$$ • U.S. Hwy. 1A, York Beach
• (207) 363-2961

It's been said that if you live in York you've probably worked at Sun and Surf. Located on York Beach, with windows on three sides overlooking the ocean and Nubble Light in the distance, the decor of Sun and Surf is light, bright and airy. Blue sponge-painted walls, light white curtain swags held back with starfish tiebacks, a bleached wooden floor and bright, cheerful artwork make this a delightful seaside stop. For those who prefer not to eat in, Sun and Surf has a take-out window and an area with round stone tables and chairs overlooking the sea.

Specials vary throughout the summer, but you may find steak au poivre, grilled marinated duck breast and fresh grilled Arctic char among the offerings. Special sandwich choices include a lobster or crab croissant or the broiled tuna sandwich. Sun and Surf is open daily in-season (May through October). Full bar service is available.

The Goldenrod
$ • Railroad Ave., York Beach
• (207) 363-2621

Since 1896, the Goldenrod has been one of the highlights of York Beach. Its Goldenrod Kisses are argued to be the original saltwater taffy you'll find throughout New England. Around 9 million pieces of this candy are made at the Goldenrod each year — that's about 65 tons of the smooth, sticky sweets!

In addition to its candy, the Goldenrod serves food, and everything on the menu is available all day long. If you want pancakes for dinner, this is the place to go. Whatever you order and whether you sit at the ice cream counter or in the dining room, you're sure to receive prompt, pleasant service. With around 100 employees, the Goldenrod is certainly never understaffed! However, because it's usually packed, you might be able to avoid a line if you have an early lunch or dinner or a late breakfast. The dining area has a traditional New England feel with a large stone fireplace, gleaming hardwood tables and chairs and a beamed ceiling. For breakfast you might want to try the homemade blueberry strudel or a fluffy omelette. The Goldenrod is open daily from late May until the middle of October.

Arrows Restaurant and Bar
$$$$ • Berwick Rd., Ogunquit
• (207) 361-1100

Critics rave over Arrows. It has been lauded in *Down East* magazine, *The New York Times Magazine*, the *Boston Globe Magazine*, *Food and Wine Magazine* and *Boston Magazine*. The gardens at Arrows are given as much attention as the decor at most restaurants. Three full-time gardeners are employed, and each day the master gardener lists the produce and flowers available for use. The menu is then planned around the list. Decor is simple, stark and elegant with crisp linen, delicate crystal and one colorful, flamboyant floral display cut from the gardens. In daylight the gardens provide a sunlit splash of color for those in the window-lined rear dining room. In the evening,

Dining al fresco is a warm-weather treat.

white lights ornament the area in fairy-like splendor.

Owned by chefs Clark Frasier and Mark Gaier, Arrows has delighted diners since 1987. You'll find inventive entrees combining fresh produce, local seafood and top quality cuts of meat. Full bar service and an wine list are available. The menu changes daily. Arrows is open for dinner from July through November. In-season it's open Tuesday through Sunday; September through Columbus Day (mid-October) it's open Wednesday through Sunday; and from Columbus Day through November it's open Friday through Sunday. Reservations are suggested, and there is no wheelchair access to the restaurant.

Capt'n Nick's Restaurant & Lounge
$$ • U.S. Hwy. 1 N., Ogunquit
• (207) 646-9653

Capt'n Nick's is famous for its lobster and prime rib. A casual, family atmosphere will make you feel right at home as you wrestle with our famous crustacean, and don't be embarrassed to wear the bib! In addition to the restaurant, Capt'n Nick's club is one of the most popular local spots for nightlife. Check out our Nightlife chapter for more information on the club. The restaurant is open from April to the end of October.

Clay Hill Farm
$$$ • Agamenticus Rd., Ogunquit
• (207) 361-2272

Chosen by *Down East* magazine as "one of the five finest and most reliable restaurants in Southern Maine," Clay Hill Farm provides fine dining in an elegant country setting. The original farmhouse at Clay Hill was built in 1780. After renovations, the tavern at Clay Hill Farm opened its doors in 1975. Expansion followed in 1977, with the addition of the Veranda Room, and in 1978, when the Foyer & Lounge were enclosed. In 1983 the new owners, who include executive chef Roberta Pomeroy and the Lewis family, added the Fireside Room.

Specialties include lobster-stuffed haddock with red pepper cream sauce and the prime rib, which comes in two sizes — an 8-to-10-ounce or a 12-to-14-ounce cut. We also suggest the Scallops Frangelico, with scallops baked with crumbs flavored with garlic, ginger chives and hazelnut liqueur. Appetizers include Maine crab cakes with hollandaise sauce, lobster bisque and Gravad lox, which features the restaurant's own salt-cured and seasoned salmon, sliced and served with onions, capers, cornichons and rye bread.

Clay Hill Farm is open daily from May 1 to the end of October. Off-season operating days vary, so it's best to call ahead. The restaurant has an extensive wine list and full bar. Live piano entertainment is featured in the lounge Wednesday through Saturday evenings in-season and Friday and Saturday evenings off-season.

Compass Rose Restaurant & Bar
$$$ • 125 Shore Rd., Ogunquit
• (207) 646-1200

Compass Rose caters to the breakfast crowd, the dinner crowd and the late-night crowd. If you're looking for lunch, you'll have to go elsewhere. In-season they offer entertainment most nights. Breakfast specialties include eggs Benedict and wonderful breakfast crepes stuffed with almonds and a mixture of seasonal berries and topped with homemade peach ice cream. Bread lovers will be thrilled to know that bread is baked daily at Compass Rose; you can buy it by the slice or have it made into French toast.

For dinner you might want to try one of their interesting appetizers such as empanadas, which consist of sautéed spinach and shiitake mushrooms baked in a phyllo dough and served on a bed of red pepper coulis. Entrees include Lobster Forestier —

shelled lobster sautéed with forest mushrooms and finished with a tarragon cream, served with basmati rice. Those who prefer meat to seafood might want to try the Twin Towers: twin medallions of beef placed on toasted bread and potato toasties, then covered with a Madeira cracked pepper demi-glaze. Compass Rose is open daily for breakfast until noon. Dinner service begins at 5 PM, and full bar service is available. The restaurant is open from May through October.

Grey Gull
$$ • 321 Webhannet Dr., Wells
• (207) 646-7501

The Grey Gull is owned and operated by the same folks that run Clay Hill Farm. Executive chef and part owner Roberta Pomeroy oversees both establishments, so it isn't surprising that you can find the famous lobster-stuffed haddock at both restaurants. Other specialties at the Grey Gull include pecan-broiled haddock and rack of lamb. The restaurant is open daily in-season. Off-season open days vary; it's a good idea to call ahead. Entertainment is offered in the lounge on Tuesdays and Sundays (see our Nightlife chapter).

Gypsy Sweethearts Restaurant
$$$ • 10 Shore Rd., Ogunquit
• (207) 646-7021

You'll enjoy a creative contemporary menu at Gypsy Sweethearts. Located in a house that dates from the 1800s in the heart of Ogunquit's Main Street area, the restaurant features locally grown produce and locally caught seafood. One of the hallmarks of the restaurant is the freshness of the ingredients used in the kitchen. All the ice cream is made fresh, and desserts, condiments and dressings are created in the kitchen using herbs, vegetables and edible flowers from the garden. For those who enjoy fine wine with dinner, an extensive *Wine Spectator* award-winning wine list is avail-

INSIDERS' TIP

Call ahead and find out if the restaurant you are interested in has a two-for-one dinner night or an early-bird special. Also, check the coupon section of the local Yellow Pages and look in the local newspaper for special deals at particular restaurants.

able for review. For early birds, a fixed-price menu is offered from 5:30 to 6 PM; cost for this dinner in 1998 was $14.95.

Gypsy Sweethearts is open for breakfast on Saturday and Sunday from 7:30 AM to noon. Dinner is served daily from 5:30 to 10 PM. Gypsy Sweethearts is open from May to the end of October. In 1998 the restaurant celebrated its 20th season, and it is still owned by the husband and wife team who opened it — Judy Clayton and Tony Tarleton.

Jonathan's Restaurant
$$$ • 2 Bourne Ln., Ogunquit
• (207) 646-4777

Jonathan's is one of the premier dinner and entertainment spots in Southern Maine. In addition to scheduled entertainment (see Nightlife), the restaurant is popular for its selection of unusual dinner entrees and appetizers. Choose from entree selections including pan-blackened duck breast with mango and chili coulis, or appetizers like artichoke hearts baked with cheddar cheese. The entree list also serves up Mediterranean Pasta, which features organic lamb sausage sautéed with garlic, mushrooms, onions and tomatoes, tossed with pasta and topped with locally produced goat cheese. Seafood choices include a variety of scallop, shrimp, lobster and haddock dishes.

Jonathan's also offers Chef's Table choices, which include a caramelized salmon fillet, marinated in a Grand Marnier vinaigrette, dusted with sugar, dill and black pepper, pan-seared and served over a lemon beurre blanc with balsamic essence. This dish is garnished with snow peas and toasted almonds. The restaurant is open year round, and full bar service is available.

98 Provence
$$$ • 104 Shore Rd., Ogunquit
• (207) 646-9898

This charming French Provencal restaurant makes a nice change from traditional seaside fare. Inside you'll find romantic, country French decor with lace curtains, crisp tablecloths, a fireplace and candlelight. Specialties of the house include lamb, venison and veal dishes. You can get lobster here, but it won't be the traditional boiled or baked dish — it will

be cooked in a French style, perhaps sautéed in olive oil in the shell.

98 Provence opened in 1994 and is frequented by year-round residents of Ogunquit. The restaurant is completely smoke-free. It's open from April to December and closed on Tuesdays. Full bar service and an extensive wine list are available.

Oarweed
$$ • Perkins Cove, Ogunquit
• (207) 646-4022

Located on the ocean in Perkins Cove, Oarweed specializes in sweet Maine clams, homemade seafood chowder and all manner of fresh seafood dishes. You should also try the wonderful stuffed baked potatoes. Visitors can sit inside or out on the deck overlooking the sea. In addition to seafood, Oarweed offers chicken and steak, and there's a special menu for the kids on a coloring place mat. Oarweed serves homemade pies, cakes, puddings and ice cream and has a full bar. They are open daily from May to October for lunch and dinner, and all items are available for takeout. Reservations are not accepted.

Bull and Claw
$$ • U.S. Hwy. 1, Wells
• (207) 646-8467

The Bull and Claw claims to offer Maine's largest lobster roll, and since it measures two-feet long we aren't going to argue with them! According to the manager, only one man has ever managed to eat the whole thing by himself — and he was so impressed that he took another home to show his wife! The restaurant has a fun, family atmosphere with cartoons and popcorn for kids (and an all-inclusive children's menu that ran $3.99 in 1998), but it also caters (with a separate dining area) to those who prefer a quieter, more intimate dinner. Thick, hand-cut steaks, pitchers of fruit daiquiris, local micro-brewed ales and pilsners and daily prime rib specials are all part of the Bull and Claw scene. You'll also be tempted by a giant breakfast buffet served daily and rotisserie chicken served family-style. The Bull and Claw is open daily from April to December. Breakfast is served daily from July 4 to the end of August, then on Sundays only during the rest of the season.

Congdon's Doughnuts Family Restaurant

$ • 1090 U.S. Hwy. 1, Wells
• (207) 646-4219

Since 1945 the Congdon family has been famous for their absolutely yummy doughnuts, but the restaurant also serves breakfast and lunch. While a variety of flavored doughnuts are available, aficionados will probably prefer the good old plain Congdon doughnut. Not many can top it. If you're on the road, take-out orders are available.

For those who prefer to sit in and dine, you'll find omelettes, fresh baked waffles, pancakes and the Congdon Special — two eggs, home fries, toast, a Congdon doughnut and your choice of bacon, sausage or ham. Lunch items include the usual variety of burgers and sandwiches as well as fish and chips and lobster rolls. Congdon's is smoke-free.

Maine Diner

$$ • U.S. Hwy. 1, Wells
• (207) 646-4441

This is your chance to visit one of those diners you've seen in movies set back in the 1950s. It's stainless steel and chrome shine throughout, and a flashy neon sign announces its presence on Route 1. Since 1986 the Henry family has welcomed scores of guests who want to enjoy the real diner experience.

In the tradition of good, simple diner food, Maine Diner offers old favorites like chicken pot pie, roast turkey and homemade macaroni and cheese. Its specialty, however, is lobster pie, which has been featured in *Yankee* magazine's *The Cook's Magazine* and *Good Food, Road Food*. The Maine Diner is open daily year round from 7 AM till 9 PM on Friday and Saturday, 8 PM on weeknights and Sunday. Its gift shop, Remember the Maine, is next door. On weekends and during the busy season, you'll probably have to wait before dining, but it's worth it. They'll present you with a little gadget that vibrates when your table is ready, so you can wander off to the gift shop while you wait.

The Steakhouse

$$ • U.S. Hwy. 1, Wells • (207) 646-4200

The Steakhouse makes you feel more like you're in Texas than along the Maine coast. Set in a large, barn-style building with an upstairs gallery overlooking the main floor, the restaurant prides itself on the quality of the meat it serves. Beef is always fresh, hand-cut and well-marbled, and it's served in a variety of cuts and sizes. For example, you can choose from an 8-, 12- or 16-ounce portion of New York strip sirloin or a 6-, 9- or 12-ounce portion of filet mignon. Surf-and-turf combinations featuring steak and scallops, jumbo shrimp or lobster tails are available along with a variety of other dishes. The Steakhouse is open for dinner starting at 4:30 PM Tuesday through Sunday. Reservations are not accepted. The restaurant is closed for the season from mid-December to April 1.

Seafare

$ • U.S. Hwy. 1 N., Wells
• (207) 646-5460

Adjacent to the Moody Post Office, Seafare is known as one of the best local fish markets around. It also has a small take-out window where you can order prepared food. Picnic tables are set on a small lawn and deck, making it a great place to stop for lunch or a quick dinner. We tried the fish and chip special, and it was terrific. Chunks of white, flaky fish in a light batter and good french fries were served in traditional paper baskets with tartar sauce and ketchup. The quality couldn't be beat and, at $2.99 in 1998, neither could the price. In addition to fish and chips you can get all manner of fried seafood at Seafare. If you like, order a "Clambake" for one (or more) with steamers (local jargon for steamed clams), lobster, fries, coleslaw, corn on the cob and chowder. Seafare is open daily in-season.

INSIDERS' TIP

Most Maine restaurants are kid-friendly, but if you have young children, make dinner a more pleasant experience for your family and other diners by eating early in the evening while there's still a chance of getting a table away from the crowd.

Federal Jack's Restaurant & Brew Pub

**$$ • Maine Hwy. 9, Kennebunk
• (207) 967-4322**

Federal Jack's is the brewpub restaurant created to serve the beer and ales brewed by the Kennebunkport Brewing Company, which is beneath the pub. All beer brewed here is for use at Federal Jack's. The company's two other facilities, which are operated under The Shipyard Brewing Company name, are here in Portland and in Orlando, Florida. (See Attractions for more information on the brewery.)

Just across the bridge from Dock Square, Federal Jack's features a water view from every table, plus brewery tours, a game room and eight ales on draught. The award-winning menu includes the freshest seafood, chowders and mouth-watering pub fare. You'll also enjoy live acoustic music three nights a week and happy hour Monday through Friday.

Among the appetizers at Federal Jack's are the unusual Goat Island Mussels (native mussels steamed in Goat Island Light Ale with fresh basil and garlic) and the standard fried seafood sampler with shrimp, scallops and calamari served with cocktail sauce. Dinner favorites include Federal Jack's Feast — a cup of chowder, a pound-and-a-quarter steamed lobster, steamers and mussels, roasted potatoes and a glass of your favorite beer (root or ale)! Pub favorites include bangers 'n' mash, a classic English-style sausage with a mushroom and brown ale gravy; and Pugsley's Cottage Pie, which features braised lamb and beef layered with whipped turnips and mashed potatoes. Federal Jack's is open for lunch and dinner daily year round.

Peppermill Steak House

**$$ • 25 Log Cabin Rd., Kennebunkport
• (207) 967-8885**

Dark beams, a fireplace and captain's-style chairs at tables with crisp white tablecloths bring out a warm, country atmosphere at this steakhouse. Known for its prime rib, the Peppermill offers three different portion sizes — 8-, 12- and 14-ounce. Another house specialty is the top sirloin served with a creamed, brandied peppercorn sauce. Fresh seafood and pasta entrees are offered, and specials change daily. On Friday and Saturday evenings in-sea-

son, you can enjoy a pianist in the Coach Room, and weekly entertainment is offered in the Peppermill Lounge (see our Nightlife chapter). Reservations are accepted. The Peppermill Steak House is open for dinner Tuesday through Saturday. The restaurant is closed from January to March.

The Colony Hotel

**$$$ • Ocean Ave., Kennebunkport
• (207) 967-3331**

The Colony Hotel is an environmentally aware hotel (see the Close-up in our Hotels and Motels chapter) that opened in 1949. It's open from the end of May to the middle of October and offers breakfast, lunch and dinner. Comfortable attire is acceptable in the restaurant, but the hotel prefers that guests not wear jeans or shorts for dinner.

Special dining events at the Colony include the Friday night lobster buffet, Sunday brunch, Sumptuous Homemade Breakfast, Saturday night dinner dancing and ocean terrace lunch. Dinner specialties include a variety of fresh fish, free-range chicken and meat dishes. All fish, chicken and meat used at the Colony are procured from local vendors. Produce, herbs and garnishes are harvested from the hotel's gardens whenever possible or purchased from local farmers. Reservations are suggested for dinner.

The White Barn Inn

$$$$ • Beach St. (Maine Hwy. 35), Kennebunkport • (207) 967-2321

The White Barn Inn is the only restaurant in Maine to hold the distinguished five-diamond award from the American Automobile Association (AAA), an honor it's held for seven straight years. In January '99, the White Barn received a top rating from *Conde Naste* for resort restaurants — one of just five restaurants in the world to receive this award – and the *Zagat Boston Restaurant Survey* named the White Barn as one of three restaurants in New England worth making a special trip to experience. It's an honor Executive Chef Jonathan Cartwright maintains with an excellence of quality and creativity. A staff member travels to Boston daily to buy fresh ingredients, and the menu changes weekly.

A fixed price four course dinner is avail-

Photo: Giselle A. Auger

Lobster shacks such as this can be found along the coast of Maine. Most markets sell fresh fish and lobster, and they will often boil the lobster for you if you prefer not to cook it yourself.

able year round for $63 per person, excluding tips, tax and beverages (except coffee and tea which are provided with dessert). The menu changes each Thursday but always includes a seafood option and a vegetarian option. One of the most popular dishes which appears on the menu regularly involves a steamed Maine lobster on a bed of homemade fettucine with carrots, ginger, snow peas and a cognac coral butter sauce.

Dinner is by reservation and a jacket is required for men. Ties are optional. Reservations are accepted 30 to 45 days in advance.

Windows on the Water

$$$$ • Chase Hill Rd., near jct. Of Maine Hwy. 9 and Maine Hwy. 35, Kennebunkport • (207) 967-3313

In 1997 Windows on the Water received the Culinary Guild of the Americas "Epicurean Plate Award." Chef/owner John P. Hughes III was inducted into the Master Chefs Institute in 1988. It's no wonder that the restaurant is favored by those looking for a gourmet meal in Southern Maine. Windows has received positive reviews from *Bon Appetit, Gourmet, Food & Wine, Down East* and *Yankee* magazines.

House specialties include farm-raised Maine salmon nicoise, California-style lobster ravioli and cedar plank-roasted day-boat codfish. The restaurant also has an award-winning lobster bisque.

Windows on the Water is aptly named — lots of windows overlooking the Kennebunk River lend a bright, airy ambiance and provide wonderful views. Dockage is available for those arriving by boat. Windows on the Water is open for lunch Monday through Saturday and dinner Tuesday through Sunday. You may also enjoy their Sunday brunch.

Old Orchard Beach Area

Buffleheads
$$ • 122 Hills Beach Rd., Biddeford • (207) 284-6000

Enjoy a walk on Hills Beach (see our Beaches chapter) before or after eating at Buffleheads. Open year round and serving breakfast, lunch and dinner, Buffleheads is a favorite of locals. In 1996 the restaurant won the Portland Chocolate Lovers Fling Best Brownie Award, which tells you a little bit about the quality of the desserts. (For more on the Chocolate Lovers Fling, see our Annual Events and Festivals chapter.)

Breakfast specialties include Buffled Eggs, which involve two eggs scrambled with cream cheese, fresh mushrooms and herbs and served with home fries and toast. At lunch you might want to try crab cakes with Cajun mayonnaise or a lobster melt. Delightful dinner selections include the duck with Maine blueberry sauce and pecan-crusted salmon. Daily specials are also featured for all three meals. Take-out service is available.

Island Wok
$ • 11 Elm St. (U.S. Hwy. 1), Biddeford • (207) 282-3838

While there are a number of good Chinese restaurants in the Saco-Biddeford area, Island Wok stands out as one of the best. With windows overlooking the Saco River and a stylish, large photograph of Hong Kong on the back wall, Island Wok avoids the fast-food atmosphere common in many Chinese restaurants. Combination plates are available for lunch and dinner and include your choice of hot and sour or egg-drop soup. We've tried many different dishes at Island Wok, and all have been expertly prepared. Among our favorites are the spicy, tangy General Tso's

chicken and the house special lo mein. Island Wok is open daily for lunch and dinner.

Lily Moon Cafe & Bakery
$$, no credit cards • 17 Pepperell Sq., Saco • (207) 284-2233

You'll find this delightful little restaurant just off Saco's Main Street in Pepperell Square. Homemade breads and pastries are featured at Lily Moon Cafe, which doubles as a bakery. Open for breakfast Tuesday through Sunday, lunch Tuesday through Saturday, and dinner Wednesday through Saturday, Lily Moon specialties include fruit-filled crepes, deli sandwiches and an eclectic selection of dinner entrees. The dinner menu includes caramelized salmon and herb-crusted chicken breast, and specialty sandwiches like the grilled roast turkey, Portobello mushroom and cheese served on a baguette show up at lunch. The Lily Moon Cafe doesn't serve alcohol.

Lucky Loggers Landing
$ • Saco Valley Shopping Center, off U.S. Hwy. 1 • (207) 283-0485

For a great homestyle breakfast, lunch or dinner in a no-frills atmosphere, don't miss Lucky Loggers Landing. Located in a strip plaza that includes Shaw's supermarket, Bookland and the Dollar Store Marketplace, Lucky Loggers Landing maintains a steady stream of business throughout the day. Its clientele leans toward the older generation, perhaps because of the type of food served. You'd bet it was your grandmother cooking when you see the meat loaf dinner with mashed potatoes and gravy go by.

In addition to homestyle dinner choices, the restaurant carries a wide selection of sandwiches including pastrami with Swiss cheese and club sandwiches. If you'd rather, you can always choose a hamburger or cheeseburger. Breakfasts are hearty and tasty and served all day. There's the usual assortment of waffles, crepes and omelettes to choose from, as well as muffins and bagels. Alcoholic beverages are not sold at Lucky Loggers Landing. The restaurant is open daily.

Silver Spoons Restaurant
$$$ • 63 Storer Ave., Saco
• (207) 286-8686

Silver Spoons has proven popular enough to bring about a move from a smaller restaurant space in Pepperell Square (which now houses the previously listed Lily Moon Cafe) to its present location, which features two dining areas and a lounge. Voted No. 1 in dining excellence in Greater Biddeford-Saco in 1997 by Market Surveys of America, Silver Spoons offers casual dining in the lounge and a more formal, romantic atmosphere with candlelight and fresh flowers in the restaurant.

A few of the restaurant's specialties include veal marsala, duck breast with raspberry sauce, and steak au poivre, which is served Madagascar-style with black and green cracked peppercorns, pan-seared and finished with a brandy and cream sauce. You'll also find a nice selection of seafood dishes including baked haddock. Silver Spoons is open year round for lunch and dinner Tuesday through Friday and for dinner on Saturday.

Wormwoods Restaurant
$$ • Bay Ave., Camp Ellis
• (207) 282-9679

Open year round, Wormwoods is well-loved by locals. Located in the heart of Camp Ellis, next to a large stone breakwater that children and adults like to stroll along, Wormwoods offers a wide selection of seafood, meat and poultry dishes. Many entrees are offered in two sizes — unless you have a hearty appetite or are very hungry, the smaller one will usually do. Both sizes come with a choice of side dishes, usually french fries, mashed potatoes or garlic potatoes and cole slaw, all of which are quite tasty.

Daily specials are offered for lunch and dinner and may include items like chicken Oscar or steak au poivre. Regular menu items include a variety of seafood pies cooked in a creamy Newburg sauce, seafood and clam chowders, boiled lobsters, baked stuffed lobster tails and garlic-baked shrimp. Wormwoods opens daily for lunch and dinner. For those visiting at Christmas time, it's worth the trip to admire the seasonal decorations.

Bell Buoy Restaurant
$$ • 24 Old Orchard St., Old Orchard Beach • (207) 934-2745

This unpretentious restaurant sits on Old Orchard Beach's main strip leading to the pier. We've heard the food is consistently good, and guests return year after year. On the menu are seaside staples like chowder, baked stuffed shrimp and boiled lobster. Other items include lasagna, chicken with broccoli and cheese, and lobster pie. A children's menu is available for those younger than 12; it includes favorites such as popcorn shrimp, chicken tenders and hamburgers. The Bell Buoy is open for lunch and dinner daily from May to September.

Captain's Galley Restaurant
$ • 168 Saco Ave., Old Orchard Beach • (207) 934-1336

It is little wonder that the parking lot of this restaurant is packed year round and they had to build a second dining and banquet room in 1998. Open daily for breakfast, lunch and dinner, the Captain's Galley offers good food at reasonable prices. Two-for-one dinner specials are featured year round at a couple of different prices — it was $12.95 or $14.95 in 1998, depending on what you ordered from a limited selection that included tender prime rib and baked haddock. (In-season these specials are available until 5 PM; off-season they're available all evening.) In addition to the two-for-ones, the restaurant has a full range of appetizers and entrees — lobster and shrimp dishes, prime rib, steaks and poultry are among the choices.

The breakfast menu includes eggs, home fries, toast and bacon, sausage or ham in a variety of combinations as well as pancakes, omelettes and other standard morning fare. Service at the Captain's Galley is always good, and the atmosphere is pleasant. You won't find tablecloths, but you will find solitaire peg games to entertain you and the children.

Danton's Family Restaurant
$ • Old Orchard Street, Old Orchard Beach • (207) 934-7701

Established in 1946, this little family restaurant is exceptionally clean and appealing for one so near to the beach. Tables are squeaky clean, service is good and the food is great. We split a turkey roll-up and a salad and had room for lemon meringue pie — but just barely! Pies and dinners are homemade and there's always a wide selection to choose from. Danton's is open for breakfast, lunch and dinner daily in-season.

Joseph's By The Sea
$$$ • 55 W. Grand Ave., Old Orchard Beach • (207) 934-5044

Joseph's offers excellent elegant dining with superb views overlooking Saco Bay. Tablecloths, candlelight and fresh flowers create a romantic, sophisticated ambiance; it's the perfect atmosphere for a special occasion or an intimate dinner for two. Creative appetizers such as lobster potato pie and wild mushroom torte set the tone for inventive entrees like the pepper-crusted filet mignon, Diver Sea Scallops and the Best of Both Worlds, which features a beef tenderloin and lobster flamed with garlic brandy sauce.

To complement the meal you can choose from an extensive wine list, and a delightful assortment of desserts will provide a sweet ending to a perfect meal. Joseph's is open from May through early September, serving dinner daily and Sunday breakfast in-season. From early September to late October, the restaurant is open for dinner Thursday through Saturday and breakfast on Sunday.

Village Inn
$$ • 213 Saco Ave., Old Orchard Beach • (207) 934-7370

Open year round, the Village Inn is popular with locals and tourists. Located at the intersection known as "Halfway," the building sprawls with a lounge area and a number of dining rooms, all of which get packed in-season. In addition, there's a small brewpub called the Whale's Tail where you can sample a variety of beers brewed on the premises. For dinner selections, choose from the whole range of lobster and seafood dishes, from twin lobsters to baked stuffed shrimp and baked haddock to the traditional fried clams, scallops and shrimp. Poultry and meat entrees round out the menu.

Though very busy, the Village Inn has a sizable wait staff and good service. The ambiance isn't particularly romantic, but it's a fun place to go with a family or large group of friends. The restaurant serves breakfast, lunch and dinner, but hours are reduced in the off-season.

Greater Portland Area

Anjon's Italian Restaurant
$$ • U.S. Hwy. 1, Scarborough • (207) 883-9562

You can't beat Anjon's winning combination of good food and great views. Located on Route 1 overlooking Scarborough Marsh, the restaurant is notable because there are no buildings in front of it — you get an unobstructed view of the marsh leading to the sea. Needless to say, it is a pleasant spot to watch the night fall.

Established in 1954, the restaurant is known for its fine Italian fare, but it also does a nice job with seafood, including boiled twin lobster. For an appetizer you might want to try the bruchetta — freshly baked bread topped with chopped fresh tomato, olive oil and basil. . . . yum! Reservations are accepted for parties of six or more; if your party is smaller and you want a table overlooking the marsh, you may have to wait. Anjon's also features early-bird specials that allow you a selection of entrees, a non-alcoholic beverage and dessert for around $7. Lunch specials start at about $4. The restaurant offers full bar service and is open from March to New Year's.

Carson's Family Restaurant
$ • 433 U.S. Hwy. 1, Scarborough • (207) 883-4400

Popular with an older crowd, Carson's offers a variety of homemade dinners you might remember from your youth — meat loaf with brown gravy and mashed potatoes, roast pork and roast turkey with all the fixins and baked stuffed chicken. You'll also find the usual favorites like hamburgers, hot dogs and club sandwiches as well as fried clams, fish and chips and baked haddock. In summer 1996 Carson's added an enclosed outdoor deck that's very pleasant in the summer, and they renovated the interior with a new entrance and additional dining space in 1997.

Chowderheads
$ • Oak Hill Plaza, Maine Hwy. 114, Scarborough • (207) 883-8333

If you've been looking forward to trying New England clam chowder (the white stuff!), this is the place to go. Chowderhead's is kind of a well-kept local secret, though people in areas north of Portland are beginning to find their way to Oak Hill Plaza. Despite being in a shopping center, the restaurant has arguably the best chowder around, and the seafood is as good as anything out there. For decor you'll find blue and white patterned linoleum squares on the floor and blue walls decorated with colorfully painted wooden fish.

While it may look like a fast-food place, Chowderhead's offers high-quality food at reasonable prices without any fuss. Its most popular dishes are the seafood platter with fried clams, shrimp, haddock and scallops; the swordfish steak and salmon fillet sandwiches; and the crabmeat roll. Dinners are served with two side orders (french fries, cole slaw, onion rings, pasta salad or rice pilaf), and we recommend the onion rings. Menu items are available for take-out. Chowderhead's is open daily year round and doesn't serve alcohol.

Clambake Restaurant
$$ • 358 Pine Point Rd., Scarborough • (207) 883-4871

The Clambake is reminiscent of a time gone by. It features a traditional, large-crowd clambake atmosphere with long trestle tables in a long building. Busloads of people come to the Clambake every year to enjoy corn on the cob, steamed clams, boiled lobster and clam chowder. It's basic, it's plentiful and it's good. Clambake is on Pine Point Road overlooking the marsh, next door to the Nestling Duck Gift Shop (see our Shopping chapter). It's open daily in-season and weekends the rest of the year.

Northern Lites Cafe
$, no credit cards • 313 U.S. Hwy. 1, Scarborough • (207) 883-6114

Whether it's time for a meal or you just want coffee and a snack, take time to stop in at Northern Lites. Everything we've ever tried has been fresh and tasty, though our favorites are the turkey, cheddar, honey mustard sandwich on french bread and the chicken Caesar salad. The muffins and pastries are mouthwateringly tempting — no doubt many a diet has been blown here. However, if you are being careful about what you eat, try the vegetable roll-ups — they're great too.

Northern Lites has an outside patio with green wrought-iron tables and chairs topped with umbrellas where you can sit and enjoy a meal or some fresh-brewed iced tea. If it gets too hot, take a seat inside where it is always cool and clean. Everything at Northern Lites is cooked from scratch, from the turkey to the soups, chowders and baked goods. In 1995 the Chocolate Mousse Cake won the best cake award at the Portland Chocolate Lover's Fling. Northern Lites is open daily for breakfast and lunch. Dinner is served Tuesday through Saturday. It is a completely smoke-free restaurant.

Two Lights Lobster Shack
$$ • Off Maine Hwy. 77 at Two Lights, Cape Elizabeth • (207) 799-1677

Since the 1920s, the Lobster Shack at Two Lights State Park has been a local landmark. Set below the lighthouse, overlooking the sea, next to the foghorn, it's an unforgettable place to enjoy lunch or dinner in a cozy dining room or outside on picnic tables. Before or after dining you can walk along the rocks shelving

---

INSIDERS' TIP

Children love the experience of eating at one of our wharf restaurants where you get to select your own lobster from the tank. Watching the lobsters is a great diversion while you wait for dinner to arrive.

out to the sea, get an up-close view of the seagulls (who know a good thing when they find one) or just sit on a bench and enjoy the view. You can also browse in the adjacent gift shop, the Candle Shack, which carries Maine souvenirs and gifts. For your meal, you can choose a lobster from the lobster pool and see it cooked, or you can order from the menu. Specialties at the Lobster Shack include clam chowder, lobster stew, fried chicken, fried clams, scallops, haddock, and clam cakes. The restaurant is open daily from April to the middle of October.

Mr. Bagel
$ • 220 Mall Plaza, South Portland
• (207) 773-3238
$ • 172 U.S. Hwy. 1, Scarborough
• (207) 883-0070

In addition to the two listed locations, this local franchise has 10 other locations in the Greater Portland area. Fresh bagels, sandwiches, bagel pizzas, soups and other baked goods are prepared daily for these stores, and it's a good choice for a lunchtime stop. Be warned, however, that some of the locations, including the two listed, get very busy at lunch. The good news is that the lines are dealt with quickly and professionally, and the quality of the food doesn't suffer for the restaurant's popularity.

Bagel varieties include poppy, garlic, salt and pumpernickel, and cream cheese comes in a wealth of choices including olive (very good), chive, plain and strawberry. Sandwiches come with your choice of a side dish (macaroni salad, potato salad or chips) and a pickle. Opening times vary by location. The listed Mr. Bagels are open for lunch and breakfast bagels and coffee daily.

Ricetta's Brickoven Pizzeria
$$ • 29 Western Ave., South Portland
• (207) 775-7400

Ask people in the South Portland area where they go for pizza, and they'll probably say Ricetta's. You'll see cooks working in full view of the dining room, with large brick ovens lining part of one wall behind them. Pizza is prepared, then placed in these ovens to come out with that unbeatable brick-oven-baked taste. A number of specialty pizza combinations are available, or you can build your own pie. Toppings include the usual pepperoni, sausage, green peppers and onions, and unusual ones like Feta cheese, blackened chicken and spinach. If you prefer something other than pizza, there are a number of different entrees and calzones. For lunch Ricetta's offers a buffet with pizza, macaroni and salad items. The restaurant is open daily year round for lunch and dinner.

Romano's Macaroni Grill
$$ • 415 Philbrook Ave., South Portland
• (207) 780-6620

Part of a national chain based in Dallas, this is the only Romano's Macaroni Grill in Maine and the first one in New England. Since opening in October 1996, the restaurant has become a popular lunch and dinner destination for residents of Greater Portland. You'll find the restaurant in the plaza next to the Maine Mall that houses the Shop 'N' Save supermarket and T.J. Maxx.

Inside you're greeted by white-topped tables in a large but intimate dining room with cooks working in full view along one side. Instead of the pre-meal bread and butter you usually receive, here you'll get a warm loaf of focaccia served with virgin olive oil and cracked black pepper.

Servers write their names on the paper table covers with crayons, and the wait staff works as a team. If your server is not available when your food is ready, another server will bring it to you so that everything reaches your table piping hot.

Popular dishes include the Farfalle con Pollo al Suga Bianco, which features bowtie pasta, chicken, pancetta and red and green onion in Asiago cream sauce, and the Scalloppine di Pollo, which has chicken breast, mushrooms, artichokes, capers and pancetta in lemon butter with pasta. Pleasant Italian background music plays while you eat, and on weekends live singers entertain guests. Romano's Macaroni Grill is open for lunch and dinner daily year round.

Snow Squall
$$$ • 18 Ocean St., South Portland
• (207) 799-2232

On the waterfront in South Portland, Snow

Squall is known for fresh seafood prepared with creativity. The restaurant is large enough to offer a wide variety of unusual dishes that cater to many different tastes. The menu changes regularly but will usually include dishes prepared with farm-raised Atlantic salmon, lobster, mussels, shrimp and top-quality beef.

In-season, the Snow Squall is recognized for its lobster stew, which you can buy by the cup or bowl. In the off-season, the stew is only occasionally on the menu. This is a tablecloth restaurant with an elegant yet casual atmosphere. There are no dress requirements to dine, but you will notice that many people like to dress up for a meal here. During summer, Snow Squall features an outdoor patio overlooking the waterfront; off-season, you can enjoy a cozy fire in the lounge.

Opened in 1981, Snow Squall is operated by David Gooch; the creative genius behind the tasteful dishes is chef John St. Germain. Snow Squall is open daily for dinner year-round, for lunch Monday through Friday and for brunch on Sunday. They can accommodate large parties on short notice and are wheelchair-accessible. Ample parking is available, and the bar offers a daily happy hour with drink specials.

Cafe Stroudwater
$$$ • 1050 Westbrook St., Portland
• (207) 775-0032

For an elegant restaurant where you can dine with linen and china and still bring the kids, we recommend Cafe Stroudwater. Rated five stars by the Maine Sunday Telegram, it features intimate two-person booths and center tables for larger groups of up to 12. White tablecloths and burgundy napkins make for pretty table settings, while the bar across the hall keeps things from getting too formal. The restaurant is at the Embassy Suites by the Portland Jetport. Come in for lunch, dinner or Sunday brunch (brunch is by reservation) and order from an American menu of steak, lobster and other seafood.

Cafe Uffa
$$$ • 190 State St., Portland
• (207) 775-3380

Multi-ethnic, homemade cuisine featuring wood-grilled fish and vegetarian dishes has earned Cafe Uffa a tasty reputation around town. The menu is filled with creative fare such as the pan-fried polenta with zucchini and cheese and the apple-wood grilled tuna with chipotle butter. The atmosphere is warm and inviting (described by one person as "Greenwich-villagey") with just a dozen tables, high ceilings, candlelight at night and a feeling of airiness. The cafe is open for breakfast Wednesday through Sunday and dinner Wednesday through Saturday. Expect to find it closed for the first two weeks of January and two weeks during the month of July.

Cotton Street Cantina
$$ • 10 Cotton St., Portland
• (207) 775-3222

Latino music, a fountain and palm trees may make you question whether south is still south when you step inside this restaurant that serves South American and Caribbean food. Lunch, served Monday through Friday, offers favorites such as the grilled tequila barbecue chicken and the lime parsley marinated chicken burrito. All week long you'll find a dinner menu with just as much spice, and you can choose between small and large plates. To go with your meal, try something refreshing from the juice and smoothie bar or the full bar specializing in rum and tequila drinks. The atmosphere is as original as the food, with hot Caribbean colors, South American art and walls covered with rusted corrugated metal.

INSIDERS' TIP

Taking apart a whole lobster is a daunting task for youngsters, and it's an expensive investment for you if they don't eat it all. Instead, let the little ones nibble your lobster's legs. They'll get a taste of the meat, and you'll get to save your money. That's what our moms did.

David's at the Oyster Club

$$$ • 164 Middle St., Portland
• (207) 773-4340

Order fresh, raw oysters and clams on the half-shell or select a shrimp cocktail at the seafood bar. David's has two separate dining rooms. Downstairs — where you can order a four-course meal for $15 per person — the atmosphere is dressier. Upstairs, where the bar is located, things are more relaxed, and there's an outdoor patio for dining during the warmer months. David's describes its food as eclectic French and American cuisine. There are lots of pasta dishes and juicy steaks on the menu, as well as seafood and nightly specials. A favorite appetizer, for which it is well known, is the lobster and scallop sweet potato cake; the goat cheese packets with leeks are terrific as well. The restaurant is open for lunch, dinner and Sunday brunch.

DiMillo's Floating Restaurant

$$$ • Long Wharf, Portland
• (207) 772-2216

When you park your car at Long Wharf and look for DiMillo's, don't be surprised if you miss it among the many boats tied up in the harbor. After all, it is a boat. In fact, the old ferry is the biggest boat at the dock, and you can sit in one of the dining rooms on its upper or lower decks and get a water view from any table. Commissioned The New York in 1941 to ferry cars and people between Delaware and New Jersey, the 206-foot boat is believed to be the only floating restaurant on the upper East Coast.

Inside you'll find elegantly set tables and a choice of lunch and dinner entrees that feature seafood, steak and pasta. The restaurant was started on land by Tony DiMillo in 1954 on Portland's Fore Street. It moved several times, then landed on the water in 1982 when DiMillo bought Long Wharf. Outside the boat are several decks for outside dining; inside there's a full bar. Some favorite Italian recipes you can try here include ziti baked with four cheeses; jumbo shrimp, lobster and scallops sautéed in fresh garlic and butter served over linguine; and boneless breast of chicken stuffed with fresh spinach.

F. Parker Reidy's

$$ • 83 Exchange St., Portland
• (207) 773-4731

Located in the original Portland Savings Bank on Exchange Street, F. Parker Reidy's is a lovely place to go to lunch with Mom or a friend. Large windows with leaded stained-glass designs frame a cobbled square and the charm of the street. Sitting in the high-ceilinged Victorian dining room and looking through those windows in winter, with large, lacy snowflakes drifting down, will make you feel as though you've stepped back in time.

F. Parker Reidy's has a separate bar and lounge area and a congenial, friendly atmosphere. The restaurant features prime rib on Friday and Saturday nights, but it is also well-respected for its seafood selections. The restaurant is open daily for dinner and Monday through Saturday for lunch.

Gritty McDuff's

$ • 396 Fore St., Portland
• (207) 772-2739
$ • Lower Main St., Freeport
• (207) 865-4321

You can expect traditional pub fare and atmosphere at one of Portland's most popular brewpubs. Calamari, meat loaf and beef, chicken and lentil burgers fill the lunch and dinner menu. Beers brewed right on the premises fill the kegs. The atmosphere is relaxed and friendly with lively conversation and plenty to drink. (For more information, see the Brewpubs section of our Attractions chapter.)

Katahdin Restaurant

$$ • 106 High St., Portland
• (207) 774-1740

A mural of the mountains greets you when you dine at this restaurant, which is named for

Maine's highest peak. You can expect the food to be just as New England as the scenery. The menu is stuffed with crab cakes, pan-fried trout, oyster stew, smoked seafood, pot roast, sirloin tip steak and vegetarian pastas. For the lighter appetite, half-portions are available, and for all diners the atmosphere is as warm and homey as the most popular kitchen in your hometown. The restaurant is open for dinner only.

The Armory
$$$$ • Portland Regency Hotel, 20 Milk St., Portland • (207) 774-4200

In the heart of the Old Port, this four-star dining room in one of the area's finest hotels (see our Hotels and Motels chapter) serves breakfast, Sunday brunch and dinner daily and lunch Monday through Friday. The intimate eatery has just more than a dozen tables. The food is cooked to perfection and elegantly served; the tables are set with linen and fine china. The menu is mostly American with fresh Maine seafood. Gulf shrimp and Maine clams with sun-dried tomatoes and salsa was the special on the night we checked it out. From the moment the hotel's glass front doors are opened for you to the end of your dining experience, this restaurant is full of romance. Dress is casual in general, though some people will likely be dressed up for special events and occasions.

Roma Cafe
$$ • 769 Congress St., Portland • (207) 773-9873

Established in 1924, this lovely restaurant is in a 100-year-old Victorian mansion and lays claim to be Portland's most romantic dining spot. When you step inside, it isn't hard to see why. The atmosphere is intimate, with private dining rooms available for parties of 10 or more and candles, fresh flowers and linens on each table.

The menu features succulent seafood and Italian cuisine. Some favorites are baked haddock with a tomato-basil sauce, roasted breast of duck and filet mignon. The seafood linguine is also very popular, and you can top it with either a marinara sauce or a white wine sauce with garlic and herbs. The restaurant is open

for lunch during the week and for dinner daily, though it does close on Sundays during the fall.

Saigon Thinh Thanh
$$ • 608 Congress St., Portland • (207) 773-2932

This is Vietnamese food at its best. You'll choose from a large menu of steamed vegetables, noodles, fresh seafood, chicken and pork seasoned as spicy or mild as your taste buds demand. Owner Thinh Bui, who emigrated to the United States in 1980, runs the business with his wife, brother and brother-in-law. The eatery can seat about 40 people at booths or tables. The atmosphere is pleasant, but the food is the main attraction. The restaurant is open seven days a week for lunch and dinner.

Street and Company
$$$$ • 33 Wharf St., Portland • (207) 775-0887

Set in a small dinning room off a backway, cobbled street, this Mediteranian fish restaurant is in a rustic building with wood floors and dried herbs and flowers hanging from the ceiling. Bottles of wine line back walls. The food is the main centerpiece, with a very simple menu offering whole fish, scallops in pernod and cream, grilled lobster on lignguine, and lobster for two. You can get tuna, salmon, halibut, sole or scallops and a variety of dishes over linguine. There are less than a dozen appetizers featuring mussels, salad, calamari and clams. It's not the variety that makes this restaurant a treat, but the flavorful preparation and freshness of the food. Street and Company is open for dinner only and is small, so call ahead for reservations.

Tandoor Restaurant
$$ • 88 Exchange St., Portland • (207) 775-4259

Here the menu features a wide array of Indian dishes, with a large selection of vegetarian, lamb and chicken entrees and hot breads. The family business combines food from the north and south of India, and cooking is done in a large clay oven for authentic Tandoor flavor. We suggest the tender, delicious Tandoor chicken! While Indian food has

a reputation for being spicy, you can get it any way you like here. Lunch is served Monday through Saturday, and the restaurant is open for dinner all week long.

The Back Bay Grill
$$$$ • 65 Portland St., Portland
• (207) 772-8833

Set in an unpretentious brick building just off a busy street in a section of town that's crowded with apartments, this intimate restaurant has been delighting patrons with award-winning food and drink for 11 years. Step inside and you'll find yourself in a warm dinning room set with intimate tables, candlelight and fresh flowers. The walls are covered with merry murals of the restaurant and city, and the kitchen is open to the front dinning room, providing an entertaining distraction while you wait for your meal.

There's no better way to try Maine lobster than by ordering the Lobster Tasting Menu, which begins with a taste of lobster stew and progresses to lobster Napoleon with grilled corn salsa, seared lobster with pesto scented goat cheese... and the lobster goes on and on.

Other items on the menu include herb crushed rack of lamb with warm figs, filet mignon and fresh duckling with roasted pepper polenta. The menu changes several times a year, and the beverage menu includes an extensive list of sparkling wines and champagne, gewurztraminer, viognier, merlot and reds, whites, ports and regional microbrews. For dessert you might find something like pecan lace cookie with peach sorbet and ginger ice cream, or dark chocolate truffle cake with mascarpone mousse and blackberry cabernet sauce. Save plenty of time to savor the full menu. The Back Bay Grill serves dinner only Monday through Saturday.

The Village Cafe
$$ • 112 Newbury St., Portland
• (207) 772-5320

A Portland institution, this Italian restaurant has been run by the same family since 1936 — some of its original customers are now bringing their grandchildren! It began when Vincenzo and Maria Reali emigrated from Italy and started the restaurant as a neighborhood tavern.

Now serving lunch and dinner, the restaurant has been expanded several times, and the menu has won the praise of Portland. Ranked Best Family Restaurant and Best Overall by readers of the *Maine Sunday Telegram* five years in a row, The Village Cafe caters to groups of all ages. You'll find favorite Italian dishes such as veal parmigiana, marsalas, scaloppines and fettuccine alfredo as well as fresh seafood and choice steaks. A children's menu is available. Best of all, if you have a hankering for a dish that's not on the menu, they can often make it for you!

The Zephyr Grill
$$ • 653 Congress St., Portland
• (207) 828-4033

Open since July 1996, this Mediteranian-Italian restaurant has carved a niche for itself in the Portland market by offering a wide array of dishes to satisfy both vegetarians and meat lovers. A self-dubbed "fusion restaurant," The Zephyr Grill combines a number of cuisines, serving up meals in its signature large white bowls. You'll find items such as marinated sirloin with a peppercorn crust, wood-grilled marinated lamb, fried corn tortillas with avocado dressing and grilled eggplant slices layered with spinach, mushrooms and squash.

The grill is open daily for dinner. Breakfast is served on Sunday with a variety of omelettes and other favorites such as Eggs From Hell — scrambled eggs with cheddar cheese on a tortilla smothered with chili. The restaurant is filled with handpainted tables and custom-painted walls, and it is totally smoke-free.

Moose Crossing Fish & Steakhouse
$$$ • 270 U.S. Hwy. 1, Falmouth
• (207) 781-4771

The first time we drove by this steakhouse looking for lunch, we were somewhat skeptical because there weren't any cars in the parking lot. Then we found out it is open almost exclusively for dinner. If you make the same mistake, make sure you return. The lounge cranks up just before the dinner hour, and the restaurant opens an hour later at 5 PM.

Inside you'll find the dining room is both casual (with tables and booths) and elegant, with dimmed lights, nicely dressed servers and twinkling white lights woven through the branches of a giant fir tree in the center of the dining room. You'll have a choice of prime rib, steak, chops and chicken served just about any way you like them. If you want to come for lunch, Moose Crossing serves it on Sunday.

Muddy Rudder
$$$ • U.S. Hwy. 1, Yarmouth
• (207) 846-3082
$$$ • U.S. Hwy. 1, Wiscasset
• (207) 882-7748

You'll get the same great service and food at either of the Muddy Rudder's two locations even though they're under different management. The Yarmouth restaurant is in a gray shingled building with country-nautical charm just off Route 1. In Wiscasset the fare comes with a view of the wide Sheepscot River. The atmosphere at both is casual and festive with candlelight. A children's menu is available, as is a diverse selection of bottled and draft beers and a select wine list.

Dinner favorites include braised apple chicken, roast prime rib and Burgundy rack of lamb. If you're lucky you'll visit when the piano bar is in full swing. The restaurant and pub are open year round for lunch and dinner, and breakfast is served on Saturday and Sunday.

The Royal River Cannery
$$ • Lower Falls Landing, Yarmouth
• (207) 846-1226

If sitting on a canopied deck overlooking the water appeals to you, we think you'll love the Cannery. Located at the site of a real seafood cannery dating back to 1913 (it's no longer in the canning business), this upscale restaurant offers casual waterfront dining on the Royal River. The inside dining room features a full wall of windows overlooking the boats tied up at the docks below, post-and-beam framing and an oyster bar. For lunch and dinner the menu offers seafood, steak and pasta made with the finest ingredients. On weekends the Cannery is also open for brunch.

China Rose
$$$ • 10 School St., Freeport
• (207) 865-6886
$$ • 42 Bath Rd., Brunswick
• (207) 725-8813

Depending on whether you go to the Freeport or Brunswick location of China Rose, you'll have two distinctly different experiences. But the food and the service are equally good at both places. In Freeport, the restaurant is an intimate affair, with a popular sushi bar as well as a full menu featuring Hunan, Szechwan, Mandarin and Cantonese food. The Brunswick location, which opened in early 1997, has three huge buffet tables from which you can sample traditional Chinese food or, if you prefer, fill up on french fries, barbecue chicken, lasagna, salad and soft-serve ice cream. A full menu is also available in Brunswick. At both restaurants you can get lunch or dinner year round.

Crickets Restaurant
$$ • 175 Main St., Freeport
• (207) 865-4005

How does a Downeast Feast sound? Lobster, steamed clams, a cup of chowder, french fries and coleslaw — you can get them all at this upbeat restaurant with open, bright dining rooms and plenty of good home-style cooking. The menu features a number of seafood specialties such as Haddock Fromage — a fresh haddock fillet topped with cheddar and Swiss cheese melted to a golden brown and sprinkled with bread crumbs. There are pasta and steak dishes, burgers (including a veggie burger), specialty sandwiches and fajitas. For little people (younger than 12), there's a children's menu. Everything is made from scratch, and there's a large selection of Maine microbrews on tap. The restaurant is open for lunch and dinner daily and is also open for breakfast on Saturday and Sunday.

Old World Gourmet Deli & Wine Shop
$ • 315 U.S. Hwy. 1, Freeport
• (207) 865-4477

Get your hot pastrami on fresh marble rye, sourdough or whatever bread you prefer at this great lunch spot, which is open until 5:30 PM in winter and 6 PM in summer. In addition to its old-style deli offering Boarshead Provision meats, you can get a steaming bowl of homemade soup, focaccia bread (made on site), homemade casseroles and fresh pastries to round out your meal. Seating is inside during the colder months; picnic tables are available during summer. Spend some extra time shopping for a gourmet bottle of wine, and be sure to check out the gift store and Christmas room.

The Lobster Cooker
$$ • 39 Main St., Freeport
• (207) 865-4349

Enjoy fresh seafood in the main dining room, which is housed in an antique barn and filled with antiques, or eat outside on the landscaped patio surrounded by flower gardens.

The Lobster Cooker menu is swimming with steamed clams, fried shrimp, native scallops, lobster any way you like it (as if there was a way not to like it!) and fresh fish and chips with hand-cut fries. The meat for the always-popular lobster sandwiches is picked from the shell on site, so you know it's some of the freshest around. A full beer and wine menu and a children's menu are available. The Lobster Cooker is open daily for lunch and dinner and serves breakfast sandwiches, bagels and coffee in the morning.

Harraseeket Inn
$$$$ • 162 Main St., Freeport
• (207) 865-9377

Enter here to experience some of the most acclaimed food in the state (and country) in The Maine Dining Room of the elegant Harraseeket Inn (for more information on accommodations, see our Bed and Breakfasts and Inns chapter). Almost all the foods used are grown at farms right here in Maine — from specialty cheeses and stone-ground flour to organic vegetables and, of course, wild blueberries. The menu also features fresh pheasant, quail, partridge, wild turkey and Atlantic salmon.

Executive chef Chris Moran oversees an ever-changing menu of earthy foods, which he has civilized to charm the most discerning palates. Some of the techniques used in Moran's kitchen date back to the Colonial era — a time reflected in the elegant furnishings displayed throughout the inn. You'll also find flavorings reminiscent of his days as a cook in New Orleans. Try the grilled Atlantic salmon with Maine crabmeat, in which the fish is treated with molasses and salt and cured overnight, or try any of the lobster, sirloin or seafood dishes. We're sure you won't be disappointed. For dessert you can sample delectable treats such as chocolate mocha cream rolls and blueberry-raspberry turnovers.

If you're in town on Sunday, reserve a table for what has been called the finest brunch in the state. For $16.95 per person, you can try a little of all the restaurant has to offer. In The Broad Arrow Tavern, which opened in 1997, you can enjoy your meal in a more relaxed, rustic atmosphere, served up with the same grace and great cooking. The tavern is open for lunch and dinner every day. The Maine

Photo: Merry Farnum

Seaside dining is a Maine tradition.

Dining Room is open for breakfast until 10:30 AM and for dinner from 6 to 9 PM.

Jameson Tavern
$$$ • 115 Main St., Freeport
• (207) 865-4196

For a meal of historical significance, eat lunch or dinner in the same room where Maine was born. This is the place where in 1820 a few brave souls converged and signed the secession paper for Maine to separate from Massachusetts. We're not sure if the food they had was this good. The Jameson Tavern is a favorite for casually elegant dining where you can get a juicy steak, fresh seafood or steaming pasta. Pull up a seat in the Tap Room, where you can have a drink or a cigarette (the rest of the restaurant is nonsmoking), or eat outside on the patio beneath a shady umbrella. The atmosphere is relaxed, with glowing candles and classical music. The undisputed specialty here is lobster — steamed, broiled or baked and stuffed with crabmeat. If you're not game for the cracking, try the Lazy-man Lobster, which is cracked for you and sautéed in cream and sherry.

The Chowder Express
$ • 2 Mechanic St., Freeport
• (207) 865-3404

Winner of the Freeport Chowder Challenge in 1996 and 1997, this small deli serves up creamy combinations to melt your heart — fish, corn, lobster and clam chowders. If you're really hungry, you can get a salad or sandwich to go along with it for a quick lunch or dinner. You'll find Syrian roll-ups, ham, turkey and corned beef. In the morning, pull up a stool for bagels and coffee.

Brunswick, Bath and Boothbay Harbor Area

Captain Daniel Stone Inn
$$$ • 10 Water St., Brunswick
• (207) 725-9898

Elegance will envelope you at this restaurant and inn attached to what was once the home of a sea captain (see our Bed and Breakfasts and Inns chapter). The choice of entrees ranges from lobster to grilled swordfish to poached salmon as well as a variety of steak and chicken dishes. Appetizers include such delicacies as a potato cake with lemon parsley sauce, and baked phyllo with garlic-roasted spinach and ginger shrimp wonton. In winter you can expect more hearty fare, with lighter dishes served during summer.

Although we found the surroundings quite refined, with painted, raised wood panels on the walls and intimate tables for dining, some guests were dressed casually while others wore dinner jackets. The inn is open for lunch during the week and dinner all week long. Smoking is allowed in the lounge.

China Pearl
$$ • 112 Pleasant St., Brunswick
• (207) 725-8686

For some good Szechuan, Mandarin and Cantonese cuisine, try this pearl of a restaurant. In 1995 and 1996 it was picked as having the best Chinese food in the Greater Brunswick area. Take-out is available, or you can eat in the glass-enclosed patio. At lunch there's an all-you-can-eat, 14-item buffet costing $5.95 for adults and $3.95 for children younger than 8. The buffet is also available evenings for $8.95. Anytime during the week, you can select items from the extensive menu that features everything from traditional favorites to a dish seafood lovers won't want to miss — Nested Seafood Delight, with lobster, scallops, shrimp and vegetables served on a bed of fried noodles.

Benzoni's Brick Oven Pizza & Italian Cafe
$ • 9 Town Hall Pl., Brunswick
• (207) 729-2800

For some of the best pizza in town, come to Benzoni's, where the atmosphere is as good as the food. Your gourmet pizza — we recommend the house specialty, "Benzoni's Original," with fresh tomatoes, mushrooms, spinach, mozzarella and ham — will be cooked in a brick oven and served steaming hot on a raised platter. Other choices we enjoy are the alfredo pizza, Grecian pizza and vegetable pizza, but whatever you choose, the result is sure to be delicious. The atmosphere is lively, and the wait staff is friendly. It's a great spot for lunch or dinner, whatever the occasion.

Bombay Mahal
$$ • 99 Main St., Brunswick
• (207) 729-5260

For authentic Indian cuisine, try Brunswick's only Indian restaurant. You can select tender lamb dishes such as the house specialty: a plate for two of steaming basmati rice cooked in butter with choice pieces of lamb, chicken and shrimp mixed with almonds, cashews and raisins. Or try any of the other variety of dishes from curries to vegetarian entrees to fresh seafood. A sampling of traditional flat and butter-baked breads go along with the meals, and for the more adventurous we recommend raita, a spiced yogurt with cucumber and tomato. The tables at Bombay Mahal are simply set (better to highlight the food), and the service is outstanding.

Fat Boy Drive In
$ • Bath Rd., Brunswick
• (207) 729-9431

When this place wipes down the grill at the end of the summer, locals know the days of glorious sun and sand are over for another year. Open from mid-March through October, this 40-year-old hamburger joint is a marker of the seasons for the folks who look forward to coming here after a day on the beach. Just find a spot in the parking lot and blink your car headlights, and a waitperson will come to your window and take your order.

For bacon lovers, we recommend the BLT with thick slices of Canadian bacon, juicy tomato and crisp lettuce (a favorite around here), and don't forget the onion rings! Fat Boys (the locals add the "s") also has a mouth-watering selection of fresh seafood made to order, lobster rolls and crab rolls. If you want to sit amid the '50s decor in the dining room, you may have to wait for one of the five booths, but that's where all the action still takes place.

The Brunswick Diner
$ • 101 Pleasant St., Brunswick
• (207) 721-1134

Put a nickel in the jukebox, give your counter stool a spin and get ready to enjoy a meal in this authentic dining car. Originally a passenger train in Norway, Maine, the car was moved to Brunswick and turned into a restaurant in 1946. It has changed hands plenty of times over the years but remains a favorite for locals and curious travelers.

The menu offers fried haddock and clam dinners, turkey sandwiches (with real carved turkey), pork dinners and jumbo hot dogs with fries. It's open for breakfast, lunch and dinner seven days a week. On weekends it is open from Friday straight through closing time on Sunday night. The diner is a favorite stop for truckers heading up U.S. 1.

Richard's Restaurant
$$ • 115 Maine St., Brunswick
• (207) 729-9673

For a steaming plate of Sauerbraten, Spoetzle and German cabbage, we recommend Richard's, an authentic German restaurant in the heart of Brunswick's downtown. The interior is casually elegant, with beer steins on the walls and intimate tables. Service is tops, and the food — delicious. For those who prefer something a little less filling than German sausage or pot roast, there are plenty of other options on the menu, from delicious soups to seafood and chicken. The restaurant is open for lunch and dinner Monday through Saturday.

Hot Dogs on the Mall
$ • Town Park, Maine St., Brunswick

For locals and summer visitors alike, stopping at the town mall in Brunswick to sit out on the grass and eat steaming hot dogs is a summertime tradition. You can get your dogs from a choice of two vendors — Danny's and Down East Dogs — that set up here from lunchtime through the early afternoon most days of the week. Both places offer a variety of toppings — from sauerkraut to chili and cheese to cole slaw. This is a great way to save money on a meal and take a break from your day; chase the seagulls that flock here, or just munch away in the sun. You'll find hot dogs here throughout the warmer months, but don't look for the vendors when the leaves are off the trees.

Cook's Lobster House
$$$ • Maine Hwy. 24, Bailey Island
• (207) 833-2818

Overlooking the world's only cribstone bridge (see our Attractions chapter), Cook's Lobster House has steamed up lobsters, clams and corn on the cob since 1955. The seafood is delivered right at the wharf below the restaurant. Before or after dinner, stroll along the dock and watch as crabs and lobsters are hauled in off the boats.

Back in the restaurant, the menu is full of local flavor with dinner items such as the Split-Tail Special — a bowl of chowder or lobster stew with three hot, boiled lobster tails, split for you and served with drawn butter. You'll also enjoy the fried and broiled seafood, a raw bar, steak and hearty sandwiches. Eat indoors or outside on the deck overlooking the rocky beach and water below. Cook's is open for lunch and dinner, but the hours may change after the summer season.

The Log Cabin Lodging & Fine Food
$$$ • Maine Hwy. 24, Bailey Island
• (207) 833-5546

If you're one of the lucky few to get a reservation for dinner at this restaurant, you'll enjoy panoramic views of Casco Bay, the White Mountains and Mount Washington. With just eight tables for guests, the restaurant offers intimate dinning by reservation only. Open April through October, it features fresh seafood favorites such as stuffed lobster, steaks, vegetarian cuisine and home-baked desserts. In cooler months you'll enjoy the fire in the open hearth. (If you want to stay for breakfast too, see our Bed & Breakfasts and Inns chapter).

Beale Street Barbeque & Grill
$$ • 215 Water St., Bath • (207) 442-9514

Summer or winter, from the moment you step out of your car, you'll smell the tangy smoke spiraling up from the outdoor barbecue set up just outside this small restaurant. This is grilling done the old-fashioned way over hickory sticks. Inside, jazz music wafts through the air, and the menu is full of finger-licking favorites: pulled pork, shredded beef, hickory-smoked ribs, jerk chicken sandwiches, teriyaki steak, smoked Italian sausage...the list goes on and on. You can get the meat on its own or order a full plate with coleslaw, barbecue beans and corn bread on the side. The restaurant is open for lunch or dinner, and take-out is available.

Kristina's Restaurant & Bakery
$$ • 160 Centre St., Bath
• (207) 442-8577

OK, when it comes to Kristina's we have to admit we're a little partial. We simply love it! And why wouldn't we? Rated one of the top 10 restaurants in Maine, this place is a favorite for locals and celebrities alike. Cher used to drop in when she visited her son at nearby Hyde School (see our Education and Child Care chapter), and Maury Povich (whose uncle lives here) is said to frequent the place when he's in town with Connie Chung.

Sit on the outside deck above the busy street or in the dining room, which looks more like a gallery than a restaurant. The work of local artists is displayed above intimate tables in the airy dining room. You're guaranteed wonderful food and great service whether you come for breakfast, lunch or dinner. In the morning, you'll choose from specialties such as The Californian, a toasted English muffin with scrambled eggs, avocado, tomato and melted Havarti cheese served with homefries. In the afternoon there's a tempting choice of seafood, sandwiches, salads and other delectable entrees, and in the evening you can pick from a wide selection of sensible food served up with elegance — from steaks to chicken to seafood.

Don't forget the other half of the name: the bakery. It's out of this world (and our guess as to why the restaurant's logo is a baker on the moon). Delicately layered cakes, creamy glasses of mousse, chewy cookies and tart pies will make your meal here (even if its breakfast — it's never too early for dessert at Kristina's) an occasion to remember.

The Cabin
$ • 552 Washington St., Bath
• (207) 443-6224

Just across the street from Bath Iron Works, one of the oldest shipyards in the nation (see the Close-up in our Area Overviews chapter), The Cabin is reminiscent of the wooden ships that were once built along the nearby banks of the Kennebec River. The exterior is kind of run-down and gloomy and inside are all sorts of odd ship trinkets, but it's not the atmosphere that makes this place so outstanding — it's the food.

Some have called the pizza here the best in the state, and once you've tried it, you can see why. For lunch or dinner you can get specialty pizzas or submarine sandwiches with a large variety of toppings or fillings — salami, pepperoni, sausage, fresh vegetables, and olives among them. Our personal picks: the loaded pizza (thickly layered with goodies) and the veg-

etable sub, which is a mix of grilled vegetables smothered with melted cheese. The only complaint we've ever heard about this place is that they put so many toppings on the pizza you have to eat it with a fork.

J.R. Maxwell & Co.
$$ • 122 Front St., Bath
• (207) 443-2014

Most people just call this place Maxwell's, and it's known for fine food and great atmosphere. We love the menu, we love the prices and we love the brick-walled, tin-ceilinged interior that's highlighted by hanging stained-glass lights.

The restaurant and pub are in the heart of Bath's downtown in an old hotel, The Elliot House, which was built in 1840. Whether you're looking for a relaxed lunch or a quiet dinner, this place is a sure bet.

There's a large menu filled with food from right here in Maine – from lobster to chicken to pasta to steak. Try the baked stuffed lobster, in which the meat is stuffed with fresh scallops and crabmeat, or order a fried seafood platter with various goodies deep-fried in the restaurant's own beer batter. There are some specials you'll want to know about as well: On Wednesday nights you can get two dinners from a special menu for the price of one, and on Friday and Saturday night roast prime rib is available. Maxwell's has a kid's menu that includes steak and broiled or fried haddock. Downstairs is The Boatbuilders Pub (see our Nightlife chapter), which has a happy hour daily.

Spinney's Restaurant
$$ • Popham Beach, Phippsburg
• (207) 389-1122

Right on the sandy shore of Popham Beach (see our Beaches chapter), this restaurant is an old-time favorite. For breakfast, lunch or dinner, you'll get good, home-cooked food at a good price in a diner-like atmosphere with great water views. The menu is loaded with Maine favorites: clam rolls, lobster rolls, crab rolls, fried clams, scallops and haddock as well as broiled seafood. Spinney's Original Northeast Clam Bake is also a favorite — steamed clams, drawn butter, clam broth, boiled lobster, french fries, cole slaw and rolls (large appetites recommended).

Robinhood Free Meeting House
$$$ • Robinhood Rd., Georgetown
• (207) 371-2188

In an old Congregational and Methodist church dating back to 1855, this restaurant offers some of the most acclaimed food in the area. The menu has 36 entrees ranging from grilled swordfish with red pepper, basil and jalapeno beurre blanc to Pork Roquefort — sautéed mignonettes of pork with Portobello mushrooms served with fettuccine and fresh vegetables. Chef Michael Gagne is the master behind the medley, and he has brought class to every corner of this once abandoned building. The fine dining is accompanied with candlelight in an unpretentious atmosphere.

While many choose to dress up for the evening out, others stop in after docking at the local marina. The restaurant is open for dinner only and has been acclaimed by *The New York Times*. Everything, from the pasta and sorbet to the sausage, is made in-house. Call ahead or ask to be added to the mailing list to learn of specially scheduled wine-tasting dinners, jazz nights and off-season cooking classes.

Georgetown Fisherman's Co-op
$$, no credit cards • Five Islands, Georgetown • (207) 371-2950

You'll find no indoor seating here, just brick-red picnic tables set out on a wharf overlooking the water (for drizzly days there is a covered area); when you experience the view, you'll know why outdoor dining is encouraged. No one in their right mind would want walls to separate them from the smell of the salty sea and the sight of the surrounding islands at the end of the Georgetown peninsula.

If you're lucky you'll see fishermen hauling in their catch right before your eyes. For fried food lovers, there's the Love Shack, where you can buy canned soda and order fried seafood, onion rings and french fries that will be brought to your table. There's a separate sea shanty where you can order lobster and steamed clams and see them brought from the back-room tank before being steamed in salt water. (Of course, the tender-hearted may not want to see their meal flipping in the scale before it's sent off to the steamer.)

The co-op is about a 25-minute drive from downtown Bath, but we don't think you can get the real Maine experience driving any less. Two warnings, however: The mosquitoes out here are ferocious, so cover up; and keep an eye on the young children, as the wharf is not well-fenced. The restaurant is open for lunch and dinner through the summer season.

LeGarage Restaurant
$$ • Water St., Wiscasset
• (207) 882-5409

For a sunlit breakfast, laid-back lunch or casually elegant dinner, try this old automotive and engine repair shop set above the Sheepscot River. Those with a flair for things mechanical will enjoy checking out the antique drills and tools set up like prized sculptures around the inside of the original building. Those with a mind for romance will love the nightly candlelight dinners, where the only electric lights shine in the entryway. (The folks at the restaurant spend about $10,000 a year on candles!)

We recommend reserving a window seat on the glassed-in deck. The food is modestly priced, and those with smaller appetites will appreciate the dinner choice of standard or full meal sizes. If you're coming in the morning, the menu will include a choice of omelettes made with eggs from a local farm and served with homemade biscuits. There's also more delicate breakfast fare such as crepes with a fresh fruit garnish. Later in the day, the menu includes delectable items such as a vegetarian baked ratatouille casserole, charbroiled lamb and Maine lobster Newburg — chunks of lobster meat combined in a sherry cream sauce and topped with a flaky pie crust. After dinner we recommend a short walk to the waterfront to take a look back up at the restaurant and see the candlelight streaming out.

Red's Eats
$ • Water St. and Main St., Wiscasset
• (207) 882-6128

When driving through Wiscasset, this eatery is a sure bet for what some have called the best lobster rolls in the state. The meat from one entire lobster is used to make each sandwich! Crab rolls, hot dogs, sandwiches and ice cream are also favorites.

You can eat at one of the outdoor picnic tables or take your food across the street to

Photo: Merry Farnum

Many of Maine's favorite meals come straight from the sea.

the public deck over the Sheepscot River. Red's is open daily for lunch, dinner and late-night snacking (till the wee hours of the morning on Friday and Saturday nights) during the summer season.

Sarah's Cafe
$ • Main St., Wiscasset • (207) 882-7504

What began in 1982 as a home-based pizza delivery service in nearby Boothbay Harbor has turned into one of the region's most popular restaurants. Come for breakfast, lunch or dinner seven days a week, and you are guaranteed great home-cooked food for a good value in a friendly atmosphere. Picture windows and an outside deck overlook the Sheepscot River with views of passing boats; inside, booths and tables are lit by hanging stained-glass lamps.

The menu features smoked meats, fresh lobster served 16 different ways, plenty of Mexican favorites and the famous triple soup buffet with your choice of stuffed breads. Sarah's never deep-fries, and low-fat entrees are available. You'll want to save room for the old-fashioned homemade desserts, and Maine microbrews are available to complement your meal. This place is also a big favorite with kids — it has balloons and coloring contests.

Boothbay Region Lobstermen's Co-op
$$ • Atlantic Ave., Boothbay Harbor • (207) 633-4900

You'll know your seafood is as fresh as it can be when you pick your own lobster from the restaurant's saltwater pool or watch a fresh load of fish or lobster being hauled off the boats at this working co-op. Indoors or at a picnic table on the dock, you'll get to choose from a menu of lobster, steamed clams, fried seafood, hot dogs, hamburgers and desserts. In its 28th year, the restaurant serves lunch and dinner and will pack lobsters and clams to go.

Brown's Wharf & Marina
**$$$ • 107 Atlantic Ave.,
Boothbay Harbor
• (207) 633-5440, (800) 334-8110**

Operated by the same family for 50 years, this motel, restaurant and marina is easy to spot with its huge statue of a lobsterman in bright yellow rain gear. Inside you'll encounter a casual dining atmosphere with a deck overlooking the water and a full bar and lounge. Painted murals of the Maine coast on the walls and a huge model ship in the center of the restaurant will warm the hearts of seafarers, and the menu will warm the hearts of all.

Choose from dinner entrees such as Mediterranean scallops with capers, kalamata olives, Feta cheese and sun-dried tomatoes with white wine and olive oil over pasta, or sample one of the lobster specials. A large selection of fresh seafood (broiled, stuffed or fried) plus sirloin and chicken are available. There is a children's menu.

Chowder House Restaurant
**$$ • 49 Townsend Ave., Boothbay
Harbor • (207) 633-5761**

Set at the harbor's edge in the old Granary Way building, this traditional Maine restaurant has been family owned for 19 years. You can eat lunch or dinner outside on the canopied deck or inside the casual dining room decorated with nostalgic pictures of the harbor at the turn of the century. Open during the summer season, the restaurant features favorites such as lobster stew, crab melts, turf-kebabs and homemade pies and shortcakes for dessert. Another favorite here is the outdoor, waterfront deck bar made out of an old boat. Some people drive great distances to Boothbay Harbor just to eat here, but if you want to you'll have to come between June 25 and Labor Day, because that's the only time it's open.

Christopher's Boat House
**$$$ • 25 Union St., Boothbay Harbor
• (207) 633-6565**

In an old boathouse perched over Boothbay Harbor, Christopher's is one of the area's most acclaimed restaurants. It's recipe for lobster succotash with lobster, onion, tomato, zucchini, fresh corn, brandy and cream appeared in the Wall Street Journal and was a favorite of the Maine Lobster Council. If you've been here before you may recall it as Christopher's 1820 House in East Boothbay; in 1997 it moved to a new location and changed the name.

The dining room, with a white oak interior and French windows and doors, is spiced with nautical flavors, while the New World cuisine reflects the Caribbean, with plenty of fruit and mango flavors. Plenty of fresh seafood, steaks with tangy glazes and vegetarian fare are offered. If you prefer, you can eat outside on the pier. The restaurant is open Monday through Saturday for lunch and dinner. In the winter it's closed two days a week.

J.H. Hawk Ltd.
**$$ • Pier One, Boothbay Harbor
• (207) 633-5589**

Gourmet entrees, Cajun specialties and plenty of fresh seafood (including a raw bar) are waiting at this summertime favorite on a pier overlooking the harbor. You can eat indoors or out, and a children's menu is available. The restaurant is open daily for lunch and dinner, and there's nightly entertainment featuring Mark Rosier on the piano. Come for the food or the fabulous harbor view. Whatever your reason, you'll come away satisfied.

Lobsterman's Wharf
**$$$ • Maine Hwy. 96, East Boothbay
• (207) 633-3443**

Sit on the deck next to the boats tied up at the wharf or pick a booth inside the rustic dining room — no matter where you sit, we think you'll enjoy your experience here. The menu is stocked with mouth-watering seafood and steak combinations such as Steak Marchard — a 12-ounce sirloin with lobster tail meat and bernaise. Other favorites include the Lazy Lobster — lobster meat sautéed in sherry and butter over linguine. There's a full bar, and the restaurant (which is open seasonally from May through mid October) is open until midnight.

The Lawnmeer Inn & Restaurant
**$$$ • Maine Hwy. 27, Southport Island
• (207) 633-2544**

Lobster boats, buoys and seagulls beyond the wall of picture windows will entertain you as you dine at this seasonal favorite overlooking a tidal cove. The main dining room of the inn is spacious and accommodating with high-backed chairs and smaller tables. The menu is filled with classic Maine fare. Appetizers feature Maine mussels steamed in white wine with garlic and tomato, and sautéed Maine crab cakes on steamed spinach with lemon butter. Entrees include pastas tossed with seafood and creamy sauces, Long Island duck, roasted lamb and choice steaks. Desserts — from homemade ice cream to chocolate torte to blueberry pie — are made right here. The restaurant, open from mid-May through Columbus Day, serves breakfast Monday through Saturday, brunch on Sunday and dinner daily.

Spruce Point Inn
$$$$ • Atlantic Ave., Boothbay Harbor • (207) 633-4152

One of the harbor's most gracious resorts (see our Bed and Breakfasts and Inns chap-ter) welcomes guests and the public to one of the finest restaurants in the region. Seated in an elegant dining room with linen and fine china, you'll enjoy a four-course meal with first-class service. You can sit in the more casual dining room or the dressier jackets-only section (children are welcome in either) and enjoy the same great food in both.

The menu begins with first-course choices such as crab cakes accompanied by remoulade, fresh tomato salsa and pesto sauce, and moves on to a selection of soups and salads for the second course. Dinner entrees range from pan-seared fresh duck stuffed with fresh spinach, wild mushrooms and walnuts to Maine lobster steamed traditionally or baked with shrimp, crab and bay scallop stuffing. For dessert, there's a selection of tarts, cheesecakes, mousse and creme broulee. We highly recommend an after-dinner walk along the point.

Since Portland is only about an hour's drive from Kittery and a little more than 90 minutes from Boothbay, it is possible to enjoy the city's nightlife regardless of where you stay.

Nightlife

With so much natural beauty around us, the daily lives of Mainers are closely tied to the seasons and elements. We like to take advantage of warm weather by spending as much time as possible outdoors. We enjoy evening walks and jogs along Baxter Boulevard in Portland's Back Bay area and along the Marginal Way in Ogunquit, and watching the sun set and moon rise above our lovely beaches.

Once the sun disappears and the stars are out, we may head out with friends to a brewpub or go for a leisurely dinner, but to be honest, we don't often go to nightclubs. In fact, we're more likely to go to a movie or have friends over for drinks and a barbecue.

But that doesn't hold true for everyone, and it doesn't mean there isn't any nightlife in Southern Maine. On the contrary, you'll find a number of nightclubs, coffeehouses, brewpubs and restaurant lounges that feature entertainment in-season. Some of the larger communities such as Portland have clubs that keep hopping all year. In addition, there are summer concerts in our parks and original stage productions in our theaters (see our chapter on The Arts).

You'll find a variety of movie theaters — from the Saco Drive-In to dinner theaters like the Keystone in Portland and Chunky's in Windham. The Movies, on Portland's Exchange Street, offers foreign and offbeat film selections, and there are a number of movie complexes that offer first-run films.

For the most part, the nightlife in Southern Maine is concentrated in Portland. Since the city is only about an hour's drive from Kittery in the south, and a little more than 90 minutes from Boothbay to the north, it's possible to enjoy Portland's nightlife regardless of where you stay. Those of you near Kittery may also want to check out the nightlife in Portsmouth, New Hampshire (just five or 10 minutes away).

To get up-to-the-minute news on what nightlife opportunities are available along Maine's Southern Coast, we suggest you pick up a local newspaper (see our Media chapter). Most papers offer movie listings and a daily or weekly calendar of events. You should also peruse our Annual Events and Festivals chapter. Many festivals and fairs feature evening entertainment that might interest you.

Along the same lines, be sure to check out the Spectator Sports and Attractions chapters; you might see evening activities there (such as minor league baseball, auto racing events or local museum fetes) to tickle your fancy. When you're looking for nightlife, you should also visit the local supermarket or bookstore and peruse the posters and flyers advertising local fund-raisers, church dinners, contra dances and fairs that may not have made it into our book. Don't be afraid to go to these events — people in Maine are receptive to those from away. They'll be delighted that you were interested enough to come to their event, and they're sure to make you feel at home. Finally, you should ask your hotelier, inn host or hostess, waitress or even the person at the gas station what they do for nightlife. They live here and work with tourists, and they might know of places we didn't hear about.

What it all adds up to is an interesting and eclectic mix of nightlife offerings, which we have listed in geographic sequence from south to north under our four main geographic headers. Note that all prices are subject to change. As always, if you find a great nightspot we missed, make sure you drop us a line or contact us at our website (www.insiders.com).

And a word of caution: When heading out for the evening, keep in mind Maine's laws regarding drinking and driving. Under Maine law, the legal blood-alcohol threshold is .08 percent. However, you can be arrested for operating under the influence (DUIs are referred to as OUIs in Maine) if you have a blood-alcohol level of .05 percent, if there is corroborating evidence to suggest you are impaired. Maine also has an open-container law that prohibits consumption of alcohol on public roadways. So, if you think you might be drinking during the evening, or if you realize you've had a bit too much, why not call a taxi?

For information on cab service in Southern Maine, flip to our Getting Here, Getting Around chapter.

Southern Beaches Area

Cap'n Simeon's Galley
Maine Hwy. 103, Kittery Point
• (207) 439-3655

You'll find Cap'n Simeon's on Route 103, overlooking Pepperell Cove. Though they don't have regularly scheduled entertainment, locals say the lounge is a nice place to go with friends to enjoy a drink. On weekends you may occasionally find a guitar duo, folk singer or other entertainment in the lounge. The restaurant is open for lunch and dinner

daily; it is closed Tuesdays during the off-season (see our Restaurants chapter).

Norton's
U.S. Hwy. 1, Kittery
• (207) 439-7892

Every night of the week there's something fun happening at Norton's. Monday is men's night — all men get special drink prices; Tuesday is acoustic open-mike night for all you aspiring singers; Wednesday is electric jam night; Thursday is ladies' night, with women receiving special drink prices; and Friday and Saturday nights put the spotlight on local live bands. There usually is no cover charge unless a bigger name band is playing. Norton's is closed off-season.

Aqua Lounge
17 Ocean Ave., York Beach
• (207) 363-7578

Located on the second floor, with spectacular ocean views over Short Sands Beach, the Aqua Lounge features dancing, with a DJ spinning discs daily in-season. In summer the place can fill up to its capacity of around 300 people, but with about 3,500 square feet, there's plenty of room for everyone. The Aqua Lounge features "under 21" dances on Monday and Tuesday nights and a karaoke night on Wednesday. In addition to its main bar, the lounge has a second bar that's opened when it gets busy. There are also nine televisions, including a wide-screen where you can watch sports, music videos and other fun stuff. In-season you can also get a bite to eat if you're hungry or have the munchies. The Aqua Lounge is open from 2 PM to 1 AM. Off-season, the lounge is open on weekends only, from around 4 PM to 1 AM.

Cape Neddick Lobster Pound
Harborside Restaurant, Shore Rd.,
Cape Neddick • (207) 363-5471

Live entertainment is featured at "The Pound" every Monday night in-season; call

Many of our night spots offer pleasant views of the ocean and shoreline.

Photo: Convention and Visitor's Bureau of Greater Portland

to see who's playing when you intend to visit. Folk guitar duos and local bands are common musical fare. If you're looking for something to do and it isn't Monday, go ahead and try here anyway; they occasionally have performances on other nights of the week.

Stage Neck Inn
U.S. Hwy. 1A, York Harbor
• **(207) 363-3850**

If you're looking for the classic ambiance of a piano bar, try the real thing at Stage Neck Inn. A pianist plays in the lounge Thursday through Sunday evenings from 6 to 10 PM. Consider getting there early enough to watch the sunset over York Harbor. (For more information on the Stage Neck Inn, see our Hotels and Motels chapter.)

Capt'n Nick's Restaurant & Lounge
U.S. Hwy. 1 N., Ogunquit
• **(207) 646-9653**

In addition to the restaurant, which features lobster and prime rib (see our Restaurants chapter), Capt'n Nick's has a nightclub that's open in-season. Cover charge for the club varies depending on what entertainment is featured, but it usually falls somewhere between $3 and $7 per person. The entertainment schedule includes live comedy on

Wednesday and Saturday nights, and Thursdays featured a disc jockey and dancing. Friday night's highlight was the Erotic Hypnotic (yes, a hypnotist), with dancing following the show.

Clay Hill Farm
Agamenticus Rd., Ogunquit
• **(207) 361-2272**

You don't have to have dinner to enjoy live piano entertainment in the lounge. In-season you can enjoy the piano bar atmosphere Wednesday through Saturday. Off-season it's offered on Friday and Saturday evenings.

Jonathan's
2 Bourne Ln., Ogunquit
• **(207) 646-4777, (207) 646-8894**

Jonathan's features concerts, shows and dinner theater year round. Some of the performers who have played there in the past include Leon Redbone, Peter Wolf, Livingston Taylor and Suede. Ticket prices vary and can be obtained at Strawberries Record Stores or by calling (800) 464-9934.

Grey Gull
321 Webhannet Dr., Wells
• **(207) 646-7501**

Sundays, enjoy the quiet, elegant music of classical guitarist Michael Silvestri. The Grey

Gull is open for dinner daily in-season (see our Restaurants chapter).

Federal Jack's Brew Pub
Lower Village, 8 Western Ave., Kennebunk
• (207) 967-4322

In addition to brewery tours (see our Attractions chapter) and good food (see our Restaurants chapter), Federal Jack's offers live entertainment with no cover charge on Friday and Saturday evenings, usually in the form of a local singer/guitarist. To find out what's going on while you're visiting, give them a call.

Kennebunkport Inn
Dock Sq., Kennebunkport
• (207) 967-2621

You'll enjoy the warm atmosphere of a traditional New England country inn while listening to piano music in the lounge at the Kennebunkport Inn. In-season, a pianist is featured each evening.

Old Orchard Beach Area

Pockets II
12 Lincoln St., Biddeford
• (207) 284-9283

Formerly known as Shelley's, this local bar changed hands in early 1997, but the tradition of offering live rock bands on Fridays and Saturdays has continued. You can usually count on Pockets II to have live entertainment on at least one weekend night year round.

Saco Drive-In
969 U.S. Hwy. 1 (Portland Rd.), Saco
• (207) 284-1016

Open in-season only, this is the real thing! You sit in your car under the stars and watch a double feature while listening to the movies from your radio. They'll tell you what fre-quency to tune in to when you enter. Cost for entrance was $10 for a car with two people in 1998.

Cocktail's
1 Staples St. (on the beach), Old Orchard Beach
• (207) 934-4068

This is the ultimate in beach nightclub fun. The dance floor is a little bit small, but you can't beat the location — it sits adjacent to Palace Playland on the beach! Live entertainment is offered daily in-season, and there is additional daytime entertainment on weekends. Cocktail's also features an oceanside patio. It's open from early June to early September. The cover charge is usually around $3.

The Brunswick
39 W. Grand Ave., Old Orchard Beach
• (207) 934-4873

Whether you want to enjoy a quiet game of pool, have a drink overlooking the beach or hear live entertainment, the Brunswick is a good choice for an evening out. Throughout the month of July, entertainment is featured daily; in August it is offered Wednesdays through Saturdays. In-season you'll also hear live entertainment on the patio on Saturday and Sunday afternoons from 1 to 5 PM.

Greater Portland Area

Beech Ridge Motor Speedway
70 Holmes Rd., Scarborough
• (207) 883-6030

Tired of piano bars and nightclubs? Why not go to the races? At Beech Ridge Motor Speedway you can enjoy auto racing from May to October on the only NASCAR-sanctioned track in the state. (See our Spectator Sports chapter for much more information.)

INSIDERS' TIP

Many restaurants stop serving around 9 PM. If you're planning on going to a movie or the theater and then to dinner, check to make sure the restaurant of your choice will still be seating diners.

Scarborough Downs
U.S. Hwy 1 or Maine Hwy. 9 (Payne Rd.), Scarborough • (207) 883-4331

For an interesting night out, consider dinner at the elegant Downs Club restaurant while watching live harness racing at Scarborough Downs. The complex features a lounge, and whether or not you feel like placing a wager, you'll be entertained by the action. Races are held Wednesday through Sunday from April until November. Starting time (called post time) is 7:30 PM, except on Sundays, when racing begins at 1 PM. Maine Highway 9 (Payne Road) offers an alternate entrance to the track. See our Spectator Sports chapter for more information.

Comedy Connection
6 Custom House Wharf, Portland
• (207) 774-5554

With stand-up comedians from across the state and country, this club will keep you laughing all the way home. Located on a wharf at Portland Harbor, Comedy Connection is the only full-time comedy club in the state and features stand-up comedians who have appeared on The Late Show with David Letterman, The Tonight Show with Jay Leno, HBO and Showtime. Shows are performed Wednesday through Sunday, and tickets range from $5 to $10.

The club has a light-fare menu during shows with shrimp, chicken sandwiches and plenty of microbrews on tap. On Wednesday nights there is improvisational comedy, and every Sunday night, local George Hamm performs and presents six other comedians.

Java Joe's
13 Exchange St., Portland
• (207) 761-5637

For a late-evening wake-up call, step into Java Joe's, where you can get specialty coffees such as Joe Jackson's (a tall latte with almond and honey) or Bazooka Joe's (four shots of espresso with hot chocolate and whipped cream). There are plenty of pastries to accompany your coffee, and chessboards and other games are scattered around

to keep you entertained. The atmosphere is very casual, and the place is filled with funky art and groovy music. Java Joe's is open weekdays and weeknights until about 11 PM and attracts a crowd from 20-somethings on up.

Keystone Theatre Cafe
504 Congress St., Portland
• (207) 871-5550

For dinner and a flick all at the same place, the Keystone Theatre Cafe will seat and serve you while you watch a first-run movie. The menu is casual and features a large selection of Maine microbrews; the food cost is additional to the show, which runs $5 for adults and $3.50 for children younger than 12 for day and evening shows. For more information, see our Attractions chapter.

Maine Ballroom Dance
614A Congress St., Portland
• (207) 773-0002

Every Saturday night you'll get to swing and waltz to your heart's content at this ballroom dance center that features a large hardwood dance floor and a DJ playing all your favorite tunes. Dress should be your Sunday best, though some people come pretty casual. There's a refreshment table with coffee, tea, cookies and chips; the dance hall is smoke-free and doesn't serve alcohol. Most of the dancers are students, but anyone is welcome. The cost is $6 per person; Saturday dances run from about 8 PM to midnight. If you need lessons, the center offers them midweek.

Olde Port Mariner Fleet
Long Wharf, Commercial St., Portland
• (207) 775-0727

Enjoy live weekend entertainment while cruising Portland Harbor on two cruise boats in the Olde Port Mariner Fleet. From Memorial Day through Columbus Day, you can enjoy dinner and dancing aboard The Casablanca. Tickets are $34.50 and get you a table aboard this floating nightclub, decorated with palm trees and featuring an upper deck with a wraparound mahogany bar. Downstairs lies the dance floor and seating for 125. Aboard The Odyssey you will set sail on a floating Irish pub complete with Irish Capt. Mulkern, an Irish band and Irish ales. The cabin of this 74-foot cruiser has seating for 25, and the boat sets sail Saturday and Sunday evenings for $10 per person. (For information on day cruises, see the Olde Port Mariner Fleet listing in our Attractions chapter).

Stone Coast Brewing Co.
14 York St., Portland
• (207) 773-BEER

This microbrewery fills three floors, including a restaurant and nightclub with live bands and pool tables. The cover charge varies depending on who's playing, but you can expect to pay anywhere from $1 to $15. (The upper end would have bought you a ticket to see 10,000 Maniacs when they played here.) The club features regional and national bands playing everything from bluegrass to rock to jazz. For a list of Stone Coast's six house brews, see the listing in our Attractions chapter.

Nickelodeon Cinema
Corner of Temple and Middle Sts., Portland • (207) 772-9751

When downtown, this is a great place to check out a movie that you might have missed when it was a first-run. All tickets at the Nickelodeon are $1, and most of the movies are scheduled just after their runs at the regular cinemas. Inside you'll find the regular movie-theater atmosphere — including popcorn and drinks — for quite a bargain. We like coming here because it is right in the center of the shopping district, making for a great end to a busy day. One word of caution, however: While the tickets are el cheapo, you'll have to pay for parking, which can run anywhere from $1 for two hours on the street to $1 an hour and up in a garage.

The Pavilion
188 Middle St., Portland
• (207) 773-6422

This upscale nightclub is in a 19th-century building graced with two-story ceilings, black and white marble floors, chandeliers and authentic moldings. Wednesday night is ladies' night; on Friday you may find a band scheduled; and on Saturday night the dance hall turns into a big party with live music. Some of the national acts that have played here are Better Than Ezra and Barenaked Ladies. There's typically a $3 cover, but national acts will cost in the $10 to $20 range. A variety of American cuisine is available.

The Top of the East
The Radisson Eastland Hotel, 157 High St., Portland
• (207) 775-5411

You'll sit high above Portland with a view of the White Mountains and the sunset to the west and Casco Bay and islands to the east from the top floor of the Radisson Eastland Hotel downtown (see our Hotels and Motels chapter). On weekends the bar features live piano music along with either folk or jazz music and a snack menu. Best of all, there is no cover charge.

Zootz Nightclub
31 Forest Ave., Portland
• (207) 773-8187

Open seven nights a week, this place is a little on the wild side, catering to a younger crowd with local bands and DJs who play everything from disco to techno. The club is open Thursday through Monday from the late afternoon to the wee hours of the morning, and there are pool tables and pinball machines. An alcohol-free night is held once a week (call for the schedule), and the dress code is anything goes. Cover charges range from $2 on up.

Southern Maine is abloom with possibilities for fun and entertainment.

L.L. Bean
Main St., Freeport • (800) 341-4341

Granted, you won't find live bands, but if you want to get away from all the music and madness, visit the L.L. Bean outdoor retail store late at night for a serene shopping experience. The store is open all night; if you come in the wee hours of the morning, you may have it all to yourselves. (For more information, see our Shopping chapter.)

Brunswick, Bath and Boothbay Harbor Area

Player's Pub and Nightclub
**Corner of Maine and Center Sts.,
Brunswick • (207) 729-6260**

Step into the basement below Richard's Restaurant (see our Restaurants chapter), and you'll find a favorite local hangout. Business people start off the night with happy hour, but Navy personnel and college students soon take over as the pub is transformed into a nightclub with dancing and Top 40 music. The

atmosphere is casual — people don't usually dress up unless it's Friday night. In fact, Friday nights are so popular, you should come by 10 PM if you want to avoid the line outside. The pub is open Tuesday through Saturday, and there's a free happy hour buffet on Friday. Usually no cover is charged, but for special occasions (like when they're raising prize money for a special event) expect to pay $1.

Winner's
**The Atrium Inn, 21 Gurnet Rd.,
Brunswick • (207) 725-6500**

At this sports grill you'll be able to catch the game (or the races) on 24 large-screen TVs and one that's extremely large-screen — it's 8 feet wide! The food is typical pub fare with nachos, burgers and plenty of beer. For more action, check out the off-track betting parlor next door. (For more information, see the Winner's listing in our Spectator Sports chapter.)

The Chocolate Church
**804 Washington St., Bath
• (207) 442-8455**

Although there are plenty of other perfor-

INSIDERS' TIP

Want to watch a video, but you don't have a VCR? Many area stores will allow you to rent a VCR as well as videos. You'll need identification and a credit card, and you'll probably have to pay a deposit.

mance centers included in our chapter on The Arts, we wanted to list The Chocolate Church here because it is one of the major nightlife venues in Bath. You'll find quality productions staged by traveling groups, and other shows ranging from folk and bluegrass music to theater, from the Bath Municipal Band to variety shows put on by the people who live here. Ticket prices vary widely: The Church has everything from free sing-alongs to high-priced shows with sellout performers. Call ahead for a schedule, and see our Arts chapter for more information.

The Boatbuilders Pub
122 Front St., Bath
• (207) 443-2014

Bath's version of TV's Cheers, this local hangout is in the basement underneath J.R. Maxwell's restaurant (see our Restaurants chapter). You'll find two pool tables, a large-screen TV, a full bar and plenty of locals (from shipbuilders to business people) to enjoy a drink with. There's no cover, and pool is 75 cents a game. If you have any trouble finding it, ask anyone where J.R. Maxwell's is located.

Carousel Music Theatre
Maine Hwy. 27, Boothbay Harbor
• (207) 633-5297, (800) 757-5297

Singing waiters will croon at your tableside while you enjoy dinner at this very unusual nightspot. Past shows have included vaudeville, vintage Broadway and plenty of old-time show tunes in a turn-of-the-century atmosphere — an old barn. Entrees include seafood, steak tenderloin, chicken and more. A full bar is available.

In this chapter we've tried to usher you beyond the corridor of U.S. 1. We take you into the towns, show you our very favorite haunts and share some of the treasures you can find.

Shopping

Shopping in Maine is a fun, somewhat different adventure. Unlike what has become the common shopping scene in much of America, we don't have a lot of malls; in fact, there are only three good-sized ones in the entire state. But that's a good thing, we promise. Some say our originality is gone, that Southern Maine is merely an extension of Massachusetts, but we beg to differ. Sure, you'll find the area along U.S. Highway 1 quite commercialized, with shops and accommodations lined up in a fairly uninterrupted stream from the New Hampshire border to Bar Harbor, but that's just Route 1, and there's a lot more to Southern Maine.

In this chapter we've tried to usher you beyond the corridor of U.S. 1. We take you into the towns, show you our very favorite haunts and share some of the treasures you can find when you go shopping in Southern Maine.

The chapter is organized by geographic area, then separated into shopping categories and arranged by town from south to north. You'll find malls and plazas first in each area, followed by a tour of the shops along our "Maine Streets." Next comes Outlet Shopping, which, for the most part, is centered in Kittery and Freeport. Antique lovers will want to check out Antiques and Flea Markets, but, remember, there are hundreds of these stores from Kittery to Boothbay along Route 1, on the back roads and in the towns. It was hard to choose among them, but we have tried to include a fair representation of the types of antique stores in our area.

In Arts, Crafts and Jewelry we list traditional country-type craft stores as well as jewelry stores that specialize in Maine gems and shops that focus on functional art created by a variety of artisans. Most of the artists and craftspeople whose work is featured in these shops are from Maine, though some of the stores carry distinctive products from other regions. This category also includes some of our finer gift stores.

Lobster pounds, bakeries and wine and cheese shops are among the businesses in our Specialty Foods section. While some of these places feature attached restaurants or coffee bars, we've focused on the shops that have distinctive food items you would be interested in taking home with you. Next is a related category, Farmers' Markets, where you can buy an assortment of fresh fruits, vegetables and flowers from local farmers.

Finally, we've written about our local bookshops. Most sell new books, but we've included our favorite secondhand bookstores as well. For rare and antique book dealers, check our Antiques section or the Yellow Pages of the local phone book.

Southern Beaches Area

Malls and Plazas

York Village Shopping Center
Long Sands Rd., York

Dave's Thrift Way IGA supermarket and Rite Aid Pharmacy are the anchors for this plaza, which also includes the Village Laundry, Cook's Hardware and Yorke's Barber Shop. Harbour House Apparel sells women's clothing, and you can get fresh pastry from Anderson's Bakery. York Stop N' Go Video and BIG Auto Parts round out the selection of stores. Additionally, there's a branch location for People's Heritage Bank.

Ogunquit Plaza
U.S. Hwy. 1 S., Ogunquit

This little plaza includes Soaps Laundromat, a hairdresser called Zanadu and a pizza place, the Ogunquit House of Pizza. There's also a surf shop here, Liquid Dreams, that sells equipment and clothing.

Wells Highlands Shoppes
U.S. Hwy. 1 S., Wells

The most notable shop in this group is Annie's Book Stop (see subsequent listing under Bookstores), though you'll also find Sharp's Dry Cleaners and Maineland Computer Center.

Wells Plaza
U.S. Hwy. 1 N., Wells

For a shopping plaza, Wells Plaza is a big one. It has an Ames department store, Shop 'n' Save supermarket and a Bookland (see Bookstores listings). You can watch the latest releases at the Five Star cinema (see our chapter on Nightlife), pick up a pizza at Paras Pizza or do your banking at Fleet Bank. The plaza includes Eat the Music music store, Video Etc. and Radio Shack to meet your entertainment needs.

Kennebunk Plaza
U.S. Hwy. 1 N., Kennebunk

This plaza offers a variety of shops to meet your personal and housekeeping needs. Along with Kennebunk Trustworthy Hardware, Courtney Cleaners and Rite Aid Pharmacy, there's Farrington's Family Clothing and Footwear and the Custom Shop. A Subway sandwich shop and an unusual Dunkin' Donuts, with a small outside courtyard, are also part of the mix. You can take care of your banking at Coastal Bank.

Shopping the Maine Streets

York Village

You'll step back in time when you take a stroll through York Village. Starting at Town Hall on Route 1A, where you can park, cross the street and you are in front of the York Historical Society buildings. To the right is Jefferds Tavern, where you can buy tickets to the museum (see the listing for Old York Historical Society Houses in our Attractions chapter); to the left is a Civil War cannon, and on the grassy hill is a set of stocks where miscreants were once punished. You can put your head (or someone else's) in the contraption. The kids will be enthralled.

Moving left, up the right side of the street, you'll pass the Olde Church, which houses three floors of gifts and crafts (see listing under Arts, Crafts and Jewelry). In the center, at the junction of Route 1A and Route 103, is the town's Civil War monument. Keep right to pass the Bergen's Bike Shop building and Manzi's barber shop, complete with the old-fashioned revolving red, white and blue striped pole. Walk until you're opposite the Bagel Basket Cafe and Coffee House, then cross the street.

As you head back toward the Civil War monument, admire the architecture and charm of the John Campbell Powder House Gallery and the large, beautifully proportioned cream-colored building that now houses professional businesses. Stop and gaze at the delightful window displays at Toys and Games — when we visited, it had a marvelously detailed jungle scene on the left and a colorful kite display on the right. Next door, you'll appreciate the quality craftsmanship found in the items for sale at River Place (see listing under Arts, Crafts and Jewelry).

Continue walking on this side of the street, and you'll pass the Cumberland Farms variety store and Whiffletree Furniture & Home Accessories, where you can find custom-made fine art, clocks, quilts and lamps as well as furniture. When you turn the corner, cross the street and you'll be back on the same side as Town Hall, where our tour began. Before you return to the car, step into the Museum Shop: It's filled with great gifts, interesting cards and beautiful decorative items.

York Beach

The charming center of York Beach on U.S. Highway 1A retains the feeling of a Victorian seaside town. The village is endearingly small, with Short Sands Beach (see Beaches) and the picturesque entrance to York's Wild Kingdom (see Kidstuff) within a five-minute walk of each other with shops and candy stores in between.

On the corner of Railroad Street sits the most famous of York Beach's restaurants and candy stores, the Goldenrod. The name is lit up in red neon lights on the roof of the building, but it doesn't make the village look honky-tonk, just quaint. The Goldenrod is famous for its Goldenrod Kisses, perhaps the original saltwater taffy. You can watch them make taffy and choose from a wide variety of flavors (as well as other candy and chocolate) inside. The Goldenrod serves a full menu throughout the day (see our Restaurants chapter).

Opposite the Goldenrod is Shelton's, with fine gifts, art, glass, clothing and its restaurant, Cafe Shelton (see Restaurants). More gifts, art and Maine-made products await you at Whispering Sands, the Blue Stocking Studio and the Tea Room, and traditional beachwear and seaside souvenirs can be bought at Bill & Bob's, Summer Memories, and Brown's. Women's clothing is available at The Clothes Way and Creative Fashions by Patti Anne, and children will love Maine-ly Kids, a fun store with children's clothes, toys and games.

If the Goldenrod is too crowded to watch candy being made, try Johnny's Potpourri, adjacent to Shelton's, where you can sometimes stand on the sidewalk and watch them make their famous "turtles" — a chocolate, pecan and caramel delight. Finally, for a laugh, have your palm read a few doors down from Johnny's at Readings By Pauline.

Ogunquit

Main Street

Despite the traffic congestion in the summer, Ogunquit remains one of the prettiest towns in Maine with its old-fashioned Main Street (Route 1), magnificent ocean views and charming Perkins Cove. It's a walkable town, and that's the best way to visit it. Leave your car elsewhere and take the trolley (see our Getting Here, Getting Around chapter). It will make your visit much more pleasant.

Main Street has lots of interesting shops and restaurants. Starting down Shore Road, at its intersection with Main Street, you'll find a few specialty clothing shops: Lido women's wear, Jeremiah's Sportswear, Mountain Tops Custom T-shirts and Seacoast Apparel and Embroidery. The Hobbit House gift store and The Golden Pearl arts shop are here as well.

Just north of its intersection with Shore Road, Main Street intersects with Beach Street. At the Main Street end of Beach Street (which, not surprisingly, leads to Ogunquit Beach), you'll find the Shops at the Betty Doon

Motel. These include Z Name Shop, where you can buy personalized items from pens to clothes; Atlantic Software, with clothes for men and women; the Cat's Meow Zoo, which has chimes, doormats, art and gifts with a nautical theme; and Lobster Republic beachwear and sweatshirts.

Continuing north, you'll pass Native Grounds and the Latest Scoop. Native Grounds is a coffeehouse that has fun stencils on the wall like "Automatic drip defines most people's personalities"; the shop sells pastries, bagels and the whole range of coffee types. The Latest Scoop sells — you guessed it — ice cream. You can get groceries, sandwiches and other deli items from the Village Food Market and souvenirs and pharmacy needs at the Ogunquit Pharmacy. The pharmacy also sells Ben & Jerry's ice cream.

Martins and Drop Anchor will solve any T-shirt, beachwear or general souvenir problems, and Harbor Candy will get that sweet tooth excited (see listing in the Specialty Foods section). Lastly, drop in to H.M. Crumpets for luxurious bath and toiletry treats for yourself or someone you love.

Perkins Cove

This lovely fishing village, with the sea spreading out toward the Kennebunks on one side and a tidy cove with sailing and fishing boats bobbing gently at rest on the other, is a lovely place to visit. Galleries, gift and jewelry shops and specialty clothing stores abound, along with a number of places to eat.

The Ocean Winds Art Gallery, The Left Bank Gallery, Paintings by George Carpenter, the Scully Gallery and the Cove Gallery are just a handful of the art galleries in Perkins Cove (see our chapter on The Arts). Women's clothing is available from stores such as Fair Skies and Upstairs at Blue Willow while children's wear is on the racks at Next Generation. Dock Square Clothiers and Atlantic Software stock clothes for the whole family.

As you wander you'll run into Perkins Cove Candies (see listing in the Specialty Foods section) and artisans shops such as Swamp John's, which features creative leather and precious metals, Perkins Cove Pottery and Coastal Candles. Among the array of interesting gift stores are Cove's End, with fine gifts, birdhouses and garden accessories; the Whistling Oyster, with select art, outerwear and seashells; and Golden Sails (see listing in the Arts, Crafts and Jewelry section).

The Kennebunks

Main Street

Main Street Kennebunk was made for strolling and stopping to browse in whatever stores catch your fancy. Pleasantly tree-shaded and lined with quality gift and clothing stores and restaurants, this Main Street defies the characteristic hustle and bustle of Route 1.

To best explore this charming street, park at the southern end of Main Street near the Lafayette Center, a renovated mill building that houses a variety of professional offices and the Tom's of Maine Outlet Store (see listing under Outlets). Cross Main Street so that you're on the right side of the road heading north. If you like fine lingerie and women's clothing, stop in at Sincerely Yours; if the thought makes you blush, move on to Hearth and Home, which carries an extensive selection of speckled blue and green pottery, painted wood and pressed tin items as well as candles, country accents and furniture. Next, be sure to admire the life-size moose made of grapevines that stands watch outside of Marlows. This store claims to carry "swell stuff and terrific things," and indeed it does (see listing in our Arts, Crafts and Jewelry section).

If you walk toward the traffic lights, you'll pass the Kennebunk Inn, then the Brick Store Museum. If you're strictly in shopping mode, cross the street at the inn to Fine Things Boutique women's clothes and accessories, the Jack & Jill Shop for children's wear and the Kennebunk Toy Company, a toy store the kids will love. Just before you reach Lafayette Center again, you'll encounter the Kennebunk System Company, which sells general merchandise, and Chadwick's women's clothiers.

Lower Village and Dock Square

Tourists absolutely love this part of the Kennebunks. They flock here in droves in the summertime; it gets quite crowded with people and traffic. This doesn't really affect the beauty of the area or your ability to enjoy its shops and amenities. Just don't expect to get a parking space easily. You might try to park along the streets or on the hill behind the church.

Enjoy the beauty of the stately homes as you travel from Kennebunk Main Street south on Maine Highway 9 to the Lower Village and Dock Square. At Firehouse Place, a small plaza in Lower Village, there's a great kitchen store called Keys to the Kitchen and The History Store, which specializes in history books, maps, prints and memorabilia. Near the intersection where Route 9 turns left (Cooper's Corner) into Dock Square, check out Jim Dionne's Northeast Angler, specializing in fly-fishing items and clothing. After turning at Cooper's Corner, notice more terrific shops — Living Arts gifts in the Yellow House (see Arts, Crafts and Jewelry) and Meserve's Market (see Specialty Foods).

The Kennebunkport Brewing Company (The Shipyard) (see our Attractions chapter) is to your right as you cross the bridge into Dock Square. If you're driving, you'll have to give the square a fleeting glance as you pass through, because you'll be looking for a place to park. A good idea may be to park in the Lower Village area and make the 10-minute walk.

Once in Dock Square, you'll enjoy a wide selection of specialty gift shops, candy stores and restaurants. Compliments and Abacus are well-known for their eclectic selections of funky, functional art and decorative pieces, while The Whimsy Shop (see Arts, Crafts and Jewelry) and Julia's Gifts sell more traditional crafts, gifts and artisans' works. For clothing, there's Lobster Republic, American Sailor clothing, Dock Square Clothiers and the Lido, to name just a few options. The Candy Man

---

INSIDERS' TIP

When shopping in Bath, be sure to stop by the front of City Hall and check out the enormous wooden map of the downtown district. It will help you find all the great shops you're looking for.

Photo: Maine Office of Tourism

Looking for bargains? Don't forget to hit the outlets in downtown Freeport.

and What's In Store can handle your candy needs, and The Chandlery and Copper Candle offer a wide selection of candles and gifts.

Union Square, just off Dock Square, hosts more gift shops, including Essence of Joy, which specializes in angel-related items; Bloomin' Baskets, which features Christmas ornaments, baskets and miniatures; Unique Craftiques; and Cottage Collectibles (see Arts, Crafts and Jewelry). Personalized Storybooks is a neat stop for the children in your life. While you wait, your choice of children's book can be customized with the name of the child, her or his hometown and three family members. When you're all shopped out, buy some Ben & Jerry's ice cream, sit out on the grass and watch the bustling harbor.

Outlet Shopping

Fifteen years ago there was next to nothing on the stretch of U.S. Highway 1 through Kittery other than the Kittery Trading Post. But when the outlet craze started to spring up around L.L. Bean in Freeport, it also hit in Kittery. Today there are more than 120 stores in a dozen or more malls and plazas along a strip of Route 1 that's only about a mile long. In this section we've listed the malls from south to north. Some companies have more than

one shop in Kittery's outlet area. These are almost always located in different malls.

Dansk Square
U.S. Hwy. 1, Kittery

It isn't surprising that this mall includes the Dansk Factory Outlet. Florsheim Shoes and Toy Liquidators are also located in this small retail grouping.

Maine Gate Outlets
U.S. Hwy. 1, Kittery

Pick up some shoes at Nine West or some sturdy outdoor fashions at Eddie Bauer. Updating your kitchen? Try the Corning Revere Factory Store or the Kitchen Collection, both of which carry a good selection of kitchenware. The Leather Loft offers a variety of handbags, wallets, and other leather goods.

Tanger Factory Outlet
U.S. Hwy. 1, Kittery

Go ahead! Buy the whole family new clothes and accessories, pick up those power tools you've been wanting at Black & Decker, then stagger into American Tourister and buy a big bag to carry all your goodies. There are women's clothes and accessories at Anne Klein, Liz Claiborne, L'eggs/Hanes/Bali/ Playtex and Gant. Children's wear can be found at OshKosh B'Gosh and Carters children's wear, and men's clothing is featured at Van Heusen. Don't forget to take strides to update your footwear: Bass Shoes & Clothing is there to help.

Kittery Outlet Village
U.S. Hwy. 1, Kittery

Bagmakers Factory Store has lots of bags and leather goods, and you'll find shoes and accessories at Etienne Aigner. Men's and women's clothing runs a gamut of styles at Executive Suite/Jones New York, J. Crew and Polo/Ralph Lauren.

Kittery Trading Post
U.S. Hwy. 1, Kittery
• (207) 439-2700

Before the outlets, there was the Kittery Trading Post. A mainstay on this portion of Route 1, people have come here for years for their outdoor outfitting needs. Three floors of merchandise beg you to explore, whether you're looking for casual clothing, footwear, outerwear or accessories. They also carry sport-specific equipment and have a gift department featuring Maine-made products.

The trading post's main competition is L.L. Bean in Freeport. In the '80s, the trading post took a jab at the mail-order giant with a T-shirt campaign asking, "L.L. Who?" The Kittery store has held its own in the region and recently completed a major expansion.

Manufacturer's Outlet
U.S. Hwy. 1, Kittery

Drool over the china and glass at Villery & Bock, sit back in comfy chairs and listen to music at the Bose Factory Store and pick up some new outdoorsy sports clothes at Chuck Roast Outerwear. If you're in the market for dressier threads, try one of the two Jones New York shops in this mall — Jones New York and Jones New York Sport. Not looking for clothes? Then stroll into the Yankee Candle Company and select a wonderfully scented present for your home.

Factory Stores of America Outlet Center
U.S. Hwy. 1, Kittery

There's an interesting mixture of shops at this mall. Two shoe stores, Converse and Factory Brand Shoes, will take care of your footwear needs, while London Fog can outfit you for staying dry. In addition, there are children's clothes at Bugle Boy, stained-glass products at the Stained Glass Factory Outlet and perfumes and cosmetics at Prestige Fragrance & Cosmetics.

Kittery Place
U.S. Hwy. 1, Kittery

This is one of the smaller clusters of shops. Get yourself some clothes at Esprit, Geoffrey Beene or Nautica, then accessorize at Sunglasses & More. You'll also find fine Japanese china at Noritake.

The Maine Outlet
U.S. Hwy. 1, Kittery

If you're looking for wedding presents or just want to update your dinner service, this is the mall to visit. Mikasa, the Oneida Factory Store and Waterford/Wedgwood are all found here, and if you want a new tablecloth to go with the china, check out Linens 'N' Things or Famous Brands Housewares. For children there are SharpKids and The Children's Place for clothes and Gund for a selection of cuddly friends. Timberland and Banister Shoe Studio provide a choice for shoes, and Tommy Hilfiger, Champion/Hanes, FILA and Jockey will fill men's sportswear and underwear needs. Other stores include Perfumania, Bag & Baggage and the Book & Music Outlet.

Kittery Outlet Center
U.S. Hwy. 1, Kittery

More china is available at this mall. Aynsley China and Royal Doulton have lovely selections if you're looking for wedding or anniversary presents or figurines for gifts. Mesa Imports Home & Garden is a good place to browse if you're looking for an unusual gift or just want something fun for the house. Outfit the teenagers at Levi's Outlet by Designs, then get them some of those shirts with the famous crocodile emblem at Izod. You'll find footwear for the whole family at Stride-Rite/Keds/Sperry Topsider. Finally, when you're tired of dishes and clothes, drop in to the Book Warehouse for a new read.

Outlet Mall of Kittery
U.S. Hwy. 1, Kittery

You can get sportswear, menswear and children's clothes at this mall. Browse through Big Dog Sportswear for fun, functional activewear for the whole family, then move on to the Casual Male/Big & Tall store to outfit the men. At Hartstrings Childrenswear there's high-quality, classic sportswear for infants and children. Cape Cod Crafters offers a welcome change from clothing with displays from more than 300 talented craftspeople.

Dexter Shoe Factory Outlet
20 U.S. Hwy. 1, Kittery • (207) 439-3667
U.S. Hwy. 1, Wells • (207) 646-7557

These low, log-cabin-type buildings house an extensive array of Dexter Shoes. Try on walking shoes, loafers and casual shoes in a variety of styles and sizes.

Tanger Factory Outlet Center
U.S. Hwy. 1, Kittery

Men will enjoy the classic suit styles at Brooks Brothers while the women check out Jones New York Country and Maidenform. Everyone will enjoy browsing through Calvin Klein before a trip to the Samsonite Outlet to get spiffy new suitcases to go with your elegant clothes. In the building behind these shops is Mainley Flags which carries (that's right!) mainly flags.

Tidewater Outlet Mall
U.S. Hwy. 1, Kittery

Housewares, again, play a big part at this mall. A Corning Revere Clearance Center, the Foreside Company, a Lenox Factory Outlet and Pfaltzgraff are among the stores at Tidewater Outlet Mall. Benetton, the Old Navy Clothing Company and the Polo/Ralph Lauren Factory Store have the name-brand clothing selections you'd expect, the Jewelry Mine can take care of accessories and Reebok/Rockport has shoes to soothe your aching feet!

Woods to Goods
891 U.S. Hwy. 1, York • (207) 363-6001

You'll enjoy the fine craftsmanship of these products made by prison inmates from Maine and New Hampshire. The inmates create fine wood products in a program designed to provide them with marketable skills, some money and a strong work ethic. Woods to Goods is an independent outlet that specializes in goods made through the prison industry programs.

While most of the products are from Maine and New Hampshire, there are some from prisons in other parts of the country. Chests, souvenirs, boat figures, jewelry boxes, benches and nautical items as well as clocks are among the pieces offered here.

Tom's of Maine Natural Living Store
U.S. Hwy. 1 and Storer St., Kennebunk
• (207) 985-3874

They started out creating a natural toothpaste, and now you can get a whole range of natural products from Tom's of Maine. The store carries the famous toothpaste, personal care products and environmental gifts.

Antiques and Flea Markets

Bell Farm Antiques
244 U.S. Hwy. 1, York
• (207) 363-8181

As you might expect from the name, this group shop is housed in a barn and made for browsing. Both floors of the barn are filled with country antiques, art, silver, china, glass and furniture. If you like primitives and Victoriana, you'll also find those items here.

There are loads of bargains to be found in Kittery's outlets.

Rocky Mountain Quilts
130 York St. (U.S. Hwy. 1A), York Village • (207) 363-6800, (800) 762-5940

A rainbow of color envelops you at Rocky Mountain Quilts. Antique quilts from the late 1700s to the 1940s, from doll-size to king-size, are always kept in stock, as are antique quilt tops and blocks in vintage fabrics from the 1780s to the 1950s. In addition to antique quilts, owner Betsey Telford sells decorating accessories like pillows, pillowcases, shams and stuffed animals. She also restores antique quilts and hooked and braided rugs. Open from May through October, this is truly a quilter's and quilt-lover's paradise. Call ahead for winter hours.

The York Antiques Gallery
U.S. Hwy. 1 S., York • (207) 363-5002

A renovated three-story barn houses this quality, multiple-dealer shop. The emphasis throughout the store is on American country furniture and accessories, and you'll see a wide selection of items relating to that theme.

Antiques Ogunquit
321 U.S. Hwy. 1, Ogunquit • (207) 641-2799

Victorian and glass lovers will enjoy this store, which features Victorian furniture and accessories and a wide selection of pre-Depression glass.

Corey Daniels
U.S. Hwy. 1 S., Wells • (207) 646-5301

Though this is a single proprietor's shop, you'll immediately see it isn't small. A large inventory in a large barn awaits you with continental, American and Oriental furniture, architectural and garden pieces and other small items and accessories.

Harding's Book Shop
U.S. Hwy. 1 S., Wells • (207) 646-8785

A member of the Antiquarian Booksellers Association of America, Harding's carries about 20,000 volumes. The shop is carefully organized to facilitate browsing, and the clerks are more than happy to assist you in your search. Harding's selection is varied, but specialties include New England, town histories, cartography, art, antiques, military topics, philosophy and children's books. They also carry a large selection of prints and maps.

MacDougall-Gionet Antiques & Associates
2104 Post Rd. (U.S. Hwy. 1 S.), Wells • (207) 646-3531

Since 1966 this 60-dealer antique center has been a must for antiquing in Southern Maine. A wide range of period antiques, both formal and country, along with appropriate small items and accessories can be found in the barn that houses this center. Note that it's closed on Mondays.

R. Jorgensen Antiques
502 Post Rd. (U.S. Hwy. 1 S.), Wells • (207) 646-9444

If you like beautiful, showroom-type antique stores, you'll love this one. R. Jorgensen is well-known for its beautiful displays found in two spacious buildings. Nine rooms are in a historic house dating from 1685; two more rooms are in the barn. Formal and country antiques and accessories from England, America, France and Scandinavia are lovingly arranged so that you can better enjoy the rich, glowing beauty and excellent workmanship of the items. The store is closed on Wednesdays.

The Arringtons
U.S. Hwy. 1, Wells • (207) 646-4124

While they do carry some new books, this store specializes in old and rare books on history — particularly military history from all periods. They also carry postcards, prints and maps. The Arringtons is a little less than a mile north of Wells Corner.

The Farm
294 Mildram Rd., Wells • (207) 985-2656

Owners of The Farm say this is one of the prettiest antique stores around, and we agree. Its specialty is 18th- and 19th-century formal and country furniture from England, France and the Orient. You'll also find Oriental and English porcelain and a large selection of antique lamps, boxes and accessories. To get to The Farm, take Coles Hill Road (across the street from the Tall Woods Motel on Route 1). Travel 2.5 miles, which may seem longer than it actually is (watch that odometer!), until you see the sign high in a tree on your left. Take a left, and the store is a few hundred yards away. The Farm is closed on Wednesdays.

Wells Union Antique Center
U.S. Hwy. 1 N., Wells • (207) 646-4551

Nine individually owned shops in a "made to look quaint grouping" on Route 1 North make up the Wells Union Antique Center. The center features a wide range of country and formal furniture as well as American, English and continental furniture, accessories and paintings. In addition, the center carries garden and architectural items, glass, china, jewelry and collectibles.

Antiques Kennebunkport
31 Western Ave. (Maine Hwy. 9), Kennebunkport • (207) 967-8033

If you like 19th-century furniture, this is a great shop to visit. The specialty here is formal and country furniture and accessories from the 19th and early 20th century.

Antiques on Nine
75 Western Ave. (Maine Hwy. 9), Kennebunk • (207) 967-0626

European and American furniture and accessories from the 18th, 19th and early 20th centuries are featured here. An eclectic mix of items including glass, paintings, quilts and garden accessories awaits in this 10,000-square-foot shop.

Antiques USA
Corner of U.S. Hwy. 1 and Log Cabin Rd., Arundel • (207) 985-7766

There are a few antique stores on this corner in Arundel, located at an intersection between Biddeford and Kennebunk. Antiques USA is a large store that specializes in glass, furniture and accessories. Glass and small items are displayed in large, well-lit cabinets.

Arundel Antiques
Corner of U.S. Hwy. 1 and Log Cabin Rd., Arundel • (207) 985-7965

There are 200 dealers displaying a wide variety of wares in this large shop. You can while away hours looking through the tables downstairs. Upstairs you'll find jewelry, Wedgwood items, toys, glass and china displayed in glass cabinets, as well as more open booths.

Arts, Crafts and Jewelry

G. Irwin Jewelry Company
436 U.S. Hwy. 1, Kittery
• (207) 439-2299

G. Irwin Jewelry Company, about a half-mile north of the Kittery outlet area on Route 1, specializes in tourmaline jewelry. Tourmaline is Maine's state gemstone and can be found in shades of green and red. There are approximately 3,000 different shades of tourmaline, which takes its color from 13 different elements. For instance, the pinker the stone, the more iron it has in it; the greener the stone, the more chromium it has.

Visitors to Maine are often surprised by the variety of tourmaline available. In addition to a number of colors and shades, you can also select tourmaline that's bi-color or watermelon-colored. Bi-colored tourmaline crystals begin as one color, then abruptly change to another. You'll find darker pinks shading to lighter pinks and greens shading to lighter greens, but a green-to-pink combination is the most common and popular of the bi-color gems. Watermelon tourmaline is a crystal that's green on the outside and pink on the inside and has been "sliced" to resemble watermelon — it's a truly distinctive stone.

G. Irwin carries tourmaline from all over the world in order to provide the largest selection of tourmaline shades and types. There's also distinctive jewelry in silver and gold, again from a worldwide selection of jewelry designers. The store is open daily year round.

ShootingStar Gallery
74 Wallingford Sq., Kittery • (207) 439-6397

Located in Kittery's Historic District, next to Gate 1 of the Portsmouth Naval Shipyard, this fine art gallery features New England artists. Opened by Fran Joseph in 1998, the gallery carries paintings in various mediums, from pastels and watercolor to oils and acrylics. Prefer functional art pieces? You can also buy contemporary craft exclusives from across the U.S., including stained glass lamps, whimsical and contemporary jewelry, turned wood items and decorative and functional ceramics.

Every six weeks a new exhibit is highlighted at the gallery, which also hosts the Annual Community Arts Show each October (for more information see Annual Events).

River Place
250 York St., York Village
• (207) 351-3266

You'll find pottery, ceramics, glass, etchings and fine-crafted wood items in this interesting gallery. River Place also has photographs and prints, jewelry, hand-woven and silk clothing and accessories, hats, books, cards, puzzles and games. Dolls, stuffed animals, science and craft sets, travel games and other creative toys for children are displayed along with capes and crowns for the little princes and princesses in your family.

The Little Red Hen Gifts 'N Things
Woodbridge Rd., York • (207) 363-4894

A little of this and a little of that can be found in the big red barn that houses The Little Red Hen. This family business was started in 1973 and has just grown and grown! The store is a delightful mix of antiques, gifts and crafts including jewelry, furniture, glass, china, Hummels and Sebastians. Upstairs you'll find a Christmas loft filled with items designed to fill you with holiday cheer regardless of the time of year. The shop is open from June to December.

York Village Crafts, Antiques & Gifts in the Olde Church
**211 York St. (U.S. Hwy. 1), York
• (207) 363-4830**

On the second and third floors of a historic 1834 church, next door to the York Historical Society, this shop displays the works of more than 125 craftspeople and artisans. Antiques, dried flower arrangements, Christmas ornaments, pottery, woodworking items and jewelry are among the items in this varied sea of merchandise. York Handcrafters and Givings Inc. is on the first floor, and it also carries crafts, gifts and artwork. You'll definitely enjoy your visit to this three-story cornucopia of goodies. The shop is open from April 1 to December 31.

Golden Sails
Perkins Cove, Ogunquit • (207) 646-6631

Owned by Ken and Gwen Michaud, Golden Sails was opened in 1984 as a jewelry and gift shop. Today, in addition to

those items, they carry Christmas ornaments, collectibles that include the works of Deb Wood, Pipka and Tom Rubel, and the shop's famous trolls!

Cole's Corner
U.S. Hwy. 1, Wells • (207) 646-3466

A charming country atmosphere pervades this unusual craft and gift shop. Close to 50 individual, room-size shops have space in this two-story barn — you'll like the "market square" feeling it brings. Local craftsmen offer many one-of-a-kind items, including pottery, hand-printed items, birdhouses, clothing, accessories and country collectibles. The store is closed on Tuesdays and Wednesdays in spring and fall.

Lighthouse Depot
U.S. Hwy. 1 S., Wells • (207) 646-0608

Lighthouse lovers, this is your store! From postcards and prints to clothing, magnets, mugs and more, everything sports a lighthouse motif. If you're into lighthouses, you'll have a wonderful time browsing through two floors of merchandise, including lighthouse collectible

INSIDERS' TIP

In mid-fall, Bath merchants have an early-bird sale where some stores open as early as 5 AM and offer great discounts. Call the chamber of commerce, (207) 725-8797, for specific dates.

series such as Harbour Lights, Lefton Lights and Spencer Collins. There are also books, guides and videos, posters, cards and prints.

Littlefield House Crafts Gallery
1544 U.S. Hwy. 1 (Post Rd.), Wells
• (207) 646-1257

A different shopping experience awaits at Littlefield House. The shop is in a building dating to 1841 that has been set up as a series of rooms with items displayed in various themes. Explore the dining room, master bedroom, children's bedroom/playroom, parlor and sun room. Peruse the handcrafted merchandise, dolls, bears, candles, ceramics, dried flower arrangements, prints, watercolors, baskets and handmade children's sweaters throughout the shop.

Shaker Valley Country Crafts & Gift Shop
Wells Plaza West, U.S. Hwy. 1, Wells
• (207) 641-0767

Stocked with goods from local crafters, this shop carries a little bit of everything. Bears, baskets, lamps, quilts, pottery and Christmas ornaments are just some of the items available. You will also find Boyd's Bear lamps here.

plum dandy craft gallery
21 Dock Sq., Kennebunkport
• (207) 967-4013

You can try, but it won't be easy to leave this shop without a purchase. Everything in it is absolutely "plum dandy" — from pottery and stoneware to raku, sterling silver and whimsical jewelry, original art and prints. Searching for that one-of-a-kind clothing item? This is the place to find sweaters, skirts or blouses. The store also has music boxes, wooden wall sculptures and paper goods such as cards, journals and napkins. Other items include Christmas ornaments, nativity scenes and blown and fused glass. Blueberry stoneware is one of their specialties.

Cottage Collectibles
Union Sq., just off Dock Sq.,
Kennebunkport • (207) 967-5170

Boyd's Bears in all their forms, from the stuffed variety to figurines, are a specialty here. In addition you can buy handmade,

handpainted items from Maine — many of which are unique to the Kennebunks. The store carries a large selection of miniatures and features handpainted gourds and birdhouses. The store is open from the last weekend in May to the third weekend in October and again for the first weekend in December.

Living Arts of Kennebunk
The Yellow House,
Lower Village, 17 Western Ave.,
Kennebunk • (207) 967-8460

Distinctive American handcrafts are the specialty of this shop, which has pottery, jewelry, candles, hand-blown art glass and chimes. You'll also notice Seagull Pewter, Southern Cross deck chairs and Hartwood Creations Secret Boxes as you browse.

Marlows
39 Main St., Kennebunk
• (207) 985-2931

The motto under the name of this store is "swell stuff and terrific things," and they back up that claim. From the life-size, grapevine moose outside the door to the thousands of interesting things inside, Marlows is a joy for shoppers. You can buy (take a deep breath) delightful wind chimes, colorful raku pottery, creative toys and puzzles, cards, special soaps and gift baskets, fine jewelry, pens, journals, notebooks, rubber stamps and ink pads, candles, stuffed animals, Boyd's Bears and Boyd's Bearstones…and the list goes on!

The Whimsy Shop
Dock Sq., Kennebunkport
• (207) 967-5105

A blanket throw illustrating some of Kennebunkport's most famous buildings is one of the unique home decorating items you'll find in this store. They also carry handmade and hand-painted furniture by English Woods of New England, hand-carved birds by Will Kirkpatrick, floral arrangements, handbags and an extensive selection of Cat's Meow houses.

Unique Craftiques
24 Ocean Ave., Union Sq., Kennebunkport
• (207) 967-3949

Open April to December, this store fea-

Photo: Merry Farnum

There are lots of interesting shops to explore along Maine's Southern Coast.

tures Maine tourmaline and sterling silver jewelry, candles, handpainted items and antiques. They also have a large display of cookie cutters.

Specialty Food Stores

Frisbee's Supermarket
Maine Hwy. 103, Kittery
• **(207) 439-0014**
   Visit what is claimed to be North America's oldest family store. Located on lovely Route 103, Frisbee's was established in 1828. Originally located in the building that's now behind it (which is now the home of Capt. Simeon's Galley restaurant), Frisbee's has been owned and operated by one family since its establishment. Warm wooden paneling and floors, turn-of-the-century wooden cabinetry and a round kitchen table and chairs give the store a homey feeling. A full range of deli items, bread, milk and sundries is available at Frisbee's, which also sells gasoline.

Hebert Candies
Shops at the Weathervane Restaurant, U.S. Hwy. 1, Kittery
• **(207) 439-3307, (800) 642-7702**
   Since 1917 Hebert Candies have been a New England tradition. This store is in the heart of Kittery's outlet area, adjacent to the Weathervane Restaurant. The white chocolate is excellent, as are the milk and dark varieties. Why not treat yourself to a mixed box of their "Genevas" so you can enjoy them all?

Yummies Candy & Nuts
U.S. Hwy. 1 (across from the Lenox Factory Store), Kittery
• **(207) 439-5649, (800) 638-9377**
   Your mouth will water just looking at the more than 10,000 pounds of candy and nuts in this shop. Homemade fudge, old-fashioned candies, saltwater taffy and gourmet jellybeans are just some of the goodies you can buy. The store also carries sugar-free candies.

Pie In The Sky Bakery
U.S. Hwy. 1 and River Rd.,
Cape Neddick, York
• **(207) 363-2656, (800) 869-2656**

You have to try one of the Stearn Family's pies. Even if you're staying in a hotel, we suggest a bit of decadence: Buy a pie (or a piece of pie), then trundle off in the car, pick up a coffee or some milk and find a nice spot to sit out on the grass under the trees and dig in. Yum! Thick, flaky crusts and fresh, juicy fillings are the key to the exquisite pies. As Nancy Stearns says, "This is not a low-fat establishment — we use fresh, unsalted butter in everything!"

Types of pie available include apple crumb, blackberry, blueberry, blueberry-raspberry, pecan, chocolate-pecan, raspberry-rhubarb and peach-blueberry. Selection varies slightly by season.

Pie In The Sky also sells cookies, sour cream coffee cake, cheesecakes, breads and muffins. The store is open daily in July and August and is closed on Mondays from September through December and in May and June. February through April it's closed on Mondays and Tuesdays, and the shop is closed throughout the month of January.

Beach Plum Live Lobster Farm
U.S. Hwy. 1 N., Ogunquit
• **(207) 646-7277**

Pick up a live lobster for dinner and take it back to your cottage, condo or campground or have it cooked before leaving the site. Cost for cooking is $2, regardless of quantity. Lobsters can be shipped overnight to all 50 states. Beach Plum Live Lobster Farm, which is actually a lobster pound on a larger farm, has an exterior deck where patrons will be able to sit outside and enjoy their freshly cooked lobsters.

Bread & Roses
28A Main St., Ogunquit
• **(207) 646-4227**

Since 1989 Bread & Roses has delighted local taste buds. The exquisite pastries, desserts and handcrafted breads will make your mouth water. Just think about cream cheese brownies, old-fashioned chocolate fudge cake, Key lime pie, coffee toffee torte and chocolate-raspberry torte. Or how about muffins, fat-free cinnamon rolls, scones or croissants?

You might also consider stopping in for breakfast on the porch or picking up something to take to the beach for lunch. The selection of vegetarian lunch specials includes garden burgers, veggie roll-up sandwiches, pizza and fresh fruit and pasta salad. If you miss out on breakfast or lunch, stop by after dinner and try one of their desserts with a cup of coffee. Light-fare dinners are served at Bread & Roses.

Harbor Candy Shop
26 Main St., Ogunquit
• **(207) 646-8078**

What a pretty store! Dark wood floors and paneling surround clear glass counters covering a delicious display of chocolates; other treats are wrapped in bright foils and piled high on tables and shelves. Mind you, they don't just look lovely, they taste great. You can buy decorative tins to hold your selections, or pick pre-packed assortments. At Christmas the store is especially beautifully decorated, but it's nice at any time of year. Drop in for a peek while shopping Ogunquit Main Street.

Perkins & Perkins Fine Wine, Food & Gifts
U.S. Hwy. 1, just north of Ogunquit Village, Ogunquit • (207) 646-0288

The motto at Perkins & Perkins is, "Life's short, drink good wine!" You'll certainly find good wine in this shop, which features hundreds of the finest domestic and imported vintages. They stock wines for all tastes and budgets and also carry sparkling wines and cider. In addition to the wine selection, the shop carries specialty gift items such as handpainted pasta bowls, wooden salad bowls and acrylic pepper mills. You'll find the right foods to go with your wine here as well — cheeses from around the world, olives, pates, salad dressings, mustards and breads. They also carry a selection of Maine-made food products.

Perkins Cove Candies
Oarweed Rd., Perkins Cove, Ogunquit
• **(207) 646-7243**

Give the kids an allowance to spend in

Perkins Cove Candies, and they'll be in heaven. While you're at it, why not treat yourself to a hazelnut meltaway or a giant turtle? The meltaway is a quarter-pound of white chocolate swirled with hazelnut; the turtle is a similar-size confection of chocolate, nuts and caramel.

Candy is displayed in attractive ranks of baskets and jars, and you shouldn't miss the extensive array of saltwater taffy. The Fitzgerald family, owners and operators of Perkins Cove Candies since 1980, pride themselves on the quality of the taffy, which has been garnering praise for years.

No preservatives and only the finest ingredients are used, and the taffy is available in a wide range of flavors from peanut butter, maple walnut and molasses to peppermint, blueberry, Key lime and watermelon.

Borealis Breads
U.S. Hwy. 1 N., Wells • (207) 641-8800

Throughout Southern Maine many food retailers and sandwich shops proudly state they sell or use Borealis Breads. Formally known as Bodacious Breads, the company was founded in 1993 and quickly grew in popularity. In 1997 a second store was added in Wells. The company's famous, rustic breads are baked in stone-hearth French ovens. Most contain no oils, sweeteners, dairy products or eggs.

Wine and Cheese Shop Ltd.
U.S. Hwy. 1 N. (Post Rd.), Wells
• (207) 646-9959

You can't miss this store. Located near the Wells-Ogunquit line adjacent to the Moody Post Office, the shop is on your right as you head north on Route 1. When you see the large, adorable grey mouse sitting on top of a yellow building, you're there.

The building, if you look closely, has been created to look like a circle of cheese with a wedge taken out. Built 35 or so years ago during Route 1's heyday — back when motor courts and drive-in movie theaters were popular — this building is a fun reminder of the type of building style used to attract tourists in the 1960s. Inside you'll find a varied and extensive selection of domestic and imported wines and cheeses as well as some gourmet grocery items.

Cape Porpoise Lobster Co.
15 Pier Rd., Cape Porpoise
• (207) 967-4268, (800) 967-4268

In addition to the usual lobsters and clams, you can also get fried seafood to go from this lobster pound. Lobsters are available live or cooked and can be shipped by next-day air to all 50 states.

Meserve's Market
Maine Hwy. 9 (Western Ave.),
Lower Village, Kennebunkport
• (207) 967-5762

An extensive wine selection is the major drawing card at this store, which has been the village market since 1865. Meserve's also carries an array of beers, liquor and soft drinks. There's also a full deli with domestic and imported cheeses and a rack of Maine-made products such as pasta, fudge, jams, jellies and taffy. Meserve's Market also features a coffee bar so you can sit back with a frothy latte after making that difficult decision on which wine to buy!

O'Reilly Lobster Co.
Mills Rd. (Maine Hwy. 9),
Cape Porpoise • (207) 967-1275

This is a Maine Lobsterman's Cooperative that sells live and cooked lobsters, lobster rolls and clams. You can also take care of dessert while your here — they sell baked goods and pies. Why not send a lobster to a friend? They can be packed for travel and shipped by next-day air.

Port Lobster Co.
Ocean Ave., Kennebunkport
• (207) 967-5412

Since 1953 this store has served the seafood needs of locals and visitors. You can buy lobsters (live, or cooked at no extra charge), lobster meat, clams, fish and other seafood as well as lobster rolls. The store offers gift certificates and next-day air delivery across the country.

Russell Acres Farm & Produce/
Orchard Dell Deer Farm
1797 Alewife Rd., (Maine Hwy. 35),
Kennebunk • (207) 985-2435

This historic farm dates to 1754. Among

its 185 acres of fields and rolling hills is Orchard Dell Deer Farm where red deer are raised. You can buy farm-raised venison, pheasant, rabbit and quail as well as free-range chicken and ice cream at the farm, which is 2 miles west of Maine Turnpike exit 3.

Farmers' Markets

Kennebunk Farmer's Market
Grove St.

This market is held on Wednesday and Saturday mornings from 8 AM to noon in-season, offering a selection of fruit, flowers, vegetables, eggs and other produce from local farms. The market is held off Grove Street, behind the Kennebunk Inn and the Texaco and Mobil service stations on Main Street (U.S. Highway 1).

Bookstores

Books Ink
Perkins Cove, Ogunquit
• **(207) 646-8393**

Look for this store near the footbridge in Perkins Cove, overlooking the park. In addition to books, you can buy imported and domestic wines, puzzles, games and toys here. Books Ink has cards for every occasion and a wide selection of mementos and gifts from New England.

Ogunquit Roundtable
24 Shore Rd., Ogunquit, • (207) 646-2332

This cozy little bookstore opened in April 1998. You can purchase new titles in paperback and hardback here, or settle down in a comfortable chair to sample a novel before buying. Ogunquit Roundtable also carries a selection of greeting cards and quality gift items.

Annie's Book Stop
Wells Highland Shops, U.S. Hwy.1, Wells
• **(207) 646-3821**

Annie's motto is to "try and have a good read for everyone at a reasonable price." To that end you'll find an extensive selection of secondhand books in all categories — from

classics and war stories to mysteries, romances and general fiction. The store has been building its children's section and it shows. You'll find a nice selection of new and used paperbacks and hardcovers in this section.Comfy chairs covered with bright blue fabric decorated with colored fish can be found in strategic locations throughout the shop, encouraging you to delve a little deeper into a book before deciding to buy. Annie's sells new books and publishers' remainders and carries a number of titles from local authors and publishers. All new books are sold at a discount.

Annie's is in the Wells Highland Shops (across from the Cannon Towel outlet) and is open year round. From the last week in June to the first week in September, the store is open seven days a week. In autumn and spring it is closed on Tuesdays, and from January through the end of March it is closed Sunday, Monday and Tuesday.

Bookland
Wells Plaza, U.S. Hwy. 1, Wells
• **(207) 646-8174**

Each Bookland has its own character. This one has large antique chairs for resting while you browse. It also carries a large line of Hallmark products, from ornaments to cards and other paper products like cups, plates and napkins.

Kennebunk Book Port
10 Dock Sq., Kennebunkport
• **(207) 967-3815, (800) 382-2710**

Located in the heart of Dock Square, this charming bookstore carries hardcover and paperback books and specializes in children's titles. The Book Port also features nautical titles and books about New England, and it has an unusual selection of calendars.

Old Orchard Beach Area

Malls and Plazas

5 Points Shopping Center
Alfred Rd., (Maine Hwy. 111), Biddeford

Staples office supply store is the anchor

for this plaza, which features an eight-screen cinema, Hoyt's Cinema 8. Shop for women's clothing at Fashion Bug, electronic goods at Radio Shack and home decorating supplies at Sherwin-Williams. Before heading back to the room, stop for an ice cream at Deering's Ice Cream store.

Saco Valley Shopping Center
Off U.S. Hwy. 1, Saco

Comprised of two main clusters of businesses, this shopping center has a little bit of everything. You can drop off your laundry at Maine Cleaners, do the grocery shopping at Shaw's Supermarket, buy a newspaper or paperback at Bookland (see listing in the Bookstores section) and pick up those everyday odds and ends from the Dollar Store Marketplace.

Ames department store anchors the center, offering just about everything to meet your household needs. Other stores in the center include Play It Again Sports and Steego Auto Supplies. Lucky Loggers Landing is a popular local restaurant in the center (see our Restau-

rants chapter). In late 1998 three new stores were added to the plaza group — Economy Drug; Mail Boxes Etc., where you can do photocopying, pick up some stamps or mail all your newly purchased goodies home; and Pet Superstore, where you can buy anything Fifi or Fido desires!

Shop 'n' Save Plaza
U.S. Hwy. 1, Saco

Shop 'n' Save supermarket is the focal point of this plaza, which also houses Poor Benjamin's clothing store, Little Caesar's Pizza, Casablanca Comics and The Book Rack (see Bookstores section).

Cascade Plaza
Cascade Rd., Old Orchard Beach

Locals know you get the best meat in town at Radley's food store (see listing in our Specialty Foods section). The plaza also contains a Key Bank branch, David's Sub Shop, a Maytag Laundromat, Coast County hardware and the Old Orchard Beach Post Office.

Shopping the Maine Streets

Biddeford

While you wouldn't call Biddeford quaint, it does have lots of character. What other town has a casket company on Main Street that sells urns for pet ashes? This is a mill city and while its industrial heyday may have peaked a half-century ago, it's still proud, with a strong chamber of commerce doing its best to maintain a traditional Main Street.

Take a right onto Main Street at its junction with U.S. Highway 1 South, and you'll pass Tony's Variety and McArthur Library on your left and Potter's furniture store on the right. Proceeding south, on the left are Reilly's Bakery and New Morning Natural Foods Market & Cafe (see listings for both businesses in our Specialty Foods section) as well as Bert's Barber Shop, complete with red, white and blue spinning pole. Carol's Gifts and Office Products carries a good selection of Yankee Candles, gifts and collectibles, plus cards, paper, pens and stationery.

Farther along on the right, you'll find the Children's Store, which (as you might expect) sells children's clothes, La Corseterie, offering women's undergarments, and Langevin's menswear. Keep to the right and you'll pass Mid-Town Music, Jack & Larry's Jewelers and York County Electric, which has a wide array of light fixtures and the bits, pieces and wires that make up lamps. Reny's, a Maine department store with furniture, shoes, kitchenware, clothes and toys, completes the tour on this side of Main Street.

Crossing the street at Reny's and proceeding north, you'll see Maine Family Films video store, Moe's Italian Sandwich Shop and, farther along, the West Point Stevens Mill Store (see subsequent listing in the Outlet Shopping section).

Saco

Park the car and stroll along this tree-lined Main Street, which retains some of its turn-of-the-century charm. Beginning at the southern end of the street by the Saco Island mills and proceeding north, you'll pass Champion's Sports

Bar and the Plaza Restaurant on your left. On the right is Saco House of Pizza, and to the right of the pizza place is Pepperell Square, which includes Maine Cleaners, the Lily Moon Cafe & Bakery (see our Restaurants chapter), A Pane of Glass (which specializes in stained-glass panels and lamps) and Butterfly Kiss Books (see the Bookstores section). There's also Tresor, an Aladdin's cave of beautiful antiques, unusual gifts and clothing.

Returning to Main Street and continuing north, consider visiting Heart's Desire, a consignment store that specializes in the finest women's clothing and accessories. If you need stamps for the postcards, stop at the post office; it precedes the Sportshoe Center, where they can help you find the right shoe for any sport. From there, walk a little farther north and cross the street to visit Saco Bay Classics, which sells men's and women's clothing. The store is lovingly laid out with handbags and jewelry, teddy bears and chests spilling a cornucopia of accessories and an excellent selection of quality wool, linen, cotton and fiber suits and separates. Unusual patterned jackets, flowery skirts with contrasting sweaters, blouses embroidered with the most delicate detail — it all can be found at Saco Bay Classics.

Next, turn around and start back the way you came. You'll soon pass Sam's Place, where you can pick up decorating items such as paint and wallpaper, the Golden Rooster Restaurant and Stone Soup Artisans, where you can choose from country and contemporary handcrafted work from 50 Maine craftspeople. Stock changes regularly within the shop but there is always a generous selection of contemporary, functional ceramics, blueberry motif ceramic items, jewelry, painted and stenciled slate wall plaques, and a small gallery of original artwork and prints. (see listing under Arts, Crafts and Jewelry). Farther along is Vic & Whit's Victualers (see Specialty Foods) and the end of our tour. Why not stop for a coffee and sit outside at one of the charming white wrought-iron tables and chairs?

Old Orchard Beach

Old Orchard Street is this town's "Maine Street." Renovated in the early 1990s, the street features Victorian-style lamp posts and brick side-

Come see what Summer looks like.

Consistently the Finest Apparel
For Men and Women

walks that lead to a square at the base of the town's famous pier. There's a fountain in the square and circular cement tables and chairs where visitors can sit and enjoy the wide variety of take-out food items sold by vendors lining the street. The ocean views are terrific.

Old Orchard Beach is a fun mix of Victorian elegance and kitschy, honky-tonk seaside stuff. There are a few bars and nightclubs, but it's basically a family vacation town. The shops lining Old Orchard Street carry your usual beachwear, accessories and souvenirs. One of the biggest is DY-NO-MITE.

Outlet Shopping

West Point Stevens Bed and Bath Mill Store
170 Main St., Biddeford • (207) 286-8255

A couple of years ago this mill store moved to its present location in a beautifully proportioned brick building nestled among the large brick mill buildings. You can redecorate bedrooms and bathrooms with the treasures to be found here, or simply purchase something as a gift. After all, everyone can use an extra blanket or a few new towels! A room full of comforters in

various sizes and styles awaits, along with towels, pillows, pillowcases, sheets, vellux blankets and sheets and vellux remnants. The discontinued trimmings and thread and polyester filling here is ideal for craft projects.

Dexter Shoe Factory Outlet
U.S. Hwy. 1 S., Saco • (207) 282-1694

Dexter Shoes originate in Maine and are known for their quality. Whatever type of shoe you're looking for, you'll find it among the selection at this outlet store. The Dexter store also carries leather belts, shoe polish and waterproofing products, and there are regular sales featuring a particular type of shoe — the loafer or the walking shoe, for example. The outlet store is about a half-mile from the junction of Route 1 and Interstate 195.

Antiques and Flea Markets

Ocean Park Antiques
12 Colby Ave., Ocean Park, Old Orchard Beach • (207) 934-9505

Poke around this little antique store and

find something different to take home as a souvenir. Located on the square in Ocean Park, next to the ice cream parlor and across from the Studio Gift Shop, this store is packed with plates, stemware, linens, tables, lamps, artwork and some Christmas ornaments as well as nautical items.

Arts, Crafts and Jewelry

The Muchmore Tree
1 Lester B. Orcutt Blvd., Biddeford Pool • (207) 282-4945

Not only will you find quality craftsmanship from New England and Maine artisans in this shop, you'll also be privy to a lovely view. The rear wall of the shop is a window overlooking the sea. Pottery, balsam pillows, handmade children's clothes and men's ties and Christmas-oriented items are just some of the things you can sort through. While it's true you will find "much more" than you might expect, owner Margaret Ayers says the name of the shop was taken from an old family name. The Muchmore Tree is open seven days a week from May through Labor Day. From Labor Day to Columbus Day (the second Monday in October), it's closed on Tuesday and Wednesday.

Stone Soup Artisans Three
232 Main St., Saco • (207) 283-4715

More than 50 artisans from the Society of Southern Maine Craftsmen display their wares in this shop. Blueberry motif pottery, pottery with heart motifs, pottery without any motifs, welcome slates, clothing items, Maine-made foods and candies, baskets, painted wood products, woodcarvings, clocks and dried flower wreaths are among the goods on display.

The shop also features a small gallery with original paintings and prints as well as handmade soaps, aromatherapy candles, handcrafted hotpacks in a variety of unusual

shapes to cover all your aches and pains, stained glass night-lights and more. The cartoon occupational plaques are sure to make you laugh as are the comical vegetable stakes. Most importantly, the shop is staffed by members of the Society of Southern Maine Craftsmen so there is always an expert on hand. And if you don't find what you'd like, most of the craftspeople will be more than happy to create custom work to your specification.

European Expressions
39 Old Orchard St., Old Orchard Beach • (207) 934-1352

You never know what you'll find in this shop located among the T-shirt stores of Old Orchard Street. Artwork, candles and candle holders, glassware and interesting pottery items as well as more traditional crafts like dried flower arrangements are all part of the mix here.

Studio Gift Shop
9 Temple Ave., Ocean Park, Old Orchard Beach • (207) 934-4811

This cheerful gift shop is at the square in charming Ocean Park, across from the old-fashioned ice cream parlor. Inside are sun catchers, glass figurines, collectibles, T-shirts and sweatshirts, mugs, notecards and postcards. A separate room houses a pretty selection of Christmas items, including sea-themed ornaments.

Specialty Food Stores

New Morning Natural Foods Market & Cafe
230 Main St., Biddeford • (207) 282-1434 York St., Kennebunk • (207) 985-6774

For more than two decades New Morning Natural Foods has sold high-quality organic products in the local area and beyond. You'll find bread, bulk organic products and spices, organic produce, meats and dairy products

from local farmers and a good selection of organic snack foods and salsa. A range of frozen and prepared foods, both dried and in cans, is also available.

In addition, you can buy books and magazines relating to cooking, health and well-being; at the Biddeford location, you can sit down for a cup of coffee, lunch or a snack in the cafe (see our Restaurants chapter). New Morning Natural Foods also carries products for people who suffer from allergies to wheat and gluten. The store is open every day but Sunday.

Reilly's Bakery
248 Main St., Biddeford • (207) 283-3731

One of the shops on Biddeford's Main Street, Reilly's has an old-fashioned charm. The eclairs are great, the flaky pastries are great, the cakes are great. What more can we say? Drop in and try some for yourself. You can also buy sandwiches to go if you're looking for lunch on the run. (They're great, too!)

Braley's
23 Main Ave., Camp Ellis, Saco
• (207) 282-5842

You can get live or cooked lobsters to go and live steamers (small clams that are steamed and eaten with drawn butter) at Braley's. If you're planning on spending the day at Camp Ellis beach (see our Beaches

chapter), it's an excellent place to pick up a lobster roll for lunch.

Pastry Gallery
17 Thornton Ave., Saco
• (207) 284-9266

"Gallery" is a good name for this shop. The pastries are so beautiful and melt so delightfully in your mouth, they truly are works of art. If you don't have a special occasion in sight, make one up so you can try one of the great cakes.

Vic & Whit's Victualers
206 Main St., Saco
• (207) 284-6710

Charming white wrought-iron tables and chairs await along the sidewalk and under the trees in an adjacent courtyard at Vic & Whit's. The store carries a wide selection of domestic and international wines and specialty, Maine-made food products. You can buy beer and soft drinks here as well as coffee and sandwiches. There are also wooden tables and chairs inside the store for your convenience.

Way Way General Store
93 Buxton Rd., Saco
• (207) 283-1362

It's worth the short drive "way way up country" to visit this general store (see the Close-up in our Kidstuff chapter). Though small, the Way

Way packs in a lot of charm, and you'll enjoy buying a quarter's worth of penny candy whether you have kids with you or not.

Emerson Candy
42 Old Orchard St., Old Orchard Beach
• (207) 934-7507

This store sure looks like a candy store! The outside of the building has been painted in bright stripes of pastel. You can sit and enjoy coffee with your fudge or candy at one of the outside tables topped by cheerful umbrellas, or you can get your goodies to go. A wide selection of candy and fudge is sold by weight, and gift packages are available.

Radley's Market
2 Cascade Rd., Old Orchard Beach
• (207) 934-4311

Buy the best meat around at this store in the Cascade Plaza. Knowledgeable butchers will gladly tell you, in detail, the best ways to cook the various types of meat. You can also buy produce, beer and wine, snacks and sundries at Radley's.

Farmers' Markets

Saco Farmer's Market
Behind Shaw's Supermarket, Saco Valley Shopping Center, off U.S. Hwy. 1

The Saco Farmer's Market is held Thursday, Friday and Saturday mornings from 8 AM to noon behind Shaw's Supermarket in the Saco Valley Shopping Center off Route 1. You can buy fresh and organic fruit, vegetables, eggs and produce as well as flowers at the market.

Bookstores

The Book Rack
532 U.S. Hwy. 1 (Main St.),
Shop 'N Save Plaza, Saco
• (207) 283-2711

Thousands of secondhand books (and some new ones) in all categories fill this small shop. Whether you're looking for science fiction, romance, adventure, classics, fiction or children's books, there's sure to be something

at the Book Rack you'll want to take away. If they don't have a used title you're looking for, they'll be glad to look out for the author or book and hold it for you.

Bookland
Saco Valley Shopping Center,
off U.S. Hwy. 1, Saco
• (207) 282-2638
5 Points Shopping Center, Alfred Rd.
(Maine Hwy. 111), Biddeford
• (207) 282-4244

Two of a chain of Maine-owned bookstores (see Bookstore listings in the other three geographical areas for more locations), these shops are individually managed but have a similar flavor. Both carry Hallmark ornaments and gift items as well as a good selection of hardcover and paperback books. Both locations have a selection of books by Maine authors, and the Biddeford store has a selection of computer books. You can pick up copies of free weekly and monthly publications (see our Media chapter) at the entrance to the Bookland stores, which also carry newspapers and magazines. There's usually pleasant music to accompany your browsing, and the staff is always very helpful.

Butterfly Kiss Books
8 Pepperell Sq., Saco • (207) 282-2552

This is a specialty bookstore featuring Christian and children's books, family videos, gifts and music. You can also get Sunday School supplies here.

Hospice Bookstore
29 Main St., Biddeford
• (207) 282-6706
111 W. Grand Ave., Old Orchard Beach
• (207) 934-5031

Whether you're looking for a novel to read on the beach or books to amuse the kids on a rainy day, there's a good chance you'll find something you like here. The Biddeford store is twice the size of the Old Orchard Beach store, but both have a good selection of used paperbacks, hardbacks and old magazines. Proceeds from the stores are used to support the hospice program of the York County Visiting Nurses Association, which provides care for the terminally ill.

Greater Portland Area

Malls and Plazas

Oak Hill Plaza
Corner of Maine Hwy. 114 and U.S. Hwy. 1, Scarborough

Whether you need to do laundry, want some fresh flowers, need a good book or are looking for a special gift, Oak Hill Plaza has what you need. The Florist at Oak Hill, Oak Hill Dry Cleaners, the Book Boutique (see listing under Bookstores) and the Golden Pheasant arts and country crafts all make their home here. In addition, Arlberg Ski & Sports Shop can outfit you with sporting goods, and you can enjoy an ice cream at Zango's Dairy Scream Soda Fountain or some great New England clam chowder at Chowderheads (see our Restaurants chapter).

Scarborough Marketplace
U.S. Hwy. 1 N., Scarborough

A varied selection of shops awaits at Scarborough Marketplace. You can get natural foods and organic produce at Lois' Natural Marketplace (see the Specialty Food Stores section), pick up a video at Captain Video and a pizza at Pizza Time. In addition, there are books at Bonnie's Books and children's clothes at The Children's Store. If you need to do laundry, stop at Scarborough Laundromat.

Jetport Plaza
Western Ave., South Portland

This is a small plaza, but it does have a Burlington Coat Factory store where you can get great deals on clothing and houseware items for the whole family. Other stores in-clude office product giant Staples and Ocean Pets.

The Maine Mall
Maine Mall Rd. and Gorham Rd., South Portland

The Maine Mall is the "main" mall for the entire state. We don't have many malls in Maine, and this is the biggest, serving the Greater Portland area and beyond. The mall, which recently celebrated its 25th birthday, has grown beyond expectations. Every year, the parking area surrounding the mall shrinks as more and more stores join retail areas along the mall's perimeter.

The mall is laid out in a cathedral shape, roughly like a cross, with 130 stores. The long, vertical portion of the mall is anchored by JCPenney at one end and a mall entrance at the other. The horizontal portion is anchored by Sears and Macy's. A second, smaller horizontal section near JCPenney has Filene's women's apparel at one end and Filene's men's apparel and furniture at the other.

In addition to the anchor stores you'll find Lane Bryant and The Avenue for larger women's clothing; Lerner and the Gap for trendy and teenage fashions; Eddie Bauer and Eastern Mountain Sports for outdoor adventure wear; plus stores for shoes, accessories, prints and framing, gifts, music and video needs. Fun stores for kids include LearningSmith, the Disney store and Kay-Bee Toys. If they're bored with shopping, a few dollars in quarters will keep them entertained for a while at the Dream Machine arcade adjacent to the outside entrance to the food court.

Speaking of the food court, you can appease your hunger with a wide selection of vendors — from fast-food places like Taco Bell and McDonald's to Chinese, Japanese and

---

INSIDERS' TIP

Looking for an out-of print book? Bring along some prepaid postcards with your name, address and a stamp on them, put the title you're looking for on the back and ask the various dealers of used, old and rare books to keep an eye out for you. If they find it, they can just note the find on the back with their phone number and send it off to you. When you receive the postcard you can call them and arrange for payment and shipping.

Portland Public Market

Picture the largest timber-frame building in New England then picture it filled with the finest fresh fruits and vegetables, the choicest cuts of beef, elk and venison, fresh seafood, home baked breads, pies, cheesecakes and more. This is what awaits visitors to the newly opened Portland Public Market.

It's a wonderful place to pick up the finest provisions, meet friends for coffee or just browse. More than 24 permanent vendors and others who set up for one day at a time are housed in the market - a two-story, lofty building with windows for walls on two sides.

Modeled after other world-class markets such as the famous Pikes Place in Seattle, the Portland Public Market opened in the fall of 1998. You'll find it on Preble Street, a quick walk down from Congress, beside a new parking garage (where two hours of parking are free to market visitors) with a sky walk to the market balcony.

The few things you won't find here include trinkets and T-shirts. The market deals exclusively in foods, wines and flowers. That's the way the late Maine philanthropist Elizabeth Noyce wanted it. Before her death in 1996, she donated $6 million to build the market - just one venture of many she funded.

Noyce became independently wealthy after her divorce from Robert Noyce, co-developer of the microchip. Moving to Maine, where she had often summered, Noyce preferred a simple lifestyle to the furs and jewels and chauffeurs she was used to in California, where she moved from.

Settling in the small fishing village of Bremen, Noyce found she liked giving away money more than she liked having it, and gave close to $75 million to state schools, museums, hospitals and charities. To this day, the Libra Foundation, which she established, continues to give millions to good causes.

The market was one step in many that Noyce took to revitalize Portland's downtown. In doing so, she also hoped to help Maine farmers. The gracious and grand market is a legacy of her success.

Italian options to soups and salads. If you want a quieter atmosphere with more service, try Thatcher's, near Sears, or any of the many restaurants around the mall's perimeter (see our Restaurants chapter).

Restrooms are located off the food court and down a hallway adjacent to Eastern Mountain Sports, and most of the big stores have public restrooms. Strollers are available from the information booth in the center of the mall between the two Filene's stores. An ATM is across from Victoria's Secret, next to Filene's women's shop.

Mill Creek Shopping Center
off Broadway, South Portland

Get your errands done at this large plaza.

You'll find a CVS Pharmacy store, Bookland, J & R Millcreek Laundromat, the Millcreek Barber Shop, True Value hardware and a Goodwill retail outlet among the lineup of stores.

Mall Plaza
Maine Mall Rd., South Portland

Ames department store is the anchor for this series of shops, which also includes the Imperial China restaurant (see Restaurants), Bookland (see our Bookstores section) and The Big Party, which sells all kinds of fun items for whatever type of party you're throwing.

Mallside Plaza
Maine Mall Rd., South Portland

You'll find the Whip and Spoon kitchen

Absolute Must See While Visiting Maine!

Absolutely the Best Place to Go for Maine Tourmaline Jewelry

Luscious. Sensuous. Colors evocative of the purest moments of nature. Tourmaline from Maine, rings, pins, bracelets, earrings, necklaces; crafted in the highest tradition of fine art jewelry. Over 700 different pieces of Maine tourmaline jewelry on display... guaranteed to delight. This is an absolute must see while visiting Maine. If time and circumstance prevent your visit this season, do call for our 225 item, full color, portfolio-catalog of Maine tourmaline jewelry.

Cross Jewelers

The Upstairs Jewelry Store   570 Congress Street
Downtown Portland, Maine 04101

1-800-433-2988

©97

shop in the parking lot of this plaza, which has Service Merchandise (household and gift items) as the anchor. The Dress Barn women's clothing, Papa Gino's pizza, Strawberry's music and Office Max are also part of the mix here.

Shaw's Mill Creek Plaza
off Broadway, South Portland

Shaw's Supermarket is the anchor to this series of shops that includes a pet store, Animal Antics, Fashion Bug women's clothing, the Carriage Lantern Hallmark store and Rite Aid. McDonald's, Pizza Hut and a number of different banks on the perimeter of the plaza parking lot round out the lineup.

Shops at Clark's Pond
Gorham Rd., South Portland

Located off Gorham Road, this grouping of stores includes Marshall's, which sells discounted designer clothing lines and housewares, Famous Footwear, a Hoyt's Cinema with eight screens showing new releases, and MVP Sports. HomeQuarters Warehouse (HQ) has its own building next to the plaza where you can buy paint and wallpaper, plants, items for gardening and house repair and other maintenance needs.

Shop 'n' Save Plaza
Preble St. Ext., Portland

At this strip shopping center you'll find a large Shop 'n' Save grocery and drug store where you can stock up for your trip. You'll also find Fleet Bank (with an ATM), Maine Photo (for one-hour film processing) and Colonial Express Cleaners. For good reading material, browse through Annie's Book Stop. To get to the center from Interstate 295, take Exit 6A and turn left at the first set of lights onto Marginal Way. Turn left at the next set of lights, crossing beneath the highway, and look for the shopping center on your left.

Falmouth Shopping Center
U.S. Hwy. 1, Falmouth

Take Exit 9 off Interstate 295, then follow Route 1 north all the way into the center of town to find this center, which will be on your right. There's a large Shaw's Supermarket, a Rite Aid drug store, an Ames department store and a Fleet Bank with an ATM located here. There's also The Book Review, which sells a wide selection of reading material.

Shop 'n' Save Plaza
U.S. Hwy. 1, Yarmouth

About five minutes north of Falmouth on Route 1, you'll come to Yarmouth and this outdoor shopping center. Among the mix of stores are a Shop 'n' Save grocery store and pharmacy, the children's retail store Toyland and Home Vision Video.

Shopping the Maine Streets

Portland

Experience Maine history while tripping through little shops stocked with everything from Maine-made soaps and candles to locally crafted jewelry and pottery, gourmet kitchenware, designer clothing and locally grown produce, flowers and specialty goods. That's just what a day spent foraging through the Arts District and the Old Port — Portland's downtown shopping area — is all about.

This network of tiny streets lined with historic buildings and museums leads right down to the bustling harbor. The majority of the buildings in which retailers are located were constructed after 1866, when a Fourth of July fire swept through the city, so most of the architecture you'll see is either Victorian or 20th century. You can tell the area was once the commercial center of Portland by the names of the streets: Cotton Street, Exchange Street, Market Street, Milk Street, Wharf Street, Commercial Street. It was transformed during the 1970s, when artists began setting up their studios here. Soon, retailers followed.

A festive mood greets you entering the Arts District, centered around Congress Square. The names of Maine artists fly on banners overhanging the square, and during summer, throngs of eager shoppers swarm the streets. If you're like the rest of us, you'll be drawn in by the brick sidewalks and the few remaining cobblestone streets. There are far too many noteworthy shops to mention here, but read on for a broad sampling of some of our favorites. And set aside a complete day (at least) to explore.

To make it easy for you to find the businesses included here, we've included addresses before or after the store names. The Arts District begins at Congress Square at the intersection of Congress and Free streets next to the Portland Museum of Art and the Portland Children's Museum (see our Attractions and Kidstuff chapters for more on these sites). Passing these, heading north along Congress Street, you'll come to Springer's Jewelers, 580 Congress Street, a 128-year-old family business that has New England's largest collection of estate jewelry. You can purchase antique brooches, pendants and rings for less money than similar items that are new. Just a few shops beyond is Cross Jewelers, 570 Congress Street, another family-owned business with a claim to fame. This one has the world's largest display of Maine tourmaline jewelry (see listing in our Arts, Crafts and Jewelry section).

At 551 Congress Street you'll come to the pottery gallery of Clay City Monroe Salt Works, which has a large selection of salt-glazed stoneware for the kitchen and house. Levinsky's, at 278 Congress, is a Maine department store that's a tradition around here for its huge stock of jeans. It's a great place to find good deals on clothes. Next door is an L.L. Bean Factory Outlet, where you can expect a bundle of bargains on clothing, household furnishings and outdoor equipment. Just ME, at 510 Congress Street, has a large collection of Maine-made items, from pottery to T-shirts, toys, books, collectibles and a large assortment of jams, pickles and condiments.

For Maine-made fashions, step across the street to Common Sense Designs (511 Congress), which showcases a large selection of matching, all-cotton clothes for children and women. Don't miss The Maine Historical Society's headquarters at 489 Congress Street; the offices have a small collection of Maine history books, gifts and children's games. Inside you'll also find a changing exhibit on local life in the days gone by. When you get to Center Street, head east and check out the specials at the Victory Deli & Bake Shop, 1 Monument Way, a favorite lunch spot

where you can get roll-up sandwiches, Asian noodles, mouth-watering desserts and gourmet coffees among other delectables.

As writers, we might be a little prejudiced about this one, but when you come to Free Street, we think you should keep an eye out for the Papier Gourmet. This store, at 6 Free, is all about its name — gourmet paper. We love the specialty stationery, journals, day planners and scrapbooks among its collection of other fine gifts.

The Old Port picks up around Middle Street. When you're here, pop into Portmanteau, 191 Middle Street, where you'ill be engulfed by the scent of leather and the rat-tat-tat of the sewing machine as an artist crafts fine handbags while you watch. The wide selection of purses, totes and backpacks are made right here and sold around the country. Joseph's Clothing Store has exquisite fashions for the most discriminating tastes.

One of our favorite streets is Exchange Street — the heart of the Old Port. You might never want to set foot in a mall again after walking through this corridor of darling shops and eateries. There are a handful of great clothing retailers such as Amaryllis (41 Exchange Street), which offers an elegant selection of women's clothing in flowing fabrics and unusual prints. You'll also find an assortment of hats, scarves and bags. Gallery 7, at 49 Exchange Street, has a variety of fine American crafts including molded wooden chairs, pottery and prints.

Italian or not, you'll savor Fresh Market Pasta at 43 Exchange, which sells a number of homemade pasta and sauces as well as salads and sandwiches to eat in or take out. Just a few steps down is the upscale breakfast and lunch spot, Java Net (37 Exchange Street), where you can surf the Internet on one of the cafe's computers while enjoying a bite to eat in an overstuffed leather armchair. Edgecomb Potters Gallery, just a few storefronts down, is a nationally acclaimed studio that crafts pottery and glassware in colors of sea and sky.

At the end of Exchange Street is Fore Street. Head right into Motifs, at 425 Fore Street, and check out a tropical collection of artsy frames, handpainted glassware and festive kitchen and bathroom furnishings. Next door is J. Nelson Collection, with a museum-

Portland

it's Cool on the Coast.

Shop 24 hours a day at L.L. Bean's main location in Freeport.

(sidebar, rotated) Photo: Convention and Visitor's Bureau of Greater Portland

quality display of fine china, glass and gifts from around the world. You'll be dazzled by the floor to ceiling collection of serving and dining pieces from Portugal, France, England, Italy and Europe. Buy a piece and have it shipped home for free within the United States.

Continue down Fore Street to Mohr & McPherson (463 Fore) and a collection of antiques from around the world. There's also an ornate selection of wooden and wrought-iron furnishings made just for the shop. Next door is the Covent Garden, which has an array of specialty bath and home furnishings.

On Commercial Street, one street down on the waterfront, don't miss The Resourceful Home (111 Commercial) and its unusual selection of environmentally friendly products — from a lemon-scented spray to keep your favorite feline from scratching your furniture to recycled stationery, glassware made from recycled Coke bottles, tire swings carved in the shapes of animals and all-cotton linens.

Yarmouth

Main Street through Yarmouth's historic downtown is Maine Highway 115, and the best place to begin your shopping tour is at Railroad Square, a little park by an old railroad station just before the train tracks. (This is also a nice place for a picnic). The shops in Yarmouth are a little scattered compared to some of the other main streets in Maine, but the town center is a very enjoyable place to stretch your legs and grab lunch away from the crowds. Heading east on Main Street and crossing under Interstate 95, a five- to 10-minute walk will bring you to Clayton's, a gourmet food shop and cafe with indoor seating and chairs outside. You'll find hardwood floors, 20-foot ceilings and antique fixtures displaying delectable foods — everything from specialty chocolate and coffee to pasta and preserves.

The old stage in the rear of the building is now Clayton's Café, a popular lunchtime destination offering overstuffed sandwiches, salads, baked goods, and, in the evening, gourmet take-away meals. Select a bottle of wine from their specialty collection and call it a day. This is one of the best places in town for lunch, and the Yarmouth Chamber of Commerce is only about a five-minute walk east of here.

If you head west from Railroad Square, you'll come to Handworks of Yarmouth, a gallery that houses work by Maine crafters featuring hand-painted furniture, pictures, collectibles and baby and doll clothes (including homemade dresses for the popular American Girls doll collection). The Natural Woman, in the same storefront, has jewelry, gifts and specialty clothing for, you guessed it, women.

Continuing up the street, a short walk will bring you to Main Street Antiques, a darling little shop in an old home with a fun collection of lamps, furniture and mirrors. One building up, the Village Thrift Shop has a large selection of used designer clothing for women and children. Queen of Hearts Cards and Gifts is one of our favorite gift shops with everything from stamp kits, collectible figurines and children's toys to baby gifts, cards and great picture frames.

Freeport

One of the most popular shopping centers in the state, Freeport has scores of cute retail shops lining its downtown streets as well as the L.L. Bean outdoor retail giant. To find out more about the amazing variety, see the following section on Outlet Shopping.

Outlet Shopping

Freeport

The transformation of this sleepy little town into one of the busiest shopping centers in the state began in August 1982, when a fire burned down the local five-and-dime store. A developer bought the property where the old Holden building stood, fixed it up and convinced the Dansk Factory Outlet to set up shop in this little Maine village. Dansk did so well that Hathaway shirts opened an outlet nearby, and within a month Dexter Shoes followed.

All three capitalized on the increasing num-

ber of outdoor lovers traveling to the L.L. Bean Retail Store at the center of town. Other retailers caught on, and soon what used to be a little country town dotted with office buildings and gas stations exploded into one of the shopping capitals of New England, with nearly 200 retail shops, restaurants and lodges along a 2-mile strip of U.S. Highway 1 (known here as Main Street).

Quaint old houses and office buildings have been converted into storefronts. Other houses were demolished to make room for parking lots. But the village charm and old buildings have preserved Freeport's small-town flavor, even as its downtown has been claimed by outlets. The L.L. Bean Retail Store, with four floors of outdoor equipment, sports gear, clothing, gifts, home furnishings and guidebooks, continues to draw increasing numbers of travelers each year (see the Close-up on L.L. Bean in our Attractions chapter). The store has created its own market, catering not only to those who truly love the challenges of long hikes and camping or hunting trips, but also to those who like the look and comfort such sportswear offers.

In summer 1997, the company completed construction of a new building aimed exclusively at children's items, L.L. Kids. Inside you'll not only find a huge collection of children's clothes and outdoor gear, but you'll also encounter interactive mountain bike and rock climbing exhibits where kids can try out the equipment. There's even a trout pond with glass windows so kids can get a fish-eye view. If the shopping's too much, you can step out on the porch and recline in a patio chair. Also, check out the deals at the L.L. Bean Factory Outlet off Depot Street, where you can purchase returns and items left over from the previous season at largely reduced prices.

With the exception of the ongoing expansion of L.L. Bean, new development in Freeport has been dormant for the last couple of years. Every winter a handful of older stores go out of business — for example, the Hathaway shirt outlet is no longer here — and new ones take their places. Still, no matter when you come, you're guaranteed to find plenty of big-time clothing designer names such as Banana Republic, Boston Trader's, Gap, Jones New York, Polo/Ralph Lauren,

Laura Ashley and Carters, all selling clothes for less than the suggested retail price. There are also familiar names for household furnishings and gifts: the Coach Factory Store, Samsonite Company Store, Cannon Sheets, Towels & More, Chaudier Cookware Factory and NordicTrack Factory Direct. It's truly a place for shop-till-you-droppers — a gluttonous selection of shops is here to consume, most within easy walking distance of each other.

Getting Around the Freeport Outlets

The best way to find your way around Freeport's shopping district is to pick up a Freeport Map and Visitor Guide, available at most downtown stores and the Merchants Association information center at the Depot Street parking lot.

Arriving in Freeport from Exit 19 off I-95 (Desert Road), the first shopping center will be to your right as you head south on Route 1. You'll see the Dexter Shoe Outlet and Village Candle side by side. Heading north on Route 1, look for the Freeport Crossing Outlet Mall, one of the few traditional shopping centers in town. This outdoor mall is full of deals on clothing and household items. You'll find the Famous Brands Housewares Outlet, NordicTrack, Golf Day, OshKosh B'Gosh, Jockey, Mostly Maine, Rockport and Reebok and Carter's Childrensware.

Continue north on Route 1 to the center of town, and you'll pass Chilton Unfinished Furniture on the left (south) and Wilbur's of Maine Chocolate Factory. Downtown is home to L.L. Bean and the rest of the shopping outlets,

referred to as "Village Stores." One of the first retail stores you'll see in the village is Eagle's Eye and Eagle's Eye Kids, on the south side of Route 1 (Main Street). Two blocks up on the same side of the street is the Gap and Gap Kids outlet, showcasing the latest styles. Across the street is The Body Shop, home to environmentally friendly soaps, bath oils and beauty products from around the world.

Banana Republic and its safari-inspired casualwear is one block north on the left side of Main Street, and next door is Maxwell's Pottery Factory, with all sorts of painted pottery and glass tableware. (Upstairs at Maxwell's is where to look for the markdowns and seconds.) Abacus American Crafts (see our Arts, Crafts and Jewelry category) is across the street, as is Maidenform and the Donna Karan Company Store. As you head north look for the Benetton Factory Store and the Jones New York Factory Store. The Polo/Ralph Lauren Factory Store is just a minute's walk up the sidewalk. Look to the left, and you'll see the front walkway leading up to L.L. Bean. When you're done exploring the outdoor outfitter's hallowed halls, don't forget L.L. Kids, which is in a separate building out back.

The streets heading east from Main Street across from L.L. Bean offer more great bargains. Off Bow Street, you'll find The North Face (with more outdoor gear), the J. Crew Factory Store, the Samsonite Company Store and the Brooks Brothers Factory Store, among others. Between Bow and Mechanic streets, continuing north along Main Street, you can hit the Dansk Factory Outlet, Crabtree & Evelyn and the Stone Mountain Handbag Factory Store. Off Mechanic Street is Brown

INSIDERS' TIP

A little bit about parking. Don't be tempted to park where it says "No Parking." You will get a parking ticket. In many towns there is a severe shortage of parking spaces both for tourists and the employees who work in the shops and restaurants that serve you. If a town has marked out parking "For Employees" and you park there, you will be ticketed. You will also find "No Parking" areas where delivery trucks load and unload, in front of fire hydrants and where space needs to be reserved for emergency vehicles. In winter there are occasional "snow bans" where vehicles need to be moved so snow-removal equipment can clear the streets. In those cases, if you do not remove your car, you will be towed.

Goldsmiths. Farther north along Main Street is the Kings Way Mall, which houses Bugle Boy, Play and Learn and the Pet Pantry.

After shopping, hit one of the nearby restaurants for a bite to eat. The McDonald's at 155 Main Street is actually worth visiting. Located in the antique Gore House, it opened for business in 1984 despite protests from a grassroots organization called Mac Attack. They deemed the golden arches inappropriate for the small town, but the restaurant was permitted and serves breakfast, lunch and dinner out of a renovated house with period moldings and glass-paned windows.

On the upscale side, Jameson Tavern, at 115 Main Street, serves juicy steaks and fresh Maine seafood for lunch and dinner (see our Restaurants chapter). It's in the original building where the treaty to separate Maine from Massachusetts was signed. Broad Arrow Tavern, at the acclaimed Haraseeket Inn at 167 Main Street (see Restaurants and Bed and Breakfasts and Inns), serves Maine cuisine in a hunting lodge setting with a wood-fired grill. For something more casual, try Chowder Express & Sandwich Shop (2 Mechanic Street), with its award-winning New England chowders and Syrian roll-up sandwiches. Or step into Gritty McDuff's, Freeport's original brewpub (see Breweries in the Attractions chapter), at 183 U.S. Highway 1, for handcrafted ales, seafood, pizza or pasta.

Be prepared to hit some traffic heading into town, especially on the weekends, which are as crowded as a summer fair. On your way into Freeport you might stop at the Maine State Information Center, at Exit 17 off Interstate 95. There you can pick up a map of the shopping district and the parking areas. Then again, you might have more fun surprising yourself with the neat little shop around the next corner.

Antiques and Flea Markets

A Scarborough Fair Antiques
**264 U.S. Hwy. 1, Scarborough
• (207) 883-5999**

This isn't one of the big warehouse-type shops. It's cozy, with jewelry, crystal, silver,

art, china, lamps, rugs and toys as well as furniture on display. They buy everything from single items to entire estates and accept items on consignment.

Centervale Farm Antiques
**200 U.S. Hwy. 1 (Oak Hill),
Scarborough • (207) 883-3443**

You'll enjoy strolling through this shop, which has the flavor of a beautifully set up museum. Furniture gleams and glows throughout the 20,000-square-foot building. The store specializes in 19th-century, Mission oak and early 20th-century furniture and accessories.

Cliff's Antique Market
**370 U.S. Hwy. 1, Scarborough
• (207) 883-5671, (800) 230-5671**

Not much furniture is displayed in this shop, but you'll find a wonderful array of small items and collectibles. This is a group shop with about 80 vendors.

Cherished Possessions
**185 Cottage Rd., South Portland
• (207) 799-3990**

Used furniture, antiques and accessories are selected for sale in this consignment shop based on quality and originality. Items get marked down depending on how long they've been displayed, but turnover is pretty steady — you take a gamble if you decide to wait for a markdown.

F.O. Bailey Antiquarians
141 Middle St., Portland • (207) 774-1479

Housed in the oldest building in Portland, this antiquer's mecca has been in business since 1819, developing a widespread reputation as one of the largest and finest antique stores in the city. You'll find furniture, collectibles and jewelry from all styles and periods including fine and country antiques.

Geraldine Wolf Antique and Estate Jewelry
26 Milk St., Portland • (207) 774-8994

Located in Portland's Old Port, you'll enjoy a dazzling collection of estate jewelry, sterling silver, fine china and period items at this shop started by owner Geraldine Wolf in 1968. Even if you're not in the market for a new brooch or pendant, come and admire the exhibit of heirlooms from days gone by.

Mohr & McPherson
463 Fore St., Portland • (207) 871-1868

You'll have a hard time distinguishing the new from the old in this store near Portland's waterfront. It has a stunning display of antique furniture from Indonesia, Japan, Morocco and China in addition to a handsome collection of cabinets made in its own woodworking studio. The cabinets come in a variety of earth-colored stains and are intermingled with pieces from around the world. You'll also find new wrought-iron canopy beds and iron fixtures for your home.

Venture Antiques
97A Exchange St., Portland
• (207) 773-6064

If you're looking for an antique table lamp or have one in need of repair, this Old Port shop makes lamps its specialty. Pick one from among the collection or bring in your own piece and have it wired for electricity. Venture Antiques also has an assortment of small home furnishings and decorative items.

Attic Treasures
270 U.S. Hwy. 1, Freeport • (207) 865-4999

Furniture, china, crystal, silver, artwork, jewelry, rugs and fine home furnishings — you'll find them all at this general antique store that showcases the treasures of about 100 dealers in a 5,000-square-foot, two-story building. Dealers specialize in costume jewelry, depression glass, antique toys, vintage pocket books and a collection of more than 200 pieces of vintage Fiesta Ware — brilliantly colored pottery released during the 1930s. The store is away from the downtown congestion, about a mile off I-95 at Exit 17 on the left side. It's open seven days a week from 10 AM to 5 PM and some evenings.

Arts, Crafts and Jewelry

The Nestling Duck Gift Shop
350 Pine Point Rd., Scarborough
• (207) 883-6705

The view from this store, which borders Scarborough Marsh, is lovely. Tall marsh grasses glow in the sunlight with a winding tidal river meandering through the marsh toward the sea reflecting the sky at high tide and revealing mud banks at low tide. Inside you can browse Christmas items in the loft and prints, Boyd's Bears, toys and stuffed animals, pottery, magnets and collectibles downstairs. The Nestling Duck has a large display of Cat's Meow houses and sterling silver jewelry. Homemade fudge is also a specialty.

Widow's Walk Gifts & Collectibles
20 Black Point Rd., Scarborough
- **(207) 883-8123**

Located in a big red barn, this gift shop carries antiques, artwork, baskets, dolls and collectibles. You're sure to find something, old or new, that you like here.

Abacus American Crafts
44 Exchange St., Portland
- **(207) 772-4880**
36 Main St., Freeport • (207) 865-6620
6 McKown St., Boothbay Harbor
- **(207) 633-2166**

This is a store you have to see to believe. Black and white polka-dotted pottery, golden end tables with swirling suns, hand-blown martini glasses in candy-colored hues, stained-glass lamps and a line of pearls set inside a golden sheath like peas in a pod — that's just a sampling of the finely crafted home furnishings and jewelry on display here. It's more of a gallery than a shop, with the fortunate exception that if you like any of the pieces on display, you can take them home. Abacus collects pieces from artists all over the country.

Cross Jewelers
570 Congress St., Portland
- **(207) 773-3107**

This family-owned business has a huge collection of Maine tourmaline jewelry and displays more than 700 pieces — every one of which you'll want to take home with you. Begun by William Cross in 1908, the jewelry store originally operated as a wholesale distributor to other fine jewelers in the city and to Masonic lodges across the country. When many workers were drafted for World War II and the company couldn't keep up with orders, it gave up the wholesale business and turned to retail.

Now owned by Ralph Pride, the great-grandson of William Cross, the store has its showroom on the second-floor of an older building in Portland's Arts District — the same showroom where the wholesale manufacturing took place. In addition to finely crafted tourmaline, it offers Maine amethyst, aquamarine and other state stones. There's also a wide selection of jewelry featuring diamonds and other precious stones. One word of warning: The shop is open only Monday through Friday from 9 AM to 4 PM and on Thursday evening until 8:30 PM.

Maine Potters Market
376 Fore St., Portland • (207) 774-1633

The works and styles of about 15 Maine potters are on display at this cooperative in Portland's Old Port. In fact, it's one of the largest pottery co-ops in the state. You'll find fine and painted pottery in modern and traditional styles and colors. The co-op has been around since 1978 and caters to the functional side of entertaining with all kinds of pieces for your dining room, kitchen and home.

Springer's Jewelers
580 Congress St., Portland
- **(207) 772-5404**
76 Front St., Bath
- **(207) 443-2181, (800) 725-2181**

With the largest collection of estate jewelry in New England, Springer's is a worthwhile Maine tradition. Locals go out of their way at lunch just to walk by the display cases in the store windows. Originally a fine jewelry and gift store operating out of Westbrook, Maine, in 1870, the store moved to Portland in 1946 and later expanded to Portsmouth, New Hampshire, and to Bath. It carries a mixed collection of new pieces and older gems from various antique periods including Victorian, Etruscan Revival and Art Deco.

Stein Glass Gallery
195 Middle St., Portland • (207) 772-9072

One of the largest glass galleries in the country, this shop sells the work of more than 75 contemporary glass artists. You'll see a full range of work, from functional and decorative pieces to glass sculpture and jewelry. The shop has been in business 25 years, having grown out of co-owner Phil Stein's own work as a glass artist. Eventually he closed his New Hampshire studio and moved to Portland with his wife, Anne, to start this nationally recognized gallery. It's open seven days a week during summer.

Maine Cottage Furniture
Lower Falls Landing, Lafayette St.,
Yarmouth • (207) 846-1430

You'll love the Maine-made painted wood

furniture in 33 colors at this recently expanded showroom. The store has a full selection of rugs, lamps and furnishings. Maine Cottage Furniture has been in business 10 years and is popular with summer folk and year-round residents. It has a "Color Book" catalog featuring its products and sells to retailers all over the country. The Color Book is $10, but the cost is redeemable if you order furniture. It's a bit tricky to find, but head east on Main Street, turning right onto Route 88 and crossing beneath the Interstate. You'll see the store on your left as soon as you get to the harbor.

Cape Cod Crafters of Maine
100 Main St., Freeport • (207) 865-1691

If you delight in baskets, flowers and wreaths, you'll love this floor-to-ceiling showroom with all sorts of handcrafted gifts and decorative floral pieces. The store is so full that when you step inside, you'll almost feel as if you've stepped into the Maine woods! You'll also enjoy a wide selection of Maine pottery, quilts and woodworking.

Blueberries & Granite
313 U.S. Hwy. 1, Freeport • (207) 865-1681

This shop features the best products of Maine, from fine selection of gifts, crafts and specialty foods to one-of-a-kind souvenirs. This is one souvenir shop that's worth an extra trip. To get here, take Exit 17 off I-95, then pull into the lot beside the large Indian statue (you can't miss it).

Specialty Food Stores

Bayley's Lobster Pound
**E. Grand Ave. Ext., Pine Point,
Scarborough • (207) 883-4571**

Locals rave about Bayley's. You can get your lobster live or have it cooked at no extra charge. If you want to send one home to a friend, Bayley's will pack it and ship it by next-day air.

Higgins Beach Lobster Pound & Fish Market
**83 Spurwink Rd., Scarborough
• (207) 883-3582**

A complete assortment of North Atlantic seafood, including lobster, cod, clams and shrimp is caught daily for sale at this fish market. Next-day air service is available for shipping the catch of the day to a special friend.

Len Libby Candy Shop
**419 U.S. Hwy. 1,
Scarborough
• (207) 883-4897, (800) 339-4897**

Want to see a 1,700-pound chocolate moose? Come to Len Libby's and meet Lenny, the "world's only life-sized chocolate moose." He's sweet, he's big and he's lots of fun, and you can watch a video showing how he was made. You can't taste Lenny, but there's lots of chocolate and great fudge to buy if he activates your sweet tooth.

Lois' Natural Marketplace
**152 U.S. Hwy. 1, Scarborough
• (207) 885-0602**

If you're looking for organic foods, this is the place to visit. Lois' offers full line of natural vitamins, an organic produce section, organic wines from California, France, Spain and Italy, organic coffees and organic canned goods. You can also purchase flour, beans, grains, rice, herbs and spices from the extensive bulk section or choose prepared dinner entrees and other prepared foods from the frozen-food section. Ice cream, yogurts and cheese are representative of the organic dairy selection, and they also carry tofu and tempeh, pasta sauces and snack foods.

Many people visit the store specifically for the extensive deli counter, where you can buy fresh soups and sandwiches. Everything in the deli is made from organic items found in the store. If a non-organic ingredient has been used (because an item is out of season, for instance), it's clearly noted. Another specialty of the store is the fresh bread baked here every day; there's also a good selection of wheat-free, gluten-free and fat-free scones and muffins.

Pine Point Fisherman's Co-op
**96 King St. Ext., Scarborough
• (207) 883-3588**

However you like 'em, that's the way you'll get your lobster at this fisherman's cooperative. They carry a wide range of seafood and lobsters, and there is no charge to have them cooked. The co-op also has a restaurant, the Rising Tide, where you can eat if you decide you aren't in the mood for doing it yourself.

Gloria Jean's Coffee Bean
Maine Mall, Maine Mall Rd. and Gorham Rd., South Portland • (207) 874-7483

Located at the junction of the long vertical corridor of the mall and the horizontal corridor with Sears at one end and Macy's at the other, Gloria Jean's carries a large selection of fresh-roasted coffee beans. In addition to whole or ground beans, you can also get a cup of cappuccino, latte, espresso or whatever coffee you like. There is a lovely selection of beautiful and whimsical mugs, tea services, coffee pots and coffee accessories.

GlenAbbey Gourmet
84 Exchange St., Portland
• (207) 773-1181

You'll find international gourmet delights from Britain, Scotland, Ireland, France, Italy, Germany and yes, Maine at this gourmet grocery store that stocks jams, mustards, teas and other fine foods as well as a selection of more than 50 hot sauces. GlenAbbey orders products from more than 50 Maine manufacturers, so stock up! If you want to send goodies back home, pick a basket or miniature lobster crate, layer the items you want inside it, and GlenAbbey will pack it up and send it off for you.

Harbor Fish Market
9 Custom House Wharf, Portland
• (207) 775-0251

One of New England's finest seafood markets, Harbor Fish Market has perhaps the widest selection of seafood available to take with you or have shipped to the people you left behind. It's right on the water where you can see the crews unloading their catches of live lobsters, shellfish and fish. Harbor Fish Market has been voted by readers of the Maine Sunday Telegram as the No. 1 fish market in Portland.

Portland Coffee Roasting Co.
111 Commercial St., Portland
• (207) 761-9525

For fine coffee blends roasted on the premises, check out this coffee shop's home brews. There's the Custom House Blend (named for the historic building next door), Peaks Island Blend (named in honor of the customers from the nearby resort community), Old Port Blend (for — you guessed it — Portland's Old Port), the house blend and a classic mocha java. There's also an assortment of flavored coffees and fine teas.

Fresh beans are roasted every morning and brewed into a stand-up cup of coffee — no wimpy stuff here. In the morning, pick out a pastry, scone or muffin to go with your fix. At lunch, choose from an assortment of fine sandwiches on fresh-baked bread. Owners Sam and Gerrie Brooke have run the coffee shop since 1990.

Sweetser's Apple Barrel and Orchard
19 Blanchard Rd., Cumberland Center
• (207) 829-3074

Connie and Dick Sweetser represent the sixth generation running this family farm, orchard and vegetable stand. You can't buy 'em any fresher than this. The farm grows more than 34 varieties of apples, including antique breeds that you won't find on supermarket shelves. In addition, there's a variety of ciders, Maine maple syrup and jams and jellies. In October you can have the family gift-pack your apples and send them to your home or to someone else's. To get here from I-295 North, turn right off Exit 10 and follow the signs for Cumberland Center. Blanchard Road will be on your left. You can also buy Sweetser's produce at the Cumberland Farmers Market (see subsequent listing under Farmers' Markets).

Clayton's Gourmet Market
189 Main St., Yarmouth
• (207) 846-1117

Come for lunch in the cafe or for a gourmet shopping spree. There are table tops lined with glass jars filled with flavorful candies and shelves of high-end pastas, specialty chocolates, coffees and much, much more.

Royal River Natural Foods
88 U.S. Hwy. 1, Yarmouth • (207) 846-1141
U.S. Hwy. 1, Freeport • (207) 865-0046

This store, open since 1994, specializes in organic fruits and vegetables as well as a wide variety of vitamins and homeopathic remedies. You can buy pre-packaged lunch foods to go or grab a bite to eat in the deli. The grocery store sells bulk herbs, rice, pasta and beans as well as other health food items. It's one of the largest health food stores around.

Old World Gourmet Deli & Wine Shop
315 U.S. Hwy. 1, Freeport • (207) 865-4477

Stop in for a sandwich and pastry at the deli, and take some time to shop for Maine gifts, fine wines and Christmas ornaments. The Old World Gourmet Deli makes its own soups and casseroles and offers a host of deli sandwiches with Boar's Head provisions. It stocks an impressive selection of wine, gourmet food products from around the state and the world, and selected gifts such as pottery. The Christmas showroom has a tree and all the trimmings year round, and there's a large display of ornaments for sale.

A. Wilbur's Candy Shoppe
13 Bow St., Freeport • (207) 865-6129

For award-winning homemade chocolates in a variety of interesting Maine shapes, bring yourself and your chocolate addiction to this much-loved shop. You'll find chocolate and peanut butter moose, shells, lobsters and sailboats as well as penny candy, fudge and gourmet jellybeans. Can't get enough? Take home their Christmas mail-order catalog. Also, check out the in-town factory at 11 Main St. where the chocolate is actually made. There are large windows where you can watch the chocolate making while enjoying a coffee or sweet from the bakery counter.

Farmers' Markets

Portland Public Market
Preble St., Portland

It might sound extreme, but this is the place to go if you want the largest selection of fresh produce as well as all kinds of specialty food items from smoked meats, fresh coffee beans, baked pies and hard-crust breads to seafood, wines and cheeses. The two-story enclosed market in downtown Portland, just off Congress Street, opened in September 1998 and has drawn drooling crowds ever since. For more details see the Close-up in this chapter.

Portland Farmers' Market
Monument Sq., Congress St., Portland

Flowers and foods galore color this outdoor farmers' market, which brightens up the whole square with its wide array of blooms and local produce tables. From May through November the vendors set up here on Wednesdays and in Deering Oaks Park (off Park Avenue) on Saturdays. The hours are 7 AM to 1 PM at both locations.

Cumberland Farmers' Market
Greely Green, 303 Main St., Cumberland

Sweet, ripened corn, juicy red tomatoes, tangy green peppers, beans, zucchini, summer squash, apples and fresh herbs — you can buy them all directly from the growers at this outdoor market in front of Greely High School. The market is open on Saturday from 8 AM to 1 PM. To get to Cumberland, take Exit 10 off I-95 and turn right, crossing Interstate 295. At the light, turn right onto Maine Highway 9. The high school is about 4.5 miles up Maine 9.

Bookstores

Logos Bookstore
450 Payne Rd., Scarborough • (207) 883-4401, (800) 339-4945

You'll find books, cards, gifts and music representing a Judeo-Christian perspective at this bookstore. At this location for the past three years, the store has served the Greater Portland area for nearly two decades. Logos also carries framed art and videos.

The Abbey
605 U.S. Hwy. 1 at Dunstan Corner, Scarborough • (207) 885-5813

This recently expanded shop features religious supplies, books and Bibles. You can also find a wide selection of religious-themed music, cards and gifts for all occasions.

The Book Boutique
Oak Hill Plaza, (corner of U.S. Hwy. 1 and Maine Hwy. 114), Scarborough
• (207) 883-3324

A few years ago the owners of this shop moved to Scarborough to live near the sea, then decided to create a job for themselves in a most pleasant way by opening this bookstore. While the store specializes in Maine authors and publishers, particularly children's books, they also carry a good selection of hardcover and paperback titles.

Bookland
Mall Plaza, Maine Hwy. 9 (Maine Mall Rd.) and Gorham Rd., South Portland
• (207) 773-4238
Millcreek Shopping Center, off Broadway, South Portland
• (207) 799-2659

As with all Bookland locations, the staffs at these stores are very helpful. They will help you find a book or give suggestions if you don't know exactly what you want to read or

give as a gift. Both locations have a wide selection of Maine publishers and authors and books about the state. The Mall Plaza location is connected to a Mr. Bagel restaurant (see our Restaurants chapter) and has a very nice area displaying writing and paper goods such as specialty journals, notebooks and notepaper, cards and pens. Bookland stores also carry a good selection of secondhand books and marked-down titles. If you aren't fussy about books being new and aren't looking for a hot-off-the-press title, check these sections for good bargains.

Borders Books & Music
430 Gorham Rd., South Portland
• (207) 775-6110

Borders is more than a bookstore. It's a big store with a cafe where you can sit down with a book and a cup of coffee, meet a friend and play a board game from the pile of choices by the coffee bar, or lounge on a comfy chair with a magazine and a cappuccino. You can listen to the newest music releases on headphones by the information desk or browse through the extensive music selection at the back of the store.

Business and computer titles, self-help books, mysteries, romance novels, children's books . . . you name it, and they'll probably have it. There are also tables at the front of the store with marked-down titles; you can

find beautiful books at good prices to give as gifts or keep for your own enjoyment. Be warned, if you have book lovers in the family, you may have a hard time getting them out of this store! Borders is next to Macy's in the perimeter of the Maine Mall.

Waldenbooks
Maine Mall, Maine Mall Rd. and Gorham Rd., South Portland • (207) 772-8166

Adjacent to Sears in the Maine Mall, Waldenbooks has a nice selection of hardcover and paperback books as well as a delightful children's section. They also carry a number of marked-down titles.

Annie's Book Stop
Shop 'n' Save Plaza, 295 Forest Ave., Portland • (207) 761-4474

Recycle your pre-read paperbacks for credit at this retail shop with more than 20,000 paperbacks for sale at half the suggested retail price. Of course, you can also browse for new books at Annie's, where they sell them at a 20 percent discount.

Book Review
Falmouth Shopping Center, 251 U.S. Hwy. 1, Falmouth
• (207) 781-4808

This locally owned general bookstore has been in business for 18 years. It carries a wide supply of about 15,000 books, all of which are new. There are no specific specialties, but there's lots to choose from.

Books Etc.
38 Exchange St., Portland
• (207) 774-0626

In the same Old Port location for 25 years, this shop is Southern Maine's literary mecca, stocking a broad array of fiction, poetry and psychology titles and one of the largest selections of literature around — about 25,000 books. Comfy chairs are set around the store, which is located in an old bank. You'll also find a great assortment of books about Maine.

Emerson Booksellers
18 Exchange St., Portland
• (207) 874-2665

This artsy bookstore stocks old and new books of every kind as well as an enlightening selection of vintage maps, railroad guides and battle plans. Downstairs there's an art gallery in the making.

Harbour Books
Marketplace Shopping Center., 438 Route 1, Yarmouth • (207) 846-6306

Newly located, this store has one of the largest marine sections in the state as well as a broad kids' section with gift items related to popular storybook characters. All hardcover bestsellers are discounted 20 percent off the suggested retail price. You'll also enjoy a large selection of books on Maine, both fiction and nonfiction.

Brunswick, Bath and Boothbay Area

Malls and Plazas

Merrymeeting Shopping Plaza
Maine Hwy. 24, Brunswick

This newer development is a popular place to go grocery shopping. It features a large Shaw's grocery store, which is open 24 hours, and a Service Merchandise, which sells all kinds of home items from jewelry to furniture. There's also a bookstore and a video rental store. The easiest way to get here is by driving north through Brunswick on Route 1 and continuing until the road winds back through the trees. Take the next exit, labeled "Cook's Corner," and keep to the right, turning right at the traffic lights. The plaza is a couple of blocks away on your left.

Cook's Corner Mall
Maine Hwy. 24, Brunswick

Just a few blocks north of Merrymeeting Plaza, this outdoor mall has a Sears retail store and the biggest bookstore in the region, Bookland. You'll enjoy browsing for books here: You can lounge on one of several antique sofas scattered around the store and thumb through your selections before buying them. This Bookland also has a small cafe in the back of the store where you can enjoy decadent desserts and coffee or grab a sandwich. The mall also has a large retail toy store, Toyland, and a Staples discount office supply store.

Bath Shopping Center
Shopping Center Dr., Bath

Many Bath residents do their shopping at this outdoor mall. It has a small Shaw's grocery store, a coin laundry, a CVS pharmacy, a local bank with an ATM, a Hallmark gift and greeting card store and a video rental store. For some good deals on used clothing head to Goodwill, which has a store here. To get to the center take the first Bath exit off Route 1. Turn right off the exit, then take your first right onto Congress Avenue. After crossing back over the highway, turn right onto Shopping Center Drive; that will take you to the center.

Small Mall
Maine Hwy. 27, Boothbay

You'll find the Video Loft movie rental store, the House of Pizza and a laundry/cleaners at this aptly named outdoor mall. There is also a Key Bank. Just across the street is a Shop 'n' Save grocery store.

Shopping the Maine Streets

Brunswick

This town's main street really is Maine Street, the only one so-named in the state. It is also our widest main street, with four lanes of traffic. Unfortunately that also makes it one of the most dangerous for pedestrians. There have been a number of auto-related accidents and fatalities, so be extremely careful.

Long before there were cars, however, Maine Street channeled through one of the area's most historic towns. It was built wide so that soldiers at the nearby river trading post could protect their wares by firing cannons down the street without hitting any buildings! Now the only invaders are tourists, and it's not hard to see why they attack — the town has many fabulous shops and restaurants and a handful of galleries (see our chapter on The Arts).

It can be difficult to find parking on the street and even harder to back out of an on-street parking space. The best places to park are in the municipal parking lot by the police station, 28 Federal Street, and in the town lot behind the fire station, 21 Town Hall Place. To find these free, two-hour spots, look for the white and green parking signs.

All the shops along Maine Street are within easy walking distance of each another; the whole district is about a quarter-mile in length. Starting at the municipal parking lot and heading south toward Bowdoin College, one of the first shops you'll come to is Jenney Station Tobacconist, a retro train station lined

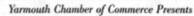

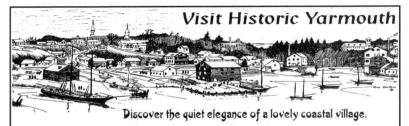

with all manner of cigars, pipes and cigarettes. There's also a wide variety of tobaccos in little glass jars and a handsome collection of tobacco boxes. Not far down the street is Paper Works Inc. Inside, beneath a large red awning, you'll find a huge assortment of whimsical gifts -our favorite is a paper doll cut-out book of the president and the entire first family! Paper Works also has two complete rooms full of greeting cards and gift paper. Upstairs you'll find specialty women's clothing.

Just a little farther down Maine Street is the Tontine Mall, a small indoor shopping center with several great gift stores, a women's resale clothing boutique, a chocolate factory, bookstore and a popular cafe, Wild Oats, where you can get scrumptious sweets and great soups and sandwiches. At the other end of the shopping center is the Evening Star Cinema, which shows art films daily.

Field's Jewelers, also on Maine Street, has a tasteful selection of jewelry, and Day's Antiques, with its large collection of antique furniture, is in an old Sea Captain's house just a little farther down the street, across from the town mall. (If you're looking for more shops, this mall doesn't have them; it's the town park.)

Crossing Maine Street to head back up the other side, you'll come to the intersection with Pleasant Street. Take a quick detour just one block down Pleasant to The Kitchen, where you can get tasty Greek and American food at great prices. Keep going down Pleasant Street, and within a few hundred yards you'll come to the Maine Writers and Publishers Alliance, which has a bookstore showcasing publications about Maine and works by state authors. Now, retrace your steps to get back to Maine Street for more shopping.

At the corner of Maine and Pleasant streets is the Wyler Gallery, which sells beautifully crafted home furnishings and clothing. Grand City, a favorite local department store, is one block north on Maine Street. This is a great place to shop for deals on household items. Behind Grand City is Benzoni's, where you can get tasty brick-oven pizza. For the gourmet cook (or the wannabe), the Mix stocks a great selection of gourmet gadgets, cookbooks, linens, foods and glassware. The Stone Soup artists cooperative is next on the block selling a wide variety of Maine-made pottery, prints, quilts, baskets, bags

and much more. Just next door is a children's resale clothing shop, and lastly you'll arrive at the Goodwill store, with used clothes for children and adults.

Bath

Built near the banks of the Kennebec River, this city's shopping district consists of storefronts strung together in historic brick buildings, each a block or more in length. The two main streets, Centre and Front, converge at a T to form the shopping district. The roads meet at City Hall, a huge granite building with carved columns, a balcony and a tower with an original Paul Revere bell. Parking is across from the police station off Water Street, which loops between Centre and Front streets.

The shopping along Centre Street begins near the bottom of the hill leading into town at R.M. Tate's, where a treasure trove of collectibles, baskets, craft supplies and discount items fills the floor of a huge warehouse. Just across the street is Morning Glory Natural Foods, a newly designed natural foods store with a wide variety of health foods and organic vegetables. A few stores up on the same side of the street, you'll come to Yankee Artisans, a popular craft cooperative with all sorts of locally-made gift items — everything from knit hats to hand-painted T-shirts, toys and home decorations.

At this point, you are at Centre Street's intersection with Front Street in front of City Hall. To the right you'll find the Bath Chamber of Commerce as well as Bath Jewelry, a local jewelry store that crafts some of its own pieces. Across the street is Mason Street Mercantile, which has wonderful country furnishings and collectibles.

Head back toward City Hall, and on the other side of Front Street you'll come to Full Spectrum, an art supply store that also carries a wide variety of prints by Maine artists such as Andrew Wyeth. Next door is The Intown Shop, a fine clothing retailer for women (Make sure to browse in the back corner of the store for bargain items at low prices). Springer's Jewelers, a family store dating back to 1870, is a couple of shops down on the same side of the street and carries a large selection of estate jewelry and new pieces.

Not much farther is Reny's, a Maine de-

Photo: Merry Farnum

You can fill a day window shopping in Portland's Old Port.

partment store that carries discounted clothes from well-known manufacturers including L.L. Bean and J. Crew as well as a broad selection of household items.

Keep heading north on Front Street, and at the far end of the downtown district you'll hit a handful of antique stores. Hunt through Brick Store Antiques (see listing in our Antiques and Flea Markets section), and enjoy the large supply of old china, glass, silver, jewelry and buttons as well as furniture. Rummage through the wall of older books in Countryside Antiques, or browse through Cobblestone & Co.'s two showrooms filled to the brim with china, furniture and clothing. Don't miss Pollyanna's Antiques and Front Street Antiques, which have an assortment of paintings, china, dolls, rugs and furniture.

Toward the north end, two great places to eat lunch or breakfast are The Kitchen, where you can get delicious and inexpensive food served quick and hot off the grill, and Front Street Deli, which has an enjoyable selection of soups and sandwiches.

Wiscasset

As you drive into town along Route 1 (which turns into Main Street), look for little, white-painted arrow signs directing you to some of the antique shops on various side streets. Wiscasset is known as a great place to go antiquing, and it claims to be Maine's prettiest village. As you drive by the Victorian houses and old Sea Captain's homes along Main Street and see the church spires poking through the trees (especially when coming into town over the bridge from the north), it's easy to see why the whole town is on the National Register of Historic Places. The quaint shops are tucked inside historic brick buildings butting up to the Sheepscot River.

Heading into Wiscasset along Route 1 North, keep an eye out for Big Al's Super Values, (207) 882-6243. You'll see it on the right side of the road before you get to the downtown shopping district. The large red warehouse is full of bargains, with prices beginning around two for $1 and not climbing much higher. There's everything from kids'

toys to household items to greeting cards. Best of all, there's free coffee while you shop and a "free table" where you can pick up a trinket or two after making a purchase. We bought our Christmas greeting cards here, saved a bundle and then snagged a free back scratcher! It's also a good place to stop and let the kids stretch their legs before heading into what can be a very congested drive through town. Give them a few dollar bills and let the fun begin.

As you come in from the south, you'll also see Wizard of Odds and Ends on the left. This is a funky antique shop: You're never sure what you'll find, but you're always sure to come away with a good deal. To the right is Treats, a gourmet cheese and wine shop. Nearby on Main Street is the Wiscasset Bay Gallery, which has a fine selection of local paintings, and Norman Antiques.

Venture down either side of Middle Street, which intersects Main Street in the center of town, and you will encounter a smattering of other specialty shops including The Butterstamp Workshop, which has a collection of antique butter mold designs and handcrafted folk art. Eliott Healy Books and Prints is nearby, and Terry Lewis Antiques is in a huge house full of antiques spilling out onto the lawn.

The road that intersects Main Street and runs along the river is Water Street. If you follow it to the right, you'll come to Sarah's Cafe — one of the most loved lunch spots in the region with everything from homemade soups to Mexican food to delicious desserts (see our Restaurants chapter). Located in the brick and granite Customs House, which was built in 1870, Area's is on the National Register of Historic Places. Just below the Customs House is the town dock, where you can grab a bite to eat or admire the boats in the harbor.

On the left side of Main at the intersection with Water Street is Red's Eats, a little red shack that sells some of the best lobster rolls around. Beside Red's is Wiscasset Hardware Company — don't pass it up just because you're not looking for a hammer. The hardware store has kites, T-shirts, Maine mementos and gifts galore. Follow Water Street to the left, and you'll come to Debra Elizabeth Schaffer Antiques, a specialty shop of fine antiques and replicas.

Boothbay Harbor

Maine Highway 27 brings you into the center of this popular tourist destination, which is the largest boating harbor north of Boston. It's famous not only for its many boat excursions, but also for its boat building industry, which goes back a couple of centuries. You'll have fun exploring the many shops in the old wooden houses that line the streets and in some of the historic buildings that form the town center. The buildings push right up to the harbor and even extend over it on several piers! Parking is tight. It's free along the street for up to two hours (then you have to move on), but there are also a couple of parking lots off Maine 27 just before the commercial center as you head into town. These charge about $5 a day.

Beginning at McKown Street, which brings you into the heart of the shopping district, you'll encounter the Edgecomb Potters Hand in Hand Gallery. There you'll see pottery from the group's main store in Edgecomb and jewelry and other American crafts from around the country. Next door is the Abacus Gallery. Its main store is in Portland, but this offshoot sells many of the same handcrafted furnishings as well as a variety of paintings by regional artists.

On Townsend Avenue, just across the street, duck into The Hutch, which has hundreds of collectibles and gifts including Hallmark, Hummels and Maine-made crafts. You'll find two complete floors of souvenirs, and the windows are filled with even more. At the corner of McKown and Commercial Street is Sherman's, a book and stationery store that sells books upstairs and toys, model ships and cards downstairs. Continue down Commercial Street and on the left you'll see The Customs House, which sells fine gifts including Maine blueberry pottery, handbags and T-shirts.

Orne's Candy Store (which has been around since 1885!) is on the right. You'll find china plates stacked high with homemade fudge, and the smell of chocolate will overwhelm you as you walk inside. Big Jack's Cigars is next door, and if you go just a bit farther, to the end of the street, you'll come to Pier One, a dock where many cruise boats pick up their passengers (see our Attractions chapter). The atmosphere here is carnival-like, with food vendors in booths selling everything from gourmet ice cream to sandwiches, hot dogs and drinks. Bridge Street, which forms a "V" with Commercial Street, will bring you back up to Townsend Avenue. Several restaurants will tempt you along this corridor, as well as Downeast Candies where you can watch taffy being made on a mechanical stretching machine.

A Silver Lining has a large display room of hand-wrought silver and gold jewelry; pieces begin at about $20, but the collection includes many fine pieces that sell for much, much more. Farther down the street you'll find beautiful handmade wreaths at Preston's. These are the same ones sold in the L.L. Bean catalog, but here you'll enjoy a much wider selection. There are plenty of great kitchen gadgets and specialty foods at The International Gourmet next door, and across the street you'll find House of Logan, which sells fine clothes for men and women (be sure to check the sales rack outside).

A few yards up the street, The Village Store is a beautiful old house that has been reconstructed to include the Children's Shop, with designer clothes for kids, as well as the main store, which sells home furnishings. Mung Beans, just a bit farther on Townsend Avenue, has a large showroom of clocks, Maine gifts, toys, pottery and T-shirts. And just across the street is Loving Hands, an artisans' gallery selling Maine-made sweaters, jewelry, toys and more.

Antiques and Flea Markets

Cabot Mill Antiques & Collectibles
Fort Andross, 14 Maine St., Brunswick • (207) 725-2855

This multi-dealer emporium has more than 140 collectors who bring their wares to this 15,000-square-foot showroom in the west tower of a restored textile mill built in 1820.

The offerings include primitive, country and fine furnishings and glassware set up in handcrafted cabinets. Dealers come from as far as Florida and New York, but 60 percent are from Maine. Cabot Mill is open year round, seven days a week, from 10 AM to 5 PM.

Day's Antiques
153 Park Row, Brunswick • (207) 725-6959

This antique store is housed in a lovely old Sea Captain's house built by the Scoffield brothers in 1819. You'll find a little bit of everything here — from the Period period (which comes before Victorian) through the Art Modern period. The shop sells American and European antiques and is across from the town park, known as the mall.

Water Front Flea Market
14 Maine St., Brunswick • (207) 729-0378

This is a treasure hunter's dream. Even if you don't find a deal that will bring you wealth, you're bound to get a good deal on something you need. Scores of dealers set up shops on the bottom floor of the old Fort Andross Mill. The inventory includes everything from garage-sale items that never sold to antiques (although you're likely to find more of the former than the latter). So bring plenty of small change and have a good time bargain hunting. You never know what you might find. The market is open weekends from 8 AM to 5 PM.

Brick Store Antiques
143 Front St., Bath • (207) 443-2790

Business partners Barbara Boyland and Polly Thibodeau run this little antique shop, which has become a favorite among locals. Inside you'll find silver, Oriental rugs and textiles as well as large and small country and period decorative pieces and furnishings. During the summer season, Polly also holds monthly antique shows in the area. Call the shop for more information.

Front Street Antiques
190 Front St., Bath
• (207) 443-8098

The oldest group shop in Bath, this store was started in 1989 and carries the collections of 14 dealers. There's a small collection of early 19th-century and 20th-century furniture, ceramics, furniture, clocks, textiles, oil paintings and prints and a large selection of new and old books. Another popular item the store stocks up on is ephemera — collectible paper — so keep all those grocery lists and memos, they might be worth something someday!

Montsweag Flea Market
Mountain Rd., Woolwich • (207) 443-2809

When Norma Scopino found herself unemployed in 1977, she decided to do something about it and turned her front lawn into a flea market. It took six years to get established,

but now the business thrives with 85 to 100 antiques dealers renting tables. Open May through October on Wednesday, Friday, Saturday and Sunday, dealers set up tables at 6:30 AM and close up at 3 PM.

You'll see plenty of antiques — Wednesday is set aside strictly for antiques and collectibles — and also some crafts and knick-knacks. There are snack and ice cream bars; the atmosphere is festive. You can often find better prices on antiques at a flea market such as Montsweag. In fact, this is where many antique shop owners come to stock their stores. U.S. Highway 1 will get you here. If you're driving north, you'll see the market on your left in a dip below the highway. It's directly on the corner of Mountain Road, but watch carefully for traffic — it's a blind intersection known for accidents.

Portside Antiques
106 Main St., Wiscasset • (207) 882-6506

One of the more formal antique stores in Wiscasset, this shop (open since 1991) sells 18th- and 19th-century high country and formal furniture of both American and English design, as well as sterling silver. Owner Skip O'Rourke keeps the shop open during the summer season, and by appointment when the thermometer starts to drop.

The Marston House American Antiques
Main St., Wiscasset
• (207) 882-6010

On the corner of Maine and Middle streets, this shop specializes in English gardening tools and accessories and early homespun linens and textiles. It also has a large selection of painted furniture. Ten years ago Sharon and Paul Mrozinski bought the old Marston house, which belonged to a local ice cream shop and pharmacy owner, and turned it into a home for their collection of antiques. They also established a small bed and breakfast inn, with two rooms in the carriage house out back. The building itself dates back to 1785.

J. Partridge Antiques
17 Dodge Rd., Edgecomb
• (207) 882-7745

For fine 18th-century English and American furniture, try the two galleries set up at this business at the intersection of Route 1 and Dodge Road. You'll admire the sophisticated sets of dining chairs, highboys and chests of drawers in mahogany, walnut and satinwood. J. Partridge also houses an exquisite collection of paintings and fine prints from the 17th, 18th and 19th centuries. What you won't find are country antiques or collectibles. The galleries are open May through October and other times by appointment. The shops have operated since 1950, when Mr. Partridge opened the business. His wife, Tatiana Partridge, now oversees the collection.

Somewhere in Time Antiques
91 Townsend Ave., Boothbay Harbor
• (207) 633-5980

This store, near the end of Boothbay Harbor's shopping district, features a large selection of sterling silver, jewelry, cut glass, lace doilies, crystal, porcelain and many fine collectibles. The 4,000-square-foot shop has been in business since 1986.

Pallabra Shops
85 Commercial St., Boothbay Harbor
• (207) 633-4225

If you're a fan of Poland Springs bottled water, come to this family-owned antique shop. It boasts the world's largest collection of Moses bottles (the glass bottles first used by the Poland Springs bottling company). Pal Vincent, who started the business in 1962, began collecting the bottles (which date back to 1876) in 1930 when she was just 13. At last count she had more than 4,000! Her daughter, Valerie Vincent, now manages the store and watches over the bottles, which come in 43 varieties and sell for anywhere from $15 to several thousand dollars each.

The shop also specializes in "antique smalls" — art glass, china, sterling, jewelry, dolls, collectibles and small-sized primitive and nautical antiques. It doesn't deal much in furniture, but it does have a large collection of duck and fish decoys. The bottle collection is out front, and there are six rooms of antiques in back. Pallabra Shops is open March through mid-December, and in the winter by appointment.

Arts, Crafts and Jewelry

Wyler Gallery
150 Maine St., Brunswick
- **(207) 729-1321**

What started out as a wholesale pottery business is now an upscale American craft store that carries not only its own lines of pottery and tile but also an eclectic collection of picture frames, home furnishings, clothing and textiles. Husband and wife John Faulkner and Sylvia Wyler both help make the pottery and run the business. Their works are characterized by organic, abstract designs highlighted by color on a dark background. Their high-end tiles are distributed in New Jersey to roughly 100 galleries across the country.

Stone Soup Artisans
102 Maine St., Brunswick
- **(207) 798-5841**

Take time to gift shop for yourself or someone else at this crafters' cooperative that carries quilted wall hangings, handmade wooden toys, dolls, stained glass, jewelry, tote bags, clothing and much more. It's a colorful collection of nicely made crafts to fit all styles.

Timeless Treasures Antiques and Collectibles
104 Front St., Bath
- **(207) 442-0377**

Owner Carol Grose sells fine jewelry, oil paintings, glass and pottery made by local crafters at this exquisite two-floor shop in Bath's historic downtown. In addition, you'll notice a small collection of antiques and fine wooden furniture made by Grose's husband, Karl Grose.

Yankee Artisan
56 Front St., Bath • (207) 443-6215

This cooperative of more than 35 crafters has been around for better than two decades delighting tourists and locals with a wide selection of locally made items. The shop offers everything from clocks to quilted wall hangings, pottery, jewelry, paintings, knitwear, carvings, stained glass and more. All those participating in the co-op are selected by a jury of crafters on the store's board of directors.

Halcyon Yarn
12 School St., Bath
- **(207) 442-7909, (800) 341-0282**

Maine's largest source for natural yarns and fibers, this downtown store is a knitter's or spinner's dream. You'll love the linen, wool, silk, rayon and other fibers, some of which are dyed and loomed exclusively for the shop. There are also rug punching, loom and spinning wheel supplies and accessories and more than 900 book titles. A variety of nearly 50 yarns and 100 spinning fibers are available through the store or by mail order. Classes are also offered.

The Center of Native Art
U.S. Hwy. 1, Woolwich • (207) 442-8399

You'll see authentic Native American jewelry, blankets, drums and flutes at this log-style building on the north side of Route 1. Some of the arts and jewelry, such as the real bear and wolf claw necklaces, are from Maine. Other pieces are from Arizona and New Mexico. The center also carries a large selection of tapes and CDs. It stands alone along this stretch of highway; the good-sized teepee out front makes it hard to miss.

Georgetown Pottery
U.S. Hwy. 127, Georgetown
- **(207) 371-2801**

For 26 years a handful of throwers, glazers and trimmers have turned out some of the finest pottery on the coast here, featuring high-fired porcelain pieces with hand-decorated brush work portraying Maine and nautical themes. The pottery is made and sold on site in a wooden lodge nestled against a Maine pine forest. To get here, take Maine Highway 127 east roughly 9 miles off U.S. Highway 1. The studio, with a large deck out front, is on the left.

Sheepscot River Pottery
U.S. Hwy. 1, Edgecomb
- **(207) 882-9410**

The china clay pottery made here resembles porcelain. It's made on site and hand-painted with designs reflecting the Maine outdoors: lupine, ladyslippers, birds, iris, Maine islands, herons. You'll find a variety of kitchen and dining pieces as well as candlesticks, tiles,

Kennebunkport is filled with lovely boutiques.

mugs and lamps. The shop, clearly visible from the highway just past Wiscasset, also carries a charming selection of jewelry, fountains, candles, toy trains and stuffed animals. It's open daily 9 AM to 6 PM Monday through Sunday during the summer. Hours are cut back during the off-season.

Edgecomb Potters
Maine Hwy. 27, Edgecomb
• (207) 882-9493
8 School St., Portland
• (207) 865-1705
10 McKown St., Boothbay Harbor
• (207) 633-4199

What began in 1976 as a small pottery studio in a one-room schoolhouse has become the state's largest American craft gallery with a modern two-story showroom, a large outside deck and, of course, the schoolhouse, which shelters the potters' finest works (you'll find cookie jars there for $150). The schoolhouse also has handcrafted stained-glass lamps starting at about $400, as well as many other fine pottery and stained-glass pieces.

The outdoor deck is where you'll see the most deals, with seconds selling for 50 to 70 percent off. It's punctuated with sometimes humorous, sometimes dramatic iron sculptures. Inside the main building, all sorts of art,

including Edgecomb Potters pottery (which is nationally acclaimed for its vibrant colors), Frank Lloyd Wright reproduction lamps, gold and silver jewelry and hand-blown glass await.

Basket Barn of Maine
Maine Hwy. 27, Boothbay • (207) 633-5532

Browse through thousands of baskets in this barn-style gallery showcasing domestic, Native American and imported work. Open since 1972, the shop has the largest basket collection in the state as well as a large sampling of basket weaving supplies, doll houses and miniatures. It's open all year; you'll find in on the left when heading east on Maine Highway 27.

andersen studio
1 Andersen Rd., E. Boothbay
• (207) 633-4397, (800) 640-4397

This family business has created stoneware sculptures, bowls and vases for more than 40 years. All the work, both decorative and functional pieces, is made in the small studio where it is also sold. The Andersen family sells its work to galleries across the country. Prices range from $20 to $400, and just after the summer season is a good time to shop for seconds. To get here, take Highway 27 to Maine Highway 96 east. Andersen Road is 2.5 miles away.

Specialty Food Stores

Morning Glory Natural Foods
64 Maine St., Brunswick
• (207) 729-0546

This shop fills two storefronts with a wide selection of health foods, vitamins and homeopathic remedies. Grab some paper bags and fill them with your choice of grains, beans or flours, or choose from a variety of natural granola mixes. You'll also find an organic produce section and a frozen-food section. Owned by Susan Tartinian, this store has operated for 16 years here. In nearby Bath, a second store by the same name at 36 Centre Street, 442-8012, is under the same ownership and carries a similar line of products.

Gilmore's Sea Foods
129 Court St., Bath
• (207) 443-5231

Established in 1958, this family-owned business sells fresh seafood — lobster, clams, shrimp and the daily catch of fish — to the public at near wholesale prices. It's open seven days a week from 7 AM to 6 PM and offers next-day air delivery anywhere in the United States.

Treats
Main St., Wiscasset • (207) 882-6192

This shop traditionally specialized in wines and cheeses, but Treats has just added a whole line of goods baked in its own kitchen. You'll want to devour the delicious pies, breads and scones. Just make sure to buy some jam to go along with them!

Boothbay Region Lobstermen's Co-op
Atlantic Ave., Boothbay Harbor
• (207) 633-4900

This working lobster pound on a dock overlooking the harbor is owned and operated by local fishermen. You can grab some lobsters and clams to go (or have them shipped anywhere by next-day air), or you can sit at a picnic table on the deck and have a feast cooked for you.

Farmers' Markets

Brunswick Farmers Market
Town Mall, Maine St., Brunswick

May through December, rain or shine, you can buy fresh produce, meats, crafts, plants and herbs at this outdoor market. About 19 local businesses bring their wares to the grassy mall in the middle of Brunswick's Maine Street on Tuesdays and Fridays from 8 AM to 3 PM. On Saturday, the market moves to the Cook's Corner Mall off Maine Highway 24 and is open during the same hours. The farmers' market, which was started to promote local agriculture, has been operating since 1977.

Bath Farmers' Market
Fleet Bank parking lot, Front St., Bath

From Memorial Day to the end of October, you'll enjoy a large selection of flowers and local produce at this outdoor market right on Commercial Street right next to the waterfront park. The market runs from 9 AM to 2 PM, and has a plethora of local produce — everything from hand-woven baskets and fresh picked flowers to organic fruits and veggies.

Bookstores

Bookland
Cook's Corner Mall, Maine Hwy. 24,
Brunswick • (207) 725-2313

Although this large chain has retail shops in other areas along Maine's Southern Coast that have already been mentioned, this bookstore is worth breaking out. You'll find more than a million books on hand, with antique sofas and side tables scattered throughout the store to help you enjoy them. At the back of the store is a cafe that serves up tasty meals, coffee and tea and scrumptious desserts.

Gulf of Maine
134 Maine St., Brunswick • (207) 729-5083

Poetry, books about the environment and books written by women are the specialties at this downtown store. You'll also find many regional and Native American titles, in addition to a modest collection of general literature.

Maine Writers and Publishers Alliance
12 Pleasant St., Brunswick
• **(207) 729-6333**

This bookstore and writers guild carries all Maine-related titles — books either printed by Maine publishers, written by Maine authors or about Maine. It has 1,800-plus titles, many of which are hard-to-find books printed by small presses. Examples include Carrying Water as a Way of Life, a homesteader's history by Linda Tateleaum, and Maine Speaks, an anthology by Maine writers that's in its fifth printing and is used in more than 100 schools and colleges around the state.

We have historical museums and houses, amusement parks, microbreweries and lighthouses as well as miniature golf courses and a multitude of boat excursions.

Attractions

Get out your walking shoes, bug spray, sunscreen and sweatshirts: There's lots to do in Maine, and you'd better be prepared! If your idea of a great vacation is having different kinds of things to do each day and not just lying on a beach, this is the chapter for you. (For all you beach bunnies out there, see our chapter on Beaches.)

Maine is known for its natural attractions: crashing surf; miles of soft, white, sandy beaches; towering pines; rivers, lakes and streams; moose, deer and sea birds. What you might not know is that there are a lot of other things to do here — stuff that's not so closely tied to the natural world. We have historical museums and historic houses, amusement parks, micro-breweries and lighthouses as well as miniature golf courses and a multitude of boat excursions.

In this chapter we've grouped attractions by our four major geographic areas, then subdivided them into categories and arranged them by town from south to north. You'll find Amusement Parks, Breweries, Cruises, Islands, Lighthouses and Historic Houses and Forts in this chapter. You won't find parks here — they have their own chapter — but we have included some nature preserves, walks and other items of interest under Odds & Ends. So go ahead, read through it. We bet there are at least a couple of things here that will get you on your feet and on your way!

Southern Beaches Area

Amusement Parks

York's Wild Kingdom
U.S. Hwy. 1, York Beach
• **(207) 363-4911, (207) 363-3025**
Entertain yourself with a visit to this friendly zoo. Elephants, tigers, kangaroos and more will

charm you as you wander through the park. Kids will also enjoy the amusement rides like the Ferris wheel and carousel located near the entrance to the park. Ticket prices for the zoo and amusements in 1998 were $12.75 for adults and teens, $9.50 for children ages 4 through 10 and $3.50 for children ages 3 or younger. (See our Kidstuff chapter for more information.)

Breweries

Kennebunkport Brewing Company and Federal Jack's Brew Pub
8 Western Ave., Kennebunkport
• **(207) 967-4311**
Though only six years old, this small brewery is growing by leaps and bounds. It may be because their ales are made from only the best natural ingredients: malted barley and yeast from England; fresh, flowering hops from Washington state; and pure spring water from Maine. Famous for its signature brand, Shipyard Export Ale, the brewery also produces Old Thumper Extra Special Ale (under a separate license), Goat Island Light Ale, Shipyard Brown Ale and Chamberlain Pale Ale. You'll also find seasonal ales like Sirius Summer Wheat and Longfellow Winter Ale as well as root beer.

The schooner featured on the labels of many of the ales is a depiction of one of the four masted ships that were built at the shipyard where the brewery and brewpub stand today. The schooner's name was Federal Jack, and it's from this that the founders of the company, Fred Forsley and Alan Pugsley, took the name for their brewpub. The Kennebunkport brewery is the original producer of Shipyard ales but doesn't do the bottling. All beer brewed here is for use at Federal Jack's, located upstairs.

The company's two other facilities, operated under the Shipyard Brewing Company name, are in Portland, Maine, and Orlando, Florida. It's at these facilities that the various brands are bottled, put into kegs and distributed throughout the Eastern Seaboard and as far west as Chicago. Shipyard ales are also shipped to England and Germany. During a tour of the Kennebunkport facility you'll learn about the brewery, the brewing process and where they find the ingredients they use. Tours are free and are offered every hour on the hour from 4 to 7 PM on Fridays and 1 to 6 PM on Saturdays.

Historic Houses and Forts

Strawbery Banke Museum
Marcy St., Portsmouth, N.H.
• **(603) 433-1100**

Follow the timeline from the 1600s to the present day at this fascinating museum. Nine furnished houses illustrate the various eras of American history that have passed since settlers came to the banks of the Piscataqua River in 1630. The river is noteworthy for separating Maine and New Hampshire. On its north bank is Kittery; on the south side is Portsmouth. Originally called Strawbery Banke for the wild berries that grew along the banks of the river, the town changed its name to Portsmouth in 1653. The museum got its start in 1958 when the old Puddle Dock neighborhood was saved from destruction to be restored as Strawbery Banke.

You can trace the history of Portsmouth from its beginning to its involvement in the Revolutionary War, then on to the prosperous 1800s and through Strawbery Banke's change into a poor neighborhood where the city's immigrant and working class families lived at the turn of the century. The 20th century is represented by Abbott's Little Corner Store, which has been restored to its 1943 wartime appearance.

The museum is open daily from May to October, during the third weekend in November (Thanksgiving weekend) and for the first two weekends in December for candlelight strolls. Admission in 1998 was $10 for adults, $7 for children ages 7 to 17, $25 for families and free for children 6 or younger. All tickets are good for two consecutive days. For groups

of 10 or more, the price drops to $7 for adults and $4 for children.

Fort Foster
Off Maine Hwy. 103, Kittery
• **(207) 439-3800**

Keep an eye out for the Lady in Red at this fort: Legend has it that a woman dressed in red haunts its waterfront. Apparently, during the Civil War a woman used to stand watch for her husband or lover to come back from the war. He never did, and today some say you can see the lady's ghost moving along the pilings to the left of the pier where a second pier once stood.

To get to Fort Foster, travel north past Fort McClary on Route 103. Take the first right after the Sunoco station, then the first right again. Half a mile along take a right onto Pocahantas Road, continue over a bridge, then take a right into the fort grounds. Cost for admission in 1998 was $2.50 per car, plus $2 per adult and teen and $1 for children 12 or younger. You'll find a bunker-type fort (erected in 1872), a pier, swimming and picnic areas and nature trails to entertain you.

Fort McClary State Park
Maine Hwy. 103, Kittery
• **(207) 384-5160**

Now named for Andrew McClary, a Revolutionary War hero who lost his life at the Battle of Bunker Hill, this fort was originally called Fort Williams and was a major defense post during that war. The first buildings on the site are estimated to have been built in the late 1600s to early 1700s. In 1808, additions were made to the fort, and it was completely rebuilt between 1844 and 1846. The hexagonal blockhouse you can visit today was the last blockhouse built in Maine. It's a nice place for kids to explore and run around. There is a $1 per person entrance fee.

Sarah Orne Jewett House
101 Portland St. (Maine Hwy. 236),
South Berwick • (207) 384-2454

Sarah Orne Jewett's (1849-1909) beautifully written, realistic portrayals of Maine in books such as The Country of the Pointed Firs, published in 1896, have made her famous not only within the state, but also throughout America and abroad. Her white clapboard home was built in 1774, and the furnishings you see inside date to that time. Admission is about $3 per person, but discounts are available for local residents and children. The home is open May through October.

Old York Historical Society Houses
Lindsay Rd. and U.S. Hwy. 1, York Village
• (207) 363-4974

Seven historic buildings make up the Old York Historical Society Museum. These include the Emerson-Wilcox House, Old Gaol Museum, Jefferds Tavern, the George Marshall Store Gallery and a one-room schoolhouse. The tavern was built by Capt. Samuel Jefferd in the 1750s and is used as the visitor center for the museum today. You'll also occasionally find hearth-cooking demonstrations here.

The Emerson-Wilcox House has an interesting history. It served as a general store, tailor shop, tavern and post office and also housed two of the town's prominent families. As part of the museum, the house now contains a series of rooms furnished in period style from 1750 to 1850. John Hancock, whose famous signature is penned to the Declaration of Independence, once owned the John Hancock Warehouse, which was used as a customs house for York.

Youngsters will delight in the chilly past of the Old Gaol Museum. Watch their faces as they view the dungeons, cells, jailer's quarters and the exhibit of instruments of torture. The jail was built in 1719 as the King's prison for what was known as the Province of Maine. It is the oldest existing English public building in the United States. The museum is open from mid-June through September but closed on Mondays. Ticket prices in 1998 (good for all of the society buildings) were $6 for adults and $2.50 for children ages 6 to 16. Children younger than 6 are admitted free. Parking is available adjacent to Jefferds Tavern.

Sayward-Wheeler House
79 Barrell Lane Ext., York Harbor
• (207) 436-3205

One of 33 properties owned and operated by the Society for the Preservation of New England Antiquities (SPNEA), this white, 18th-century wood-frame house was once the

See What's Historic About Portland!

Tate House
Built in 1755 in Historic Stroudwater

Home of Main Mast Agent, Capt. George Tate
1270 Westbrook St., P.O. Box 880, Portland, ME
Telephone (207) 774-9781
Open June-October, Tues.-Sat. 10-4, Sun. 1-4

Wadsworth-Longfellow House

Childhood home of poet Henry Wadsworth Longfellow, built 1786
1489 Congress Street, Portland, ME 04101
Open June-October, Daily 10-4
(207) 897-0427 www.mainehistory.com

Victoria Mansion

109 Danforth St., Portland, ME 04101
A magnificent Victorian Mansion built 1858-60 with original furnishings. Visit the Museum Shop!
portlandarts.com/victoriamansion
Open May to October, Tues.-Sat 10-4, Sun. 1-5
Group tours by arrangement (207) 772-4841

home of Jonathan Sayward. Sayward was a merchant and politician known for trading in the West Indies. His home reflected his prosperity. You'll find the house on the banks of the York River just a half-mile from the ocean in York Harbor.

Inside, you'll see pre-Revolutionary furnishings and decorative arts, including Chinese export Imari wares brought back by Sayward from the conquest of the French fortress of Louisburg in Nova Scotia in 1745. The property is open on Saturdays and Sundays from the beginning of June to mid-October. Entrance fees in 1998 were $4 for adults and teens, $3.50 for senior citizens and $2 for children ages 12 or younger.

Meetinghouse Museum
U.S. Hwy. 1 S. and Buzzel Rd., Wells
• (207) 646-4775

Operated by the Historical Society of Wells and Ogunquit, this museum explores how the tradition of religious freedom was born. There's a nautical room that displays photos and artifacts relating to shipbuilding, a room of furnishings from the Littlefield family and special events. A National Registered Landmark, the Meetinghouse, which was once a church, has a large auditorium where educational and cultural events are still held. Upstairs you can view a variety of displays including quilts, stencils and other artifacts detailing 350 years of history. The Meetinghouse is open Thursdays all year and also on Tuesdays and Wednesdays from June 1 to November, but it's a good idea to call ahead and check on opening hours.

Willowbrook at Newfield Restoration Village
Off Maine Hwy. 11, Newfield
• (207) 793-2784

Though a bit off the beaten track, we thought this might interest some of you. It's a restored 19th-century village consisting of 27 buildings. You'll enjoy learning about life in the 1800s while walking the beautiful grounds, complete with a mill pond. A carpenter's shop, the unmarried maidens' room and vehicles of the younger set, as well as a saw house and print shop, are just some of the exhibits to explore. From May 15 to September 30, the museum is open daily. Cost for admission in 1998 was $7 for adults and $3.50 for children ages 6 to 18. Children younger than 6 are admitted free.

Newfield is about 45 minutes from the Kennebunks. To get to Willowbrook from the Southern Beaches area, take Maine Highway 109 west from Exit 2 of the Maine Turnpike. You'll pass through Sanford and Springvale. At Emery Mills take Maine Highway 11, which branches off to the right. You'll pass through Shapleigh and North Shapleigh, then intersect with Maine Highway 110. Stay on Route 11, bearing right, and you'll reach Newfield.

Cruises and Charters

Apollo Charters
Town Dock No. 2, Harris Island Rd. off Maine Hwy. 103, York Harbor
• (207) 351-1961

Feel the wind in your hair as you enjoy one of two sailing trips offered by Apollo Charters. On Monday, Wednesday and Friday from July through mid-September, you can take a two-hour sailing trip. Departure times in 1998 were 10:30 AM and 1:30 PM; cost for the trip was $28 per person. Alternately, you can choose a Sail & Seal tour that takes place on Tuesdays and Thursdays beginning at 9:30 AM. This three-hour trip in search of seal sightings is offered from July to mid-October and costs $35 per person. There is a six-person maximum on all sailing trips. Reservations with deposits are recommended though walk-ons will be accommodated if space is available. All trips depart from York Town Dock No. 2 on Harris Island Road, off Route 103.

Lobstering Trips on The Boat
Town Dock No. 2, Harris Island Rd. off Maine Hwy. 103, York Harbor
• (207) 363-3234

If you've ever wondered how Maine lobsters are caught, this is your chance for a close-up view. You'll cruise along the mouth of York Harbor in a 25-foot solid fiberglass lobster skiff, standing within 10 feet of the action at all times. Learn about lobstering and lobsters while seeing traps hauled and lobsters caught. Capt. Tom Farnon is a Coast Guard-licensed Master of Near Coastal to 200 Miles Off Shore and has been lobstering for more than 25 years. Note that there are no facilities on board The Boat. Trips last approximately 50 minutes, and there are hourly departures from 10 AM to 2 PM Monday through Friday. Cost for the ride is $7.50 per person for 1999. There is a six-person maximum per trip, and private charters are available.

Finestkind Scenic Cruises
Perkins Cove, Ogunquit • (207) 646-5227
A variety of cruises are offered by Finestkind. You can take a scenic breakfast cruise, complete with hot coffee and a freshly baked muffin, to the Island Ledges, which are popular with harbor seals. You can also take a 14-mile round-trip cruise to Nubble Light, a cocktail cruise or even a lobstering trip. Prices in 1998 ranged from $8 for the lobstering trip to $13 for the Nubble Lighthouse cruise for adults and $6 to $9 for children ages 4 to 11. Finestkind Cruises begin operating weekends from the end of April through the end of May, then daily from June to mid-October.

The Cricket
Perkins Cove, Ogunquit
• (207) 646-5227
Tired of motor-driven boats? Take a ride on a sailboat! The Cricket is a locally built wooden boat designed more than a century ago. Captain Grant Hubbard, a Perkins Cove native, will sail you along the beautiful coastal waters of Ogunquit. Four cruises are offered daily. Each lasts 1½ hours and departs from the Finestkind dock at Barnacle Billy's restaurant in Perkins Cove. There's a six-passenger maximum per trip, and reservations are recommended. Cost to sail in 1998 was $17.50 per person. The Cricket begins operat-

ing weekends at the end of April through May. From June to mid-October, it operates daily.

The Indian
Ocean Ave.,Kennebunkport
• (207) 967-5912
Your whale watching trip aboard The Indian is led and narrated by an experienced whale researcher. With your participation, data is collected for the Cetacean Research Unit. Some of the whales you might see include finback, humpback, and minke. Other sightings include rare right whales, Sei whales, harbor porpoise, sunfish, sharks and seals.

The boat is a 75-foot Coast Guard inspected passenger vehicle that includes a galley for hot and cold food and drink. Captain Dick Brindle has more than 40 years experience in the passenger vessel service and strives to provide a fun, memorable experience. Cost for tickets in 1998 was $30.

Nautilus
Western Ave., Lower Village (at the bridge), Kennebunkport
• (207) 967-0707
You can't help being excited by the sight of a whale, and the Nautilus can help you see one — or more. While the crew can't guarantee sightings of any particular type of whale, they claim to have a 99 percent sighting record since 1986. The ship offers upper- and lower-deck viewing and sells refreshments. Four-hour trips depart daily at 10 AM and 4 PM. Reservations are strongly recommended. Cost in 1998 was $30 for adults and teens and $15 for children ages 3 through 12. Between the end of May and the Fourth of July and between September 1 and the middle of October, adult prices drop to $25.

Second Chance Inc.
4-A Western Ave., Lower Village
(at the bridge), Kennebunkport
• (207) 967-5507, (800) 767-2628
Take a scenic lobster cruise aboard the Second Chance or head out to sea on a whale-

watch expedition aboard the First Chance. Lobster cruises are 1½ hours long and depart every other hour from 11 AM until 5 PM. Price per person in 1998 was $15 for adults and teens and $6 for children ages 3 to 12. Whale Watch trips will take you out to Jeffrey's Ledge, a feeding area approximately 20 miles from shore. Among the several species of whale that frequent the ledge and might be seen are finbacks, humpbacks, right and pilot whales. You might also see minke whales, white-sided dolphins and harbor porpoises.

Whale Watch expeditions on the First Chance are narrated by naturalists from the Maine Whale Study. Your trip is guaranteed: If for some reason you don't see any whales on your trip, you'll receive a free ticket for a future trip. Cash refunds are not given once the trip is under way. Whale Watch trips are offered twice daily, at 10 AM and 4 PM, and last approximately four hours. Reservations are recommended. Cost for the trips in 1998 was $30 for adults and teens and $15 for children ages 3 through 12. Both the First Chance and Second Chance operate from Memorial Day (end of May) to Columbus Day (mid-October).

Islands

The Isles of Shoals

Part of the Isles of Shoals belong to New Hampshire and part belong to Maine. Duck, Appledore, Smuttynose, Malaga and Cedar islands are Maine's, while Lunging, White, Seavey and Star are New Hampshire's. During the summer Appledore and Star are accessible to visitors, but the others are uninhabited or privately owned. None of the islands have public boat landings.

The largest of the islands, Appledore, was settled shortly after John Smith's visit of 1614. It became a thriving fishing village after the American Revolution and exported a great deal of fish to the West Indies. In the mid-1800s a hotel was built on the island by Thomas Laighton, father of New Hampshire poet Celia Thaxter. The hotel became a popular vacation destination for such literary figures as Nathaniel Hawthorne and John Greenleaf Whittier.

Star Island has a history of contrasts. In the 1600s the island was linked to religious activities, but later fell into a period of decadence around the time of the Revolutionary War. You will hear stories about pirates like Bluebeard frequenting Star Island and the Isles of Shoals, and of buried treasure. To date, the only treasure that has been found was four bars of silver discovered in the early 1800s. Since 1916 the island has been owned by the Unitarian Church, which uses it as a convention center for its own and other religious groups.

You can get to Star Island through the Isles of Shoals Steamship Company, 315 Market Street, Portsmouth, New Hampshire, (603) 431-5500. They offer various cruises that view or stop at the island. Appledore Island is operated by the Shoals Marine Laboratory of Cornell University. The Isles of Shoals Steamship Company travels to the island, but you must have advance reservations made through Cornell University, SML, G-14 Stimpson Hall, Ithaca, New York, (607) 255-3717.

Lighthouses

Cape Neddick Lighthouse
Nubble Rd., (off U.S. Hwy. 1A), York

Popularly known as the Nubble or Nubble Light because it sits on a "nubble" at the end of a rocky promontory, this lighthouse was built in 1879. Located on an island, separated from shore by just a narrow channel, the Nubble is one of the most photographed and well-known lighthouses on the Eastern Seaboard. Its red-roofed white buildings and the little red oil house make a pretty grouping that's well-loved by locals and tourists alike. In fact, when the Coast Guard once painted the oil house white to match the other buildings, they received so many calls of complaint that they repainted it red!

Until 1987 Nubble Light was maintained as a family light. Generations of families and children lived there from the time it was built until the time it was automated. To attend school, children would often be carried piggyback across to the mainland at low tide by their fathers wearing hip boots; they were ferried across in a dory at high tide. If you're interested in learning more about life at a family light, pick up Lucy Glidden Burke's ac-

Using the Ol' Bean:
From Boot Idea to Freeport Phenomenon

Anyone who's hiked with wet feet knows it's annoying, if not downright painful - water sloshing around your feet, blisters forming on your soles. Leon Leonwood Bean knew this too. But in 1912 all the outdoorsman could find were leather boots, which sucked up water like a thirsty moose. So Leon set out to make his own, combining lightweight leather tops with waterproof rubber bottoms.

The resulting boots worked so well, he took out an ad and sold 100 "guaranteed" pairs through the mail. Ninety were sent back. The stitching had given way, but true to his word, Leon refunded his customers' money and started on an improved boot. You've probably seen some like it. Or maybe you have a pair sitting in your closet. Today Leon Leonwood Bean's boots are sold all over the world under the name L.L. Bean.

You can find many varieties of these most-loved "Bean boots" in Freeport's colossal retail store that still bears Bean's name. Bean boot likenesses come in the form of chocolate. They come as Christmas tree ornaments. They come on keychains. You can even find them as doorstops. You can find some of these spinoffs at L.L. Bean, but that's not all you'll find there. Not by a long shot.

As Bean's boots became more and more popular, he expanded his line of merchandise to other outdoor products, and in 1917 Bean opened a little showroom next to his Freeport workshop. Today that store is one of the most popular tourist destinations in the state, ranking right behind Acadia National Park several hours to the north. More than 3.5 million people visit the store each year.

To give you some idea how big a deal it is, the store doesn't have a street number . . . it has its own zip code! L.L. Bean distributes 115 million mail order catalogs every year. Telephone orders account for 80 percent of the company's business, and on its busiest week in 1996 it received more than a million calls. More than 16,000 different items are kept in stock at any given time, and of those more than 90 percent carry the L.L. Bean label. Wow.

The retail store on Freeport's Main Street - with four floors of clothing, sporting equipment, a stocked trout pond (no fishing!) and souvenirs - has been open 24 hours a day, 365 days a year since 1951. The decision to "throw away the keys," as Bean put

Photo: L.L. Bean

L.L. Bean's main retail store is on Main Street in Freeport. Today, the 90,000-square-foot store sits on the site of Leon Leonwood's original store.

— continued on next page

it, was made to accommodate sporting types who'd appear at the store at any hour of the day or night en route to their favorite fishing hole or hunting ground.

When Bean died in 1967 at the age of 94, his grandson, Leon Gorman, became president of the company. Through aggressive marketing, he has built L.L. Bean into one of the world's leading international mail order businesses. Like his grandfather, Gorman is an outdoor enthusiast who tests the company's products on outdoor trips such as his 1990 ascent to the base camp of Mt. Everest. He has also climbed Mt. Rainier and Mt. Kilimanjaro.

At the retail store, you'll find everything from outdoor men's and women's clothing to the latest camping and backpacking equipment, bicycles, kayaks, cross-country skis and fitness gear. The recently completed L.L. Kids retail store, just behind the main store, carries children's clothing and outdoor gear. Here you will also find interactive exhibits where kids can flex some muscle while you shop (see more in the Outlet Shopping sections of our Shopping chapter). And, for bargain hunters, the company has 12 factory stores selling seconds at reduced prices. They're located in Maine, New Hampshire, Delaware, Oregon and even Japan!

counts written in 1919. She was the daughter of one of the keepers of Nubble Light.

The Cape Neddick Lighthouse has a red beacon, which flashes every six seconds and is visible for 13 miles. The tower is 88 feet tall from mean high water and 41 feet tall from the ground to the beacon. While you can't visit the island where Nubble Light stands, you can see it very well from the rocks on either side of the Sohier Park parking area. To view Nubble Light from the sea, take a cruise offered by Finestkind Cruises in Ogunquit (see the previous Cruises section). You can also see the Nubble outlined in white lights if you visit the area in December. Special lighting ceremonies usually take place at the beginning of that month.

Museums

Kittery Historical and Naval Museum
Intersection of U.S. Hwy. 1 and Maine Hwy. 236, Rogers Rd., Kittery
• (207) 439-3080

You can trace the history of naval shipbuilding from the American Revolution to the present at this museum founded in 1975. The museum features a 10-foot replica of the USS Ranger, on which John Paul Jones sailed when he received the first foreign salute to a ship bearing the American flag. Opening days

and times vary by season, so call to find out when the best time is for you to visit. Admission is free.

Portsmouth Naval Shipyard Museum
Naval Shipyard base, off Maine Hwy. 103, Kittery • (207) 438-2320

The United States' first shipyard, the Portsmouth Naval Shipyard, was established in Kittery in the late 1700s. In 1777 the USS Ranger — famous as the first man-of-war flying the American flag to receive a foreign salute — was built and launched. Many other Civil War ships, including the USS Raleigh, were built here, as was the country's first submarine, the L8, which was launched in 1917. In the Command Museum you can view exhibits detailing the history of the shipyard. Visits to this museum are arranged by appointment only. At the time of writing, there was no charge for admission.

Wells Auto Museum
U.S. Hwy. 1 N., Wells
• (207) 646-9064

Car enthusiasts, get ready to have a good time! You'll find 45 makes of automobile on display at this museum, including models by Stanley, Rolls-Royce, Pierce Arrow, Chrysler, Ford, Stutz, Baker Electric and Avanti. A parade of technological progress, from steam to gas and electric, is displayed. In addition, you'll find a large collection of operating nickelodeons, picture machines, Orchestrions and Regina Hexaphones to entertain you.

The museum was founded in 1950, but its inception began four years earlier, when Glen C. Gould Jr. was given a Stanley Steamer found in an uncle's barn cellar in Vermont. From a one-car hobby, it soon grew. Today the museum has more than 70 antique automobiles (as well as motorcycles and bicycles) on display. It's a nonprofit organization — memberships are welcome and volunteers always needed.

The Wells Auto Museum is open daily from mid-June to mid-September and weekends from mid-September to mid-October and mid-May to mid-June. Admission in 1998 was $4 for adults and teens and $2 for children ages 6 through 12. There is no admission charge for children younger than 6.

Brick Store Museum
117 Main St., Kennebunk
• (207) 985-4802

Founded in 1936 by Edith Cleaves Barry, the Brick Store Museum was originally housed on the second floor of William Lord's store, built in 1825. Today the museum has expanded to incorporate the Brick Store and three adjacent 19th-century buildings. All four buildings are part of Kennebunk's National Register District.

While the museum focuses on the maritime history of the area, it also carries excellent displays on its social history and the local history of fine and decorative arts. Permanent exhibits include the William Lord Gallery, which houses Federal period furniture and accessories. You'll also find exhibits on local authors and artists like Booth Tarkington. In addition to the Brick Store Museum complex, the museum includes the Taylor-Barry House, home of the museum's founder. This elegant shipmaster's home at 24 Summer Street dates to 1803. Four period-furnished

rooms and a turn-of-the-century artist's studio can be seen here as well as the home's original hallway stenciling. Those interested in architecture should consider taking one of the Brick Store Museum's architectural walking tours, offered Wednesday at 10 AM and Friday at 1 PM.

Cost for admission to the museum in 1998 was $3 for adults and teens, with children younger than 12 admitted free. The architectural walking tours were also $3, but you can buy a combination ticket for $5. The museum is open year round from Tuesday through Friday. From April 15 to December 15 it's also open on Saturday.

Seashore Trolley Museum
Log Cabin Rd., Kennebunkport
• (207) 967-2800

If you like the ding-ding-ding sound of trolley bells and still thrill to riding these old-style cars, you must visit this museum. You can take a ride on an authentic electric trolley, visit car barns housing 40 trolleys and watch artisans in the restoration barn. Entrance fees (including unlimited rides) in 1998 were $7 for adults, $4.50 for children ages 6 to 16 and $5 for senior citizens. Children younger than 6 are admitted free. The museum is open daily from May to the second weekend in October. From the second weekend in October to the second week of November, it's open on weekends and by chance or appointment on weekdays, weather permitting. (See our Kidstuff chapter for more information.)

Odds & Ends

Ghostly Tours
250 York St., U.S. Hwy. 1A, York Village
• (207) 363-0000

Why not do something a little bit different after dinner and join one of these candlelit walking tours through historic York Village? A hooded guide will escort you through the village while recounting ghost stories, witch tales and folklore of the 18th and 19th centuries. Whether you get spooked or not, you're sure to have fun. Reservations are strongly suggested for the hour-long tours, which take place from the end of June until October 31. From June to August 31, tours are Monday through Saturday at 8 PM. From September 1 to Halloween, they take place on Saturdays at 7 PM. Cost for the tour in 1998 was $6 per person. Group rates are available, and bus tours are welcome.

Mount Agamenticus
Mt. Agamenticus Rd., York

Why don't you take a hike! That's right, stretch your legs and climb to the top of Mount Agamenticus; the view from the top is worth the effort. The top of a three-hill area, Mount Agamenticus reaches 692 feet and can be seen for miles around. There's a road from the base to the top and trails for walking and mountain biking. From the summit you'll have great views that extend to the White Mountains to the west and the ocean to the east. (For more information, see our Parks and Recreation chapter.)

Parsons Family Winery
60 Brixham Rd., York • (207) 363-3332

You'll get a pleasant surprise at Parsons Family Winery. Not only can you tour the winery, but you'll also learn the history of this 200-year-old farm, which was first settled by Zebulon Preble, a veteran of the Battle of Louisburg.

The winery produces varietal apple wines that you can taste at the tasting bar following the tour. The gift shop features a selection of Maine-made craft items, including some with hard-to-find apple designs. Free winery tours and tastings are offered Monday through Saturday from 10 AM to 5 PM and from noon to 5 PM on Sunday. Tours and buses are welcome.

Marginal Way, Perkins Cove and Pedestrian Footbridge
Ogunquit

Stretch your legs and take a walk from Ogunquit center to Perkins Cove along the Marginal Way footpath, which skirts the edge of the sea. In 1923, local farmer Josiah Chase grew concerned that seafront property was being scooped up by the wealthy and decided to deed the path (along which he used to herd his cattle to feed on the marsh grass of Wells) to the town.

The 1.5-mile path has a number of benches where you can rest your feet or simply admire the view. At Perkins Cove (see "Shopping the Maine Streets" in the Southern Beaches Area section of our Shopping chapter), you'll find a delightful pedestrian footbridge. Children and kids-at-heart will love pushing the button to raise and lower the bridge to allow boats to pass through.

Wells National Estuarine Research Reserve at Laudholm Farm
342 Laudholm Farm Rd., Wells
• (207) 646-1555

Nature buffs and bird lovers will enjoy a visit to the Wells National Estuarine Research Reserve at Laudholm Farm. It preserves 1,600 acres of varied field, forest, wetland and beach. Laudholm Farm is the center from which human contact can be made with the estuarine ecosystem. There are 7 miles of trails throughout the reserve where you can spot endangered wildlife such as peregrine falcons and piping plovers. In addition to a Discovery Program, the Wells Reserve offers a variety of specialty tours. The farm is open seven days a week, year round. Cost for tours is $3 per person or $6 for families. Some trails are handicapped-accessible. A parking fee of $7 is charged in July and August, except on Tuesdays. (For more information see our Kidstuff chapter.)

INSIDERS' TIP

When visiting Fort Popham you'll see a long line of cars parked along the road beside "No Parking" signs. Don't be fooled into thinking it's OK; we personally know the cop who makes ticketing these cars a summer hobby. And don't hold it against him either - the road must be kept clear for emergency vehicles.

Photo: Kevin Brusie

Youngsters enjoy a carousel ride.

Wonder Mountain Miniature Golf
U.S. Hwy. 1, Wells • (207) 646-9655

From the end of May until mid-October you can test your skill at this two-course miniature golf center. Both the Nautical Nightmare and the Mountain Mania courses have 18 holes centered around waterfalls and tunnels on "Wonder Mountain." The course opens at 9 AM, and the last players are allowed on at 10:30 PM. Cost to play is $5.50 for adults and teens for one round on one course, or $8 to play both courses. Children younger than 12 are $4.

Old Orchard Beach Area

Amusement Parks

Aquaboggan Water Park
U.S. Hwy. 1, Saco • (207) 282-3112

Yes, it can get very hot in Maine in the summer. If you want a change from the beach, take the kids to this fun park filled with water-based activities. Try the Dual Yankee Ripper, the bumper boats, the wave pool or the Grand Prix Race Cars. The park also offers a recently expanded toddler splash and play area and souvenir and concession stands. (Please see our Kidstuff chapter for more information.)

Funtown/Splashtown USA
U.S. Hwy. 1 S., Saco
• (207) 284-5139, (800) 878-2900

Roller-coaster lovers from across the country welcomed Excaliber to Funtown/Splashtown USA for the 1998 season. The first traditional wooden roller coaster in Maine since the last such coaster burned down in 1948 at Old Orchard Beach, Excaliber has a total height of 100 feet, an 82-foot first drop and a top speed of 55 mph. Total length of the coaster is 2,700 feet, and the ride lasts for about two minutes. Excaliber was constructed by Custom Coasters, and has a capacity of 24 riders per train.

In addition to the new coaster, Funtown added a castle-like entrance to the ride, complete with a gift shop and medieval-looking bridges. Funtown opens weekends in May, then daily beginning in mid-June until the last week in August. It's also open some weekends in September. (See our Kidstuff chapter for more information).

Palace Playland
1 Old Orchard St., Old Orchard Beach
• (207) 934-2001

You can see for miles from the top of the SunWheel at this funpark on the beach. Buy some cotton candy or fried dough and remember childhood as you enjoy the sights and sounds. Actually, there's a wide variety of yummy take-out options including gyros, chop suey, pizza, clams, fudge and Pier Fries. The park is open daily from the end of May to the beginning of September and some weekends in May and September, weather permitting. (For much more on Palace Playland, see our Kidstuff chapter.)

Lighthouses

Wood Island Light
Biddeford

Located on an island at the entrance to Wood Island Harbor off Biddeford Pool, Wood Island Light is famous for its ghost. According to legend, a resident lobsterman killed the deputy sheriff and then committed suicide on the island in 1896. Since that time people say the ghost of the murdered man haunts the island.

The light was built in 1808 near the mouth of the Saco River. It has a green-and-white beacon that alternates between colors every 10 seconds and can be seen for 14 and 16 miles, respectively. It also has a foghorn. Like Nubble Light, Wood Island was a family light before it was automated in 1986. While you can get there only by boat, you can see the green-and-white light clearly from the beaches in the area.

Museums

York Institute Museum
371 Main St. (U.S. Hwy. 1), Saco
• (207) 283-0684

You'll discover the interesting heritage of northern York County when you visit this museum. An extensive regional decorative arts collection including paintings and portraits can be found here, as well as exhibits detailing the growth of the county from its earliest settlement in the 1630s to its importance as Maine's first industrial center. The museum is open year round but closed on Mondays. Admission in 1998 was $4 for adults, $3 for senior citizens and $1 for students. Children younger than 6 are admitted free. Family rates are also available.

Odds & Ends

East Point Sanctuary
Maine Hwy. 208, Biddeford Pool
• (207) 781-2330

Leave your canine friends behind and go for a stroll through this 30-acre bird sanctuary operated by the Maine Audubon Society. The views from the sanctuary are spectacular, and you'll see a wide variety of shore and sea birds including black-backed gulls, terns, several varieties of sandpipers, red-winged blackbirds and snowy egrets. You'll also get a picture-perfect sighting of Wood Island light from here.

Saco Drive-In
969 U.S. Hwy. 1 (Portland Rd.), Saco
• (207) 284-1016

Open daily from May to September, this is the real thing. You sit in your car to watch a double-feature of recent releases, and you can walk over to the concession stand to buy popcorn and pizza, just like it used to be! Instead of using the speakers that attach to your windows, the drive-in now broadcasts on AM radio — they'll tell you where to tune in when you get there. Saco Drive-In is open from the end of May to early September. Cost for admission in 1998 was $10 per car with two people, $2.50 for each additional person.

Saco Heath
Off Maine Hwy. 112 (Buxton Rd.), Saco
• (207) 729-5181

If you drive too quickly you'll miss the parking lot to the Heath. As you head west, the entrance will be on your right, about a mile or so from the Way Way General Store (see the Close-up in Kidstuff). You'll enjoy walking through the woods at the start of the trail and then along wooden planking through the heath.

Five hundred acres of wild grasses, sedge and reeds stretch to either side, and you'll see birds and maybe even a deer or moose (sightings have been reported, though we admit we've never seen one here). Saco Heath is operated by the Nature Conservancy and is open from dawn to dusk. Dogs are not permitted on the heath because they tend to scare away the indigenous wildlife.

Schooner Miniature Golf
58 Ocean Park Rd., Saco • (207) 284-6174
Eighteen holes of various difficulties will entertain and challenge you. There are also batting cages to test your skill. In 1998 a round of golf cost $3.50 per person and 10 balls in the cages were $1.

Vacationland Bowling and Recreation Center
U.S. Hwy. 1, Saco • (207) 284-7386
If you've never tried candlepin bowling, here's your chance. The center has 32 lanes as well as billiards and bumper bowling for the kids. (See our Parks and Recreation chapter for more information, including an explanation of candlepin bowling.)

Pirates Island Adventure Golf
70 First St., Old Orchard Beach
• (207) 934-5086
Round up your friends and challenge them to a game of championship miniature golf. Pirates Cove features two 18-hole courses, intricately set around a mountain, complete with waterfall and tunnel. You can dress up like a pirate if you want to, but you might find it difficult to get a hole-in-one with a patch over your eye! In 1998 the cost to play the lower course, Captain Kidd's, was $5 for adults and $4.50 for children 12 or younger. The Challenge course was $5.50 for adults and $5 for children.

Greater Portland Area

Breweries

The Shipyard Brewing Co.
86 Newbury St., Portland
• (207) 761-0807, (800) BREW-ALE
Tour this microbrewery any day of the week between 3 and 5 PM to see the com-

plete process of how beer is brewed and bottled. This is the largest brewery in the state, and on a guided walk through the plant, you'll see the entire process from beginning to end and even get to sample the finished product! Children younger than 7 are not allowed in the brewhouse but can watch a free movie while they wait. Tours are free and run every half-hour with the last one beginning at 4:30 PM. Make sure to arrive at least 10 minutes early and dress lightly — the temperature in one production room is about 120 degrees! You can buy beer in the gift shop, but you're likely to find it anywhere along the coast from Maine to Florida. Some of the beers crafted here include Shipyard Export Ale, Shipyard Brown Ale and Chamberlain Pale Ale, named for former Maine governor and Civil War hero Joshua Chamberlain.

Gritty McDuff's
396 Fore St., Portland • (207) 772-2739
One of Portland's smaller brewpubs, you can tour this microbrewery's production rooms on weekends by appointment or grab a bite to eat in the restaurant any day of the week (see our Restaurants chapter). On tap are a few of their specialty brews such as Portland Head Light Ale; other labels include Black Fly Stout and Best Brown. Gritty McDuff's sells its beers in Maine, Vermont and Massachusetts.

D.L. Geary's Brewing Co.
38 Evergreen Dr., Portland
• (207) 878-2337
Tour guides will take you through the manufacturing side of this brewhouse Monday through Friday at 2:30 PM. You'll see everything from the ingredients that go into the brew to the holding tanks and the bottling line, although you should call ahead to arrange a tour. The tour is free, and if you're lucky, you can even taste raw beer straight from the tanks. D.L. Geary's is sold in Maine and New Hamp-

shire. The company's beers include D.L. Geary's Pale Ale, London Style Porter and American Ale.

Stone Coast Brewing Co.
14 York St., Portland • (207) 773-BEER

Call for a walk-through appointment to get an inside look at this brewery, or just come for lunch or dinner and see the kettle and fermenters through two walls of glass bordering the dining room. Most beers made here are sold locally. You'll find seasonal brews such as Octoberfest and five other beers including Red Stone Ale, Sunday River Ale and Black Bear Porter. The microbrewery occupies three floors and includes a nightclub with live music (see Nightlife).

Historic Houses and Forts

Fort Preble
Fort Rd., South Portland • (207) 799-6337

This fort dates to the early 1800s and was used until the 1950s. (For much more information, see the Spring Point Museum listing that follows in our Museums category.)

Fort Williams
Fort Williams Park, Shore Rd. (Maine Hwy. 77), Cape Elizabeth

You'll find Fort Williams to the right of the Portland Head Light as you face the sea. Built into the hillside, this bunker-type fort was a military outpost for coastal defense that developed next to the lighthouse. Construction on the fort started in 1872 and wasn't completed until 1892. (See Portland Head Light in the subsequent Lighthouses section for more information.)

Tate House
1270 Westbrook St., Portland
• (207) 774-9781

Built in 1755 in historic Stroudwater, the former home of Capt. George Tate, British

celebrity and Maine Mast Agent, makes for a wonderful tour. Tate supervised the cutting of white pine trees in Maine to ensure that only the best wood would be used for the masts of British fighting ships. Best-known for its elegant furniture, the house is a National Historic Landmark. It's open for tours June through October. Hours are Tuesday through Saturday from 10 AM to 4 PM and Sunday from 1 to 4 PM. Admission is $5 for adults, $4 for seniors and teens and $1 for children 12 and younger.

Victoria Mansion
109 Danforth St., Portland
• (207) 772-4841

New England's foremost historic house museum of the Victorian era, Victoria Mansion is the only surviving commission of New York designer Gustave Herter. It's a stunning piece of Italianate architecture, built between 1858 and 1860 as a summer home for New Orleans hotelier Ruggles S. Morse. Also known as the Morse-Libby Mansion, the house is resonant with fresco paintings, stained glass and many original furnishings. You'll find it open May through October (and open and decorated for the Christmas season in December). Hours are Tuesday through Saturday from 10 AM to 4 PM and on Sunday from 1 to 5 PM. Guided tours are offered at a quarter before and after the hour, and admission is $5 for adults and $2 for children ages 6 to 17. Children younger than 6 are admitted free.

Wadsworth-Longfellow House
485 Congress St., Portland
• (207) 774-1822

The childhood home of poet Henry Wadsworth Longfellow, this house is full of the original furnishings of the Wadsworth and Longfellow clans and memories of an era gone by. The first brick house in Portland, it was built in 1785 by the poet's grandfather, Gen. Peleg Wadsworth. The family continued to live

INSIDERS' TIP

Be warned: Even though many of our towns are geared toward summer tourists, the shops still tend to close pretty early. Even during the summer, stores shutting down at 5 to 7 PM is pretty common.

there until 1901, when the house was taken over by the Maine Historical Society and opened as the first historic house museum in the state. Longfellow himself lived in the house from the age of 8 months until he turned 15 and left for college, but even as an adult, he loved to visit. Now more than 15,000 people visit his house (along with the beautiful Victorian-era gardens behind it) each year.

Founded in 1822, the Maine Historical Society is the fourth-oldest historical organization in America. Both Aaron Burr and Daniel Webster contributed to its collection of more than 100,000 books, 2 million documents, 70,000 photographs and 10,000 artifacts. Gen. Joshua Chamberlain was one of its original trustees! It's currently embarking on a $3.1 million capital campaign to create a Center for Maine History at its current location that will make its collections more accessible to the public. The house and gallery of the Historical Society, just next door, are open June through October. Admission to the house and gallery, which has changing exhibits, is $5 for adults and teens and $1 for children younger than 12. To tour just the gallery, admission is $2 per person.

Neal Dow House
714 Congress St., Portland • (207) 773-7773

Civil War Gen. Neal Dow is best known in Maine for having spearheaded the prohibition law here. He became quite a well-known and controversial figure after the liquor ban passed in 1850 (it wasn't rescinded until 1934). But his house, built in 1829 and run by the Women's Christian Temperance Union, is best known as a fine example of Greek Revival architecture.

All the furnishings are original, including family portraits and paintings and Civil War memorabilia. Book lovers will gawk at the extensive library. Admission is free, but donations are accepted. The house is open Monday through Friday from 11 AM to 4 PM year round, and the average tour lasts 30 minutes.

Greater Portland Landmarks Inc.
165 State St., Portland • (207) 774-5561

If you want to know more about the historic buildings that line the city's downtown area, pick up a free walking tour brochure that points out the fine architecture of the surrounding buildings. Five different booklets focus on the development of different areas of the city such as the Old Port, Congress Street and the west end. Guided tours are also available twice a week in summer; the price in 1997 was $7 per person. Portland Landmarks also maintains a research library for designers and developers.

Cruises and Charters

Casco Bay Lines
Custom House Wharf, 56 Commercial St., Portland • (207) 774-7871

Hop on a mail boat and cruise to the outer Casco Bay Islands — Little Diamond, Great Diamond, Great Chebeague, Long and Cliff — or take a romantic sunset or music cruise and get carried away by the sounds and sights of the Atlantic. Reservations aren't necessary, but you can make them to be sure you won't miss the boat. Ticket prices range from about $9.50 to $13 for adults and teens and $4.25 to $6.25 for children between 5 and 9 years old. Children younger than 5 sail free.

Chebeague Transportation Co.
314 Cousins Island, Yarmouth • (207) 846-3700

This boat travels exclusively between Cousins Island (which you can drive to) and Great Chebeague Island. Reservations are not required for the 15-minute trip, and ticket prices each way are $4.50 adults and teens and $1 for children up to age 12.

Olde Port Mariner Fleet
Long Wharf, 170 Commercial St., Portland • (207) 775-0727

For whale watching, deep-sea fishing or scenic cruises, this fleet can meet all your nautical needs. The boats run every day from Memorial Day through Labor Day, then weekends only until Columbus Day. For cruises from two to seven hours in length, the cost is between $8.50 and $40 for adults and teens, $7.50 and $25 for children 12 and younger. The fishing trips tend to be the longest and the most expensive — but hey, if you're lucky they come with dinner (just remember, you have to eat what you catch!).

Palawan Sailing
DiMillo's Marina, Portland
• **(207) 773-2163**

This 58-foot racing yacht Palawan hosts private and open sails May through October. For three hours on the open ocean, the cost is $35 for adults and $15 for children; for a two-hour evening sail, it's $25 for adults and $10 for kids. No experience is necessary, just cruise and enjoy the ride around the islands of Casco Bay. For a private charter, you can expect to pay $300 or more.

Prince of Fundy Cruises
International Ferry Terminal, 468 Commercial St., Portland
• **(207) 775-5616, (800) 341-7540**

Cruise to Nova Scotia overnight on this car ferry equipped with a restaurant, casino, air-conditioned cabins and duty-free shopping. (See much more on this in our Daytrips & Weekend Getaways chapter.) The MS Scotia Prince departs Portland nightly. The round-trip cost for the 11-hour ride for two adults and a vehicle is $416 during July and August (the peak summer season) and $370 during the off-season. Meals are additional. For $235, you and another passenger can eat two meals onboard, share a cabin and simply sail the round trip without a car. Many other packages are available.

Atlantic Seal Cruises
25 Main St., Freeport • (207) 865-6112

You'll be able to cruise to Eagle Island, watch for island seals, see a lobster trap demonstration or relax for a sunset cruise aboard this 42-foot boat with an open cabin and outside seating. Cruises depart three times daily from the downtown wharf, and reservations are required. The boats run from June through October, and the cost is $20 for adults and teens and $15 for children 12 and younger. If you want to eat, you'll need to bring your own food. There is space to store coolers.

Freeport Sailing Adventures
P.O. Box 303, Freeport 04032
• **(207) 865-6399**

Participate in a crewed sailing charter on Casco Bay or just relax and enjoy the experience of wisping over the water on a half- or

full-day cruise along the Maine coast. Various cruises include island histories, island stops and seal watches. The cost is typically $35 per person for a half-day cruise and $75 for a full day. A private charter in 1997 started at $220 for a half-day. Children sometimes get a cheaper fare. Call for more information.

Islands

Eagle Island

Famous as the home of Adm. Robert E. Peary, the first explorer to reach the North Pole, Eagle Island is today owned by the state. You'll love the study of Peary's home, with its diamond-paned glass windows framing the sea. The house (the only one on the beautiful island) is on the National Register of Historic Landmarks, but it retains the comfy feeling of a summer home. Large, enclosed porches, comfortable chairs and lots of bookcases give you insight into how the Pearys lived. You'll find photos of his pre-expedition training with sled dogs on a nearby island and other exploration memorabilia.

The 17-acre island has walking paths and little pebble coves for exploring. Bring a picnic and make a day of it. There are no concession facilities on the island though an outside toilet facility is available in the woods to the rear of the house. You can reach Eagle Island by private boat or via excursions that depart from both Portland and South Harpswell. There's no fee to visit the house.

From Portland, Eagle Tours, (207) 774-6498, operates one trip daily at 10 AM, which leaves from the waterfront on Commercial Street. Cost for the trip in 1999 is $15 for adults, $12 for seniors and students and $9 for children. The boat waits at the island for around an hour so you can tour and picnic, then returns. For information on how to get there from South Harpswell, contact Dolphin Marina at (207) 833-6000.

Cliff Island

This rocky island off the coast is a part of Portland and has about 80 year-round residents. You may have seen the island without knowing it if you saw the movie The Whales of August, which was filmed here. There aren't many organized attractions, but just walking the island's roads and along its shore is enough to satisfy most visitors.

There are no accommodations or restaurants, but lobster rolls and hot dogs are available beside the ferry landing. The island has struggled to keep its one-room schoolhouse going by trying to lure mainlanders to relocate here. Not too long ago, when the schoolhouse was about to close for lack of students, the locals pooled their money to fix up an abandoned house and gave it to a low-income city family with three children!

To get here, board the Casco Bay Lines mail boat at Custom House Wharf in Portland, or reserve a ticket by calling (207) 774-7811. (For more information, see Cruises and Charters in the Greater Portland Area section of this chapter.)

Great Chebeague Island

This five-mile island off the coast of Freeport first became a popular tourist attraction in 1870, although bands of traveling Native Americans used it as a rest stop long before that. It is the largest of the Casco Bay Islands and remains a popular destination today because of its sandy beaches and its mini-resort, The Chebeague Island Inn, which has 21 rooms and a large veranda overlooking the bay.

The island is inhabited by scores of summer folk; about 300 year-round residents stick it out during the colder months. You'll find a handful of shops to browse through and more fun on Little Chebeague, just a hop, skip and a jump over. No one lives here, but it has nice sandy beaches and old stone foundations of where houses used to be.

One of the easiest ways to reach the island is by purchasing a boat ticket with Chebeague Transportation of Yarmouth, (207)

846-3700. (For more information, see Cruises and Charters in this chapter.)

Long Island

You won't find any freeways or traffic jams here — this is definitely not Long Island as in New York! Off the Portland coast, it is one of the largest of the Casco Bay Islands, and one of the most popular for its lush foliage and stretching, state-run beaches: Andrews Beach and Singing Beach. There's also Big Sandy Beach, which doesn't offer restrooms.

The year-round population of about 100 jumps to 10 times that number in the summer. Many come to watch the fishermen at work in Long Cove. When you get hungry, check out The Spar for a lobster dinner. To get to Long Island, use the Casco Bay Lines mail boat, (207) 774-7871 (see Cruises and Charters in this chapter).

Jewell Island

To get here you'll have to charter a boat or have one of your own, but this is the only one of the Casco Bay Islands where camping is allowed. The island, off the coast of Portland, is unoccupied, although it is the home of many legends. It was supposedly the place where pirate Captain Chase was murdered and where Captain Kidd hid his treasure — no one's found it yet! The swimming is good in the Punchbowl, a semicircular cove where you're protected from the waves, and there is anchorage on the island's northern tip and a pier on the western shore. To charter a boat to Jewell Island, try Palawan Sailing, (207) 773-2163 (see previous listing in the Cruises and Charters section of this chapter).

Peaks Island

Farthest south of the Casco Bay Islands, this one is easily accessible by boat. Take a

---

INSIDERS' TIP

Take a sweatshirt and a bottle of water if you're going out on a boat. It may seem hot on land, but when the boat gets moving and you're a good way out to sea with the wind blowing, you'll be glad for the warmth. Some boats don't sell food items, so you should bring your own water and snacks. The wind may be cold, but the sun is hot; you can get dehydrated if you don't drink enough.

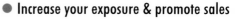

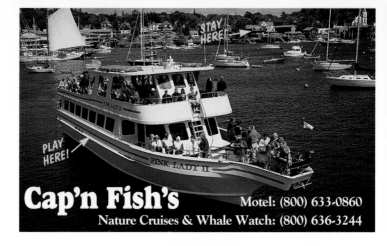

Boothbay Harbor Region

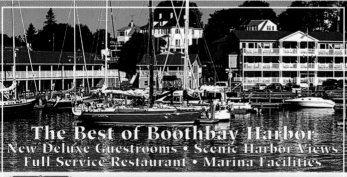

Boothbay Harbor Region

17-minute ferry ride from Portland and arrive on this 2-mile-by-3-mile haven. It's a favorite summering spot for nearly 6,000 people and a year-round residence for about 1,500.

Enjoy beautiful sandy beaches or explore an old fort with two World War II batteries, Steele and Craven. Bring a picnic to the nearby public tables. For a taste of history, stroll through Bracket Cemetery, the oldest on the island, and see if you can find the oldest grave, which dates back to the 1700s.

Before you leave, check out Whaleback Rock. Its crashing breakers and spraying mists have been the subject of many photographers and artists. Literary buffs may know that writer Henry Wadsworth Longfellow, who grew up in Portland (see previous listing in this chapter for the Wadsworth-Longfellow House), based his ballad, "The Wreck of the Hesperus," on the destruction of the Helen Eliza, which crashed off this island's shore in 1869.

Lighthouses

Cape Elizabeth Light (Two Lights)
**Two Lights State Park,
off Maine Hwy. 77,
Cape Elizabeth**

Don't ask anyone how to find the Cape Elizabeth Light; they probably won't know where you mean. Ask for Two Lights and they'll be more than happy to assist.

Until 1924 the Cape Elizabeth Light had a fixed light in its east tower and a flashing light in its west tower. As the only twin light on that portion of coast, it was a welcome landmark for sailors. However, in 1924 the government ordered all twin lights in the country converted, and the western tower was dismantled and the eastern light converted to a flashing beacon. The Cape Elizabeth Light has a white beacon that flashes every 30 seconds. It's visible for 27 miles, and there is also a foghorn.

You can visit the area surrounding the light but not the light itself, which has been automated and is now maintained by the Coast Guard. The lightkeeper's dwelling is now privately owned.

Portland Head Light
**Fort Williams Park,
Cape Elizabeth
• (207) 799-2661**

George Washington commissioned the building of this, the oldest lighthouse in Maine, completed in 1791. It's one of the best-known and well-loved lighthouses in the world. Pictures of its white tower and red-roofed, white painted buildings with green trim grace walls worldwide.

Poet Henry Wadsworth Longfellow, a Portland native, frequently visited the light and its keeper, Capt. Joshua Stout, who served at the light from 1867 until well into the 1900s. You'll find a plaque bearing some of the poet's lines to the right of the buildings as you face the sea. The Portland Head Light Museum is in the former lighthouse keeper's quarters. Permanent exhibits chronicle the history of the lighthouse and Fort Williams, which you'll find near the light. The museum is open daily from June to the end of October and weekends in April, May, November and December. Cost for admission in 1998 was $2 for adults and $1 for children ages 6 to 18.

The lighthouse is easily accessible. Located in Fort Williams Park off Route 77, Portland Head Light has plenty of parking space. Restroom facilities are available in the parking areas.

Spring Point Ledge Lighthouse
Fort Rd., South Portland

You can reach Spring Point Ledge Lighthouse by walking along a breakwater. Built in 1897, this caisson-style light is one of the few of this type that you can reach by foot. The lighthouse was built at the request of seven steamship companies that regularly served Portland in 1897. Before it was built, many ships foundered on the partially submerged ledge.

A caisson-style light has a cage-like structure around its base, and the tower itself is squat (Spring Point Ledge Light is only 54 feet tall). Spring Point has a white-and-red alternating beacon that can be seen for 14 miles. The breakwater was built in 1954. (For more information, see the subsequent Spring Point Museum listing).

Museums

Spring Point Museum
Fort Rd., South Portland • (207) 799-6337

Located at Fort Preble, amid the grounds of Southern Maine Technical College (see our Education and Child Care chapter), this museum incorporates the fort, a gift shop, Spring Point Ledge Lighthouse and the Spring Point Shoreline Walkway. The museum is housed in the former cannon room of the fort, which was begun in 1808 and used through the 1950s. You'll see many coast artillery gun emplacements dating from both world wars along the Civil War-era casements lining the shore. In addition, you can walk out along the breakwater for a close-up view of Spring Point Ledge Lighthouse (see previous listing).

In the museum you'll see exhibits illustrating the region's maritime history with photographs, models and artifacts from Maine's seafaring past. The Spring Point Shoreline Walkway is well-notated, with descriptions of interesting historical facts about the area. From here you'll also have great views of Casco Bay, the Portland Head Light and the Portland Breakwater (Bug) Light as well as the early harbor fortifications on nearby islands. Within easy access of the walkway are Willard Beach and the 17th-century Old Settler's Cemetery.

The Shaker Museum
707 Shaker Rd. (Maine Hwy. 26), New Gloucester • (207) 929-4597

You can see the White Mountains in the distance from this beautiful museum village. Located about 40 minutes north of Portland, the museum is part of the Sabbathday Lake Shaker Community village, the last existing Shaker community in the world. For the uninitiated, the Shakers believe in simplicity, and they are a religion of celibacy. People with children may join, but they must remain celibate after joining. It makes for a somewhat difficult belief system to sustain.

Famous for their furniture, baskets and textiles, the Shakers have a fascinating history. Learn about their inventions and see how their furniture and fancy goods evolved through the years as you tour the various buildings of the village. The museum is open Monday through Saturday from Memorial Day to mid-October (Columbus Day). It's closed on Sunday. Recently, introductory tours were $5 for adults and teens and $2 for children 12 or younger. An extended tour was $6.50 for adults and $2.75 for children.

Maine Narrow Gauge Railroad Co. & Museum
58 Fore St., Portland • (207) 828-0814

You can view the smallish trains that traveled on Maine's 2-foot tracks at this museum, which is open year round from 10 AM to 4 PM. Trains run daily from May through October and on weekends only for the rest of the year. Or take a ride in a train along Casco Bay. (For more information, see our Kidstuff chapter under "Things in Motion.")

The Jones Museum of Glass & Ceramics
Douglas Mtn. (off Maine Hwy. 107), Sebago • (207) 787-3370

Enjoy the beauty of the Sebago Lake region (with views of the White Mountains in the distance) as you visit this extensive decorative arts museum. Located about 45 minutes from Portland, the Jones Museum features more than 7,000 pieces spanning 3,000 years. Sandwich Glass, Chinese and English Porcelain, Baccarat crystal and Wedgwood are just some of the groups you will find. Paperweights, vases, stemware and dinnerware represent the diversity of items on display.

In addition to its permanent exhibits, the museum creates four special exhibits each year. Its glass collection has been ranked in

INSIDERS' TIP

Traveling with kids or dogs? Plan your day around a picnic lunch at one of the many forts or parks so the kids and your furry friends can burn off steam after a morning of shopping or visiting sites.

the top 10 of U.S. museums. And you may want to consider bringing a picnic lunch to eat at the top of Douglas Mountain. The view from the summit, from the seacoast to the mountains, is spectacular. The Jones Museum, which is at the base of the mountain, is open from May to mid-November. Entrance fees in 1999 are $5 for adults, $3 for students and $3.75 for senior citizens. Children younger than 12 are admitted free.

Odds & Ends

Keystone Theatre Cafe
504 Congress St., Portland
• (207) 871-5500

Crowd around a table set for four and enjoy dinner or lunch from a casual dining menu while watching a movie at this theater cafe. The seating is lounge-style, and you can be served before or during the show — saving you all those annoying trips to the concession stand. The cafe serves pizza, burgers, hot dogs and sandwiches as well as fries, popcorn and other good food you know you shouldn't eat. It also has a large selection of microbrews and wine. The movies are all current, and the cost of admission is $5 for adults and $3.50 for children younger than 12. Tickets are $3.50 for all ages at matinees. Crawlers get in free. This place is pretty popular, so we recommend you arrive at least 30 minutes before the show. The matinees are Saturday and Sunday only.

Portland Fish Exchange
2 Portland Fish Pier, Portland
• (207) 773-0017

Show up just before noon Monday through Thursday, and you'll get a true glimpse into the local fishing industry at this fish auction. It's the only nonprofit, all-display fish auction in the country. You'll see fishermen hauling their freshest catches right off the boat, sorting them by species and size and stocking them away in the coolers to be bid on by wholesalers from around the state.

Don't expect a formal tour. The basic procedure after you step through the door is a little speech on staying off the working piers, staying out of the way of trucks and watching

Photo: Merry Farnum

You can spend a whole day exploring Two Lights State Park.

your footing, as the floors get pretty slippery. The auction takes place in a huge warehouse filled with crates of fish; if you don't like the smell, this might not be your best bet for a fun afternoon. Auctions also take place every Sunday at 11 AM.

The Desert of Maine
Desert Rd., Freeport • (207) 865-6962

It may sound kind of corny to explore a desert in Maine — kind of like visiting a saltwater lobster pound in the middle of Saudi Arabia. But don't pass this one by too quickly. These 300 acres of inland sand and dunes are 100 percent authentic and well worth the trip. (For more information, check out our Kidstuff chapter under "Kids in Motion.")

The DeLorme Mapping Company
2 DeLorme Dr., Yarmouth
• (800) 452-5931

Come to one of the biggest map-making companies in the nation to visit the world's largest globe, a hulking monument located in the company's entryway. It's 41 feet in diameter, weighs 5,665 pounds and is made of 720 removable panels. Driven by two electric motors, the globe rotates at a top speed of one rotation every two minutes. You can see the elevation

and contour of the land and check out the detailed markings of countries and regions.

When you're done ooohing and ahhhing, stop in the company store and check out the great maps of regions all over the United States. DeLorme maps are famous for providing travelers with the intimate details of the regions where they are traveling. They include listings and map markers of nature preserves, historic sites, campgrounds and other places of interest.

The maps are also famous for their whimsy. Each has a made-up guide symbol marking an imaginary place. For example, the Kansas map has an icon showing where you can go to see a tornado, and the New Hampshire map has the marking for a hamster! Those are the only ones we can tell you about though; hunting for the silly stuff is half the fun!

The globe, by the way, was designed by DeLorme and was completed in 1998. DeLorme Drive is just off Route 1, and the company store is clearly visible from the road.

L.L. Bean
Maine St., Freeport • (800) 341-4341
542 Congress St., Portland
• (800) 341-4341

This is the granddaddy of all outdoor shopping stores and one of the biggest tourist attractions in the state! You'll find everything from camping, fishing and hunting gear to men's, women's and children's clothing, fur-

niture, Maine gifts, shoes and famous L.L. Bean boots. This place is a galaxy all its own (there's a trout pond in the store) and has many discount outlets in various locations throughout the state. For much more information, check out our Close-up on L.L. Bean in this chapter, or look in the Outlet Shopping sections of our Shopping chapter.

Brunswick, Bath and Boothbay Harbor Area

Historic Houses and Forts

Joshua L. Chamberlain
Civil War Museum
226 Main St., Brunswick • (207) 729-6606

Known as the "fighting professor," Joshua Chamberlain had no formal military training when he led the 20th Maine regiment to triumph at Gettysburg in the Civil War's Battle of Little Round Top. Chamberlain was a Bowdoin College professor of writing and rhetoric when he joined the Union Army during a feigned sabbatical and became a national legend.

During the three days of fighting in 1863, he led the 20th Maine in a bayonet charge that routed a Southern force superior in number, thus helping lead the North to victory at the Battle of Gettysburg. In fact, Chamberlain received the Congressional Medal of Honor for his valor and was given a signal honor by Union Gen. Ulysses S. Grant: Chamberlain was chosen to accept the Confederate surrender at Appomattox. He stunned friend and foe alike by ordering his troops to attention to salute the vanquished Southern foes. After the war experience, Chamberlain went on to become governor of his home state.

At Chamberlain's house, just down the street from the college where he taught and later served as president, you can stroll down the halls where he walked and glimpse many of his personal belongings — chairs, china, and goblets among them. You'll get a good feel for his decorating tastes, from the vibrant mural hand-painted on his parlor ceiling to the massive spiral staircase in the hall and the Maltese crosses displayed on his chimneys.

The Pejepscot Historical Society runs the museum and is carefully restoring the house to its original splendor — peeling back layers of wallpaper, repairing the roof and buying back as many of the general's original furnishings as possible. After walking through the house, peek in the adjoining gift shop for Civil War memorabilia. Admission is $4 for adults and teens and $2 for children ages 6 to 16. The museum is open from June 1 to mid-October on Tuesday through Saturday from 10 AM to 4 PM, although you'll need to arrive by 3:15 PM to tour the house.

The Skofield-Whittier House
161 Park Row, Brunswick
• **(207) 729-6606**

Step inside this Italianate house, and you'll be stepping into the life and times of a Victorian-era family living in Brunswick. Not only are the furnishings perfectly preserved, so are the accessories, right down to the original toothpaste and soap in the bathroom. The 17-room mansion was kept under lock and key from 1925, when the last family member moved out, to 1982, when it was opened by the Pejepscot Historical Society.

The other half of the Park Row duplex houses the Pejepscot Museum and has changing exhibits reflecting the way life used to be in Brunswick, Topsham and Harpswell before the modern era. The Pejepscot Historical Society is among the oldest in the state, founded in 1888. It draws from a collection of more than 100,000 local historic artifacts and 20,000 photos to form its exhibits. The museum and house are open from June 1 to mid-fall, Tuesday through Saturday from 10 AM to 3 PM. Admission is $4 for adults and teens and $2 for children ages 6 to 16.

Architectural Tours
Bath-Brunswick Region Chamber of Commerce, 49 Front St., Bath
• **(207) 443-9751**

Take a self-guided walking or driving tour of historic Bath by picking up a brochure at the Chamber of Commerce for the Bath-Brunswick Region. There you'll find architectural sketches of the various house styles around the town — Georgian, Federal, Greek Revival, Gothic Revival, Italianate — as well as a map and written descriptions of the houses and buildings you'll see.

They're spread out all over the city, so it will take a little work if you want to see them all, but a one-mile stroll or drive north along Washington Street from the center of town to Beacon Street will bring you by many of the nicest buildings, most of which are privately owned. Several must-sees are the Gothic Revival Chocolate Church at 804 Washington Street (see more on this in our Arts chapter); the Winter Street Church, which has the highest steeple in the city; the Patten Free Library, which looks just like a miniature castle; and York Hall, a magnificent Georgian Revival with cascading verandas.

INSIDERS' TIP

Keep bug spray, a bathing suit and towel, a spare pair of sunglasses and a sweatshirt or windbreaker in your car. That way you'll be prepared if you decide to have an adventure or go for a swim at the spur of the moment.

Photo: Giselle A. Auger

Pleasure boats and fishing boats bob gently at anchor in Perkins Cove, Ogunquit.

Fort Popham
Maine Hwy. 209, Phippsburg

You'll love exploring this two-story, semi-circular granite fort at the mouth of the Kennebec River. Building began in 1861 during the Civil War, but the war ended before it was complete, so the fort was never finished. Modifications were made during the Spanish-American War and during both World Wars, but the fort never saw any real fighting action. Today it makes a great place to roam or have a picnic. You can't miss it, because the fort is at the very end of Highway 209 — to go beyond it, you'll need a boat.

Entrance is free, and you can guide yourself through the fort's dark corridors or peer through granite gun holes over the water and look for enemy ships as the salty Atlantic laps at the granite walls below. Historians believe this was the same site on which a wooden fort was built to protect inland settlements during the Revolutionary War. And inland, just

across the cove on Sabino Head, is where the English sent their first colonists to form the Popham Colony in 1607 — that was 13 years before the pilgrims landed at Plymouth Rock! Unfortunately these brave souls didn't have much luck, and after one bitter winter they called it quits and headed home on The Virginia, the first wooden ship built in the New World. You can walk around the cove to get to this site, but you'll have to look carefully. It's marked only with a stone slab on a bluff of grass near the shoreline.

Fort Baldwin
Maine Hwy. 209, Phippsburg

Built between 1905 and 1912, there are three batteries for your exploration hidden high up on heavily wooded Sabino Hill. A road takes you to the top, but most visitors opt to park at nearby Fort Popham and walk. The fort has been part of the Popham State Park since 1924, and in 1942 the adjacent fire control tower was built — climb it for great views of the surrounding forest and sea. The fort is near the very end of Highway 209, just across the cove from Fort Popham.

Castle Tucker
2 Lee St., Wiscasset • (207) 882-7169

Built in 1807 by Judge Silas Lee — a man with a reputation for living beyond his means — this Victorian mansion was sold to Capt. Richard Tucker in 1958 and has been in his family ever since. You'll admire the house's original furnishings and wallpaper as well as its elliptical, freestanding staircase and wall of glass overlooking the Sheepscot River. Tucker added a glass, two-story portico on the corner of Lee and High streets when he purchased the mansion.

After you're done touring the house, walk out to the barn, where there's an antique carriage and sleigh display. Capt. Tucker's heir, Jane Tucker, acquired the house through a will in 1960. When she couldn't find a buyer to preserve it, she opened it to the public. Jane Tucker continues to live in the mansion, although she handed its care over to the Society for the Preservation of New England Antiquities in 1997. The house is open to the public from July through August, Tuesday through Saturday from 11 AM to 4 PM. Admission is $4 for adults and teens and $2 for children ages 6 to 12. The house is open from June through Oct. 15, and tours run every hour on the hour with the last tour starting at 4PM.

Nickels-Sortwell House
121 Main St., Wiscasset • (207) 882-6218

This elegant mansion towers over Wiscasset's Main Street, telling the tale of the town's prosperity during the era of wooden shipbuilding here. Capt. William Nickels, a wealthy ship owner and trader, built the house between 1807 and 1808. But when he lost his fortune several years after the Embargo Act

of 1807, which crippled the shipping industry, the private palace became a hotel. In 1895 it caught the eye of Foye Sortwell, the mayor of Cambridge, Massachusetts, who refurbished the house in the Colonial Revival manner for his summer residence.

Sixty years later it was given to the Society for the Preservation of New England Antiquities, which now maintains it. Tours of the house and grounds, which have period gardens, are offered every hour on the hour from 11 AM until 4 PM from June 1 through Oct. 15. Admission is $4, but Wiscasset residents get in free. The house is open from Wednesday through Sunday with tours running on the hour.

Old Lincoln County Jail and Museum
Federal St., Wiscasset • (207) 882-6817

Built in 1811 and used to house prisoners until 1953, this old jail house still has original graffiti from its prisoners on the walls! Explore the prisoners' cells with 41-inch-thick granite walls, and tour the jailer's house with its Victorian Christmas parlor and antique tool shed. Operated by the Lincoln Country Historical Association, the site is open from 11 AM to 4 PM, Tuesday through Sunday during July and August. Admission is $2 for adults and teens and $1 for children younger than 13.

Fort Edgecomb
Off Rt. 1, to Old Fort Rd., Edgecomb • (207) 882-7777

On Davis Island, overlooking a strategic passage in the Sheepscot River, this octagonal blockhouse was built in 1808 as the nation looked toward war with England. It was one of three forts in Maine authorized by Congress just before the outbreak of the War of 1812. The blockhouse and surrounding earthworks, which show the layers of construction, are original. You can explore the fort and grounds every day between 9 AM and 5 PM from Memorial day through Labor Day. The cost is $1 per person. Children younger than 12 get in free.

Cruises and Charters

The Captain's Watch Sail Charter
2476 Cundy's Harbor Rd., Brunswick • (207) 725-0979

For an afternoon sail or a cruise of up to five days, set sail on Symbion, a 37-foot, center-cockpit sloop. Coast Guard-licensed Capt. Ken Brigham will take your private group on a tour of Maine's sheltered coves and rivers or out to the open ocean. You can even charter a sail to nearby Eagle or Seguin island. Day sails are limited to six passengers; the cost in 1997 was $45 per person for a half-day sail or $65 for a full day. Reduced rates are available for guests of The Captain's Watch Bed and Breakfast (see our Bed & Breakfasts and Inns chapter for more information.

Appledore V
Fisherman's Wharf, Commercial St., Boothbay Harbor • (207) 633-6598

Set sail aboard the 64-foot windjammer Appledore V for a 2½-hour cruise to the Outer Islands and Seal Rocks from mid-June through October. Keep an eye out for lighthouses, lobstermen and wildlife on remote islands accessible only by boat. Skipper and crew Herb, Doris, Tom and Lisa Smith have sailed around the world twice onboard the same boat. The cost is $20 per person, and half price for children younger than 12. Call ahead for reservations.

The Argo
Pier 6, Commercial St., Boothbay Harbor
• (207) 633-7200

This excursion boat will take you on a one-hour cruise to Cabbage Island, where you will enjoy a succulent lobster bake cooked up the old-fashioned way by the Moore family. They've been holding bakes on their private island for about nine years, steaming lobsters, clams, corn on the cob, onion and egg in seaweed for their guests' delight and serv-

ing up fish chowder and blueberry cake on the side. The cost, which includes the sail and food, is $37.50 for adults and teens (this gets you two lobsters, by the way). Children younger than 12 can sail for $8 and share the meal with an adult or pay $12.50 for the ride and a couple of hot dogs on the island. You'll spend a little more than two hours on the island, with time to browse the gift shop, play a game of croquet, horseshoes, badminton or volleyball and hunt for an osprey nest. The boat, which is the only way to get to the island, departs once a day Monday through Friday at 12:30 PM and twice Saturday (12:30 and 5 PM) and Sunday (11:30 AM and 1:30 PM).

Reservations are recommended at least one week in advance, and the season runs from mid-June to the end of September.

Balmy Days Cruises
Pier 8, Boothbay Harbor
• (207) 633-2284, (800) 298-2284

Set sail for Monhegan Island or just view the sparkling harbor lights during an evening cruise aboard one of this company's two motorized cruise boats. Some cruises include dinner or lunch and even jazz music. Prices range from $29 per adult and $18 per child for Monhegan Island cruises to $8.50 and $4.25 for one-hour harbor cruises. For a little quiet, set sail on the Bay Lady and experience the sun glinting off the Atlantic Ocean or watch it slowly set over the horizon while aboard this 31-foot friendship sloop. The boat departs five times daily, and the cost is $18. Private charters are available, and the boat operates until Columbus Day.

Boothbay Whale Watch
Commercial St., Fisherman's Wharf, Boothbay Harbor
• (207) 633-3500

Looking for whales? Depart Boothbay Harbor aboard The Harbor Princess, a custom-designed, high-speed aluminum vessel with a spacious heated cabin and full-service galley. If you don't see a whale, your next trip is free. Call ahead for reservations. Trips run from May through late October, and the cost is $25 for adults and teens and $15.00 for children ages 6 to 12. Children younger than 6 sail free.

Festival-goers show off a stuffed animal.

Cap'n Fish's Cruises
Pier One, Boothbay Harbor
• **(207) 633-3244**

For more than 71 years, Cap'n Fish's has chartered Boothbay Harbor visitors around the coast. There are three boats that take out large groups of tourists as well as smaller private charters, which run $500 per hour. Try the nature cruise "Seafari," where you're likely to spot seals, blue heron and maybe even a whale. There are sunset cruises, lighthouse cruises, cruises of summer colony homes, river trips and more. Tickets are sold at the bright red ticket booth at Pier One. The same family has captained Cap'n Fish boats since Cap'n Ray Fish started it all. His grandson, Cap'n John Fish, now carries on the family tradition.

Hardy Boat Cruises
Shaw's Fish and Lobster Wharf, Maine Hwy. 32, New Harbor
• **(207) 677-2026, (800) 278-3346**

This one's a little north of the rest of the attractions, but it's worth the trip if you want to go on a puffin and seal watching cruise aboard the Monhegan Island Ferry. Take a day-long Ocean Safari cruise for $30 for adults and $18 for children younger than 12, or an afternoon seal watch for $8 for adults and $5 for children. The Monhegan Island Express will take you to the island for the day or overnight for $26 for adults and $15 for children. There are also sunset lighthouse cruises, puffin watches narrated by an Audubon naturalist and fall foliage cruises. A portion of each fare supports wildlife and the local environment.

INSIDERS' TIP

Why not get both your brain cells and your blood cells moving? Combine a visit to one of the area's museums with a walk on a beach, through a park, along a nature trail or up a nearby mountain. See our Beaches and Parks and Recreation chapters for some suggestions on where to go. You might want to check out Odds & Ends in this chapter, too.

Reservations are recommended. To get here, take U.S. Highway 1 to Damariscotta, turn right onto Maine Highway 129, then bear right onto Maine Highway 130. Go 9 miles before turning left onto Maine Highway 32. Parking is a half-mile ahead on the right.

Islands

Seguin Island

This uninhabited island off the coast of Georgetown is little more than a grassy hill rising out of the ocean, but it does have a lighthouse, and during the summer season it has two brave caretakers who will show you around. To get to Seguin Island, you'll need to book a charter. We suggest The Captain's Watch Sail Charter out of Cundy's Harbor in Brunswick. For information, see the previous listing in this chapter's Cruises and Charters section. (For more on Seguin Lighthouse, see this chapter's Lighthouses section.)

Monhegan Island

This one is way out there, 9 miles off the coast of Boothbay Harbor to be exact, and despite the raging civilization on the mainland, you'll find nothing of the sort here. Instead look for kerosene lamps at night when the generators run low. It is believed that Vikings were the first travelers here, based on the runic figures carved on the ledges of Manana, a little dot of an island nearby.

Disney fans and history lovers will like knowing that Capt. John Smith, who fell in love with the Native American princess Pocahontas, helped settle the island 400 years ago, calling it his fishing headquarters. Now it is inhabited by a stoic band of painters, writers and escapists who just prefer the tranquility of island life. There are plenty of trails for hiking and steep cliffs for gawking. Check out the granite lighthouse tower, built in 1850, which sits on the top of a hill in the center of the island. There you will also find the Monhegan Museum, a collection of island his-

tory, which is housed in the former lighthouse keeper's house.

You'll find a small collection of restaurants here, but believe us, only the island itself will satisfy your cravings. Many cruise boats will take you to Monhegan, including Balmy Day Cruises out of Boothbay Harbor (see previous listing under Cruises and Charters).

Lighthouses

Seguin Light
Off the coast of Georgetown

One of the oldest lighthouses on the East Coast, Seguin Light was built off the Georgetown coast in 1795 and commissioned by President George Washington. Set in a grassy field above the towering cliffs of rocky Seguin Island, the lighthouse stands 1,800 feet above water, making it one of the highest beacons in the state.

It was rebuilt in 1820 and in 1857, when the first Fresnel lens was installed in the lantern of a Maine lighthouse tower. Rumors of buried treasure caused the Bureau of Lighthouses to hire someone to spend an entire year searching the island; none was ever found. Twelve men from the Coast Guard were stationed on the island to care for the light during World War II, and the number dropped to three until the light was automated in 1986. Now summer caretakers keep watch here, maintaining the tower and the small house beside it and showing tourists around one of the foggiest locations in the state.

While you're here, don't forget to check out the massive conveyor belt used to transport goods from the boat dock at the bottom of the island to the top. The lighthouse is about 2 miles out from Reid State Park, and from the beach on a clear day it can be viewed as a pencil sticking out on the horizon. Tours are free. The only way to get to the island is by boat, and the Maine Maritime Museum in Bath sometimes offers excursions here.

Ram Island Light
Maine Hwy. 238, Boothbay Harbor

Tradition has it that before this lighthouse was built, area fishermen rowed out to the island each night to light a dimly flickering lantern to keep area fishermen from wrecking their boats on the jagged reefs below. A number of near catastrophes, including shipwrecks in which villagers risked their own lives to save others who ran aground on the island, finally led to the construction of this lighthouse in 1883.

Visible from shore, the gray stone tower stands on a small outcrop of rock and is joined to Ram Island by a walkway. Just south of Ocean Point, the small island was often used for grazing sheep, although many locals feared the ghosts who were said to inhabit it. The light marks the passage between nearby Fisherman's Island and the mainland.

Museums

Pejepscot Museum
159 Park Row, Brunswick • (207) 729-6606

Run by one of the state's oldest historical societies (dating back to 1888), the Pejepscot Museum showcases changing exhibits on life the way it used to be in Brunswick, Topsham and Harpswell. It has a collection of more than 100,000 area artifacts that are selected and arranged in seasonal displays. There is also a small research gallery for people wanting to dig into their family roots.

The museum is housed in half of a 19th-century sea captain's house that was once the home of Civil War Gen. Joshua Chamberlain. The other half of the house is being restored to the way it looked when Chamberlain lived there. For more information on this, see the Joshua Chamberlain Civil War Museum listing in the Historic Houses and Forts section. During summer, the museum is open Monday through Friday from 9 AM to 4:30 PM and on Saturday from 1 to 4 PM. Admission is free.

The Peary-MacMillan Arctic Museum
Hubbard Hall, Bowdoin College, Brunswick • (207) 725-3416

Relive the famous expedition of Admiral Robert Peary and Admiral Donald MacMillan, the first explorers to reach the North Pole. At this exhibit on the first floor of Hubbard Hall, you'll see artifacts, carvings, costumes, paintings, photographs and journals from the trip. Both men were Bowdoin College graduates, and to this day the polar bear is the school's mascot (see our Education chapter for more on Bowdoin).

Most striking about their journey is that the men traveled in true Arctic style, bringing along typical provisions of food and fuel, wearing Eskimo garb, riding on dog sleds and hunting whales and musk ox along the way. On subsequent journeys, Peary's wife, Josephine, accompanied her husband on his Arctic explorations, even giving birth to their daughter — nicknamed the Snow Baby — on the way! For more history on Peary, visit his house on Eagle Island. You'll find more information in the Islands category of the Greater Portland section of this chapter. To visit the museum, stop by from 10 AM to 5 PM Tuesday through Saturday or from 2 to 5 PM on Sunday. There is no admission charge.

Maine Maritime Museum
243 Washington St., Bath • (207) 443-1316

Chronicling the history of shipbuilding in Maine, this museum has an outdoor exhibit replicating an old-fashioned, wooden shipyard as well as an indoor gallery. Boat rides from here are also available on the Kennebec River. The museum is open year round from 9:30 AM to 5 PM. (For more information, see listing under "Minds in Motion" in our Kidstuff chapter.)

Musical Wonder House
18 High St., Wiscasset • (207) 882-7163

This internationally acclaimed music box museum has a huge collection of rare musical boxes and mechanical musical instruments displayed throughout a gorgeous Greek Revival sea captain's home. You'll find all sorts of highly decorated antique disc players from around the world as well as forte piano boxes, candy dispenser machines with bells, drums and dancing dolls, painted drum phones, a 1912 Steinway Grand piano and much more. You'll even be able to see many of the pieces played.

They are all displayed in rooms furnished

Photo: Merry Farnum

Portland Observatory on Munjoy Hill was built in 1807.

with antiques of the period. See the stunning flying staircase in the entrance hall and play the coin-operated music boxes on display. Come for a guided tour from 10 AM to 5 PM daily from May through Labor Day and on a limited basis until October 31. The cost for a one-hour tour is $12 for adults and teens and $7.50 for children younger than 12, although you can view just the coin operated antique music boxes in the front hall for $1 and then choose whether to go and see the rest of the house. A 30-minute tour is also available for $6.50. The longer the tour, the more rooms you get to see, but at any time you can choose to switch to the higher-priced long tour. A three hour tour for $25 lets you see the whole house and includes live demonstrations on the instruments.

Odds & Ends

Brunswick Fishway
Brunswick-Topsham Hydro Plant, Maine St., Brunswick • (207) 725-5521

On the dam over the Androscoggin River, this fish ladder is open weekends from 10 AM to 2 PM and on Wednesday evenings from 7 to 9 PM during May and June. That's the season when salmon hurl themselves up through the fishway to spawn upstream. You can catch all the action from a viewing room that's under the water level. (For more information on this unique attraction, see listings for "Things in Motion" in our Kidstuff chapter.)

Cribwork Bridge
Maine Hwy. 24, Orrs Island

Built in 1928, this bridge is the only one of its kind in the world! It's constructed of criss-crossed granite blocks allowing the tide to flow through. The bridge is impossible to miss as you drive from Orrs Island to Bailey Island on Maine 24, and the curve of the road gives you a great view of the architecture as you go across.

Land's End
Maine Hwy. 24, Bailey Island

For a panoramic view of Casco Bay, Halfway Rock Light and Eagle Island, drive to the end of the land on Maine 24. You'll know you're there when the road stops. At low tide you'll be able to walk along a small beach area where sport anglers cast for mackerel and bluefish off the rocks and tourists hunt for sea treasures. You'll also be able to hunt for Maine souvenirs and Christmas decorations at the Land's End Gift Store just above the shore. From downtown Brunswick, Land's End is about a 20-minute drive, and there is plenty of beautiful scenery along the way.

Don't think for a minute these activities will leave you grownups bored — most of our Kidstuff suggestions are equally enjoyable for adults.

Kidstuff

In Maine we've got plenty to keep young bodies and young minds in motion, from long stretches of nature trails to long aisles of interactive exhibits in museums tailored to kids.

In this chapter, we've arranged the outings under three subject headers: Kids in Motion, Things in Motion and Minds in Motion. And don't think these activities will leave you grownups bored — most are equally enjoyable for adults.

For more diversions to keep you and the kids going, check out our Attractions chapter as well as the one on Parks and Recreation. For several entries, we refer to complementary listings in other chapters where you can get more information, usually including prices. Now, just select what you want and have a ball — or a train ride, or a museum tour, or a nature walk...

Kids in Motion

Southern Beaches Area

Fort Foster
Off Maine Hwy. 103, Kittery
• (207) 439-3800

Sit on the beach, walk along the nature trails and explore this bunker-type fort. Kids will be wide-eyed at the ghost story associated with this fort. (See our Attractions chapter for directions and more on the story.)

Fort McClary State Park
Maine Hwy. 103, Kittery • (207) 384-5160

Kids of all ages will enjoy roaming this large hexagonal blockhouse by the sea. Eat lunch and relax as they explore, or join them! (See our Attractions chapter for more information.)

Ellis Park
Short Sands Beach, U.S. Hwy. 1A,
York Beach

Sit in a white-painted gazebo while the kids exercise their skills on the climbing toys and play on the swings at this little park by the sea. Or toss a ball around with them on the beautifully maintained lawn.

Wiggly Bridge
Maine Hwy. 103, York

Get out the camera and snap a picture of the kids as they cross what is believed to be the smallest suspension bridge in the world. You'll find the bridge off Route 103 as you head from York Village to York Harbor. From Kittery, heading north on Route 103, the bridge is on the left just past the York Town Dock.

Old York Historical Society Houses
Lindsay Rd. and U.S. Hwy. 1, York Village
• (207) 363-4974

Children will be ghoulishly entertained by the Old Gaol ("jail") at this museum. The one-room schoolhouse will also fascinate them (see Attractions for prices and more information).

Marginal Way, Perkins Cove and Pedestrian Footbridge
Ogunquit

Everyone will enjoy the walk from Ogunquit center to Perkins Cove along the Marginal Way, a 1.5-mile footpath that skirts the sea. Kids can burn off some of their youthful energy hopping, skipping and jumping along the way, and if they get tired, there are plenty of benches for them to take a rest.

At Perkins Cove you'll find perhaps the only double-leaf pedestrian drawbridge in the United States. This third version of the bridge was built in 1939, and kids will delight in pushing the button and hearing the alarm bell ring as they raise and lower the bridge to let sailboats pass through.

Laudholm Farm
342 Laudholm Farm Rd., Wells
• **(207) 646-1555**

Self-guide your way through Wells Reserve with the help of Annie Otter, Mitchell Mummichog and eight other "tour guides," part of the Discovery Program designed especially for kids. Each young explorer receives (to keep) a special guidebook that describes the five trail loops created for children. They can also borrow a backpack complete with a compass and binoculars to help them in their exploration.

The Wells National Estuarine Research Reserve at Laudholm Farm preserves 1,600 acres of varied field, forest, wetland and beach. Laudholm Farm is the center from which human contact can be made with the estuarine ecosystem without danger to the wildlife there. Both children and adults will enjoy the 7 miles of trails throughout the reserve, where you might see such endangered wildlife as peregrine falcons and piping plovers.

In addition to the Discovery Program, the Wells Reserve offers a variety of specialty tours such as bird walks, human history tours (which explore the evolution of Laudholm Farm from a Native American encampment to the present), nocturnal wildlife walks, research tours, skywatch and wildflower tours. Guidebooks and backpacks are available from the visitors center in the historic restored house of Laudholm Farm. The farm is open seven days a week, year round. Cost for tours is $3 per person or $6 for families. Tours are free on Community Day (Tuesdays). The gate to the parking lot is open from 9 AM to 5 PM, seven days a week, year round. You are free to use the trails during these hours, and some trails are handicapped-accessible. A parking fee of $7 is charged in July and August, except on Tuesdays.

Wonder Mountain Miniature Golf
U.S. Hwy. 1, Moody, Wells
• **(207) 646-9655**

Take your little explorers with you as you play through a most interesting miniature golf course. Kids will be thrilled by the gushing waterfall, caves and secret places on this mountain of wonder that features two 18-hole challenges. The course opens at 9 AM, and the last players are allowed on at 10:30 PM. Cost to play in 1998 was $5.50 for adults and teens for one round on one course, or $8 to play both courses. Cost for children younger than 12 was $4 (see our Attractions chapter).

Willowbrook at Newfield Restoration Village
Off Maine Hwy. 11, Newfield
• **(207) 793-2784**

Kids will delve into history with glee at this restoration village. Pretty grounds including a mill pond will attract them, along with the wonder that comes with learning how people lived in the 1800s. They'll be amazed by the Fenderson School House, so different from our schools of today, and overjoyed to choose from penny candy at the Amos Straw Country Store. (See our Attractions chapter for directions and prices.)

INSIDERS' TIP

Children will be enchanted by the whale painting on the wall opposite the Casco Bay Lines parking lot on the northern end of Commercial Street in the Old Port District of Portland. A series of these paintings was done on the sides of buildings in cities along Interstate 95 by artist Robert Wayland in the early 1990s. You'll find two more of them in New England — one in Boston and the other in Providence.

Orchard Dell Deer Farm
**1797 Alewife Rd. (Maine Hwy. 35),
Kennebunk • (207) 985-2435**

Children love visiting this farm where red deer are raised. These large, antlered animals originated in Europe; they're the type of deer Robin Hood would have hunted. There's plenty of room for the little folks to stretch their legs, and once they've slowed down a bit, you can buy them an ice cream. The deer farm is off Highway 35, 2 miles west of Maine Turnpike Exit 3. There's no charge to visit.

Cape Porpoise Pier
Off Maine Hwy. 9, Cape Porpoise

This adventure is about 3 miles north of Kennebunkport. You'll find a quiet village by the sea with a working fishing pier that's perfect for walking. The kids will enjoy the beautiful views of the harbor, with its fishing boats, and the lighthouse on Goat Island. Get them to listen to the music of the harbor: the chug-chug of boats, the raucous crying of the seagulls, the slap of the waves on the shore and the occasional dinging of boats' bells. The children can lean over the rails of the pier (carefully!) to watch lobstermen unloading their catches.

Old Orchard Beach Area

Schooner Miniature Golf
58 Ocean Park Rd., Saco • (207) 284-6174

Let your little sluggers practice their batting skill at the batting cages, then get the whole family involved in a miniature golf contest. In 1998, a round of golf was $3.50 per person; 10 balls in the batting cage were $1. (See our Attractions chapter for more information.)

Pirates Island Adventure Golf
**70 First St., Old Orchard Beach
• (207) 934-5086**

"Yo ho ho, me maties!" Grab a golf club and follow the twisting, turning paths of this creative miniature golf center that features two 18-hole courses. Kids will love the waterfall, tunnel and ponds that surround the site. (See our Attractions chapter for more information and prices.)

Shuffleboard in Ocean Park
**W. Grand Ave., Ocean Park,
Old Orchard Beach**

There's no need to take a cruise to get the chance to play shuffleboard. The whole family will enjoy playing on these shady courts just off the square in Ocean Park on W. Grand Avenue. Cost to play in 1998 was 50¢ for children and 75¢ for adults.

Covered Bridge in Ocean Park
**Temple Ave., Ocean Park,
Old Orchard Beach**

Walk along Temple Avenue from the beach or pull over (there's room to park) and let the kids explore this charming, green-painted covered bridge under the pines. It's lovely to walk on a thick carpet of pine needles beneath the tall trees on a hot day, and the little bridge is absolutely picture-perfect.

Greater Portland Area

Smiling Hill Farm
**781 County Rd. (Maine Hwy. 22),
Westbrook • (207) 775-4818**

Don't miss out on visiting this small, working dairy farm if you have small children. They'll love seeing and petting some of the more than 250 animals in the barnyard, including rabbits, cows and pigs. The farm also has an ice cream stand, sandwich bar and picnic tables set out on the grassy hillside. Cost for admission to the barnyard in 1998 was $5 for adults and $3.50 for children younger than 15. Children younger than 1 are admitted free. There is no charge for admission to the picnic area.

The Game Farm and Visitors Center
Maine Hwy. 26, Gray • (207) 657-4977

Kids will love this wild game farm operated by the Maine Department of Inland Fisheries and Wildlife. The animals you see at the farm are kept there for a variety of reasons. They may have been orphaned, might be suffering from injuries due to accidents or could be human-dependent from being raised (sometimes illegally) in captivity. You might see raccoons, squirrels, deer or porcupines, among other animals. In addition to the game farm, you'll find nature trails, picnic areas and a Nature Gift Store operated by the Maine Audubon Society. Dogs and other pets are not allowed beyond the parking area. Cost for admission in 1998 was $2 for children ages 4 through 12, $2.50 for seniors 60 or older and $3.50 for adults and teens. Children 3 or younger are admitted free.

Children's Theatre of Maine
Various locations, Portland
• (207) 878-2774

Children of all ages can experience the creation of live theater either by participating in a play or watching others their age put on a production at one of the oldest children's theaters in the country. The company usually produces two spring and two summer shows, allowing participating children to write, act, advertise and even make sets for the theater. In summer, you'll also find acting and play writing workshops. In May the winning entries from the theater's annual playwright's contest are performed. Tickets for all ages are $5. Show locations vary; call for information.

Deering Oaks Park
Park Ave., Portland • (207) 774-5514

Enjoy walking through this lovely, multi-faceted city park, designed by the same man who built New York's Central Park, and then take the kids on a paddleboat ride around the large duck pond. Deering Oaks also offers a restaurant and winter ice skating. (For more information, see our Parks and Recreation chapter.) The cost of boat rental is $3 for a half-hour. To get here, take Exit 6A off Interstate 295. That will take you to Forest Avenue, and the park will be on your right.

Fore River Sanctuary
Rowe Ave., Portland

You'll enjoy roaming 2.5 miles of trails that wind through this 76-acre preserve within the city limits of Portland. The trail follows the historic Cumberland and Oxford Canal, winding over a salt marsh and through the woods

to the city's only waterfall, Jewell's Falls. To get here, take Exit 8 off Interstate 95 and go three blocks east on Brighton Avenue to Rowe Avenue. The path begins at the end of Rowe Avenue and follows an old railroad track until the trails split into color-coded paths. The sanctuary is open dawn to dusk.

Joker's
510 Warren Ave., Portland
• (207) 878-5800

This is a great place for the kids to unwind — especially if the weather's bad. Inside this mega-complex of fun, you'll find indoor go-carts, a train and Ferris wheel as well as a three-story high "A-Maze-Zing" playhouse. There are more than 150 arcade and video machines, plus laser tag, spaceball and trampoline volleyball. If that isn't enough to get rid of extra energy, we don't know what will! Enjoy all this while eating lunch or dinner on the premises. You get in free, then pay for individual rides and games.

Maine Audubon Society
Gilsland Farm, U.S. Hwy. 1, Falmouth
• (207) 781-2330

Hunt through forests, salt marshes and meadows and spy on the pond at this nature preserve at Gilsland Farm. Or come for a weekend program and have a guide take you on the trails or help you make arts and crafts out of natural materials. You'll also catch seminars on everything from loons, snow and recycling to animal adaptations.

The Discovery Room has changing interactive exhibits where children can put their hands in covered boxes and guess what's inside, or try on moose and deer antlers to see what it's like to wear them. Justin the turtle is a favorite at the pond exhibit, and brave youngsters can lift the lid off an enclosed beehive and watch the honey-making process. A $1 donation is requested for the Discovery Room. The year-round attraction is open Monday through Saturday from 9 AM to 5 PM and Sunday from noon to 5 PM. The sanctuary is open dawn till dusk. To get here

Let Us Show You the Way Way

Don't worry about not being able to find the Way Way. You can't miss it. In fact, the first time we saw it, we couldn't believe our eyes. "What is that?!" we said, and immediately stopped to investigate. You'll want to, too.

Located on Route 112 (the Buxton Road), the building is made of red-and-cream-painted stone with columns holding up an overhanging carport that covers disused gas pumps. Behind it and across the street, woods form a backdrop behind fields of waving tall grass.

Close-up

Inside you'll find beautiful wooden cabinetry with glass tops and sides displaying a colorful selection of penny candy. For a penny kids can choose from sourdrops and Swedish fish, sour patch kids and gum, to name a few. There's a selection of candy for five¢ and 10¢ and more expensive stuff as well. Still, for a quarter, your little ones can walk away with a pleasantly filled bag of sweets. There's even a wooden box for little legs to stand on so children can peer through the glass.

Whether they have a dime or a dollar to spend, children's transactions are taken seriously by Catherine Cousens and her sister-in-law, Margaret "Peggy" Tyrell. They never rush the children but let them take their time, choosing one of this or two of that - whatever their little hearts' desire. It can be quite a serious matter for a small child to choose how to spend 10¢, and Catherine and Peggy know it!

Owned by Catherine and Maynard "John" Cousens, the Way Way was built by John Cousens' father in the 1920s. Despite the Great Depression, he made his own cement and hauled rocks and gravel to build the store. Catherine laughs when she says he wouldn't tell anyone what the name of the store was going to be. He wrote it in cement above the doorway, hid it until the building was complete, then unveiled the "Way Way."

Why was it called the Way Way? Well, Catherine explains, at the time it was built, the store was "way way up country," with about six farms between it and Saco's Main Street. It was a true general store carrying lamp chimneys, boots and rubbers, axes, nails, bolts and all the things local farmers needed. There was even a resident mechanic at the Way Way.

Today the Way Way is on the National Register of Historic Buildings. It's still a general store, but it doesn't carry axes and lamp chimneys any more. Instead you'll find regular grocery staples and canned goods, souvenirs and the famous candy counters. The Way Way is open year round. Tour buses and children are always welcome.

The Way Way General Store is on the National Register of Historic Buildings. You won't be able to miss its unique exterior.

from Interstate 295, take Exit 9, and after crossing the bridge, look for the Maine Audubon Society sign on the left.

The Desert of Maine
Desert Rd., Freeport • (207) 865-6962

A desert in Maine? When William Tuttle moved to this 300-acre farm in 1797 to plant hay and potatoes, he couldn't imagine it either. But when severe soil erosion exposed sand hidden beneath the soil, Tuttle and his family were forced to move away. It wasn't until this century that Henry Guldrup saw the potential of this seeming wasteland, and it was preserved as a natural phenomenon.

Geologists believe the sand and mineral deposits were left behind by a melting glacier 8,000 years ago. What was bad luck for Tuttle will be great luck for you as you explore the trails weaving through the woods edging this giant desert. If the walking is too much, you can opt for a narrated coach tour of the dunes. Spend some time in the 1783 Barn Museum, where a collection of antique farm tools, sand paintings and a sand collection are housed in Tuttle's old shingle barn, or check out the Desert Dunes Gift Shop, which sells Native American pottery, Maine-made crafts and unique sand designs and paintings. Open May through October, the price of admission is $6.50 for adults, $5.75 for seniors, $4.50 for teenagers ages 13 to 16 and $3.50 for children ages 6 to 12. You'll find a picnic area here, and camping is available at the Desert of Maine Campground (see our Camping chapter).

Perham's
Maine Hwy. 26, West Paris
• (207) 674-2341

OK, this one's a little west of the coast, but for rock hounds (and jewelry lovers) of all ages, it will be well worth the trip. Maine's Western Mountains are full of semi-precious gems and minerals, and you will find plenty of them at this mineral store and museum about an hour northwest of Portland.

At Perham's there is a display of the various gems and minerals you might find if you visit one of the four Western Maine quarries where you and the kids can dig for free! Whispering Pines has rose quartz, the Harvard Quarry has rare purple apatite and the

Nubble Quarry has garnet, mica, quartz and feldspar. All it takes is a small pick or hammer (the common hardware store variety will do), a magnifying glass and luck to uncover a find. There's also a jewelry store featuring Maine gems and a store that sells rock-hounding equipment.

The easiest way to get here from the south is to take Exit 11 off the Maine Turnpike in Gray. Turn right at the exit, at the light go left, then turn left again onto Maine Highway 26. Perham's is open everyday from 9 AM to 5 PM.

Brunswick, Bath and Boothbay Harbor Area

Josephine Newman Wildlife Sanctuary
Maine Hwy. 127, Georgetown
• (207) 781-2330

You'll find easy walking trails on this Maine Audubon Preserve on a peninsula off Woolwich. It takes about 20 minutes to get here from Route 1, but the walk is free and will take you through meadows, woods and along Robinhood Cove. A booklet on the history of the sanctuary is available from the society at the number listed.

Turn onto Highway 127 just before the Dairy Queen in Woolwich after crossing over the Kennebec River in Bath. Look for the sanctuary on your left about 10 miles down the peninsula. Parking is in a little alcove cut into the trees just beside the road. If you reach Reid State Park, you've gone too far, but that's also a great place to explore with the kids (see our Parks and Recreation chapter for more).

The Morris Farm
156 Maine Hwy. 27, Wiscasset
• (207) 882-4080

Come meet the animals and explore the fields and streams at one of the last working farms in Wiscasset. Kids will enjoy seeing and learning about the laying hens and chickens (there is a difference), ducks, turkeys, Jersey cows and a pair of rare American Guinea Hogs. There are summer workshops on subjects such as making tomato sauce from scratch (with fresh pasta to go along with it) and exploring and investigating the farm's various streams and critters. And the farm itself is always open for self-guided tours.

During July and August, come for kids camp. The farm was established as a non-profit in 1994 when a group of local citizens raised money to buy it and save it from future development. Now area school children and adults can come help out and learn about agriculture. See how organic gardening is done, have a picnic by the waterfall or visit the farm store to purchase locally grown fruits, veggies, meats and cheeses. There's also a great spot for picnicking inside a little knoll with a waterfall and boulders.

You'll find the farm just next door to the Wiscasset Primary School, and that's a good place to park when school is out. The farm is open daily during daylight hours. Call ahead for a tour schedule or pick up a self-guided tour map. Admission is free, but donations are welcome.

Boothbay Railway Village
Maine Hwy. 27, Boothbay • (207) 633-4727

This old-fashioned railway museum is set up like an early New England village on 8 acres of land, so there's plenty of space for the kids to romp as you walk from one exhibit to another among the 27 buildings. Check out early toys in the Village Toy Shop, then stroll through a bank, hotel, barber shop, millinery and more while learning what village life used to be like.

You can also hop on a narrow-gauge steam train, the Boothbay Central, for a 20-minute ride around the village, through the woods and over the kissing bridge. The train stops at Summit Station, and passengers can get off to take a short walk to a 15,000-square-foot antique auto and truck display. Ticket prices are $7 for adults and teens, $3 for children ages 3 to 12 and free for children younger than 3. During the third weekend in August, all children get in free. Beginning in mid-June, the village is open daily from 9:30 AM to 5 PM,

and it remains open until Columbus Day weekend. All the attractions are included in the admission, and the train departs every half-hour.

Things in Motion

Southern Beaches Area

Lobstering Trips on The Boat
Town Dock No. 2, Harris Island Rd. off Maine Hwy. 103, York Harbor
• (207) 363-3234

Your kids will love being close to the action on a real lobster boat. They'll watch as traps are set and lobsters are caught while learning about these popular crustaceans from experienced lobstermen. (See our Attractions chapter for prices and more information).

Narrated Historical Trolley Tour
New England Trolley Company, York

This hour-long historic tour of the Yorks will entertain the whole family. Smaller children will merely enjoy the ride while older ones may actually learn some interesting historical facts! You'll pass Jefferd's Tavern, the Old Gaol (jail) and other historic points of interest. Tours depart on the hour from Dave's Thriftway Shopping Center on Long Sands Road. Cost for the tour was $3 per person in 1998, regardless of age. Tour tickets allow a free reboarding during the same day, space permitting. A partial-loop local ride was $1.50 per person. The trolley operates from the end of June to Labor Day (the first Monday in September).

York's Wild Kingdom
U.S. Hwy. 1, York Beach
• (207) 363-4911, (207) 363-3025

Lions and tigers and bears, oh my! Kids will see these animals and many others as they explore this "wild kingdom." They'll enjoy close encounters with small animals like goats and rabbits in the petting zoo, laugh as

Funtown offers reduced admission prices after 6 PM. You can ride from 6 until closing for $13.

they watch the "Talk to the Animal Show" and be awed by the elephant show. The whole family will be fascinated by the white tiger lecture: You'll learn about Maine's only white tiger, which lives at this zoo. Kids will also enjoy the amusement rides like the Ferris wheel and carousel located near the entrance to the park. There's also a large picnic area at Wild Kingdom. Ticket prices for the zoo and amusements in 1998 were $12.75 for adults and teens, $9.50 for children ages 4 through 10 and $3.50 for children ages 3 or younger.

Seashore Trolley Museum
Log Cabin Rd., Kennebunkport
• **(207) 967-2800**

Take a ride on an old-fashioned trolley at the Seashore Trolley Museum. The oldest and largest mass transportation museum in the world, it houses more than 40 of the finest trolleys in existence. Children will enjoy the thrill of riding in an authentically restored, open-sided electric trolley complete with the well-known ding-ding trolley bell sound.

In addition to the car barns that house the trolleys and the ride, you can also visit artisans in the restoration workshop or browse through the museum store. Entrance fees (including unlimited rides) in 1998 were $7 for adults, $5 for senior citizens and $4.50 for children ages 6 to 16. Children younger than 6 are admitted free. The museum is open daily from May to the second weekend in October. From the second weekend in October to the second week of November the museum is open on weekends and by chance or appointment on weekdays, weather permitting.

Old Orchard Beach Area

Funtown/Splashtown USA
U.S. Hwy. 1 S., Saco
• **(207) 284-5139, (800) 878-2900**

Scream, yell, laugh and smile as you enjoy the thrills at these two parks, filled with a multitude of rides and amusements. Originally two parks on one site, the two merged in 1996. Splashtown incorporates all the water-based rides (except the log flume), while Funtown is where you'll find traditional rides like the roller coaster and tilt-a-whirl.

In May 1998 Funtown celebrated the opening of the largest wooden roller coaster in New England. Called "Excaliber," the coaster generates lots of thrills, but it isn't the only attraction in this wonderful park. (For more information on Excaliber, see Attractions). A castle-like entrance gate, beautifully maintained grounds and neat paths lead you through a wonderland of color, lights and sound. You'll find Grand Prix racing cars, a pirate ship swing ride, an antique car ride and a unique scrambler ride called the Astrosphere, where you enter an airlocked dome and get twirled around in the dark amidst a laser light show and music. The lines are long for the Astrosphere, but it's worth the wait.

Funtown opens weekends in May and daily from late June until the last week in August. It is also open some weekends in September. Splashtown operates daily from mid-June to the end of August. You can purchase discount ride passes for either park or a combination pass. Individual tickets are also available as well as a booklet of 10 kiddie ride tickets. In 1998, entrance fees were $20 for adults and some teens (those 48 inches or taller) and $14 for children (shorter than 48 inches) at Funtown. Splashtown tickets were $15 for adults and $12 for children. A combination pass for both parks was $28 for adults and $20 for children. Those ages 2 and younger are admitted free but must have a ticket or bracelet to ride. Children shorter than 48 inches tall must be accompanied by a paying adult in the water park.

There is a $3.50 fee to enter the parks. If you don't want to spend a whole day, special evening rates apply if you choose to visit Funtown from 6 PM to closing (Splashtown isn't open in the evening). During those hours you can get an all-inclusive ride pass for $13. Opening days and times for the parks are weather-permitting.

Aquaboggan
U.S. Hwy. 1 S., Saco
• **(207) 282-3112**

When the kids are cranky and bored with the beach, take them along to Aquaboggan. This large water park offers a variety of water-based amusements and other attractions sure to entertain the whole family. Challenge a friend

Photo: Merry Farnum

The Children's Museum of Maine is great for a rainy day.

to see who'll get to the bottom first on the Dual Yankee Ripper, bump each other into the fountain on bumper boats, toss and turn in the wave pool or take to the track and race each other around in the Grand Prix race cars. When you're tired of splashing, play a round of miniature golf. The park also offers a recently expanded toddler splash and play area, plus souvenir and concession stands.

A Super Ticket, which includes one ride on the special attractions like the bumper boats and race cars, was $23.95 in 1998. A Senior Ticket, which does not include special rides, cost $16.95. A Junior Ticket was $11.95 and a Pool Ticket was $10.50. There are no children's rates as such, though height restrictions may determine which ticket you can buy. Kids must be under 4 feet tall, for instance, to get in on a Junior Ticket.

Palace Playland
1 Old Orchard St., Old Orchard Beach
• (207) 934-2001

In true summer resort style, this amusement park sits right on the beach. Next to the town's famous pier (be sure to grab an order of Pier Fries!), Palace Playland offers a good selection of adult and kiddie rides, the largest pinball and video arcade in New England, games, food and an enormous water slide. The whole family will love the view from the top of the SunWheel, and kids will laugh as they traverse Sheik Abdulla's funhouse and dodge each other in the Dodgem cars.

Ride passes in 1998 were $16.95 for adult rides including the water slide and $11.95 for a kiddie-ride pass. Tickets are also available individually for 75¢, and in books; the number of tickets required varies by ride. The park is open daily from the end of May to the beginning of September and some weekends in May and September, weather permitting.

Greater Portland Area

Scarborough Marsh Nature Center
Maine Hwy. 9 (Pine Point Rd.), Scarborough
• (207) 883-5100, (207) 781-2330

Learn about Maine's largest salt marsh while paddling in a red or green canoe along the tidal river that twists and turns through the marsh to the sea. Red-winged blackbirds, cormorants and egrets are among the host of bird species to be seen. Cost for a variety of different tours in 1998 was $9 for adults and teens, $7 for children 12 or younger. (For more information, see our Attractions chapter.)

Portland International Jetport
Western Ave., Portland (about 1 mile from the Maine Mall)

If you've been shopping and the kids are restless, take them to the airport to watch planes taking off and landing. The runway is easily visible through a large chain-link fence. (There are official airport parking areas, but they can make the fun more expensive.) The kids will get a thrill as planes swoop down for landing or take off just beyond the fence, and you can't beat the price.

Maine Narrow Gauge Railroad Co. & Museum
58 Fore St., Portland • (207) 828-0814

Once you take a 3-mile train ride along scenic Casco Bay on a set of tracks that are just 2-feet wide, you'll know why they call it the "narrow" gauge railroad. The smallish trains and 2-foot tracks were unique to Maine from the 1870s through the 1940s, hauling wood, slate and farm produce to wider, standard-sized trains that would then haul the items around the country.

At this year-round museum, you'll find authentic narrow gauge trains including the Rangeley, which was the only such parlor car ever made. You'll also get to see the inner workings of a disassembled locomotive and view videos on the trains' histories. The museum is open daily from 10 AM to 4 PM. Train rides are available daily from May 15 through October 15 and on weekends during the offseason. The museum is free to visit, but tickets for the train are $5 for adults and teens, $4 for seniors and $3 for children ages 4 to 12.

The Maine Bear Factory
Maine Hwy. 1, Freeport
• (207) 846-1570

The things in motion at this teddy bear factory are the teddy bears themselves! Get ready to build your own bear from the fur up. You can pick the shade of fuzz and what color his (or her) eyes will be, and even determine how much he will eat before stuffing him on the stuffing machine. Then watch as stitchers sew and groom your bear right in front of your eyes. Give your new-found friend a "bear bath," pick his outfit and accessories, and he is ready to go.

The factory is open Monday through Saturday from 10 AM to 5:30 PM and Sunday from noon to 5 PM. The price of the bears ranges from $28.95 to $64.95, and this is the only place (besides the Internet) where you can get them.

Brunswick, Bath and Boothbay Harbor Area

Brunswick Fishway
Brunswick-Topsham Hydro Plant, Maine St., Brunswick • (207) 725-6621

Didn't think fish could climb ladders? Atlantic salmon, alewives and shad can, if it's the fish ladder at the Androscoggin Dam in Brunswick, and you can watch them through a viewing room above the holding pool. Attracted by the large stream of water flowing out of the powerhouse, the fish climb the 40-step underwater ladder to get over the dam to spawn upstream. When they get to the top, they are counted and sorted. Some are placed back in the water to continue their journey, and others are trucked to other rivers. You can watch it all through aquarium-like windows at the side of the holding pool on May and June weekends from 10 AM to 2 PM and Wednesday evenings from 7 to 9 PM. Admission is free.

Maine Coast Railroad
U.S. Hwy. 1, Wiscasset
• (207)882-8000, (800) 795-5404

Whooooo, whooooo! Travel the coast of Maine in a diesel-powered coach from the 1920s or '30s as you chug over tidal rivers and wildlife marshes. Look for osprey, eagle and heron nesting grounds and scan the woods for moose during your 100-minute journey. Trains run from May through December and include spectacular fall foliage tours. Lunch is available on board. Tickets for adults and teens are $10; it's $9 for seniors and $5 for children ages 5 to 12. Kids 4 and younger get in free. Trains leave three times a day; call ahead for departure times. Special train rides also take place during the fall months to see the breath-taking change in the color of the Maine woods. In October there's a special haunted train ride.

Owls Head Transportation Museum
Maine Hwy. 73, Owls Head • (207) 594-4418

Call ahead for the schedule of events at this auto and airplane museum. It's about 45 minutes north of Wiscasset, but your reward will be great. On various weekends, the museum hosts fly-ins, aerobatics shows, antique truck and tractor meets, classic car auctions, motorcycle festivals, a car parts flea market and a bicycle/pedal-powered vehicle meet and air show.

The museum itself is known internationally for its collection of pioneer aircraft, historic automobiles, bicycles, motorcycles, carriages and engines. It's open daily April through October from 10 AM to 5 PM. From November to March, it's open weekdays 10 AM to 4 PM and weekends 10 AM to 3 PM. Pack a picnic and enjoy the eating area, or explore the 60-acre nature park. You'll also find a museum gallery and store and a theater showing transportation films.

To get here, follow U.S. Highway 1 through Thomaston. After driving through town, turn right on Buttermilk Lane just after the cement factory. At the end of the lane, turn left. The transportation museum will be on your right. The cost of admission is $6 for adults and teens, $5 for seniors older than 65 and $4 for children 5 through 12, or $16 per family. Children younger than 5 get in free.

Minds in Motion

Southern Beaches Area

Hackmatack Playhouse
538 Maine Hwy. 9, Berwick
• (207) 698-1807

From the beginning of July to mid-August, this theater near Kittery holds children's productions every Friday and Saturday at 10 AM.

The 1998 season featured magic shows and mystery and drama productions. Prices in 1998 were $5 for all seats.

Greater Portland Area

Creative Resource Center
1103 Forest Ave., Portland
• (207) 797-9543

This nonprofit organization collects and sells clean, safe, inexpensive scrap materials for just about any craft project you can imagine. It's filled floor to ceiling with recyclables in brightly painted barrels and clear plastic bins. You'll find a paper corner stocked with all sizes and colors of paper, a fabric area with canvas, wool, ribbons, wallpaper, yarn and zippers as well as other materials including buttons, rope, cardboard, wood, metal and plastic. Call ahead and check out their offerings for creative workshops. The center is open year round Tuesday through Saturday.

Portland Public Library
2 Monument Sq., Portland
• (207) 871-1700

Explore the kids' room in this four-story library in Portland's downtown district. The library has been serving children for more than 100 years! Award-winning authors will mesmerize children and adults alike with storytelling and concerts. Stop in for a schedule of events.

The Children's Museum of Maine
142 Free St., Portland
• (207) 828-1234

Haul traps on a Maine lobster boat, soar in a space shuttle, milk a cow or run your own grocery store — these are some of the activities you can try in the many interactive, hands-on exhibits at The Children's Museum. Both adults and children can explore science and the arts in a colorful, open atmosphere while letting their imaginations run wild.

Make sure to see the Camera Obscura and optics room, where you can gather around a table lit up with moving images of Casco Bay and downtown Portland. The show is done using Renaissance technology involving a large mirror and a 12-inch lens. Check out the

gifts in the Flights of Imagination museum gift shop or enjoy lunch in a cafe that welcomes children.

General admission is $5, with children younger than 1 getting in free. Admission is free on Friday evenings from 5 to 8. Museum hours are Monday, Wednesday, Thursday and Saturday from 10 AM to 5 PM, Sunday from noon to 5 PM, and Friday from 10 AM to 8 PM. Parking is in the garage a block and a half past the museum. Keep your museum ticket stubs for 2 hours of free parking.

Brunswick, Bath and Boothbay Harbor Area

Maine Maritime Museum
243 Washington St., Bath • (207) 443-1316

Open year-round from 9:30 AM to 5 PM, one of the state's most popular tourist attractions affords youngsters the wonder of exploring Maine shipbuilding. Located at the site of the old Percy & Small Shipyard, which built 41 schooners between 1894 and 1920, the museum has refurbished the original shipyard buildings with exhibits on how wooden ships were built. Everything from lofting the design lines to launching day is accurately reconstructed.

Shipyard tours are available only from April 15 through October. Also, throughout the summer, visiting ships tie up at the museum docks along the Kennebec River. But if you happen to come at an off time, there's still plenty to see and do. The lobstering exhibit lets you walk down a mock pier and take in displays on how lobstermen prepare and can lobster meat. You can watch a video about the industry from your perch on the gunwale of a lobster boat. And if you call ahead to find out the time, you can catch a live lobster demonstration discussing the anatomy, lore and typical habits of lobsters and the history of lobstering.

The museum itself has a library research room and a wide collection of ship paintings and memorabilia. Admission is $8 for adults and $5.50 for children ages 6 to 17. Kids younger than 6 get in free. The museum is open daily from 9:30 AM to 5 PM. Don't miss

---

INSIDERS' TIP

You don't have to spend much money to have fun with the kids. Why not challenge them to a sandcastle building contest at the beach? Let the winner choose where to have dinner that night.

the gift store, which is stocked with a great selection of nautical gifts and books. You'll find tasteful picnic spots and a children's play area in a giant sandbox shaped like a ship. If you're going to be in town for awhile, be sure to find out about the various summer and winter camp programs for children 6 and younger. River rides in the museum's excursion boat are an additional fee and should be reserved ahead of time. Mooring is available for people who prefer to sail here.

Marine Resources Aquarium
McKown Point Rd., W. Boothbay Harbor
• (207) 633-9542

Sponsored by the Maine Department of Marine Resources and the U.S. Fish and Wildlife Service, this just-completed aquarium has tanks of fish and shellfish common to the Gulf of Maine. Search for crabs, sea urchins, sea cucumbers and sea stars in the indoor tidal pools or step outside for a picnic lunch right on the harbor. To get here follow Maine Highway 27 and take the first left after St. Andrew's Hospital onto the McKown Point Road. The aquarium is at the end of the road.

If you are coming during July or August, we strongly suggest you ride the Rocktide trolley at the Small Mall directly across from Shop 'n' Save. The trolley is free, but bring along some change to tip the driver. Trolley pickup runs on the half-hour from 10:30 AM to 2:30 PM. The aquarium is open weekdays from Memorial Day to Columbus Day from 10 AM to 5 PM. Admission is $2.50 for adults and $2 for seniors and children between 5 and 18. Children younger than 4 get in free.

We have everything
from agricultural shows
and arts festivals to
concerts, carnivals,
craft fairs and
competitions.

Annual Events and Festivals

In Southern Maine we're proud of our festivals and annual events and how long we've been holding them. The Topsham Fair, for example, began in 1854! In this chapter you'll find many other events that have grown over the years, and some that are still enjoying infancy.

We have everything from agricultural shows and arts festivals to concerts, carnivals, craft fairs and competitions. And, of course, there's always entertainment that's just plain silly — such as an April event in Boothbay Harbor where you can run across a row of lobster crates strung together in the harbor. Hey, we've got to have some way to amuse ourselves when the weather gets cold. (Yes, it's still that cold in April.)

With so many small towns sprinkled along our coastline, there are many local events that aren't mentioned here such as Memorial Day parades and small church craft fairs (it seems that just about every church has one). But we've tried to give you a mix of big-crowd drawers and small-town get-togethers. That way you can pick whatever you're in the mood for — long lines and loud festivities or pocket audiences and evening serenades.

Many of the bigger events are spectacular, but don't pass up the others just because they're small. You'll get a great feel for our communities and what it's like to live here and be one of us. There's plenty to do during the summer months, our biggest tourism season, when the weather is spectacular. Come here in the off-season and there may not be as much going on, but you'll get a great taste of true Maine life as we hunker down for the winter and cozy up in our cabins. Around

Christmas time craft fairs are the big socializers, with plenty of home-baked goodies, knickknacks and stocking stuffers. Some are even juried, where a committee votes on who gets to participate.

There are two terrific categories of events you won't find in this chapter. If you're looking for an outdoor concert to attend during the summer, there are plenty. Many places such as Portland and Boothbay Harbor have special concert series where different artists play free to the public on certain nights of the week. We have chosen to include these in our Arts chapter, so look for them there. There are also great farmers' markets where you can buy fresh, locally grown produce and flowers. They begin early in the growing season and last through September. We've written those up as a category in our Shopping chapter.

Remember to dress for the weather. In the summer bring a hat and sunscreen if you're going to an outdoor event, because it gets pretty hot and there might not be much shade. And dress really warmly for any outdoor winter activities. No matter how good the entertainment, you won't enjoy it if your ears and toes are numb. We can't stress this enough.

As you read through this chapter, know that the cost of admission is free unless specified. However, if you're going to a fair or carnival, you should still expect to pay for rides, games and food. Listings are not grouped using our four geographical areas but are instead arranged in loose chronological order, with early-month activities coming first and late-month happenings last.

January

L.L. Bean Cross Country Ski Center
Freeport Country Club, Old Country Rd., Freeport • (800) 341-4341 ext. 2666

Pack your cross-country skis or plan to rent a pair when you arrive at this golf course turned ski club. Whether you're a pro or a newcomer, you'll have a great time getting out in the crisp winter air and gliding over nearly 15 kilometers of groomed trails. You'll find plenty of flat terrain for ski-skating (a sport that requires shorter skis that maneuver like ice skates) and rolling hills and woods for cross-country-style skiing.

The center is run by the L.L. Bean retail store, and ski lessons are available on site. Weather permitting it's open from November through mid-March; just make sure there's a foot of solid snow cover or skiing here won't be possible. Expect to pay about $8 for an adult ski ticket and $6 for kids. Lessons are from $15 to $30 and are available for all skill levels. You'll get here by taking Interstate 95 to Exit 19 in Freeport. Turn right onto U.S. Highway 1, follow it 1.4 miles, then turn right onto Old Country Road, passing back over the interstate. Turn right again and follow the road until you see the Freeport Country Club on the left. The course opens mid-morning and closes in late afternoon — remember, it gets dark early in the winter.

February

Winter Carnival
Parson's Field, Kennebunk • (207) 985-6890

If it's the beginning of February and the kids are tired of indoor activities and bored with sledding and skating, bring them to this weekend event, organized by the Kennebunk Parks and Recreation Department and co-sponsored by the Portside Rotary Club. Events include a variety show, spaghetti supper, children's games, sleigh/hay rides, ice skating and a petting zoo. If you think you make a prize-winning chili or chowder, enter the chili/chowder contest. If cooking isn't your strong point, get the whole family involved in the snow sculpture contest and the annual snowball championship.

February Is For Lovers
Various locations, Kennebunks • (207) 967-0857

Kennebunk and Kennebunkport join to host this month long celebration with a romance theme. Special events include a Valentine Gala, Opera for Lovers and a Winter Carnival. Romantics can keep warm by participating in winter sports such as cross-country skiing and ice skating, or they can cuddle up in a sleigh or on a carriage ride. For those who prefer indoor activities, museum visits, shopping and antiquing are also available. Fall in love again while you enjoy romantic accommodations and intimate, candlelit dinners at local restaurants.

The Southern Coast in Winter
Various locations

This is the time of peace, reflection and easy parking. While many of our hotels and restaurants (and some shops) close during this slowest time of year, plenty of bed and breakfasts stay open (see our Bed and Breakfast Inns chapter). Design your own vacation package and pay much lower off-season accommodation rates. Then pick a beach and enjoy the seclusion of being one of the only people walking along the shore.

Visit the coast after a recent snowfall, and you'll see the wonder of pure white beaches

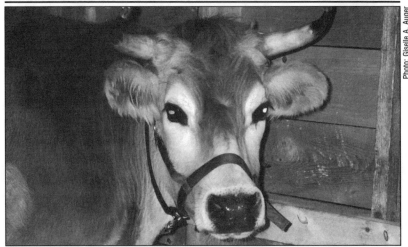

From September through October, farmers and breeders from across Maine and New England flock to agricultural fairs to display their prize livestock, compete for prizes and buy and sell animals.

and foaming surf crashing over the snow. On some days the ocean breeze is cold enough to take your breath away, but the stark beauty of the coast at this time of the year is well worth the trip. Then stop in at a country store on your way back and pick up a cup of hot chocolate. Your mind will be clearer, and you'll be ready to face civilization again.

March

Annual Home, Food & Juried Craft Show
Kennebunk High School, Fletcher St., Kennebunk • (207) 967-0857

Held the next-to-last weekend in March, this show draws more than 100 local business displays. Each year the focus of the show is geared to a particular theme. In 1998 the theme was "Ten Years of Commitment to the Community." Guest appearances by state celebrities like Miss Maine, the official Portland Pirates mascot ("Crackers"), Renzo the Clown and local radio personalities make the event even more fun. There's a children's corner featuring Maine authors and children's literature, and you can take part in raffles held

throughout the weekend. It may be too early to think about Christmas shopping, but at the craft show you'll find dried floral arrangements, woodwork, crochet items and pottery that will make you reach for the checkbook.

Fill up on pancakes at the pancake breakfast, held on Saturday morning from 8:30 to 10 AM, and you won't be hungry until late in the day! Cost to put away hotcakes is less than $5 per person. Proud of your chili or chowder? Then enter the chili/chowder contest held on Sunday or merely enjoy the competition as a bystander. Entertainment is held throughout the weekend, with a special concert featuring local rock bands held on Saturday night from 6 to 9 PM.

Kennebunk Fun Run
Kennebunk High School, Fletcher St., Kennebunk • (207) 985-3870

Walk or run this 5K road race, but do it for fun! Proceeds from the race are used to help a seriously ill child from the local community. Pre-registration for the event is available beginning in January. For a registration form send a self addressed stamped envelope (SASE) to Record Rendevous, 8 York St., Kennebunk, ME 04044. The race begins at 8

AM and goes off regardless of rain, snow or shine. T-shirts will be given to the first 300 registered participants.

Dinners for the Arts, the Annual River Tree Arts Fund-raiser
Various venues, Kennebunks
• **(207) 985-4343**

Toward the end of March the Kennebunks host a social and culinary celebration, also known as a "progressive dinner" (due to the "progressing" of participants from one venue to another), to raise funds for River Tree Arts. You'll begin your evening with the entire group of about 150 diners gathered for cocktails at an oceanfront home. While there, you'll receive an envelope telling you at which fine home you will eat dinner. Each of 15 to 20 hosts welcomes six to 12 guests for an intimate homemade dinner. Following dinner you'll move on to the Victorian Club, where the entire group reconvenes for desserts and entertainment. The event is dressy but not black-tie, and it is open to anyone who would like to participate (up to a limit of about 150 people). Cost for the evening was $35 in 1998.

River Tree Arts is a community arts organization that runs a music school and sponsors performances throughout the year. The group also operates an art gallery in the Depot Building in Kennebunk (see our Arts chapter).

L.L. Bean Fly Fishing Expo
L.L. Bean, Main St., Freeport
• **(800) 341-4341 ext. 26666**

If you love fly fishing, you'll love this extravaganza, which takes place at the L.L. Bean retail store toward the end of March. Leading makers of fly-fishing gear set up booths throughout the store to display their products and show people how to use them. You'll get free lessons in fly-tying and see a live demonstration — in the store's indoor trout pond — of how to properly catch and release a fish. In the conference room you can listen to speakers, who will fill you in on the area's best fishing grounds and on what equipment to take along.

April

Ogunquit's Patriot's Day Weekend Celebration
Ogunquit Beach, Ogunquit
• **(207) 646-2939**

Maine and Massachusetts are the only two states in the nation that celebrate Patriot's Day (the second or third Monday each April). If you aren't running in the Boston Marathon, why not join the fun in Ogunquit? Tents are set up on Ogunquit Beach, where you can browse through vendors' wares in the bazaar tent, try your luck in the casino tent or enjoy restaurant tastings and ongoing entertainment.

Chocolate Lover's Fling
Holiday Inn By the Bay, 88 Spring St., Portland • (207) 799-9020

Wear an elastic waistband to this chocolate feast held every April as a fund-raiser for the Sexual Assault Response Services (SARS) of Southern Maine. Tables of luxurious chocolate pies, cakes, creams, soufflés, pâtés and tortes fill the room where this event takes place. Expect a complete loss of control, and plan to eat until you get carried out.

More than 50 restaurants, hotels and chocolatiers participate, and the event draws more than 1,000 people. Many local celebrities attend, and some of them help judge. Last year there was standing room only. It's no mystery when you consider the lengths bakers go to win the People's Choice Award for the best chocolate dish. Past winners have included the Chocolate Mountain — a chocolate, chocolate-filled cake smothered with chocolate. Another big winner: strawberries dressed in chocolate tuxedos. Then there was the chocolate pâtés with raspberry sauce and the 30-pound cake built to replicate the hotel where it was baked.

Exactly when the all-you-can-eat event takes place varies year to year, so call the SARS center at the listed number to find out the dates for this year. The cost is $15 a person; children younger than 5 get in free. Dress is black-tie and mud boots, which basically means you can wear whatever makes you feel comfy. The event generally takes place from 1 to 4 PM and includes a chocolate and non-chocolate auction, where you can bid on everything from waist-expanding delectables to ski packages, trips, golf equipment and whatever else someone happens to donate.

Fishermen's Festival
On the water and at Boothbay Region High School, Maine Hwy. 27, Boothbay Harbor • (207) 633-2353

If you think the water off the Maine coast is chilly in the summer, try it at the end of April as a contestant in this lobster-crate run. The object is to run across a string of 40 crates tied together between two floats in the harbor as many times as possible before falling in! And have no doubt, you will fall in. Sixth-grader Jon Farrin holds the record for running across more than 600 crates in 1996! It took him about 20 minutes. The run takes place on the harbor, and nearby is the annual codfish relay in which high school students don foulweather gear and form teams that race through the downtown area holding a codfish by the tail.

Once you've had your fill of downtown fun, head to Boothbay Region High School, where you can watch the fastest fish filletcutters and clam shuckers compete and see the judges sample entries in the fish chowder contest. For grammar schoolers, there is the coronation of Miss Shrimp. No, the prize doesn't necessarily go the shortest girl.

May

Opening of the Arts District
Congress Square, corner of Congress and High St., Portland • (207) 772-4994

Come watch as young and experienced dancers from The Portland School of Ballet weave colorful ribbons around a May pole to the rhythms of Celtic music. This pre-Christian ritual to welcome spring is performed toward the end of May as an opening celebration for the downtown Arts District. If you're one of the luckier members of the audience,

you may even get picked to take part! Also on hand are jugglers and musicians. The event usually takes place on a midweek afternoon and draws spectators from the street and the downtown office buildings. (See our Arts chapter for more on The Portland School of Ballet and the downtown Arts District.)

June

Old Port Festival
Old Port District, Portland • (207) 772-6828

Kick off the summer with this family festival in early June. It started 25 years ago as a block party to celebrate the arrival of the season and grew into what some believe is the best one-day festival in New England. Stroll down the cobblestone streets of Portland's historic waterfront while strains of music from a nearby band dance in your ears. Catch a horse-drawn wagon ride or peek into one of the district's many quaint shops (see our Shopping chapter). From great dining to great deals, there's fun for everyone.

Six music stages — each dedicated to a different style — are set up throughout the Old Port. You'll find country, rock, jazz, contemporary tunes and more. Two children's areas are set up in Tommy's Park for face-painting, games and kiddie rides. Food vendors display their goodies along the street, and at 11 AM there's a parade that includes more music and string puppets. One word of caution: Some specialty shops such as clothing boutiques close to avoid confrontations with sticky fingers, but to make up for it, others set up shop outside.

Scottish Festival
Boothbay Railway Village, Maine Hwy. 27, Boothbay • (207) 633-4727

Trains and tartans may not seem to have much in common, but here they do during the first weekend in June, when Scottish folk singers and bagpipers descend on the area's rail museum. The two-day event includes a "kirkin' of the tartan service," where you can get your kilt blessed, and a knobby knees contest, in which blindfolded judges feel for the knobbiest of the men's knees. There are also historical displays.

It all takes place in a re-created early New England village, where you can catch a ride on a narrow-gauge steam train or check out an antique auto display (see more on this in our Kidstuff chapter). The cost to get in is $2 for adults; children younger than 12 are free. Tickets for the train ride are an additional $3 each for children and adults.

Bed & Breakfast, Inn and Garden Tour
Various locations, Kennebunks
• (207) 967-0857

Spend an English type of afternoon touring some of Kennebunk and Kennebunkport's finest and most charming properties. The tour takes place on the first or second Sunday in June from noon until 5 PM, beginning at the Nott House on Main Street in Kennebunkport.

On the guided tour you'll have the opportunity to visit up to 20 properties, including Nott House. In previous years the tour visited the Arundel Meadows Inn, the Captain Fairfield Inn, Captain's Hideaway, The Captain Jefferds Inn and the Christmas Tides Inn. Also included were stops at the Cove House Bed & Breakfast, the 1802 House Bed & Breakfast Inn, The Green Heron Inn, the Harbor Watch Restaurants & Inn and The Kennebunk Inn, among others.

The event is sponsored by the Kennebunk/Kennebunkport Chamber of Commerce. Cost for the tour in 1998 was $10.

Back Cove Family Day
Payson Park, off Allen Ave., Portland
• (207) 874-8793

Ever dream of building your own boat? Turn out for this outdoor fair, and you'll get your shot for just $10 — supplies included. Granted, you'll have only 45 minutes to complete your work. And your building materials? Cardboard.

Nearly 5,000 people turn out for this local event held on a Sunday in early June, but amazingly, only about a dozen compete in the boat-building competition. It might have something to do with the fact that after building your cardboard canoe, you have to paddle it around a 150-foot course in the nearby harbor. About half the boats actually make it (we won't mention the other half), and the winner goes home with an engraved paddle and bragging rights.

Family games, entertainment of every kind and food vendors are scattered throughout the park, and biking and in-line skating demonstrations take place at nearby Baxter Boulevard. General admission is free.

The Portland String Quartet
Newagen Seaside Inn, Maine Hwy. 238, Southport Island
• (207)633-2353, (888) 337-2710

For an outdoor summer concert, try this one on an island. Admission to this mid-June event is $15 for adults and $6 for students, but you'll get more than music for your money. You'll also get plenty of scenery. Stroll across the landscaped grounds or take a quick dip in the ocean before relaxing in the inn, where you can buy lunch or a picnic basket to go. The cool ocean breezes and the sweet music will whisk you away at this evening event.

Lobster Boat Races
On the water, Maine Hwy. 27, Boothbay Harbor
• (207) 633-2353

OK, they may not churn up the waters like some speed boats, but you'd be surprised how many people show up at Boothbay Harbor for the lobster boat races in mid-June. Starting at noon, dozens of these boxy work boats and their crews compete in the harbor to see who can pull and set a lobster trap fastest and return to shore. Awards are given out at Gray's Wharf following the races. For the best view, head to the east side of the harbor or to McKown Point.

St. John's Bazaar
St. John's, 37 Pleasant St., Brunswick • (207) 725-8756

If you're looking for a great place to amuse the kids, hunt for crafts and sneak in a little local history, this carnival — held in the shadow of one of the town's historic churches — is a great place to go. Rides, games, craft tables, food, live music and all kinds of dance groups fill the church parking lot for three days during the third weekend in June.

Beat the summer heat by stepping inside the towering stone church, built at the turn of the century, and checking out its Italian murals, stained-glass windows and marble detailing. General admission is free, but tickets for the rides and games are $3 for four rides if you purchase them in advance. Tickets are $1 each once you're there. All proceeds benefit local charities.

Greek Heritage Festival
Holy Trinity Greek Orthodox Church, 133 Pleasant St., Portland • (207) 774-0281

You don't have to be Greek to enjoy this four-day celebration put on by the Greek Orthodox Church, but it does help if you love Greek food. You'll taste gyros, loukanikos, dolmathes, spanakopita and, of course, baklava at this late June event where food is the main attraction. If you want to find out what all those delicious, hard-to-pronounce foods taste like, come try them out. You can also dip into the Greek wine. There's plenty of music and dancing to go along with it. It all takes place under a tent in the church parking lot. . . . Well, at least it's supposed to — some years, people dance in the street.

La Kermesse Festival
St. Louis Alumni Field, West St., Biddeford • (207) 282-1567

Insiders know that while this is one of the largest Franco-American festivals in the United States, the word "kermesse" is actually Dutch for "gathering or meeting." This three-day celebration of Franco-American culture takes place on the last full weekend in June. Festivities are launched Thursday evening with a fan-

tastic half-hour fireworks display on the Saco River waterfront. The 1998 display was arguably the best in the state, and its popularity is growing. You can see the fireworks from vantage points in both Biddeford and Saco, but the most popular place to view them is from the Saco Island area on Saco Main Street. Police close the street for the event, so be prepared to park at a distance and walk, and expect traffic when it's time to go.

A gala parade headlines the opening of the Festival Grounds on Friday evening at 6 PM. To watch the parade, line up along the route, which begins on Main Street at the corner of Jefferson Street in downtown Biddeford, continues along Main Street, turns right up Alfred Street to Graham Street and finally empties onto West Street to the St. Louis Alumni Field. Residents begin placing chairs and staking out viewing points as early as noon, so you shouldn't wait until the last minute to find a place to park and view.

While the fireworks and parade are free, there's a charge to enter the Festival Grounds. A three-day pass was $9 at the gate and $7 in advance in 1998. You can buy advance purchase buttons from most local stores in Biddeford. Within the grounds you'll find a midway with carnival-type food, games and rides along with tents featuring entertainment, crafts, casino games and traditional Franco-American food such as tourtiere (pork pie) crepes and boudin (blood sausage).

Beachfest
Town Square and Beach, Old Orchard Beach • (207) 934-2500

Old Orchard Beach celebrates summer on the last weekend in June, when you can join in a giant sand castle building contest, strut your stuff in a bikini contest or merely enjoy live band entertainment and a fireworks display.

The Sandcastle Contest is held on Saturday morning, with cash prizes for winners. For inspiration, take a look at the giant sand sculpture to the right of the pier as you face the ocean. Since 1995, businesses from the town have hired Tom Morrison, a professional sand sculptor, to build a 70-foot-high (or larger) creation. In 1995 Tom created a rendition of the Lion King; in 1996 he built a wonderful castle with spiral turrets, a curving

Boothbay Harbor Windjammer Days are held at the end of June.

bridge and little houses down below; and in 1997 he replicated the Portland Head Light. His most recent creation, in 1998, was a splendid rendition of the Titanic. Who knows what might be created for 1999!

Sidewalk Arts Festival
Main St., Saco
• (207) 282-6169

Stroll along one of the prettiest Main Streets in Maine as you view the works of more than 160 artists in Saco. On the last Saturday in June, the sidewalks overflow with paintings in oils, watercolors, acrylics and mixed media, etchings, photography and sculpture. As you meander through the parking lots and squares adjacent to Main Street, you'll find more artists' exhibits as well as a display from the Southern Maine Craftsmen.

In addition to the artists' displays, you can enjoy entertainment from musicians, cloggers and magicians, and children will be thrilled by clowns and balloons. Concession stands offering lemonade and other goodies are available.

Strawberry Festival & Auction
St. Phillip's Episcopal Church, Hodge St., Wiscasset • (207) 882-7184

Get your strawberries any and every way you like them — fresh-picked from the field or piled high on a biscuit topped with real whipped cream. This homegrown festival is served up by church parishioners, and people from all over the state and New England come to dig in. Some even plan their vacations around it.

You'll find craft tables, a used-book sale, children's activities and everyone's favorite — an all-day auction to sell off gift certificates and gifts donated by local merchants. It lasts from 10 AM to 2:30 PM on the last Saturday of June. Remember, while admission may be free, the calories are not.

Annual Windjammer Days
On the waterfront, Boothbay Harbor
• **(207) 633-2353**

July

For a sailing extravaganza, follow Maine Highway 27 to the waterfront and watch as more than a dozen windjammers (that's a multi-masted sailing boat, in case you were wondering) sail into harbor. Many of these beautiful wooden vessels are designated historic landmarks, and all are graceful as they ply through the harbor as reminders of days gone by when such ships were common here.

The four-day event was started 36 years ago by Capt. David Dash and his wife Marion, who was the first woman to get her captain's license off the coast of Maine. It takes place near the end of June. Watch a parade of antique boats, listen to the bands, indulge in good food and participate in free on-board tours of a number of vessels including Navy and Coast Guard ships, which tie up for the celebration. There's also a block party, a waterfront concert and fireworks.

Blessing of the Fleet
Various locations, Kennebunkport
• **(207) 967-0857**

This annual event features the Chamber of Commerce Sunset Cocktail Cruise, Quaint Town Trivia contest and the Blessing of the Fleet ceremony. Other events include canoe and kayak races, a band concert on the Green and the Goat Island Cup regatta.

Edible Auction
River Tree Arts, 12 Depot
St.,Kennebunkport • **(207) 985-4343**

Sometime in June or July, River Tree Arts holds an Edible Auction to benefit their programs. Cost to take part is usually about $35 and includes dinner and the chance to bid on items in both a silent and live auction. Items that were auctioned in the past include dinner for 10 cooked at your home; a cocktail party for 20 at your home; cookbooks; wine; gift certificates to area restaurants and all kinds of baked goods and specialty food items.

Annual Concert and Picnic on the Green
Village Green, Kennebunkport
• **(207) 967-0857**

Part of the town's Independence Day celebrations, the annual concert begins at 5:30 PM on the Village Green, in front of the Captain Lord Mansion. In case of rain the event will be held at the Sea Road School.

Fourth of July Fireworks Displays
Towns along the Southern Maine coast

Most towns have their own way of celebrating Independence Day. Some have local parades, and most have fireworks displays beginning as soon as it's dark (around 9:15 PM), all preceded by entertainment. Heading from south to north along the coast, Ogunquit, Kennebunk, Old Orchard Beach, Portland, Freeport, Bailey Island, Bath, Wiscasset and Boothbay Harbor produce fireworks displays of 10 to 20 minutes. Call the local chambers of commerce for more information. In Portland, call Parks and Recreation.

Week of July 4th Celebrations
Various locations, Kennebunks
• **(207) 967-0857**

The Kennebunks celebrate Independence Day with a week-long series of events including a picnic and concert on the green on July 3 and fireworks and craft fairs on the Fourth. For more information on specific events, contact the chamber of commerce at (207) 967-0857.

Parade of Trolleys
Seashore Trolley Museum,
Log Cabin Rd., Kennebunkport
• **(207) 967-2800**

On the Fourth of July, the Seashore Trolley Museum runs 15 or more of its trolleys before a seated audience while exhibitors describe the history and function of each car.

INSIDERS' TIP

For outdoor events where you will be watching a show or performance, bring a folding chair or blanket to sit on.

Visitors learn why each trolley is unique and the impact that trolleys have had on society. Before and after the parade, trolley rides are available. This special event is included in the price of admission to the museum, which in 1998 was $7 for adults and $4.50 for children ages 6 to 16. Children younger than 6 get in free. (See our Attractions chapter for more on the Seashore Trolley Museum.)

Heritage Days
Various downtown locations, Bath
• **(207) 443-9751**

This Fourth of July celebration has it all: dozens of nifty craft booths nestled under the trees in Library Park, a whirling carnival of rides along the bank of the Kennebec River, a parade of fire trucks, Brownies, Boy Scouts and all the locals who want to dress up for their neighbors (even some tourists jump in). You'll also find children's events, bands, a triathlon and — to top it all off — fireworks over the waterfront.

Bring money for the food and rides and a little extra for the Maine crafts you just won't want to leave behind. This is a small-city celebration at its best, and people come from all over to get in on the four days of festivities. The parade itself is always held on the holiday. You won't want to miss it.

BCA Annual Fourth of July Celebration
Town common, Maine Hwy. 27, Boothbay
• **(207) 633-4250**

The Boothbay Civic Association heads up this one-day fair that includes craft tables, music, games for the children and a chicken barbecue, which is served at noon. The event is always held on the lush town common on the Fourth of July, and lunch is served until the food is gone.

New England Craft and Specialty Food Fair
Beach Ball Field, York
• **(603) 755-2166**

Rain or shine, during the first week of July nearly 175 craftspeople from New England gather in York to display and sell their wares. This is a traditional country folk and craft exhibition with a screening committee selecting craftspeople based on their workmanship. Live music and craft demonstrations take place throughout the days as you browse through the extensive array of displays.

Absolutely yummy stuff like jams and jellies, honey, bread, muffin and cake mixes, handmade candy, specialty salsa and chips, mustards and maple products are displayed alongside pottery, wood carvings, woven baskets, jewelry and paintings. So if you're in the mood, you can buy a lovely salsa and chip pottery set to go with the specialty salsa and chips you buy!

Annual Art Show
York Art Association Gallery, U.S. Hwy. 1A, York Harbor
• **(207) 363-4049**

Take a cultural break and view this month-long exhibit, which features the work of the 300-member York Art Association. Whatever your taste in art, you're sure to see something you like, as amateur and professional artists display new works in a variety of categories including sculpture, oils, pastels, watercolors, mixed media and collage. The York Art Association Gallery is open from 10 AM to 4 PM Wednesday through Sunday.

Annual Craft Fair on the Green
Village Green, Kennebunkport
• **(207) 282-2023**

Set on a pleasant, tree-lined green that's a shady walk from Dock Square, this fair is held the first week of July and includes juried exhibits, gourmet food and live music. This fair is well-respected and always well-attended. The event is presented by School Around Us, a small, alternative, parent-run educational cooperative (see our Education and Child Care chapter). A second Craft Fair on the Green is held in August, and a winter fair is held in November at Kennebunk High School.

York Summerfest
Village Green, York Village
• **(207) 363-4422**

Throughout the second weekend of July, the York Village Green takes a step back in time, becoming a colorful, bustling, old-fashioned marketplace. The celebration begins on Friday with a pancake breakfast, tours of historic houses and children's events. From 10 AM to 4 PM on Saturday, vendors create an old-fashioned marketplace, filling the green with booths featuring antiques, collectibles, art, jewelry and crafts, T-shirts and other general merchandise and food. Sunday, a juried crafts show takes place from 10 AM until 4 PM. During the celebration you might also want to join the arranged tours of the Old York Society buildings adjacent to the green.

Summer Solstice Craft Shows
Wells Junior High School,
U.S. Hwy. 1, Wells
• (207) 646-5172

For three consecutive weekends in July, more than 60 artisans from throughout New England exhibit at this juried craft show. Among other crafts, you'll see quality stained glass, glass blowing, gold jewelry, silver work, herbal products, herbal wreaths and swags, knitting, woodwork and leather work. This show is set apart by allowing only two or three entries in any given category.

Gourmet lunch offerings are available. In past years the selection has included pasta salads with organic basil pesto or a feta cheese dressing, corn or clam chowder, veggie pita sandwiches with hummus or pesto, peanut butter brownies, lemon verbena-glazed pound cake and angel-food cake. For the kids there are peanut butter and jelly sandwiches. Lunch items are usually priced at less than $5.

Kittery Seaside Festival
Fort Foster Park, Kittery Point
• (207) 439-3800

Enjoy sea breezes and marvelous views at historic Fort Foster Park on the Kittery Peninsula while joining in the fun at this one-day festival held on a weekend toward the middle of July. Musicians, dancers and children's entertainers take to the stage throughout the day, with a featured group performing at approximately 7:30 PM.

Typical fair food like fried dough, hot dogs, cotton candy and fries will fill you up as you stroll though the many vendors' displays. Pony rides, children's games, crafts and handiwork round out the list of attractions, and the evening

closes with a fireworks display at about 9:30 PM.

Maine Antique Dealers' Annual Show
University of New England,
Hills Beach Rd., off Maine Hwy. 9,
Biddeford • (207) 882-4200

This is the place to visit whether you like antique glass, jewelry, furniture, linens and plain ol' "stuff"; you're looking for a period piece to finish off a room; or you're just looking in general. Sprawling throughout the auditorium and spilling over into the halls and adjacent rooms, this show takes place in the middle of the month and features about 60 dealers. Be warned, however, this isn't a yard sale. These dealers know their merchandise and may give you a good deal, but you probably won't find a steal. This is the show to attend if you're serious about antiques and are looking for good quality pieces sold by professional dealers. The show has been run annually since 1929. The entrance fee in 1998 was $6.

Moxie Day
Seashore Trolley Museum, Log Cabin Rd.,
Kennebunkport • (207) 967-2800

Before today's soft drinks were invented, there was Moxie. Reportedly the first popular soda, or "pop," Moxie is a derivative of the early patent medicines that supposedly "cured-all." According to our sources, Moxie was invented by a man from Maine, and today a group of Moxie lovers, known as the Moxie Congress, is trying to preserve Moxie memorabilia.

On the second or third Saturday in July, the Moxie Congress gathers in Lewiston, Maine, where there is an old-fashioned soda fountain that serves Moxie on tap. The following day, they drive down to Kennebunkport for a Moxie Day at the Seashore Trolley Museum. All of the orange trolleys are brought into service for the day because, we are told, orange is the color associated with Moxie. The group displays antique advertising gimmicks used by Moxie, including an automobile built to look like a horse. They give talks to the public to promote the love and preservation of their favorite drink. Free Moxie is available throughout the day — we'd love to tell you what it tastes like, but you'll have to try it for yourself! You can buy it in area supermarkets.

Moxie Day activities are included in the price of admission to the museum. In 1998 admission was $7 for adults and $4.50 for children ages 6 to 16.

Yarmouth Clam Festival
Memorial Green, Main St., Yarmouth
• (207) 846-3984

Battered, buttered, crumbed, stuffed, fried and boiled in a creamy stew, clams are definitely the highlight of this three-day outdoor festival in mid-July. If you don't think you like the slimy, long-necked creatures, you haven't tried the ones here. There are clams to satisfy everyone's taste, and there is plenty of other food around too: lobster dinners, crab cakes, corn on the cob, strawberry shortcake, pizza, hot dogs, snow cones, sodas — you crave it, it's yours. But even if you don't come for the food (you should), come for the carnival, craft fair, music and activities. Look for signs advising where to park, as this popular event draws thousands to this little town. If you can't find a spot near the green, there are shuttle buses from designated parking areas.

Great State of Maine Air Show
Brunswick Naval Air Station, 551 Fitch Ave., Brunswick • (207) 921-2000

For a hair-raising, breathtaking time, come to this mid-July air show put on in many years by some of the best Navy and civilian pilots in the country. The names of the stunt teams change, but the talent keeps coming back. Be prepared for crowds — the two-day event is the biggest in the state and drew 200,000 people the last time it was held.

Little kids and big kids alike will love walking among the more than 50 military aircraft on display. If you don't mind waiting your turn, you can even sit in some cockpits. Bring plenty of sunscreen because there isn't much shade on the tarmac, and bring your appetite — lunch is sold by various vendors. You'll also want to arrive early to avoid the miles-long traffic jam on Route 1, which gets you here. The gates open at 8 AM, but the aerobatics don't start until about 10.

Maine Antique Power Days
Seashore Trolley Museum,
Log Cabin Rd., Kennebunkport
• (207) 967-2800

Children and adults love this event! Even if you aren't into machinery, you'll find this weekend display, held toward the end of July, fascinating. Before the internal combustion engine became the sophisticated gadget surrounded by electronics that's parked in your driveway, single-cylinder engines powered most of our industrial world. During this weekend the Seashore Trolley Museum displays approximately 50 of these early engines, some of which have flywheels up to 6 feet in diameter. Some engines are displayed dormant while others are operating, with knowledgeable exhibitors available to explain how the engines were used. Museum hours are 10:30 AM to 5:30 PM, and the cost for admission in 1998 was $7 for adults and $4 for children ages 6 to 16.

Aucocisco: A Celebration of Casco Bay
Along the waterfront, Commercial St., Portland • (207)772-6828

Want to know what it's like to live the life of a sailor while forgoing the hardships? You won't need sea legs or motion-sickness pills to have a good time walking through some of the many boats that tie up in Portland Harbor during this 10-day celebration toward the end of July.

You'll find Navy and Coast Guard ships as well as research vessels and sailboats, with crew members on board to answer your questions and show you around. Call ahead and discover when and where various maritime-related lectures will be held. It's all free, and who knows, you might enjoy it so much that you'll take to the sea yourself! If you're already a pro, you'll still enjoy checking out the large variety of boats. Oh, and in case you want to impress your fellow travelers, "Aucocisco" is a Native American word for "bay."

Summerfest
Town common, U.S. Hwy. 1, Wiscasset
• (207) 882-7544

This late-July celebration in front of the First Congregational Church draws an even mix of locals and out-of-towners. If you're looking for good old-fashioned fun, spend the day on the grassy Wiscasset town common listening to the bands and barbershop quartets after placing your bids for local gift certificates at the silent auction. Make sure to catch the frog-jumping contest, then poke through the craft tables, play some games and, when you're done, stroll downtown and enjoy the waterfront shops and restaurants there — it's a walk of less than 10 minutes and well worth the effort. Summerfest, which is put on by the church, opens at 9 AM and runs until 2 PM.

August

York Days
Various locations, York
• (207) 363-1040

Come join in the fun on the first weekend in August. Parades, crafts, races, concerts and fireworks are just some of the activities you'll enjoy amid the cheerfully decked-out town.

Great Inner Tube Race
Ogunquit Beach, Ogunquit
• (207) 646-2939

Get your feet (and the rest of you!) wet in this fun family event. Contestants launch inner tubes and group rafts from the Tidewater Hotel at the Footbridge near the Blue Waters Inn, then paddle and float to the Beach Street bridge. There are prizes for different age groups, and every year a good crowd gathers for the fun. The cost to enter the event, held the first weekend of the month, is $5 for an individual and $25 for a group raft, with all proceeds benefiting Ogunquit Performing Arts (see our Arts chapter). Following the race is an auction, which also benefits Ogunquit Performing Arts. You can obtain entry forms for the Great Inner Tube Race at the Blue Waters Inn.

Annual Kennebearport Teddy Bear Show & Sale
Sea Road School, Sea Rd.
(off Maine Hwy. 35), Kennebunk
• (207) 967-0857

We dare you to go to this show and not come away with a cuddly new friend! Held the

Photo: Merry Farnum

The Old Port Festival in Portland gets summer off to a rousing start.

first week of August and sponsored by the Kennebunk/Kennebunkport Chamber of Commerce, the show features more than 40 exhibitors and bear artists from across the United States.

Bears of every size and description and teddy bear-related items fill the auditorium. New teddy bears, old teddy bears, artists' teddy bears, manufactured teddy bears, bear clothing, teddy bear-making materials and bear furniture are displayed.

On the day preceding the show, Sally Winey of Winey Bears holds a Bear Making Class from 10 AM to 4 PM. Admission to the show in 1998 was $3 for adults and $2 for senior citizens and students at the door. All advance purchase tickets were $2, and children 3 and younger were admitted free. Cost for the Teddy Bear Making Class, including your completed bear and lunch, was $100 in 1998.

Lobster Festival
South Freeport Church, S. Freeport Rd.,
Freeport • (207) 865-4012

Crack open a steamed lobster and get your corn on the cob, coleslaw and dinner roll on the side at this local gathering during the first weekend in August. Lunch is served from noon into the evening and costs about $9. For those who are a little squeamish about eating something with eyes staring back from your plate, try a chicken dinner, and don't forget the strawberry shortcake for dessert.

Before or after your meal, rummage through other people's "attic treasures" at a huge garage sale and enjoy musical entertainment in the evening. The road to the church is off U.S. Highway 1, right after the huge carving of the Indian (the locals call it the FBI: Freeport Big Indian). The church is 1.8 miles from the highway.

Cumberland Craft Show
Cumberland Fairgrounds, off I-95, Cumberland • (207) 621-2818

More than 20,000 people show up for this event, the largest craft show in Maine. It's four fabulous days of great food and handmade crafts during the first week of August. Some 350 crafters put on the show that features pottery, fiber, wood, dolls, jewelry, glass, metal, toys and folk art. There's also a supervised children's play area. The cost of admission is $3 for adults and teens; children younger than 12 get in free.

Annual Topsham Fair
Topsham Fairgrounds, Elm St., Topsham • (207) 725-2735

By far the oldest event in the area, the Topsham Fair is a mix of agricultural exhibits, carnival rides, harness racing, high-wire circus acts and a fireworks display. It all takes place in a large field with a grandstand and a raceway during the second week of August.

You'll gawk at the strength of the work horses as they strain against heavy loads in one of the animal competitions and grow envious at the displays of local produce (that is, if your garden doesn't produce the same fruits). At night the fair is a great place to schmooze with a sweetie-pie as the sweet scents of fried

dough and trampled hay fill the warm evening air and glittering carnival lights glow in the night sky.

Topsham is the town just north of Brunswick. You can get to the fair by following Maine Street north over the bridge into Topsham. At your first set of lights, turn right, then take a left after the sign for the Topsham Municipal Building. Admission costs $4 for adults and teens; children younger than 12 are admitted free.

Italian Street Festival
St. Peter's Catholic Church, 72 Federal St., Portland • (207) 773-0748

If you want to entertain your taste buds, bring them to this two-day festival of Italian food and music held the second weekend of August. If you don't want to go home feeling guilty after a day of pasta, pizza and cannolis, join the 4-mile road race; youngsters can participate in a fun run around the block. There are plenty of children's games at 25 cents each; the adults can take part in raffles and games of chance where they might walk away with some money.

Maine Festival
Thomas Point Beach, 29 Meadow Rd., Brunswick • (207) 772-9012, (800) 639-4212

Your senses will be blown away by this four-day feast of music, dance, art and food staged in early August beneath numerous tents in a sprawling field next to Thomas Bay. Groups come from across the nation and around the world to perform here at Maine's largest and most diverse arts and culture event.

The action begins at 10 AM daily, with music, theater and dance groups performing on seven different stages. Once you've had your fill of entertainment, satisfy your stomach with international cuisine and microbrews from around the state. Children of all ages will en-

INSIDERS' TIP

Though Kennebunk and Kennebunkport are separate towns, they are closely united and share a chamber of commerce. Including Cape Porpoise and Goose Rocks Beach, the towns are frequently referred to as "The Kennebunks."

joy field games and art workshops, and adults will enjoy shopping at tables filled with Maine-made products.

Started by nationally acclaimed storyteller Marshall Dodge in 1976, this festival will give you plenty of stories to go home and share with your friends. Admission is about $12 for adults and teens, $6 for children younger than age 13 or $30 for a family of two adults and up to three children. If you want to volunteer and help out, a six- or eight-hour shift will get you free admission. You can also pitch your tent in the Thomas Point Beach campground for $20 a night (see our Camping chapter). It's all right here.

Annual Beach Olympics
Beach area, Old Orchard Beach
• (207) 934-2500

Join the people who have been coming to Old Orchard Beach for years as they participate in the town's Beach Olympics held in mid-August. There is a whole series of fun and zany events to join including a bubble-gum-blowing contest, ice cream eating contest, frog bog, volleyball tournament and a three-legged race. Bands and other entertainment perform throughout the event. In 1998 a $3 advance ticket (button) allowed you to participate in everything, with the cost jumping to $5 on the day of the games. All proceeds benefit Maine's Special Olympics.

Tidewater Craftsman Fair
Tidewater Mall, U.S. Hwy. 1, Kittery
• (603) 755-2166

More than 75 artisans gather under the big top at this fair in the middle of August. Held under a big white tent in the parking lot of the Tidewater Mall, the event features hourly door prizes, live music and craft demonstrations. You'll find lots of coastal-themed crafts, from lighthouses and sand-dollar art to beach glass and Salt Marsh pottery. A shopping atmosphere prevails at this show, which is held rain or shine.

Annual Sidewalk Art Show
Streets of Ogunquit
• (207) 646-2939

For one Saturday in the middle of August, Ogunquit turns into an open-air art gallery as more than 80 artists set up booths and tables to display their work. Seascapes, landscapes, animals, flowers, people and houses are just some of the subjects depicted in the works, which include a representation from most art media. As you stroll the streets, you'll see a colorful display of paintings in oils, acrylics, watercolors, mixed media, charcoal and pen and ink. Sizes from miniature to large in both original artwork and prints (framed and un-framed) are available for sale. Prices begin at about $7.50 and move up to several hundred dollars.

Annual Highland Games
Thomas Point Beach, 29 Meadow Rd., Brunswick • (207) 364-3063

Want to flex some muscle or just watch others show off their athletic prowess? Try this Scottish festival in mid-August, where people of all ages can compete in traditional athletics. Toss the caber (that's a 120-pound log resembling a telephone pole), put a stone or hurl a sheaf. There are also dancing and bagpiping contests. In fact, there's so much to do at this one-day event, the entire family will love it: a parade of pipers and clans, plenty of children's games, Scottish livestock on display, a border collie herding demonstration and Scottish food and history. If you're Scottish, you can even research the background of your clan. Parking is easy, and all the events take place on the park's sprawling fields that stretch right down to the beach. The cost of admission is $9 for adults and teens and $4 for children ages 6 through 12. Tickets are a little cheaper if you buy them in advance. Proceeds from the festival go toward educational scholarships.

Antique Show & Sale
Bath Middle School, 6 Old Brunswick Rd., Bath • (207) 767-3967

Antique sellers from around New England haul some of their nicest finds to this event, which is worth going to even if you are not looking to buy any of the gorgeous pieces on display. You'll find everything from ornate tea-cup collections to beautifully carved captain's chests, all from the 18th to the early-20th centuries. Display booths on the gym floor turn the basketball court into a museum during this mid-August event. Admission is $3.50, and all the proceeds benefit the local YMCA, which provides athletic opportunities for people of all incomes. A homemade lunch is sold during the show.

Annual WCSH 6 Sidewalk Art Festival
Congress St., Portland
• (207) 828-6666

This one-day art show includes 350 participants from all over the country who display their original watercolors and oil paintings in booths all along Congress Street. The outdoor exhibit runs from One Congress Square, in the center of the shopping district, to Monument Square. The event takes place from 9 AM to 5 PM on the third Saturday of August and typically draws around 50,000 people. There's no admission; the rain date is the following Sunday. While the show is strictly about art, there are plenty of other shopping opportunities within easy walking distance, and a large variety of restaurants for a bite to eat. (For more information, see our Shopping and Restaurants chapters.)

Annual Great Falls Balloon Festival
Downtown riverfront, Main St.,
Lewiston-Auburn • (800) 639-6331

OK, this one is a little out of our coverage area, but chances are you've never seen anything like it. In late August, more than 50 hot-air balloons fill the sky over the Androscoggin River. Some even come in unexpected shapes: Last year there was a giant eagle, a rendition of the Flying Purple People Eater and a giant birthday cake. The balloons range in height from 6 to 8 stories tall. And on the last night of the festival, the balloons are tethered together so they'll hang above the river while a luminescent substance makes them glow.

If that's not enough to keep you busy, there are balloon and helicopter rides, children's games, craft tables, a carnival, music groups from around the world and plenty of good food, making it one of the biggest festivals in the state. Best of all, admission is free, and money raised at the booths goes to support nonprofit organizations. The festival runs Friday, Saturday and Sunday. To get here, take Exit 12 off

Interstate 95 and turn left. From there it's easy: Just follow the bright pink balloon signs all the way to the three giant fields where the activities take place. Balloon launches are at 5:30 AM and 5:30 PM because it gets too hot during the middle of the day for them to take off. Getting here early in the morning is the best bet as the show draws upwards of 150,000 people during the time it's open.

Thomas Point Beach Bluegrass Festival
Thomas Point Beach, 29 Meadow Rd.,
Brunswick • (207) 725-6009

This musical celebration on Labor Day weekend will set your feet tapping to the sounds of some of Nashville's favorites. Well-known bands from the country music capital of the world and around the country come to this park for New England's leading family bluegrass festival. Past participants have included Mac Wiseman, Ralph Stanley and the Clinch Mountain Boys, the Lonesome River Band, Jim & Jesse and the Virginia Boys and the Lewis Family.

Take in all the sounds from Thursday through Sunday and explore the beach's 80 acres of fields, woods and shore. Swimming in the sandy bay is a great way to cool off (and a lot more comfortable than a frigid plunge in the Atlantic). Food booths will keep you eating all day and night, and security and medical services are available on site.

If you want to stay more than one day, consider renting a campsite right in the park for $17 a night (see our Camping chapter for more on campground amenities). Tickets for the festival range from $15 for an adult for a single day to $80 for a four-day pass. You'll pay more for a one-day pass if you're planning to come on the weekend. Children younger than 12 get in free.

September

Craft Fair on the Green
Village Green, Kennebunkport
• (207) 282-2023

See the previous listing under July events. This event also takes place on the first weekend in September.

Annual Fiddle Contest & Folk Festival
Kennebunk Town Hall, Kennebunk
• (207) 985-4343

This Kennebunk tradition will have you clapping your hands and kicking up your heels! Sponsored by River Tree Arts, the event takes place in early September and spans an entire weekend. A folk concert on Friday evening launches the festival, and on Saturday you can attend a series of workshops in the morning and the finals of a songwriting contest in the afternoon. On Saturday evening you'll enjoy the central focus of the weekend as approximately eight junior and eight adult fiddlers get their strings humming as they compete for first place.

If you're wondering what to do for dinner between the workshops and fiddle contest, you can join the locals at an Old Fashioned Baked Bean Dinner sponsored by the fire department's ladies' auxiliary. All events for the festival take place in and around Town Hall.

A weekend ticket for the festival in 1998 (not including the Bean Dinner) was $40 for adults and $35 for senior citizens and students (including college students with an ID). Children are charged if they're big enough to need their own seat. The Bean Dinner will run

you about $4.50 per person. Tickets for individual parts of the festival are also available; those for the contest were $10 for adults, $8 for senior citizens and $7 for children, but tickets sell out quickly and there's never an empty seat — make your calls early.

Tow Truck Meet and Parade
Memorial Park, First St.,
Old Orchard Beach
• (207) 934-2500

In early September close to 100 trucks roll into Old Orchard Beach for a giant truck meet. Truck lovers of all ages will thrill as they watch the trucks drive from the Town Square up East Grand Avenue and West Grand Avenue to First Street, where the meet takes place.

Old Port Equinox Art Fair
Exchange St., Portland • (207) 772-8766

More that 150 artists display and sell their works at this outdoor street fair on a Sunday in mid-September. Enjoy the work of some of the area's finest artists — among the works displayed are oils, pastels and photographs — while being serenaded. The Portland String Quartet usually stages a concert (see our Arts chapter), as do jazz groups and barbershop quartets.

Photo: Giselle A. Auger

At many local fairs throughout Maine you'll find midway attractions such as this one, as well as presentations of livestock, harness racing, pig scrambles and entertainment.

Art for Art's Sake
**Newagen Seaside Inn, Maine Hwy. 238,
Southport Island • (888) 337-2710**

Check out this art show and sale in early September. Admission is free, and the location is a beautiful island inn. On display are watercolors, oil paintings and sculptures by more than 50 Maine artists. The show lasts three days and is followed by a concert by The Portland String Quartet on the final afternoon. The concert is a separate event, and in 1998 tickets were $15 for adults and $6 for students.

Tri-State Fishing Tournament
**Beau Rivage Motel, 54 East Grand Ave.,
Old Orchard Beach
• (207) 934-4668**

On the second weekend of September, fishermen from Maine, Massachusetts and Rhode Island compete for points in a 10-hour tournament beginning at 12:01 AM and ending at 9 AM on Sunday. Other events include a cookout on Saturday and fishing gear exhibitions.

Classic Car Show and Go-Cart Grand Prix
**Memorial Park, First St.,
Old Orchard Beach
• (207) 934-2500**

More than 200 classic car owners exhibited at this show in 1998, and the numbers are growing. Held in middle to late September, the event draws owners of classic cars and trucks from New England and beyond. Categories include cars from the 1950s, 1960s and 1970s, plus Corvettes, Mustangs, Mopars, and classic and antique cars and trucks. There are also awards for Best of Show and People's Favorite.

To watch the parade of cars, which begins at 6 PM on Friday, pick a spot along Old Orchard Street, First Street, East Grand Avenue or West Grand Avenue. First Street is turned into an obstacle course with hay bales marking the paths for the go-kart portion of the event. This is a professional go-cart race with corporate-sponsored drivers and other professionals, and though you can't participate, it's a lot of fun to watch as a local radio station blasts tunes and the cars rev and vroom!

Annual Ogunquit Antiques Show
**Dunaway Center, School St., Ogunquit
• (207) 646-2939**

Start your holiday shopping early and support the Historical Society of Ogunquit and Wells. This popular show is held on the second-to-last weekend in September to benefit the society and draws more than 80 vendors from the combined towns. You'll find glass, furniture from the 18th, 19th and 20th centuries, books and postcards at the show.

Cumberland Fair
**Cumberland Fairgrounds, off I-95,
Cumberland • (207) 829-5531**

This is one of the oldest and biggest fairs in the area. There is everything you might expect at an agricultural event: pie-baking contests, flower-growing and produce competitions, livestock judging, harness racing, a carnival and plenty of food. The horse- and ox-pulling are world-class, and you'll oooh and ahhh as you watch teams pull against a heavy load.

For the young there are calf and pig scrambles, and for the young at heart there are antique tractor and four-wheel-drive pulls, in which vehicles are hitched to heavy loads. The weeklong event takes place during the end of September. In 1998 weekend tickets were $5 for adults (the price dropped to $4 during the week), and it's $2 to park. To get here, take Exit 10 off Interstate 95, take a left off the exit, then follow the signs to the fairgrounds.

October

Fryeburg Fair
**Fryeburg Fairgrounds, Fryeburg
• (207) 935-3268**

We know this is outside our book's coverage area, but we felt we had to include it. Set amid the foothills of the White Mountains, the venue for this fair is beautiful — if you go to only one fair, go to this one. Arguably the best of the many agricultural fairs held throughout Maine, the Fryeburg Fair runs for a week. It's usually the first week in October, but it occasionally begins the last week of September.

While at many fairs the livestock are set apart, at Fryeburg everything is intermingled. You can walk through the cow barns or watch children scamper after piglets in a pig scramble, then take a few steps and be in the middle of a carnival-type midway with games, cotton candy and bloomin' onions. Walk around a little bit more, and you'll find yourself watching a harness race or meandering through the agricultural museum.

Events take place throughout the day, with ox pulls and livestock judging. Oxen, sheep, cows, pigs, goats, horses and other livestock, from prize-winning adults to young animals at their first show, are judged in a variety of categories. If you're interested, you can watch the owners bathing and primping the animals in the barns before judging. At the Fairground's agricultural museum, you can watch craftspeople as they make furniture using hand- and foot-powered lathes, build a canoe, and bake Early American goodies and churn butter in an old-time kitchen. Children are often fascinated by this part of the fair and enjoy the lectures about Early American education held at the one-room schoolhouse adjacent to the museum.

To get to the fair, take Maine Highway 302 west from Portland or use Exit 8 off the Maine Turnpike. Fryeburg is about 90 minutes away. Insiders know this event is popular and the fair coincides with the best of "leaf-peepin'" season, so traffic is congested. In fact, we recommend going early on a weekday and avoiding the weekend altogether. Even then, expect to be in traffic for at least 15 minutes. Parking is available at the fair, and residents along the roads leading to the fairgrounds also offer parking for a fee. Parking will probably cost about $4, even in the fairground lots, and you can expect a walk of at least five minutes before you get to the grounds. Admission to the fair was $4 per person in 1998 for Monday through Thursday; it was $5 on Friday, Saturday and Sunday. Tuesday is Senior Citizens Day, when folks 65 and older are admitted free.

Harvestfest
Various locations,
York Village, York
• (207) 363-4422

Have you ever been to an ox roast? Whether you have or not, you'll probably want to visit York's Harvestfest on the weekend following Columbus Day in mid-October. The festivities are launched on Friday with an old-fashioned marketplace featuring crafts, food and entertainment. You might try homemade apple pie or lobster stew.

On Friday evening preparations are begun for the Ox Roast and Baked Bean Supper. Two giant bean pots are lowered into the ground where they simmer all night until they're deemed ready by the Bean Master, Fred Flanders of Flanders Baked Beans. While you're sleeping, the Ox Roast will begin with a veteran crew supervising the roasting throughout the night. Carving for the famous Ox Roast sandwiches begins at 11 AM on Saturday. Be aware that lines form early, but from all accounts, it's worth the wait. If Ox Roast sandwiches aren't your thing, try the food tent sponsored by the Ocean National Bank. Here you can sample a wide selection of food including lobster rolls, chowder, chili, turkey sandwiches, homemade pies, pastries, coffee, fried dough, pork strips, lo-mein and more.

In addition to food, Harvestfest features an old-fashioned church fair on Saturday, where you'll find things such as baked goods, novelty items, jams and jellies and floral arrangements. Kids will enjoy special entertainment

INSIDERS' TIP

If you'd like a different kind of fireworks-viewing adventure, drive or walk a couple of miles south of Old Orchard Beach. You won't be able to hear the booms, but the sound of the waves on the shore will accompany your display. From this distance the fireworks don't look as large in the sky, but you can view at least two other area displays along the distant horizon.

and activities in the kids' tent. If you appreciate fine crafts, you'll be impressed with the juried craft show, which features a diverse selection of products from 100 quality craftspeople. The show is held throughout the weekend.

Saturday evening you can feast on those baked beans, complete with fixin's and pies. Supper is served on a first-come, first-served basis beginning at 5 PM. The event is always a sellout, so don't be late! Cost for dinner is usually around $5.

Throughout the three days of Harvestfest, the York Art Association hosts its annual Art Show and Exhibit (see our Arts chapter). As the craft fair closes, preparations begin for the event's Native American Pow Wow. Here, a dozen or so dancers in authentic dress entertain with traditional Native American music and dance. You will also learn how the drum, central to the dance, is used to draw upon the teachings of the elders.

Annual Community Arts Show
ShootingStar Gallery,
74 Wallingford Sq., Kittery
• (207) 439-6397

Hosted by the gallery, the Community Arts Show allows residents of town to display their artwork for a month and does not charge the artists commission for sales made during that time. You'll be able to view artwork in a wide range of styles and mediums from seascapes

and still-life to modern style and small sculptural pieces.

Annual Fall Foliage Festival
Boothbay Railway Village, Maine Hwy. 27,
Boothbay • (207) 633-4727

This mid-October festival offers Maine-made crafts, entertainment, country music and plenty of food, and takes place during the height of the state's leafy splendor. There isn't any place to hike and take in the fall foliage at the festival, but there are plenty of glorious trees along the road to town. Admission for adults to this two-day event is $2. Children younger than 12 get in free.

Ghost Trolley
Seashore Trolley Museum,
Log Cabin Rd., Kennebunkport
• (207) 967-2800

Give your children a Halloween treat and bring them on a Ghost Trolley adventure. You'll ride the 1.33-mile main line on a ghostly dark trolley past spooky scenes acted out along the trail — and you might even encounter a surprise goblin or ghoul on board. Held from 7 to 9 PM on the two weekends preceding Halloween, the rides are very popular. Reservations are not accepted, and lines start forming well before opening time, so be prepared to come early and wait. Cost for adults in 1998 was $4; children ages 6 to 16 were admitted for $3.

Photo: Merry Farnum

Your children will enjoy Maine's many special events.

November

Maine Brewers Festival
Portland Exposition Bldg.,
239 Park Ave., Portland
• **(207) 874-8200**

On the first Saturday in November, buy a ticket to the premier gathering of brewers from across the state. More than 20 brewers participate in a tasting with some 80 microbrews. The Shipyard Brewing Company and Gritty McDuff's are just two local favorites you might be familiar with (see Breweries in our Attractions chapter).

In 1998 a $19 ticket got you in the door with a tasting glass and 15 tickets to sample the brews of your choice. Additional tickets were five for $1. A food court is available, and soda and water are offered for designated drivers. Children younger than 2 are allowed at the festival, but it is against policy for older children to attend because of the alcohol. Ticket holders must be 21 and older. Each ticket is good for a four-hour session at the expo, and live bands perform all day long. Last year, some 4,000 people participated.

Annual Great Osprey Ocean Run
Wolfe's Neck State Park,
Wolfe's Neck Rd., Freeport
• **(207) 865-6171**

Want to jog down some of Maine's backcountry roads and across a farm? This 10-kilometer run takes place on the third Saturday of November and usually draws about 200 runners. You must call ahead to register, and if you do so by November 1, you'll get a free, long-sleeved T-shirt commemorating the event. The registration fee should be about $15. Parking is limited.

Tree Lighting and
Old Port Window Walk
Monument Sq., Portland
• **(207) 772-6828**

This historical rendition of Christmas during Victorian times takes place at 5:30 PM on the first day after Thanksgiving. After watching the tree-lighting in Monument Square, stroll the Old Port streets and listen to carolers dressed in Victorian costume or watch the jugglers and stilt walkers. There are also free horse-drawn carriage rides and plenty of dazzling stores where you can begin your Christmas shopping. You can even vote on your favorite store window. The carriage rides and carolers are around every weekend (Friday through Sunday) until Christmas, and Father and Mother Christmas are in Post Office Park to meet believers.

Old Fashioned Christmas
Downtown Bath
• **(207) 443-9751**

This is about as old-fashioned a Christmas as you'll find, and it offers a great time to shop if you want all the yuletide atmosphere without the crush of the crowds. Imagine walking down brick sidewalks beneath iron lampposts and glittering white lights in the trees overhead. The store windows will be decked for the season, and you can vote on who did the best job decorating. Don't forget to take an evening walk through Library Park, where there are more lights and a Christmas tree inside a wooden gazebo.

This trip has all the makings of winter romance, and there are several great restaurants within easy walking distance. In addition to the great atmosphere, which lasts all season long, the city puts on a Christmas parade and has caroling on this special weekend in late November. You can usually pick up a free cup of hot cider and treats for yourself while your children visit with Santa.

Craft Fair
Kennebunk High School, Fletcher Rd., Kennebunk • (207) 282-2023

Similar to the Craft Fair on the Green (see our July listings), this holiday-themed event is also held to support School Around Us.

Victorian Horse and
Carriage Parade
Downtown Portland • (207) 772-6828

On the first Sunday following Thanksgiving, you'll be enchanted by this parade of horse-drawn carriages and their passengers as it winds down and around Congress Street and the Old Port. Other Victorian folk roam through the Old Port and the Arts District, minding their own business and reminding admirers of days long gone. When it's all over, take your time to do a little shopping. (For more information on shops in the Old Port, see our Shopping chapter.)

December

Annual Christmas Prelude
Various locations, Kennebunks
• **(207) 967-0857**

The Kennebunks welcome you to join them in a magical season of shopping and special events. Enjoy the charming towns dressed in their Christmas finery as you shop and attend concerts, caroling and other seasonal events. You can take a trip back in time on an old-fashioned sleigh ride (or hay ride if there's no snow!), during which it will be easy to imagine it's the turn of the century in these lovely towns. Or you can stroll along beautifully decorated streets where lights sparkle and reflect from every window.

In previous years special events have included Wassail By The Sea (featuring music and pageantry), Christmas Trees of the Victorian Era at Nott House, U.S. Post Office Commemorative Prelude Station Cancellation, craft fairs, candlelight caroling, concerts, luncheons and lobster suppers. Cost for individual events, most of which are held during the first two weeks in December, varies.

Annual Ski Sale
Kennebunk Town Hall Auditorium, Kennebunk • (207) 985-6890

If you've been thinking about buying some used ski equipment, this is the time to do it. On the first weekend of December, this ski sale is sponsored by Sunday River Ski Resort (see our Parks and Recreation chapter) from 9 AM to 5 PM. If you'd like to have your old ski-related items sold at the sale, you can deliver them to Town Hall during specified hours on the preceding day.

Annual Christmas by the Sea
Various locations, Ogunquit • (207) 646-2939

A weekend of activities designed to launch you into the holiday spirit begins at around 6 PM on the second or third Friday of December. Events scheduled for the weekend include tree-lightings, caroling, a chowder fest, a bonfire on the beach, hay rides and a crafts fair. You can also enjoy a stroll by Ogunquit inns, children's games and entertainment, concerts, theater and, of course, visits by Santa. The Ogunquit Chamber of Commerce sponsors the event.

Sparkle Weekend Celebration
Various locations, Freeport • (207) 865-1212, (800) 865-1994

The first weekend in December is one of the prettiest times to do your Christmas shopping in Freeport. You'll find lots of big-name retailers selling things at their outlet stores for less than you might expect. During Sparkle Weekend (sponsored by the Freeport Merchants Association) you'll also encounter carolers on various street corners, a giant talking Christmas tree, horse-drawn carriage rides and storytelling for the children. Be prepared for crowds and a tough time finding parking. And remember, this is not the mall — shops tend to close around 6 PM (except L.L. Bean, which is open 24 hours). (For more information on the shops in Freeport, see the Outlets section of our Shopping chapter.)

Holiday Craft Show
University of Southern Maine Gym, 96 Falmouth St., Portland • (207) 621-2818

Holiday shopping is a treat at this craft show where the work of Maine jewelers, basket makers, toy makers, woodworkers, potters, carvers and bakers is displayed in two different college gymnasiums. You'll find a large selection of ornate, handmade Santas as well as collectible teddy bears, and all your gift-wrapping is free! The show takes place in mid-December and is sponsored by the United Maine Craftsmen, a group that provides scholarships for young people who want to pursue careers in crafts. Admission is $2 for adults and teens, and that will get you into both facilities. Children younger than 12 get in free.

New Year's Portland
Various locations, Intown Portland • (207) 772-9012

Put on your woolies, wrap up in a scarf, bundle up in a warm jacket and get ready to party the night away at this nonalcoholic New Year's celebration. There's something for everyone, with children's events and a parade earlier in the day and numerous musical performances, comedians, dance groups and more for the entire family in the evening.

A New Year's Portland button ($10 for adults and teens, $6 for children 12 and younger) will get you into all the events, but remember to bring some extra cash for hot chocolate or cider. This is a great way to ring in the New Year. Most events take place indoors, but you'll have to walk from one to another, and it can be quite cold. Gather with the rest of the crowd at Monument Square for the countdown to midnight and a jubilant fireworks display. Dress extra warmly, and don't forget about your feet — treat them with comfy shoes (or boots) and super-warm socks so you can keep going all night long. In 1998 there were 150 artists and 7,000 spectators.

Some of the writers associated with Maine include E.B. White, Sarah Orne Jewett, Nathaniel Hawthorne, Harriet Beecher Stowe, Henry Wadsworth Longfellow and Stephen King.

The Arts

Since the 1800s Maine has been a popular destination not only for the casual tourist, but also for artists of all types. Consider this short list of well-known authors, poets, musicians, thespians and other artists, and you'll begin to see what we mean.

Among the famous painters associated with the state are Winslow Homer, Rockwell Kent, Frederick Church, Edward Hopper, Alex Katz and Andrew Wyeth. Some of the writers and poets who were born, lived or vacationed in Maine include E.B. White, Sarah Orne Jewett, Nathaniel Hawthorne, Harriet Beecher Stowe, Henry Wadsworth Longfellow and Edna St. Vincent Millay. Contemporary writers include Stephen King, Tabitha King, Carolyn Chute and Tess Gerritsen. You'll recognize the names of actors Jeff and Lloyd Bridges, Leslie Caron, Dabney Coleman, Mary Astor, Bonnie Franklin, Ann B. Davis, Bob Denver and Gene Wilder, all of whom have appeared in summer productions in Maine at one time or another. Musical groups that have performed here in recent years include Counting Crows, John Hiatt, Van Halen, Bruce Hornsby and the Range and Aerosmith, whose lead singer, Steven Tyler, lives in Portland.

While Portland is certainly the center for performing arts in the state, there are wonderful productions at other Southern Maine theaters like the Hackmatack Playhouse in Berwick and the Ogunquit Playhouse, as well as venues like the Saco River Grange in Bar Mills, west of Saco. In summer you'll find free concert series held on both the Eastern and Western Promenades in Portland, on the South Congregational Church lawn in Kennebunkport, at the Harbor Park gazebo in Wells and at Music on the Mall in Brunswick (see listing in this chapter's Music section).

Venues in Southern Maine vary from Portland's large, somewhat characterless Cumberland County Civic Center to church halls, parks, restaurants and the newly renovated Merrill Auditorium. Soaring ceilings, gilded trim and an otherwise elegant interior combined with excellent acoustics are fast making this Portland auditorium a well-loved venue for performing artists and audiences. Productions range from typical summer theater mysteries and musicals to Shakespeare, Kotzschmar Organ Concerts, big-name rock bands and classical string quartets. There are also opportunities to enjoy dance performances, from classical ballet offered by the Maine State Ballet and the Portland Ballet Company to contemporary dance from Ram Island Dance Company.

As for the visual arts, you'll find them everywhere. Works by local artists often are displayed on the walls of coffeehouses and restaurants as well as in museums and galleries. In fact, many of our galleries resemble museums with large, airy spaces and a diversity of media displayed — from watercolor to sculpture.

To help you find what you're looking for, we've divided this chapter into categories (Visual Arts or Performing Arts, for instance), broken those into appropriate subcategories (such as Art Galleries or Theater), then organized it all using the book's four geographic regions — the Southern Beaches Area, the

INSIDERS' TIP

Call the Portland Visitors' Information Center at (207) 772-4994 for a free Portland Summer Concert and Events guide. That way you'll know when various groups are scheduled to perform in our area parks.

Old Orchard Beach Area, the Greater Portland Area and the Brunswick, Bath and Boothbay Harbor Area. We lead off with Visual Arts, which includes Art Museums and Art Galleries, followed by Literary Arts. After these you'll find Performing Arts, with subcategories of Dance, Music and Theater. At the end of the chapter, you'll find listings for area venues.

Visual Arts

Art Museums

Southern Beaches Area

Ogunquit Museum of American Art
Shore Rd., Ogunquit • (207) 646-4909

When you visit the Ogunquit Museum of American Art (OMAA), you'll understand why it has been referred to as "the most beautiful small museum in the world." Built in 1952, the museum was enlarged in 1992 and 1996 and today houses some of America's most important 20th-century paintings and sculpture. Its extensive permanent collection includes paintings from Marsden Hartley, Edward Hopper, Gertrude Fiske, Charles Burchfield and Peggy Bacon. Special exhibitions are also regularly on display.

It's not just the collection that makes this a lovely museum, it's also its location. Situated in a meadow overlooking a rocky cove and the ocean, with a reflecting pool on the grounds to mirror the sky and movement of the clouds, you couldn't choose a more ideal spot for a museum. OMAA is open daily from July 1 to the end of September. It is closed on Labor Day. Admission is $4 for adults and $3 for senior citizens and students 12 and older. Children younger than 12 are admitted free.

Greater Portland Area

Portland Museum of Art
7 Congress Sq., Portland
• (207) 775-6148

The state's oldest art institution, dating back to 1882, offers an extensive collection of fine and decorative art from the 18th century to the present. You'll find native works by Winslow Homer, Rockwell Kent and Andrew Wyeth as well as a selection of works by European artists representing styles from Impressionism through Surrealism. The exhibits change from month to month, so call to find out what you'll be able to see during your visit.

One of the most captivating works you'll encounter, regardless of the timing of your visit, is the museum itself. Constructed in 1983 with many dramatic open spaces and grand stairways, the building has won awards for its architecture. In addition to its showrooms, the museum has a lunch cafe and a museum shop with fine gifts. Both are open to the public with no admission charge. The cost to enter the museum itself is $6 for adults, $5 for seniors and students and $1 for youngsters ages 6 to 12. Children younger than 6 get in free. If you want to save money, come on Friday night from 5 to 9 PM when everyone gets in free. From Columbus Day to July, the museum is closed on Mondays.

Brunswick, Bath and Boothbay Harbor Area

Bowdoin College Museum of Art
Walker Art Bldg., Bowdoin College, 9400 College Station, Main St., Brunswick
• (207) 725-3275

Past exhibits at Bowdoin College's art museum have included European works from the 14th century to the present as well as cross-temporal exhibitions of American art. It also features rotating contemporary exhibits and a collection of more than 13,000 objects, many of which are Mediterranean, American portraits and Syrian relief pieces. The works of Winslow Homer are also displayed from time to time, but you should call ahead to see whether they are being exhibited when you plan to visit. The museum is housed in the Walker Art Building, and admission is free.

Farnsworth Art Museum
352-356 Main St., Rockland
• (207) 596-6457

It's a little out of the way, but for a true sense of Maine art you shouldn't miss the Farnsworth Art Museum. Featuring images of

America with a special emphasis on Maine, its permanent collection is filled with master works by important artists such as Winslow Homer, George Bellows, Edward Hopper and the Wyeth family — Andrew Wyeth, his father, N.C. Wyeth, and son, Jamie Wyeth. The museum also collects and exhibits works by the state's leading contemporary artists.

Due to an expansion, most sections of the museum were closed in the winter of 1998, but when the museum fully reopened, guests were thrilled with an entire gallery of Wyeth paintings. The first traveling exhibit scheduled after the reopening was a show of paintings collected by the late Maine philanthropist Elizabeth Noyce.

Rockland is about 45 minutes north of Wiscasset. To get to the Farnsworth Art Museum, follow U.S. 1 north to Rockland. At the last traffic light on the corner of Park and Main streets as you enter town (the ocean will be directly in front of you), turn left onto Main Street and drive three blocks. The museum will be on your left. The main gallery is open year round but is closed on Mondays during the winter. Admission is $5 for adults, $4 for seniors and $3 for students ages 3 through 18.

Art Galleries

Southern Beaches Area

Kittery Art Association
8 Coleman Ave., Kittery
• **(207) 438-9332**
In the original firehouse in Kittery Point, off Maine Highway 103 just south of Pepperell Cove public landing, the Kittery Art Association gallery is open Wednesday through Sunday from noon to 6 PM. Inside you'll find inter-generational exhibits of artists' works from every level of experience. Paintings in most media and sculpture are showcased in the

gallery. The most popular exhibit is a shrine exhibit called "Dia De Los Muertos (Day of the Dead)," which takes place in October every year.

In addition to the gallery the association sponsors workshops; painting, color, composition and drawing classes; and art studio classes for kids.

Founded in 1958, the association hosts an annual exhibit throughout the month of September that reflects the membership of the association through the years. Other special exhibits are scheduled throughout the year. A number of special activities are offered through the Kittery Art Association. Those interested might want to consider taking part in the Collective Eye Group, which meets monthly. Group members challenge one another to respond artistically to an idea, concept or question that has been posed by a member. You can also sign up for Feng Shui workshops led by Mary Trainor-Bringham or watercolor classes to be led by Edward Winslow on a boat in Portsmouth Harbor. For more information on membership, exhibits and special events, contact the association at the listed number.

ShootingStar Gallery
74 Wallingford Sq., Kittery
• **(207) 439-6397**
The ShootingStar Gallery features New England artists in all mediums. In addition to regular displays, the gallery highlights a new exhibit every six weeks. For more information see their listing under Arts, Crafts & Jewelry in our Shopping chapter.

BlueStocking Studio
5 Railroad Ave., York Beach
• **(207) 363-7336**
Open daily May through October, BlueStocking Studio features functional pottery and original works of art on paper. Many

---

INSIDERS' TIP

Many area civic, church and school groups hold in-season theater, music and dance productions featuring local talent. For an up-to-date listing of what is happening while you're visiting, pick up a local newspaper. For information on what newspapers are available, see our Media chapter.

of the etchings, linocuts and watercolors are local views by gallery owner Nancy R. Davison. BlueStocking opened in 1985 and adds new artists and potters to its collection each year. In addition to Davison's work, you'll find pastels by Louis Frechette, etchings by Brian Cohen, Jean Lau and Laura Stowe and paintings by Edward Betts and Diana Shank. Handmade porcelain by Bill Campbell, Lynda Katz and Karen Howell is also available.

The Powder House Gallery
276 York St., York
• **(207) 351-2979**

In the heart of York Village in a 200-year-old, cottage-style building that was used as a powder house during the American Revolution, the aptly named Powder House Gallery contains the works of JoAnne Campbell. Campbell, who is self-taught and has been painting for 10 to 15 years, paints exclusively in watercolor. Approximately 200 paintings of all sizes are displayed in the gallery, which features high-beamed ceilings and a large fireplace. She uses loose, bright colors and paints all manner of subjects from landscapes and florals to seascapes. The Powder House Gallery is open almost year round since JoAnne lives in the building that houses the gallery.

George Carpenter Paintings
Oarweed Rd., Perkins Cove, Ogunquit
• **(207) 646-5106**

For 30 years George Carpenter has maintained a studio in Ogunquit. You'll find this world-renowned artist's place just across from the Footbridge in the Cove. George offers a selection of his finest works in oils and watercolors, all on display in a gallery evocative of old-time fishing shacks. Stop in and say hello. The gallery is open from May through October.

June Weare Fine Arts
Shore Rd., Ogunquit
• **(207) 646-8200**

In summer 1997 June Weare Fine Arts moved to its new location at the corner of Israel Head Road and Shore Road. Since 1977, Weare has been selecting the best work from the choice group of artists she displays. At one time she displayed the works of close to two dozen artists, but today she focuses

on 15. Among them you'll find Canadian watercolorist Pierre Tougas and Kennebunk's Ed Betts. Others include Joan Griswold, George Kunkel and Dean Minor. By representing fewer artists, Weare is able to maintain a larger body of knowledge on each one — from little personal tidbits about them to which societies they belong to. There are bright florals, landscapes and seascapes, sculpture, oils and watercolors in the bright, airy gallery. The gallery is open from mid-April to mid-October.

Ogunquit Arts Collaborative Gallery
Bourne Ln., Ogunquit
• **(207) 646-8400**

Founded in 1928 by Charles Woodbury, this contemporary fine art gallery features work by members of the area's highly respected professional arts organization. Formerly the Ogunquit Art Association Gallery, the gallery became a charitable corporation with a new name in 1997. Paintings, graphics, sculpture and photographs are displayed. In addition, the gallery hosts lectures, panel discussions, workshops and demonstrations. It's open from Memorial Day to the end of September.

Maine Art Gallery
Maine Hwy. 9, Kennebunkport
• **(207) 967-2803**

The Maine Art Gallery focuses on high-end limited-edition prints. The prints carried by the gallery are predominantly from New England artists, though you'll find selections from across the United States. The gallery also acts as a custom framing shop.

Next door there's a sister shop called Kennedy Studios, which offers posters and prints. Both shops are owned by Francesca and John Spain, who also own the Gallery on Chase Hill (see subsequent listing). Call before you visit in the off-season.

Mast Cove Gallery
Mast Cove Ln., Kennebunkport
• **(207) 967-3453**

It's not surprising this wonderful gallery has been written up in *The New York Times* travel section as well as *Travel & Leisure* magazine. The largest privately owned group gallery in Maine, Mast Cove Gallery represents more than 90 artists. You'll find paintings, graphics

Portland: Organ Donor to the Arts Scene

Music lovers will want to stop in Portland to hear the city's municipal organist, Ray Cornils. For most it may be the only chance they get to see someone with such a title, as Cornils is one of just two people in the country to hold the job of municipal organist.

In 1990 Cornils, of Woolwich, was appointed the city's 10th municipal organist. If

you're lucky and you're traveling through Portland during summer, you can hear him play the city's 50-ton, 6,600-pipe Kotzschmar Memorial Organ. (See more on the Kotzschmar Concerts in this chapter's Music section.) The instrument fills an entire wall of Portland's Merrill Auditorium, with gilded pipes running from the stage nearly to the top of the ceiling.

After Portland's first city hall burned to the ground in 1908, a new hall was constructed and the organ installed in 1912. It was a gift of publishing giant Cyrus Curtic, the man who published the Saturday Evening Post, and it was given in memory of Hermann Kotzschmar, an organist and musician who played in Portland for 50 years.

The Kotzschmar was the first municipal organ in the country, and it remains the largest one in the state. The instrument is a marvel, with pipes ranging in length from 32 feet to one-quarter of an inch. In the 1920s and '30s, when big city entertainment options such as symphonies began replacing the grand organs in terms of popularity, instruments such as the Kotzschmar fell into disrepair. Portland kept hiring organists to play "The Mighty Kotzschmar," but by 1980 only 25 percent of its pipes worked. That's when a group of citizens banded together and raised the money needed to fix it.

Cornils is helping keep the love of organ music alive by sharing it with the public. The Illinois native began studying

Ray Cornils is Portland's municipal organist.

piano at age 7 and organ at 13. He received a bachelor of music degree from Oberlin Conservatory and a master of music degree from the New England Conservatory. He has served on the faulty at Tufts University and Brookline Music School.

Since 1990 Cornils has been organist and music director for the First Parish Church of Brunswick (see our Worship chapter), where he directs five of the church's seven choirs.

and sculpture displayed in an older home in Kennebunkport's Historic District next to the Graves Memorial Library. There's also a delightful sculpture garden that includes such whimsical items as a salamander that's 5 feet long and a 14-foot-tall giraffe. The gallery will be entering its 20th season in 1999. It's open daily in summer, but you should call ahead in winter.

River Tree Arts Gallery
12 Depot St., Kennebunk
• (207) 985-4343, (800) 336-7856

River Tree Arts is a nonprofit community arts organization that offers a wide variety of performances and hands-on opportunities to promote artistic growth and understanding. They also have an art gallery where artists can display works not dictated to by the local market. This allows artists to pursue new, possibly risky roads in their art and to create works they might not be able to display elsewhere. The gallery is open Monday through Friday year round.

The Gallery on Chase Hill
10 Chase Hill Rd., Kennebunkport
• (207) 967-0049

One of three galleries owned by Francesca and John Spain, the Gallery on Chase Hill contains original artwork with a focus on representational and realistic subjects. You'll find artwork in all mediums, from oils and watercolors to pen and ink. Twenty-six different artists are represented in the gallery, which is open daily in season. Off-season, call first to make sure they'll be open. For the Spain's other galleries see Maine Art Gallery, above.

The Wright Gallery
5 Pier Rd., Cape Porpoise
• (207) 967-5053

If you're visiting the Kennebunks, you should make time for a visit to Cape Porpoise; once there, be sure to drop by the Wright Gallery, a fixture in the village since 1985. Located in a 19th-century post and beam

building with paintings, carvings and sculpture displayed on two floors, the gallery features a view across the harbor. You'll enjoy the sounds of a concert guitarist as you browse through the representational New England works of 30 artists from across the country. The Wright Gallery is open year round — daily most of the year and by appointment in January, February and March.

Greater Portland Area

Bayview Gallery
75 Market St., Portland • (207) 773-3007

Original paintings, sculpture and open- and limited-edition prints by Maine artists are displayed at the Bayview Gallery. Set in the heart of the Old Port, the gallery, which showcases works of traditional representation, is open daily July 4 through Columbus Day. An attached framing shop, The Pine Tree Shop, is open year round.

Danforth Gallery
20-36 Danforth St., Portland
• (207) 775-6245

From the traditional to the experimental, the Danforth Gallery showcases the works of Maine artists in an unpretentious atmosphere. With more than 200 members statewide, the gallery's exhibits change frequently. Past shows have ranged from digital art to photography to the sculpture of local high school students.

In 1998 the gallery celebrated its 10th anniversary with special exhibits such as "The Healthy Mind," in which five curators will present interpretations of the workings of the mind. The Danforth Gallery is run by The Maine Artists' Space, founded in 1988 to present art that transforms and enriches life. It's named for Thomas Danforth, the first governor of Maine, who was a strong supporter of the arts. In 1999, the Danforth Gallery celebrates the 300th anniversary of Danforth's death. Special events include drama, music, and the exhibition, "The Way Mayne [Maine]

Was." Admission to the nonprofit gallery is free. Hours change seasonally, so call ahead to find out when it is open. For most of the year, the Danforth Gallery is open during the afternoon from Wednesday through Sunday.

Greenhut Galleries
146 Middle St., Portland
• **(207) 772-2693, (888) 772-2693**

In business since 1979, Greenhut showcases the work of contemporary Maine artists. You'll find a large variety of works from landscapes to the abstract. The gallery is located in Portland's quaint Old Port and is open Monday through Saturday and by appointment.

The Institute of Contemporary Art
Maine College of Art,
522 Congress St., Portland
• **(207) 775-5152**

Regional, national and international artists display contemporary works here at the main gallery of the Maine College of Art. Past displays have included the work of Yvonne Jacquette, Robert Indiana and Alex Katz. Housed in a historic building with large, arched windows and a Romanesque facade, the gallery building is a piece of art itself. Formerly known as the Baxter Gallery, it often features contributions by the school's students and staff. Educational programs such as lectures, symposia and panel discussions are offered throughout the year. The gallery is free and open to the public Tuesday through Sunday, with evening hours on Thursday. (For more on the Maine College of Art, see our Education and Child Care chapter.)

The Stein Gallery of Contemporary Glass
195 Middle St., Portland
• **(207) 772-9072**

See glass sculptures that push the limits of the medium at this contemporary glass gallery. More than 85 percent of the gallery's visitors are from out of state — glass is an art medium that not all Mainers have accepted. However, once you step inside and see the pieces by 65 artists from around the country, you'll have no doubt that these works, both functional and decorative, are truly art. Each piece is hand-picked, and you'll be surprised

at the many forms glass can take as you view the wide variety of works presented here. Call for operating hours and more information.

Brunswick, Bath and Boothbay Harbor Area

O'Farrell Gallery
58 Maine St., Brunswick
• **(207) 729-8228**

Praised by *The New York Times* and local art lovers alike, the O'Farrell Gallery occupies a prominent place in the ranks of regional galleries. You'll find exhibitions ranging from contemporary painting and sculpture to limited-edition prints by internationally known artists. Among those who have displayed their works here are Neil Welliver, Alex Katz, Robert Indiana, Andy Warhol and Louise Nevelson. The works are displayed in a traditional showroom with high ceilings and hardwood floors. The gallery is open year round, Tuesday through Saturday, from mid-morning until evening. In summer it is also open on Monday.

The Chocolate Church Arts Center
804 Washington St., Bath
• **(207) 442-8455**

The works of Maine artists are on display at The Chocolate Church gallery. All media are represented, and shows range from juried competitions to invitational group shows to individual shows. Many artists have national and international reputations. It is open Tuesday through Friday.

Wiscasset Bay Gallery
Maine St., Wiscasset
• **(207) 882-7682**

Specializing in paintings by noted Maine artists and antique works from Europe and the United States, the Wiscasset Bay Gallery offers artistic gems from the past and present. Paintings are hung against the rough red brick of the gallery's walls, and displays change monthly during summer. Varying shows exhibit a wide range or watercolors and oils. "At Home and Abroad: American and European Works from Two Centuries" is an example of a recent exhibit. The gallery has a well-known reputation and has been around since 1984.

It's open daily from mid-April through Christmas.

Boothbay Region Art Foundation
7 Townsend Ave., Boothbay Harbor
• **(207) 633-2703**

This community-supported public gallery presents the works of some of the best artists in the Boothbay region and includes the work of people who live in Maine only during summer. You'll find traditional art, oils, watercolors, photographs and pencil drawings by the 140 artist members. The gallery is open daily from late May through Columbus Day weekend, and art classes are offered during fall and winter.

Gleason Fine Art
15 Oak St., Boothbay Harbor
• **(207) 633-6849**

Set in a stately brick house overlooking the downtown shopping area, Gleason Fine Art has eight rooms full of antiques and oriental rugs, as well as a collection of contemporary, regional and early 20th-century paintings and sculpture. During a recent summer season, the gallery featured watercolors from the estate of modernist James Fitzgerald and landscapes painted by Fairfield Porter during his summers in Maine. Nationally known sculptors Cabot Lyford and Don Meserve also have works here. The gallery is open year round Tuesday through Sunday.

Literary Arts

Maine Authors

Sarah Orne Jewett (1849-1909)

Famous for her portrayal of Maine life in the late 1800s, Sarah Orne Jewett hailed from Berwick, and you can visit the house where she lived (see our Attractions chapter). Her most famous novel is The White Heron, but perhaps her best-loved book is *The Country of the Pointed Firs and Other Stories*, which was once required reading for many U.S. high school students. We've even bumped into people abroad who've said, "You live in Maine? Have you read *The Country of the Pointed Firs?*" If you are interested in Jewett, you might want to seek out her third book, Deephaven.

Kenneth Roberts (1885-1957)

Author of historical novels such as *Arundel, Northwest Passage, Rabble in Arms* and *Oliver Wiswell*, Kenneth Roberts' work was so popular that North Kennebunk changed its name to the name Kennebunkport had held from 1719 to 1821 — Arundel. A Kennebunk native, Roberts was also famous for campaigning against the placement of billboards along Maine highways.

Nathaniel Hawthorne (1804-1864)

Those familiar with Hawthorne may be saying, "Hey, I thought he lived in Massachusetts," and indeed he did for some time. What you might not know is that from about age 12 he lived just off Maine Highway 302, near Sebago Lake in Raymond. He also attended Bowdoin College in Brunswick. As an adult he lived in a house with seven gables in Salem, Massachusetts. There he wrote *The Scarlet Letter* and *House of the Seven Gables*, a title he surely must have garnered from his own residence, which you can visit today. Salem is about a two-hour drive south of Portland.

Kate Douglas Wiggin (1856-1923)

About 30 miles west of Saco on Route 112, or about the same distance southwest of Portland on Route 22 (Congress Street), you'll reach the village of Bar Mills. Just south of Bar Mills on Route 117 is Salmon Falls. Both villages lie on the banks of the Saco River, which is wide, tree-lined and quite beautiful. At Bar Mills you'll find the waterfalls for which its neighboring village is named. A cheerful green bridge crosses the falls, allowing both pedestrian and vehicular access. This is the background around which the beloved children's classic *Rebecca of Sunnybrook Farm* was set. Author Kate Douglas Wiggin lived in the area, and it isn't difficult to see "Riverboro" in these two villages nestled on the banks of the Saco.

Stephen King (1947-)

Technically, Stephen King doesn't fit into our area, but he's certainly the best-known

Photo: Merry Farnum

Maine is inspirational to artists from all over.

literary figure from Maine. Raised in Lewiston, King resides in Bangor, a couple of hours north of Portland, where he churns out the spine-tinglingly scary novels for which he is famous. He occasionally incorporates place names from Maine, such as Ogunquit, into his work. King fans will know Ogunquit is mentioned in *The Stand*. Other titles you might recognize include *Cujo, Carrie, Thinner, The Shining, Pet Sematary* and *The Running Man*. He also has published under the name Richard Bachman.

Henry Wadsworth Longfellow (1807-1882)

Born in 1807 in a rented house off Fore and Hancock streets along the Portland waterfront, famed American poet Henry Wadsworth Longfellow spent many of his days in Maine. He is rumored to have written his first poem behind his grandfather's barn in Gorham. Longfellow came from a long line of highly educated folk, and his father, Stephen Longfellow Jr., was a distinguished juror and legislator.

The poet was born at his aunt's rented home, a large house at 161 Fore Street in Portland, but most of his childhood was spent at the large Georgian home on Congress Street now known as the Wadsworth-Longfellow House (see our Attractions chap-

ter for information on visiting). Back then it was tucked between woods and fields on the outskirts of the city, but today it's in the center of the downtown district. It was the first brick house built here.

In this historic mansion, Longfellow wrote his first literary papers at the age of 3. He entered Bowdoin College in Brunswick at age 14, graduating with classmate Nathaniel Hawthorne in 1825. Longfellow went on to teach at Bowdoin, then at Harvard in Boston, where he eventually settled. Still, he frequently returned to his family's Portland home, last visiting in 1881. Many of his poems such as "A Rainy Day," written in 1841, were penned here. Others such as "Evangeline," "My Lost Youth" and "The Building of the Ship" reflect Maine themes. By his death, Longfellow had become one of the most celebrated poets in the world and one of the most beloved. His verse is still widely read and published today.

Harriet Beecher Stowe (1811-1896)

It was noon, and Harriet Beecher Stowe, the little-known wife of a Bowdoin College professor, was sitting at the family pew of the First Parish Church in Brunswick when it happened. A vision unrolled before her eyes as if painted on a scroll: a black man knelt on a wooden floor as two white men loomed over him, lashing him to death with two large whips. As Mrs. Stowe knelt in awe, she heard the voice of Jesus urging her to help the oppressed. On that day — March 2, 1851 — she returned home and began penning the words of a story that helped lead to the Civil War and, ultimately, to the freeing of America's slaves. It was *Uncle Tom's Cabin*.

The home in which Mrs. Stowe wrote this classic is also in Brunswick, at 63 Federal Street, and was auctioned off in January 1999. Its new owners plan to open a restaurant and bed & breakfast. Born in 1811, she didn't come to Bath until May 22, 1850, when she joined her husband, Dr. Calvin Stowe, who was a professor of mental and moral theology at Bowdoin. Brunswick itself was a station on what became known as the Underground Railroad, a chain of houses and people providing shelter for fugitive slaves fleeing from the South. Mrs. Stowe was introduced to the abolitionist movement by her friend, Phoebe Lord Upham, who lived in the house where the Brunswick Elks Home is today. It's on Park Rowe just above the Brunswick Town Mall. Mrs. Stowe lived in Brunswick with her six children until 1852.

Uncle Tom's Cabin was first published as a series of magazine stories, then as the now-world-famous novel. In addition to that book, she wrote *The Pearl of Orr's Island*, a novel based on the lives of people who lived on the nearby island, which is part of Harpswell.

Writing Groups

The Kennebunk Writers Group
12 Depot St., Kennebunk
• (207) 985-4343,
(800) 336-7856

The Kennebunk Writers Group meets twice a month at River Tree Arts. Writers share works in progress, tips and experiences. Meetings are held on the second Saturday of each month at 10 AM and the fourth Wednesday of each month at 7 PM.

Maine Romance Writers of America
• (603) 471-0289, (207) 782-2697

The Maine Romance Writers of America (MERWA) meet every third Saturday of the month at Bookland in Brunswick at Cook's Corner (see the Bookstores section of our Shopping chapter). At meetings you'll enjoy presentations on topics associated with writing, such as how to interpret a rejection letter and other related subjects. Annual dues for MERWA are $20, but you need to belong to the National Romance Writers of America in order to join. Dues for the national group are $60 per year. At present there are about 10 published writers in MERWA. You don't need to be a writer of romance to join.

Maine Writers and Publishers Alliance
12 Pleasant St., Brunswick
• (207) 725-0690

Maine's foremost writing association, this alliance has 1,500 members from across the state and nation. It offers a wide variety of writing courses on topics ranging from how to get published to actual writing techniques. The group produces a monthly newsletter called Maine in Print. A one-year membership is $30 and gets you discounts on workshops and seminars.

Performing Arts

Dance

Greater Portland Area

Maine State Ballet
91 Forest St., Westbrook • (207) 856-1663

Although this ballet company is based just outside Portland, it often performs at the Portland City Hall auditorium along with various venues around the state. The professional dance company attracts more than 20,000 spectators each season and works with acclaimed choreographers from around the country. Recent productions have included *A Midsummer Night's Dream, The Nutcracker* (accompanied by the Portland Symphony Orchestra), and *Sleeping Beauty*. General ticket prices range from $10 to $30, with a $2 discount for children younger than 12 and seniors older than 60.

Ram Island Dance Company
Portland Stage, 25A Forest Ave.,
Portland • (207) 773-2562

When this contemporary dance company opened in 1968, it was the first professional dance company north of Boston. In addition to producing a lively array of performances, it offers residencies and classes in modern dance and ballet. Show tickets are $10 for adults and $8 for students and seniors.

The Portland Ballet Company
25A Forest Ave., Portland • (207) 772-9671

Famous for its annual Victorian production of *The Nutcracker*, this professional ballet company tells the traditional story with sets inspired by Portland's Victoria Mansion (see our Attractions chapter) and characters named for well-known people from the Portland area. Guest artists from the Russian Ballet appear in the performance. In addition, The Portland Ballet usually schedules spring and fall productions. In 1998 it did a sampler of six pieces based on music by Schubert. Ticket prices range from $10 to $30 for *The Nutcracker* and $12 to $15 for smaller-scale productions. Discounted tickets are available for children and seniors.

Music

Southern Beaches Area

Jonathan's Restaurant
Bourne Ln., Ogunquit • (207) 646-4777

Upstairs at Jonathan's Restaurant you can enjoy music and cabaret shows throughout the summer. Previous seasons have featured performers such as Suede, The Shaw Brothers, John Gorka and Peter Wolf. Theater programs included *Tony 'N' Tina's Wedding*, by Shenanigans Productions (see subsequent listing), and *Park Your Car In Harvard Yard* by Ogunquit Productions. Tickets for shows at

Jonathan's can be purchased at Strawberries Record Stores or by calling (800) 464-9934. Cabaret (dinner) seating is reserved for guests as tickets are purchased, and dinner is served a little more than two hours prior to showtime. Cocktail (show) seating is general admission, and doors open 45 minutes before showtime. No smoking is allowed during performances at the restaurant.

Meetinghouse Museum
U.S. Hwy. 1, Wells • (207) 646-4775

During the summer season the Meetinghouse Museum holds a series of free concerts. In 1998 there were two concerts in July and two in August. Music varies from local singers to classical string quartets. (For more information on the museum, see our Attractions chapter.)

Wells Free Concerts
Hope Hobbs Gazebo, Harbor Park,
Harbor Rd., Wells

A series of free concerts is held at Harbor Park in Wells throughout summer. Performances begin at 7 PM, and have included such diverse offerings as Peruvian folk music, a Beatles tribute group and a country-western band. To get to the park, take a right on Harbor Road as you head north toward Kennebunk on U.S. 1.

River Tree Arts
12 Depot St., Kennebunk
• (207) 985-4343, (800) 336-7856

Formed in 1982, River Tree Arts is a nonprofit organization founded with the dream of offering high-quality artistic programs and experiences for the entire community. In 1997 the organization was able to purchase this Depot Street location, enabling it to bring together all of its programs under one roof. River Tree Arts offers productions year round, held at a variety of venues — from Kennebunk Town Hall to the South Congregational Church in

Photo: Convention and Visitor's Bureau of Greater Portland

Portland's Merrill Auditorium hosts the Portland Symphony
Orchestra and the Portland Concert Association.

Kennebunkport. In years past, performances have included the Annual Fiddle Contest (see our Annual Events and Festivals chapter), a Rock 'n' Roll Showcase featuring local rock bands, Wayne from Maine (children's music) and Libana (a feast of world music).

River Tree Arts also offers music lessons for all ages and runs a folk club. The folk club is open to anyone who wants to share a song or just drop in and listen. They meet on the last Friday of the month at 7:30 PM at the Community House on Temple Street in Kennebunkport. A $2 donation is appreciated. (For information on River Tree Arts' gallery, see this chapter's Art Galleries section.)

River Tree Arts/WBQQ
Summer Concerts
**South Congregational Church lawn,
Kennebunkport**
• **(207) 985-4343, (800) 336-7856**

In-season you can enjoy free concerts sponsored by River Tree Arts and the radio station known popularly as "W-Bach." Con-

certs are held at 7 PM on Thursdays and range from Big Band-era music to a women's chorus and a saxophone quartet. Donations are accepted.

Old Orchard Beach Area

Saco River Grange Hall
Salmon Falls Rd., Bar Mills
• **(207) 929-6472**

Located about 30 miles west of Saco off Maine 112, or about the same distance southwest of Portland on Maine 22 (Congress Street), the Saco River Grange Hall hosts musical performances year round. Cost for admission varies by performance but usually ranges from $5 to $10 for adults and a couple of dollars less for students and senior citizens. Some of the performers seen at the Grange include concert pianist Allan Barker, Bernhard Hartog and Sevimbika Eilbay, and the Northeast Winds. (For more on the Saco River Grange Hall, see the subsequent section on Venues.)

Ocean Park Temple Series
Temple Ave., Old Orchard Beach
• **(207) 934-9068**

Just south of Old Orchard Beach center you'll find the community of Ocean Park. In-season the Ocean Park Association hosts concerts at The Temple, one of three green and white buildings nestled under very tall pines on Temple Avenue. Held on Sunday nights at 7:30 PM, concerts in 1998 were $5 for adults and $2 for children ages 6 through 18; children age 5 or younger were admitted free. Some concerts do not have an admission charge but instead a "free-will offering." If you expect to attend many concerts in the series, a season pass is available at $25 for adults and $10 for children. Types of concerts offered have included a singalong with the Ocean Park Band, cast members and apprentices from the Portland Opera Repertory Theater singing music from Tosca, the Bellamy Jazz band and the Temple Choir.

Greater Portland Area

Chandler Band Concerts
Eastern Promenade, Portland
• **(207) 874-8793**

Spend a day playing on the promenade, then listen to whichever band is playing afterward. On Thursday evenings from July through August, the Eastern Prom is the site of the Chandler Band Concerts, which generally begin at 7:30 PM. The 68-acre promenade overlooks Portland Harbor and Casco Bay and includes tennis courts, a boat launch, a ball field, East End Beach and a bathhouse. The free concerts take place at historic Fort Allen and feature old-fashioned band music.

Deering Oaks Park
Forest Ave., Portland
• **(207) 874-8793**

Free evening concerts for all ages are held at Portland's largest downtown park on Tuesday evenings, and children's performances are held on Thursday afternoons at the park bandstand. The park covers 58 acres, so there's lots of room to roam afterward. The summer productions are offered by Portland Parks and Recreation; call them at the number listed for more information.

Kotzschmar Organ Concerts
Merrill Auditorium, 20 Myrtle St.,
Portland • **(207) 874-8200**

In summer, sit in the cool of recently restored Merrill Auditorium as you listen to the music bellowing from one of the world's greatest Austin organs. The Kotzschmar has 6,613 pipes, and visitors have enjoyed its music here since 1912. Organists from around the country hold evening concerts from mid-June through the end of August. Evening concerts begin at 7:30 PM and are held on Tuesdays. There is no admission charge, but the suggested donation is $5. At noon, free demonstrations are sometimes given, again for a suggested donation of $5, but these are sporadic. Special concerts such as a Christmas spectacular are also scheduled throughout the year. Call ahead to find out when the concerts will take place. (For more information, see this chapter's Close-up.)

Noontime Summer Performance Series
Various downtown locations, Portland
• **(207) 772-6828**

Portland's downtown district offers free lunchtime concerts that will get your feet tapping no matter how tired they may be from a morning of sightseeing. Jazz, country, folk and rock bands perform in Tommy's Park, on Congress Square and at Post Office Park. Occasionally, children's shows and dance performances are also scheduled. Past shows have featured Portland's Ram Island Dance Company (see listing above), country folk singer Slaid Cleaves and teenagers with the Maine Summer Dramatic Institute performing scenes from Shakespeare. Performances are held weekdays at noon from late June through August.

Portland Symphony Orchestra
477 Congress St., Portland
• **(207) 842-0800**

World-class artists with the Portland Symphony Orchestra perform the classics and the pops each season at Merrill Auditorium. Directed and conducted by Toshiyuki Shimada since April 1986, the orchestra performed more than 41 concerts during its 1997-98 season. Toshiyuki is the former music director of the

Nassau Symphony Orchestra and the Cambiata Soloists, a contemporary music ensemble in Houston.

The symphony is in its 73rd season, and its 1998 performance schedule included "The Astounding Voices of Brahms" in March, "Jambalaya Fever!" with the Jim Cullum Jazz Band in May and the annual Independence Pops series in July. Most events take place at Portland's recently renovated Merrill Auditorium, but the orchestra holds other performances around the state. In addition it presents Kinderkonzerts, music aimed at preschool and primary grade children (see our Kidstuff chapter), and it has three youth ensembles made up of more than 200 elementary, middle and high school students from across the country. Ticket prices generally range from $14 to $30.

Sunset Folk Series
Western Promenade, Portland
• (207) 874-8793

On the banks of Portland's Western Promenade, you can take in views of the surrounding countryside and the White Mountains while relaxing to acoustic music in this free, outdoor summer series. Concerts take place on Wednesday nights from mid-June through mid-August.

Brunswick, Bath and Boothbay Harbor Area

Bowdoin Summer Music Festival
Various locations, Brunswick
• (207) 725-3322, (207) 725-3895

From July 3 to August 7, this festival of chamber music is presented by the faculty and students at Bowdoin College and by guest artists. The college's music students and faculty are drawn from the leading conservatories in America, Asia and Europe. Some events are scheduled at Brunswick High School's Crooker Theater, while others are held at the Kresege Auditorium on the Bowdoin campus.

Upbeat!, a concert series with small chamber ensembles, is typcially held at Bowdoin one night a week from early July through August. Other special events take place throughout the year, and the school orchestra often

presents summer performances. Tickets for the various productions range from $17.50 to $22.50 for adults and teens and $8 to $10 for children younger than 10. The outdoor family concert is $5 for adults and $2 for children. The festival is in its 35th year.

Music on the Mall
Brunswick Town Mall, Maine St., Brunswick • (207) 725-8797

Various area bands put on free outdoor family concerts every Wednesday evening in July and August. The events are sponsored by the local chamber of commerce, and past participants have included the Bath Municipal Band, the Merrymeeting Community Band and the Royal River Philharmonic Jazz Band. Concerts generally begin at 7 PM.

Summer Organ Concert Series
First Parish Church, Maine St., Brunswick
• (207) 729-7331, (207) 443-6597

Sit in a pew once occupied by Joshua Chamberlain or Harriet Beecher Stowe as you listen to a noontime recital on the restored 1883 Hutchings-Plaisted tracker organ of the First Parish Church. The church itself is an area monument, with cloud-gray pinnacles pointing toward the sky. The recitals are free (a donation is accepted at the door) and are followed by a church tour. They are offered on Tuesdays from early July through the middle of August and begin at 12:10 PM. Civil War buffs should note it was in this church that Gen. Joshua Chamberlain married the minister's daughter and where writer Harriet Beecher Stowe had the vision that inspired her to pen Uncle Tom's Cabin (see previous listing on Mrs. Stowe in this chapter's Maine Authors section). Children are welcome.

Lincoln Arts Festival 1998 Summer Series
Various locations, Boothbay Harbor
• (888) 337-2710

From the Portland String Quartet to jazz duos, there are plenty of summer concerts indoors and out in Boothbay Harbor. Grouped under the name of the Lincoln Arts Festival, the concerts take place at churches, boatyards and inns from mid-June through early October. Tickets are available through the Boothbay Harbor Region Chamber of Commerce or by writing to the Lincoln Arts Festival, P.O. Box 391, Boothbay Harbor, ME 04538. Past performers have included Maine composer Thomas Bucci, organist David Maxwell and the Lincoln Quartet from the Lincoln Center in New York City. The Portland String Quartet and the Portland Brass Quintet are also popular performers. Ticket prices vary widely.

Theater

Southern Beaches Area

Hackmatack Playhouse
538 Maine Hwy. 9, Beaver Dam, Berwick • (207) 698-1807

A diverse array of productions was selected for the Hackmatack Playhouse's 1998 summer season. Productions included *Nunsense, Camelot, Phantom, Annie* and *No Sex Please We're British*. Regular tickets usually go for around $20; a season ticket is $64.

Ogunquit Playhouse
U.S. Hwy. 1, Ogunquit • (207) 646-5511

Since its founding in 1933, the Ogunquit Playhouse has been regarded as "America's Foremost Summer Theater." In addition to a wealth of Tony and Emmy award-winning actors and actresses, the playhouse has also hosted 29 Academy Award winners in various productions through the years. Some of the familiar actors who've taken to the playhouse stage include Christopher Plummer, Walter Matthau, William Shatner, Olympia Dukakis, Ed Begley, Bette Davis, Keir Dullea, Will Geer, Merv Griffin, Jeff Bridges, Lillian Gish, Gene Wilder and Cybil Shepherd.

The 1998 season was the first under the ownership of the Ogunquit Playhouse Foundation. Founded in 1933 by Walter and Maude Hartwig, the playhouse passed to the ownership of John Lane in 1951. In 1994 Lane began searching for the best way to preserve the playhouse for future generations, and the concept of a tax-exempt foundation was generated. After the foundation raised $500,000 as an endowment to maintain the building and

gained tax-exempt status, Lane deeded the playhouse to the group on September 17, 1997.

Each year four or five productions are held at the Ogunquit Playhouse, depending on when Labor Day falls in September. Performances are held Monday through Saturday at 8 PM, and there are matinees on Wednesdays and Thursdays at 2:30 PM. Cost for a single ticket was $24 for the 1998 season.

Shenanigans Productions
Ogunquit • (207) 646-6825

Shenanigans Productions is a professional, non-equity company presenting live theater in a casual atmosphere. Based in Ogunquit, the group uses the talents of local actors and others from Portsmouth, New Hampshire, to Portland. In the past few years, Shenanigans has produced such popular shows as *Girl's Guide to Chaos, Psycho Beach Party* and *Tony 'N' Tina's Wedding*. For information on this season's shows, call the number listed. Prices vary depending on the venue for the performance.

Old Orchard Beach Area

City Theater
Main St., Biddeford • (207) 282-0849

In 1996 the City Theater in Biddeford celebrated its 100th anniversary. Designed by renowned architect John Calvin Stevens, the theater opened its doors in 1896The 500-seat venue is on the National Register of Historic Sites and is acknowledged as one of the finest Victorian theaters in America. You can enjoy performances at the theater year round. Ticket prices are usually around $10 for adults.

Greater Portland Area

Portland Players
420 Cottage Rd., South Portland • (207) 767-6208, (207) 799-7337

Together since 1931, the Portland Players are the oldest community theater group in Maine and the second oldest known in New England. Originally founded as the Portland Dramatic Guild, the group stages five productions a year between September and June. Past performances have included *West*

Side Story, Jesus Christ Superstar and *Brighton Beach Memoirs*. More than 10,000 people are estimated to attend Portland Players' productions each year. Regular ticket prices for performances are $10 for opening night and $13 for all other nights. Season series rates are available.

Mad Horse Theatre
Oak Street Theater, 92 Oak St., Portland
• (207) 775-5103

From the whimsical to the dramatic, this resident professional theater ensemble offers productions from October through July. In summer it provides a special children's' theater that is done for and by kids. Tickets range from $8 to $20, with a $2 discount for students and seniors. The company performs Thursday through Sunday.

Portland Stage Company
25A Forest Ave., Portland
• (207) 774-0465

There's almost always a production to enjoy with this professional theater company, which produces six shows in a season that runs from October through May. In 1998 the works included *Spunk*, by Zora Neale Hurston; *The Loman Family Picnic*, by Donald Margulies; and Anne Bogart's *Culture of Desire*. Tickets ranged from $23 to $29 for adults and $18 to $24 for seniors and students.

Brunswick Bath and Boothbay Harbor Area

Maine State Music Theatre
14 Maine St., Ste. 109, Bowdoin College, Brunswick • (207) 725-8769

Maine's only professional music theater offers acclaimed performances all summer long at Bowdoin College's historic, 610-seat Pickard Theatre. Since 1959 the group has thrilled audiences with timeless classics, rediscovered musical plays and new works. The theater's 1998 summer performances included five of the following: *A Funny Thing Happened on the Way to the Forum*, *Big River*, *Chicago*, *Grease*, *Guys and Dolls*, *Man of La Mancha* and *Smile*. Single show ticket prices range from $15 for a preview or special matinee to $30 for some of the best seats in the house.

The Theater Project
14 School St., Brunswick
• (207) 729-8584

From October through July, The Theater Project offers well-known and quality new productions at affordable prices. They have recently presented *Death of a Salesman*, *Rumpelstiltskin*, *The Skin of Our Teeth* and *Bits and Pieces*, a selection of short original pieces by high school performers. At $6 to $12, tickets aren't much more than at the movies, and you'll get a lot more atmosphere for your buck. Ticket prices are the same for all age groups.

Venues
Old Orchard Beach Area

Saco River Grange Hall
Salmon Falls Rd., Bar Mills
• (207) 929-6472

In the picturesque village of Bar Mills on the banks of the Saco River, the Grange Hall hosts a variety of performances year round. You can take part in contra dancing (which is somewhat like square dancing), watch theater productions or listen to world-class musicians — it all depends on the schedule. Admission costs vary by performance but usually range from $4 to $10 for adults. To get to the Grange Hall take Maine Highway 112 west off U.S. 1 in Saco, or follow Congress Street (Maine Highway 22) southwest out of Portland. It's about 30 miles from either city.

Greater Portland Area

To find out what performances are coming to Portland, contact the Portland Concert Association, one of New England's major international arts presenters. Events handled by PCA Great Performances include dance, opera, musical theater and jazz, folk and classical music. The group is located at 477 Congress Street in Portland; the phone number is (207) 842-0800.

Merrill Auditorium
20 Myrtle St., Portland
• (207) 874-8200

With seating for 1,800 people, Merrill Auditorium is one of the larger concert halls in the state. It is also one of the most historic and commanding with its domed, gilded ceilings, plush theater chairs, two balconies and world-renowned Kotzschmar organ. The Portland Symphony Orchestra performs here as do other crowd-pleasers such as Itzhak Perlman, Peter Schickele, Lyle Lovett, Sinead O'Connor, Crosby, Stills and Nash and Broadway shows such as "Stomp."

Portland Performing Arts Center
25A Forest Ave., Portland
• **(207) 761-0591**

This 296-seat theater, once the local Oddfellows Hall, is on the National Register of Historic Places. In 1983 it was rebuilt by the Portland Stage Company and now houses that theater group as well as three dance studios used by the Ram Island Dance Company

and the Portland Ballet (see previous listings for all three organizations). The center is one of the largest performance centers north of Boston and is handicapped-accessible. For information on scheduled performances, call the Portland Stage box office at (207) 774-0465.

Brunswick, Bath and Boothbay Harbor Area

Pickard Theatre
Bowdoin College, Maine St., Brunswick
• **(207) 725-3344**

The summer performance facility for the Maine State Music Theatre, this theater has seating for 610 and hosts more than 30 school-sponsored events annually.

Southern Maine's natural world contains inspiration for the artist, solitude for the introspective and romance for the amorous.

Maine's Natural World

A large number of artists flock to Maine every summer, setting up studios in small shacks and pulling palettes from the trunks of their cars to try to transfer our world's natural beauty to canvas. Buying such a piece is a wonderful way to bring the sounds and sights of our Southern Coast home with you.

Those of us lucky enough to live here adorn our walls with art of a different type: windows. Through inexpensive glass we get ever-changing works of art impossible to capture on canvas: tall pine trees swaying in a summer breeze one season and bowing under blankets of snow the next; moonlight shimmering off a tranquil sea that by morning might churn into frothing waves swallowing up the rocky shore; fields of flowers, darting birds, wandering moose and deer, squirrels and chipmunks galore; golden fall leaves dancing off trees, milky white fogs swirling over ponds and valleys and a blur of distant mountains challenging us to climb.

Southern Maine's natural world contains inspiration for the artist; solitude for the introspective; romance for the amorous; furry, slippery and winged beasts for the animal lover; and endless outdoor fun for the adventurous. To deepen your appreciation and expand your knowledge of nature as we know it, we have devoted this chapter to the animals that live on our land and in our sea and air and the environment that supports them.

Our Land and Animals

One of the first things you might notice when driving into Southern Maine is the deep green forests of pine trees that rise above the edges of our highways and roads. Roughly 90 percent of Maine is covered with trees. In the early days, trees meant fuel, shelter and masts for sailing ships. Pine was the preferred wood for ship masts, and Mast Landing in Freeport still bears reference to its heritage and the masts it provided for the British Navy during early Colonial days.

Today trees mean jobs for the many woodcutters and paper mill workers here; they also mean plenty of rich habitats for animals. They mean tourists, too. Every fall, droves of "leaf peepers" drive to Maine to view the explosive colors of our fall foliage. Northern red oak, red maple, sugar maple, birch and elm trees display a show of orange, golden yellows, reds, greens and even purples during the fall months beginning in early October. To find preferred places to view the action, check out our Parks and Recreation chapter.

The Northern red oak is the most common oak found here. You can identify it by counting the number of points on its leaves — each should have seven to 11. This and other deciduous trees are the kind that drop their leaves in the fall, but others such as the white pine, our state tree, retain their leaves year round. To identify the white pine, count the number of needles in each bundle: The white pine will have five.

In winter, snow lays heavy on the deep green quills of our spruce, balsam fir and pine trees, weighing down giant limbs. After a severe ice storm, such as the one that showered down on the state for nearly a week in January 1998, tree trunks and limbs are coated with as much as three inches of ice. The magnificence of the sun shining through the cold crystal was breathtaking when the storm finally eased up. However, the sheer weight of the ice bent the tips of even the thickest trees in giant "U's" toward the ground, snapping complete trees and telephone poles in half and leaving thousands without electricity for more than three weeks! At the peak of the storm, half the people in the state were in darkness. It was the most brutal ice storm in memory.

Our Southern Coast is fairly flat compared to the steep inclines found in the White Mountains inland to the west and in Acadia National Park to the northeast. The "mountains" we claim might not be thought of as such by the active hiker, but they do offer tranquility, deep forests and rewarding views of the sea.

The coast is the real attraction here. While you'll find smooth, sandy beaches as long as a mile in length (see our Beaches chapter), most of our coastline is a jumble of jagged rocks heaved up against the shore, with smaller rocks and then pebbles leading to the shore.

In summer, wild roses line roadways along the coast, scenting the air with sweetness. Tall lupines with clusters of bell-like flowers at their tips sprout up all over the Southern Coast. Fiercely orange tiger lilies dot the landscape, and enormous bushes of lilac unfurl their color on front yards, wafting perfume to people passing by. The richness of our Southern Coast's fields and forests provide ample feeding grounds for deer, moose and other wildlife.

Moose

One of the best-known and best-loved animals here in Maine is also the largest antlered animal on earth: the moose. Standing on average from 8 to 10 feet in height, the lumbering moose can weigh up to 1,400 pounds. This makes them somewhat of a hazard to motorists, and as you drive along our highways you'll see yellow "Moose Crossing" signs from time to time warning you to keep a sharp eye out. Every year there are hundreds of collisions with these hulking beauties.

Moose get their name from the Algonquin Indians, who called them "mong-soa," meaning "twig eater." You won't usually see them traveling in groups of more than two because they keep to themselves, and you might not see them at all. It took us more than 10 years of living here to encounter one. Moose antlers, used for self-defense, take up to six years to reach full size — sometimes they span as much as 6 feet in width. However, you need not fear the beasts; just keep your distance and do not provoke them. Moose attacks, while not unheard of, are extremely rare.

Something that might surprise you for an animal this size is that moose are good swimmers and have been seen swimming for up to 12 miles without stopping. They can also dive down to a depth of about 20 feet where they feed on lake-bottom vegetation. Because they can stay underwater for a minute or two, they sometimes scare canoeists when they pop back up.

Moose eat up to 60 pounds of food a day, and it's a diet even the strictest doctor would probably approve of — plants and herbs. Because of overly aggressive hunting, the moose almost became extinct in Maine during the 1940s. Moose hunting was prohibited for many years and has only recently been allowed on a limited basis to help control the now thriving population. The best place to spot moose is — not surprisingly — in the Moosehead Lake Region, about two-and-a-half hours northwest of Brunswick. You're just about sure to spot one there, and we've given you some tips in the up-close box included in this chapter. Many people come to Maine with the sole intention of sighting a moose. The best time of year is June, when the bugs drive the defenseless animals out of the woods. They also like to lick the salt (scattered to melt snow and ice) off the sides of the roads. Moose are very visible in western Maine up until the end of fall. Good luck!

INSIDERS' TIP

Bring along a good pair of binoculars for birdwatching or whale-watching.

Photo: Convention and Visitor's Bureau of Greater Portland

Southern Maine's craggy coastline is legendary.

Bears

When many outdoor enthusiasts think of Maine, they think of bear country. The thought comes to mind for good reason: There are somewhere around 23,000 bears here, the most common of which is the black bear. All but the occasional garbage-eating kind stick to the thicker portions of the state's woods. So if you want to see one (or bag one), you'll have to head north. Bears thrive in heavily forested lands that are thick with spruce, fir, maple, beech and birch trees. Beechnuts make up a large part of their diet. It's unlikely that you'll spot a bear along our Southern Coast because the trees in our tip of the state's forest are predominantly white pine and oak.

Hunting enthusiasts who are interested in traveling a few hours northwest can contact the Maine Department of Inland Fisheries and Wildlife about a bear-hunting license. The hunting season is during fall, and the annual limit is one bear per hunter. Nearly 60 percent of bears killed here are taken by out-of-staters, but most of those who are successful are led by experienced guides.

Deer

White deer are also prevalent here and are more common game for hunters. It's always possible to see deer along the sides of the road or in a backyard. Maine bucks have weighed in at well over 400 pounds, but females are much lighter. Maine deer have a reddish coat from June to September, but it turns thick and grayish during the harsh winter. Most fawns are born in early June and are marked by Bambi-like white spots until they begin to grow their winter coat at about three months of age. By the end of its first week, a baby deer can easily outrun a person. Still vulnerable, however, a fawn is virtually odorless for its first month of life, making it practically undetectable to predators.

In our state, the deer have no major natural enemies, and that's one reason why hunting is encouraged. Without it, larger numbers of deer would succumb to starvation from lack of food during the long winter.

Maine Coon Cat

The Maine Coon Cat, with its tufted ears, thickly furred tail, double paws and larger-than-normal body, is also a much-loved Maine animal. Only you're much more likely to find this one sitting on a friend's couch than in the great outdoors. Many rumors revolve around the origin of the Maine Coon, which is kept by many as a barn cat and by others as a show animal. Some speculated that the breed originated when a domestic cat bred with a bobcat — a myth.

While the origin of the species remains somewhat of a mystery, the adoration of this larger-than-life kitty is well-known. If you want to take one home with you, you are just as likely to find a Maine Coon in a barnyard litter as an upscale pet store.

Our Waters

For more information on fishing charters and regulations, see our Parks and Recreation chapter. To learn more about the dwindling numbers of fish here, see History.

Fish

Maine has 2,500 miles of seacoast and about the same number of lakes and ponds. Anglers are fond of the state because most of its waters are teeming with fish. In fact, it has the only rivers in the country that support the glistening, silver-sided Atlantic salmon. From spring through fall, adult salmon swim up coastal rivers to spawn, and in some places it's possible to watch them as they travel on their journey (see the Topsham Fish Ladder listing in our Kidstuff chapter). Salmon eggs hatch in early spring, and the young stay in our rivers two to three years before returning to the ocean, where they will repeat the spawning cycle. Maine is also the original home of the fighting, landlocked salmon. Other popular freshwater fish include bass and trout.

Also prevalent in our waters is the Atlantic cod, a reddish-brown fish that was a choice food of early coastal settlers. It's still an important food species sought by commercial fishers, and it is a popular sport fish. Bluefish, a saltwater prize for anglers, are found in Maine's tidal rivers and are especially prevalent in the lower portion of the Kennebec River, which runs through Bath. Haddock is another important commercial fish, though overfishing has led to dwindling catch numbers and increasing restrictions.

Lobsters

The first report of lobsters being caught off the Maine coast was in 1605 when some of the earliest explorers threw nets to catch them. The commercial lobstering industry has changed a lot since then, with traps of wood and netting replacing fish nets. As an industry, lobstering began in the mid-1800s and continues today as a highly regulated and important part of the Maine economy.

Lobsters are also one of the reasons tourists head to Maine, making a summertime ritual of feasting on their sweet meat. Connoisseurs should know that hard-shell and soft-shell lobsters are of the same variety; the softer shell just means the lobster has recently molted. When lobsters outgrow their hard-

INSIDERS' TIP

See our Parks and Recreation chapter to find out about places to get out in our wilds and enjoy our wildlife. To get out on the water, see Attractions to find out about charters.

ened shells, they shed them and begin building a new one in its place. It can take up to seven years and 20 new shells before a lobster reaches adult size.

If you go to buy fresh lobster or order one in a restaurant, you may notice large rubber bands pinching its claws together. This is for the safety of the person handling the lobster and the protection of the other lobsters kept in the tank. Lobsters are cannibalistic and will fight one another until one backs down. If a lobster loses a claw in a fight, it can grow a new one, but that takes several years. If you look at a lobster closely, you'll also notice that it has two differently shaped and sized claws. The sharp, pointed claw is used for ripping food apart, and the larger claw is the crusher claw used for crunching food.

To tell if a lobster is male or female (even if it's on your dinner plate), turn it over on its back. Look at the little flaps, called swimmerets, behind the lobster's legs. If the flaps are hard and bone-like, you've got a male; if they are soft and feathery, it's a female. One other word about lobsters: Contrary to rumors, they do not let out high-pitched screams when they're cooked. Lobsters have no vocal cords.

Whales and Seals

Virtually all the world's great whale species, as well as most families of dolphins and porpoises, can be found swimming off the coast of Maine. You might not get to see many of them, but one good way to try is by taking a whale-watching tour (see our Attractions chapter). Whales are mammals with complex brains that use sound waves to find food and "see" their way around in the dark ocean depths. Hearing is one of their greatest assets; it is believed they can pick up sound waves over hundreds of miles.

In early Colonial years, humpback whale sightings were commonplace along the coast of Maine. Until 1946, when whaling became internationally regulated, they were aggressively hunted for their skins and blubber. This layer of fat may be an inch thick in porpoises or dolphins and up to a couple of feet thick in larger whales. It is used not only to keep the mammals warm, but also to help them regulate their buoyancy. During and before Colonial times, blubber was boiled down to make oil for lamps. More recently it has been used as a food additive.

Whaling along the Gulf of Maine ceased in the 1900s. Along our coast you are most likely to see harbor porpoises, white-sided dolphins and pilot (or pothead), finback, humpback or minke whales. The finback can swim up to 26 mph, and at 70 feet long is the second largest of the whales (the blue whale being the largest). The humpback is famous for its moaning songs, playful leaps and slapping the water with its flippers. It is the second-most commonly sighted whale here and is easily identifiable with long white flippers. Finback whales are the ones you are most likely to spot in Southern Maine.

Seals also have been aggressively hunted. During the late 1800s, Maine offered a $1 bounty on harbor seals to reduce their population because they were eating so much of the local fishing stock. The campaign was so successful that by the early 1900s Maine's harbor seals were nearly exterminated. When the bounty was lifted this century, seals made a quick comeback and now can be frequently spotted bobbing in our harbors. They are colored in various shades of gray and brown, and a male can be as large as 6 feet long and 300 pounds. Most seals weather the winter in Maine, though some do head south to the Gulf for warmer waters. Maine's most famous is the now deceased Andre the Seal, who wintered in the gulf and swam back to Rockport every summer. He is immortalized in a monument by the town dock. If you are going out on a whale or seal watch, a good companion is *Maine Geographic Whales & Seals*, by the DeLorme Mapping Company. (For more on DeLorme, see our Attractions chapter).

Other Aquatic Creatures

Our waters hold numerous treasures for the curious. Along rocky sections of the shore, look for barnacles. These grayish-white pyramids are about the size of a fingernail and attach themselves to the sides of rocks. Low tide (which occurs about six hours after high tide) is the best time to spot them — they won't be underwater.

Mussels, with purplish-black oval shells, are not only common along our rocky shores, they are also delicious to eat (according to some). These are attached to the rocks by "byssal" threads, which look a lot like small grisly beards. Not as common but still observable are sea stars or starfish. These actually feed on mussels by wrapping their arms around the shell and pulling until the shell begins to split open. These creatures then squeeze their soft stomachs out through their mouths (which are in the middle of the underside of their bodies) and suck the mussel meat out of the shell! You're also likely to spot plenty of seaweed along our shore (especially at low tide), sea urchins, periwinkles and crabs.

You'll know there is a clam underfoot if you see water squirt out of a small hole in the ground. You need a license to harvest clams, and they are hard to come by because of regulations. Most licenses are issued through lotteries. You can get more information by calling the town hall of the town where you plan to dig. Each town regulates its own mud flats.

Our Air

Climate

True Mainers keep four different wardrobes, and if you rifled through our closets you would see the almost absurd extremes of our seasons. You'd find heavy parkas, insulated knee boots, wool socks, mittens and full-faced hats for the winter; shorts, tank-tops and bathing suits for the sultry summers; lightweight cotton sweaters, long-sleeved shirts and mud boots for spring; and heavier sweaters for fall.

Our summers are hot and our winters can be frigid, but the old saying often holds true: "If you don't like the Maine weather, wait a minute." Or, wait a couple of months. It's not unheard of to have 60-degree days in the middle of winter — or to have it dip down to the 60s in summer. So whether you're coming to Maine to ski, to sunbathe or to live, bring a good range of gear. Storms frequently blow in off the coast, then blow out to sea again a couple of days later. While powerful weather storms such as tornadoes are extremely rare here, a good Nor'easter can do quite a bit

of damage by whipping up some furious winds. If you're going out on the water, you'll need to keep an ear turned to the forecast and use caution.

However, we hope our climatic mood swings won't scare you. Average temperatures hover in the low 80s for most of the summer from about the beginning of June through August. The beginning of August tends to be our hottest time. We usually keep the thermostat turned up for most of May to take the chill out of the air, turn it off completely for summer, then turn the heat back on in September. Our window of opportunity to leave jackets and long sleeves behind and run around barefoot is pretty short compared to many climates.

Some people might think this takes away from the time to enjoy the sun. In reality, it makes us appreciate it even more. April tends to be our rainiest month, and July the driest. Snow usually starts to accumulate around Christmas, though there have been many years when the ground was white by Thanksgiving and others when December's earth was covered only by dry, frozen grass.

Snow makes the backroads a bit tricky to navigate, and those unfamiliar with such driving conditions should plan to stay in for a day after a heavy snowfall to allow the plows to clear, sand and salt the roads. There's no reason to take the risk.

And don't think the cold means an end to outdoor fun. There are plenty of opportunities for skiing, sledding, ice skating and romantic evenings with firelight, old movies and parlor games. Winter is a time for hearty recreation, steaming bowls of stew and family togetherness. See our Parks and Recreation chapter for some suggestions.

Birds

Wild turkeys, ruffed grouse, pheasant, gulls and terns, sandpipers, great blue herons, ducks, geese, loons, osprey and songbirds — Maine's skies and trees, sands and marshes are home to some 200 species of birds. Our nature conservatories and coasts are a birdwatcher's dream come true. For information on which birds you are viewing, we recommend checking in with the Maine Audubon

Society, 118 U.S. Highway 1, Falmouth, (207) 781-2330, or picking up a copy of *Maine Geographic Coastal Birds*, a handy pocket guide produced by the DeLorme Mapping Company.

Whether you're on the coast or several miles inland, one of the first prevalent bird species you will notice here is the seagull. Most breed in large colonies along ocean cliffs and are easily recognizable from their white and gray plumage. They're just about everywhere you look. Some gulls swim underwater and dive to catch food. Most have a loud cry, and the most common in this area is the herring gull, immortalized in *Jonathan Livingston Seagull* (which, by the way, is a great book to pick up as you're headed for a day on the beach).

The largest bird on the Maine coast is the great blue heron. With its folded neck, long legs and beak it stands 4 feet tall. You're likely to spot one in a tidal inlet or marshy area, standing among the grasses and scooping for small fish in shallow water. The best time to see them is from April through October. Sandpipers, with their small, sparrow-like bodies and black feet and bills, are another Maine coastal favorite. You'll find them from mid-July through mid-September poking their beaks into the sand to dig for larvae and other small bug fare.

If you're out on our lakes or streams, the loon is fun to keep an eye and ear out for. Diving to depths of more than 200 feet, these birds can stay underwater for some time and pop up when you least expect them. Their call resembles a mournful howl and can be a bit eerie at night. But peek out your window or tent screen, and you are likely to see the still shape of a duck-like bird with a long, needle-like beak floating by on the water.

Thirty-six different species of shorebirds have been recorded along Maine's coast, which has been recognized as a very important area for migratory shorebirds. A variety of birds use our coast as a rest area to eat and store up fat before departing on a nonstop flight across the ocean to warmer wintering areas in South America.

If you're visiting a marsh or wetland, keep an eye out for the red-winged blackbird. Our fields and pastures are home to various sparrows, the eastern meadowlark and the eastern bluebird. Wood thrushes and black-capped chickadees (with a call that sounds a lot like the name) are common in our forests.

The Mosquito

One of the least of our winged creatures but among the most feared is the common mosquito. We don't want to scare you, but mosquitoes can turn the most enjoyable outing into a nightmare. We recall a beach walk one hot summer day when we had to cut through the woods to reach our car. What should have been a leisurely half-mile walk turned into a half-mile mosquito feeding frenzy. We ended up running as fast as we could, tripping on thorny vines and undergrowth and swatting at our backs and legs all the way back. There were literally clouds of mosquitoes all around us.

To make your outdoor experience a bit more enjoyable, bring along long-sleeved shirts (pants, too, if you can stand it) and plenty of bug repellent. Mosquitoes are less prevalent in the sunshine and on windy days, and are most dense in the woods or near the water. Even with this knowledge, you are bound to end any summertime trip with at least one bite. So consider it a souvenir, and feast on a little knowledge to better appreciate your trophy.

Mosquitoes live in nearly every nation the world over and can grow to be 2 inches long (they only seem that big in Maine). Although they tend to lay their eggs in a moist environment, their eggs can remain viable even when dry — some for as long as five years! A single mosquito can lay up to 400 eggs at once, but luckily for us, only one or two of those will survive to breed as adults.

It's the females that do the damage. There's no blaming males here because only female mosquitoes can puncture human skin. To stay aloft, mosquitoes beat their wings anywhere from 250 to 600 times per second, but they can't fly in a breeze that's stronger than a few miles per hour. That haunting humming you hear warning you of the mosquitoes' approach is made by the wings, but only females are loud enough to be heard. And only if they are near your ears.

Fall Foliage Tour

Autumn in Maine is a technicolor vision of delight. Red, yellow, orange, green, brown and rust spread as far as the eye can see. The grandest old oak to the lowliest shrub garb themselves in finery to send out the year. For a truly New England experience, walk hand-in-hand with your sweetie under the spreading branches of trees in the fall. As you walk, kick through drifts of fallen leaves and enjoy the musty, evocative scent of autumn — not to mention the fun of it!

Close-up

Here we've listed some of the best places to see foliage displays in Southern Maine, both on foot and through the windshield of your car. But don't hold yourself to these, go out and explore — everywhere is beautiful in the fall in Maine. You may also want to check out our Parks and Recreation chapter for walking and cycling routes you can enjoy in any season.

Maine Hwy. 101 & Maine Hwy. 91
Kittery to York

From Kittery, take Maine Hwy. 101 (off U.S. Hwy. 1) toward South Berwick. At the intersection with Maine Hwy. 236, take a right. Another right onto Maine Hwy. 91 will bring you back to Route 1 at York Village.

Mt. Agamenticus
Mountain Rd., York

Mount Agamenticus is a former skiing area with a height of around 800 feet. The hike to the top is reasonably easy and well worth the effort. From the top you'll get fantastic views of the surrounding area with trees spreading out towards the White Mountains in the west and toward the sea to the east.

Maine Hwy. 35 to Maine Hwy. 111
Kennebunk to Biddeford

This route will take you northwest from Kennebunk to Biddeford. From U.S. Hwy. 1 in Kennebunk, head toward I-95 on Maine Hwy. 35, but don't get on the Interstate. Stay on Maine Hwy. 35 until it intersects with Maine Hwy. 111. Take a right onto Maine Hwy. 111 and you will be heading into Biddeford where you will once again intersect Route 1. Take a right onto Route 1 to head back to Kennebunk.

Ferry Beach State Park
Bay View Rd., Saco • (207) 283-0067

Ferry Beach State Park is a pretty place to enjoy the foliage. Here you can meander along wooden boardwalks under the trees, or head onto the beach for an invigorating blast of sea air.

Saco Heath
Maine Hwy.112, Saco • (207) 729-5181, (207) 490-4012

At Saco Heath you can enjoy the autumnal colors of grassland and trees. After a short walk through pines you'll find boardwalks leading over the grassy bog sheltered by a variety of trees, including rare white feeder trees. A round-trip walk through Saco Heath is about 1.5 miles. Dogs are not permitted on Saco Heath.

In this chapter we've provided listings on parks and nature preserves as well as general recreational opportunities.

Maine Hwy. 35 to Maine Hwy. 112
Saco Country Loop

From Saco, take Maine Hwy. 5 west. At the intersection with Maine Hwy. 35, take a right towards Hollis Center. At Hollis Center you will take Maine Hwy. 4A towards Bar Mills which is famous as the setting for the children's classic, *Rebecca of Sunnybrook Farm* by Kate Wiggan Douglas. At Bar Mills you will cross the bridge then take a right onto Maine Hwy. 112, which will bring you back into the center of Saco.

Bradbury Mountain State Park
Hallowell Rd., Pownal • (207)725-4571

We've often enjoyed the leisurely climb up Bradbury Mountain. It may be one of the highest spots in the area, but its really not much more than a big hill, which is great for young children or those feeling not so spry (see the Parks and Recreation chapter for more details). Getting there is also an enjoyable drive, and you're sure to see some beautiful foliage on the way. Take exit 20 off I-95 (that's a Freeport exit) and signs will direct you toward the countryside and the mountain.

U.S. Hwy. 1
Freeport to Brunswick

For a colorful and un-congested route to Brunswick after shopping in Freeport, we suggest following Route 1 north. You'll weave by some nice bed & breakfasts as well as several old farmsteads while getting to glimpse some colorful scenery. It's also a nice change of pace from the Interstate.

Land's End
Maine Hwy. 24, Cook's Corner, Brunswick

From the bustling center of Cook's Corner, follow Maine Hwy. 24 south all the way to the tippy-tip of Orr's Island. Once you get on the main route, just stay on it. You'll weave through trees and around the shore on either side of the peninsula, cross over the world's only cribstone bridge — a balancing act of giant rocks — through quaint fishing villages and by lobster shacks galore. It's about a 25-minute drive to the end, but there are plenty of trees, and at the end of the journey — literally a dead end — breathtaking ocean views, a small pebble beach and the Land's End gift shop.

Maine Hwy. 209 south
Bath to Phippsburg

Heading south of Hwy. 209 from Bath, you'll wind through the trees and alongside the Kennebec River. At Phippsburg Center, marked by a large flagstaff and a general store, we recommend turning left onto the Parker Head Road, which runs through one of the most charming villages in the area. But be sure to take it slow, as the road follows an old carriage trail that cuts around rock ledges and river inlets. At the end of Parker Head Road, which again intersects Hwy. 209, you may turn left (south) to get to Popham Beach and take a wind-swept stroll, or turn right (north) to loop back to Bath. Without stopping at the beach, the drive is about 30 minutes.

Parks and Recreation

Whether you are seeking new challenges or searching for wooded tranquillity to ease your cares away, Maine's Southern Coast is a treasure trove for outdoor types.

One trip to Maine and you'll know who put the "great" in the "great outdoors." Towering groves of pine, lush tidal inlets, cascading waterfalls and crashing surf along the rocky coast will meet you round many bends of the road.

For the less athletic we have popular spots where you can park and have a picnic, and for the rugged we have narrow trails weaving through the woods. We also have lakes and streams for fishing, paths for walking and biking, ponds and pools for swimming, endless possibilities for cross-country skiing and much, much more.

Whether you are seeking a new challenge or searching for wooded tranquillity to ease your cares away, the Southern Coast is a treasure trove for outdoor lovers.

Mountains are a little scare along our Southern Coast, although "real" hiking can be had farther north in Acadia National Park (see our Day Trips chapter). With so much else to keep you busy, though, we don't think you'll miss it.

In this chapter we've written up parks and nature preserves as well as recreation opportunities. We've grouped the information under category headlines with listings in order from south to north. Because there are so many categories to choose from, we left out geographic headers.

If you don't find what you are looking for, we recommend calling the municipal recreation department of the town in which you are staying. Many town rec departments offer excursion trips and sometimes offer classes

for other outdoor activities. Another good bet is to call the state Bureau of Parks and Lands at (207) 287-3821. This agency can provide you with information on state parks and historic sites, public lands, boat sites and off-road vehicle trails. And one last thing: Remember that all prices listed, unless noted, refer to 1998 rates.

Parks and Nature Preserves

Southern Beaches Area

Vaughn Woods Memorial State Park
Off Maine Hwy. 236, South Berwick
• (207) 384-5160

Inside the park, a 250-acre forested tract along the scenic Salmon Falls River includes an authentic Indian trail. Amenities include picnic facilities and hiking trails through old-growth stands of pine and hemlock. To get to Vaughn Woods take Route 236 toward South Berwick from Kittery. Take a left opposite the junior high school onto Vine Street, then a right onto Old Fields Road. The entrance to the park will be on your right. In the off-season the information telephone number is (207) 624-6080.

Rachel Carson National Wildlife Refuge
Off Maine Hwy. 9, Wells • (207) 646-9226

For the most part, this wildlife refuge is in a coastal marsh area, though the trail leads through a white pine forest. You'll find a mile-long wheelchair-accessible trail beginning at the refuge headquarters off the parking area. An information board with brochures at the trailhead will help you guide yourself through the wildlife area. Limited parking is available but there is no cost for admission. Donations are welcome.

Wells National Estuarine Research Reserve at Laudholm Farm
Laudholm Farm Rd., Wells
• **(207) 646-1555**

The Wells area preserves 1,600 acres of varied field, forest, wetland and beach. Everyone will enjoy the 7 miles of trails found throughout the reserve where you may see such endangered wildlife as peregrine falcons and piping plovers. There are a variety of specialty programs, such as Human History Tours and Skywatch, offered year round.

Guidebooks are available from the visitor center in the reserve's restored farmhouse, which is open daily year round. Cost for tours is $3 per person or $6 for families. The gate to the parking lot is open from 8 AM to 5 PM daily, and you are free to use the trails during those hours. Some trails are handicapped-accessible. In-season there is a $2 per person fee for parking though children aged 14 or less are free. (For more information on Laudholm Farm and the Wells Reserve, see our Kidstuff chapter.)

Kennebunk Plains
Off Maine Hwy. 99, Kennebunk
• **(207) 729-5181, (207) 490-4012**

Also known as the Blueberry Barrens, this coastal sand plain grassland is home to an enormous number of blueberry bushes. It's about 3 miles west of West Kennebunk, with the entrance just off Route 99. In late August, a trip to Kennebunk Plains will reap rewards of beauty — in the form of the world's largest population of blazing star flowers carpeting the grassland with their purple blooms. If

you're lucky when visiting, you may also spot the grasshopper sparrow, an endangered bird that lives here. The Nature Conservancy manages Kennebunkport Plains.

Vaughn Island Preserve
Off Ocean Ave., Kennebunkport

There's limited parking and a public boat launch area near Turbat's Creek crossing off Ocean Avenue in Kennebunkport. The 40-acre mixed hardwood island with nature trails is separated from the mainland by two tidal creeks. At one time settled, you can still see the remains of cellar holes. You can access the preserve by foot for the three hours on either side of low tide or by boat during the three hours on either side of high tide.

East Point Sanctuary
Off Maine Hwy. 9 (also Maine Hwy. 208), Biddeford Pool

You'd have to search pretty hard to find an area more beautiful than that occupied by this Audubon bird sanctuary. Trails lead along 30 acres of rocky shore, pebble beaches and meadows. Open from dawn to dusk, the sanctuary is regarded as one of the best birdwatching spots in Southern Maine. It is also a wonderful spot to view Wood Island lighthouse (see Attractions). Keep your eyes peeled for arctic tern, black-backed gulls, Bonaparte's gulls, yellowlegs, sandpipers, killdeer and piping plovers. Limited parking is available, but there is no fee for admittance. Bicycles and pets are not allowed in the sanctuary.

Old Orchard Beach Area

Ferry Beach State Park
Bay View Rd., Saco • **(207) 283-0067**

Enjoy 2 miles of nature walks along boardwalks and wooded trails that meander past a pond and marsh area in this 100-acre state park that also features a wonderful, sandy

A runner gets her exercise with the Portland skyline as a backdrop.

Photo: Convention and Visitor's Bureau of Greater Portland

swimming beach, bathhouses and picnic areas. The nature trails are particularly pretty in the fall, and you should keep an eye out for a stand of tupelo (black gum) trees, which are rare at this latitude. For more information about the beach, including admission prices, see our Beaches chapter. The off-season telephone number for the park is (207) 624-6080.

Saco Heath
Maine Hwy. 112, Saco
• **(207) 729-5181, (207) 490-4012**
Managed by the Nature Conservancy, Saco Heath features some 1.5 miles of trails and raised wooden boardwalks through the heath. The heath is noted as one of the only places in the world where Atlantic white feeder trees are found on a raised bog. Dogs are not permitted in the heath because their scent will deter wild animals from the area.

Greater Portland Area

Scarborough Marsh Nature Center
Pine Point Rd., Scarborough
• **(207) 883-5100**
Scarborough Marsh is the largest salt marsh in the state and is important for wildlife as a resting, feeding and breeding ground.

The Department of Inland Fisheries and Wildlife, (207) 657-2345, manages the marsh, but the Maine Audubon Society operates the nature center. Summer programs at the center run from the end of June to the beginning of September. You'll find indoor exhibits and a nature store as well as a naturalist on hand to answer questions.

Programs include canoe rentals (see Canoeing in this chapter's Recreation section), nature walks, a summer wildflower walk, full moon canoe tours, edible and medicinal plant tours and birding by canoe. There is also fabric painting with natural objects, viewings of the summer night sky and sunrise canoe tours. Cost for programs in 1998 ranged from $4 to $10.

In addition to the programs, there is a self-guided tour along the nature trails. A brochure of trails is available at the nature center. Some of the birds you might see in the marsh include several different species of sandpipers, herons and ducks, red-winged blackbirds, willets and snowy egrets.

Crescent Beach State Park
Maine Hwy. 77, Cape Elizabeth
• **(207) 767-3625**
About a half-mile from Two Lights State Park and only about 8 miles south of Port-

land, Crescent Beach offers a wide, sandy swimming beach, a bathhouse with cold-water showers and a snack bar. You'll also find a children's playground area, picnic tables and grills on site. (For information on admission rates, see our Beaches chapter.)

Fort Williams Park
Shore Rd., Cape Elizabeth
• (207) 799-5251

This park features a small crescent beach, the Portland Head Lighthouse and Fort Williams. There's plenty of room to run around, trails to follow along the cliffs, and wonderful breezes in which locals love to fly kites. Swings for the kids are near the beach, and you'll find a museum gift shop at the lighthouse and portable toilets in the parking area. There is no cost for admission to the park. (For more information on the lighthouse and fort, see our Attractions chapter.)

Two Lights State Park
Off Maine Hwy. 77, Cape Elizabeth
• (207) 799-5871

Before becoming a park, the area at Two Lights served as a World War II coastal defense installation, and you can still see remains of the installation today. At the park you can stroll along the much-photographed rocky headland and enjoy great views of Casco Bay and the crashing surf. Picnic tables and grills are available, and you can view the Cape Elizabeth Lighthouse (privately owned) from the park. (For more information on the lighthouse, see our Attractions chapter.)

Mill Creek Park
Between Ocean St. and Cottage Rd., South Portland

Despite its location amid busy roads such as Ocean Street, Cottage Road and Broadway, Mill Creek Park is pretty — a pleasant place to take a short stroll. The park includes 10 acres of land with a rose garden, a bandstand and a pond for winter skating.

Deering Oaks Park
Between Forest Ave. and Deering Ave., Portland • (207)772-4994

Portland's largest public park is a haven from the bustling downtown center. We've fin-

ished off more than one day of shopping by reading a book beneath one of the old-growth, white oaks or watching ducks in the paddleboat pond. There are several nice walking trails, ball fields, basketball and tennis courts, a play area for children and a small footbridge. Gardeners will admire the award-winning rose gardens. In the winter the pond is open for ice skating.

The land was deeded to the city in 1879 by the Deering family and is designated as a National Register Historic Landscape District. You might recognize it from the movie *The Preacher's Wife* featuring Whitney Houston. The ice skating scene was filmed here. The park's history, however, goes back long before the silver screen. It was once the scene of a confrontation between local colonists and Indians! The 53-acre park is about a 20-minute walk from the shops along Congress Street, or you can get here by taking the Forest Avenue exit off of I-295. The park will be on your right. Dogs are allowed on leashes.

Payson Park
Ocean Ave., Portland
• (207) 772-4994

For views of Back Cove and the downtown and for a plethora of recreational opportunities, check out Payson Park. The sweeping 48-acre lawn slopes down from Ocean Avenue to Baxter Boulevard's walking and bike path. An isolated arboretum is located on the southwest corner of the park and overlooks a small pond. You'll also find a lighted softball field, three tennis courts, excellent ice skating on the pond in winter and a basketball court.

Dogs must be leashed.

Baxter Woods
Forest and Stevens Ave., Portland
• (207) 772-4994

A great place to walk, picnic, bike or let your dog off his leash for a run is this 30 acre bird sanctuary. The heavily wooded park was a gift of Governor Baxter and now serves as an outdoor recreation facility. There's a dirt loop trail near Evergreen Cemetery for walking and a special off-leash area for cooped up dogs. Parking is along Forest Avenue on the park side of the road or at Evergreen Cemetery. Well-behaved dogs are allowed to roam off a leash as long as they are beside their owners.

Gilsland Farm
118 Route 1, Falmouth • (207) 781-2330
Run by the Maine Audubon Society, this 70-acre preserve offers self-guided trails along the Presumpscot River estuary. As you walk around a pond and by the salt marsh, keep an eye out for birds, which abound here. When you've completed the easy walking trail, visit the Audubon Society children's Discovery Room, which is also right here (see more under Kidstuff).

Bradbury Mountain State Park
Hallowell Rd., Pownal • (207) 688-4712
This is a lovely little park with winding trails gently weaving through Maine forest to a rocky outlook. From the top of the mountain (more of a large hill in terms of difficulty) you can see Casco Bay to the east and the White Mountains to the west. It is an especially enjoyable trip in the fall and one of the best places in this area to view the fall foliage. The park also includes a small camping area, softball field, picnic area and toilets. There is generally plenty of parking, which costs $2 per adult and .50 for children ages 5 through 11. Children younger than 5 are admitted free. The park is open year round and allows cross-country skiing and snowmobiles in the winter. Horseback riders and mountain bikers are welcome, and dogs are allowed on a leash.

Winslow Memorial Park
Staples Point Rd., So. Freeport
• (207) 865-4198
Pack a picnic and sit on a grassy peninsula watching the boats glide by on Casco Bay at this 90-acre municipal park. It's a ter-

rific place for kids with a huge grassy area, a well-maintained playground, bathrooms and a sandy beach for swimming. However, be sure to check the tides if you plan on taking a dip. Because the bay is tidal, at low tide you'll have to practice you're stroke in the mud. At the gate expect to pay about $1.50 to get in. Freeport residents pay half that, and people younger than 6 and older than 62 get in free. If you want to camp here, check out our Camping Chapter. The park is open from Memorial Day weekend through October.

Mast Landing Sanctuary
Off Bow Street, Freeport
• (207) 781-2330
Hike through fields and forests and along rivers and tidal marshes at this 150-acre preserve run by the Maine Audubon Society. Pines from the area were once used as masts for ships in the British Navy, which is how it got its name. The sanctuary is open year round from dawn to dusk, and has several self-guided trails. Picnic areas are also available, and parking is free.

www.insiders.com
See this and many other
Insiders' Guide
destinations online.
Visit us today!

Wolfe's Neck Woods State Park
Wolfe's Neck Road, Freeport
• (207) 865-4465 (April through October), (207) 624-6080 (November through March)
More than 200 acres of woods and self-guided walking trails along Casco Bay and the Haraseeket River provide plenty of outdoor fun at Wolfe's Neck. Amazingly, this secluded vista is just 4 miles from the busy outlet shopping district. You'll find picnic areas with tables and charcoal grills, wheelchair accessible parking, bathrooms and five miles of hiking trails. From Memorial Day through Labor Day, you'll have to pay to get into the park. The cost to get in is $2 for adults and .50 for children ages 5 to 12. Those older

INSIDERS' TIP

Novice fishermen should be wary of bluefish. While exciting to catch, the fish can weigh in around 18 pounds and have hundreds of razor-sharp teeth.

than 65 and younger than 5 get in free. After Labor Day the park is closed to vehicles but remains open to foot traffic.

Call the park for information on guided walks and lectures offered to the public. Last fall the park offered a walk along the bay guided by the park manager, a "Stories in Stone" program to learn about the types, origins and history of the park's stones, and "Ready, Set, Sleep," a program for children teaching the ways in which plants and animals prepare for winter. The park also held group writing and painting days.

Popham Beach State Park
Maine Hwy. 209, Phippsburg
• **(207) 389-1335**

Three miles of sandy white beach stretch along the Atlantic at this state park located at the tip of the Phippsburg peninsula. It is a favorite with locals and visitors for swimming (see more under Beaches) and for its proximity to Fort Popham (see Attractions), which is just a 30-minute beach walk away.

In the wooded area of the park are picnic tables and charcoal pits. A bathhouse with freshwater showers is also available. The beach itself has tidal pools and natural rock outcroppings.

History buffs will be interested in knowing that building posts, door steps, broken pipes and gun balls have been excavated at nearby Sabino Head where the Popham Colony was established in 1607 — 13 years before the Pilgrims landed at Plymouth. Englishman Sir John Popham — hence the name of the beach — paid for the passage of two ships to cross the Atlantic. Three months later they arrived at the mouth of the Kennebec River and built Fort George. No one knows exactly where the fort existed. Some have said it was built

where Fort Popham stands today. More recent excavations, however, point to the tip of land on the other side of the cove.

Around the turn of the century this beach was a favorite destination of wealthy travelers who lodged in elegant hotels perched near the shore. The old hotels have long since been destroyed, but the beach hasn't lost its allure.

Getting in the park will cost you $2.00 per adult and 50¢ for kids ages 5 to 11. Seniors 65 and older are free. The park itself is open from April 15 through Oct. 30, however, you can walk the beach any time of the year by parking at Fort Popham at the very end of Highway 209 (you can also park there free of charge during the in season).

Josephine Newman Wildlife Sanctuary
Maine Hwy. 127, Georgetown

Walk through a meadow of tall grass down a trail leading into the woods and you'll be in the thick of Maine with ocean inlets peeping at you through the trees. The sanctuary is full of birds and even has a cattail pond. The 400-acre preserve is marked by a small sign on the right hand side of the road as you travel south on Highway 127. If you pass the turn off for Reid State Park, you have gone too far. Parking is scarce, at the top of a dirt road, but the easy walking trail is well worth the hunt.

Reid State Park
Seguinland Rd., Georgetown
• **(207) 371-2303**

Famous for its rugged coastline, sandy beaches and tall sea grass, this state park is the jewel of our Southern Coast. It has two sandy beaches — Half Mile Beach and Mile Beach — backed by beautiful salt marshes, dunes, rocky coves and trails. The 766 sur-

Whitewater Rafting

If you have an adventurous spirit, don't mind getting wet and can work as part of a team, whitewater rafting could be just your kind of thing. You can round up your own group of fellow adventurers or join a trip organized by one of the established rafting companies in Maine. There are no whitewater rafting companies along the Southern Coast, but a couple of hours' drive north will get you to river country.

Close-up

Whitewater rafting in Maine takes place on three rivers: the Kennebec, the Penobscot and the Dead. Most adults and children ages 8 and older can participate in the sport as long as they are reasonably fit. However, height and size restrictions may bar children from some trips.

The company you select for your adventure will usually supply life jackets, helmets and dry bags to stow your (limited) stuff. Rafts are generally self-bailing, a feature you will learn to appreciate when you see adventurers in non-self-bailing rafts vainly trying to keep the river out of the raft. Wetsuits are usually available for rent and will occasionally be included in your trip price (for instance, as an added incentive in May and June). Mind you, we rafted the Kennebec at the end of July, and while it was great to swim and play in the lower reaches of the river, it got a bit cold toward mid-afternoon.

The Rivers

The Kennebec River is one of the most popular whitewater rafting sites in the state. Access to the put-in site is at The Forks (that's a town!), north of Skowhegan. Classified as a Class IV-V river, the Kennebec features high action in the Kennebec Gorge at the beginning of your trip. You are barely in the raft when the action begins. The downside to this is that once you get used to the raft, the most exciting parts are already over.

Still, it is a fun river to travel. You'll hurtle through sections of the river with names like Rock Garden, Big Mama and Alleyway Rapids, where you lurch across 7 and 8-foot waves. Before the river calms, you'll pass through Magic Falls, which provides a world-class drop you won't forget. The length of the trip from the Harris Station put-in to West Forks is about 12 miles.

The Dead River provides Maine's longest whitewater rafting experience. You'll find 16 miles of class III and IV whitewater along the Dead, and during the peak spring run-off and special fall dam releases, this river will net you the most whitewater. If you're looking for the most adventure, you'll need to call ahead - the high releases always sell out fast, and some trip providers run the Dead River only at high-water release.

During your adventure you'll experience the stunning scenery of a narrow wooded valley and mountain views. You'll also get your thrills as you experience the mile-long series of rapids known as Poplar Hill Falls.

The most challenging whitewater experience is the one at the Penobscot River. Just south of Baxter State Park, near Millinocket, the Penobscot features spectacular scenery, wildlife and yell-inducing class V rapids.

As you travel the Penobscot, you'll wind your way around the base of Mt. Katahdin in the heart of Maine's woods and tumble your way through the famous Cribworks rapids and the Ripogenus Gorge. If you're feeling a little timid about your first whitewater adventure, you might want to try the Kennebec or the Dead first and save the Penobscot for future exploration. Those of you who want to experience nature at its most rambunctious will love the Penobscot.

— continued on next page

Whitewater rafting offers an exhilirating workout.

Trip Operators

Downeast Whitewater Center
Conway, N.H. • (603) 447-3002, (603) 447-3802

Downeast Whitewater offers trips on all three rivers. The base of operations for Dead and Kennebec trips is in The Forks, where you'll find a choice of accommodations from riverfront log cabins and the Dew Drop Inn to campsites and cabin tents.

One- and two-night packages are available, but two-night stays are usually required for weekends. A weekday one-night package, including breakfast and a riverside steak lunch, starts around $90 for a campsite and moves up to around $115 for a room in the inn; it's about $20 more for a weekend stay, when available. A two-night package includes accommodations, one all-you-can-eat buffet dinner, a riverside steak lunch and two breakfasts. Weekday prices start at around $118 for a campsite, and rates go as high as $175 for a weekend stay at the inn.

Accommodations for the Penobscot trip are less varied. You can choose from a campsite, cabin tent or a room at the Atrium Hotel in Millinocket. Or, if you prefer, you can book your own lodging at a different hotel. Cost for a two-night package with one dinner, riverside lunch and two breakfasts starts at around $118 for a tent site, $128 for a cabin tent and $145 for the Atrium Hotel on weekdays, and prices move up to $135, $155 and $160, respectively, for weekend stays. The Atrium Hotel price does not include dinner.

North Country Rivers
East Vassalboro • (207) 923-3492, (800) 348-8871

North Country Rivers offers a variety of packages on all three rivers. On the Penobscot, you have the opportunity to enjoy the "ultimate" whitewater experience via multiple passes through the Ripogenus Gorge and the Cribworks rapids, or to select a two-day adventure where you experience the usual Penobscot trip on day one and the "ultimate" trip on day two. Another option gives you the chance to explore two rivers in two days.

— continued on next page

Kennebec packages range from $77 to $97 for one night camping, and $97 to $117 for a cabin tent. Two-night packages raise prices to $84 and $104 and $124 and $144, respectively. You can also opt to stay at the Colony House Inn Bed & Breakfast for $102 to $122 for one night, or $134 to $154 for two nights. Packages include rafting, riverside lunch and lodging. The inn's packages also include breakfasts. Accommodations for Dead River trips are the same as for the Kennebec trips. Prices for Dead River packages range from $112 for camping to $137 at the Colony House for one night, and $119 to $169 for two nights.

Penobscot packages range from $82 for midweek camping to $112 for camping on Saturday, and from $89 to $117 for cabin tents. Two-night packages increase the cost by about $10. For the "ultimate" trips, and for Saturday trips in July and August, add $10; for "ultimate" trips on available Saturdays in July and August add $20. Packages are also available for lodging at the Atruim Hotel in Millinocket. Cost for a single-night package ranges from $105 to $135; for a two-night stay, the range is $135 to $165. Triple and quadruple occupancy lowers the price by up to $25 per person. For those not rafting, room-only rates are also available. Camping packages include lodging, rafting and riverside lunch. The Atrium package also includes breakfasts.

Northern Outdoors
Maine Hwy. 201, The Forks Plantation
• (207) 663-4466, (800) 765-7238

Northern Outdoors uses custom-designed, self-bailing Maravia rafts on all their whitewater rafting adventures. They also create in-house videos featuring more than 30 minutes of action from your rafting adventure, taped by video kayakers that come along on each trip. In addition to whitewater rafting, you can also create your own personal adventure getaway by combining any of Northern's programs such as rafting, bass fishing, a ropes course and rock climbing.

Cost for rafting the Kennebec or Penobscot, Monday through Friday during the shoulder season, is $79, and it's $99 on weekends. In-season, rates are $94 for Monday through Friday, $114 on weekends. The cost for rafting the Dead River at high water ranges from $99 to $114.

Accommodations rates for the Kennebec and Dead river trips range from $8 per person for a campsite to $60 for a two-bedroom cabin, based on double occupancy. You can choose from four-bedroom condos and cabins to lodge rooms and cabin tents or campsites. Though we've based rates on double occupancy, some options (such as the lodge room, which takes up to five) can sleep more per room for reduced rates.

Accommodations for Penobscot trips are limited to camping or cabin tents. You can opt to stay in a hotel in Millinocket if you prefer, and the staff at Northern Outdoors will be glad to help you with your reservations.

rounding acres of rustic property are astoundingly beautiful and prime examples of Maine coast (see more on Reid State Park under Parks and Recreation).

After walking along the rocky shoreline, one of our favorite things to do here is to look through the viewfinders perched high up on Todd's Point to look for ships on the horizon.

In 1946 the park was donated to the state by millionaire Walter Reid, a businessman who made his fortune in the railroad. Reid was a part-time Georgetown resident, and some of his relatives still live here.

Park fees are $2.50 for adults and .50 for children ages 5 to 11 (children younger than 5 and seniors older than 65 get in free). The price will get you parking and all-day use of the park, which is open from 9 AM to sunset.

The park is open year-round and has lifeguards from the middle of June to the end of

August. Restrooms with flush toilets and changing areas are available. Come to the park after Sept. 30 and before May 15 and you can get in for free, although we can guarantee the water will be freezing! People older than 65 get in free all year.

In the off-season the park remains open to foot traffic, and a fee is not charged.

Linekin Preserve
Maine Hwy. 96, East Boothbay
• (207) 633-4818

This 94-acre preserve stretches from highway 96 to the Damariscotta River with a little more than 2 miles of trails for you to enjoy. Some 650 feet of the trail system borders the river. Parts of the trail are steep, and you'll pass a beautiful wooded area and walk along the edge of the Damariscotta River. Beyond the rocky shore lie wooded islands.

Oven's Mouth Preserve
Dover Rd. Extension, Boothbay
• (207) 633-4818

Two peninsulas make up this 146-acre preserve of scenic shoreline and swift tidal water, coves and salt marshes. On the east point there are 1.6 miles of easy walking trails and on the west point, 3.1 miles of rugged hiking trails. Check out the salt marsh for signs of the old icehouse that once stood there. You'll have to chose one route or the other as the two do not connect, or you could take both trails one at a time. Dogs are allowed on leashes. Note that this is not a safe area for swimming as the current is strong.

Recreation

Ballooning

Balloons Over New England
Kennebunk
• (207) 499-7575, (800) 788-5562

If you see a lovely purple balloon lofting gently above the trees in either the Southern Beaches or Old Orchard Beach area, it probably belongs to Balloons Over New England. Though it does use other colors, the company uses purple as a theme, and its most popular balloon carries up to four passengers. Groups of up to 19 people can be accommodated by the company in a flotilla of balloons, and they cater to special events like weddings.

Balloons Over New England operates from a half-dozen launch sites in the Southern Beaches and Old Orchard Beach areas. Wind direction will determine which site is used for launching. The company operates seven days a week, year round, weather permitting. Cost for a ride is $175 per person.

Bicycling

Bicycling is one of the most popular outdoor activities along the Southern Coast. In this section, we'll point out some of our favorite riding routes, throw in a brief snippet on mountain biking and provide information on where you can rent a ride if you left yours at home.

For visitors who would like to meet other cyclists, the Casco Bay Bicycle Club meets every third Tuesday of the month at 7 PM at the Dana Center at Maine Medical Center in Portland. This is the largest recreational cycling club in Maine. At meetings they plan trips and host speakers on cycling-related topics. The core of their cycling season is April through October, but there are die-hards who cycle year round. Evening rides, after-work rides and weekend day and overnight trips are organized by the group, which has also hosted two century rallies (for non-cyclists, that's a 100-mile event). Most trips average 20 to 50 miles, depending on the leader. For more information on the coming month's activities, call the group's hotline at (207) 828-0918. You can join the group for $15 per year, and you'll receive a newsletter each month highlighting upcoming activities.

The Bicycle Transportation Alliance of Portland offers three self-guided bicycle tours of Maine. The maps are $1 each, and you can get one or all of them by writing to the alliance at P.O. Box 4506, Portland, ME 04112. The tours explore Maine islands, historic Portland or Maine lighthouses, and the maps include historic information.

Fort McClary to Cape Neddick Lighthouse

For some, this might be a more pleasant way to become acquainted with Kittery and York than by car. The ride will take you from Fort McClary on Kittery Point to Cape Neddick Lighthouse and back again, for a total of around 20 miles. Your trip begins at the fort on Maine Highway 103, then you head north on Route 103 toward York. As you enter York you'll pass the town dock area with the Wiggly Bridge to your left (see our Kidstuff chapter).

Continue along Route 103 until you reach Route 1A. Take a right onto Route 1A and you will ride through York Harbor and along Long Sands Beach. At the end of the beach, bear right toward Cape Neddick Lighthouse (there should be a signpost). When leaving the lighthouse, take a right. After about a half-mile you'll be at the intersection with Route 1A. Take a right into the village of York Beach, where you'll find Short Sands Beach, shops and places to eat (see Restaurants and Shopping).

From York Beach, take a left at the intersection of Ocean Avenue and Railroad Avenue toward York's Wild Animal Park (see Kidstuff). Bear right at the park onto Ridge Road. Stay on Ridge Road, and you will pass Dave's IGA plaza just before you reach York Village. At York Village bear right, and you will again be on Route 1A. Take a left on Organug Road and go straight over the river, bearing left onto Bartlett Road. Follow the road until it ends and take a left. In just about a mile you should intersect with Route 103. Take a right, and you will be back where you started at Fort McClary.

Dock Square to Goose Rocks Beach

Your destination for this trip is one of the nicest beaches in Southern Maine (see our Beaches chapter for details on Goose Rocks). The round-trip journey involves around 25 miles of legwork, with a few slightly tough hills.

Beginning in Dock Square in Kennebunkport, head east on Ocean Avenue (take a right from the center of the square). The Kennebunk River will be on your right as you pedal, and you'll pass the Colony Hotel on your left and former President Bush's summer home on Walker's Point on your right. Just before you reach the firehouse on your right, take a right onto Wildes District Road.

After about a mile you'll intersect with Maine Highway 9; again, take a right, this time into the village of Cape Porpoise. (For a slight detour, go straight onto Pier Road in Cape Porpoise and follow the road to the fishing pier there. When you've finished exploring the pier, return to the intersection of Route 9 and take a right.) After about 5 miles, you will see the turn for Goose Rocks Beach Road. Take a right to enter this charming summer community and lovely beach area.

Once you've finished with the village and beach, return to Route 9 and head back the way you came until you reach Cape Porpoise. At this point you can retrace your steps along Ocean Avenue or take a shorter route by staying on Route 9, which will take you back to Dock Square.

Saco River Loop

On this cycling trip you will head up the Saco River on the Biddeford side, then down the river on the Saco side in about a 15-mile loop. There are some hills, but they should be manageable. The ride begins and ends at the Saco Valley Shopping Center (see our Shopping chapter), which is just off U.S. Highway 1 in Saco. From the shopping center, take a right at the traffic light at Key Bank onto Route 1. Follow Route 1 past Dunkin' Donuts on your left, through the intersection with Main Street and up a slight hill to the next traffic light. Take a right onto South Street, which leads you out of town.

Bear right on South Street where it becomes River Road, and follow the road until you reach the intersection with Maine Highway 5. Take a right. After you cross the Saco River, you should take a right onto Boom Road. From here, simply follow Boom Road until it intersects with Route 1. Take a left, and you will return to the shopping center off Route 1 to your left.

The Pier to Camp Ellis

If you want a nice bike ride along mostly flat terrain with a couple of nice places to stop along the way, this is the trip for you. The ride begins and ends at the pier in Old Orchard Beach. Facing the pier at the beach end of Old Orchard Street, take a right onto West Grand Avenue (Maine Highway 9) heading south. You will pass through the Ocean Park area of town and along to Camp Ellis in Saco (about 3.5 miles from the pier). There you can get a bite to eat, take a walk along the breakwater or stroll on the beach.

Leaving Camp Ellis, take a left onto Ferry Road, which is still Route 9. If you haven't eaten or you still have room for dessert, make sure to stop at Garside's Ice Cream stand, which you'll encounter about 1.5 miles from Camp Ellis on your right. Garside's makes its own ice cream, and we bet you'll consider a stop here the highlight of your bike trip!

From Garside's, continue along Ferry Road. From this point it is acceptable and recommended that you use the cycle path/ sidewalk on the left side of the road. About 2 miles from Garside's, take a right onto Old Orchard Road, which will lead you past the Biddeford-Saco Country Club. About a quarter-mile from the country club, you will reach a dangerous intersection referred to as "Half-Way" by locals. You have a stop sign, and the traffic coming from your left has the right of way. When it is clear, go straight ahead. (Christy's should be on your right, and Maine Cleaners should be on your left.) You are now on Saco Avenue, which will take you to the Town Hall end of Old Orchard Street in about 2 miles.

For an alternate route, take a right onto Temple Avenue at the Half-Way intersection and follow the road until you reach the traffic light in Ocean Park. Take a left, and you are once again on West Grand Avenue, heading towards the pier.

Oak Hill Plaza to Higgins Beach or Two Lights State Park

This ride starts and ends at Oak Hill Plaza in Scarborough. Getting across the intersection to begin your ride down Black Point Road is a bit tricky, but the plaza is definitely the best place for you to park. From the shopping center, cross at the intersection so that Amato's restaurant is on your right and the gas station is on your left. You are now on Black Point Road. Follow the road until it ends at Prout's Neck. The views are wonderful, and you can lock your bike and explore the Prout's Neck Bird Sanctuary and Winslow Homer's studio if you feel so inclined. There is no parking here for automobiles.

From Prout's Neck, retrace your route to the point where Maine Highway 77 veers to your right. Follow Route 77 until you see the turn for Higgins Beach on the right. Once you've explored this small seaside village, return to Route 77 and take a right. Soon you'll need to take a left onto Pleasant Hill Road and follow it until you reach Highland Avenue. At this point, take a left and follow the road until it intersects with Black Point Road. Take a right and you'll return to Oak Hill where you began. The total mileage for the tour is about 6 miles.

If you prefer a longer trip, continue on Route 77 after leaving Higgins Beach until you get to turnoffs for Crescent Beach State Park and Two Lights State Park. You can explore either or both parks and return along Route 77 until you reach Pleasant Hill Road on your right, then continue as above, or you can retrace your steps completely. Adding both Crescent Beach and Two Lights will tack on 5 miles or so to your trip.

Cape Elizabeth State Parks Loop

For folks who enjoy cycling and like lighthouses, there's a great ride in Cape Elizabeth. Beginning at Fort Williams Park, where you'll find the Portland Head Lighthouse (see our Attractions chapter), take a left on Shore Road until it intersects with Maine Highway 77. Take a left and follow Route 77 to Two Lights State Park, and the Cape Elizabeth Lighthouse (see Attractions), the Lobster Shack (see Restaurants) and a gift shop.

Return to Route 77 and take a left. You will soon see signs for Crescent Beach State Park, which features a small, pleasant swimming beach (see our Beaches chapter). Continue on Route 77 to Spurwink Road, which is on your right about a half-mile from Crescent Beach. Take a right onto Spurwink, continue until you reach Scott Dyer Road and take another right. This will lead you back to the intersection of Shore Road and Route 77. Cross Route 77 to Shore Road and return to Fort Williams. The loop is about a 10-mile trip.

Portland's Back Cove Trail
Baxter Blvd., Portland
• **(207) 874-8793**

You won't have to dodge cars on this 3.5 mile trail circling Back Cove. The paved walk-bike path is a perfect way to pedal a lap or two while staying near the water and out of traffic. It's also a good bike path for children. Parking is a bit tricky, and one of the best spots is in Payson Park, directly across from Shop n' Save on the Preble Street Extension. Dogs must be kept on a short leash.

The Bicycle Transportation Alliance of Portland
P.O. Box 4506, Portland (no phone)

Order one of three self-guided bicycle tours of Maine for $1 each by writing to The Bicycle Transportation Alliance of Portland. You'll have the option of touring Maine islands, historic Portland or Maine lighthouses by bike and have all the historic information to go along with them.

Yarmouth's Royal River Park
West Elm St., Yarmouth

Park across from the Water District and follow the pathway along the bank of the Royal River as it weaves by embankments where old mills used to be. The park is set between two waterfalls and has a wooded picnic area, bike path and fish ladder. The pathways are lined with flowers and meet up with the Beth Condon pathway, which will take you all the way to Yarmouth's downtown shops (see more under Shopping the Maine Streets in our Shopping chapter). The pathway, which is about 1 mile, was constructed in 1997 in memory of 15-year-old Beth Condon who was struck and killed by a drunk driver as she walked along Route 1.

Brunswick to Freeport Loop
The town mall, Maine St., Brunswick

Beginning at the gazebo on the Brunswick town mall, head south on Maine Street, turning south onto Pleasant Hill Road. You'll fol-low this road past fields and beautiful Maine pines all the way to Mast Landing in Freeport where you will turn left onto Flying Point Road. Flying Point will bring you along Maquoit Bay and back into the center of Brunswick. All told the loop is 20 miles with a few hills to keep you challenged on the way.

Brunswick Bike Path
Maine Street in Brunswick

Just completed in October of 1998, Brunswick's bike path takes cyclists, walkers, joggers and rollerbladers meandering on a safe route alongside the Androscoggin River. The 2.5-mile paved trail begins at the north end of Brunswick, just after you drive over the bridge on Maine Street. There's little parking here, but you can also park across the street at the Fort Andross Mill. The path will take you alongside the river and Route 1 and ends just beyond Cooks Corner, a bustling shopping district with restaurants and a 10-screen movie theater. The path is a smooth and easy ride with safety rails, bathrooms along the route and park benches to rest and watch the river.

Historic Northern Washington Street
Library Park, Washington St.,Bath

Beginning at Library Park in Bath (you can park along the street) pedal north up Washington Street for a leisurely tour of some spectacular architecture. You'll pass a gothic church, Federal and Greek-Revival homes and some beautiful inns and gardens along the way. The most magnificent house on the street is York Hall at the corner of Washington and Edward streets. Once you reach the hall, we recommend turning around and going south a dozen yards to connect with Bowery Street on the east side of Washington Street. Turn down Bowery Street toward the Kennebec River and then turn right onto Front Street, which will take you back toward the city center. You'll be able to peek at the river through the trees. When you come to Linden Street on your left, that will take you back up to Library Park. The full route as we recommend it is a little over two miles. For more information on the buildings you'll see along the way, first stop by the Chamber of Commerce at 45

Photo: Merry Farnum

Little people enjoy playing amidst the always-hungry birds.

Front Street and pick up the self-guided walking and driving architectural tour published by the Sagadahoc Preservation Society, Inc.

Phippsburg Peninsula
Maine Hwy. 209, Phippsburg

Park at the municipal parking lot just across from the Phippsburg Elementary School and head south of 209 for a bike ride to Popham Beach. You'll avoid the fight for a parking space once you get there. There are two possible routes to the beach, one is by following Highway 209 to the very end. The other, and the more scenic route, is by taking a left onto the Parker Head Road, which is marked by a tall flag pole. Parker Head Road meets back up with Highway 209 after five miles, and at the intersection you will turn left. We particularly like the second route because it winds through Parker Head Village, a historic little neighborhood of summer cottages and fishermen's homes. It also has some

beautiful views of the Kennebec River. Round trip either route is about 17 miles. Sections of the route are quite windy, however, and bikers should keep a sharp ear tuned for cars.

Bath Cycle & Ski
Route 1, Woolwich • (207) 442-7002

Experienced cyclists from this full-service bike shop lead mountain bike rides on Sundays and Tuesdays from early spring through late November. A whole range of trips are offered from rugged trails in the back woods, to logging roads to beach trails. The tours are free, and the advantages are that you won't get lost and you'll be able to go on properties that we can't tell you about because they are privately owned. Call ahead to check on the time of the ride and to make sure one is scheduled. Some rides are canceled due to lack of participation. For information on renting a bike throughout the shop see our Bike Rentals category.

Boothbay Ocean Point
Maine Hwy. 96, Boothbay

Leave your car at the Small Mall on Highway 127 and you'll see the intersection with Highway 96 just across the street. This popular bike route will take you winding past quaint houses and inns through East Boothbay village and on out to the ocean, where you will get some great views. Like most Maine country roads, this one is narrow and windy, and we recommend heading out early in the morning to avoid traffic. To the end of the point and back is about 15 miles.

Mountain Biking

Mount Agamenticus
Mountain Rd., York

About 5 miles from York Village, Mount Agamenticus is a former skiing area that tops out at between 700 and 800 feet. There are miles of trails to explore on and around the mountain. For the most part, you'll find lots of double-track trails about as wide as a four-wheeler, though there are single-track trails and fire trails. The terrain is pretty rough, with streams, rocks and roots, but it should be manageable for intermediate cyclists. If you went back and forth on every trail, you could probably get in around 40 miles of riding, but an average ride will net you about 20 miles. You'll find a parking lot at the base and the top of the mountain. A paved road also leads to the top, for those who prefer a smoother trip.

Bike Rentals

Cape-Able Bike Shop
Town House Corners, Arundel Rd., Kennebunkport
• **(207) 967-4382, (800) 220-0907**

You can rent anything from a basic three-speed bike to all-terrain bikes at Cape-Able. Daily rentals (9 AM to 6 PM) for 1999 are $10 for a three-speed, $15 for a 10- to 12-speed

racer, $18 for a comfortable cross-country bike with 18 to 21 speeds, $20 for 21-speed mountain bikes and all-terrain bike rentals start at $20. Rental costs drop to half-price after 1 PM. Those who need baby seats can rent them for an extra $5, and all rentals include free helmet rental. Weekly rentals are available at four times the daily rate. After Columbus Day the shop is open Tuesday through Saturday. It is closed in January and February.

Kennebunkport Marina
Ocean Ave., Kennebunkport
• **(207) 967-9808**

In addition to the full-service marina (see this chapter's Boating section), you can rent single-speed and 10-speed bikes, canoes and fishing equipment from Kennebunkport Marina. Cost for bike rental in 1998 was $15 for a half-day and $20 for a full day. Rental cost includes a lock and helmet. The marina is open from 8 AM to 6 PM daily.

Joe Jones Ski & Sports
456 Payne Rd.,
Scarborough
• **(207) 885-5635**

Both front-suspension and non-front-suspension mountain bikes are available from Joe Jones. Cost for bike rental in 1998 was $15 for a half-day, $25 for a full day and $75 for a week. Rentals come with a helmet and are available from around April through October.

Bath Cycle & Ski
Route 1, Woolwich
• **(207) 442-7002**

With one of the largest selections of mountain bikes in New England, this funky little shop on the northbound lane of Route 1 has both road and mountain bikes for rent. It also does a complete range of bike repairs on site. For information on weekly trail rides led by shop guides, see our biking section.

INSIDERS' TIP

Ice fishing and snowmobiling can be treacherous for the inexperienced. We recommend finding a qualified guide who knows the area.

Harborside Bike Rentals
Boothbay House Hill, Boothbay Harbor
• (207) 633-4303

See the harbor or the surrounding countryside by bike. You can cruise the area with your whole family outfitted by this rental shop. Half-day rates begin at $12 for a single bike and go up to $79 a week. Child trailers and two-person bikes are also available. Helmets are free with each rental. The shop is located across from the Town Landing. Bike sales and services are also available.

Boating

You'll find many points of access to Southern Maine's waterways. Almost every town on a major river or harbor along the Southern Coast has a public launch, though parking is sometimes limited. For information, contact some of the marinas we've listed, town halls or the local chamber of commerce (listed in our Area Overviews chapter). State law requires that all watercraft carry at least one Coast Guard-approved floatation vest per person and that all motorboats be registered in Maine or in a state with which Maine has a reciprocal agreement. For more information on boating laws or to register a motorboat, contact the Maine Department of Inland Fisheries and Wildlife in Augusta at (207) 287-8000.

Badger's Island Marina
27 Badger's Island West, Kittery
• (207) 439-4456

From Badger's Island Marina, it's only a five-minute walk into downtown Portsmouth, New Hampshire (see our Daytrips and Weekend Getaways chapter for more on Portsmouth). Some 30 slips are available and are open to vessels of most sizes. You'll find full laundry and shower facilities here, but there is no fuel for sale. Year-round wet or dry storage is offered at this full-service boatyard with railways. Island Marine Service across the street is part of the company and handles boat sales and repairs. To reserve a transient slip, call the marina on Channel 9 or Channel 16 of your citizens band radio, or use the telephone number listed. Unless it's full, the marina will accept same-day slip rental. Badger's Island is open from May to the end of October.

Kennebunkport Marina
Ocean Ave., Kennebunkport
• (207) 967-9808

Most of the slips at this marina are rented by the season, but there are typically three to five slips available for visitors with boats of up to 40 feet. Showers and laundry facilities as well as a full-service boatyard are available on the premises, but the marina does not sell fuel. A marine store offers boating supplies, soda, bait and a small line of gift items. Located about a half-mile from Dock Square, the marina also offers boat and canoe rentals, and you can rent a rod and reel for fishing at $15 per day (see appropriate headings for more information). Kennebunkport Marina is open from April to November.

Norwoods Marina Inc.
9 Fore St., Saco • (207) 282-7411

At Norwoods Marina, slips and moorings are often available for transients with boats up to 45 feet. Located close to the town dock in Camp Ellis, the marina is handy for those who would like to be able to walk to the beach and local restaurants. Showers are available at the marina, and you can buy bait in Camp Ellis. When we spoke to them, the owners were also considering providing bicycles to get marina guests to Old Orchard Beach amusements, which are about 3.5 miles away.

South Port Marine
14 Ocean Ave., South Portland
• (207) 799-8191

Open year round, this full-service marina is just a five-minute walk from the Mill Creek shopping area (see Shopping). There are about 15 slips for transients with boats of up to 110 feet. Shower and laundry facilities are available as are fueling services for gas and diesel. Crane service, wet and dry storage and hauling are also offered on site. You can reach the marina on CB channels 9 and 16 as well as by phone.

DiMillo's Marina
Long Wharf, Portland • (207) 773-7632

Just five minutes away from Portland's historic Old Port and just below DiMillo's floating restaurant (see our restaurants chapter), this full-service marina has 120 slips on Portland Harbor. Diesel and gas and electric and water hook-ups are available, as are washers and dryers and showers. For guaranteed good times, the marina also has local microbrews for sale near the dock. The marina is open year round.

Handy Boat
215 Foreside Rd., Falmouth
• (207)781-5110

A full-service marina, Handy Boat offers 35 moorings and a dock with gas, diesel, water and ice. It also has a ship's store and restaurant, The Galley, serving lunch and dinner. The marina is open year round, although dock services are available only from mid-May to Columbus Day. The marina is located on Falmouth Foreside 4 miles from the open ocean. A public launch at the Falmouth Town Landing is just .5 miles away on the Foreside Road, also known as Maine Hwy. 88.

Casco Bay Rowing Center
Yankee Marina, Route 88, Yarmouth
• (207) 846-3277

Expert rower Hargy Heap offers private and group rowing lessons from his base at Yankee Marina. This is real ocean rowing — the kind you do in a shell — and Heap also sells boats. The more experienced may want to venture out on a three-night rowing vacation. Stay at the nearby Chebeague Island Inn and spend your days rowing to the surrounding islands. The less experienced can take a shorter row around the harbor. Heap doesn't have a storefront, so you're best to call before trying to go out on the water. Group lessons are offered in May and June, with private lessons commencing later in the summer.

Strouts Point Wharf Company
Main St., South Freeport
• (207) 865-3899

In business since 1987 on the Haraseeket River, this full-service marina has 90 slips and 15 moorings. Boaters will also fine a fully stocked marine store, fuel, ice and a complete range of boat repair services. The marina is about 8 miles from the open ocean but about only .5 miles from sailing waters. Shoppers will enjoy the convenience of the company's shuttle bus, which runs from the wharf to L.L.Bean in downtown Freeport seven days a week from late spring through early fall.

New Meadows Marina
Bath Rd., Brunswick
• (207) 443-6277

At this full-service boat yard you'll find boats for rent, a year-round marine store and 75 slips. Boat storage and boats for sale are also available. Nearby is the Sawyer Park Launch, where the public can slip boats into the New Meadows River. The marina docks are open from mid-April through November 15.

C&B Marina
Maine Hwy.96, East Boothbay
• (207) 633-0773

Diesel, gas, 52 slips, and 18 moorings are available at this full-service marina. People on longer voyages will also appreciate the laundry and shower facilities. On the dock water and electric hookups are also available.

Bowling

Bowling in Maine is a little bit different than in other parts of the country. Here you're more likely to find candlepin bowling than 10-pin bowling. Candlepin differs from 10-pin in that you are trying to knock down the 10 pins over the course of three turns by using balls that weigh around 21/2 pounds, rather than taking two turns with heavier balls that weigh between 10 and 17 pounds. Another difference: In candlepin bowling the downed pins remain on the deck so that you can use them to knock down more pins. In 10-pin, the downed pins are removed after each ball is thrown.

Vacationland Bowling and Recreation Center
U.S. Hwy. 1 S., Saco • (207) 284-7386

This candlepin bowling center features 32 lanes with full-color automatic scoring. Twelve lanes have bumper features that eliminate gutter balls; this makes the sport more fun for your little ones. The center is completely handicapped-accessible. Cost for bowling ranges from $1.50 to $2.10 per person per game. Shoe rental is mandatory and costs $1.25 per person.

In addition to bowling you can enjoy a game of pool at one of six regulation tables or play video games in the arcade. Use of pool tables costs from $6 to $8 per hour. On evenings and weekends, a snack bar opens. For those interested in honing their bowling skills, the center offers lessons and leagues for all ages and abilities. A birthday party room is also available if you're looking for a new party venue. Vacationland Bowling & Recreation Center is open daily year round.

Big 20 Bowling Center
U.S. Hwy. 1 N., Scarborough
• (207) 883-2131

The Big 20 Bowling Center features 20 lanes with automatic scoring, a snack bar, pro shop and small lounge area. Bumper bowling is available at all times to make the game more fun for children, and leagues are in ac-

tion every night except Saturday and every morning except Sunday. In winter the center offers all-you-can-bowl specials from 2 to 5 PM on Wednesday. Cost for bowling is $2 per string per person, and there is a $1 mandatory shoe rental fee. Senior citizens get free shoe rentals. Cost for bumper bowling is $13 per lane for an hour; kids can bowl as much as they like in that time. Free lessons are available anytime at the Big 20.

Yankee Lanes
867 Riverside, Portland • (207) 878-2695

With 32 lanes, this is one of the largest 10-pin bowling lanes in the area. Prices range from $3 per string or $14 per hour during the week to $2.90 per string or $17 per hour on the weekends and evenings. Shoe rentals are an additional $2 per pair. Friday night is ladies' night in the accompanying bar, and Saturday night is the weekly Karaoke contest. Friday and Saturday nights, "Galactic Bowl" begins at 10 PM complete with disco lights, a D.J. and smoke. The lane also has a game room with pool tables, and it has a snack bar.

Yankee Lanes of Brunswick
Bath Rd., Brunswick • (207) 725-2963

Here bowling ranges from $1.99 to $2.90 for a string, and you're just about confined to playing during the weekends because leagues claim all the lanes on weeknights. Shoe rentals run an additional $2 per pair. Just like its Portland counterpart, Yankee Lanes of Brunswick hosts "Galactic Bowl" on Friday and Saturday nights after 10 PM. There is also a snack bar, game room and lounge open during the evenings.

Canoeing and Kayaking

Saco River

The Saco River begins in the White Mountains, which run between Maine and New Hampshire, and continues southeast until it empties into the sea at Camp Ellis in Saco. The best place to access the river within our coverage area is at Union Falls in Dayton. To get there, take Maine Highway 5 west from the center of Saco, take a right onto the Hollis Road and then your first major right to the public boat ramp. From there you can paddle to Biddeford along a quiet stretch of river bordered by trees. The total length of the trip is about 10 miles.

Mousam River

For quiet paddling on a wide, dammed part of the river, try Estes Lake in Sanford. The lake is actually a part of the river that has been widened and deepened by a small hydroelectric dam. No power boats are allowed here, which makes for pleasant paddling. To get to the Mousam, take Exit 3 off the Maine Turnpike (the Kennebunks exit) and turn right onto Alfred Road as you exit the toll booth. Take a left onto Wichers Mill Road, then the first right after you cross the river. There will be a barricaded dirt road on the right that leads to a boat access. You'll have to carry your canoe past the barricade, but it isn't far to the river.

Scarborough Marsh

Scarborough Marsh is the largest salt marsh in Maine, with 3,100 acres of tidal marsh, salt creeks, fresh marsh and uplands. You can explore the meandering marsh creek by renting a canoe from the Scarborough Marsh Nature Center on Pine Point Road in Scarborough, or launch your own canoe or kayak from beside the bridge you'll find a few hundred yards from the nature center.

You should note that this is a tidal creek, so water levels will depend on the tide. High tide reaches the nature center about an hour after it reaches the coast. The current changes with the tide, so that if the tide is coming in, you will be riding with the current if you paddle upstream. If you plan it right, you can actually turn around when the tide changes and thus ride the current in both directions. (For rental rates, see the subsequent Canoe and Kayak Rentals section.)

Royal River Canoe Route

You'll enjoy smooth water for a good 5.5-mile paddle (one-way) when you slip your canoe into the Royal River at the bridge near Dunn's Corner off Maine Highway 9 in Yarmouth. The Royal River flows through one of the most developed areas of the state, but the scenery here is all farmland. When you cross beneath two railroad bridges, you can either pull out at the Yarmouth Waterworks or do a U-turn and head back (upstream) to your starting point.

Canoe and Kayak Rentals and Services

Kennebunkport Marina
Ocean Ave., Kennebunkport
• **(207) 967-9808**

You can rent a canoe at this marina, which also rents bicycles and fishing equipment. Cost for a half-day canoe rental on the Kennebunk River was $20 in 1998; a full day was $30. Life preservers are included with your rental.

Scarborough Marsh Nature Center
Pine Point Rd., Scarborough
• **(207) 883-5100**

In-season you can rent canoes from the nature center for $10 an hour or $30 for a half-day. Life preservers, paddles and self-guiding brochures are included in your rental. The last canoe rental of the day is made at 4 PM.

Seaspray Kayaking
78 Dessert Rd., Freeport
• **(207) 865-4189, (888) 349-SPRAY**

Whether you need to rent a kayak or if you have one of your own, Seaspray Kayaking will get you out on the water. The company offers private trips and guided tours including sunrise and sunset paddles and moonlight beach trips. Lessons are also available. Tours are led by registered Maine guides and take place in the calm waters of the New Meadows River. You might even spot a harbor seal!

H2 Outfitters Canoe & Kayak Instruction & Trips
P.O. Box 72,Grassy Rd.,
Orrs Island 04066
• (207) 833-5257, (800) 649-5257

Whether you're looking for a two-hour course on the basics of paddling or for an overnight kayaking or canoe trip, H2 Outfitters has the gear and instructors to get you going. Group clinics range from $25 to $35, and private lessons are available for $35 and up. Lake, ocean and river tours are also offered. You can paddle to a coastal island, run rapids or surf the coastal waves. Rates for trips begin at $50 per person for half a day and increase to $100 a day for an overnighter, which includes meals and equipment. Special family and children's programs are also available.

Climbing

Maine Rock Gym
127 Marginal Way, Portland
• (207) 780-6370

The Southern Coast may not have many jagged cliffs for climbing in the wild, but it does have an indoor-outdoor climbing gym with 25 feet of vertical artificial ledge inside and 40 vertical feet of concrete outside. Equipment rental and instruction are available. The gym is open to all ages and includes a full pro shop. The cost is $20 for four hours of climbing. Anyone younger than 18 must have a parental signature to participate. If you're up for the real thing, the gym, which is open Tuesday through Sunday, does schedule trips to ledges in New Hampshire.

Diving

York Beach Scuba
Railroad Ave., York Beach
• (207) 363-3330

York Beach Scuba blends the service and convenience of your favorite dive center with the charm and adventure of a resort destination. The experts there maintain that you'll find great visibility year round in our clear northern waters. Diving opportunities with the company include dives with seals, shipwreck sites and acres of grooved ledges with colorful soft sponges, sea stars, anemones and other northern species.

All levels of instruction are available, from introductory scuba through open-water diver to instructor. York Beach Scuba specializes in open-water training, referrals and specialty and technical certifications. Dive clinics offered by York Beach Scuba include rebreather, Northeast Underwater Photo and dry suit clinics. Cost for instruction ranges from $20 for a guided daytime dive from the shore to $500 for re-breather instruction. Boat dives range in cost from $30 to $80, and rentals are available.

Fishing

There are three types of fishing in Maine: open-water fishing on inland waters, ice fishing and deep-sea fishing. For open-water and ice fishing, you need a license. Open-water season is generally defined as April 1 through September 30, though you may not fish while standing on ice during that time. By definition, the water body has to be naturally free of ice. Ice fishing season runs from ice-in (when lakes and ponds are suitably iced over) to March 31. Most brooks, streams and rivers are closed to ice fishing. You can fish in the sea from most beaches, or you can take a fishing charter (see listings). Ocean fishing does not require a license.

Cost for a non-resident fishing license (including a $1 agent fee) was $51 for the 1998-99 season, $39 for 15 days, $35 for seven days or $10 for a single-day license. A one-day junior license for kids ages 12 through 15 was $8. You can also buy a combination non-resident fishing and hunting license for $124. Resident license fees were $20 for the season or $37 for the combination. Licenses are available at local town halls and most sporting outfitters.

On inland waters you are most likely to find salmon, trout, bass and togue. In general, minimum legal lengths for keeping fish from rivers, brooks, streams, lakes and ponds are 18 inches for togue, 14 inches for salmon and 6 inches for brook trout. Brown and rainbow trout must be 6 inches in rivers, brooks and streams or 12 inches in lakes and ponds. You may also catch smallmouth or largemouth bass with a minimum length of 12 inches and a maximum length of 14 inches. Other species you are likely to find include pickerel, whitefish, perch and smelt. The length limits are also valid for ice fishing. In addition, there are bag limits restricting the number of fish you may take in a day. When purchasing your license you will be given the handbook of fishing regulations that identifies by county those water bodies with special regulations. There is also a page in the handbook illustrating the proper way to catch and release fish.

In the sea, you can catch mackerel, flounder, bluefish and striped bass from the shore or cod, haddock, pollock, wolf fish, tuna and shark from off shore. The yearly migration of fish into the waters of Southern Maine begins in May with striped bass, which are followed in June by mackerel. When the mackerel are running you will see crowds of anglers dipping many-lured lines into the sea and emerging with buckets of fish. In late June, July and August the bluefish will follow, but, unlike the mackerel, there is a three fish per day limit on bluefish.

Fishing Tours and Charters

Mainely Fishing
Town Dock No. 2, York Harbor
• **(207) 363-6526**

From May to November you can go sportfishing with Capt. Richard C. Witham aboard either the 22-foot Linesider or the 35-foot Linesider II. From July 1 to Labor Day, half-day fishing trips on the Linesider II depart

at 7 AM or 12:30 PM. Cost per person (including rod, reel and bait) was $40 in 1998. The Linesider is available by advance reservation to take you fishing for stripers and bluefish. Mainely Fishing also offers stand-up shark fishing, night fishing and fly-fishing for bass, blues and mackerel. Private charters are available or you can request an early-morning fishing trip before sunrise.

Seabury Charters Inc.
Town Dock No. 2, York Harbor
• **(207) 363-5675**

Capt. Herb Poole will take you sportfishing for giant bluefin tuna, sharks, bottom fish and bluefish. Half-day trips depart at 7:30 AM and 12:30 PM on Tuesday, Wednesday and Friday through Sunday from July 1 to August 31. Cost for the trip in 1998 was $40 per person with a six-person maximum per trip.

Shearwater Fishing
Town Dock No. 2, York Harbor
• **(207) 363-5324**

Fish for striped bass and bluefish on half-day trips from May 15 to October 1st. All trips depart at 7:30 AM. Half-day trips return at noon and full day trips return at 2 PM. There is a maximum of four people on half or full-day trips. All bait and tackle are furnished, and there is no charge for filleting your catch. Cost for the four-hour trip in 1998 was $50 per person. Private charters are available at $300 per day. Shearwater Fishing also offers fly fishing charters with a maximum of 2 people at a cost of $200 for half a day or $300 for a full day. Fly casting instruction is also available. They are open daily.

Bunny Clark
Perkins Cove, Ogunquit • (207) 646-2214

Full-day, half-day and private charters are

INSIDERS' TIP

Maine's boating law requires that all watercraft have at least one Coast Guard-approved personal floatation device (life jacket or vest) per person. You may need more, depending on the size of the boat. All watercraft equipped with motors must be registered in Maine or in a state with which Maine has a reciprocal agreement. For more information on safety and registration, call the Department of Inland Fisheries and Wildlife at (207) 287-2043.

available on the Bunny Clark, which is captained by Tim Tower. On full-day trips, the 40-foot deep-sea fishing boat departs at 7 AM and returns at 3 PM; for half-days, it leaves at 4 PM and returns at 8 PM. Cost in 1998 was $50 per person for full-day trips and $30 per person for half-day trips. Captain Tower also offers pre-set dates for marathon trips, which last from 12 to 16 hours at a cost of $90 per person. The Bunny Clark operates from the end of March to early November.

Ugly Anne
Perkins Cove, Ogunquit • (207) 646-7202

Full- and half-day deep-sea fishing trips are offered on the Ugly Anne. Full-day fishing trips are scheduled from April to mid-June and from Labor Day to November 1. These trips depart at 7 AM and return at 3:30 PM for a cost (in 1998) of $45 per person. From mid-June to Labor Day, half-day tours are available daily, departing at either 8 AM or 1:15 PM for a cost of $30 per person. All prices include rod, reel, bait and having your catch filleted. The Ugly Anne can accommodate up to 35 people.

Venture Inn II
Performance Marine (by the bridge), Kennebunkport • (207) 967-0005

The Venture Inn II offers half-day fishing trips Sunday through Tuesday and full-day trips Wednesday through Saturday from May 15 to October 15. Half-day trips depart at 8 AM and 1 PM; full-day trips leave at 7 AM. Cost for adults in 1998 was $30 per person for a half-day and $50 for a full day. The Venture Inn II is captained by Sam Bavely and can accommodate up to 85 people. Use of equipment is included in your ticket, and you'll find a full galley on board.

Go Fish! Charters
Spring Point Marina, South Portland • (207) 799-1339

Pursue stripers and bluefish along the ledges and islands of Casco Bay and Saco Bay with Go Fish! Charters led by Capt. Ben Garfield. Full-day, half-day and custom charters are available. You can cast live bait toward the ledge, troll wire along the dropoffs or cast a fly into the foam — it's your choice. Stand-up shark fishing is also available. While fishing offshore, you might have the opportunity to catch sight of whales, porpoises, bluefin tuna and pelagic sea birds. Cost for a four-hour inshore trip in 1998 was $195 for up to three people; eight hours inshore was $295, and eight hours offshore was $395 (again, for up to three people).

Devil's Den Charter
DiMillo's Marina, Portland • (207) 761-4466

If you want to book a sportfishing charter for your family or friends, this 33-foot boat will supply all your gear (you need to bring your own food). A full day fishing for blues, stripers and shark will coast you about $600 for up to six people. A half-day runs $350, but you'll have to do without the shark — the boat doesn't get far enough out for you to catch 'em.

Olde Port Mariner Fleet
Long Wharf, 170 Commercial St., Portland • (207) 775-0727

Set sail aboard the Indian II and cast your line. Beginning on weekends in April, and operating daily from mid-June through September, this fishing boat takes groups of up to 35 people out on the Atlantic for half- and full-day deep-sea fishing trips. Equipment and bait

INSIDERS' TIP

If you're interested in birds and intend to visit any of the nature preserves in Southern Maine, you might want to pick up DeLorme Mapping Company's booklet on Coastal Birds. The guide will help you distinguish the various types of seagulls (from the herring gull to the great black-backed gull) as well as other types of birds found along the Maine coast. Entries are accompanied by full-color drawings. You can buy the book at most bookstores (see Shopping) that carry a selection of DeLorme titles.

are included, and ticket prices range from $25 to $75 for adults. A full day of fishing is $35 for children 12 and younger. The boat has a small galley with snacks and beverages, but you should pack your own lunch.

Ashley F. Charters
P.O. Box 231, Brunswick
• (207) 751-2740

Fish for bluefish, stripers, mackerel, shark, tuna and groundfish aboard the Ashley F II, a 26-foot sportfisherman that charters daily from May through November. Captain Paul Farrington, a licensed Maine guide and paramedic and former L.L. Bean outdoor instructor, will take you out on the open ocean from either Brunswick or Bath. The boat is equipped with the latest electronic equipment and has a full head and galley. Lunch, cold drinks and coffee are provided on full-day charters, and drinks are provided on half-days. Tackle and bait are provided, and the cost of a full-day trip begins at $200 for up to three people and increases to $500 for a dawn-to-dusk tournament charter. Sightseeing and history tours are also available for $45 per hour for a minimum of two hours.

Sportfishing Aboard the Breakaway
Pier 6, Fisherman's Wharf,
East Boothbay • (207) 633-6990

Beginners and experts will enjoy a half-day of sportfishing off the Maine coast aboard the U.S. Coast Guard-inspected Breakaway, equipped with fish-finding electronics to track schools of fish. The boat has a covered cabin and roomy fishing cockpit, and all tackle and fishing gear is provided. Drop a line for bluefish, stripers, mackerel and shark from May through October. Ticket prices are $45 per person, or you can rent a private charter.

Golf

Highland Links Golf Club
301 Cider Hill Rd., York • (207) 363-4677

At Highland Farm Golf Course you'll find a nine-hole, par 35 course, plus a driving range, putting green, practice sand trap and a fully stocked pro shop. Golf clinics are offered for all skill levels, and private and group lessons

are available. The club also offers a swim club and tennis courts and future plans call for a back nine addition. Greens fees for 1999 are $15 for nine holes or $25 for 18 holes (played on alternate tees). Carts are $10 for nine holes, $20 for 18.

Cape Arundel Golf Club
Old River Rd., Kennebunkport
• (207) 967-2222

This semi-private, par 69 course is closed to the public between the hours of 11 AM and 2:30 PM. Greens fees are $35, and carts cost $20 more. Dress codes (collared shirts, no "short" shorts or cut-offs) are enforced at this club, and tee times are available 24 hours in advance. Mandatory starting times apply.

Webhannet Golf Club
9 Central Ave., Kennebunk
• (207) 967-2061

Webhannet Golf Club features an 18-hole par 71 course. Amenities include a snack bar, pro shop, lessons and carts. The greens fees in 1998 were $40, not including cart. The course is closed on Tuesday.

Dutch Elm Golf Course
Brimstone Rd. off Maine Hwy. 111,
between Biddeford and Lyman
• (207) 282-9850

The Dutch Elm Golf Course is a par 72, 6300-yard track. We're told that No. 2, a 440-yard par 4, is the most difficult hole on the course. It doglegs to the right with water on the left. Club and cart rentals are available at this course, which also features a full pro shop and snack bar. Calling ahead for tee times is recommended. The course is open daily from 7 AM to dusk, and greens fees were $28 in 1998. Off season, before it snows, you can play 18 holes for $20, nine holes for $12 or, after 2 PM, as many holes as you like for $12.

Salmon Falls Golf Club
Salmon Falls Rd. (Maine Hwy. 117),
Hollis • (207) 929-5233

Both nine- and 18-hole play are available at Salmon Falls, where the course is par 72. Open from 6:30 AM to dusk, the club offers rentals, a snack bar and pro shop. The course features only nine holes, but alternate tees are used to allow 18-hole play. We understand the 12th hole is a difficult one. It is a 230-yard par 3 over water, and the raised green is surrounded by sand traps. Cost to play nine holes in 1998 was $13. For 18 holes it was $20, or $17 for golfers age 65 and older. Cost for two players and a cart was $50. The course is open from April to October, depending on the weather. On weekends and holidays, you will need to call for starting times.

Biddeford-Saco Country Club
101 Old Orchard Rd., Saco
• **(207) 282-5883**

The 18-hole course at Biddeford-Saco Country Club is much more difficult than the scorecard might make it appear. It's a par 72, but you'll find a whole string of holes (8, 9, 10, 11 and 12) that are very pretty and very difficult. No. 11 is regarded as the most difficult hole on the course. A par 4, it features Goosefare Brook running through its center, long yardage and a difficult green.

Public tee times are available for reservation three days in advance. The course is open from 6 AM to dusk from April through November, weather permitting. The clubhouse is open to members year round. You'll find a pro shop, lounge, snack bar and practice range at the club. Greens fees in 1998 were $35, and lessons were offered at $25 each or $100 for five.

Old Orchard Country Club at Dunegrass
Cascade Rd., Old Orchard Beach
• **(207) 934-4513**

You have a choice of two courses at Old Orchard Country Club. A nine-hole course, built in 1920, was joined in the 1998 season by an 18-hole back course. Designed by Dan Maples, who designed Pinehurst in North Carolina, the new course features lots of water and trees. Par is 35 on the nine-hole course; the new course is a par 71.

For $22 in 1998 you could play the nine-hole course all day. A single round is $14, and no tee times are necessary. Greens fees for the 18-hole course during peak season are $55, which includes use of a golf cart. In addition to the new course, you'll also find a newly built clubhouse that features a pro shop, snack

bar, banquet facility and lounge. The club is open from 6 AM to dusk from April to November. The 18-hole course had its grand opening in May, 1998. For those who are interested, the country club is offering "play and stay" packages that will include greens fees and accommodations in the area. Call the club for details.

Nonesuch River Golf Club
304 Gorham Rd., Scarborough
• **(207) 883-0007**

Formerly known as Eagle Brook, the golf course at Nonesuch River Golf Club has been upgraded to a fully irrigated, high-end course with 18 holes, a practice range and bentgrass greens and fairways. We're told that No. 16 is probably the most difficult hole. This par 5 dogleg left tempts golfers with a high-risk second shot: If you miss the green to your right, you could be looking at a double-bogey; if you get in a good shot, you're looking at a birdie or definitely par. Each hole is unique, and the course offers a challenge to golfers of all abilities. Cost to play 18 holes is $28 midweek and $35 on Fridays, weekends and holidays. Cart rental is $12 per person for 18 holes. The club also offers a pro shop and lessons and has a restaurant, lounge and snack bar. Tee times are recommended at Nonesuch, which is open from April to November from 6:30 AM to dusk.

Willowdale Golf Course
Willowdale Rd., Scarborough
• **(207) 883-9351**

Located opposite the Scarborough Downs Race Track entrance on U.S. Highway 1, Willowdale offers a 6000-yard par 70 course that is both fun and forgiving. No. 10 is the most difficult hole — it is flanked on both sides with trees, involves water and has a small, elevated green with two tiers.

The course is tree-lined with areas bordering salt marsh. For weekend or holiday play, you should call by Wednesday at 7 AM to obtain a starting time. Greens fees in 1998 were $13 for nine holes, $23 for 18 holes and $10 after 5 PM for as many holes as you could play before dusk. Carts were $10 for nine holes and $20 for 18. Amenities include a snack bar and pro shop.

Photo: Merry Farnum

Derring Oaks Park, in Portland, has a great jogging trail.

Riverside Municipal Golf Course
1158 Riverside St., Portland
• **(207) 797-3524**

You'll find a driving range, full-service pro shop and a Par 72, 18-hole course at Riverside. There's also the option of playing just 9 holes, which are par 35. Cart and equipment rentals as well as lessons are available. After your game there's a restaurant and lounge for relaxing. The course is flat with a few hills in the back. Several holes run along the river and one is over a pond. Greens fees in 1997 were $18-$22 for 18 holes and $9-$15 for nine holes. Call ahead for a tee time on weekends.

Val Halla Golf Course
Val Halla Rd., Cumberland
• **(207) 829-2225**

This 18 hole, Par 72 course is open from mid-April to the end of October. The front nine, which opened in 1964, are hilly and open and the back nine are flat and narrow. From the white tees, the course is 6,200 yards, and water comes into play on five holes. The back nine opened in 1986. The course also offers a pro shop, cart rentals, snack bar, putting green and driving range. Greens fees are $17 for nine holes, offered mid-week. Eighteen holes are $22 mid-week and $28.50 on weekends. Call ahead for a tee time.

Brunswick Golf Club
River Rd., Brunswick • (207) 725-8224

The 18 holes at the Brunswick Golf Club wind around tall pines and a couple of ponds. You'll enjoy the scenery while playing a challenging par 72 championship course. The club has a pro shop, rental carts and equipment and is open to the public. Call for tee times. Greens fees range from $18-$35 for 18 holes and $9 to $20 for nine holes.

Bath Country Club
Whiskeag Rd., Bath • (207) 442-8411

This course used to be known as the best nine-holer in the state. Since adding nine more holes in 1994, it is building its reputation all over again as a par 70, 18-hole course. The original holes were designed in 1930, and the newer holes have been integrated among the hills, ponds and wetlands. The clubhouse has a full-service restaurant, and the pro shop offers club and cart rentals. Greens fees recently were $25 for 18 holes and $15 for nine. Call ahead for a tee time.

Shore Acres Country Club
Sebasco Harbor Resort • P.O. Box 75, Sebasco Estates, Phippsburg
• **(800) 225-3819**

This nine-hole, Par 36 course with 18 sets of tees is part of the Sebasco Harbor Resort (see more on this under Hotels and Motels). The greens are just lovely, and several overlook the adjoining bay, river and ocean. With an additional nine tees being developed over the next several years, the course will include views of the Portland skyline. The course is 2000 yards, and lessons are available from the club pro. You'll experience play on 10 bunkers, and water comes into play on three holes. Greens fees for visitors are $19 for a full day and $12 for resort guests. The newly named Shore Acres is open from May 1 through Nov. 1.

Boothbay Region Country Club
Country Club Rd., Boothbay
• **(207) 633-6085**

Respected as one of the nicest nine-hole courses in the state, the Boothbay Region Country Club is a 562-yard course that celebrated its 75th year in 1997. The club includes a pro shop, a lunch counter and a bar with tables indoors and out. Call ahead to reserve a tee time.

Greens fees are $17.50 to $25, and drop to $12 for a whole day in the fall. The club is beginning work on an additional nine holes, which it expects to open in the spring of 2000. The club opens in mid-spring and remains open until Nov. 1.

Fore Season Golf
1037 Forest Ave., Portland
• **(207) 797-8835**

Golf in Maine year-round at some of the most prestigious courses in the country at this simulated golf club. Pick a course to match your skill and tee up to the ball. When you whack it toward a video screen, the ball drops out of sight and sensors around the room pick up the exact flight of the ball to simulate it flying through the air on a video screen. The club has five simulators and offers 17 different courses including California's world-class Pebble Beach. The cost is $26 an hour. Food, beer, wine and soda are available for an additional cost. A free nine-hole putting green is also on the premises. The club is closed Monday and Tuesday during the summer season.

Hiking

Mount Agamenticus
Mountain Rd., York

The view from the top of Mount Agamenticus is great! On a clear day, you can see the White Mountains to the west and the ocean to the east. You can walk or drive to the top, but since you're investigating "hiking," you'll probably want to do it on foot. A former ski slope, Mount Agamenticus is 700 to 800 feet high. You'll find a parking area at the base of the mountain and another at the top.

Fore River Sanctuary
Off Rowe Ave. and Frost St., Portland
• (207) 781-2330

You'll be captivated by this 85-acre preserve of salt marshes, woodlands and a natural 25-foot waterfall, all maintained by the Maine Audubon Society. There are several dirt loop trails to choose from. Most have moderate slopes, though the trail to the waterfall is somewhat steep. In all, there are 3.5 miles of hiking opportunities, and there is limited wheelchair access. You can get a map of the trail system from Maine Audubon by calling the number listed. There is parking off Rowe Avenue or on Frost Street in the Maine Orthopedics lot.

Bradbury Mountain State Park
Hallowell Rd., Pownal • (207) 725-4571

For a moderately easy hike that's perfect for families and hikers of all fitness levels, Bradbury Mountain has well-marked trails that gently slope upward through Maine pines to a rocky overlook. Don't expect breathtaking vistas, but you will get a good look at the surrounding countryside and a breath of fresh air. The climb is most exhilarating during fall, when you can look out over an ocean of or-

ange trees (see more in this chapter under Parks and Nature Preserves). Admission is $2 per adult and 50¢ for children ages 5 through 11. Children younger than 5 are admitted free. The park is open from May 15 through October 15.

Wolfe's Neck Woods State Park
Wolfe Neck Rd., Freeport
• (207) 865-4465
(April through October),
• (207) 624-6080
(November through March)

Five miles of hiking trails wind through this 200-acre park. You'll get to walk along Casco Bay and the Haraseeket River while enjoying Maine's outdoors. The paths are fairly flat and are well-marked. (For more information, check out the Parks and Nature Preserves listings earlier in this chapter.)

The Arnold Trail
Fort Popham, Phippsburg

Follow the path Col. Benedict Arnold and his troops forged along on their historic march to Quebec in 1775. Beginning at Fort Popham, the 194-mile Arnold Trail goes all the way to Coburn Gore at the Canadian border. For a more moderate trip, we suggest hiking just a few miles of it. The trail begins at Fort Popham, at the mouth of the Kennebec River, and travels northwest. Col. Arnold led his troops from the fort in at attempt to overcome the British and failed.

Horseback Riding

Horseback Riding Plus
338 Broadturn Rd., Scarborough
• (207) 883-1600, (800) 883-6499

Located at Long Horn Equestrian Center, Horseback Riding Plus offers trail and beach rides. No lessons are required for trail riding, but beach rides are not recommended for children younger than 12. Reservations are suggested for both trail and beach rides. Rates for trail riding in 1999 are $12 per person for a half-hour or $18 for an hour. Off-season the hour rate drops to $15. (In -season and off-season a $3 surcharge is applied if there is only one rider.) Beach rides are $35 per person for an hour, with a $15 surcharge for a party of one. Beach rides are available from September through May, beach conditions permitting.

Horsefeathers Stable
178 County Rd., Gorham
• (207) 839-2243

For trail rides that will take you clopping over the river and through the woods, check out this stable in Gorham. Guided rides are $15 an hour, and the trail is 3 to 4 miles long. Children younger than 10 are not allowed on the trail ride, but pony rides are available at the barn. Rides are offered during spring, summer and fall, but only on Sundays during hunting season, which begins the first Saturday in November.

Worff Stables
1133 Lewiston Rd., Topsham
• (207) 353-2122

This horse farm offers trail rides back through the Maine woods for $25 per person per hour. Call anytime to schedule a ride. If you're lucky you might see some Maine wildlife on the trail.

Ledgewood Riding Stables
Bradford Rd., Wiscasset
• (207) 882-6346

This stable offers one and two hour wooded trail rides by reservation for people 7 and older. A short section of the ride takes place on the road, and then weaves back into the trees where if you are lucky you might spot a deer or even a moose. The cost is $20 an hour or $35 for two hours.

Running and Walking

While just about all of our back roads include scenic routes for running and walking, we've listed some of the more popular areas. If you're looking for a track, however, we suggest calling a school department in the area where you'll be staying. Many schools have outdoor tracks they open to the public after school hours and on weekends. In winter, outdoor exercise can be somewhat treacherous due to snow and ice. Some people head to a nearby mall or school to walk, or you might try a YMCA or fitness club.

The Yorks

For those who don't mind running or walking upwards of 10 miles, you'll get a more personal view of the Yorks that way than traveling by car. Beginning in York Village, head south toward York Harbor on U.S. Highway 1A. Follow Route 1A along Long Sands Beach, and take a right at the end of the beach toward the Nubble Lighthouse. Continuing away from the lighthouse, follow the road to the right until it intersects with Route 1A and take a right into York Beach. Make a left onto Railroad Avenue at Shelton's and bear right after the animal park. You are now on Ridge Road, which you should follow past the Dave's IGA Plaza and back into York Village.

Wells Mile Road Loop

If you're in Wells and in the mood for a walk or run of 4 miles or so, head down Mile Road toward the sea and take a right onto Church Street. Run or walk along Church Street, and it will become Webhannet Drive. Follow the road to Moody Point, then make a right onto either Ocean Avenue or Furbish Road. Take another right onto U.S. Highway 1 and continue until you reach your starting point. Or, if you prefer to stay off Route 1, retrace your steps.

Dock Square to Beach Avenue

From Dock Square in Kennebunkport, head over the bridge to Lower Village and take a left at the light. Walk or run past St. Anthony's Franciscan Monastery (where you can detour and explore the grounds) or continue along Beach Avenue, which traverses the length of Kennebunk Beach. At the end of the beach, stay to the right on Sea Road, take a right at the traffic light, go straight and you're back in Dock Square. The total length of the trip is about 5.5 miles.

Old Orchard Beach Pier to Goosefare Brook

At low tide the sand at this beach area is firm and great for walking or running. Beginning at the pier, run south along the beach until you reach Goosefare Brook, then turn around and head back. You'll find a good running surface during the 2½ hours on either side of low tide. The total round-trip mileage is about 3.5 miles, but remember it's a little more difficult running on sand, no matter how firm.

Cape Elizabeth State Park Loop

Described in this chapter's Biking section, this loop involves about 10 miles of cycling, running or walking from Fort Williams Park to Two Lights State Park and Crescent Beach State Park.

Baxter Boulevard
Payson Park, along Baxter Blvd. and Ocean Ave., Portland
• (207) 874-8793

One of the most popular spots for walking and running, 4-mile Baxter Boulevard wraps around Back Cove. You'll be able to keep an eye on the water while getting your exercise on this paved pathway. You'll find parking in little lots dotting the route or directly across from the Shop 'n' Save parking lot on Baxter Boulevard. Bikers and roller-bladers are discouraged from using the path.

Brunswick Bike Path
North end of Maine Street, Brunswick

Check out the write up under bike-paths for another great place to jog. It is a favorite with locals for safety, ease and convenience.

Skating

For our skating category, we have included indoor and outdoor ice rinks — always fun in the winter — and roller-skating rinks. One word of extreme caution when it comes to unsupervised outdoor rinks: Make sure you do not skate if there is any open water, if there has been a thaw or if you see any warning signs. A good rule: Don't be the first one on the ice. There is also information on rental outlets for in-line skating, which can be done just about anywhere.

Ice Skating

Biddeford Ice Arena
Alfred Rd. (off Maine Hwy. 111), Biddeford • (207) 283-0615

You can skate at Biddeford Ice Arena from 9:30 to 11:30 AM Monday, Tuesday, Thurs-

day and Friday for $6. The arena also offers Friday evening or Sunday afternoon sessions weekly for $3, but you'll have to call to find out which is on offer when you want to skate. The Friday night session runs from 6:30 to 8:30 PM and the Sunday session runs from 1:00 to 3:00 PM. Wednesday morning is reserved for figure skating only. The arena does not rent equipment.

West Brook Skating Rink
234 Pool Rd., Biddeford
• (207) 284-9652

This 2-acre pond with a warming house was renovated in the winter of 1996-97. Cost to skate is $2 per person, and the pond is open for skating when the ice is suitably thick.

Ferry Beach State Park
Seaside Ave. (Maine Hwy. 9), Saco

Though closed for the winter season, you can access the pond in Ferry Beach State Park from Route 9. When the ice is ready, you'll see cars parked along the side of the road and skaters on the pond.

Deering Oaks Park
Between Forest Ave. and Deering Ave., Portland • (207) 772-4994

One of the most popular outdoor skating ponds in the area is in Deering Oaks Park. You'll find a sizable rink lit up by overhead lights. For more on Deering Oaks, check it out under our Parks category.

Portland Ice Arena
225 Park Ave., Portland • (207) 774-8553

Want to try out your skill on the ice in summer? Try the Portland Ice Arena. Built in 1984, the indoor rink has skate rentals, a concession area, pro shop, four locker rooms and a regulation-size rink. It is open to the public for a limited time during the afternoon on Monday through Wednesday, Friday and Sunday. Group lessons are also available for ages 4 through adult.

Outdoor skating in Yarmouth
Behind Key Bank,
Maine St., Yarmouth • (207) 846-2406

This lighted pond, which is located just off Maine Street behind Key Bank, is maintained by Yarmouth Community Services and is open when weather permits. To find out about pond conditions, call the phone number listed in the headline for this entry. Hockey players will be happy to know they are allowed on rear section of pond.

The Downtown Mall
Maine St.,Brunswick

Every winter Brunswick's downtown park, known as "The Mall," is flooded to make an outdoor skating rink. Skaters glide over the smooth ice while white lights twinkle overhead in the surrounding trees and around the perimeter of a romantic wooden gazebo.

In-line Skate Rentals

The Skate Stop
**Alfred Rd. (off Maine Hwy. 111),
Biddeford • (207) 284-1500**

You can rent all forms of Rollerblade brand in-line skates from the Skate Stop. Aggressive, hockey, race or recreational skates are available from a shop that is dedicated to being one of the best in-line dealers anywhere. Cost for rentals in 1998 was $10 for two hours, $15 for four hours, $20 for a full day and $25 for 24-hour rental. All rentals include elbow and knee pads, wrist guards and a helmet. You must be 18 years old or accompanied by an adult to rent equipment, and all rentals require MasterCard or Visa coverage. You will be responsible for any damage or loss to rented items.

Joe Jones Ski & Sports
**456 Payne Rd., Scarborough
• (207) 885-5635**

In addition to mountain-bike rentals, Joe Jones also handles in-line skate rentals and Alpine and cross-country ski rentals. Cost for Rollerblade brand in-line skates, pads and a helmet is $8 for a half-day and $10 for a full day.

Roller Skating

Happy Wheels Skate Center
**441 Payne Rd. (Maine Hwy. 9),
Scarborough
• (207) 883-3713, (800) 883-3713**

Both all-age skating and special age-group skating is offered at Happy Wheels Skate Center. On Wednesdays from 6:30 to 8:30 PM, all ages can skate for $3. On Thursday afternoons, after-school skating for all ages is offered from 4 to 6 PM for $3 admission and no rental fee. Thursday night is adults-only night for folks 18 and older; admission for this session, which runs from 7:30 to 10 PM, is $4. On Friday evening from 8 to 11 PM all ages are welcome, but the crowd is predominantly made up of teenagers. Cost for this session is $4.50.

Saturdays bring a choice of sessions. All ages can skate from 10:45 AM to 1:15 PM or 2 to 4:30 PM for $3.50, or from 8 to 10:30 PM for $4. On Sundays you again have a choice of sessions: You can skate from 1 to 5 PM for $4.50, or from 1 to 3:30 PM or 2:30 to 5 PM for $3.50. Cost for skate rentals is $1. In-line skate rental is $3 at all times.

Skateboarding

Old Orchard Beach
Skateboard Park
T-for Turn Rd., Old Orchard Beach

If you're looking for a great place to work your flips and turns, check out the skateboard park located between the Fire Station and Old Orchard Beach High School on T-for Turn Road, just off Saco Avenue. The park was built in 1997 through the efforts of skateboarders and skaters who petitioned the town and raised money for the project.

Zone Skateboarding
33 Allen Ave., Portland • (207) 878-7589

For indoor skateboarding, Rollerblading and BMX biking, check out the Zone. The center is full of jumps and ramps and has a street course to try out your latest moves and get an eye on the competition. The center has a full pro shop that sells equipment and rents pads and helmets. It's open Tuesday through Sunday, and the cost of admission is $6 per person. You will need to bring along your own board, skates or bike.

Skiing

Maine is well-known for fabulous skiing. There are a half-dozen large downhill slopes within a half-day's drive of our Southern Coast. We recommend calling the Ski Maine Association, (207) 761-3774, for information on some of our better known resorts such as Sunday River in Bethel. For cross-country skiing, check out the listings we have included. If you don't mind breaking your own trail, refer back to our Golf section — nearly all the courses we know allow cross-country skiing in winter. Best of all, if the trails aren't groomed you can count on skiing free.

Old Orchard Country Club at Dunegrass
Cascade Rd., Old Orchard Beach
• (207) 934-4513

In addition to the new 18-hole golf course at the country club, there are 25 kilometers of cross-country ski trails and a clubhouse that features a snack bar, lounge and banquet facilities. Cost for skiing had not been determined at the time of this writing.

Beech Ridge Cross Country Ski Center
193 Beech Ridge Rd., Scarborough
• (207) 839-4098

At Beech Ridge Ski Center you'll find 150 acres of historic farmland with 22 kilometers of groomed trails for cross-country skiing, skate-skiing and snowshoeing. Open daily in winter, the center's amenities include a warming shed and snack bar. Cross-country ski and snowshoe rentals were available for $10 per day in 1998. Cost for use of the trails was $10 per day on weekends and $8 on holidays and weekdays.

Lessons were available at $10 for a group lesson and $25 for a private lesson. A Polk sled, which you tow behind you as you ski, is available for parents with small children at a rental rate of $2 per hour. The center is open from 9 AM to dusk daily and until 9 PM on Fridays, when trails are lighted by lanterns. Trails are marked by wooden signs, and visitors receive a trail map when they buy a ticket.

Beech Ridge also offers a "Choose and Cut Christmas Tree Plantation" during the Christmas season with 20,000 trees of all sizes. Cost for a tree of any size is $25 per tree; most trees are balsams or blue-tip spruces. A saw is provided for you to cut your tree.

Joe Jones Ski & Sports
456 Payne Rd., Scarborough
• (207) 885-5635

Joe Jones Ski & Sports doesn't have ski trails, but they do rent Alpine and cross-country skis. Cost for Alpine rentals, including boots and poles, is $15 for the first day, $10 for the second day and $5 per day after that. For cross-country skis the first day will run you $10, the second day is $5, and subsequent days are $3 each.

Ski-A-Bit
Maine Hwy. 112, West Buxton
• (207) 929-4824

About 20 miles west of Saco and Scarborough on Route 112 in West Buxton, Ski-A-Bit features 40 kilometers of cross-country fun. Trails run mostly through woodlands, and there is a warming shed and snack bar. A free mini-lesson is given to get beginners on their way. Cost for skiing in 1998 was $10 for a full day, $8 for a half-day. Students and senior citizens pay $7, children ages 7 through 12 pay $4, and children younger than 7 ski free. Ski rentals will run you $10.

Smiling Hill Farm Cross Country Ski Center
781 County Rd. (Maine Hwy. 22), Westbrook • (207) 775-4818

Single-track, double-track and skate trails are available for winter fun at Smiling Hill Farm. Approximately 35 kilometers of trails through woodlands and fields make cross-country skiing, skate-skiing and snowshoeing a pleasure. Full-day and half-day ski rates are available, and you can rent skis, skate-skis and snowshoes. Cost for a full day of skiing on weekends and holidays in 1998 was $10 for adults and $6 for children ages 7 through 17. There is no charge for children younger than 7. Weekday rates drop to $8 for adults and $4.50 for children. Cost for ski and skate-ski rental was $10; it was $8 to rent snowshoes.

Evergreen Cemetery
672 Stevens Ave., Portland

At 239 acres, Evergreen is the largest cemetery in the state and a favorite place for cross-country skiing. You'll be able to glide around four ponds, a wooded area with trails and miles

of paths. An expansive area of the cemetery is lawn, although on parts you will have to contact with a moderate slope. The cemetery has been around since 1855 and has many noteworthy headstones to pique your interest as you exercise. Trails are not groomed, but you may be able to follow in someone else's tracks.

L.L. Bean Cross Country Ski Center
Freeport Country Club,
Old Country Rd., Freeport
• (800) 341-4341 ext. 26666

Ski on groomed trails maintained by the L.L. Bean retail store. You'll find nearly 15 km. of groomed trails with flat terrain, rolling hills and lush woods. Ski rentals and lessons are also available. The center is open from January through mid-March, and tickets prices run around $8 for adults and $6 for children ages 6 to 17. Lessons are from $15 to $30 and are available for all skill levels.

Sleigh Rides and Hay Rides

Rockin Horse Stables
245 Arundel Rd., Kennebunkport
• (207) 967-4288

Experience the beauty of New England while being pulled in a wagon or sleigh through woodlands and fields by lovely Belgian horses. Rates per hour for wagon rides in 1998 were $7 for adults and $5 for children 4 through 12. For groups of ten or more cost is $5 per person for wagon rides. There is no charge for children 3 or younger. Sleigh rides cost $10 for adults and $6 for children. For groups of 10 or more the rate is $1 less per person. Rockin Horse Stabes also offer rides in their beautiful "Wedding Carriage" which features a white carriage with burgundy interior. Rides leave from Ocean Avenue in front of the Landing Restaurant and are available, weather permitting through the Christmas Prelude in mid-December. Rides last 20-25 minutes and cost $10 for adults and $5 for children. If you're interested in having the carriage for your wedding, call the stable for details.

Smiling Hill Farm
781 County Rd. (Maine Hwy. 22),
Westbrook • (207) 775-4818

When there's snow on the ground, you can enjoy a sleigh ride at Smiling Hill Farm. On weekends and holidays, sleigh rides are $3.50 per person, but you can also hire a sleigh for large groups for $4 per person ($50 minimum). A small sleigh is also available for you romantics at heart. Cost for the small sleigh is $50, and it will accommodate up to four people. Rides generally last around 45 minutes, with private group rides lasting a little longer because they include the use of a warming shed with hot chocolate.

Throughout October you can enjoy hay rides at the farm for $3.50 per person. The pumpkin patch tour includes a trip to the pumpkin patch, where you get to select a pumpkin to take home with you. In addition to the ride, small children will love exploring the kids' maze made of hay bales. Evening "haunted hayrides" are also offered.

Horsefeathers Stable
178 County Rd., Gorham
• (207) 839-2243

You'll jingle over the river and through the woods on a horse-drawn sleigh ride at Horsefeathers Stable. If there's not enough snow, take the hay ride. Trips are 30 minutes in length, seven days, and the cost is $40 per ride for groups of up to 10. Groups with more than 10 people pay a $5 per person flat fee. Bring a picnic or a thermos of hot chocolate to enjoy after your ride in one of the stable's private cabins where a fire will be waiting for you after your trip. A one-hour use of the cabin is included in the cost of the ride, and if you have something special planned they'll spiffy it up for you.

Snowmobiling

Thousands of miles of snowmobiling trails cut across our fields, lakes and woods and can take you from the tip of the southern coast all the way to Canada! The network of interconnecting trails is growing due to the cooperation of snow-mobiling clubs, private landowners, the state and local towns.

In this category we've included snowmobile outfitters where you can rent or service your equipment. For more detailed information on our trails, contact the Off Roads Division of the Bureau of Parks and Lands at (207) 287-3821. Or call the Maine Snowmobiling Association at (207) 622-6983. Local chambers of commerce are also a good point of contact for trail maps or for local snowmobile clubs (you'll find them in Area Overviews).

Swimming

Check out our Beaches chapter for those

long stretches of sand where you can lounge in the sun. Of course, the water is very cold off most beaches, and that's why we are also including pools and freshwater swimming holes for the less daring.

Northern York County Family YMCA
Alfred Business Park (off Maine Hwy. 111), Biddeford • (207) 283-0100

Public swimming times vary at the YMCA but are usually Wednesday from 7:30 to 9 PM and Saturday and Sunday from 1 to 3 PM. Cost for swimming is $5 for adults and $2 for children 18 or younger and senior citizens. A family of five is $10.

South Portland Municipal Pool
21 Nelson Rd., South Portland
• (207) 767-7655

The South Portland Municipal Pool is Olympic-size at 25 meters in length. The water temperature is kept at 82 degrees. Amenities include showers and dressing rooms with lockers (you'll need to bring your own lock) and a hot tub that holds up to 10 people and is maintained at 104 degrees. In addition to swimming, the center offers adult, child and preschool swimming lessons, and on Monday, Wednesday and Friday evenings they offer a deep-water fitness program. You can also drop in for water aerobics classes, which cost $3.

The pool has a ramp to provide easy access for those who have difficulty getting in and out, and there is also a diving board. Cost to swim for non-members is $2; members pay $1. A membership for residents of South Portland costs $30 and allows them to purchase a pass for 20 swim sessions for $15. If you are interested in renting the pool for birthday parties or other special events, it is available from 4 to 6 PM on Saturdays and Sundays at a cost of $40 for up to 25 people.

East End Beach
Eastern Promenade, Along Commercial and Cutter St., Portland

Portland Harbor's East End Beach might not be much in the way of beaches because of its small size, but it is a place where you can take a saltwater dip without experiencing the full chill of the Atlantic. Located on the shore of the Eastern Promenade, the small beach has seasonal restrooms.

Kiwanis Pool
Douglas St., Portland • (207) 772-4708

Right off the Congress Street exit and across from the Portland Water District, this 25-meter outdoor pool offers scheduled lap time and family recreation. The pool is open from July through August at $2 per-person for residents and $2.75 for non-residents. There will be a lifeguard on duty.

Winslow Memorial Park
Staples Point Rd., South Freeport
• (207) 865-4198

Our favorite aspect of swimming at the small sand beach at this municipal park is that you might be able to feel your toes when you get out. The water stays markedly warmer than other saltwater swimming holes. For more information on the park look under our Parks category in this chapter. Open from Memorial Day through the last weekend in September, the park charges $1.50 for people ages 6-62. Also, swimming is best at high tide — unless you like a mud bath.

Coffin Pond
River Road, Brunswick
• (207) 725-6656

An ideal place to bring children, this town-owned pond has a small sandy beach and life guards seven days a week from late June through August. Parents will like that it is small enough to keep an eye on their little ones, and children will like that it has a 55-foot-long water slide, playground, concession area and changing rooms. Admission is charged and day or season passes are available.

Thomas Point Beach
Off Maine Hwy. 24, Cook's Corner,
Brunswick • (207) 725-6009

This tidal beach on the New Meadow's River has a small beach for swimming where the water is a little cloudy but much warmer than the ocean. Surrounding the beach are 42 acres of lawns and groves with picnic tables and charcoal grills. The cost to get in is $3 for adults and $2 for children younger than 12. The park is open from 9 AM to sunset, Memo-

rial Day through Labor Day. (See our Camp-grounds chapter for more on this location.)

Charles Pond
Maine Hwy. 127, Georgetown

One of the best swimming holes in the area, Charles Pond has clear water and a rim of pine trees surrounding the waterline. It's also long and narrow with a 25-yard girth and a 300-yard stretch. You'll find it by driving roughly half a mile past Reid State Park on Route 127.

Tennis

In most towns along Maine's Southern Coast, you'll find public outdoor tennis courts near town or city schools. There is usually no cost to use the courts, but you may have to put your name on a sign-up sheet to get on. In general, if no one is using the courts and they aren't reserved by anyone else or for school use or lessons, go ahead and play.

In York, you'll find courts at the high school and behind the middle school. In Wells four courts are located at the Town Recreation Park on Maine Highway 9A, and in Kennebunk there are courts at the high school, at the West Kennebunk Recreation Field on Old Holland Road, and on Park Street.

Biddeford has courts at Clifford Park on Pool Street and at Memorial Field on May Street; in Saco, you'll find courts at Memorial Field off Beach Street and at Young School and Saco Middle School, both of which are on Maine Highway 112.

In Scarborough, courts are across from the library off Route 114 at Oak Hill, and in South Portland there are courts at the high school on Highland Avenue.

There are 11 outdoor courts, open dawn until dusk, at Deering Oaks Park, (207) 874-8793, Portland's largest outdoor recreational facility. It is located between Forest and Deering avenues. For more information, see this chapter's Parks and Nature Preserves listings. There are also courts in Portland at Deering High School and in Payson Park. The Donna Hall Memorial Courts at Yarmouth High School, West Elm Street, Yarmouth, provide four lighted courts, but you may have to compete with practicing students.

In Bath, try the courts below the middle school off Congress Street. In Boothbay Harbor, there are courts across from the YMCA off Maine Highway 27.

Whether you want to stroll quietly or splash in the surf, build sandcastles or castles in the air, there is a beach to suit your needs.

Beaches

"I must go down to the seas again, to the lonely sea, and the sky...."
—from "Sea Fever" by John Masefield

*"The tide rises, the tide falls,
The twilight darkens, the curlew calls;
Along the sea-sands damp and brown
The traveler hastens toward the town,
And the tide rises, the tide falls."*
—from "The Tide Rises, The Tide Falls" by Henry Wadsworth Longfellow

Throughout the ages, poets, painters, novelists and philosophers have pondered the endless mysticism of the sea. From jagged rocks and cliffs jutting out to sea to gently sloping acres of powder soft sand, the ocean's beauty and grandeur have held generations spellbound.

Each summer thousands of visitors continue this tradition as they converge on Southern Maine's beaches to share in the state's wealth of beautiful shoreline. From the north, the south and inland they rush to the sandy, rocky, pebbly coast. Whether you want to stroll quietly or splash in the surf, build sandcastles or castles in the air, there is a beach to suit your needs.

Despite the number of people visiting the area in summer, there are quiet stretches of beach where you can walk slowly, enjoying the feel of cold water against your feet and ankles. You probably won't find total solitude on the beaches during summer, but if you walk a hundred yards or so down the beach from the main parking areas, the crowds will thin out and you'll find yourself in the company of relatively few people.

For those of you who like to go swimming, you'll find our water reasonably warm from July through September. By the Fourth of July, the water usually reaches about 68 degrees, and it stays in that neighborhood until late September. You'll find some of the die-hards swimming until then, but most people stop rushing into the sea in late August.

The tide can make a difference in the warmth of the water as well. If the tide has been in all day it will be quite warm, especially in the shallows as the tide recedes; if the tide doesn't start rolling in until around noon, it will probably feel a little chilly.

If you plan on walking the beach or just finding a sandy spot to lounge, check the tide charts before going. If you happen to show up at high tide, you might not find any beach at all. The local newspapers should have tide charts (see Media), and local television stations and The Weather Channel also provide tide information.

As a natural attraction, there is little to top a beach. You can swim, walk, run, surf (yes, a few hearty souls even brave the waves in winter), build castles, doze, get buried in sand, or stroll hand-in-hand with a loved one as the sun sets. But there are always a few basic rules you must follow, and the rules vary by city and town. In this chapter we've followed our four major geographic headings, then subdivided our listings based on the towns and cities in each area that have beaches. Under the town name you'll find an introductory paragraph explaining the parking situation, rules regarding animals on beaches and other relevant information.

Note that in areas where lifeguards are provided, they will be on the beach from the end of June to the last week in August. Alcohol is not allowed on public beaches. Overnight camping and overnight parking in public lots are also prohibited. If you want to build a fire, you'll need to get a permit from the local fire department. Some beaches allow animals at specified times. During hours when dogs are allowed on the beach, it is the owner's responsibility to pick up the animal's waste and dispose of it properly. If you don't pick it up and are caught, you can be fined. Think of it this way: You could be spoiling the privilege for other pet owners. Many towns are banning animals on their beaches because people have not been following the "pooper-scooper laws."

Southern Beaches Area

Kittery

Permits are not required for non-resident parking at Kittery beaches, but you must not park where it is posted "Residents Only." Resident permits (or "dump stickers, " so named because you need a sticker in some locales to prove you are a resident and access the local transfer station or landfill) allow residents to park in specified lots. If you do not have a dump sticker and park in the resident areas, you could receive a ticket, and we are told the police are vigilant. Dogs are allowed on the beaches but must be leashed from 9 AM to 5 PM in-season.

Crescent Beach and Seapoint Beach
Seapoint Rd., Kittery

These two beaches lie on either side of a small peninsula that you reach by taking Chauncy Creek Road off Maine Highway 103, then taking Seapoint Road from Chauncy Creek Road. The beaches are backed by salt marsh, and each is about half a mile long. There are no lifeguards or facilities.

Fort Foster Park
Off Maine Hwy. 103, Kittery
• **(207) 439-3800**

At Fort Foster you can enjoy picnic areas with grills, a pier and scenic walks through the woods. Cost for entrance for the 1998 season is $2 for adults and $1 for children younger than 12. There is an additional charge of $2.50 per vehicle. The park is open weekends in May and daily from the end of May to the end of August. Off-season, it is OK to walk under the barrier gate to enjoy the park. Dogs are allowed in the park provided they are leashed and the pooper-scooper laws are obeyed. (For more information on Fort Foster, see our Kidstuff and Attractions chapters.)

Fort McClary State Park
Maine Hwy. 103, Kittery
• **(207) 384-5160**

A small swimming beach is part of this state park that houses Fort McClary (see Attractions and Kidstuff). In addition to the beach area, you'll find picnic tables, nature trails and restrooms. Dogs are not allowed on state park beaches. Lifeguards are present from the end of June to the last week in August. Cost for entrance to the park in 1998 was $2 for those 12 and older, 50¢ for those ages 5 through 11; children younger than 5 are not charged. You can also purchase an individual season pass for $20 or a family/vehicle pass for $40 a season. The latter will allow your vehicle and all passengers into all the parks in the state system. Permits for those age 65 and older are free, and these also allow entrance to all state parks.

York

Wherever you are in the Yorks, there's a beach to explore. At York Harbor there's the Harbor Beach. Following U.S. Highway 1A, you'll discover both Long Sands Beach and Short Sands Beach. Dogs are not permitted on York beaches from May 1 to September 30, and there is metered parking at all beaches. Facilities are available at Long Sands and Short Sands beaches, and there is a portable toilet in the Harbor Beach parking lot. There is a shower for rinsing off at Short Sands. Lifeguards are provided at all three beaches.

Harbor Beach
Harbor Beach Rd., York Harbor

This is a small, crescent beach with hard, dark sand at the end of Harbor Beach Road, which is off Route 1A. If you prefer smaller, more intimate beaches, you'll like this one. From here you can watch boats coming into the harbor and easily walk to the York Harbor village shops. There is a parking lot with meters that take quarters (there's a two-hour limit), but you can walk to this beach from nearby hotels and bed and breakfast inns in the village.

Long Sands Beach
U.S. Hwy. 1A, York Beach

There's plenty of room to run on this aptly named long, sandy beach. The fine sand is

Photo: Maine Office of Tourism

Families enjoy the sun, sand and activities at Old Orchard Beach.

hard and shelves gently into the sea. Parking meters line Route 1A, which runs the 1.5-mile length of the beach. Surfers will find a designated spot to pursue their passion here. Both a bathhouse and lifeguards are provided at Long Sands, and regardless of where you place your blanket on the beach, you'll find a wide selection of spots that sell food within a short walk.

Short Sands Beach
U.S. Hwy. 1A, York Village

Crescent-shaped and at the heart of York Beach village, Short Sands Beach has a large metered parking lot. Located adjacent to Ellis Park, which features a pavilion and fenced-in playground, Short Sands is popular with families. Amenities include a bathhouse and lifeguards at the beach and lots to do in the village.

Ogunquit

Ogunquit's two public beaches are really two sections of one stretch of sand: Ogunquit Beach is the southern end, and Footbridge Beach is the northern end. Take the trolley to the beach or park in one of five municipal lots. Cost to park in the Beach Street parking lot was $2 per hour in 1998. Parking in three other municipal lots is $8 per day. The lower lot on River Street, off Beach Street, is convenient to Ogunquit Beach, and you can access Footbridge Beach from the Ocean Street (Footbridge) and Ocean Avenue (Moody) lots. A fifth parking lot, Obeds, costs $7 and is located off Shore Road on Obeds Lane about three-quarters of a mile from the main beach. Dogs are prohibited on Ogunquit beaches from May to October. Both beach areas have restrooms and lifeguards.

INSIDERS' TIP

To find out about the sea creatures that inhabit our beaches, see our chapter on Maine's Natural World.

Ogunquit Beach
Beach St., Ogunquit

Soft, white sand and the sparkling sea await at this beach. It's at the end of Beach Street, which you'll find at its intersection with Route 1 (Main Street). An interesting feature of both Ogunquit and Footbridge beaches is that they are located on a large sandbar between the Ogunquit River and the sea. You can swim in either the river or the sea.

Footbridge Beach
Ocean St., Ogunquit

This beach is at the eastern end of Ocean Street, off U.S. Highway 1. To reach the beach, you cross a footbridge over the Ogunquit River. You can also access this portion of the beach by taking a right onto Bourne Avenue at its intersection with Route 1 at the Ogunquit Trading Post, north of Ogunquit center. Following Bourne Avenue to its intersection with Ocean Avenue, take a right and turn into the Moody parking lot. As you face the ocean, Footbridge Beach is to your right; to your left is Moody Beach, which is not open to the public.

Wells

The town of Wells has miles of beaches with soft, white sand. Parking fees are charged from 8 AM to 3:30 PM during the summer. Daily non-resident fees in 1998 were $7, plus an extra $1 for RVs and campers (in the lots that can accommodate them). After noon the fee dropped to $4. If you prefer a weekly pass, they were $25 in 1997; a monthly pass was $50, and a season pass was $75. You can purchase permits at the parking lots. You'll find lifeguards and restrooms at the Wells beaches, and food is available near the Mile Road parking lot. If you want to surf, you need the permission of the lifeguards, who will point you to the designated surfing areas.

From July through September dogs are allowed on the beaches but they must be kept on a short leash. Dog waste must be picked up and disposed of properly.

Wells Beach
Mile Rd., Wells

Wells Beach is similar to Ogunquit's, with water on both sides. It is bordered on one side by the sea and on the other by the Webhannet River and salt marsh, where you will often see snowy egrets, great blue herons and a wealth of sea birds.

You can get to the beach by taking Mile Road (across the street from McDonald's). There are parking lots at the end of Mile Road and the end of Atlantic Avenue, which runs the length of the beach. Atlantic Avenue is to your left at the end of Mile Road. Though Atlantic Avenue has been built up with motels and condominiums, Wells Beach is still wide, sandy and beautiful. The Mile Road parking lot does not accept RVs or campers.

Drake's Island Beach
Drake's Island Rd., off U.S. Hwy. 1, Wells

If you prefer a quieter location than Wells Beach, you'll probably like Drake's Island Beach. You can reach this beach by taking a right onto Drake's Island Road off U.S. Highway 1 N., then following it to the end. Limited parking is available for this sandy beach, which becomes Laudholm Beach at its northeastern end. Laudholm Beach is part of Laudholm Farm (see our Attractions chapter), and you are asked not to swim along that portion of beach; the staff tries to maintain an undisturbed habitat for shore-dwelling animals and sea life. Restroom facilities are available at Drake's Island Beach.

Kennebunk

Kennebunk's main beach is commonly referred to in three sections: Gooch's Beach, Middle Beach and Mother's Beach. If you're in the mood for a stroll and for people-watching, a convenient sidewalk stretches the 1.5-mile length of the beach. Parking for the beaches is on-street, by permit only, from the middle of June to the middle of September. You can get permits from the Town Office and police station during the week or the police station on weekends. Both offices are at the corner of Route 1 and Maine Highway 35. Permits are also available from the chamber of commerce in the Lower Village.

Cost for non-resident permits in 1998 were $5 per day, $15 per week and $30 for the season. If your vehicle is longer than 18 feet, it may require additional fees. Guest permit stickers are available for $1, but a resident must buy the pass. Resident permits are $3 for the entire season. Dogs are not allowed on the beaches between 9 AM and 5 PM from June 15 to the day after Labor Day (which is usually the first Monday in September). Lifeguards and restroom facilities or portable toilets are provided at Kennebunk beaches.

Mother's Beach
Beach Ave.,
Kennebunk

So called because it has a colorful playground as well as a sandy beach in a sheltered cove where mothers (and fathers!) like to take their children, Mother's Beach is the southern end of the town's main beach. You can reach it by taking Sea Road to the right at its intersection with Maine Highway 9. Sea Road becomes Beach Avenue, which stretches the length of the beach.

Middle Beach
Beach Ave., Kennebunk

Though this is a continuation of Mother's Beach and leads to Gooch's Beach, Middle Beach has a very different character. Middle Beach is characterized by its half-mile rocky shoreline, which is far better for walking than for sunbathing or swimming. Children will enjoy searching the puddles and pools of water left among the rocks as the tide recedes.

Gooch's Beach
Beach Ave., Kennebunk

Stretching from the rocky end of Middle Beach to the breakwater at the Kennebunk River, Gooch's Beach has fine sand and is popular for walking, swimming, sunbathing and surfing. It's a busy beach, but there is plenty of room for everyone. When you get tired of playing in the surf and sand, take a walk to the river at the beach's northern end, where you can watch the boats heading upriver

and out to sea. During summer, there is access to portable toilet facilities.

Parson's Beach
Brown St., off Maine Hwy. 9, Kennebunk

This small, private beach features hard sand backed by soft dunes covered with dune grass. The beach is private, but the Parson family allows public access. If you walk to its southern end, you'll find the beach is adjacent to the Rachel Carson Wildlife Center. As a result you may see a variety of sea birds along the shore. To reach the beach, take a right onto Maine Highway 9 (Port Road) from U.S. 1. About 2 miles down Route 9, take another right onto Brown Street. You'll find limited free parking at the end of the road. There are no lifeguards or facilities at Parson's Beach.

Kennebunkport

Permits are required for on-street parking at Kennebunkport's Goose Rocks Beach. Permit fees are the same as those for Kennebunk (see above) and may be purchased at the same places. In addition, you can get permits at the Kennebunkport Police Station on Route 9. As in Kennebunk, dogs are not allowed on the beach between 9 AM and 5 PM from June 15 to the day after Labor Day.

Colony Beach
Ocean Ave. and King's Hwy., Kennebunkport

This beach belongs to The Colony Hotel across the street (see our Hotels and Motels chapter). It's small, but the whole family will enjoy scrambling among the rocks, searching for tidal pools to watch (but not touch!) the life in these miniature sea worlds. You can swim here from the hard sand crescent or sit on a bench above the dunes and rocks, watching the sky, the sea and passing boats.

It's a great place to watch the sunset (the beach is on a little peninsula that actually faces southwest). Limited on-street, free parking is available for this beach, which has no lifeguards or facilities.

Goose Rocks Beach
Kings Hwy., Kennebunkport

If you're looking for peace and quiet — a place where you can lie in the sun and listen to the call of the gulls and the sound of breaking waves against the shore, interspersed with the happy cries of children splashing in the shallows — Goose Rocks Beach is the place to be. You'll find 3 miles of soft, white beach in the form of two crescents, fringed with gently waving sea grass in the dunes and separated from the road by a stone wall. At low tide you can walk to Timber Island at the north end of the beach, searching for sand dollars and other treasures as you go. You won't find amusement arcades, bathhouses or other facilities here, but you may encounter true seaside peace and tranquillity. Lifeguards are provided from late June to late August.

To reach the beach, take Dyke Street off Route 9 about 3 miles northeast of Cape Porpoise. Dyke Street will intersect with Kings Highway, which traverses the length of the beach. From Memorial Day to Labor Day you may have trouble finding a place to park, and you will need a permit (see information in the Kennebunk section).

Old Orchard Beach Area

Biddeford

Biddeford has a number of beaches concentrated in the Biddeford Pool area of town off Maine Highway 9, south of Biddeford center and north of Cape Porpoise. No unleashed dogs are allowed on the beaches from 9 AM to 8 PM from May 25 to September 15. Parking permits are required for much of the on-street parking. Cost for an annual permit in 1998 was $5 for residents and $50 for non-residents. Permits are available at City Hall on Main Street.

Biddeford Pool Beach
Maine Hwy. 208, Biddeford Pool

The largest of the town's beaches, Biddeford Pool Beach is 2 miles of wide, white sand and surf. You'll find a bathhouse and lifeguards at this beach. The entrance to the parking lot is across from Hattie's Restaurant, on Route 208 as you head into the Pool.

Fortune's Rocks Beach
Maine Hwy. 208, Biddeford Pool

Though on the small side, Fortune's Rocks Beach is sandy and gets some great surf. It is popular with surfers and also with people who prefer less-crowded beaches. Limited on-street parking is available by permit. In addition to swimming and surfing, you'll find good bird-watching opportunities nearby at Lily Pond. The beach is on Route 208 off Route 9 and has lifeguards and portable toilets.

Hills Beach
Hills Beach Rd., Biddeford Pool

You'll find fine sand and a tidal basin here as well as good bird-watching opportunities on this half-mile beach. To get here, take Hills Beach Road off Maine Highway 9 at the University of New England. There are no facilities or lifeguards and limited on-street free parking.

Rotary Park Beach
Main St., Biddeford

For those who prefer freshwater swimming, this is a treat! Rotary Park Beach is off Main Street (north) in Biddeford, on the banks of the Saco River. The Saco is a beautiful river stretching from the New Hampshire border near the White Mountains to its outlet at the sea at Camp Ellis in Saco. At Rotary Park the river is wide and shallow enough for pleasant swimming near the banks. This unusual town beach offers restroom facilities, lifeguards and a picnic area.

INSIDERS' TIP

If it's hot and humid inland, head to the coast — the temperature can be as much as 10 degrees lower.

Saco

Saco beaches are part of a 7-mile stretch of sand that runs from Camp Ellis to Pine Point. Leashed dogs are allowed on town beaches in-season, and lifeguards are provided at Camp Ellis, Bay View and Kinney Shores. Ferry Beach State Park beach sits between Camp Ellis and Bay View beaches, on the same stretch of sand, and also has lifeguards. But keep in mind that dogs are not permitted on state park beaches.

Camp Ellis Beach
End of Maine Hwy. 9, Saco

At the terminus of Maine Highway 9, at the mouth of the Saco River where it meets the sea, Camp Ellis Beach gets smaller each year because of extensive erosion. Still you'll find deep, soft, white sand. At mid-tide, very shallow water stretches a great distance. As a result, Camp Ellis is a great place for small children to swim; the water even stays a bit warmer because of the shallows. You'll find limited on-street parking, but pay careful at-

tention to the street signs that designate where parking is allowed. In other words, if it says, "No parking this side, " you shouldn't park there. Parking is also available for a fee in Camp Ellis center.

Ferry Beach State Park
Bay View Rd., off Maine Hwy. 9, Saco
• (207) 283-0067

Amenities at Ferry Beach include lifeguards, a bathhouse and nature trails as well as the sandy beach that is reached by crossing a wide, wooden boardwalk over the dunes. To get here, take Maine Highway 9 (Beach Street) at its intersection with Route 1 on Main Street. Follow Route 9 for about 3 miles, then take a left onto Bay View Road. The Camp Ellis Fire Station sits at the corner. Ferry Beach State Park is about one-tenth of a mile ahead on the right side.

Cost for entrance to the park in 1998 was $2 for those 12 and older and 50¢ for those ages 5 through 11; there is no charge for children younger than 5. You can purchase an individual season pass for $20. A $40 family/

Photo: Convention and Visitor's Bureau of Greater Portland

Kids can spend hours digging in the sand.

vehicle pass will allow your vehicle and all passengers into all the parks in the state park system. Permits for people age 65 and older are free, and these also allow entrance to all state parks.

Bay View Beach
Bay View Rd., Saco

If instead of turning in at Ferry Beach State Park you continue along Bay View Road for another half-mile, you will reach an intersection with a dirt parking lot on both sides. These are free parking areas for Bay View Beach. To hit the beach, cross the street and walk past Bay View Villa convent. Parking is also available adjacent to the convent. If the parking lots are full and you park in a posted no-parking area, you will get a ticket. A portable toilet is available, and lifeguards are provided. In-season there is a hot dog and cold drink vendor who sets up by the entrance to the beach.

Kinney Shores Beach
Bay View Rd., Saco

Very limited on-street parking is available for this beach, which extends from Bay View Beach to Goosefare Brook. The brook separates Saco beaches from Old Orchard beaches. Lovely dunes and the winding brook make this end of the beach a joy to explore, but you may be better off parking at Bay View and walking the mile to the brook from there.

Bird lovers might like to know that the rare piping plover can be found nesting in the dunes along Goosefare Brook. If you choose to swim here, be aware of the occasionally strong, variable currents, undertow and riptides at this portion of the beach, especially when the surf is up. Lifeguards will usually put up warning tapes to prevent you from swimming where it is dangerous, but you should take care.

Old Orchard Beach

Old Orchard Beach is a very popular summer destination, particularly for visitors from Quebec, Canada. There are plenty of parking lots in town, which should cost you around $5 per day. Metered parking is available on First Street, Staples Street, along Old Orchard Street and on E. Grand Avenue. Dogs are al-

lowed on Old Orchard beaches after 6 PM in-season. Lifeguards are provided on town beaches during the summer.

Ocean Park Beach
Off Maine Hwy. 9, Old Orchard Beach

You'll find Ocean Park Beach at the southern end of Old Orchard Beach, extending to Goosefare Brook. On-street parking is available, though some spaces are limited to two hours. You won't find any restroom facilities, but lifeguards are provided. Like Kinney Shores, this section of beach will sometimes have strong currents, undertow or riptides. In addition to the soft, white sand, you'll find a variety of things to do in the Ocean Park community. There are a few shops, a shuffleboard court (see Kidstuff) and an old-fashioned ice cream parlor.

Old Orchard Beach
Old Orchard St., Old Orchard Beach

Old Orchard Beach is a center for summer fun. As a result, the beach around the pier can be a bit crowded during the season. Still, the sand is white, wide and soft. Palace Playland Amusement Park (see our Attractions chapter), the pier and arcades are adjacent to the beach, and dozens of take-out, pizza and fast-food places surround the square where Old Orchard Street meets the beach.

Amenities at this portion of the beach include a bathhouse, which is on W. Grand Avenue across from Palace Playland, lifeguards and showers for rinsing where the square turns to beach. Note that this area of ocean occasionally sees strong currents and an undertow, so be cautious. Parking is plentiful, though you'll probably have to pay $4 or $5. There is also limited on-street me-tered parking.

Greater Portland Area

Scarborough

A wealth of fine beaches can be found in Scarborough. Public parking lots are available at Pine Point Beach and Ferry Beach, but you'll have a hard time finding anywhere to park if

Photo: Giselle A. Auger

A wealth of treasures from the sea awaits beachcombers.

you want to visit Higgins Beach. Costs for parking permits in 1998 were $50 for a non-resident season pass, which allows access to both beaches, or $5 per day. Resident permits were $10 for one beach, $15 for both. A second-vehicle permit for residents was available for $2. Restrooms are available at Pine Point Beach, and a portable toilet is provided in-season at Ferry Beach. There are no lifeguards on Scarborough town beaches, and dogs are prohibited from 9 AM to 3 PM from June 15 to September 1.

Pine Point Beach
E. Grand Ave., Scarborough

Sometimes referred to as Grand Beach, Pine Point is a continuation of Old Orchard Beach. It features the same soft, white sand for sitting and, at low tide, a wide expanse of hard-packed sand perfect for walking and running. In addition to a public parking lot, you'll also find free on-street parking along E. Grand Avenue. These spaces are outlined with white borders and fill up quickly in-season.

Scarborough Beach Park
Black Point Rd., Scarborough
• (207) 883-2416

On Black Point Road, as you head towards Prout's Neck from Oak Hill Corner, Scarborough Beach was once a state beach. Today it is privately owned, and there is a fee to access the beach. Dogs are not allowed on the beach from May to September 15 from 8:30 AM to 8 PM. Cost for a day pass to the beach is $3 for adults and $1 for kids ages 5 five through 11. A season day pass valid for all occupants of a vehicle during operating hours is $50, while an individual season pass, valid 24 hours a day, is $30. Amenities at this beach include lifeguards, a snack bar, toilet facilities and a rinse shower. In addition to the sandy beach, there are dunes, a bathhouse and picnic areas.

Ferry Beach
Black Point Rd., Scarborough

Also known as Western Beach, Ferry Beach is a lovely curve of sand near the Prout's

INSIDERS' TIP

Visit our beaches in the off-season, and you'll get free parking and plenty of space to think and roam.

Neck Country Club golf course on Black Point Road. There is a small parking lot (with fees as outlined above), little surf and no lifeguards, but the view across the bay — with Pine Point, Old Orchard and Saco beaches stretched like a white ribbon along the shore in the distance — is breathtaking on a sunny day.

Higgins Beach
Maine Hwy. 77, Scarborough

Located in the small community of the same name, Higgins Beach is a small crescent of sandy beach frequented mainly by those who live in the area. Parking is problematic, but if you stay at one of the local inns or rent a cottage, you can simply walk to the beach (see our Summer Rentals and Bed and Breakfasts and Inns chapters for more information). You get to Higgins Beach by taking Route 77 from Black Point Road. The Higgins Beach turnoff is a couple of miles on your right and is well-marked.

Cape Elizabeth

Cape Elizabeth has some wonderful parks, both town and state managed, that include swimming beaches. Remember, dogs are not allowed on beaches in state parks.

Crescent Beach State Park
Off Maine Hwy. 77,
Cape Elizabeth • (207) 767-3625

With its proximity to Portland, it isn't surprising that this is one of the most popular family beaches in the area. In addition to its wide, beautiful swimming beach, there are picnic areas, a snack bar and bathhouse. Cost for entrance to the park in 1998 was $2 for those 12 and older and 50¢ for those ages 5 through 11; there is no charge for children younger than 5. As with the other state parks listed, individual season passes are $20, and

$40 family/vehicle passes will allow your vehicle and all passengers into all the parks in the state system. Permits for those age 65 and older are free and also allow entrance to all state parks.

Fort Williams
Shore Rd. (Maine Hwy. 77), Cape Elizabeth • (207) 799-7652

There is no fee to enter this town maintained park, which is home to the Portland Head lighthouse and Fort Williams (see our Attractions chapter). In addition to the lighthouse and fort, you'll find a playground area for children and a crescent beach between two headlands. There are lots of rocks to climb on and a large lawn — a nice place to sit and read the Sunday paper while the kids use up their energy on the playground's swings and slides. Restroom facilities are available in the parking lot nearest the lighthouse. There are no lifeguards.

South Portland

From May through September, dogs are not allowed on Willard Beach from 9 AM to 9 PM. Limited free parking is available for the beach, and lifeguards and facilities are provided.

Willard Beach
Beach St., South Portland

Despite the fact that this is the closest beach to Portland, it remains primarily a neighborhood beach. It is a sandy, slightly curving beach that's about a mile long, with Southern Maine Technical College and Fort Preble at its northern end.

Portland

You might be surprised to find that a city surrounded by water on three sides has only one public beach, and it's a small one at that.

But the beach and surrounding promenade make for a relaxing afternoon, so pack up your picnic and head there.

East End Beach
Eastern Promenade, E. Cutter St., Portland • (207) 774-1066

The sandy beach below Portland's Eastern Prom is just a few hundred yards long, but it's the only place you can go for a dip in the harbor on Portland's side of the water. Parking along the street or in the lot is free, just like entrance to the park and beach. Dogs are allowed on the prom but are excluded from the sand. No lifeguards are on duty, but the promenade does have bathroom facilities and park rangers.

Brunswick, Bath and Boothbay Harbor Area

Brunswick

Since most of Brunswick isn't on the ocean, you might not expect to find a beach here. It does have one, Thomas Point Beach, which is just big enough to build a sandcastle on and dip your toes in the water. Actually, you may want to dip a lot more. Because the beach is on a tidal inlet, the water is much warmer than the Atlantic. Also, you won't have to worry about waves or strong ocean currents.

Thomas Point Beach
29 Meadow Rd., Brunswick • (207) 725-6009

Just off Maine Highway 24 in Brunswick, this small beach is on Thomas Bay, an inlet of the salty New Meadows River. The privately owned beach is part of a larger camping and park complex. (If you want to stay the night, see Thomas Point Beach Campground in our Camping chapter.) There is plenty of parking, rolling fields, picnic and play areas and bath-

rooms. Open mid-May through October, visitors are welcome from 9 AM to sunset. However, pets are not allowed at any time. The cost is $3 for adults and $2 for children. Look for Meadow Road just off Maine Hwy. 24. Signs point the way to the beach.

Phippsburg

Because Phippsburg is a peninsula with wide, saltwater rivers on either side and the Atlantic at its tip, it has some of the best beaches around. However, most of its shore is either too rocky to swim off of or is covered with pine trees. We'll point out the two public beaches where you can go for a long stroll or a cool (and we mean cool) dip.

Head Beach
Small Point Rd. • (207) 389-1827

This small stretch of beach connects the peninsula with Hermit Island and has water on either side. It's owned by Myron Wyman who lets the public use it for a fee of $3 per car to get in; parking is along the beach once you drive through the gate.

One nice thing about Head Beach is that it's easier to keep track of children here than at the much larger Popham Beach (see subsequent listing). At one end of the parking area, a small camp store and take-out restaurant belong to Hermit Island Campground (see Camping). The beach has a fresh-water shower to get rid of the sea salt and has a bathroom. To get here, take Maine Highway 216 all the way to its end, then bear right onto Small Point Road. The beach entrance will be on your right. Leashed dogs are allowed on the beach.

Popham Beach/Hunnewell Beach
Maine Hwy. 209, Phippsburg • (207) 389-1335

One of the largest stretches of sand around, this beach wraps around a finger of land at the tip of the peninsula and is part of

Photo: Pauline Dimino

Fine feathered friends flock to a beach party.

Popham Beach State Park. The sandy, 2-plus mile beach begins at Fort Popham (see our Attractions chapter) at the mouth of the Kennebec River and winds its way around the point to face the open ocean. If you walk to the northernmost tip of the beach, where the fort is, look across the river and you'll see historic old houses in the fishing village of Georgetown. This is also a good place to watch fishing boats and sailboats as they glide into the mouth of the river or sail out to the open sea.

While very popular for swimming, the beach isn't overcrowded, even during the sum-mer season. However, it is best to come bright and early if you want to find parking. There are several different parking areas to choose from. If you're lucky, you'll find a free parking spot in front of the fort at the very end of High-way 209. If you find a spot in the state parking lot, which is clearly marked on the right side, you'll also be doing well. A spot there will cost $2 per adult and 50¢ for kids ages 5 to 11. It's free for folks older than 65. The park is open from April 15 through October 30. During the off-season, you can park along the road and walk the beach for free.

The park is open from 9 AM to sunset.

Dogs are not allowed. One word of caution: Because of the beach's location, it often has strong undercurrents and a riptide. So don't go in deep unless you're a strong ocean swimmer. (For more information on Popham Beach State Park, see our Parks and Recreation chapter.)

Georgetown

The beaches here are at Reid State Park, about 20 minutes east of U.S. Highway 1. You'll have to pay to get in, but, like many beaches in this area of Maine, it shouldn't be overly crowded.

Reid State Park
Seguinland Rd., Georgetown
• (207) 371-2303

This state park has two sandy beaches — Half Mile Beach and Mile Beach — backed by beautiful salt marshes, dunes, rocky coves and trails. The 766 surrounding acres of rustic property are astoundingly beautiful and serve as prime examples of the Maine coast. It costs $2.50 for adults and 50¢ for children ages 5 to 11 to enter the park (children younger than 5 are admitted free), but the price will get you parking and all-day use of the park, which is open from 9 AM to sunset. Currents and undertow are occasionally strong at Reid, so be careful.

The park is open year round; lifeguards are posted from the middle of June to the end of August. No dogs are allowed on the sandy areas, though they can be walked on a leash in other areas of the park. Restrooms with flush toilets and changing areas are available. Visit the park after September 30 and before May 15 and you'll get in free, but we can guarantee the water will be freezing! People older than 65 get in free all year long. (For more on Reid State Park, see our Parks and Recreation chapter.)

Boothbay Harbor

There are two good swimming areas in Boothbay Harbor. Because this area of the coast is mostly rock, you won't find the stretching canvases of sand common in the southernmost area of the state. But kids will love lifting up pebbles and rocks from the beaches to search for small crabs and other sea life. None of the swimming areas in the harbor have lifeguards, but dogs are allowed. For more information on any of the Boothbay Harbor beaches, call the chamber of commerce at (207) 633-2353.

Barrett Park
Lobster Cove Rd., Boothbay Harbor

On the east side of the harbor, this small beach is sandy at low tide (the best time to come) and is surrounded by a small park with picnic areas and outdoor grills. It's got a nice big lawn above the water, so this is the better beach in Boothbay Harbor to bring your dog for a game of Frisbee.

Grimes Cove
Ocean Point, Maine Hwy. 96,
Boothbay Harbor

This small pebble beach is on the left as you round the tip of Ocean Point. You'll know you've found it when you see water for the first time since heading out to the point. Parking along the road is free. There are no facilities.

In 1997 more than 1.2 million people bought tickets to watch the Portland Sea Dogs play Class AA Eastern League baseball at Hadlock Field.

Spectator Sports

Ask someone what the area's most popular spectator sports are and you're likely to hear, "Watching the tourists." We don't have Major League teams, and we only have a couple of large sports stadiums.

But what we don't have in prestige and renown, we make up for with a lot of enthusiasm. Last year more than 1.2 million people bought tickets to watch the Portland Sea Dogs play Class AA Eastern League baseball at Hadlock Field. The Sea Dogs drew more spectators than just about any other baseball team in their class. And every year the Portland Pirates draw sellout crowds to their ice hockey games.

If you're looking for more local action, watch our college teams play basketball, soccer, lacrosse or a wide variety of other sports. If that doesn't interest you, place a few bets at a harness racing track, or, for more comfort, try one of our off-track betting parlors where you can sit in a cozy lounge and watch horse racing simulcasts from tracks across the nation. Brunswick and Bath each have an OTB, as they're known, just a few minutes apart.

To make it easy to find what you're looking for, we've organized the events in this chapter according to the category of competition and then from south to north along the coast. So find your favorite sport, put on a baseball cap and some sunscreen, pack a couple cans of soda and the kids, buy your peanuts and popcorn and give a cheer for our home teams. We've got plenty to keep you busy, and chances are you'll have much more fun than you would watching us.

Auto Racing

Beech Ridge Motor Speedway
70 Holmes Rd., Scarborough
• **(207) 883-6030**

This is the only NASCAR (National Association of Stock Car Auto Racing) sanctioned track in the state. Of the 800 to 900 auto racing tracks in the country, only 100 are official NASCAR tracks. The oval at Beech Ridge is semi-banked and one-third of a mile. The speedway, opened in 1949 by Scarborough local Jim McConnell, is now in its 50th year in operation. McConnell sold the track to Calvin Reynolds of Gorham, who ran it from 1973 until 1980, when he sold it to the Cusack family. Today the speedway is owned by Andy and Glenn Cusack, who took over ownership from their parents a couple of years ago.

You might not know it, but stock car racing is a popular family spectator sport. The bleachers at Beech Ridge hold up to 6,500 fans in the grandstands and 2,000 in the pit area. This isn't just a guy thing. Families with small children fill the bleachers, bringing cushions and blankets and carrying binoculars. They even come out on cold, gray evenings when it looks like rain.

In 1997 the track began a "Thursday Thunder" series where amateurs race in six divisions: Beetle Bugs (four-cylinder compact cars), Mad Bombers (full-size stock cars), Ladies League (full-size stock cars driven by women), Truck Series (full-size stock trucks), Go-Karts (kids' caged race carts) and Legend

Photo: Convention and Visitor's Bureau of Greater Portland

Scarborough Downs is a safe bet if you're looking for excitement.

Cars (sanctioned specification cars). Amateurs are defined as anyone who has not raced professionally and holds a valid driver's license. For people who dream of being race-car drivers, this is a place where they can make the dream a reality. It is a kind of farm league for Daytona. Successful big-time drivers proceed through four levels of racing, beginning with tracks like Beech Ridge, then moving up to a Regional NASCAR tour, progressing to the Busch Grand National Series, and finally, when they are one of the top 50 drivers, advancing to the Winston Cup tour.

While stock car racing began as races using basic "stock" cars (not significantly altered from what you might see on the streets), the sport, even on the scale you'll see at Beech Ridge, has become highly specialized. The closest you'll get to races involving unmodi-

fied, road-legal cars at Beech Ridge is on amateur nights. Thursday night ticket prices are only $3 for adults and teens, with children 12 and younger admitted free.

Regular races take place on Saturdays from 7 to 9 PM. The racing season runs from April to mid-September, and sometimes stretches until the beginning of October if there have been a lot of rain-outs. Entrance costs $9 for adults, $5 for children ages 6 to 13, and children younger than 6 are admitted free. For special events, like the Busch North races, ticket prices rise to $25 for adults and $6 for children 6 to 13.

Oxford Plains Speedway
877 Main St. (Maine Hwy. 26), Oxford
• (207) 539-8865

OK, this one's a little west of the coast, but

since it is the largest auto racing track in the state, we thought we'd include it. With a three-eighths-mile track, open bleachers for 15,000 people and a 65-acre parking lot, there is plenty of room for both racers and fans.

Oxford Plains holds 15- to 35-lap races in five divisions, with mini stocks, late-model stocks and amateur stocks among them. The season runs from late April through October, with most races scheduled for 7 PM Saturday night. Special shows also take place on Sunday. The track's most popular event is the Oxford 250, which is scheduled around the Fourth of July and wraps up with a fireworks display. If you're hungry, hit the concession stand; if you're thirsty, try the track-side lounge for cold beer and wine. Tickets to regular events during the 1997 season were $10 for adults and $5 for children between the ages of 7 and 16. Kids younger than 6 get in free.

Wiscasset Raceway
W. Alna Rd., Wiscasset • (207) 589-4780, (207) 882-4271 (when track is open)

The 6,000 seats at this track fill up fast, so be sure to get here a little early on race day. Six classes of drivers compete on this raceway's one-third-mile track every Saturday from April through September. You can bring your own food or buy it at the concession stand. There is also a lounge that serves beer. General admission tickets are $8 for adults, $6 for seniors and students and $3 for children. Kids younger than 5 get in free.

Baseball

Portland Sea Dogs
Hadlock Field, 271 Park Ave., Portland
• (207) 879-9500, (800) 936-3647

Before the Sea Dogs, Portland was without professional baseball for 35 years. But now in their fifth season here, the Sea Dogs, AA affiliates of the Florida Marlins, have been hitting and pitching away within our borders at Hadlock Field.

They've made quite a name for themselves. With 229 wins in the past three years, they have been victorious in more regular season games than any other Eastern League team. They also won back-to-back Northern Division regular season championship titles in 1995 and 1996.

More than two dozen Sea Dogs players have gone on to play for the Marlins, including Charles Johnson, Edgar Renteria, Jay Powell, Luis Castillo, Billy McMillon and Livan Hernandez. Because so many people crowd the 6,500-seat, open-air stadium to watch the team play, a stadium expansion project is in the works. Ticket prices range from $4 to $6 for adults and $2 to $5 for children ages 2 through 16 and seniors. Kids younger than 2 get in free if they sit on a lap, and group rates are a little less. And, just in case you're wondering, a "sea dog" is another name for a common harbor seal.

College Sports

University of Southern Maine
37 College Ave., Gorham • (207) 780-5434

Spring, fall or winter, you can find some great Division III NCAA athletic events at this college campus just 15 minutes west of Scarborough.

In autumn you'll find men's and women's soccer, tennis and cross-country matches, as well as men's golf and women's field hockey and volleyball. In spring get ready to watch the defending NCAA Division III champions play baseball. The school also fields teams in softball, men's tennis and men's and women's outdoor track and field. Indoor winter events include men's and women's basketball and track and men's ice hockey and wrestling. The women's basketball team holds an NCAA record for all divisions for winning 20 or more (of roughly 25) games each season for the past 17 years.

The vast majority of events take place on the Gorham campus. All the playing fields are

within easy walking distance of each other, and a new, Olympic-size ice hockey rink and a $5.5 million fieldhouse were completed in early 1998. Fall and spring sports take place in the daytime throughout the week, and most winter events take place on weekday evenings or Saturday afternoons.

Admission for all events is $4 for adults and $2 for students and seniors. Kids younger than 6 get in free. To get here take Exit 6 off Interstate 95 and turn left at the light after paying the highway toll. At your second traffic light, take another left onto Maine Highway 114 and follow it all the way to the school.

Bowdoin College
5 Bath St., Brunswick • (207) 725-3000

With one of the top-ranked college athletic programs in the country, Bowdoin College provides free, year-round entertainment for its fans.

In spring you'll enjoy baseball, softball and men's and women's lacrosse and tennis. Catch football, golf, cross-country, sailing and soccer as well as women's field hockey and volleyball in the fall. And come for men's and women's basketball, ice hockey, skiing, squash, swimming and indoor track in the winter.

The women's squash team has been ranked No. 5 in the nation. Most of the teams at Bowdoin are NCAA Division III except the ski team, which is Division I. Because squash and sailing are not typical college sports, they are also ranked separately.

Out of 250 Division III schools in the country during the 1995-96 season, Bowdoin ranked ninth for sending the most teams to NCAA championships and advancing farther in the competition than most. When the teams are playing at home, the games are on campus — either out on the school's expansive fields, in its ice hockey rink or basketball court or at the covered Farley Field House, which has a track and seating for 1,000. Games are played most days of the week, and you can call the school to get a schedule.

Harness Racing

Harness racing is an old tradition in Maine. Its roots go back to the start of agricultural fairs when people would meet to compare the best of their produce, their jams and jellies, cakes and pumpkins. As a matter of course, they also began to compare their animals — "I'll bet your horse can't run as fast as mine" — and they began to race. Today you can still find harness racing at country fairs and at Maine's two commercial harness tracks, Scarborough Downs and Bangor Raceway.

Called harness racing because the horses are harnessed to simple, two-wheeled carriages called sulkies, races usually take place on half-mile tracks, which competitors circle twice to complete a mile. The type of horse raced is called a Standardbred (as opposed to the thoroughbreds you see in the Kentucky Derby). Following are listings for our harness track and a couple of off-track betting parlors in the area.

Scarborough Downs
U.S. Hwy. 1 and Maine Hwy. 9 (Payne Rd.), Scarborough • (207) 883-4331

Whether you feel like making a wager or two or not, you'll be entertained by the action at Scarborough Downs. Live harness racing is held Wednesday through Sunday from April until November. Starting time (called post time) is 7:30 PM, except on Sundays, when racing begins at 1 PM.

You'll find a choice of two atmospheres at Scarborough Downs. You can either watch and bet on races from the large, circa 1950s grandstand, where white picnic tables and wrought-iron benches with wooden seats give a country fair feeling, or you can watch from the newer clubhouse, which features a nice

restaurant on its upper level. The clubhouse is open year round from 11 AM until midnight for simulcast racing. With television sets at each table, you can sit in comfort and watch simulcast races from across the country.

Entrance to the grandstand was $2 in 1997 with clubhouse entrance costing an extra 50¢. The minimum wager you can place is $2.

Winner's
The Atrium Inn,
21 Gurnet Rd., Brunswick
• (207) 725-8801, (800) 386-1127

Come to this off-track betting parlor and watch the nation's biggest harness and thoroughbred races from the comfort of a lounge booth with a big plate of what could be New England's best nachos (management claims they are) in front of you.

The center features 36 wide-screen televisions, hand-painted, large-as-life horse murals and a VIP lounge, where the more serious bettor can sit at a private booth with a private television set and the controls to go with it. Winner's broadcasts horse racing every day of the week from noon to midnight.

Just next door to the OTB, you'll find Winner's Sports Grill, a family restaurant equipped with 24 TVs that show every imaginable type of sporting event. It also has one screen that is about 8 feet in diameter. You can stay the night in one of The Atrium's 186 rooms and enjoy the indoor pool, volleyball court and gym (see our Accommodations chapter).

The Lower Deck
Rafters Restaurant, 737 Washington St., Bath • (207) 443-6631

More than 35 large-screen TVs light up the lower level of this Greek, Italian and American cuisine restaurant, where an off-track betting parlor broadcasts live horse racing from tracks across the country. You can lounge at a sporty black table and enjoy lunch or dinner — or

INSIDERS' TIP

If you're going to the raceway, pack a picnic lunch or dinner and save some money. But don't bring glass bottles, which aren't allowed, or alcohol, which is only permitted if it's purchased on site.

The Portland Pirates are the city's AHL hockey team.

just have a drink in between at the fully equipped bar — while watching the spectacular display of strength as the racers rumble down the track.

The parlor, which is just a couple of years old, is open from 11 AM to midnight. Greek friends and co-owners Peter Bisiass and Nick Papadopolous opened the restaurant 12 years ago and in the upstairs section have served a feast of their favorite dishes to loyal customers ever since.

Ice Hockey

Portland Pirates
85 Free St., Portland • (207) 828-4665

Part of the American Hockey League, the Pirates are the training affiliate of the National Hockey League's Washington Capitals. Their first season here (which goes from October through April) was 1993-94, and they wowed home crowds by winning the Calder Cup for being the best team in the league. In the 1995-96 season, they returned to the AHL Championships but lost game 7 by a score of 2-1.

The team formerly played in Baltimore and was known as the Skipjacks. It moved to Maine's biggest city when the hockey team that used to play here left town. Tom Ebright, the majority owner of the Pirates, died in July 1997, leaving his share of the team to his wife, Joyce Ebright. The team was put up for sale in February '98, and was later purchased by partners Chet Homer and David Fisher. The Pirates play at the Cumberland County Civic Center (see listing in this chapter under Venues for directions).

Games are usually pretty packed, and ticket prices are reasonable, ranging from $8 to $13 for adults, $5 for children younger than 12 and $7 for seniors. Call the box office to order.

Venues

Cumberland County Civic Center
1 Civic Center Sq., Portland
• (207) 775-3458

The largest all-season, climate-controlled sports and entertainment complex in northern New England, the Civic Center seats close to 9,000 people. The arena floor easily converts from an ice hockey rink to a basketball court or a concert stage depending on what is needed. Convention and trade shows also rent the center.

The Portland Pirates regularly play ice hockey here (see listing under Ice Hockey section of this chapter), but other events, from the Ice Capades to Harlem Globetrotters basketball, are common. The Boston Celtics sometimes play exhibition games at the center, which has at other times, hosted figure skating, an Olympic volleyball exhibition, WWF wrestling, the All American Rodeo and the Shrine Circus.

Call the box office to find out what is going on during your visit. To get to the center from Interstate 295, take Exit 7 onto Franklin Street and proceed through four traffic lights. At the fifth light, turn right onto Middle Street. Drive through two more lights, and you will see the center on the right. The parking garage is just beyond the center.

Boston is a beautiful, historical city that's closer to Maine than you might think.

Daytrips & Weekend Getaways

While we hope there's enough in Southern Maine to keep you happily entertained, we understand that some of you might want to take advantage of other fun or educational opportunities that aren't too far away from here. To that end, we've included this chapter on Daytrips and Weekend Getaways, featuring a variety of places to visit that you might not have realized were so close — places like Yarmouth, Nova Scotia; Boston; and our state capital, Augusta. In addition you'll find information on Portsmouth, New Hampshire, as well as the Sebago Lake Region west of Portland and Bar Harbor to the northeast.

Each daytrip is organized with an introduction, general directions to the destination, a rundown of some of the attractions available and a selection of accommodations and restaurants. So if you have the urge to explore beyond our Southern Coast, read on — there's bound to be something in here to get you going!

Boston

Boston is a beautiful, historic city that's famous for its early role in our country's struggle for independence, and as the home of some of the finest universities in the world. It's also closer to Maine than you might think. From Portland, Boston is only about a two-hour bus or car ride south.

Once in the city, your options are limitless — from shopping at Fanueil Hall Marketplace or in the downtown shopping district to exploring the Freedom Trail and its historic sites or checking out some of the city's many museums. You might also want to visit the observation deck of the John Hancock Tower, or take a peek at quaint Trinity Church right next door. The tower, a modern building sided with panes of glass that reflect the sky, provides a striking contrast to the old stone facade of the church. From Trinity Church you can stroll along Newbury Street and check out the funky, arty stores there, or stop for something to eat or a drink at one of the street's many cafes. If you've always wanted to visit Harvard Square, take the Red Line subway to Cambridge and have a look around. You'll find shops and restaurants around the square, amid the beauty of the old brick buildings and beautiful trees of the university.

Like most major metropolitan centers, there's much to do in Boston at night. Theater shows and those hard-to-find artsy movies, nightclubs and big-name music events are just some of the options you can choose from for evening entertainment. For more information on the city and what's going to be happening when you're there, call the Greater Boston Convention and Visitors Bureau at (617) 536-4100. It's located at 2 Copley Place.

Getting There

You can get to Boston by bus, plane or car. Since 1996 the city has been undergoing a major road restructuring program. As a result, many roads are under construction, which can cause long delays. People in the area refer to the road project as "The Big Dig." When you get there, you'll see why.

Because of the current hassles of negotiating Boston by car, we suggest you take a bus to the city and save yourself the stress of dealing with traffic in an unknown and confusing city. If you must drive, it will take about two hours from Portland, barring traffic delays. Take the Maine Turnpike (Interstate 95) south and remain on I-95 for about 90 minutes (100 miles). You'll have to pay a 50-cent toll getting on the turnpike, a $1.25 toll at York and another $1 toll in New Hampshire.

From I-95 in Massachusetts you'll see signs for Boston and U.S. Highway 1. Follow the signs. Once you're in the city, we suggest you park in a parking garage as soon as possible and use the subway to get around. All-day parking usually costs around $10. A single ride on the subway, referred to as the "T," costs 85¢.

Two bus lines operate between Boston and the Southern Coast area of Maine — Concord Trailways and Vermont Transit Lines. Both travel to the city daily. You can take Concord Trailways, (207) 828-1151, (800) 639-3317, from Bath, Brunswick and Portland year round. In-season, you can also pick it up in Biddeford, Kennebunkport, Ogunquit and Portsmouth, New Hampshire. (For more information on buses to Boston, including fares, see our Getting Here, Getting Around chapter.)

Unless you're staying very near the airport, flying to Boston will probably take as long as driving or taking the bus. For extensive information on flight services and other amenities at Boston's Logan International Airport, see our Getting Here, Getting Around chapter.

Attractions

Freedom Trail

There's a lot to do in Boston. For those who don't mind walking, we suggest you start your visit with a stroll along the Freedom Trail, which begins at the information booth at Boston Common, near the Park Street subway station on the Green and Red lines. The Trail incorporates a 2.5-mile walk that brings you to 15 historic sites in the city including Boston Common, Paul Revere's house and Fanueil Hall. Here we highlight some of the places you'll visit on the Trail.

The tour begins at Boston Common, the first United States National Park. Land for the Common was purchased in 1634 by Puritan settlers for use as a communal grazing area for the residents' sheep, oxen and cattle. Later it served as a campground for British soldiers just before the American Revolution. Today the Common is a popular gathering place for Bostonians on fine sunny days.

From the Common you'll have a good view of the "new" gold-domed State House, which sits across from the park. Though 200 years old, the State House is termed new to distinguish it from the Old State House, which also lies along the Freedom Trail. The State House was designed by architect Charles Bullfinch, who went on to design the U.S. Capitol in Washington. Its cornerstone was laid in 1795 by Samuel Adams on the site of John Hancock's pasture. Originally covered in wood shingles painted white, the dome of the State House was gilded in 1861 and has remained so ever since.

Also along the Trail you'll have the opportunity to see the Old North Church. It's famous for the "one if by land, two if by sea" signal that launched Paul Revere's warning ride from Boston to the towns of Lexington and Concord. The British were, indeed, coming to arrest Hancock and Adams and to seize or destroy patriot military supplies. The church was chosen for the signal because at that time it had the tallest spire in Boston. For those of you who've forgotten your American history, two lanterns were hung in the spire that night! The Old North Church is the oldest church building in Boston, and it houses the oldest church bells in the United States. They were cast in Gloucester, England, in 1744.

At Fanueil Hall you can combine history with shopping and eating. In addition to the meeting hall, with its Grasshopper weather vane, there's a long building filled with all kinds of food and drink vendors, and two more buildings filled with specialty shops selling all kinds of goodies. Charming vendor carts are also displayed in the cobbled courtyards, and you'll often find street entertainers (from musicians to magicians) enthralling the crowds.

Other sites along the Freedom Trail that you might find of interest include the USS Constitution, the Bunker Hill monument and The Boston Tea Party Ship. We would suggest, however, that you stop your walking tour at Copp's Burial Ground and take a taxi to see the USS Constitution and Bunker Hill. The Trail becomes somewhat isolated at the Burial Ground, and you may feel safer retracing your steps and taking a cab.

Museum of Fine Arts

If the weather isn't conducive to walking or you'd simply prefer a museum, you can choose from several world-class venues in Boston. Art lovers will be delighted by the world-renowned Museum of Fine Arts, 465 Huntington Avenue, (617) 267-9300. Children will enjoy the art of the pharaohs of Egypt (there are thrilling mummy cases and exotic pottery) while older folks will enjoy the wide selection of paintings — from Rembrandt and El Greco to Sargent, Van Gogh and Picasso. Those of you who are fond of the Impressionists will be happy to learn the collection here is known as one of the best in the world.

If you're hoping to see a particular painting, however, you should call ahead to make sure it will be on display. Because of its reputation, the museum often sends well-loved pieces on tour with various exhibitions. Most recently this included a number of their paintings by Monet. Regardless of what might not be on display, there is sure to be some work of art in this extensive museum that will take your fancy. You'll find room after room of paintings well-placed for pleasant viewing, though the polished stone floors may get a little hard on your feet after a while. Benches in many rooms afford the opportunity to sit and gaze.

For a more sustaining break, you can enjoy a drink and some food in the Fine Arts Restaurant, the Galleria Cafe or the court-level cafeteria, which offers value-conscious family fare and outdoor seating in good weather. Admission to the MFA is $10 for adults and $8 for seniors and college students. During West Wing-only hours on Thursday and Friday after 5 PM, these rates are reduced to $8 and $7, respectively. Museum members and young people aged 17 and younger are admitted free. Those on a budget will be glad to note that on Wednesday evenings from 4 to 9:45 PM, admission to the museum is by voluntary contribution.

Depending on the exhibit, there may be an additional charge for special Gund Gallery exhibitions, regardless of the daily admission price. There's no admission charge for visitors who are using only the museum shop or libraries. The Museum of Fine Arts is open daily, except for Thanksgiving and Christmas.

Museum of Science

Visitors who prefer a more interactive museum experience or who are interested in the sciences should try the Museum of Science, Science Park, McGrath/O'Brien Highway, (617) 723-2500. You'll find the Museum of Science 200 yards from the T's Science Park station on the Green Line "E" train (Lechmere Line). Exact change (85¢) or tokens are required for the train.

Six men interested in natural history founded the Museum of Science in 1830. Since then it has grown to embrace all the sciences, with exhibits on space exploration, electricity and telecommunications, anatomy and physiology and the natural world. Children will enjoy the wave machine and the perpetual motion pendulum, which creates nifty drawings in sand when you give it a push. It's hard for anyone not to be awed by the Tyrannosaurus Rex skeleton that rises through two floors of the museum's central entrance. Many interactive exhibits can keep the whole family entertained for hours.

In addition to the exhibits, the museum is home to the Charles Hayden Planetarium and the Mugar Omni Theater, which opened in 1987. At the theater, state-of-the-art film technology projects larger-than-life images onto a five-story high, domed screen, creating a "you are there" experience for viewers.

The Science Museum is open daily except Thanksgiving and Christmas. Cost for admission to the exhibit halls is $9 for adults, $7 for senior citizens and children ages 3 through 14. There's no admission charge for children younger than 3. Admission to the Omni Theater is $7.50 for adults and $5.50 for senior citizens and children 3 through 14. Admission to the planetarium is $7.50 for adults and $5.50 for seniors and children. Discounts are available on combination tickets.

New England Aquarium

If you have an interest in the creatures of the sea, you shouldn't miss the New England Aquarium, Central Wharf, (617) 973-5200. Located a few minutes' walk from Fanueil Hall, the aquarium (subway stop: Blue Line, "Aquarium") features an enormous, circular central tank with a teeming multitude of fish. You'll see octopi, sea turtles and sharks as well as eels and other nifty creatures. We bet it won't be just the kids with their noses glued to the glass!

In addition to the main exhibit, you'll also find seals, dolphin shows and the opportunity to take a harbor or whale-watching cruise (costs are detailed below). When the New England Aquarium opened in 1969, it was the first of the nation's modern aquariums. Today it is working to maintain its modernity. In September 1996 the Aquarium began the "Aquarium 2000" program that will triple the size of the facility. The expanded aquarium will feature technological innovations such as high-definition TV and virtual-reality and other computer interactions that will allow visitors to experience the full range of aquatic life.

Admission to the aquarium is $12 for anyone age 12 and older, $11 for seniors and $6 for children age 3 through 11. Children younger than 3 are admitted free. Cost for admission in combination with the purchase of a Whale Watch ticket is $5 for adults, $4.50 for senior citizens and $4 for children. Whale Watch tickets are $24 for adults, $19 for seniors and college students, $17.50 for students ages 12 through 18 and $16.50 for children from 3 to 11. Combination tickets are also available for the aquarium and the "Science at Sea" harbor cruises. This combination is $15.50 for adults, $13 for seniors and children aged 12 through 18 and $10.25 for children 3 through 11. For more Whale Watch information, call (617) 973-5281.

Accommodations

There are many places to stay in Boston, but as in most metropolitan areas, you're not likely to find a room for less than $100 a night. Here, we recommend a few hotels scattered in various parts of the city.

Near Back Bay you might want to try The Lenox Hotel, at 710 Boylston Street, (617) 536-5300. Views of the Charles River and Back Bay are excellent, and Boston Marathon aficionados should note that Room 1100 has the best view of the finish line for the annual, mid-April, Patriot's Day race. Amenities at the Lenox include an exercise room, bar and restaurant. Room rates run from about $190 for a single to $235 for a double and $450 for a suite. The nearest subway stop is at Copley (Green Line).

If you prefer staying near the Public Gardens, you might try the Tremont House Hotel, 275 Tremont Street, (617) 426-1400, or The Ritz-Carlton, 15 Arlington Street, (617) 536-5700. From the Tremont House you'll have views of Boston Common and the Public Gardens. On site are two nightclubs, the Roxy and the Jukebox, along with the Tremont Deli restaurant. Room rates run about $134 for a single or double and start around $174 for a suite. The nearest subway stop is Boylston (Green Line). All guest rooms on the front of the Ritz-Carlton offer a view of the Public Gardens. The hotel features a pool, health club and a choice of restaurants. Room prices start around $245 for a single and move up to $285 for a double and $325 for a suite. The nearest subway stop is Arlington (Green Line).

Near Boston Harbor, you'll find the Boston Marriott Long Wharf, 296 State Street, (617) 227-0800. Located on a wharf overlooking the

www.insiders.com

See this and many other **Insiders' Guide**® destinations online.

Visit us today!

INSIDERS' TIP

When you visit Boston's State House, you might want to take a look at the Robert Gould Shaw Memorial across Beacon Street. The memorial was sculpted by Augustus Saint-Gaudens to honor the 26-year-old son of a Boston family who led the first black regiment to fight in the Civil War. The movie Glory recounted the regiment's story.

harbor, the Marriott Long Wharf's location is ideal for exploring Fanueil Hall. Amenities include a pool, health club, bar and restaurant. Room rates begin around $249 for a single or double and move to $285 for a suite. The nearest subway stop is Aquarium (Blue Line).

Restaurants

Boston is a diverse city that is home to a wide variety of cultures. As such, it has a wealth of dining opportunities to explore. Here we've selected a few of the most noteworthy.

No Name Restaurant, at 15½ The Fish Pier, (617) 338-7539, has served locals since 1917. It's argued to be the oldest restaurant in the city that has been owned by the same family in the same location. It was opened by the present owner's father and originally catered to local fishermen. Today it seats around 150 people and has hosted many famous people, including President John F. Kennedy. Throughout its history No Name has received many awards and has frequently been listed by various publications among the "Best of Boston."

Not surprisingly, the restaurant, which is open daily, specializes in fresh seafood. Cost for seafood entrees other than lobster run around $10 per person; for lobster, it will be around $16.

Whether or not you decide to stay at the Ritz-Carlton, 15 Arlington Street, (617) 536-5700, you might want to consider dining there. This fine hotel's rooftop restaurant was renovated in 1997. Thursday through Saturday the restaurant offers dinner and dancing with a live orchestra, and on Sunday there's a live jazz brunch. Diners will love the view and atmosphere at this 17th-floor establishment that overlooks the Public Garden and Beacon Hill. A four-course, fixed-price dinner at the Ritz-Carlton runs about $75 per person.

For fantastic views of the city, day or night, there's no better place to go than the Top of the Hub, located in the Prudential Tower at 800 Boylston Street, (617) 536-1775. The Top of the Hub is on the 52nd floor and has both a restaurant and a lounge. As you might expect, window seats are best, but the view from all tables in the restaurant is great. During the day, you can have fun spotting landmarks; at

night, the sparkling city is a setting for romance. Dinner entrees average in the mid-$20s, but you can enjoy the same view in the lounge, where there's live jazz nightly.

Yarmouth, Nova Scotia

We think the best way to get to Yarmouth is aboard The Scotia Prince (see information below). Not only will you save 1,716 miles of round-trip driving from Portland, but you're also likely to have a great time and arrive feeling rested and ready to explore.

The second-largest port in the province of Nova Scotia, Yarmouth was founded in 1761. From its founding, the town enjoyed prosperity due to its proximity to New England ports and its trade with the West Indies. Today it's famous as an entrance point to Nova Scotia and the site of the terminal for two ferries: The Scotia Prince and the MV Bluenose, which sails from Bar Harbor, Maine.

Strolling through town, you'll see vestiges of the town's early prosperity in its architecture, with graceful Sea Captain's mansions and stately buildings. To get information on Yarmouth and Nova Scotia prior to your visit, drop by the Nova Scotia Visitor Information Center in the International Marine Terminal on Commercial Street in Portland. To get yourself grounded once you've made the journey, stop in at the visitors center at 228 Main Street in Yarmouth. Both are open from May through the end of October. You can also call (800) 565-0000 for information on the province.

If you go to Yarmouth on a Scotia Prince package and don't have a car at your disposal, you may want to take the Rodd Grand Hotel Local Tour, which offers a two-and-a-half-hour overview of the area as well as visits to the working waterfront, Cape Forchu and the Yarmouth Lighthouse. Your guide will also point out the Yarmouth County Museum and Research Library and the Firefighters Museum of Nova Scotia (see more information below). Please note that the costs of attractions, unless we say otherwise, are listed in Canadian dollars. At the time of this writing, the exchange rate was about $1.50 in Canadian money for every U.S. dollar.

Photo: Pauline Dimino

The *Scotia Prince* sails every night from Portland to Nova Scotia.

Getting There

Prince of Fundy Cruises —
The Scotia Prince
International Marine Terminal,
468 Commercial St., Portland
• (207) 775-5616, (800) 341-7540

You don't have to go to Florida to sample the delights of a full entertainment cruise with great dining, a casino and onboard shopping. From Portland you can enjoy the fun of a 23-hour, weekend-long or extended getaway aboard the *Scotia Prince*, which (with few exceptions) sails daily from Portland to Yarmouth.

The ship operates from May to the end of October. It can be used as a ferry to transport you and your car to Yarmouth, thus saving 858 miles of one-way driving, or it can be enjoyed as a mini-vacation in itself. If you're looking for a mini-vacation, you can opt for a 23-hour round-trip package called the Overnight Sensation, which includes a night sail from Portland, arrival in Yarmouth in the morning with about an hour to visit the city, then a return cruise to Portland. The package includes an economy cabin on the outbound journey, breakfast, a day cabin on the return journey and a dinner buffet.

Onboard you can enjoy a late-night floor show, try your luck in the casino or at one of

INSIDERS' TIP

On daytrips, allow a little extra driving time, as you will be less familiar with the area you are visiting. Also, be sure to make hotel and restaurant reservations in advance.

200 slot machines or relax in one of the lounges. You'll also have an opportunity to watch a movie, take part in a trivia quiz, play bingo and shop in the duty-free gift shop. Children can enjoy supervised activities (from the end of June to mid-September) in the Kids Club, where they can take part in fun and games with the cruise staff or watch cartoons and videos. If you like live entertainment, you'll be glad to know the ship offers two different programs, one on the outward journey and one on the return trip.

For those who prefer a longer trip with time available to explore Yarmouth, *Scotia Prince* offers a variety of packages. The Great Getaway takes 47 hours over three days. The package includes everything that comes with the Overnight Sensation, but instead of departing an hour after arriving in Yarmouth, you stay overnight in one of three hotels — the Rodd Colony, Rodd Grand or the Manor Inn (see more information in Accommodations). Then you'll have continental breakfast and a whole day to explore Nova Scotia.

Those who select the Royal Getaway package (also covering three days) receive a welcome basket onboard with a half-bottle of champagne, fruit and a box of chocolates. In Yarmouth you'll receive a two-hour tour of the city, dinner (or a dinner theater show in-season) and breakfast. On the return trip Royal Getaway participants get to visit the ship's bridge and meet the captain and crew. Longer packages include the Beach Retreat, which features three nights and four days at the White Point Beach Lodge (see this section's Accommodations listings).

In 1998, cost for the Overnight Sensation from the end of June to mid-September began at $117.50 per person, based on double occupancy. The Great Getaway started at around $173.50, and the Royal Getaway was $257.50 per person. From May to the end of June and from mid-September to the end of October, rates drop to around $89.50 for the Overnight Sensation, $129.50 for the Great Getaway and $220.50 for the Royal Getaway.

Attractions

The town of Yarmouth is a good size to walk around and explore. For attractions you might want to visit the Firefighters Museum of Nova Scotia, 451 Main Street, (902) 742-5525, or the Yarmouth County Museum, 22 Collins Street, (902) 742-5539.

Anyone who has ever dreamed of being a firefighter will love the Firefighters Museum. You'll find just about every type of firefighting apparatus ever used in Nova Scotia and beyond, including Canada's oldest fire engine — a horse-drawn Amoskeag steamer dating from 1863. Cost to visit in 1998 was $2 for adults, $1 for students and 50¢ for those 14 and younger. A family pass was $4. The museum is open year round.

The Yarmouth County Museum is also open year round and highlights the area's seafaring past. Period rooms and displays of china, glass, dolls, paintings and heritage costumes are featured. Cost to enter in 1998 was $2.50 for adults, $1 for students and 50¢ for those 14 or younger. A family pass was $5.

If you'd rather explore the town than take in a museum, consider the Walking Tour of Yarmouth. You can pick up a brochure detailing the walking tour from the Tourist Information Center at 228 Main Street. The brochure includes a suggested walking route and information on the area's history and architecture. Anywhere from one to four hours will be needed to complete the tour, depending on how long you decide to stay at museums and other sites of interest.

For those who've brought a car, take a drive out to Yarmouth Light, on Cape Forchu, Canadian Highway 304 (7 miles from Yarmouth). In addition to the lighthouse, you'll find a fishing village, walking trails and sandy beaches. Unlike many lighthouses, this one is easily accessible. You can walk around the base and enjoy scrambling over the rocks and trails nearby. The site is open year round, but the gift shop is open only from May 1 to October 31. To get there, drive north on Yarmouth's Main Street and take a left at the Horse Fountain, which you can't miss. That puts you on Vancouver Street. After the hospital, take a left onto Grove Road and follow the signs to the lighthouse.

Accommodations

Most of you will probably be staying at

one of the hotels that participate in the overnight packages available through The Scotia Prince. Two of these are near the Ferry Terminal — The Rodd Colony Harbour Inn, 6 Forest Street, (902) 742-9194, and the Rodd Grand Hotel, 417 Main Street, (902) 742-2446. The toll-free number for both hotels is (800) 565-9077. Amenities at the Rodd Colony Harbour Inn include a game room, on-site restaurant and lounge, meeting room facility and gift shop. At the Rodd Grand Hotel, there's a heated indoor swimming pool, an exercise and fitness center and a dining room and lounge.

North of Yarmouth is The Manor Inn, Canadian Route 1, (902) 742-2487. Located in Hebron, 4.5 miles from the Ferry Terminal on 9 acres of landscaped grounds bordering Doctors Lake, The Manor Inn features 53 rooms in a choice of four buildings. Amenities include an outdoor heated pool, hot tub, a children's play area, horseshoes, badminton, croquet and tennis. You can also enjoy lake swimming, table tennis, pool, darts and video games. Some rooms have fireplaces and whirlpool baths.

Considerably east of town is the White Point Beach Lodge, Canadian Route 103, Hunt's Point, (902) 354-2711, (800) 565-5068. This resort is 96 miles east of Yarmouth and features a sandy beach, children's playground, nature trails, a restaurant, lounge and an indoor heated pool. There's also an outdoor children's pool and a freshwater lake where you can enjoy swimming, fishing, paddle boats and water slides. The resort features a Canadian Professional Golf Association-rated golf course, tennis courts, rainy-day activities and exercise and youth programs.

Restaurants

Those who don't have dinner included in the overnight Scotia Prince package might want to try eating at Captain Kelley's, the Ship's Bell Restaurant in the Rodd Grand Hotel or Five Corners Restaurant.

Captain Kelley's, 545 Main Street, (902) 742-7821, is in a restored Sea Captain's home that still contains many of the original fixtures and amenities from its turn-of-the-century design. In addition to the restaurant, which was opened in 1976, you'll find the Lower Deck Lounge (added to the original house in 1984) and the sports bar, Kelley's Pub (established in 1988). Captain Kelley's offers three levels of dining, accommodating everyone from the very casual (T-shirts and shorts) to those attending formal functions. Entree prices begin around $10 in the restaurant, but you can get burgers and appetizers for less in the pub.

At the Rodd Grand Hotel, 417 Main Street, (902) 742-2446, you can enjoy a dinner theater production while feasting on fresh salmon, chicken Kiev or roast beef, as well as fresh steamed mussels, salads, breads, coffee and dessert, all for around $19 U.S. dollars. Theater performances are presented Tuesday through Sunday in-season.

Only the freshest ingredients are used at the Five Corners Restaurant, 624 Main Street, (902) 742-6061. Entrees include grilled salmon, Nova Scotia-style lobster finished in cream or sauteed in butter, and the seafood crepe filled with a delicious blend of haddock, scallops and lobster simmered in a creamy herb sauce with a hint of lemon. Cost for entrees runs between $10 and $15 American dollars.

INSIDERS' TIP

The Boston subway system is referred to as the "T." There are four major lines to the system — Red, Blue, Green and Orange. Some of these lines, particularly the Green Line, have a number of different branches that are referred to by letter: For example, the Green Line has A, B, C, D and E trains. Many branches may leave from the same tracks, so make sure you get on the right train. Cost for a single ride on the T is 85¢. You can change lines without paying again, providing you don't exit the subway system.

Sebago Lake Region

Less than an hour's drive from much of Maine's Southern Coast, you'll find rolling hills and clear blue lakes waiting to be discovered. The largest of the nearby lakes is Sebago, which covers close to 45 square miles, or 29,000 acres. Sebago is, in fact, the second-largest lake in the state — only Moosehead Lake in Greenville is larger, covering approximately three times as much area.

In the Sebago Lake region you can enjoy watersports like boating and canoeing as well as other outdoor activities like camping and biking. Indoor pursuits might include a visit to the Jones Museum of Glass (see this section's Attractions listings).

Smaller bodies of water around Sebago Lake include Little Sebago, Panther Pond, Crescent Lake and Long Lake. In this section, we discuss the amenities and activities you can enjoy on Sebago Lake and Long Lake. To explore other area lakes and ponds, we suggest you pick up the DeLorme Maine Atlas and Gazetteer (see our Media chapter), which highlights access roads and public boat-launch areas.

Getting There

From Portland, take Maine Highway 302 West. This road leads through Windham and Raymond to Naples, which is some 45 minutes from Portland. At Naples, you'll find a causeway with restaurants and activities such as the Songo River Queen II (see information below). Both Sebago Lake State Park and Point Sebago Resort, which are discussed below, are accessible from Maine 302.

Those coming from south of Portland might want to consider using alternate routes to reach Naples. Maine Highway 35 and Maine Highway 202 are both good roads that lead through pleasant countryside. If you intend to use these back roads, it's again a good idea to get the Maine Atlas and Gazetteer. Alternately, Sebago Lake area visitors can take the Maine Turnpike to Exit 11 (Gray/New Gloucester). From there take Maine Highway 115 (at this point the road is also Routes 202 and 4) toward North Windham. At North Windham, take Route 302 north to Naples.

Attractions

The main attractions in the Sebago Lake region are, of course, the lakes. Unfortunately, accessing them isn't as easy as you might think. Waterfront property commands a high price whether it's on the ocean or on a lake, and Sebago is one of the most popular choices for lakefront homes in Maine. There are public boat launches at a number of sites along the perimeter of Sebago Lake, but these aren't places where you can go swimming or picnicking.

For recreation on the lake, we suggest you visit Sebago Lake State Park or Point Sebago Resort. You can also take a ride on the Songo River Queen II or go parasailing. Sebago Lake State Park, (207) 693-6613, is off Maine Highway 302 between South Casco and Naples. Both day-use facilities and camping sites are available at the park. Sandy beaches, picnic tables, grills, lifeguards and bathhouses are among the amenities you'll find at Sebago Lake State Park. There's also a boat ramp, and anglers can go after salmon, freshwater bass and togue, but they'll need a license (see Fishing in our Parks and Recreation chapter).

The cost for day-use entrance to the park in 1998 was $2.50 for anyone 12 and older, 50¢ for children ages 5 through 11. For day-use of the park, seniors 65 or older and children younger than 5 are admitted free. You can also buy a $40 vehicle pass, which allows entrance for all people in a given vehicle, or an individual pass for $20. Both passes are accepted at all parks in the state park system.

Point Sebago Golf & Beach Resort, (207) 655-3821, (800) 655-1232, is also on Route 302. Guests at the resort can enjoy amenities including an 18-hole championship golf course, boat rental marina and boat slip rentals, tennis courts, minigolf, bingo, horseshoes and shuffleboard. You can also go canoeing, kayaking or waterskiing or simply take it easy in a paddle boat. Day and evening cruises are offered on the Point Sebago Princess.

Those who aren't staying at the resort but want to enjoy a cruise can opt for the Songo River Queen II, (207) 693-6861, which offers trips on a 90-foot-long sternwheeler that looks like the sort of boat you'd find on the Mississippi River. Two cruises are available on the Songo River Queen II. You can take a one-hour cruise on Long Lake, or a two-and-a-half-hour cruise that will take you across Brandy Pond and through Songo Lock, the only surviving lock from a canal built in 1830. After negotiating the lock, you'll travel along the Songo River to the mouth of Sebago Lake.

The Songo River Queen II operates daily from July to the beginning of September and on weekends in June and the balance of September. Cost for the longer ride is about $10 for adults and $6 for children ages 4 through 12. The shorter Long Lake ride is $7 for adults and $4 for children. There's no admission charge for children younger than 4. The Songo Locks trip departs twice daily, at 9:45 AM and 3:45 PM, while the Long Lake trip leaves at 1, 2:30 and 7 PM daily.

For a bit more excitement, you might want to try parasailing from the causeway in Naples. An eight-to-10-minute flight behind a commercial parasailing boat was $35 in 1998. Owner Tim Allen also offers bumper boat rides and boat rentals from M.M. Boat Rentals, which is adjacent to Hi-Fly Parasailing, (207) 693-3888. The bumper boat ride lasts around 10 minutes and cost $5 per person in 1998. Boat rentals begin at around $45 a day. Parasailing, bumper boats and boat rentals are available from June through mid-September, weather permitting.

In addition to the water-based activities, you might also consider a visit to Seacoast Fun Park, (207) 892-5952. Located on Route 302 in Windham, the park offers miniature golf, bumper boats and go-cart racing. For the super-daring there is also the SkyCoaster swing, which winches one to three people 100 feet into the air, then lets them free-fall into a swinging motion. This is certainly not for the faint of heart, but those who've done it say it's great! The price for individual activities at Seacoast Fun Park is around $5 per person per activity, except for the SkyCoaster, which costs $20 per drop for one person, $35 for two people and $45 for three people.

From mid-December to mid-March, Seacoast Fun Park becomes a winter activity center with snow tubing, snowboarding and ice skating. It is an all-terrain park where they make and groom snow. Special events include a Big Air Snow Boarding contest, held each Friday evening during winter operation.

For more traditional entertainment you can take in a movie at Chunky's, (207) 892-4777, which offers seating in car seats from old Thunderbirds and a chance to dine on pizza or other fun fare while you watch a first-run flick. Located on Route 302 in Windham center, Chunky's always runs different films at its two showtimes: One is suitable for adults; one is geared to the kids. Shows start at 6:45 and 9:45 PM, but lines start forming an hour before showtime — you'd better plan on getting there early.

If you're searching for an indoor activity or have an interest in glass, check out the Jones Museum of Glass & Ceramics, off Maine Highway 107 at Douglas Mountain in Sebago, (207) 787-3370. There are displays featuring glass in all its forms, from paperweights and vases to stemware and dinnerware. In addition to permanent exhibits, the museum creates four special exhibits each year. Its glass collection has been ranked in the top 10 among U.S. museums. The Jones Museum is open from May to mid-November. Entrance fees in 1998 were $5 for adults, $3 for students and $3.75 for senior citizens. Children younger than 12 are admitted free. (For more information on the Jones Museum, see our Attractions chapter.)

Accommodations

Visitors enjoying the amenities at Sebago Lake State Park can also take advantage of overnight camping. Many sites are available on a first-come, first-served basis, but others can be reserved. On in-season weekends, it's recommended that you call ahead to reserve a site. From June 20 to Labor Day, call (207) 693-6613 for reservations. In the off-season, call (207) 693-6231. The cost per night per campsite in 1998 was $13 for state residents and $17 for non-residents. There's also a $2 per night, per site reservation fee.

Point Sebago Resort, (207) 655-3821, (800) 655-1232, offers a choice of camping, resort cottages, park homes or travel-trailers for rent. Costs range from $39 for a basic campsite to $154 per day for a resort cottage in peak season. Weekend packages and off-season rates are available.

Those looking for a bed and breakfast atmosphere can try the Sebago Lake Lodge & Cottages, on White's Bridge Road in North Windham, (207) 892-2698. Rooms and cottages are available at the lodge, which features a beach and picnic tables as well as boat and canoe rentals. Prices range from around $50 per day for a simple room to $120 for a housekeeping unit/efficiency.

Restaurants

The Sebago Lake region is a sprawling area, and there are small local restaurants in the towns and villages around the perimeters of the lakes. We've highlighted a couple on the Naples causeway and another one close by. All are central to the parks and attractions we've listed.

Rick's, (207) 693-3759, is the place to go to enjoy a summer cocktail or burger while overlooking Long Lake. Sitting in the sun under colorful umbrellas, watching the world go by, you'd almost think you were in the Florida Keys. You can choose from appetizers (the nachos are great), burgers, sandwiches, salads and entrees at Rick's. Prices for burgers and such are less than $10, and entrees average in the $10 neighborhood. A word to the wise: Don't be in any hurry when you sit down at Rick's. The service is fine, but you'll find it mighty difficult to get motivated to move once you've relaxed with a drink and some food at this Caribbean-inspired retreat. Rick's is open from May to September.

Charlie's On the Causeway, (207) 693-3286, also offers fine views of Long Lake and Songo Lock, and you might prefer its slightly less-crowded atmosphere to Rick's. Entrees run from $10 to $15, and we hear their lobster alfredo is out of this world! The restaurant is open from May to October.

At Bray's Brew Pub, (207) 693-6806, which is at the intersection of Maine Highway 302 and Maine Highway 35, you can enjoy American ales brewed on the premises by crafters using North American grains and malted barley, Oregon yeast and Washington hops. Owned by Mike and Rich Bray, the restaurant is open daily year round for lunch and dinner.

Daily specials are offered, and you'll find entrees in the $10 to $15 range. A lighter pub menu is also offered all day.

Portsmouth, New Hampshire

Just across the Piscataqua River and only a five-minute drive from Kittery, Portsmouth is a historic city with a bustling downtown filled with coffee shops, restaurants, brick storefronts and cobblestone streets. It's a fun place to shop (there's no state sales tax) and a great place to dine — in summer, music wafts from the porch of one restaurant to the next.

The first settlers arrived in Portsmouth in 1630 and founded the community known as Strawbery Banke (see more on this in our Attractions chapter). Because of the city's position at the mouth of Portsmouth Harbor, fortifications were built to protect the city and its shipbuilding trade. The Portsmouth Naval Shipyard, which is actually on the Kittery side of the river, played an important role here. Many famous ships were built here, including The Ranger, which was sailed by John Paul Jones. In 1905 the city was chosen for the signing of the Treaty of Portsmouth, which ended the Russo-Japanese War.

But it's the city's beautiful gardens, the atmosphere of arts and antiques, and its harbor location that now draws people to visit and live here. With more than 100 restaurants in the area, Portsmouth has a reputation as the "Restaurant Capital of New England." For more detailed information, we suggest you visit or call the Greater Portsmouth Chamber of Commerce, 500 Market Street, (603) 436-1118.

Getting There

Getting to Portsmouth is simple. From Kittery, follow U.S. Highway 1 south until you cross the Piscataqua River. Downtown Portsmouth is on the other side. The other option is to take Interstate 95 south from Kittery, get off at Exit 7 and turn left onto Market Street. Market Street will take you directly into downtown. Parking is available along the street or in a parking garage that you can access by turning onto Hanover Street.

The one thing about visiting Portsmouth that can be confusing is that just about all the streets are one-way. If you can't seem to get where you want to go, we recommend driving one street past your destination and turning around the block. Or you could try what works best for us: Park the car and walk.

Attractions

Porstmouth is full of historic places to see, and many of them are open to the public. A good place to start is the Portsmouth Harbor Trail, a self-guided walking tour that will take you from the waterfront through the gorgeous flower gardens in Prescott Park and through the most historic areas of the city. The guide is available at the chamber of commerce office.

Once you've familiarized yourself with the history of Portsmouth, set off for Strawbery Banke, a 10-acre waterfront neighborhood and museum rebuilt and restored to commemorate one of the nation's first urban neighborhoods (see our Attractions chapter). The community is on Marcy Street; small signs will point you in the right direction. It's open seasonally, from April through autumn and for special holiday events. For ticket prices call (603) 433-1100 — in 1998 they ranged from $8 for kids ages 7-17 and $12 for adults. Children younger than 7 were admitted free.

The John Paul Jones House, at the corner of Middle and State streets, (603) 436-8420, is a National Historic Landmark where the famous captain lived while supervising the outfitting of The Ranger. It's open from May through the summer. If you're looking for an outdoor activity, call the Prescott Park Arts Festival, (603) 436-2848, and see what's scheduled. The festival offers more than 100 events each year with Broadway-style family entertainment in the park (don't forget your picnic). The Music Hall, 28 Chestnut Street, (603) 436-2400, also offers a selection of popular and classical music concerts, dance and theatre in a historic 1878 hall. The chil-

dren can explore at The Children's Museum of Portsmouth, 280 Marcy Street, (603) 436-3853; admission is $4 for adults and $2 for children older than 2. For even more adventure, take them aboard the USS Albacore — a retired Navy submarine at 600 Market Street, (603) 436-3680. Admission to tour the sub is $4 for adults, $3 for seniors and free for children younger than 7.

The second weekend in June, Portsmouth is home to Market Square Day, a family celebration of booths, crafts and games that floods the entire downtown district. For winter fun, try First Night Portsmouth, a New Year's Eve celebration of the arts that takes place indoors at locations throughout the city. And don't forget that there's shopping, shopping, shopping. The downtown is loaded with specialty clothing shops, gourmet groceries, galleries, collectors' shops, jewelry studios and more.

Accommodations

Because of its popularity and proximity to the ocean, Portsmouth is a gold mine of cozy bed and breakfasts, historic inns and comfortable hotels. As in Maine, the busiest tourist season is from late June through August and at major holidays such as New Year's Eve. There are far more places to stay than just those we've included, but this will get you started.

Sheraton Portsmouth was built to blend in with the brick style of the historic downtown buildings. The hotel and conference center at 250 Market Street, (603) 431-2300, is in the heart of downtown within sight of the harbor. The atmosphere is elegant, and there are condo suites, an indoor pool, a fitness facility and sauna. A standard room at the Sheraton begins at $128 during the peak season; suites range as high as $450. Courtyard by Marriott, 1000 Market Street, (603) 436-2121, is a large downtown hotel with a guest exercise room. Rates begin at $129.

Sise Inn, 40 Court Street, (603) 433-1200, is an elegantly restored Queen Anne-style Victorian inn with private baths. A light breakfast is included with your stay. Prices at Sise Inn start at $135. The Wren's Nest Village Inn, 3548 Lafayette Road, (603) 436-2481, is farther away from the shopping district, but its upscale country atmosphere and Jacuzzi suites make up for the distance. The motel has a variety of accommodations and cottages, with prices starting at $99 for a standard room. For other places to stay near Portsmouth, check our chapters on Hotels and Motels and Bed and Breakfasts and Inns and look for accommodations in Kittery and York in the Southern Beaches Area.

Restaurants

In the heart of Portsmouth, Cafe Brioche, 14 Market Street, (603) 430-9225, is a favorite any time of the day. You can get mile-high veggie sandwiches, steaming cups of coffee and some of the most scrumptious pastries around. The Portsmouth Gaslight Co., 64 Market Street, (603) 430-9122, is a happening place for brick-oven pizza and beer. The restaurant has an outdoor patio where live bands perform during summer. For Mexican with an attitude, try poco diablo, 37 Bow Street, (603) 431-5967. The atmosphere is kind of brooding, but the spicy fare is some of the best around.

If you're looking for more intimate, elegant dining we recommend The Library Restaurant, 401 State Street, (603) 431-5202. You'll be surrounded by mahogany shelves lined with old books in a building that dates to 1785. These are just a few recommendations. As we mentioned, the streets of Portsmouth are teeming with restaurants, and we are sure you will find just what you like. Reservations are strongly recommended during summer, and almost without exception, attire is comfortably casual.

Augusta

Maine's capital city, Augusta, is dotted with historic buildings and museums and makes a great educational daytrip for the whole family. Set in the Kennebec Valley, Augusta spreads out on both sides of the Kennebec River. It was selected as Maine's capital in 1827, just seven years after the state was admitted to the Union (Portland was the first capital). The city began as a trading post and slowly developed into the center of trade and industry you'll find today. Downtown redevelopment has taken shape slowly over the past couple of decades, but one-by-one more retail shops have begun to move back into Augusta's brick storefronts.

Getting There

Just 60 miles north of Portland, Augusta is an easy trip from just about any community along our Southern Coast. I-95 North will get you there. We recommend taking Exit 30 onto Western Avenue, which will bring you to the city center and the downtown traffic circle. For maps or more detailed information, call the Kennebec Valley Chamber of Commerce, (207)623-4559, or contact the attractions you wish to visit and ask for more specific directions through the city.

Attractions

The State House, at U.S. Highway 201 (State Street), (207) 287-2301, is an ideal place to begin your historic wanderings through Augusta. The stately building that houses the state legislature and government offices was constructed of Maine granite in 1829. Look for the Roman goddess of wisdom, Minerva, standing atop the dome 185 feet in the air. Free tours are available weekday mornings from 9 AM to 1 PM, but we think the outside of the building is more impressive than the interior, which is in the middle of renovations. Still, there are exhibits of stuffed moose and bear, and you'll see the hall of flags and the areas where the state senate and legislature meet. The Italian tile floor, which took more than a year to put in place, is exquisite.

The governor's mansion, known as the Blaine House, (207) 287-2121, is on the corner of State and Capitol streets. The Federal period house was built in 1833, but it was later remodeled in the Victorian and Italian styles and was finished off with a Colonial look in 1919. The house has been the official residence of Maine's governors since its last remodeling, and it is open to the public for free tours Tuesday through Thursday from 2 to 4 PM. Incidentally, Maine's current governor, Angus King, has bucked the long tradition of living at the Blaine House; he resides at his own home in Brunswick, where he and his family rent out rooms for a little extra income.

You'll get the full spectrum of Maine history, free of charge, while visiting the Maine State Museum, (207) 287-2301. With exhibits on the state's natural environment, social history and manufacturing heritage, the museum is in the State Capitol complex. It's open seven days a week, but only during the afternoon on Sunday. After learning about Maine's heritage, visit it at Old Fort Western. Built in 1754, it's New England's oldest surviving wooden fort. You'll see the original main house (comprised of barracks and a store) and reproductions of blockhouses, watchboxes and the palisade. The fort is on the banks of the Kennebec River on Cony Street and is open Memorial Day through Labor Day. Admission in 1998 was $4.50 for adults and $2.50 for children older than 6. Call (207) 626-2385 for tour information.

The Pine Tree State Arboretum is a great place to take to the outdoors. This 200-acre preserve is perfect for birdwatching, picnicking, hiking, biking and cross-country skiing, and it's open to the public free of charge. You'll find it at Hospital Street and Piggery Road; the visitors center phone number is (207) 621-0031. Look for the 68 white pines planted in honor of each of Maine's 68 governors. If you're in the mood for a concert, other performance or trade show, check with the Augusta Civic Center, Community Drive, (207) 626-2405, to see what's in town. The auditorium can seat 7,000 people.

Accommodations

Most of the hotels in Augusta are cen-

tered around the Civic Center. We've included a handful that have reputations for good service and a comfortable night's stay. Reserve early to make sure the hotel isn't booked for a Civic Center event.

Just off Exit 31 from I-95, the Holiday Inn, 110 Community Drive, (207) 622-4751, (800) 694-6404, has 102 rooms, an outdoor pool, a fitness center and banquet and meeting facilities. Holiday Inn rooms range from $89 to $120. Nearby is a Comfort Inn, 281 Civic Center Drive, (207) 623-1000. Here you'll enjoy a heated indoor lap pool, hot tub and health club with exercise room. Again, rates begin at $89 and range to $109. The Senator Inn & Restaurant, Western Avenue (off Exit 30A of I-95), (207) 622-5804, (800) 528-1234, is a Best Western property that is another fine choice. A room with one double bed is $99; the rate for a larger room with a king bed is $129. We've listed the inn's restaurant as a good dining option.

For more intimate accommodations, we highly recommend one of the six guest rooms at The Inn at Bachelder's Tavern. The gracious main house has an elegant dining room where you'll receive a complimentary breakfast, and each of the rooms has a private bath. In 1998 rooms were either $75 or $95. We provide directions in our subsequent Restaurants listing.

Restaurants

Many of the better area restaurants are actually in the small towns surrounding Augusta, but if you're just visiting for a day, we don't want to get you lost meandering down the back roads. Here are a couple of choices within the city. For other options that are easy to get to in time for dinner, look in our Restaurants chapter for our favorite picks in Brunswick, about 30 minutes south of the capital.

The Senator Inn & Restaurant, off Exit 30A

of I-95, specializes in seafood, steaks, crab cakes and its own pastries and breads. It has been a favorite area restaurant since 1962 and serves breakfast, lunch and dinner. An espresso bar and a lounge are also available. It's on outer Western Avenue, (207) 622-5804. Captain Cotes, directly across from the Augusta Civic Center on Civic Center Drive, (207) 622-4625, is a family restaurant where you can choose from a menu of seafood and ribs. It's open daily for lunch and dinner. Mike's Restaurant, 15 Bangor Street, (207) 622-3221, has been serving prime rib, steaks, seafood and an extensive salad bar since 1935. It's open for lunch and dinner daily and serves breakfast on weekends.

The one exception we'll make to our promise not to spin you down any backcountry roads is to recommend the fine dining at The Inn at Bachelder's Tavern, Maine Hwy. 126, Litchfield, (207) 268-2572. The restaurant and inn are housed in a beautiful historic tavern in a country setting overlooking a pond. The restaurant features fresh seafood, veal, steaks, vegetarian cuisine and game dishes such as venison and buffalo! To get there, take Exit 28 off I-95 and head 6.5 miles west on Maine 126. Reservations are suggested.

Bar Harbor and Mt. Desert Island

The first settlers arrived in Bar Harbor in 1825, carving a fishing and shipbuilding community out of the tall pines along the bays that surround Mt. Desert (pronounced like "dessert"). Soon after their arrival, droves of artists discovered the island's stark beauty and captured it on canvas, bringing it back to high society across America.

Because of the publicity provided by the artists, the wealthy began streaming to Bar Harbor to play their summers away. The first hotel was erected in 1855; soon after, the steamer Lewiston began depositing tourists on the island. Before long, it became known as the Queen of American Summer Resorts. The wealthiest American families built summer mansions, which they referred to as "cottages." The Vanderbilts, Pulitzers, Fords and Rockefellers were among the most prominent. It was John D. Rockefeller who built roads, carriage paths and trails on the island and launched a campaign to preserve it for the public. In 1916, President Woodrow Wilson declared it a national monument.

Then tragedy struck. The Great Fire of 1947 destroyed more than 17,000 acres and most of the town's summer cottages and grand hotels. The beauty of the island, however, still draws tourists from across the country and the world, and the trails and paths once built by Rockefeller are still available to the public today. (For much more information on Bar Harbor, Mount Desert Island and the surrounding Maine coastline, pick up a copy of *The Insiders' Guide to Maine's Mid-Coast.*)

Getting There

By car, Bar Harbor is roughly two hours north of Wiscasset along U.S. Highway 1. That's the best driving route if you're coming from Wiscasset or the Boothbay Harbor area. If you're driving from any town south of Bath, we recommend following I-95 north to Augusta. Take Exit 30 and head east on U.S. Highway 202, which will merge with Maine Highway 3. Follow Maine 3 through Belfast and Ellsworth, where it merges with Route 1, and all the way to the center of Bar Harbor. If you are arriving by boat, there are many mooring points to choose from. Call the Harbormaster's Office at (207) 288-5571 for suitable locations.

Attractions

Biking, hiking, canoeing, rock climbing and sailing are the most popular activities on Mt. Desert; the mountains and surrounding sea

INSIDERS' TIP

While you're in Nova Scotia, you should try "rappie pie." This delicious concoction is an Acadian dish made of grated potatoes, meat and spices.

are the main attractions. Maine's largest island, Mt. Desert provides great opportunities to explore the wilds at Acadia National Park. The 40,000-acre park absorbs half the island.

Check in at the Hulls Cove Visitor Center, Maine Highway 3, Hulls Cove, (207) 288-3338, and pick up a map to start your adventure. The park has a plenitude of trails for walking, hiking, biking and horseback riding, and the visitors center or area chamber of commerce can put you in touch with outfitters that can help you enjoy them. The Acadia Information Center, (207) 667-8550, (800) 358-8550, is another great resource for visitors. It's off Maine 3 in Trenton, just before you reach the bridge to Mt. Desert.

Park fees are $10 for a carload of people for one week. Many trails, however, are accessible for free from roadways outside the park. If you're not up to scaling Cadillac Mountain, the island's highest peak, we recommend driving up it. The Park Loop Road winds through the park and past some of its most inspiring vistas. Keep an eye on the road for pedestrians and mountain bikers who also prefer this route. If you're feeling nostalgic, catch a carriage ride through the park. Wildwood Stables, Park Loop Road, Bar Harbor, (207) 276-3622, offers one- to two-hour carriage rides through the park daily during summer. Rates start at about $12 per person per hour.

For attractions outside the wilds, visit the Bar Harbor Historical Society at Jesup Memorial Library, 34 Mt. Desert Street, Bar Harbor, (207) 288-3807. It's a great way to familiarize yourself with the island and its history. It is open year round, but you'll have to make an appointment during the winter months. Then see Bar Harbor's remaining historic homes with a one-hour tour by Jolly Roger's Trolley. It leaves Testa's Restaurant, 53 Main Street, Bar Harbor, (207) 288-3327, several times a day during summer and offers a narrated tour.

For a closer look at Maine's sea creatures, spend a day at the Mount Desert Oceanarium, (207) 244-7330. At its location off Maine 3 in Bar Harbor, you can see young lobsters and their kin up close; inside the museum you can learn all about lobstering and its history. (Did you know that lobster was once considered such loathsome fare that Maine had a law that prisoners could only be fed lobster twice a week?) The museum also has a salt marsh and a seal demonstration. It's open every day except Sundays from mid-May through Columbus Day. Ticket prices range from $4.50 to $11.95 for adults and $3 to $8.75 for children, depending on which exhibits you see.

For shopping, check out downtown Bar Harbor, which is lined with cute harborside buildings filled with ice cream and chocolate shops, souvenirs, outdoor clothing and gift stores.

Accommodations

The peak tourist season on Mt. Desert is summer and fall, though more and more people are looking to the island for quiet winter getaways. Reservations are recommended, but there is such a variety of places to choose from — hotels, motels, inns and campgrounds — you're just about guaranteed to find a place to stay. (However, it might not be your first choice.)

For spectacular ocean views in elegant surroundings, from April through November try the Bar Harbor Inn, Newport Drive, (207) 288-3351, (800) 248-3351. The main lodge is quaint and old-fashioned with a wraparound porch facing the harbor. More room choices are available in the adjacent Oceanfront Lodge and the Newport Motel. Outside there is plenty of room to roam on 8 landscaped acres of lawns and gardens. The inn also has an outdoor pool and Jacuzzi and complimentary memberships to a nearby health club. Summer room rates start at about $139 and include continental breakfast.

Luxury abounds at Bar Harbor Hotel and the Bluenose Inn, 90 Eden Street, Bar Harbor, (207) 288-3348, (800) 445-4077, a resort that's one of the island's most honored accommodations. There are oversized rooms and two-room suites (some with fireplaces), a heated indoor pool surrounded by large windows and columns and an elegant great room where you can relax and meet other guests. Rates begin at $108, and gourmet dining is available at the resort's Rose Garden restaurant. Graycote Inn is a charming year-round bed and breakfast inn offering extra-large rooms with private baths, canopied beds, fireplaces and private sun porches. A full hot breakfast and afternoon refreshments are included in the room rate. The inn is at 40 Holland Avenue, (207) 288-3044, and rates range from $95 to $150 a night. For another bed and breakfast in the downtown center, try Stonethrow Cottage, 67 Mt. Desert Street, (207) 288-3668, (800) 769-3668. Open from May through mid-October, this newly restored 1860 cottage is tucked behind a stone wall and flowering gardens. It really is just a stone's throw from the shopping district. Rates start at $155.

If you want to spend more time with nature, there are plenty of campgrounds to choose from on Mt. Desert Island. Campsites range from $14 to $30 per night, and many campgrounds offer swimming pools, hot showers, playgrounds and stores. A few options include Barcadia Campground, RR1 Box 2165, Bar Harbor, (207) 288-3520; Bar Harbor Campground, RFD1, Box 1125, Bar Harbor, (207) 288-5185; and Mt. Desert Narrows, Maine Highway 3, Bar Harbor Road, (207) 288-4782. To find out about camping at sites operated by the state Bureau of Parks and Lands, call (207) 287-3821. Sites at state parks tend to be less expensive and more rustic. Also check out the campgrounds located in Arcadia National Park by calling the visitors information center.

Restaurants

On Mt. Desert you will be well catered to, no matter what kind of food you're craving. The largest section of restaurants is in down-town Bar Harbor, although some of the more memorable restaurants are spread out over the island. One such lunch and dinner spot is The Jordan Pond House, off the Park Loop Road in Acadia National Park, (207)276-3316. It is renowned for its mouth-watering, buttery popovers served up hot for afternoon tea. Reservations are strongly recommended, and the Jordan Pond House is only open May through October.

Also out of the way but worth the trip is Redfield's, Maine Street, Northwest Harbor, (207) 276-5283, which has been praised in national gourmet magazines for its French bistro-style fare. In the downtown area, Cafe Bluefish, 122 Cottage Street, (207) 288-3696, is run by a fourth-generation native chef. Enjoy international flavors mixed with local seafood at this year-round restaurant, which has garnered recommendations in several national publications. George's Restaurant, 7 Stephen's Lane, (207) 288-4505, has been a Bar Harbor favorite since 1979, serving Mediterranean cuisine in a quiet atmosphere.

For a relaxed meal among locals, we recommend Acadia Restaurant, 62 Main Street, (207) 288-4881, where you can get a creamy, steamy bowl of some of the best chowder around (though you'll have to pay in cash). The Island Chowder House Restaurant, 38 Cottage Street, Bar Harbor, (207) 288-4905, is a lunch or dinner favorite for its lobster, chowder and blueberry pie.

Following the coast from
Kittery to Boothbay,
you'll find oceanfront
and oceanview
properties ranging from
$250,000 to well
over $1 million.

Neighborhoods and Real Estate

Maine is filled with streets of dreamy properties: Large, turreted Victorians, Queen Anne-style "painted ladies," sea captains' houses with widows' walks, sprawling New Englanders with extensive porches, turn-of-the-century farmhouses boasting big barns and green fields, stately Colonials and endearing little houses with no land but great locations near the sea. There is also a profusion of classic Cape Cods (generally called Capes) and ranch-style homes.

The towns in our guide's coverage area sprawl from Kittery to Boothbay. While they're individually charming and unique, the towns share some general features when it comes to real estate. Basically, the closer you are to the sea or river, the more expensive the property. Many people from outside Maine live under the misconception that property here is inexpensive. Depending on where you're from you might agree with that assessment, but you might find prices here way beyond what you expected. In any case, it's very unlikely that you'll find an oceanfront or oceanview property for less than $200,000.

To our north and west in Maine, you'll find less expensive property, but you'll also find less employment opportunity and lower wages. In the south, particularly along the coast, real estate prices are higher, with rarely anything less than $100,000. The reason for the higher price tag on property in the south relates to a number of factors: denser population and, therefore, higher demand for property; lower unemployment and higher wages; proximity to Boston; and the attraction of living near Portland, Maine's largest city.

The geographic area covered by this guide — which is, for the most part, east of Interstate 95 (Maine Turnpike) — is seacoast. Following the coast from Kittery to Boothbay, you'll find oceanfront and oceanview properties ranging from $200,000 to well over $1 million. The full range of housing types is available, from condominiums and cottages to a variety of houses and mobile homes. While some towns have very little new development going on, others are being developed almost to the bursting point.

At this writing, the most expensive house on the market in our area was listed at $2.5 million. Located in Ogunquit, the house is a contemporary Victorian featuring 9 rooms: three bedrooms, two-and-a-half baths and a fireplace. The property has ocean frontage and is on close to three acres.

At the other end of the spectrum, you can get a mobile home in a park for less than $20,000 and a two-bedroom condominium for under $50,000. Your best bet for somewhat lower-end house prices will be in the Bath-Brunswick area and the Old Orchard Beach area. You should be aware, however, that property prices are on the move, and the more affordable homes are being scooped up quickly.

Each town or city along the coast has its own character, its own special features that will make you fall in love with it and want to stay. There are dozens of real estate agencies in each area to help you find and buy the house of your dreams. In this chapter, we summarize some of the various neighborhoods within our towns, and provide sample listings that were available at the time of this writing. Toward the end of the chapter we list a selection of realty companies for each of our four main geographic sections.

Once you know where you'd like to live, you can also find agency listings in the Yellow Pages of the local telephone book and obtain referrals from the local chambers of commerce. Be sure to check out the local newspapers as well — the Maine Sunday Telegram is a great resource for classified listings throughout Maine's Southern Coast. Free publications containing property listings are available at the entrances of most grocery stores. In particular, you should check out Homes For Sale, which has regional editions and is published twice a month and the Maine edition of REBO (Real Estate By Owner) which is published monthly.

Maine Real Estate Disclosure Form No. 1

Before contacting an agent, there are a few things you should know about shopping for real estate in Maine. Real estate agents are required by law to have clients sign a disclosure form, generally referred to as "Form No. 1," the first time a property is discussed.

Many people feel hesitant about signing the form, but it is not a contract, it's merely a form saying that the agent has informed you whether the agency represents buyers only, sellers only or both. They should also explain what their relationship is to you.

In brief, unless you sign a separate form hiring the agent as a "buyer broker" (see section below for more information), the agent represents the seller, and you are simply the agent's customer. That doesn't mean they won't deal fairly with you, but it does mean they can't tell you anything about the sellers that they have not been authorized to tell. However, they must disclose any information regarding any problems with the house, including whether it contains lead paint — that's

state law. They also cannot suggest an offering price to you, but they will (in fact, they are required to) present any offer that you wish to make to the seller.

Multiple Listing Service (MLS)

Most real estate agencies in Maine belong to the Multiple Listing Service (MLS). The service is a computerized listing of all the properties that are available in the state through agents of the MLS.

What this means is that you can walk into any MLS-affiliated agency in any town, and they can pull up a list of properties for you based on the criteria you give them. This can include the town or towns you are interested in, the price range, number of bedrooms and any amenities you would like (i.e., fireplace, water view or attached two-car garage). They can also arrange to show you any property in the system.

Buyers' Agents and Brokers

Buyer brokerages are a fairly new phenomenon, and they are causing a lot of confusion. While there are a few agencies that have no property listings and deal exclusively with buyers, most agents, regardless of agency, will work as buyers' agents.

When you hire an agent as a buyers' broker, you sign a contract with them. Most of the time the contract will state that the agent will receive their commission from the seller. It is common practice for the listing agent and the selling agent to receive a percentage of the commission (usually a 50-50 arrangement) paid by the seller. However, you should be aware that some buyer broker contracts state what percentage the agent will receive.

INSIDERS' TIP

If you are looking for real estate, it's handy to know that any agent affiliated with the Multiple Listing Service (MLS) can show you any property within that service. You do not need to call the listing agent for each property you'd like to see.

For example, if the commission is 6 percent and the split is 50-50, then the buyers' agent will receive 3 percent. However, if your contract says that the agent is to receive 3.5 percent, then you will have to pay the extra 0.5 percent yourself.

To be fair, if you have hired an agent as a buyers' broker, do not call other agents and ask them to show you property. In fact, the contract you sign may prohibit you from making other agent contacts. If you are interested in meeting with another agent, ask your buyers' agent to set up an appointment. If you do call another agent, make sure that you inform them that you have a buyers' agent.

Area Neighborhood Overviews

Southern Beaches Area

Kittery

It would be unfair to think of Kittery as merely a strip of outlet malls located on U.S. Highway 1. True, this is the part of town most people see as they travel up the coast, but it isn't all of Kittery by a long shot.

If you get off U.S. 1 and take Maine Highway 236 south to Kittery Foreside at the junction of Maine Highway 103, you'll see more of the character of this town. Maine 103 runs along a branch of the Piscataqua River, which flows between Seavey Island and Portsmouth Harbor. Along it you'll find a nice gathering of 19th-century homes built when Kittery was known for its shipyards.

As you head north on Maine 103 past Fort McClary, you'll cross into Kittery Point, known for its fine old Sea Captains' homes and other distinguished properties. Kittery Point and adjoining Gerrish Island are where you'll find the most expensive properties in this town. The nearest point in Maine to Boston, Kittery oceanfront property commands prices beginning around $200,000. A two-bedroom waterfront Cape in need of some work, for example, would cost about $225,000. Still on the Point but not on the waterfront, a three-bedroom Cape with a wraparound deck and

fireplace might go for $230,000. This area has some of the highest property and resale values in the state.

Following Maine 103 towards York, you'll pass into a less-populated area of farmland sandwiched between this road and U.S. Highway 1. In this area, three-bedroom houses (split-entry raised ranches and gambrel-style homes) are being offered for between $130,000 and $180,000. South of Route 103 (Brave Boat Harbor Road), a nine-room Colonial with two fireplaces goes for about $390,000.

Condos: There isn't much in the way of condos in Kittery. At Twin Birches you can get a three-bedroom, one-and-a-half bath place with cathedral ceilings for around $125,000, or you can get a similar-size condo in the center of town on the water for $185,000.

York

The town of York is comprised of four areas: York Village, York Harbor, York Beach and Cape Neddick. The population rises from about 14,000 in the winter to more than 40,000 in summer. Many of the more expensive waterfront properties are owned by out-of-staters, though there are a good number owned by year-round Mainers.

York Village is the business hub of the town, with several historic buildings, including the seven owned by the Old York Historical Society. Heading west from York Village on Maine Highway 91 (Cider Hill Road) is the Cider Hill Road area, where there has been some recent development. Houses in this area tend to fall in the $150,000 to $200,000 range and are set amidst the fields and trees of old farmland.

Heading south on U.S. 1 from York Village is York Harbor. As you would expect from the name, York Harbor faces the Atlantic. Many of the stately old homes in this upscale neighborhood are now bed and breakfasts and inns (see a sampling of these in our Bed and Breakfasts chapter), and the character of this part of town, with its river and rugged coastline, is quite different from the more commercial York Beach area.

The Green Acres Drive development, found off Orchard Farm Road, is also a recent addition. Here you'll see two-story Colo-

388 • NEIGHBORHOODS AND REAL ESTATE

nial style homes close to the village with access to the river for around $140,000. Nearer to the sea, Woodbridge Estates in York Harbor will run you between $260,000 to $330,000 for a home on a half-acre lot. Larger lots are available at the Meadows Estates subdivision off of Southside Road. Newer than Woodbridge Estates, the Meadows Estates development features homes in the $280,000 to $400,000 range. Houses within these developments vary somewhat in style from Colonials and garrison Colonials to Victorian cottage styles and expanded Capes, but they usually have a minimum of three bedrooms and two baths and upwards of 2,000 square feet of living space.

The northernmost sections of York are York Beach and Cape Neddick. York Beach was once a part of Cape Neddick, but it now has a completely different atmosphere. It is the commercial part of town where tourists flock and summer rentals abound. You can buy condos, houses and cottages here at a wide range of prices, depending on proximity to the beach, age and state of repair of the property and what type of place you're looking for. At the low end, $90,000 will buy you a two-bedroom ranch. For $130,000, you can get a three-bedroom ranch or a two-bedroom bungalow with skylights. A seasonal cottage with three bedrooms and one bath will also run about $130,000.

Cape Neddick is a rural area surrounded by magnificent views of the Atlantic, and it features the picturesque Cape Neddick Lighthouse (known as Nubble Light; see our Attractions chapter). Here you'll find old farmhouses as well as large oceanfront and oceanview properties with great character and price tags to match. At the time of this writing, a 12-room antique Cape, dating from the 1800s, was available for $195,000; an eight-room, four-bedroom, multilevel contemporary home with access to a rocky private beach was listed at $250,000.

Condos: Condominiums range from around $45,000 to $200,000 in York. Spring Point Estates, a new development for seniors,

is at the high end, while a two-bedroom, one-and-three-quarter-bath condo (a three-quarter bath includes a shower, sink and toilet but no tub) on Ocean Avenue across from Short Sands Beach, with amenities like a pool, sauna, hot tub and exercise room, costs around $160,000. You can get a three-bedroom, one-and-three-quarter-bath condo with a fireplace on Rosewood Lane for $144,900 and a fully furnished motel unit at Gray Gull condos for $46,900.

Ogunquit

Ogunquit has been a magnet for artists since the late 1800s, and it's little wonder. The village, with its awning-dressed shops and flower bedecked houses is picture-perfect pretty, while Perkins Cove, with its harbor filled with boats, charming pedestrian drawbridge and fishing village atmosphere (albeit a dressed-up fishing village), just begs to be painted or photographed.

Driving around Ogunquit is problematical in the summer. To see this town, it's best to park in one of the public parking areas and take a trolley to get around (see our Getting Here, Getting Around chapter). You can also walk from the village to Perkins Cove along the Marginal Way, a 1.5 mile-long oceanfront path from which you can enjoy views of the beach and the sea.

As of this writing, the least expensive single-family, year-round property available in Ogunquit was a two-bedroom house with one bath at a listing price of $139,500. The majority of available properties were in the $200,000 to $350,000 range.

Condos: If you're looking for a condominium in Ogunquit, you'll find prices ranging from $59,900 for a three-room condo with access to a pool at Ocean Towers, to $289,000 for a four-room unit at Briarbank that overlooks Marginal Way with panoramic views of the ocean.

Wells

People who travel along U.S. Highway 1 rarely see the greatest part of the Town of Wells. They see the Wells Beach area, Moody

Beach and the commercial stretch along the highway, but that's only a fraction of the town. Heading west of Wells away from the sea, there are woodlands and farmlands with lovely subdivisions. These developments have good-sized lots — some over two acres with trees and privacy. Strip subdivisions, where houses are set close together and most trees are cleared away, are not allowed.

Some of the developments in this western part of town include Sherwood Forest, with prices from $90,000 to $150,000; Webhannet Woods, in the $125,000 to $180,000 range; and Penny Meadows, which offers 2- to 3-acre lots, blueberry bushes and a deer walk (through the woods and meadows, where you can see deer in their natural habitat) for $150,000 to $250,000. A smaller development closer to town is Spice Bush, with properties around $160,000. Then there is Moody Estates, which is closer to the beach with prices around $260,000.

Wells Beach and Moody Beach are the commercial parts of town that you run through along U.S. 1. There are plenty of houses and condos in this area in a variety of prices depending on proximity to the ocean, views and amenities.

Drake's Island is a strictly residential island between Wells Harbor and Laudholm Farm Estuary. There are no condos here, only single-family homes that share community tennis courts and a community center. The island is surrounded by a tidal river and salt marsh connected to the mainland by a little bridge over the river. At low tide you can walk across the river; it's a mere half-mile off U.S. 1. A two-bedroom, contemporary gambrel on Drake's Island will cost you about $225,000.

The agents we talked to said that if you're looking for property in Wells, you really need to ask a real estate agent for help. There are no convenience stores or other businesses to use as reference points as you head into the backroads, and you'll find it difficult to find places without their assistance.

Condos: Condominiums abound in Wells — from single-room motel/condos to seven-room units overlooking the sea. At Village by the Sea, a resort-type condo complex, you can own a fully furnished, three-room unit with one bedroom and two bathrooms (but no ocean view) for $48,500. Similar to this are Langdon's Resort and East Winds, with prices in the high $40,000s to low $50,000s.

Misty Harbor is a motel/condo where a two-bedroom unit will run you about $80,000. At Flintlock Village you can get a six-room, two-bedroom, one-and-three-quarter-bath condo with a fireplace for $114,900. Moving to the high end, Running Tide on Ocean Avenue will cost you around $210,000 for a unit with three levels, three decks and balconies, some furnishings and ocean views. Sea Hawk, also on Ocean Avenue, has seven-room units with three bedrooms and one-and-three-quarter baths as well as a rose arbor, flowers and lawns. They run around $300,000.

Kennebunk and Kennebunkport

Though frequently grouped together, these two towns, along with Cape Porpoise and Goose Rocks Beach, have very distinct personalities.

Kennebunk has a main street with a couple of old brick mill buildings now converted into shops, large Colonial houses and a number of buildings on the National Historic Register. It is the first part of the Kennebunks that you see as you come in off Interstate 95 (Maine Turnpike) at Exit 3, or along U.S. 1. From the Turnpike, drive along Fletcher Road past the high school into town, and on either side of the main road are streets shaded by large maples and oaks with a variety of house styles — from ranches and Capes to older New Englanders and Colonials. Property prices in this

---

INSIDERS' TIP

Before looking for real estate you should talk to your local lending institutions about being pre-qualified for financing. They will tell you how much you can afford to buy, so you don't get disappointed by looking at overly expensive properties or look too low when you could be considering more expensive options.

area begin around $120,000 for a two-bedroom Cape with an attached garage.

Along Kennebunk Beach you'll find an upscale neighborhood with a few Victorians and contemporary houses, but most houses are in the Queen Anne cottage style or are Colonial reproductions. Prices range from $200,000 to around $500,000.

From Kennebunk center, if you drive down Maine Highway 9 (Sea Road) towards Kennebunkport, you'll pass the Sea Road School area, where subdivisions branch off the main road. Here house prices range from $150,000 to $260,000 for anything from a three-bedroom cottage with one bathroom and a deck to a 12-room, five-bedroom, three-bathroom Cape with a heated two-car garage. Woodside Drive, across from Sea Road School, is perhaps the oldest subdivision in town, with smaller houses and prices in the $110,000 to $140,000 range.

From Kennebunk Beach back up Maine Highway 35, you'll find Kennebunk's Historic Preservation District. The town's Historic Preservation Ordinance is meant to keep houses appropriate to their style and age. Big, fancy Colonials, Sea Captains' houses and the famous "Wedding Cake House" with its gingerbread trim are some of the properties you'll see. Listing prices for these houses vary depending on their age, size and how faithful restoration, if any, has been.

Between Kennebunk and Kennebunkport is a new development called River Locks, with houses in the $300,000s. Some of these houses have river frontage, while others overlook the Cape Arundel Golf Course. Next comes Lower Village, with old Colonial Capes painted pretty colors and many buildings that have been turned into shops. Dock Square in Kennebunkport, with a picturesque cluster of shops and restaurants backed by docks with fishing and lobster boats, is reached by crossing a bridge from Lower Village.

Heading out of Dock Square on Maine 9 (Maine Street) towards Cape Porpoise, you'll pass large Colonials with attached barns and other distinctive features. Some of these have been converted into inns or shops, but many are still family residences. An alternate route between the two locales is the Wildes District Road. If, instead of crossing the bridge into Dock Square you continue down around the coast on Ocean Avenue, then you'll pass large oceanfront properties including Walker's Point, where former President Bush has his summer home. Just beyond Walker's Point, Ocean Avenue curves northward and intersects with Wildes District Road. Take a right and you're heading to Cape Porpoise; take a left and you're heading towards Dock Square.

As you'd imagine from its delightful name, Cape Porpoise is a wonderful little village. Whitewashed houses line the road that circles the harbor, and you can find property here from $140,000 to around a half-million dollars. At $140,000 is a two-and-a-half-story, hip-roofed Colonial with three bedrooms and a three-car garage. At the high end, $550,000 will get you a seven-bedroom, 13-room home with perennial gardens and a view across the harbor. That's where lobster and fishing boats come in to unload their catch; you might enjoy watching them from Cape Porpoise's large dock. Though only minutes from the tourist bustle of Kennebunkport in summer, this is a quiet place where you can sit on a rock and listen to the gulls or watch the sky turn pink.

Goose Rocks Beach is farther along Maine 9 heading away from Kennebunk. While it has a large number of houses used only in the summer, there are properties lived in year round. Prices vary depending on whether the houses are oceanfront or not, but you'll be lucky to find anything lower than $150,000. The beach here has been rated one of the best in Maine, and it can get a bit crowded in summer (see our Beaches chapter). In winter it is beautifully empty.

Condos: Prices for condominiums in the Kennebunks run from $62,000 to $289,000. At the high end, you can try Christensen Lane

Photo: Maine Office of Tourism

Most Southern Coast communities provide handy access to area waters.

condos, where some units have a bird's-eye view of the river and Kennebunkport. Dock Square West will run you around $220,000 for a five-room, two-bedroom with one bath and a porch overlooking the river and water access. At the lower end of the spectrum you'll find Brown Street Condos at $67,500 for a three-level unit, and Leeside condos on Ocean Avenue at $74,900 for a studio unit in the heart of Kennebunkport.

Old Orchard Beach Area

Biddeford

Biddeford is an anomaly along our coast. It is a city with two distinct parts — Biddeford Pool and Biddeford center. "The Pool," as Biddeford Pool is called by locals, is on the coast where Maine Highway 9 bends like an elbow to travel westward up the Saco River. It is little more than a five-minute drive from

Goose Rocks Beach in Kennebunk and incorporates Fortunes Rocks Beach. Biddeford center, by contrast, is an old mill town with large brick factory buildings and many multi-family properties.

Houses in Biddeford Pool are pricey. For $650,000 to $800,000, you can get ocean-front homes with four or five bedrooms. For about $160,000 you'll find a three-bedroom ranch that backs up onto the salt marsh. In recent years there has been a movement for the Pool to secede from the city. Some residents argue that the limited number of properties in the Pool generate a high proportion of the property taxes collected in Biddeford, yet residents get little in return. Others argue that the Pool has always been a part of Biddeford and want it to remain so. They don't want to have to build schools or pay other towns to take their children in for schooling, and they don't want to deal with forming a government.

Biddeford, Saco and Old Orchard Beach are the least expensive places to buy a house along the coast from Kittery to Portland. Biddeford is not as picturesque as a village by the sea, but the red-bricked factory buildings and turn-of-the-century multi-family homes here have their own style of beauty. The city is predominantly French-Canadian in origin. Canadians emigrated here to work in the factories, and their heritage endures to this day. Single-family homes are available here for less than $100,000. An older New Englander or two-bedroom ranch will run about $75,000; a new three-bedroom Cape with an unfinished upstairs costs just under $100,000.

The city has a viable main street with a Reny's department store, sandwich shops and a number of hair salons. Properties vary in type from single-family Capes with small yards to large multi-family homes and sprawling properties along the river off Maine 9 (Pool Road). Driving along South and Main streets north off U.S. 1 (Elm Street), you'll find a wonderful country atmosphere. Just a minute from the busy center you can suddenly hear birds singing as you travel on winding, tree-lined roads. This, too, is Biddeford.

Condos: Condominiums in Biddeford range from $49,000 to $234,900. At the high end you can get a beachfront townhouse condo overlooking the ocean with a spa tub, fireplace, deck, three bedrooms and three-and-a-half baths near Biddeford Pool. For $134,000 you can buy a unit in the center of Biddeford Pool at Colgate House with four rooms, two bedrooms and one bath. Lower down the price scale, you'll find the Western Avenue condos, located off South Street, with two skylights, cathedral-ceilinged bedrooms, one-and-a-half baths and a bay window in the open-plan living room/kitchen area for around $50,000.

Saco

The Saco River separates Saco from Biddeford, but the cities are divided by more than mere geography. Originally called Pepperellboro, this city has a very different character from its neighbor. Main Street and Pepperell Square are lined with brick and wood-framed buildings, ranging in style from the Plaza Restaurant with its wrought-iron bench sitting outside to the imposing brick building housing the U.S. Post Office on the other side of the street.

Farther along sit several large Colonials, New Englanders and Victorians, some maintained as residences and others holding offices for dentists, doctors and lawyers. If you continue north to the intersection of Main and Beach streets, Main Street ends and becomes U.S. Highway 1. Heading away from Main Street, you'll find the road lined with beautiful, large Victorians and Colonials painted turquoise, pink, red, yellow and traditional white. Some of these houses are now bed and breakfasts; prices range from $165,000 to more than $300,000 depending on the amount of land available with the property and its condition.

On the side streets lining Main Street to the left, and on the streets west of U.S. 1, lies the historic district of Saco. Including Main Street, parts of U.S. 1 and parts of Beach Street, this area features houses that are set on small lots but have much turn-of-the-century character. In this area two- or three-bedroom ranches, New Englanders and Capes generally range from $75,000 to around $125,000 .

If you turn right on Beach Street (Maine 9), you head toward Camp Ellis, following the Saco River on the side opposite Biddeford. There are a number of schools along the portion of Beach Street near its intersection with U.S. 1, and the residential neighborhoods around the schools tend to have tree-lined streets and houses set on good-sized lots. Prices in this area generally run from $100,000 to $150,000 for a two- to three-bedroom home. Beach Street turns into Ferry Road at the intersection of Old Orchard Road as you head south. Both Old Orchard Road and Ferry Road have good-sized houses on large lots with plenty of grass, flowers and trees. These streets and the developments off of them are desirable neighborhoods and property sells quite quickly. Prices range from $100,000 for a two-bedroom ranch to more than $300,000, but the average is in the $150,000s.

A couple of miles down Ferry Road is an intersection with Bay View Road. If you take a left down this road, you'll pass the entrance to Ferry Beach State Park (see our Parks and Recreation and Beaches chapters). In recent years an upscale subdivision called Plymouth Settlement has been developed off Bay View Road. Large Colonials, expanded Capes and other styles of homes are set on large, treed lots in this development. It's a quiet neighborhood close to the beach and is quite popular. House prices range upwards of $175,000.

Camp Ellis is at the end of Ferry Road. This charming fishing village where the Saco River meets the sea is a popular tourist spot. But it isn't just tourists who come to buy fried clams and french fries and walk out on the breakwater to eat. Locals do it, too. Unfortunately, Camp Ellis has its problems. That large breakwater has caused the sea to erode what was once an extensive beach. The houses that you see lining the sea-front today were once a couple of streets back. Whole sections of this village have been taken by the ocean. The threat to the village is real, and residents have launched an S.O.S. (Save Our Shore) campaign. However, at this writing, the town of Saco (citing costs and the fact that shoring up appears to be a lost cause) had decided to no longer subsidize the shoring up of Camp Ellis.

Like Biddeford, Saco has roads leading out of the city, namely Maine Highways 5 and 112 (North Street), which quickly bring you into more rural country. Flag Pond, Broadturn and Beech Ridge roads can be found branching off U.S. 1 to the left as you head towards Scarborough. These roads will bring you into sparsely developed, wooded country. You'll find everything from two-bedroom ranches (priced around $100,000) to horse farms (more like $300,000) along these roads.

Condos: Condominium prices in Saco range from $35,000 to $275,000. At the Ocean Park East condos, you can find a single-floor unit with two bedrooms, a bath and a large kitchen/living room area for less than $50,000. Saco Island, in the converted mill buildings between Saco and Biddeford, has one-bedroom, single-floor units from around $35,000 and two-floor units with two bedrooms starting around $50,000. At this writing, Baywood housed the area's most expensive condo — an oceanfront, tri-level townhouse unit with seven rooms, built-in bookcases, three bedrooms, three-and-a-half baths, hardwood floors and a garage for $275,000.

Old Orchard Beach

In the late 1800s (and at the beginning of this century), Old Orchard Beach rivaled Newport, Rhode Island, as the place to be in the summer in New England. Oceanfront grand hotels, a long pier jutting out into the sea, miles of sandy beach and a seaside amusement park made it a fun, popular place to visit. Today the grand hotels have been replaced by dozens and dozens of hotels, inns, motor courts, condominiums and guest houses, but the town still has the pier jutting out to sea (don't miss the famous fries with salt and vinegar), miles of sandy beach and a seaside amusement park.

About five years ago the town spent $3 million to renovate the downtown area. They built red-bricked sidewalks, put in a large fountain and a square with semicircular stone benches and tables at the foot of the pier, bought Victorian-looking black iron lampposts and completely refurbished the impressive Town Hall building at the corner of Old Orchard Street and Saco Avenue. The street is now an endearing mix of old-fashioned charm and honky-tonk. T-shirt and bathing suit shops line the sidewalks, but there is also a cute coffee shop with umbrella-topped tables, and the town is making an effort to get a variety of vendors to fill their shop fronts.

Old Orchard Beach is roughly divisible into four residential sections: Ocean Park, East and West Grand Avenues, the Saco Avenue area and the Cascade Road area.

Ocean Park is somewhat separated from the main town. It is south of the town square along West Grand Avenue (Maine Highway 9). While it shares the same government with the rest of Old Orchard Beach, it has its own post office and library. Houses here tend to have porches (often screened-in), some are oceanfront, and others are on the streets leading off West Grand Avenue and amongst the tall pine groves off Temple Avenue, a main road branching right from West Grand. House prices in Ocean Park range from $115,000 (if you're lucky) to $300,000, depending on how close to the water they are and how big. A three-bedroom ranch runs around $165,000; three-bedroom Capes start at about $145,000.

The Salvation Army has a campground in the tightly built-up area to the right off Saco Avenue as you head into the town center. The houses here were originally built as summer homes, and they tend to be small and very close together. The Salvation Army campground is in a tall pine-shaded depression among these homes. You can find houses here in the $60,000 range and some that are higher. To the left of Saco Avenue, you'll find more houses, but this neighborhood has larger lots and homes. Still, you can find properties for less than $100,000 here.

East Grand and West Grand avenues are also Maine Highway 9. They run from south of Old Orchard in Ocean Park (West Grand) to the town square, then north towards Scarborough (East Grand). On either side of these streets, you'll find hotels, motels and condominiums interspersed with houses. The farther you get from the town square, the less congested it is; the nearer you get, the more built-up. This is less of a residential area than a tourist haven, but people do live here year round in houses and condos.

Cascade Road (Maine Highway 98) loops up to meet U.S. 1 from Town Hall. There are a number of subdivisions along Cascade and on the streets branching from it. Orchard Hill is a development of 35 lots with house prices ranging from $105,000 to $165,000. Cascade Heights has about the same number of lots with prices running from $95,000 to $135,000 for three-bedroom gambrels, Capes and contemporaries.

Dunegrass, also off Cascade Road, is the newest development in Old Orchard Beach, with a series of neighborhoods sprouting up around a premier 18-hole golf course designed by Dan Maples, one of the top course architects in the United States. Water is the predominant feature in this development, with houses nested among the trees alongside the vibrant greens of the course. At this writing, house lots were being sold for a development of properties in the $175,000 range as well as small, single-family homes on zero lot lines (in other words, these have very little land). These properties were being advertised in the $85,000 range.

Condos: Old Orchard Beach has a variety of condominiums. These range from $47,000 for a condo at Smithwheel Farm (not far from Exit 5 off I-95) to $230,000 for an oceanfront unit at Sea Scape, one of the few high-rise condo buildings on the beach. The unit at Sea Scape has four rooms, two bedrooms, two baths, marble flooring in the bathrooms and balconies off every room. You can get a three-room, one-bedroom, one-bath unit with a balcony but no ocean view for $105,000 in the same building. At Danton Towers, another high-rise, a five-room, two-bedroom unit with two bathrooms and an ocean view costs $132,500, while a corner unit with ocean views at The Diplomat, also a high rise, will run you about $140,000.

Not all condos in Old Orchard Beach are high-rises. You'll find plenty of other developments, from Beaver Creek, which features sunken living rooms with fireplaces and prices in the $50,000s, to Ocean Park Meadows off West Grand Avenue, which offers two-bedroom, townhouse-style units amidst beautiful grounds with winding paths and foot bridges over a stream for around $175,000.

Greater Portland Area

Scarborough

Scarborough is a sprawling town with a variety of neighborhoods from exclusive oceanfront communities to wooded areas and farmland. It's the fasting-growing town in Maine; in most areas of Scarborough, development is rampant. Houses and streets are being built so quickly, it would be impossible to describe them all here. In fact, growth has been progressing at such a rate that the town's new middle school, built to accommodate the growing number of students, had to be changed and expanded while it was being built in order to cope with an even greater influx of new families than was originally predicted.

Development sizes vary from those with fewer than 10 lots to those with 25 or more; some have half-acre lots while others have larger ones. The east side of Scarborough is separated from the west side by U.S. Highway 1. Two main intersections that are key geographical locators for the town occur at junctions of U.S. 1. In the south, at its intersection with Maine Highway 9 (Payne Road), is Dunstan Corner, and in the north, at the intersection of U.S. 1 and Maine Highway 114, is Oak Hill.

The stretch of U.S. 1 that runs between Dunstan Corner and Oak Hill crosses Scarborough Marsh, which separates Pine Point to the south from Black Point and Prout's Neck to the north and east. These three — Pine Point, Black Point, and Prout's Neck — are joined by Higgins Beach as the oceanside communities in the town. Most houses in Pine Point have ocean or marsh views, and house prices run from around $115,000 to $500,000. A full range of house styles are available in this area, from contemporaries to ranches and cottages. This is an older community with very little building taking place today.

Black Point Road heads east with neighborhoods branching out on either side; you can find houses from $90,000 for a four-bedroom Colonial in need of some cosmetic work to $179,000 for a three-bedroom Cape with hardwood floors. Prout's Neck, at the very end of the point, is a very upscale neighborhood with elaborate oceanfront properties for $300,000 and up. Its claim to fame is that painter Winslow Homer had his studio here. Higgins Beach is a quiet, small community with neatly laid-out streets and a lovely, curving little beach. You'll find property less expensive than in Prout's Neck, but not much is available in the low $100,000s.

On the Black Point side of the marsh heading north, Fogg Road runs between Black Point Road and Pleasant Hill Road. Quite a bit of development has been taking place in this area on Pin Tail Drive and at Grondin Pond, Settlers Green and Coultard Farms. Most houses in these developments run in the $200,000-and-up range, while houses in the Portland Farms Road area developments tend to be a bit lower. Arbor Place and Serenity Place run in the $140,000 to $170,000 range, and Autumn Pond will cost you between $170,000 and $220,000. West of U.S. 1, Regal Pines off Payne Road starts around $140,000 and Old Blue Point Woods, off Blue Point Road south of Dunstan Corner, starts around $125,000.

Condos: The range of condo prices in Scarborough isn't as wide as it is in the other towns. Here they go from $64,000 to $162,000. For $64,000 you'll get a four-room, two-bedroom unit at Sandpiper Cove off Black Point Road. At a little less than double that you can buy a six-room, freestanding unit with two bedrooms, two baths and amenities such as pools, tennis courts and stables.

At Cedarbrook East a three-bedroom, two-and-a-half-bath unit with a spa tub, cathedral ceilings and a fireplace costs $123,000. A similar unit at Teal Point Drive costs about 10 percent more, while on Oceanwood Drive in Higgins Beach you can get a seven-room condo with three bedrooms, two-and-a-half baths, a garage and deck for between $150,000 and $162,000.

Cape Elizabeth

In contrast to Scarborough, Cape Elizabeth has very little new development. Most of the development here took place between the 1960s and 1980s. House prices run the gamut from $90,000 to close to $2 million, and agents tell us there are currently more buyers in the $200,000 range than there are properties for them to purchase in this town. Architect Calvin Stephens designed many of the older oceanfront homes, when Cape Elizabeth was a colony of shingled summer properties for wealthy city dwellers.

For a small city, Cape Elizabeth has a wealth of parks: Two Lights State Park, Crescent Beach State Park and Fort Williams Park (see our Parks and Recreation chapter), which contains the famous Portland Head Light (see our Attractions chapter). Its neighborhoods are roughly grouped around these parks. There is Broad Cove, near Two Lights; Oakhurst, off Shore Road near Fort Williams in the older part of town; and the Casino Beach area, so named for the casino that operated here during the war. It's now a day-care facility.

Condos: At the two extremes in Cape Elizabeth, you'll find Great Pond Terrace — with seven-room, three-bedroom, one-and-a-half-bath townhouse units for $89,000 — and a Canterbury Way condo with seven rooms, three bedrooms, two-and-a-half baths, a fireplace, tennis courts and pool for $274,000. In between is Wildwood Drive, where a six-room, two-bedroom condo with two-and-a-half baths goes for $149,900.

South Portland

Once a part of Cape Elizabeth, this town is difficult to chart. It sprawls considerably and has two distinct characters — the commercial and the residential. The Maine Mall area, so named for the shopping mall and strip malls surrounding it, is mainly non-residential. South Portland Gardens is an apartment complex overlooking the Stroudwater River on Western Avenue near the mall area, but most houses are located around Broadway, the city's main thoroughfare.

If you're near the Maine Mall, you can get to Broadway from either Maine Highway 9 (Westbrook Street) or U.S. Highway 1 at Cash Corner. Traveling east on Broadway toward the sea, you'll intersect Cottage Street and, later, Preble Street. These three form a large triangle within and around which are formed the residential areas of South Portland. Alternately, if you're in Cape Elizabeth you can follow Shore Road until it forks: to the left is Cottage Road and to the right is Preble Street.

The Meeting House Hill area can be found to the right of Broadway or south of Cottage Road and is a popular family neighborhood. Willard Beach is another popular spot, with a residential area bordering the closest beach to Portland. House prices throughout South Portland range from the $80,000s to around $350,000. For $87,000, a four-bedroom Colonial on Broadway can be yours, while $350,000 will get you a four-bedroom home on Danforth Cove with a private beach and a tennis court.

Condos: In South Portland you can get a condo with a private entrance, skylights, sliding doors onto a deck, five rooms, two bedrooms and a bath for about $70,000 at Harbor Place, or you can get a single-floor, four-room, two-bedroom unit at the Breakwater for $89,900. A larger unit at the Breakwater, on Pickett Street, with five rooms, two bedrooms, two-and-a-half baths, a Jacuzzi and views of Casco Bay will run you $192,900. At a price between these two you'll find the Karynel Drive condos, with a solarium overlooking gardens, a fireplace, three bedrooms

and two baths with an attached garage for $109,900.

Portland

A compromise of city and country, Portland is a place where you can catch a symphony or a ballet and cruise down quiet neighborhood roads on your way there. With 64,000 people spread out over 26 square miles, there is still enough room for everyone even though more and more people are choosing to relocate here.

Most come for the quality of life Maine's largest city has to offer. There is swimming and sailing in Portland Harbor, bicycling, walking, skating and jogging on a 3-mile path around Back Cove and plenty of ice skating in the pond in Deering Oaks Park (in the summertime, the pond is full of paddle boats). Then there is the art museum, the children's museum and the Old Port with its novelty shops, pubs and restaurants. Modern office buildings line the streets of the state's financial and commercial center alongside historic brick buildings that form the city's core. Church spires poke through the skyline, and yachts and commercial vessels fill the harbor.

Getting to work is a breeze in Portland compared to living and working in the nation's larger cities. Although the roads are full during the morning and afternoon commutes, traffic jams are rare. There are plenty of parking garages, and you'll often see a smile when people pass on the sidewalks. If you're looking to move here, you'll find plenty of options, from oceanside houses to in-town condominium complexes to small neighborhoods where people still know each other.

The market has picked up since the beginning of the decade when things were kind of sluggish. In the early 1990s people were staying put, and most who were buying were first-time homebuyers. But with 4,000 houses on the market in the summer of 1997 in the Greater Portland Area, the average time it takes to sell a house has plummeted from 180 days to 109. It is even common for people to offer more than the asking price of a home on the first bid, just to be sure they get it.

The average selling price of a home in Portland is roughly $130,000. Back in the middle of the decade, the average was about $108,000. That statistic, however, can be misleading. Selling prices haven't increased that significantly, people are just buying nicer homes. Instead of fixing up the ones they're in now, they are shopping for larger houses.

There really are homes here for every price range. Expect to pay more for houses in the popular West End of town, which has many historic buildings. A 16-room house with seven fireplaces, antique moldings, a wraparound porch and three-car garage recently listed for $537,000. The Stroudwater area, on the riverfront, is also popular. Houses there have a little more space between them. A beautifully restored antique with three fireplaces and a studio in the barn recently listed for $175,000. Houses with water views are always priced a bit higher than the rest of the market because of constant demand. They also typically have higher resale value.

If you're looking for a great family neighborhood, try North Deering, Woodfords or the Back Cove area. Houses are often close together, but many have nicely fenced backyards, making them a popular buy. Trees dot the sides of the streets, and the neighborhoods are generally well-kept. A recent listing of homes in that area included a nicely maintained, three-bedroom Cape with vinyl siding and a fenced-in backyard for $85,000. Another four-bedroom bungalow with maple floors listed for $84,000.

Condos: You can find in-town condos in all price ranges. A two-bedroom unit in a historic brick building with water views and on-site storage and parking recently listed for $57,000, while an Italianate townhouse with hardwood floors, French doors and high ceilings near the Portland Museum of Art (see our Arts and Culture chapter) listed for $189,000. If you want a nice rental, good luck. Many downtown shops have small apartments on the upper floors, but there are generally so few rentals around that most real estate companies don't even work with them. Owners of rental properties can get rid of them for the cost of one advertisement in the newspaper, and that's a good place for you to begin your hunt.

Falmouth and Yarmouth

Side by side, these towns, with a combined population of 16,300, are two of the hottest on the real estate market. New subdivisions are booming. One 20-lot subdivision recently sold out within three months.

What's the draw? The area, which is mostly rural, is just 10 minutes north of Portland on U.S. 1, and the schools have a reputation for excellence. There are plenty of grand, old houses scattered along the woodsy roads, which used to be carriage paths, and there are modern, new homes popping up in rural developments. The resale value of houses here is quite high.

Both towns have plenty of history. Settled in 1632, Falmouth was the start of what is now known as the Greater Portland area. And Yarmouth, just a few minutes north on U.S. 1, came to be a few years later in 1658.

The majority of the people who live here are executives and retirees. Expect to pay from $100,000 to $400,000 for a new three- or four-bedroom house in a subdivision. Cape-style homes with attached garages are very popular designs, as are imitation Colonials. Lot sizes are large, and it's common to get a couple of acres with a house. But if it is in a development, you may have restrictions that would limit future building.

As for existing property, a nicely landscaped four-bedroom garrison with a formal dinning room, finished basement and a private backyard recently listed in Falmouth for $185,000. And a charming, antique, gambrel-roofed home with hardwood floors, a large country kitchen, hearth, orchard and water frontage on the Piscataqua River listed for just $135,900.

A Yarmouth Colonial on 1.33 acres with oak floors, a cherry kitchen and two-car ga-

INSIDERS' TIP

Did you know that Ogunquit used to be part of Wells? The towns were always quite separate in character, but it wasn't until 1980 that Ogunquit officially seceded from Wells.

Bountiful autumn harvests are a prelude to Maine's demanding winter.

rage listed for $179,000. Out here that comes with plenty of privacy and quiet. There are a couple of main roads through town where you'll find some large apartment complexes, and many more back roads with houses spread out. These communities are largely made up of homeowners, and while you may find a house to rent for about $1,000 a month or more, there are only a few apartment complexes.

Condos: Falmouth and Yarmouth have a handful of moderately priced and executive-quality condos. Some even have water access. In the first six months of 1997, 15 condos sold in these two towns. The average selling price in Falmouth was $122,000; in Yarmouth it was $172,000. Condos stayed on the market an average of 172 and 107 days, respectively.

An oceanfront, three-bedroom unit at Bayside Condominiums in Falmouth recently listed for $214,000. The owners are likely to get close to what they're asking — most condos in this market go for 97 percent of the asking price. In Yarmouth you could buy a nine-room, four-bedroom unit at Foxglove Court for about $189,900. In March 1997, a six-room, two-bedroom unit with a fireplace, vaulted ceilings, built-in bookshelves, a master bedroom and frontage on the Royal River at Blueberry Cove sold for $245,000.

Freeport

This town's worldwide claim to fame is the outdoor retail store L.L. Bean, which sells everything from camping gear and fishing poles to designer wool sweaters and long underwear. You'll find more about L.L. Bean, and the nearly 250 outlet stores that feed off its reputation, in our Shopping and Attractions chapters.

But Freeport's history goes back quite a bit further. It was chartered in 1680 and became a free port, hence the name. Trees from its forests were hewn for the masts of tall ships and stocked at Mast Landing to be shipped to England. One of the city's most noteworthy historic events occurred at the Jamestown Tavern, now a restaurant off Main Street (see our Restaurants chapter). It was there in 1820 that a few brave men signed a treaty to separate from Massachusetts, and Maine was born.

Freeport draws tourists from all over the world. They drive up U.S. Highway 1, which runs right through the center of town, for the great shopping deals. But despite the summertime and weekend crowds, it also draws people looking to get away from such things. With plenty of lovely, wooded back roads, shorefront property along Casco Bay and a top-notch school system, it's a wonderful place to live. Two more pluses: The town is

Photo: Merry Farnum

just 20 minutes from Portland, and the retail stores help offset the tax rate by contributing their share to the town budget.

Generally, the farther north you are from Portland, the less you can expect to pay for real estate. So while buying a house in Freeport might be less expensive than in Falmouth or Yarmouth, it is still a little more expensive than Brunswick. In Freeport a nearly-new, double-wide mobile home with three bedrooms and two bathrooms on 2 acres of land recently listed for $63,000. A two-bedroom house closer to the shopping district listed for $66,000, and that included hardwood floors, a formal dining room and pine cabinets in the kitchen.

The Wolfe's Neck area of town, right on Wolfe's Neck Cove, is where many of the higher-priced homes are located. There a two-bedroom house with three fireplaces and an in-law apartment listed for $374,500. But the views? Worth every penny!

Condos: You won't find much here in the way of condos, but the few to be had are priced lower than those in Falmouth and Yarmouth. In 1997 there were just three condominium projects. A five-room, two-bedroom unit at Summerset recently listed for $56,000, and at nearby Cushingwood, a two-bedroom unit with a combined living room and dining room and a kitchen listed for $64,900.

Brunswick, Bath and Boothbay Harbor Area

Brunswick

Brunswick is a town of 21,000 that has its fingers dug deep in the soil of the nation's history. A walk through the downtown will take you past the clapboard home of Civil War hero Gen. Joshua Chamberlain, past the white, wood-framed house where Harriet Beecher Stowe lived while her husband taught here at Bowdoin College, and past the college itself, where ivy-lined buildings rub shoulders with newly built dormitories. (See our Attractions chapter for more on the Chamberlain and Stowe homes; see our Education and Child Care chapter for more on Bowdoin.) It was at the college that American author Nathaniel Hawthorne and former U.S. Sen. George Mitchell both studied and graduated.

Brunswick is history. But it is also the present: a modern mix of eclectic bookstores and coffee shops, gift nooks, specialty clothing stores and restaurants and cafes of every flavor. It is a place where college students play hacky-sack, Frisbee and stringed instruments on the town green, and business people stop to chat in the shade of brick storefronts. Cook's Corner, one of the fastest-growing commercial developments in the state, is just up Maine Highway 24. It offers a sparkling new 10-screen movie theater, two outdoor shopping centers and a Wal-Mart amid a slew of other stores.

If you plan to stay a while, you might rent an inexpensive apartment above a storefront beginning at just $300 — depending on whether you want more than one room. Or you might step back one block and rent an apartment in a historic house along Federal Street for about $475 and up. (Believe it or not, this usually includes heat, which can be quite expensive in the winter.)

Federal Street has some of the most desirable houses in town. Most have good-sized lawns and are historical, in immaculate shape and within easy walking distance of the town center. A carefully restored Greek Revival home with six fireplaces, period moldings and a separate two-bedroom apartment recently listed for $325,000. Federal Street also stands out for the care and forethought that went into its planning. Some of the homes built here date back to the early 1800s. Residents of the neighborhood got together and, in an interesting example of early urban planning, decided that all the houses had to be set back from the road by 20 feet, and that they all had to be at least two stories. That's part of the reason the street is so distinguished today.

More interested in country living? Pick property off a back road between here and Freeport, or head out toward one of the adjoining peninsulas. In the wooded countryside a typical three-bedroom farmhouse might start for as little as $125,000. Oceanfront land, of which there is very little left, sells for $100,000 to $200,000 for as little as a half-acre. If you purchase land facing a bay you'll end up paying quite a lot less, starting at about $65,000 an acre. Remember, the demand for housing is high due to the Brunswick Naval Air Station and the nearby Bath Iron Works.

After passing Bowdoin College, head south on Maine Highway 123 and 15 minutes later you'll come to Harpswell, a rural peninsula town with some pretty hot-selling property. The main attractions here are trees, rocky coves and the swelling sea, but expect to pay quite a costly admission fee. A nine-room ranch overlooking a cove lists for $259,000, while an 11-room contemporary with water views from each room lists for $495,000. A two-bedroom camp on the water with no insulation and no heat recently sold for $99,000.

Harpswell is a popular spot for retirees seeking scenic summers, but most head to a more civilized retreat where they spend the winters to avoid the 30-minute drive to the nearest grocery store. Getting back to Brunswick can be a hair-raising experience for newcomers when the roads are slick with snow and ice.

Harpswell's main claim to fame is that it has more coastline — 150 miles of it — than any other town in the state! The peninsula itself is 10 miles long, and surrounding it are more than 200 islands, although some aren't much more than rocks poking their heads out of the ocean. Out here you'll find lots of lobster traps, fishnets and boats — fishing is the main industry — and many lovely homes from charming Capes to grand Colonials.

Condos: Up until the last few years, "condominium" was a dirty word here. Now they are selling faster than ever, as two-paycheck families look toward simplified living and older people look for summer or retirement homes. You'll generally find two condo classifications: more affordable units and executive-quality

properties. In the lower end of the market, about $60,000 to $90,000 can get you a two-bedroom, planned development unit, where each living space has its own outdoor entryway. Coastal Estates in Cook's Corner, where open-concept condos have vaulted ceilings, is one of these complexes. Willow Grove, off McKeen Street, has larger condos with up to three bedrooms for $80,000 to $130,000. These prices are a little higher because there is less development and less traffic to contend with in the area.

Upper-end properties such as Appletree, off Maine Street, and The Pines, in the Meadowbrook neighborhood, sell for between $160,000 and $225,000. There you will typically find more floor space, up to three bedrooms and special features such as hardwood and tile floors.

Bath

On the west bank of the Kennebec River and just off U.S. Highway 1, Bath is a community rich in maritime history. Back in the 1600s, the river marked the border between territories owned by France and England. Later it became one of the most prolific shipbuilding centers in the world, at one time having more shipyards than any comparable strip of waterfront in North or South America. Now it has only one shipyard, Bath Iron Works, which has 7,000 workers, making it the largest employer in the state.

The men and women who work at the shipyard live in the many surrounding communities and come here daily to pound and weld steel into naval destroyers. In addition to producing some of the finest fighting ships on the water, the yard lays claim to one of the largest moving cranes in the Northern Hemisphere. Its red and white striped neck towers above the city skyline and is visible from just about any point in the downtown.

The city itself has a population pushing 10,000 and was recently named among the best small cities in the nation for its quality of life. Its downtown center is just one block away from the river and is made up of two crisscrossing roads: Centre and Front streets. It is a menagerie of great lunch spots and well-loved restaurants, specialty boutiques, gift stores and offices (see the Shopping the

Maine Streets section of our Shopping chapter). Walking down the brick sidewalks beneath centuries-old brick buildings is like stepping back in time. You almost expect a horse-drawn carriage to rumble by.

The housing market is very active due to the constant influx of people at the shipyard and the nearby Brunswick Naval Air Station. There are a large number of houses in Bath, which on the south end of town has one of the most densely populated neighborhoods in the state. You can generally buy a house for 10 percent less than in the surrounding communities.

In the current market, $120,000 to $200,000 will buy a really lovely in-town home within walking distance to nearby marinas. But if you're looking for a deal, look no further. We actually know people who bought an 1800s Colonial here for $15,000! Granted, they had to put in new windows and plasterboard and put on a new roof, but they did much of it themselves and saved a bundle of money. A four-bedroom house also dating back to the 1800s recently sold for $60,000. For that price, you won't get much land to speak of, but it's a great opportunity to buy a first home.

Drive north on Washington Street if you want to view some of the grander homes here. Many are enormous old Sea Captains' houses with Greek columns and windows that stretch from floor to ceiling. Those, and other houses in the historic district, start around $180,000 and climb into the $400,000 range. But for the lower price, you can get a fully restored Victorian with a wraparound porch, living room, dining room, parlor and sunroom as well as a large backyard.

In addition to the downtown section, Bath has rural areas made up of old farms and some new construction, although few people actually build because there are so many good buys already on the market. If you're in the market for land, it goes for about $25,000 an acre in these areas.

Bath also has more rentals than just about any other small community in the state. They run anywhere from $300 a month for a one-room efficiency to $800 or so for an entire house with two or three bedrooms.

If you want a little more peace and quiet than Bath has to offer, head out to one of the nearby peninsulas for plenty of tranquility and shore frontage. The wooded peninsulas of Phippsburg, south on Maine Highway 209, and Georgetown, south on Maine Highway 203, have tax rates nearly half those of Bath, but you'll have to use your own well and septic system and drive 20 minutes to get to a shopping center. Out on the peninsulas, three-bedroom houses start at about $80,000 and quickly climb several hundred thousand dollars or more for water views.

To see a quaint Maine village, drive north on U.S. 1 to Woolwich, a rural town of 3,000 residents, and take your first left onto Maine Highway 127 after crossing over the Carlton Bridge. Take another left onto Maine 128 and slow down to enjoy Days Ferry, one of the earliest settlements here. When you gaze at the Colonial houses and tiny Capes knit together along the east bank of the Kennebec River, you'll want to pack up and move here. But before you do, beware: A tiny brick Cape with just a speck of land underneath recently listed for $225,000.

Keep going up U.S. 1 another 10 minutes and you'll arrive in Wiscasset, which claims to be the prettiest village in Maine. You'll find out why and discover plenty of rural buys at great prices when you drive around the country roads or along the Sheepscot River, which runs through town. There is a large historic district downtown. One house, built in 1804, is a display-case example of what you might find. The property was completely restored to museum quality in 1985 and boasts an elegant main house with six fireplaces, three bedrooms and a library, an attached guest house with three bedrooms, an in-ground pool and a three-car garage all for $595,000.

INSIDERS' TIP

The Casco Bay Islands, off the coast of Portland, are part of the much larger Calendar Islands. There are approximately 365 of them; that's how they got their name.

Condos: There aren't many condos in Bath, and they are typically a slow part of the market due to the number of inexpensive houses available. However, one condominium complex, Schooner Ridge, does overlook the Kennebec River. The building has a central entryway, which makes it less desirable to some, but the two- and three-bedroom units are nicely constructed and typically sell for $70,000 and up.

The Boothbays

This area is largely made up of the tiny towns stretched out along the Boothbay Harbor peninsula on either side of Maine Highway 27. The closer you get to the harbor, the more you can expect to pay for real estate.

On your way toward the tip of the peninsula, you'll drive through North Edgecomb, Edgecomb and Boothbay. All offer very rural properties and access to the water. There really aren't any set neighborhoods here because until you get to the town center of Boothbay, which has a grocery store and several other shops. The land is fairly undeveloped.

The Harbor itself, however, is another story, with scores of tourist-oriented shops sitting shoulder to shoulder along every inch of road and bed and breakfasts and apartments squeezed in between. Properties come in every shape, size and price range. A two-bedroom bungalow set in the woods on an acre of land in Edgecomb recently listed for $49,999, while a nearby antique Cape built in the 1780s listed for $122,500.

From the beginning of the peninsula to the harbor is roughly a 15-minute drive. But just wait until you get there. . . . Imagine neighborhoods of stately old Victorians, small Capes and sharp condominiums wound around a sparkling harbor of bobbing sailboats and sea gulls. Picture darling shops set in old-style homes and a wooden foot bridge stretching from the shopping district across a narrow cove. Smell the warm, salty air. Listen to the band playing at the library park. Want to own a piece of it? Picture yourself writing a check for a couple hundred thousand dollars — at least if you want the water views.

Boothbay Harbor is one of the premium vacation centers in the state. Its population during the colder months is just 2,300, but in summer the number of people living here doubles, and that's nothing compared to the hoard of 7,000 visitors who descend on the peninsula daily. Some call it the boating capital of New England — more than 25 excursion boats sail out of here during the summer (see our Attractions chapter).

Boothbay Harbor is the largest boating harbor north of Boston, and it used to be a major shipping and shipbuilding center. Many of the people who buy property here are looking for a home away from home — a place where they can dream away the summer while drinking iced tea on their porches.

Shorefront houses sell from $200,000 to $700,000, partly because waterfront property retains its value better than any other during market declines — there is always great demand for it. A less expensive way to get near the water is to buy something on a river or with tidal frontage. Because undeveloped land is so plentiful here, new subdivisions are becoming quite popular, and at least 10 were developed during the 1980s. For a three- or four-bedroom house there, plan to pay anywhere from $275,000 to $400,000.

Condos: Hot! Hot! Hot! Condos are among the fastest-selling properties on the peninsula. You'll find them tucked in town, hiding out in the trees and leaning down toward the waterfront. In Boothbay Harbor a two-bedroom unit at Harbor Front Condominiums — set among oak trees with a back yard sloping down to the water — will run you about $160,000. That includes a common deep-water dock and a swimming area. Less room means less money — a one-bedroom condo at Harbor-Side Condominiums is $42,000 to $62,000.

Some condos on the harbor sell in as few as 30 days. Where the property you're looking for is located makes a huge difference in the price — even within the same condominium complex! For instance, one two-bedroom townhouse with two floors of living space and a loft overlooking the marina in Boothbay Harbor recently listed for $169,900, while another townhouse with the same amount of living space but with ocean views listed for $249,000.

Real Estate Agencies

Regardless of where you want to buy along Maine's Southern Coast, there are several real estate companies with eager agents ready to assist you. The list we offer here is not meant to be all-inclusive, but it does give a good representation of the number and high quality of the agencies in our area.

Southern Beaches Area

Anne Erwin Real Estate
281 York St., York • (207) 363-6640

The local affiliate of Sotheby's International Realty, this agency has listings that vary from historic to contemporary and from ocean or river to the center of town. For two decades the agency has been the local leader in selling waterfront, water-view and distinctive properties in all price ranges. The agency has seven full-time agents with an extensive knowledge of the Yorks, Kittery, Kittery Point, the Berwicks and nearby communities. The agency is part of Maine's Coastal Connection, a referral network of independent agencies along the coast from New Hampshire to Bar Harbor.

Stone & Stone Real Estate Services
Rt. 1, Meadowbrook Plaza, York
• (207) 363-7283

Cliff and Joanne Stone saw a need for a service-oriented real estate company and opened for business in 1990. As experienced real estate specialists, the Stones guide their clients through the often turbulent complexities of today's real estate sales. They understand the current legal and financial issues involved in an ever-changing market. Today the agency has grown to include two agents in addition to the Stones.

Drown Agency
U.S. Hwy. 1, Wells
• (207) 646-5131
75 York St., Kennebunk
• (207) 985-6176
169 Main St., Sanford
• (207) 324-2622

The first Drown Agency was founded by Lawrence Drown in 1973. Today there are no Drowns in the business, but the three owners have affiliated offices in Wells, York, Kennebunk and Sanford. Each office has its own manager and a total of about 25 agents working among them. The agencies are strong on all types of residential property from traditional and motel condos to single-family homes.

Garnsey Brothers Real Estate
510 Webhannet Dr., Wells
• (207) 646-3091

Not surprisingly this agency was founded in 1965 by two brothers named Garnsey. Several years ago a group that included the son of one of the original Garnseys purchased the agency, but today, ownership has passed into the hands of Luke Guerrette. The number of agents working at Garnsey Brothers varies by season. In the summer when the agency handles vacation rentals, there are about 50 agents (see our Summer Rentals chapter), while in the winter the number drops to about 10. Garnsey Brothers is a full-service agency that lists and sells real estate, handles vacation rentals and offers property management services.

Aiello & Co. Real Estate
183 Port Rd. (Maine Hwy. 35),
Kennebunkport
• (207) 967-5338

Barbara Aiello entered real estate in 1976 and in 1985 founded this agency. She is a past president of both the Maine Association of Realtors and the York County Board of Realtors. The combined experience of the agency's 11 agents totals more than 125 years, and it is little wonder they are one of the top agencies in the area. Aiello & Co. is an affiliate of Sotheby's International. They offer a full range of professional services from residential and commercial brokerage to long-term and seasonal rentals. The company is also an active member of the Coastal Connection, a referral network of 11 independent agencies covering coastal communities from Hampton, New Hampshire to Bar Harbor, Maine.

Old Orchard Beach Area

Classic Realty
365 Elm St., Biddeford
• **(207) 283-4100**
345 Main St., Saco
• **(207) 282-0100**

When Sue Poirier entered the real estate business in the soft market of 1990, people told her she wouldn't last four months. Today she's one of the leading movers and shakers in the area's real estate market. Eight full-time agents work in the two offices. Both offices handle listing and selling of real estate, and the Saco office has recently started providing a rental service.

ERA Agency 1
326 Elm St., Biddeford
• **(207) 282-5000**
185 Saco Ave., Old Orchard Beach
• **(207) 934-5194, (800) 595-5194**
152 U.S. Hwy. 1, Scarborough
• **(207) 883-5135**
349 Oceanhouse Rd., Cape Elizabeth
• **(207) 799-2244**
347 E. Main St., Gorham
• **(207) 839-2747**

One of five offices serving Greater Portland and York County, ERA Agency 1 has close to 60 agents located among these offices. They list and sell a full range of residential real estate from homes to land and new developments.

Great American Realty
One Park Place, Ste. 33, 445 Main St., Saco
• **(207) 284-4500**

One of the largest listing and selling agencies in York County, Great American Realty has seven full-time agents. The company specializes in residential, land and new development and was founded in 1988 by David and Sue Greaton, who continue to run it today.

Prudential Prime Properties Bay Realty
445 Main St., Saco
• **(207) 282-7552**

In terms of volume of business, Prudential Prime Properties (with 20 agents on staff) is one of the largest agencies in York County. Owners Bob and Lisa Ouellette bought a portion of the business in 1985 when it was a Drown Agency affiliate. In 1989 they purchased the balance of the business and the large 1800s-era building where the offices are located. Following an extensive selection process a decade after first buying into the business, Bob and Lisa decided to affiliate themselves with Prudential. Bob is a past member of the York County Board of Directors. His company's philosophy is a strong commitment to people, with agents matching up buyers and sellers and providing informed, quality service.

Signature Realty, LLC
One Park Place, Ste. 38,
445 Main St., Saco
• **(207) 283-9000**

In early 1997 five well-established brokers decided to break away from their various agencies to form their own agency. Signature Realty is dedicated to providing quality real estate service for people who like the comfort of working with a local, non-affiliated company.

Cheryl Filliger, Ken Lane, Sandy O'Connor, Jay Clark and Norm Guerrette carry a variety of listings from oceanfront condos to lakefront houses.

Patry Family Realty
133 Saco Ave., Old Orchard Beach
• **(207) 934-4432**

Patry Family Realty was launched in December 1985. Because of a strong belief in service and integrity and a can-do attitude, this father and son team (Dan Sr. and Dan Jr.) has built a recognized standing in the area. Dan Sr. was president of the Old Orchard Little League for four years and served on the town's Planning and Budget Committee. Both he and Dan Jr. keep an active interest in town events. The company handles residential and commercial listings and provides summer and long-term rental services (see our Summer Rentals chapter).

Greater Portland Area

Curry Agency
362 Pine Point Rd., Scarborough
• **(207) 883-6444**

This team of brokers deals with property in the Pine Point area of Scarborough. They list and sell property and also handle short- and long-term rentals as well as some property management (see our Summer Rentals chapter). In business since 1969, they are very familiar with the range of properties available in Pine Point.

Properties By The Sea
299 Ocean House Rd., Cape Elizabeth
• **(207) 799-1234**

This small agency, launched in 1994, has two full-time agents. They focus exclusively on oceanfront and oceanview properties.

RE/MAX Coastal
72 Atlantic Pl., South Portland
• **(207) 773-6400**

RE/MAX Coastal is part of the RE/MAX International Referral Network, composed of RE/MAX offices in 13 time zones from St. Thomas in the Virgin Islands to Hong Kong. While internationally affiliated, the agency is locally owned and staffed by individuals who are familiar with Southern Maine. The agency currently has 11 full-time agents willing to service all of your real estate needs from residential brokerage and relocation to new construction to income and seasonal properties.

Cape Realty
339 Cottage Rd., South Portland
• **(207) 799-6969**

As a licensed Realtor for more than 50 years, Robert Tinsman, the owner of this 12-person office, is one of the longest-working real estate agents in the area. When he was just 21, Tinsman started the company with a partner. Soon after, the partner retired, and Tinsman continued building the company on his own. Eight years ago Tinsman's son, Greg, a former police officer, joined him in the company's management. Another son, Douglas, handles commercial listings for the office, and a third son, Thomas, has his own real estate business in nearby Cape Elizabeth. All the agents who work with Cape Realty are licensed, and the company's primary focus is selling houses in Greater Portland.

ERA Home Sellers
118 Maine Mall Rd., South Portland
• **(207) 774-5766, (800) 698-8361**

With more than $37 million in sales for 1996, this independently owned franchise is among the top 100 ERA affiliates nationwide. Its 25 Realtors handle listings from Biddeford to Freeport and carry a total of 200 residential, investment and commercial listings. For the past five years, a regional survey of homebuyers has singled out the company as having the highest level of customer satisfaction in its market area. The agency was founded in the 1960s and has been owned by Alan Peoples for the past 10 years. ERA's national headquarters are in New Jersey, and it has more than 3,000 affiliates spread across the country.

Flynn & Company
372 Cottage Rd., South Portland
• **(207) 767-0022**

Husband and wife team Jeff and Jane Flynn run this four-year-old office with one buyers specialist to help them. They offer individualized service for people looking to buy or sell residential or investment property in the Greater South Portland Area. For the most part, Jane Flynn manages the office while her husband is in the field as the primary selling and listing agent. The properties they handle range in price from $39,000 to $300,000. "We are not just out there seeking the higher end," Jane Flynn says.

INSIDERS' TIP
You'll often hear Boothbay and Boothbay Harbor referred to as "The Boothbays." These also include West and East Boothbay.

Century 21 Balfour

295 Ocean House Rd., Cape Elizabeth
- **(207) 799-5000**

449 Forest Ave., Portland
- **(207) 774-2121**

95 India Rd., Portland
- **(207) 774-7715**

Owned by one family since its inception, this agency was founded in 1959 by I. Alan Balfour to service his building and development activities. In 1974 Alan's son, Scott, became, at 18 years old, the youngest sales agent in Maine. Four years later father and son formed a partnership that lasted until Alan's retirement in 1983. Today, Scott is president of the company, which has grown to include a number of offices, including one in South Portland and another in Falmouth Foreside.

Balfour recently expanded its Cape Elizabeth office to service commercial listings as well as residential properties. The Forest Avenue office in Portland focuses on residences. The other Portland office deals solely with commercial real estate. Among them all, there are 45 agents who are licensed Realtors. With about 200 current listings, the agency covers a geographic area from Biddeford to Brunswick. The business has received awards from Century 21 for providing a high quality of service and for its agents, who often individually sell more than $1 million in property a year. Century 21 has its headquarters in New Jersey and has more than 6,000 offices nationwide.

Buyer's Resource

1321 Washington Ave., Portland
- **(207) 878-7770**

This agency is the only one in Portland that represents buyers only. Because it isn't trying to sell houses, it avoids what could potentially be a conflict of interest in representing both a buyer and a seller for the same property. Its three brokers get paid by the listing agencies, so their services are free to clients (but remember to be very clear on the percentages involved in order to avoid any extra out-of-pocket expenses). Bill Gardiner, the manager of this franchise, and the other Realtors review for-sale properties by connecting to a statewide computer listing service. Buyer's Resource is a national franchise with roughly 60 offices. It was founded in Denver in 1989. This office is the only one in Southern Maine and has been in operation since 1994. Gardiner has 25 years of experience and was at one time an exclusive sellers' agent. This agency covers the Greater Portland area and as far north as Brunswick.

Coldwell Banker Harnden Beecher

Maine Hwy. 9, Kennebunk
- **(207) 967-9900**

1065 Broadway, South Portland
- **(207)799-1501**

949 Brighton Ave., Portland
- **(207) 775-6055**

301 Foreside Rd., Falmouth
- **(207) 781-2216**

This four-office, 85-agent real estate company has been active for 45 years and covers towns from Kittery to Freeport. The Falmouth office was the first to open, with others following in Portland and Kennebunkport. Harnden Beecher lists properties from $29,000 to more than $1 million in value. Several of its associates have been named Realtor of the Year by the York County Board of Realtors, and the company prides itself on being active in community affairs and raising money for various causes.

Greater Portland Realty

400 Allen Ave., Portland • (207) 797-7777

Selling house lots and building packages from $100,000 to $400,000 are this firm's specialties. It was started by Jake Webb in 1961, and for the past seven years his daughter, Pam Audet, has managed it with her husband, Willie J. Audet Jr. In addition to handling new development, the eight agents who work here oversee residential, commercial and business sales. The most active areas of development for Greater Portland Realty are in Falmouth, Cumberland and North Yarmouth.

Harbor City Realty

500 Woodford St., Portland
- **(207) 775-1991**

Offering one-on-one service, Jean Russo, the owner of this one-person company, says she specializes in giving personal attention to her clients. With 15 years of experience, she sells homes, condos, apartment houses and

land in the Greater Portland area and is part of the Multiple Listing Service. Portland itself, however, is her specialty — she was born and raised here. Russo averages more than $1 million in real estate sales each year. She worked for a real estate attorney and for a brokerage firm with more than 40 agents before deciding to start her own business so she could spend more time with clients.

Mark Stimson Associates
312 Elm St., Biddeford • (207) 282-5988
53 Baxter Blvd., Portland • (207) 773-1990
37 Depot Rd., Falmouth • (207) 781-4220
253 Main St., Yarmouth • (207) 846-6429
173 Park Row, Brunswick • (207) 865-6221

With more than 200 licensed Realtors in the Greater Portland area, Mark Stimson Associates sells an average of 2,000 houses a year. That's more than double the number sold by its closest competitor. Founded in 1966, the company has seven branches and 12 affiliates listing all types of properties from the Southern Maine border all the way north to Bangor. A whopping 34 percent of the houses sold in this section of the state are sold by Mark Stimson agents. However, there are so few rental properties in the Portland area, this agency doesn't handle them. Since 1984 Mark Stimson has also financially supported nonprofit organizations that help people find housing, emergency shelter and special care. Agents contribute to the fund by donating money from their listings and sales, and the company contributes. Some of its company branch offices are located in Biddeford, Falmouth, Yarmouth and Brunswick.

RE/MAX By The Bay
281 Veranda St., Portland
• (207) 773-2345, (800) 707-7214
50 Depot Rd., Falmouth
• (207) 781-8700, (800) 707-7214

An independently owned franchise of one of the largest real estate companies in the world, RE/MAX By The Bay has its main office in Falmouth and a second office in Portland. Its 27 agents handle listings from Saco to Brunswick and in 1996 had a total of $83 million in sales. Owner David Banks started this affiliate in 1994 and one year later won a regional company award as broker-owner of the year for the amount of new business he generated. When this franchise opened its Falmouth office, styled after a Colonial house, the company won an international design award for the architectural plans, which several associates drafted. The company primarily handles residential properties, although it also deals with commercial and income properties. The RE/MAX parent company has more than 44,000 associates in 2,811 offices scattered across every state in the nation and throughout Canada, the Caribbean and Europe. One thing the company prides itself on is the experience of its brokers, most of whom average 12 years in the business.

Bay Properties Realty
16 Lafayette St., Yarmouth
• (207) 846-9224

If you're looking for a historic home to fix up yourself or one that has already been restored, this father-son real estate team is a good place to start. The company is run by Bill Honan and his son, Will, who started it in 1987. The two handle residential sales from Portland to Freeport, and, through a separate business called Bay Properties, they also buy and renovate historic homes before putting them back on the market. Bill Honan lives in one antique home he refurbished. The pair has fixed up several houses, from Portland to about 60 miles north in Richmond.

One Portland landmark the two had their hand on was the Zebulon Babson House, one of the few buildings to survive the Portland fire of 1866. In restoring a home, the Honans are careful to maintain its historic integrity by using as much of the original materials as possible. As you might expect, many of the clients who come here are searching for old homes.

INSIDERS' TIP

Maine has one of the highest rates of home ownership in the country with more than 70 percent of the people statewide living in their own homes.

Brunswick, Bath and Boothbay Harbor Area

Moore Realty Group
5 Rosemary Ln., Freeport • (207) 865-0707

Janet Moore, a Realtor for more than 12 years, just started this company in 1996 to go along with a construction business she and her husband, Brian Moore, own together. Janet Moore specializes in new construction, helping people locate land on which to build. Moore Homes Inc., the building end of the business, will design and construct a house for you for $225,000 to $400,000. Moore Realty's primary market is the Greater Freeport area, with most of their new construction centered in Harpswell and Yarmouth.

Brunswick Realty Group
Fort Andross, Brunswick • (207) 729-2820

This local firm, which handles real estate from Freeport to Wiscasset, is jointly owned by the seven Realtors who work here. The company, started in 1988, deals with many waterfront properties, but its primary business is residential.

CHR Realty, Better Homes and Gardens
37 Mill St., Brunswick • (207) 725-4384
823 Washington St., Bath • (207) 443-3333

The second-largest listing agency in the state and the largest real estate company in its market, CHR Realty has been selling houses in the Greater Bath-Brunswick area since 1973. Owner Al Austin joined the company a year after it started and recently bought out his partners. The company has 26 licensed agents divided between its Brunswick and Bath offices. Its primary focus is residential property, listing everything from houses for first-time buyers to elegant mansions. It also handles commercial sales and some subdivisions. Part of the Better Homes and Gardens franchise since 1990, CHR Realty won a national award in 1996 for designing the best-looking free guide to homes. And for two years in a row, an independent auditing firm found that local people rated this affiliate as the best agency in the area. One of the special features offered by CHR Realty is free home ownership counseling for people who need to straighten out their finances before being ready to own a home.

Coldwell Banker Gleason Real Estate
82 Pleasant St., Brunswick
• (207) 725-8522, (207) 865-9446 (toll-free from Portland and Freeport)

Owned by David Gleason, this company was started in 1970 and has 15 full-time licensed brokers. It is one of the dominant players in the Greater Brunswick and Topsham areas. With an average of 150 residential listings, it has consistently maintained a large share of the market. Gleason Real Estate sells everything from house lots in the $20,000 range to $600,000 waterfront homes. Its annual sales were $23 million in 1996. Both Gleason and business manager Rick Baribeau are former presidents of the area chamber of commerce and pride themselves on their activity in the community. The agency is a member of the Coldwell Banker national franchise, which in 1996 was named by Success magazine as one of best franchises (regardless of type of business) in the country.

Morton Real Estate
240 Main St., Brunswick • (207) 729-1863

Deborah Morton is co-owner of this seven-person agency, which she started in 1974. Since its inception, the company has won a couple of local awards, including one for Small Business of the Year in 1987, given by the local chamber of commerce. Morton Real Estate sells residential, commercial and development property and helped develop the Appletree and Birch Meadow planned-unit developments in Brunswick. Morton's eldest son, Paul H. Clark, is a partner in the company and specializes in business development.

Century 21 Baribeau Agency
51 Pleasant St., Brunswick
• (207) 729-3333, (800) 882-5681
38 Centre St., Bath • (207) 443-2121

This agency is among the five top-performing Century 21 affiliates in Maine and has been owned by the same family since its start in

1927. Founded by Henry M. Baribeau, the company was handed down through the generations to his grandson, Michael Baribeau, who is the current owner. As a Century 21 affiliate, the Baribeau Agency offers a nationwide referral service, though it is independently owned and operated. It has 15 licensed agents who sell residential, coastal and country property. The agency also operates a property management service called Rentex, which handles seasonal and year-round rentals.

Roebuck-Boynton Real Estate
1027 Washington St., Bath
• (207) 442-7988

If you want to buy a house and fix it up, this company can help you do both. Lynn Roebuck has owned it since 1985, but just last year her husband, Chris Boynton, came on as a partner. While Roebuck and the company's four other Realtors handle listings, Boynton specializes in renovations and restorations. For example, one client who recently bought a waterfront home through the agency is also having the roof and kitchen completely redone by Boynton. Roebuck-Boynton handles existing homes in the Merrymeeting area, which includes Bath, Brunswick, Wiscasset and the nearby peninsulas. It does not work with new developments and prides itself on being a small agency offering more personal service.

Sharon Drake Real Estate
136 Front St., Bath
• (207) 443-1005, (800) 561-1005

This local company has been in business here only since 1995, but it has quickly climbed to the top of the field. Owner Sharon Drake has more than 23 years of real estate experience, and her fledgling company has a solid track record of selling more properties in Bath and Brunswick than any other in the market. The offices are located in the downtown center, in what used to be a boxing arena on one floor and a house of ill repute on the second floor. Sharon Drake Real Estate has eight licensed agents, one of whom is Sharon's husband, Ted Drake, a retired doctor who joined the business soon after they were married. As of 1997 the company offered the only accredited buyers' brokers in the area. They specialize in historic homes and waterfront properties and also handle long-term rentals. The agency is also a strong supporter of community activities.

Harbor Realty
2 McKown St., Boothbay Harbor
• (207) 633-4803

Specializing in condominium sales and rentals, Harbor Realty was started in 1980 by owner Mary Lee Brown. The four other licensed agents who work here, including Brown's son, Ted Brown, handle all types of real estate along the Boothbay Harbor peninsula. Condos are a particularly hot item for this company because Harbor manages three in-town complexes. Mary Lee Brown grew up here, left and came back 20 years later. She has been in real estate since 1972 and tries to hire other agents with similar experience. In addition to running her own company, Brown sits on the town Board of Selectmen.

Lewis & Pottle Realty
1 Townsend Ave., Boothbay Harbor
• (207) 633-6911

From summer and long-term rentals to mobile homes, waterfront property and subdivisions, this downtown agency has six licensed brokers who handle all types of real estate properties throughout Lincoln County. In business since 1986, it has 100-plus listings. The partners who started it are Clayton Pottle and Roy Lewis. The company also handles real estate insurance.

INSIDERS' TIP

If you're a first-time homebuyer in Maine, you may qualify for a mortgage with a super-low interest rate through the Maine State Housing Authority, based in Augusta. The same agency also offers a program where qualifiers can pay as little as a $1,000 down payment for a bank mortgage.

Tindal & Callahan
32 Oak St., Boothbay Harbor
• (207) 633-6711

First in sales in the Boothbay region, this company says it finds buyers for more properties than all the other agencies on the peninsula combined. Partners Bruce Tindal and Judy Callahan started the business together in 1985 and now have more than a 50 percent market share in their area. With four other licensed agents, they handle a little bit of everything, from affordable properties for first-time home buyers to upscale shorefront properties in the $200,000 to $700,000 range.

Some of our public
schools are outstanding,
with as many as 96
percent of their kids
going on to college.

Education
and Child Care

Education

You'll find a broad cross-section of schools on our Southern Coast, from public schools to religious and secular private schools to technical colleges, business schools and universities. You'll also find plenty of specialty schools for adults offering everything from ballet and music to how to write your own book or build your own house.

Many communities along Maine's Southern Coast are trying to keep their public schools open for extended hours so taxpayers can get the most for their money. Instead of locking up what is often the town's biggest building at the end of the school day, townspeople get together for adult education classes, computer labs and community meetings. In winter it's not unusual to find people walking the halls for a little ice-free exercise.

Some of our public schools are outstanding, with as many as 96 percent of their kids going on to college. But unfortunately, recent polls have shown that many more graduates want to go to college than can afford to. Statewide, only about 58 percent of Maine students go on to higher education. On the brighter side, public schools in Maine have been nationally recognized for providing students with a positive learning environment due to our low incidence of violence and our close-knit learning environments. Some smaller towns you'll read about in this chapter have student-teacher ratios as low as 12-1 and fewer than 100 students in their schools.

You'll find all manner of private schools here, and a growing number of parents are

choosing them. One private all-boys school in Portland, Cheverus High School, has grown more than 50 percent in the last five years! Because tuition prices are so volatile, we haven't listed the cost of attending these schools. But we can tell you they vary from about $1,200 for an entire school year all the way up to about $12,000 (and we're not talking room and board). Parents interested in homeschooling need to call the Maine Department of Education at (207) 287-5922 to request a registration form. At the end of each year parents of homeschoolers must have their children independently evaluated to see how they are performing. Although Maine has far fewer homeschoolers than many southern states, the trend is rapidly increasing here.

Most of our technical colleges and universities are in the Portland area, and we've included a sampling of those as well as a variety of specialty schools for continuing education. In addition, we've topped this chapter off with summer camps and child-care centers. You'll find the schools you're interested in organized by categories, and for some we've included a brief introduction to give you additional information where necessary.

Public Schools

While some larger Maine towns contain their own school system from kindergarten through high school, it's also common for towns to pool their finances and kids in one regional school. Towns that educate their children independently are known as "school departments," while towns that pool their resources and their kids have a group number and are known as School Administrative Districts.

In Maine you'll also find school unions, which consist of individual towns with their own elected school boards and a single administrator to keep an eye on things. Often towns in school unions have their own elementary schools but send their kids to joint facilities for middle school and high school.

In Maine the academic requirements to graduate from high school vary from town to town. The programs offered in various schools also vary widely. Although every town is required under federal law to provide adequate education for students with special needs, not all schools have gifted-and-talented programs or even music and art. If a certain program is important to you, check to make sure it is available. Another way to compare Maine schools is to ask how their students performed on the Maine Educational Assessment test. Every school is required to administer the test in grades 4, 7 and 11 to gauge students' competency in math, reading, writing, science and social studies.

Southern Beaches Area

Kittery School Department, 22 Shapleigh Road, (207) 439-6819, encompasses the town of Kittery and Kittery Point. Approximately 1,300 students were enrolled in the district in 1998-99 from kindergarten through grade 12. There are four schools in the district, each of which has its own principal, and secretarial, nursing and guidance services. Additionally, each school has a library, physical education program, music program, art program and computer lab. The average student-teacher ratio across the district is 17-1. In addition, the school department provides a gifted and talented program for all grades and a special-services program for children with disabilities.

The school department strives to generate an enthusiasm for knowledge and a desire in students to reach their personal best. The department is committed to providing students with a strong academic foundation, a sense of personal health and well being, a sense of responsibility and productivity, effective and creative communication skills, creative and practical problem-solving skills and

technological proficiency. To this end, the department added a Curriculum Coordinator to its staff beginning in the 1998-99 school year.

The York School Department, 300 York Street, (207) 363-3403, is noted for having a high percentage of students continue on to further education. Providing education to York Village, York Beach, York Harbor and Cape Neddick, the York School Department had more than 2,000 students enrolled in the two elementary schools, and the middle and high schools in 1998.

Both the Village and the Coastal Ridge Elementary schools handle kindergarten to 4th grades, with approximately 400 students in each. Built in 1977, York High School is a quarter mile from the ocean on 72 acres of land. It caters to all levels of ability from Honors and Advanced Placement College Preparatory to Skill Building. The school follows a block-scheduling format with classes meeting for 80 minutes every other day.

It is not surprising that Ogunquit and Wells share a school district since the two towns were one until 1980. The Wells Ogunquit Community School District, 1470 Post Road, (207) 646-8331, had 1,473 students enrolled in the 1998-99 school year in grades kindergarten through 12. Each town has its own elementary school, and they share a junior high school for 5th through 8th grades, and a high school. Student-teacher ratios in the district drop as low as 15-1 for kindergarten to 2nd grades, and go as high as 27-1 in high school.

Kennebunk and Kennebunkport have a combined school district known as Maine School Administrative District 71, 10 Storer Street, (207) 985-1100. The acronym for the district is referred to as MSAD 71 or SAD 71. It incorporates four elementary schools that serve between 226 and 456 students each, a middle school, and a high school. A total of approximately 2,500 students were enrolled in the district for the 1998-99 school year.

SAD 71 has a reputation for excellence and strong local support of its educational programs. One of its most highly regarded programs is the community service program where high school students select a service to provide based on their interests. For example, they may help combat erosion along a stream, read to the elderly, tutor younger stu-

dents or volunteer at a local animal shelter. All high school students are required to earn community service hours, and most students exceed the minimum requirement by a significant amount.

Old Orchard Beach Area

The Biddeford School District, 205 Main Street, (207) 282-8280, prides itself on meeting the needs of a diverse student population. The success of its students and the schools is attributed not only to the district, but also to the strength of parental and community support of school programs. Both Biddeford High School and Biddeford Middle School have been recognized as National Schools of Excellence by the Blue Ribbon Commission in Washington, D.C. In addition, the two schools have won numerous music awards.

Serving close to 3,000 students, the district incorporates one elementary school for kindergarten through 2nd; another elementary school for 3rd to 5th grades; a middle school for 6th to 8th grades; and high school for grades 9-12. The district also features a center for technology for high school students who prefer to pursue technical, rather than strictly academic careers. The average student-teacher ratio across the grade levels 18-1.

School Union #7, 56 Industrial Park Road, (207) 284-4505, serves the City of Saco and the Town of Dayton. In 1998-99 there were 2,168 students enrolled in kindergarten through 8th grade in four elementary schools and one middle school. Students from both communities attend Thornton Academy (see Private Schools, below) for 9th to 12th grades.

Students in School Union #7 typically score above the state average on the Maine Educational Assessment tests administered in grades 4, 8 and 11. Class sizes in the elementary grades range from 17 to 20 from kindergarten through 2nd grade and 22 to 25 in 3rd to 8th grades. School and recreational programs provide children with a wide variety of activities on a year-round basis.

The teaching staff reflects a blend of veteran and new professionals dedicated to achieving excellence and implementing Maine's Learning Results. School Union #7 sees education as a collaborative adventure in lifelong learning that requires a partnership between home, school and the community. To further that end, the system has a dynamic teacher development program.

In 1991 Old Orchard Beach School District, 28 Jameson Hill Road, (207) 934-5751, was chosen as one of 12 schools from across the United States highlighted in a book titled Twelve Schools That Succeed. In 1996 it was one of 26 school systems in the United States to be awarded a Competitive Technology Grant, which it received in partnership with the University of Southern Maine. In 1998-99 there were 1,130 students enrolled in the district, which has one school for kindergarten through 3rd grade, one school for 4th through 8th grades, and a high school, which has been a National School of Excellence Blue Ribbon winner. The school district has an excellent band program with winning jazz and marching bands as well as a very successful football team and debate, drama, yearbook and other extracurricular activities.

The district hosts a Cooperative Education Program where students learn valuable skills while working in the community and all senior class students are required to do a community service project. At the elementary level, Old Orchard Beach has begun an innovative music program for kindergarten through 3rd grade where every student is taught to play the violin.

Greater Portland Area

The Scarborough School District, (207) 883-4315, incorporates six schools — three elementary schools for grades kindergarten through 2nd; one elementary school for 3rd to 5th grades; one middle school for 6th to 8th grades; and one high school. In the 1998-99 school year 2,767 students were enrolled in the district. Due to the rapid expansion of Scarborough, the town boasts a brand new middle school, and recently completed renovations to the elementary schools.

Extracurricular activities offered by the district include track, cross-country, soccer and baseball as well as yearbook, a school newspaper and a debate team. In addition, there are independent swimming and hockey teams that are funded through the efforts of team boosters. For about the past 11 years the school has had the distinction of being the State Academic Decathlon champions, and approximately 85 percent of students go on to pursue post-secondary education.

There are three schools in Cape Elizabeth, 325 Ocean House Road, (207) 799-2217: Pond Cove Elementary with kindergarten to 4th grades, the Cape Elizabeth Middle School with 5th through 8th grades, and the Cape Elizabeth High School. Approximately 1,800 students are enrolled in the school district with

class sizes averaging around 18 to 21 students per elementary school class, 21 students per class for grades five and six and 22 students in grades 7 through 12. Average tenure of teachers is around 10 years.

In addition to 45 sports teams, the school district features an "Artists in the Schools" program and a Portland string quartet residency. There are also extensive community service opportunities for students.

The South Portland School Department, Wescott Road, (207) 871-0555, is one of the largest on the Southern Coast with close to 3,500 students enrolled from kindergarten through 12th grade. There are seven elementary schools, two middle schools and one high school in the city. Student-teacher ratios range from as low as 15-1 to as high as 26-1 across all grades, and the average teacher's tenure is 15 years.

Highlighted programs in the department include the reading recovery program, an all-day kindergarten opportunity and multi-age classes at five elementary schools. A comprehensive co-curricular program is offered to students in the district from grades 6 through 12. The most successful of these programs include instrumental and choral music programs and athletic teams such as baseball and football. In addition, a new performing arts center was completed in 1997 for the high school.

Public education in Portland rests with the Portland School Department, 331 Veranda Street, (207) 874-8100, which oversees 12 elementary schools (three of which are on islands), three middle schools with about 600 students each and two high schools, each with 950 students. It provides an alternative education program for special-needs students from grades 6-12 and a variety of adult education courses. Portland Arts & Technology High School also offers vocational classes to students from Portland and the surrounding communities.

Just a few miles north on Route 1, the Falmouth School Department, 51 Woodville Road, Falmouth, (207) 781-3200, has roughly 1,700 students divided between three schools. Falmouth High School is well known for its theater group, mock trial team and soccer team. Academically it's rated as one of the top high schools in the state, and each year between 70 and 80 percent of its graduates pursue higher education.

The Yarmouth School Department, 8 Portland Street, Yarmouth, (207) 846-5586, oversees 1,575 students housed in four school buildings. Here students consistently score above the national and state averages on basic skills tests, and at least 86 percent of high school graduates go on to pursue higher education. Yarmouth High School, well known for its drama program (more than a quarter of the student body participates), was named a National School of Excellence by the U.S. Office of Education.

Twenty minutes north of Portland, the Freeport School Department, 17 West Street, Freeport, (207) 865-0928, consists of four schools with a total of 1,300 students. There is a kindergarten through 2nd-grade early childhood center, a 6th to 8th grade middle school and a high school. A handful of students from nearby Durham and Pownal also attend Freeport schools, because those towns are so small they have none of their own.

Freeport High School regularly wins awards for its choral program, math team, athletic program and academic initiatives. In 1995, 53 percent of its high school graduates went on to higher education.

Brunswick, Bath and Boothbay Harbor Area

With 3,400 students, the Brunswick School Department, 38 Union Street, Brunswick, (207) 729-4148, oversees four elementary schools, a middle school and a newly completed $9 million high school, each with a program of traditional subjects and music and art. The school system also has an alternative education program at Maine Vocational Region 10 with work-study courses for kids in 6th through 12th grades.

More than 50 percent of the town's teachers have advanced degrees, and all high school students are required to perform 20 hours of community service in order to graduate. As many as 96 percent of its students said they planned to pursue higher education.

Bath, just a few minutes north of Brunswick along Route 1, has a school system with 2,100 students. The Bath School Department, 2 Sheridan Road, Bath, (207) 443-6601, has a kindergarten center, two elementary schools, a high school and a newly built regional vocational center. High school students come from Bath and the surrounding communities of West Bath, Phippsburg, Georgetown, Woolwich and Arrowsic. Vocational students also come from Wiscasset and Boothbay Harbor. Roughly half of the graduating seniors go on to pursue higher education. One highly unusual middle school program is the Shariki Exchange in which participating students spend a couple of weeks visiting the city's sister city in Shariki Japan.

School Union 47, Witch Spring Hill Road, West Bath, (207) 443-1113, is made up of five small towns — West Bath, Phippsburg, Woolwich, Arrowsic and Georgetown — and their four elementary schools (Arrowsic students go to school in Georgetown). Over the past five years, each school has scored at or above the state average on the MEAs, and each has a fairly low student-teacher ratio (West Bath and Georgetown are about 12-1). Unique programs include researching, seeding and monitoring clam flats and visiting a logging town up north. Most students transfer to Bath for middle and/or high school, but some towns will help pay for older students to attend private, secular schools.

Wiscasset School System, Gardiner Road, (207) 882-6303, in 1997 separated from the surrounding towns, which now pay tuition to send their older students here. In the past it has spent more than most schools in the state per student, but with the recent closing of the Maine Yankee nuclear power plant, the town is facing financial cutbacks. Wiscasset itself has a primary school, middle school and high school, and has been widely recognized for an outstanding gifted-and-talented program.

School Union 48, located at the Dresden

Middle School, (207) 737-2559, is made up of Dresden, Alna and Westport island and used to include Wiscasset. Dresden has its own elementary school, and Alna has no school of its own. Most older students attend Wiscasset schools, and there are a total of 550 students in the union.

The Boothbay-Boothbay Harbor Community School District, or School Union 49, Wiscasset Road, Boothbay Harbor, (207) 633-2874, consists of an elementary, middle school and high school in Boothbay and schools in Edgecomb and Southport, which go from kindergarten through 6th grade. In all the school system has about 1,000 students. Roughly 70 percent of the graduating high school seniors plan to pursue some form of higher education. In September 1997, the Boothbay Region High School completed a $2 million expansion including a new library, computer lab, art and music rooms and additional classroom space.

Private Schools

Private schools in Maine have a long and proud tradition, and you're just about guaranteed to find whatever method you're looking for, from Christian- and Catholic-based schools to Montessori schools and college-prep schools. The class size at private schools tends to be smaller than public schools, although that sometimes means the schools have fewer facilities. So check for the resources that interest you.

Southern Beaches Area

Berwick Academy
31 Academy St., South Berwick
• **(207) 384-2164**
Founded in 1791, Berwick Academy is the oldest educational institution in Maine. Enrollment is kept at a total of around 500 and incorporates grades kindergarten through 12. As a result the school has low student-teacher ratios. Berwick Academy students regularly attain combined scores of 1200 on the SATs.

The academy has three parts: the lower school for grades K to 4, the middle school for 5th through 8th grades and the upper school for 9th through 12th grades. Each school has its own curriculum. Math, music, art, foreign language and computers are taught from the lower school to the upper school. Middle school students are also taught library and study skills. At the high school level students enjoy the option of advanced placement courses and activities periods where they may work on the yearbook or the school newspaper or take part in music or drama rehearsals. In 1997 the school opened the new, fully equipped Kozlowski Athletic Facility. Sports at the academy include soccer, golf, skiing, swimming, baseball, lacrosse and tennis.

Kennebunk Christian Academy
Sea Rd., Kennebunk
• **(207) 985-2415**
The Kennebunk Christian Academy (KCA) a nondenominational school that was founded in 1979 by a group of professional educators and parents under the aegis of the Kennebunk Advent Christian Church. It's governed by a school board that is self-perpetuating and approved by the State's Department of Education.

Thirty-three students from 4th to 8th grade are taught by four full time teachers and one teachers' aide. In addition, special courses like art, gym, music, Spanish and computer studies are taught by outside professionals on a regular basis. The school regularly exceeds the national average at every grade level under the Stanford Achievement Tests. The Academy is housed in a modern building on several acres. In addition to classrooms, it features a multipurpose room complete with a kitchen, gymnasium, eating area and a stage. You'll also find a library, computer room and science laboratory amongst the facilities.

School Around Us
281 Log Cabin Rd., Arundel
• **(207) 967-3143**
Founded in 1970, this cooperative school offers preschool through 8th grade education. It is accredited by the state and limits enrollment to a maximum of thirty students with a student-teacher ratio of about 8-1. The school is supported by tuition, donations, fundraising and parent involvement. In addition to

paying tuition, parents are expected to contribute to the operation of the school by assuming a job in administration, maintenance or teaching. Moreover, adults associated with the school share a concern about the health of the environment. Set on four acres of field and woods with a brook, School Around Us students also enjoy access to a library, kitchen, art center and science area. The playground is complete with a student-built fort. In addition to full-time enrollment, School Around Us provides programs for students who are partially home-schooled.

Old Orchard Beach Area

St. James School
25 Graham St., Biddeford
• (207) 282-4084

At St. James School, students in kindergarten through 8th grade receive instruction in Catholic faith and values in addition to traditional subjects. Computer studies and French are offered for 1st through 8th grades, and all grades receive music, art and physical education studies.

Notre Dame de Lourdes School
50 Beach St., Saco • (207) 283-3111

For more than 60 years Notre Dame de Lourdes has strived to meet the educational and spiritual needs of students from kindergarten through 8th grade. Approximately 200 students are enrolled at the school, which prides itself on individual attention; all students and their families will be known by name. The educational program at Notre Dame de Lourdes includes faith formation as well as moral and physical growth. Extracurricular activities at Notre Dame De Lourdes include student council, journalism club and full participation in Saco Public Middle School Sports Program.

Thornton Academy
438 Main St., Saco
• (207) 282-3361

Thornton Academy is a private day school founded in 1811. Though private, the academy has an agreement with School Union #7 to accept its high school students since Saco doesn't have its own high school. Approximately 1,000 students attend the Academy, which sits on an 80-acre parcel with 10 buildings, some of which are part of the City's Historical Preservation District. It has earned the Maine School of Excellence distinction and in recent years has had two teachers named National Teachers of the Year — one in visual arts and one in English. Typically, 65 percent of students from the academy go on to pursue some form of secondary education.

In addition to its extensive sports offerings, Thornton Academy has a 148-member Boy's Choir and is very strong in visual arts such as drama. In 1996 the school opened a new 492-seat auditorium that has hosted alumni and school productions to sold-out houses since opening night. Visitors who would like more information on Thornton Academy can visit the school's Alumni and Public Affairs Office, which is open year round.

Greater Portland Area

Aucocisco Day School
Rear 700 Main St., South Portland
• (207) 773-7323

The Aucocisco School is a state-approved special-purpose school for ages 5 through 16 that provides short-term (2-4 years), intensive remedial schooling focusing on skills and language for students with average to gifted ability levels. Aucocisco doesn't serve students with primary behavioral or psychological disorders.

At Aucocisco, each child's educational pro-

INSIDERS' TIP

If you're planning on moving to an area, contact the school department for the most up-to-date information on the schools your children will be attending. If you're considering a private school, call for an appointment to visit. Most schools welcome visits from prospective parents and students.

gram draws from as many different approaches as needed. No single specific remedial technique or philosophy is followed at the school. The basic student-teacher ratio at Aucocisco is about 5-1 for younger children and 8-1 for older children. In addition, adjunct teachers regularly come into the classrooms to provide courses such as karate, swimming, bowling and other physical education as well as computer science, math and music.

Greater Portland Christian School
1338 Broadway, South Portland
• **(207) 767-5123**

Students from kindergarten through 12th grades are taught at the Greater Portland Christian School. Enrollment usually falls between 100 and 120 students total. The philosophy of the school is such that every area of knowledge is related to God — in other words, science is recognized as the investigation and use of God's eternal purpose and the arts are viewed as reflections of God's creations. Eighty-five to 90 percent of students from the Greater Portland Christian School go on to pursue some form of post-secondary education. Extracurricular activities offered by the school include soccer, softball, basketball, drama, music, chorus, competitive singing and yearbook.

Learning Achievement Center
Rear 700 Main St., South Portland
• **(207) 773-7323**

The Learning Achievement Center seeks to help children become competent and confident in after-school, evening, weekend and summer programs. Students are given diagnostic tests and take part in a family conference so an individualized learning program can be developed to improve the student's skills.

Breakwater School
856 Brighton Ave., Portland
• **(207) 772-8689**

This independent elementary school for children from preschool through grade 5 strives to create a strong partnership between parents and teachers while encouraging children to think creatively and independently. It was founded in 1958 and moved to its current brick building in 1982. The day school tries to tailor its curriculum to each child's pace and natural learning style. Students come from diverse backgrounds from 15 surrounding communities. Traditional subjects as well as French, art, music and community service are offered. After-school care and a summer day camp are also available (for more information see our Day Camps section).

Catherine McAuley High School
631 Stevens Ave., Portland
• **(207) 797-3802**

Girls in grades 9 through 12 attend this private day school sponsored by The Sisters of Mercy. With roughly 250 students, the school has a full gymnasium and auditorium and fully equipped science and computer labs. An average of 97 percent of its students go on to college, and the student-teacher ratio is 10-1. The only all-girls school in the state, Catherine McAuley has a graduation rate of 99 percent.

Cheverus High School
267 Ocean Ave., Portland
• **(207) 774-6238**

The 382 male students enrolled at this college-preparatory day school come from all over Southern Maine. It's one of 47 Jesuit high schools across the country, and the nearest one east of Boston. The school focuses on whole character education based on the five ideals of the Jesuit order: intellectual competence, openness to growth, being loving, being religious according to one's own traditions and being committed to justice for others. The school occupies several buildings on a 40-acre campus complete with full athletic facilities and playing fields. An average of 96 percent of its students go on to four-year colleges, and the average student-teacher ratio is 11-1. In the last five years the school's admissions have grown 52 percent.

Photo: Merry Farnum

High-quality education and child-care options are available for youngsters in Maine.

Waynflete School
360 Spring St., Portland • (207) 774-5721

The largest independent day school in Northern New England, Waynflete teaches more than 500 students in kindergarten through 12th grade. Founded in 1897, the school campus is on 3 acres in Portland's West End. The school also owns 30 acres of athletic fields and walking trails on the nearby Fore River. Beginning in the elementary school, students are encouraged to develop their own work and learning plans that become increasingly complex as they progress through the school. Community involvement is an integral part of the middle and upper school program, and students participate in food drives and volunteering. Waynflete is highly regarded for its arts and music programs, and students are encouraged to participate in sports.

North Yarmouth Academy
121 Main St., Yarmouth • (207) 846-9051

This college-preparatory, coeducational day school is on a 25-acre campus in the middle of Yarmouth village and schools 250 students in grades 6 through 12. Dating back to 1814, the school is one of the oldest private schools in the state and provides a traditional liberal arts curriculum complemented with computer courses, visual and performing arts and a wide range of extracurricular activities. Athletic participation is required each trimester and social-service opportunities are encouraged. The average class size is 12, and in the past several years 100 percent of the school's graduates have gone on to further their education.

The Merriconeag Waldorf School
57 Desert Rd., Freeport • (207) 865-3900

The Waldorf method was developed in 1919 to integrate traditional learning with a more natural, playful environment using art, dance, handwork, drama and music. It was the reaction of Austrian philosopher Rudolph Steiner to the chaos following World War I and was his effort to create a more peaceful, caring society. The Merriconeag Waldorf School, on 17 acres off a back road in Freeport, was established in 1984 as a nursery-kindergarten. In 1992 it was expanded to include a full program through 8th grade.

You'll find a strong academic program sans electronic teaching aids. Another unusual aspect of the program: One teacher oversees each class with students from age 7 through 14. Other teachers provide specific instruction in foreign languages, music and other areas. Subjects such as zoology, botany, mineralogy, astronomy, chemistry and environmental studies are part of the curriculum, as well as German and French.

Brunswick, Bath and Boothbay Harbor Area

St. John's School
39 Pleasant St., Brunswick
• (207) 725-5507

Established in 1883, St. John's School is in a stately brick building in downtown Brunswick. Its initial mission was to provide a Catholic education for the young people in its own parish, but with more people seeking alternatives to public education it opened its doors to the surrounding communities for children in kindergarten through 8th grade. The school is overseen by the Diocese of Portland, and has been administered by the Ursuline Sisters and the Marist Fathers since 1911. On standardized tests, its students typically score well above the national average with 8th graders scoring at a 12th-grade level. The curriculum is designed to not only provide a solid academic program but also to promote the growth of the whole person, helping students think creatively, reason logically and accept responsibility. Parents play a part in the education as well, with each family required to donate 25 hours of service to the school each year.

Children's School of Arts and Science
185 Harding Road, Brunswick
• (207) 443-4771

Founded in 1981, the Children's School of Arts and Science seeks to link creativity with learning from pre-kindergarten through 8th grade. The school is set in a quiet brick building away from the city center and offers a full academic program including art, drama

and music for its roughly 25 students. Every child works in every subject at his or her own level, and some of the school's priorities are to teach children to value themselves and their own creativity and to build study skills that suit them. The student-teacher ratio is 6-1.

Hyde School
224 High St., Bath • (207) 443-5584

Committed to character-based education, Hyde School has 218 students at its Bath campus and 250 at its secondary campus in Woodstock, Conn., which opened in 1996. The private, coeducational boarding school for 9th through 12th grade and post graduate studies was founded in 1966 with an emphasis on the whole family in the learning process. Parents are required to meet in regional groups once a month, and also attend twice-yearly seminars at the school, which is on the historic estate of an old Bath shipbuilder, Thomas Hyde.

Ninety-five percent of the students at Hyde School go on to four year colleges, and about 30 percent of the students who attend the Bath campus come here from California. The school doesn't consider any activities extracurricular and requires that all students be involved in athletics as well as the performing arts and community service. The student-teacher ratio is 12-1. The school recently built a new performing art center and a new dormitory.

Chop Point School
Chop Point, Woolwich
• (207) 443-3080

Located off a dirt road far back in the woods, in a farmhouse and barn on the bank of the Kennebec River, this Christ-centered day school seeks to motivate children to learn through love. The facilities include tennis courts, sailboats, canoes and a library in the old boathouse. The school attracts students from both religious and non-religious backgrounds. Most classes have less than 12 students, and teachers think of themselves as servants rather than authority figures. The school teaches traditional subjects through the A-Beka curriculum as well as music, art and drama. High School students also have the opportunity to participate in a mission trip to Mexico. Founded by Peter Willard in 1967, the school continues under Willard's leadership.

Colleges and Universities

Southern Beaches Area

York County Technical College
112 College Dr., Wells
• **(207) 646-9282**

York County Technical College (YCTC) is a two-year accredited public institution. Though it has been around for years, in the fall of 1997 YCTC opened its new campus on College Drive. It offers seven associates of applied science degrees within an innovative, hands-on learning environment. The curriculum is designed specifically to meet the needs of York County businesses and to better provide employment opportunities for YCTC graduates. Among the degree programs offered at YCTC are business administration, computer-aided drafting and design, computer applications technology, culinary arts and hospitality management. Courses are offered in spring and fall semesters and two summer sessions. Two evening terms are offered each semester for those pursuing a degree after work hours. Federal financial aid is available.

Old Orchard Beach Area

University of New England
Hills Beach Rd., Biddeford
• **(207) 283-0171**

The University of New England (UNE) was chartered in 1831. It is an independent, co-educational university with two campuses. One is on a beautiful oceanside site in Biddeford, while the Westbrook College Campus is on the outskirts of Portland. The University of New England has degree programs focused on the health and life sciences, human services, management, education and the liberal arts. It also includes Maine's only medical school, the University of New England College of Osteopathic Medicine, which emphasizes the education of primary-care physicians. On two occasions UNE has been ranked one of the best universities in America by *U.S. News & World Report*.

Greater Portland Area

Southern Maine Technical College
Fort St., South Portland
• **(207) 767-9500**

On a 60-acre campus with 40 buildings, Southern Maine Technical College (SMTC) offers more than 30 fully accredited one- and two-year career-oriented programs. Most academic credits from SMTC are transferable to the University of Maine and other four-year colleges. Among the associates degree programs in applied science offered at SMTC are applied marine biology and oceanography, automotive technology, early childhood development, culinary arts and surgical technology. Diploma courses and certificate programs are also available.

Campus accommodations are here for those wishing to enjoy "on-campus" living, and the college offers a wide range of athletic pursuits. For those who want to complete high school-level courses, SMTC offers NovaNET as an alternative to adult education. NovaNET is a computer-based educational system that provides connections to educational, informational and communications services for students using satellite links and modems. Using this system, students can work from home at their own pace.

Andover College
901 Washington Ave., Portland
• **(207) 774-6126, (800) 639-3110**

With both day and evening courses, this junior business college offers an associate's degree in applied science in seven major areas of study: accounting, business administration, computer science, criminal justice, office management, medical assisting and paralegal studies. Historically the school has maintained a 95 percent placement rate for its graduates. More than 600 students attend the school, which was founded in Portland's downtown center in 1967 as the Andover Institute. The school year is divided into six eight-week modules, allowing students to enroll at various times from September through July. The student-teacher ratio averages 21-1. Students who enroll in the school after 1997 and graduate are guaranteed "free education for life;" they may come back to the school at any time for an unlimited number of courses for the cost of supplies.

Casco Bay College
477 Congress St., Portland
• (207) 772-0196

Founded in 1863, Casco Bay College was the first business school in Maine and remains one of the oldest in the United States. The college, which operated under another name, merged with the Plus School of Business in 1966 to become the Plus-Gray School of Business before the name was changed in 1974 to the current moniker.. The school's goal is to help students earn an associate's degree and to help them pursue further education in their field. In addition to competency in their chosen field, students are required to show achievement in basic subjects such as math, reading, language arts, communication skills, keyboarding, computer skills and economics. Majors range from business administration to office management to legal administrative assistance. The college offers a life-time placement service for its students and alumni. A 1995 survey showed that 90 percent of the graduates who responded were either working in their field or pursuing higher education.

Maine College of Art
97 Spring St., Portland • (207) 775-3052

Founded in 1882, this nationally accredited four-year art and design college grants bachelor's degrees in ceramics, graphic design, metalsmithing and jewelry, painting, photography, printmaking and sculpture, as well as a minor in art history. About 300 students from around the United States and abroad are enrolled, and it's the only independent professional art institution in northern New England. The college is made up of six buildings in the center of Portland's Downtown Arts District. Facilities include student dorms, several galleries, a library, studios and classrooms. The library, in the MECA Building, is the largest art library open to the public in northern New England with more than 18,000 volumes and 45,000 slides. The Baxter Gallery exhibits works from the state and region (for more on this see our Arts chapter).

University of Southern Maine
96 Falmouth St., Portland
• (207) 780-4000, (800) 800-4876
37 College Ave., Gorham
• (207) 780-5670

A member of the Maine state college system, the University of Southern Maine is home to nearly 10,000 students, the majority of whom are pursuing undergraduate degrees. The university is split between two campuses, one in downtown Portland and the other in the countryside of Gorham, about 15 minutes west. Both have classroom facilities, and the Portland facility has a new, state-of-the-art library.

More than 40 majors are available in the following areas: College of Arts and Sciences, College of Education & Human Development, School of Applied Science, School of Business and the College of Nursing. Day, evening and weekend classes are available at both the Portland and Gorham campuses. At the Lewiston-Auburn campus, about 20 minutes west of Brunswick, students can enroll in arts and humanities, leadership and organizational studies, natural and applied sciences, social and behavioral sciences and occupational therapy.

At its Portland and Gorham centers, the university also has graduate programs in subjects such as law, business administration, computer science and nursing. The school has a library with more than 1 million books, documents, journals and microfilms for student research; computer centers equipped with Internet access; and a university career service to help students choose their major and find a job.

The school also has an active NCAA Division III sports program (for more information see our Spectator Sports chapter) with 21 intercollegiate and three club sports. Women's ice hockey was added to the program as a varsity sport in 1998-99.

World Affairs Council of Maine
P.O. Box 9300, University of Southern Maine, Portland • (207) 780-4551

Offering international education programs for teachers, students and the public, the World Affairs Council of Maine is a nonprofit, nonpartisan organization promoting the understanding of world events and issues, foreign policy and international trade, and other countries and cultures. Managed by a committee of staff, teachers and international affairs professionals, it offers breakfast and dinner lectures and school enrichment programs. Past speakers include Maine's governors, former U.S. ambassadors and other prominent leaders. Call for a calendar of events and for more information.

Brunswick, Bath and Boothbay Harbor Area

Bowdoin College
5010 College Station, Brunswick
• (207) 725-3000

Established in 1794, Bowdoin College is one of the nation's oldest schools of higher education. Since its founding, it has graduated national heroes such as Civil War General Joshua Chamberlain in 1863, writer Nathaniel Hawthorne in 1825 and Arctic explorer Admiral Peary in 1909. Many of its professors have been equally renowned, including Henry Wadsworth Longfellow (also an alumnus) and Calvin Stowe, the husband of Harriet Beecher Stowe. The private liberal arts college now enrolls students from every state in the country and 30 countries around the world, drawing them to its vast campus of historic brick buildings set around a grassy quad.

Academic programs available to students include humanities, interdisciplinary studies, natural sciences and mathematics and social and behavioral sciences. The school's resources include a library established by the school's founding father, James Bowdoin III, more than 200 years ago; the Bowdoin College Museum of Art, with a permanent collection of more than 13,000 art objects; an interdisciplinary science center completed in 1997; a visual arts center with studios and exhibition space; and student dorms.

The college also has a full athletic program (for more information see our Spectator Sports chapter). The school accepts about 25 percent of the students who apply. Most of those who apply are in the top 10 percent of their class.

New Hampshire College
Building 20, Brunswick Naval Air Station, Brunswick
• (207) 725-6486, (800) 427-9238

This division of New Hampshire College offers classes toward associate and bachelor's degrees in business and liberal arts. Certificate programs in everything from accounting and aviation to education and the family to healthcare administration are available. Founded in 1932, the college is a private, nonprofit and coeducational institution. In 1998 enrollment in day programs was about 1,200. The Graduate School of Business has an enrollment of roughly 1,700 students. The school's new technology-based network allows students to access the Shapiro Library via computer, and undergraduate and graduate courses are available through the Internet.

Specialty Schools

If you don't find the course of study that interests you in this section, don't give up. This is just a sampling of the many learning opportunities available along Maine's Southern Coast. If you're looking for hobby classes, such as cooking, sewing and upholstery, or life-skill classes, such as investing or small-engine repair, call the school department in the area that interests you and ask for the phone number to the nearest adult education center.. We've included one or two of them here, but there are plenty more. Still can't find what you want? We recommend the Yellow

Pages or browsing the bulletin board at the nearest library.

Southern Beaches Area

Days Meadow Science Center
Maine Hwy. 35, Kennebunk
• **(207) 985-7323**

Science is fun. Science is neat. Science is wacky. At least that's what Claudia Berman is saying to children in the Kennebunk area. A former teacher in alternative schools like School Around Us (see the previous listing), Berman opened the Science Center in 1996 to provide science classes to students from kindergarten through high school. The aim of the center is to help students develop a personal connection with nature and to have fun while gaining scientific process skills and learning science concepts. She teaches physics, biology and chemistry and offers an astronomy class for families. Delightfully titled courses include Kinderscience, Flights of Imagination, Science Tricks and Toys, Funny Physics and Wild and Wacky Chemistry. One 12-week or two six-week sessions are offered in spring and fall. In summer, one- and two-week day camp sessions are available (see Summer Camps, below).

Landing School of Boatbuilding & Design
River Rd., Arundel • (207) 985-7976

The Landing School of Boatbuilding and Design is a full-time vocational school that specializes in teaching people skills to work in the marine industry as boat builders and designers. Students range from age 18 to the mid-50s and come from across the United States and around the world.

Programs begin in September and end in June. The Design Program is an intensive 10-month program that prepares students to work in the modern marine industry by teaching them about yacht and small commercial craft design, including principles of naval architecture. Drafting and Computer Aided Design (CAD) are also covered. Enrollment is limited to 20. Students wishing to attend the Boatbuilding Program have a choice of two 10-month courses, the Small Boats Course

and the Cruising Boat Course. Each involves intensive, hands-on training in traditional or contemporary wooden boat construction techniques. Students in the Small Boats course work in teams of three or four and complete both a traditionally planked Maine Peapod and a round-bottom daysailer. Cruising Boat students devote 10 months to building two boats up to 30 feet in length using modern construction methods.

Old Orchard Beach Area

The Environmental Schools
1 Randall Ave., Old Orchard Beach
• **(207) 934-7374**

The goal of the Environmental Schools is to help students develop a greater understanding of and respect for the natural environment, an appreciation and respect for their peers, greater confidence in themselves and the background needed to make informed decisions on environmental issues. Four sites are available for study, two of which are in Southern Maine: Ferry Beach in Saco and Ocean Park in Old Orchard Beach. The other two sites are west of the coast, in Bridgton and Stockton Springs. All sites are administered through the executive director, Duane Bond, at the listed address.

The Environmental Schools' programs are five-day, residential programs. They're available to students from 4th through 8th grades and enrollment, depending on site, is limited to 60 to 165 students. Programs are offered from September through November and from February through June. In addition, Summer Sessions in Canada are offered for students ages 12 through 18. The Canadian program takes place in Alberta, British Columbia or Nova Scotia and involves an environmental adventure including backpacking, hiking and camping.

Greater Portland Area

Baxter School for the Deaf
P.O. Box 799, Mackworth Island,
Portland, ME 04104 • (207) 781-3165

What began in 1876 in a one-room classroom with four students has grown into a comprehensive program for infants, children and adults who are deaf or hearing impaired, helping them to better understand themselves and the world around them. Set on private Mackworth Island (which is accessible by car), the school offers educational, residential, transitional and outreach programs while promoting deaf culture. Many young people who attend the school are from public schools throughout the state; others come for the preschool program. The school offers an adult education center, a library/media center, diagnostic testing, sign language training, therapy and a full-time and part-time residential program where participants learn to live independently while in a family-style setting.

Portland Conservatory of Music
44 Oak St., Portland
• (207) 775-3356

Here students of all ages and abilities can receive instructions on all manner of instruments, from orchestral instruments to piano, guitar, voice, harpsichord and organ. Classes include private lessons but don't stop there. You'll find classes like Kindermusic, in which children as young as 18 months can experiment with music through songs, chants, moving and playing. Other classes include children's choir, music theory classes, music history, jazz improvisation and special classes focusing on speaking English without an accent and overcoming lisps and stuttering.

The conservatory is a nonprofit organization. A small amount of financial aid is available, and there are discounts for multiple family members participating in the same class. The instructors at the conservatory have performed with such groups as the New York City Symphony, the Boston Pops and the Portland Symphony Orchestra (see more on this under Arts). Continuing studies courses for adults who are not pursuing a degree and an early college program for gifted high school students are available.

Portland School of Ballet
25-A Forest Ave., Portland
• (207) 772-9671

Students of all skill levels from age 4 through adult can enroll in classical ballet for recreation or professional study at the Portland School of Ballet. Established in 1980, the school also runs the Portland Ballet Company, which puts on four productions a year (see our chapter on The Arts). The school has two studios, and its instructors are all former professional dancers from around the country and the world.

SALT Center for Documentary Field Studies
17 and 19 Pine St., Portland
• (207) 761-0660

Established in 1973, this center serves as a school, gallery, archive and publisher of nonfiction writing and photography. The school offers one-semester accredited courses for advanced undergraduate and graduate students to put together a literary magazine of their photographs and essays. Students participate in independent research projects and document their work in words or on film. If you want in, call early — the center enrolls a maximum of 24 students per semester. The student body is pretty evenly split between graduates and undergrads. SALT faculty members are field professionals like Maine author Willis Johnson, who wrote the collection of short stories *The Girl Who Would be Russian* and traveled as a journalist in Korea, Australia, Vietnam and Maine. For more information on the students' publication, see SALT in our Media chapter.

INSIDERS' TIP

More and more high schools across the state are promoting positive interaction between students and the community through service programs. Students are required to consider various community service options, choose one, then go out and work for a specified number of hours. The good news is that most students greatly exceed the number of hours required.

Brunswick, Bath and Boothbay Harbor Area

Maine Writers and Publishers Alliance
12 Pleasant St., Brunswick • (207) 729-6333

Would-be authors can participate in any number of writing workshops put on by this alliance with more than 1,500 people from across the country. Classes range from outdoor writing and field trips to how to get your first magazine article published. The alliance also publishes its own monthly newsletter, *Maine in Print,* which includes upcoming literary events such as workshops and seminars. Look for it in area libraries.

Bailey Evening School
826 High St., Bath • (207) 443-8255

Adults can finish their high school degree or take any number of self-improvement and craft classes at one of the state's oldest adult education schools. Located at Morse High School, the evening school offers everything from classes on how to invest in the stock market to chair caning, basket weaving and quilting. It was founded in 1913 with a $74,473 donation from Lucinda Bailey, a prominent Bath resident. New course listings are available in September and January. To pick up a school brochure, stop by the high school guidance office.

Shelter Institute
38 Centre St., Bath • (207) 442-7938

People from all over the country and the world come to the Shelter Institute to learn how to design and build their own homes. Courses, which are as short as two weeks, cover everything from timber framing to understanding heat loss. The institute offers 17 lectures and workshops and has a complete library of building and design books that showcase everything from world-class tree houses to working with stucco. Weekend classes are also available.

Coastal Enterprises Incorporated
P.O. Box 268, Water St., Wiscasset, ME 04578 • (207) 882-7552

This private, nonprofit community development organization provides financing and training to people interested in starting their own businesses. Since 1979 it has financed more than 800 projects with $42 million, leveraged another $120 million and counseled more than 8,000 young businesses. You'll find assistance and courses in everything from how to develop a business plan to the best ways for women to break into the world of micro-enterprise. In addition, CEI runs first-time home-buyer classes for the public.

Summer Camps

Maine is famous for its summer camps. We have hundreds of them. In fact, you'll often hear tourists saying, "I used to go to camp up here when I was a kid." While most of these camps are located to the north and west of our geographic area, there are a handful along the southern coast that we've included for ytour convenience.

Maine's summer camps offer it all — from sports and backpacking to arts and theater. Day camps and overnight camps offer a full spectrum of learning and fun while giving kids a great way to meet new friends.

Southern Beaches Area

Days Meadow Science Center
Maine Hwy. 35, Kennebunk • (207) 985-7323

A variety of summer day camp programs are available for children 4 through 14. For the little ones, there is a Kinderscience camp. For the older ones there is a survival skills

---

INSIDERS' TIP

If you want to send your child to a private school but aren't sure you can afford it, you might consider a move to a town that doesn't have its own school. Often, the town will help foot the bill.

camp. In between ages enjoy the science potpourri, discovery camp, and nature camp. You'll even find a camp "For Girls Only" ages 7 through 12, designed for those girls who tend to shy away from science. For more information on Days Meadow, see the previous write-up under "Specialty Schools."

Old Orchard Beach Area

Northern York County Family YMCA
Alfred Rd. Business Park, Biddeford
• **(207) 283-0100, (207) 283-3778**

This is a summer day camp run by the Northern York County Family YMCA for children 3 to 17. The program is held in weeklong sessions at the center's facility in Biddeford, which features 26 acres of fields and woodlands. In addition to a camp lodge where arts and crafts programs are held, kids can take part in other pursuits like archery and swimming. You don't need to be a resident of York County to participate in the YMCA programs. The Northern York County Family YMCA also offers "Vacation Camps" which are held during the weeklong school vacations in February and April.

Greater Portland Area

Camp Ketcha Day Camp
336 Black Point Rd., Scarborough
• **(207) 883-8977**

Camp Ketcha is a summer day camp with adventure-based programming. The camp operates in one-week sessions from the end of June to the end of August, though they will accept campers for fewer than five days if space is available. Before- and after-camp care is also available from 7:30 AM to 9 AM and from 4 PM to 6 PM. Camp sessions are available to children 4 to 16. Some of the activities offered at Camp Ketcha include swimming, canoeing, arts and crafts, archery, environmental education, a ropes course, outdoor skills and theater and music. A horseback riding program is available for children 8 to 16, and a discovery challenge program is offered for children 6 to 16. A transportation

schedule provides rides for campers from the greater Portland area.

Toddle Inn Daycare & Nursery School
605 U.S. Hwy. 1, Dunstan Corner, Scarborough
• **(207) 885-0848, (207) 883-4563**

Summer day camp is available at Toddle Inn for children 3 through 10. The focus of the camp is the environment, and activities are based on field trips to many of the natural areas in southern Maine. The program runs on a weekly basis for eight weeks. For more information on Toddle Inn, see this chapter's section on Child Care.

Kennebec Girl Scout Council
138 Gannett Dr.,South Portland
• **(207) 772-1177**

Kennebec Girl Scout Council offers both resident and day camps at a number of sites in Southern Maine. Activities include swimming, arts and crafts, canoeing and climbing practice using a treadwall. You don't have to be a Girl Scout to attend camp.

Breakwater Summer Camp
856 Brighton Ave., Portland
• **(207) 772-8689**

Run by the Breakwater School, this nature camp is for children 4 through 10. Children get to explore marshes, beaches and Maine forests as they search for the small critters that live in them and learn about our local flora and fauna. Daytrips include visits to area museums and island cruises. On rainy days there are crafts, games, drama, computer activities and signing. Campers are grouped by age, and each two-week program is geared to meet the needs of the kids in it. The program runs from Monday through Friday and after-camp care is available for an additional charge. For more information on Breakwater School, look under our "Private Schools" section in this chapter.

Portland YMCA Summer Camp
70 Forest Ave., Portland
• **(207) 874-1111**

With 14 different day camps and an overnight camp at Otter Pond in Standish, the Port-

Kids learn about weighing and measuring at the Children's Museum of Maine.

land YMCA provides plenty of summer opportunities for young people ages 4 through 17. The Otter Pond Wilderness Day Camp takes place in 10 one-week sessions on a 280-acre preserve. Children ages 6 through 12 can participate in the whole program or for one week at a time. The Out Post Camp on the same preserve takes young people on overnight camping, fishing and hiking trips while teaching outdoor safety. Back in town, kids can sign up for everything from sports camps to skateboarding and fishing camps to whitewater rafting camps. Transportation and some financial aid are available, and the staff is first aid

and CPR certified. An EMT is also available full-time at Otter Pond.

University of Southern Maine Sports Camps
37 College Ave., Gorham
• **(207) 839-8200**

Held on the Gorham Campus of the University of Southern Maine, this sports camp provides a wide variety of training for young athletes. Both boys and girls will have a chance to participate in basketball, baseball, soccer, softball, field hockey and tennis camps, and for adults there's The Maine Referee Academy. Activities are organized into both day and overnight camps and are led by coaches from across the country and Europe. In addition to meeting new friends from all over the state, children learn athletic skills that they can bring back to their schools in the fall.

Maine Audubon Society
20 Gilsland Farm Rd., Falmouth
• (207) 781-2330

Maine Audubon Society offers a wide variety of one- to two-week nature and outdoor day and overnight adventure camps. Every year the itinerary changes, but to give you an idea of the programs offered recently, there was a course on painting nature's diverse patterns, colors and textures for children in 2nd through 4th grades. For older campers there were hikes around the 140-acre Mast Landing sanctuary complete with an evening camp-out beneath the stars. A camp focused on the water gave 3rd- through 5th-graders the chance to explore Maine's marshes, streams, rocky coasts and sandy shores all along the coast. At Gilsland Farm there are day camps focusing on natural craft projects, outdoor survival, canoeing and hiking. And for older campers there are plenty of overnight adventure camps from island expeditions to wilderness canoeing. Camp director Lynn Forsyth holds a master's degree in environmental education. The staff of counselors and trip leaders is trained in first aid and CPR, and many have advanced wilderness training. Enrollment is first come, first served, and partial financial aid is available on a limited basis.

Brunswick, Bath and Boothbay Harbor Area

Camp Davenport
26 Summer St., Bath
• (207) 443-4112

This YMCA day camp for boys and girls ages 7 through 12 sits on a 50-acre campsite in wooded West Bath, just a few minutes south of Bath. Children will have the opportunity to play field games such as soccer, lacrosse, baseball and field games in addition to enjoying crafts, drama and music inside rustic cab-

ins. The pool at the Bath YMCA is used for swimming lessons and games, and the gymnasium for recreational gymnastics.

The camp is in nine one-week sessions, each with a different theme. Past themes have varied from "Land and See" to "Recycle" to "Woods and Wilderness." Children don't need to be members of the YMCA to participate, and there's a 10 percent discount if you register by April 30. Families with more than one child attending the camp can get an additional 10 percent discount. The camp generally runs from late June through mid-August. Before- and after-camp care is also available.

Chop Point Camp
Woolwich • (207) 443-5860

Teenagers from across Maine and as far away as France have enrolled in Chop Point Camp's bicycling, canoeing, kayaking, sailing and hiking trips, which take them all over the state and up into Canada. The Christian-based overnight camp for youngsters ages 12 through 18 is affiliated with the Chop Point School (see more in our "Private Schools" section of this chapter). Campers get to choose which trips they want to go on during their three-week camp session, as well as which activities they want to try. Some include water skiing, tennis, sailing (for all abilities) and a Red Cross advanced water safety course. The camp itself is on a 50-acre farm on the bank of the wide Kennebec River (the city of Bath is on the other side). Camp equipment includes a 17-foot Boston Whaler, 10 canoes, a sailboat and power boat. Since many campers come from non-religious homes, Christianity is presented in a relaxed atmosphere with a short morning devotion and open discussions.

Camp Chewonki
485 Chewonki Neck Rd., Wiscasset
• (207) 882-7323

Located on a 400-acre peninsula, this outdoor camp dates to 1915 when it was an all-boys summer camp. Since the 1980s, however, it has been run as a year-round non-profit camp for boys, girls and adults and offers summer day and overnight camps for kids and adventure programs for adults. During the school year kids can participate in special day programs or in a semester-long environmental course through participating schools.

The summer program consists of three- and seven-week overnight camps with an emphasis on natural history, sailing and wilderness trips for boys ages 8 to 15, and overnight programs for boys. Coed sailing, sea kayaking, canoeing and hiking expeditions are also available for teenagers 13 to 18. Family groups can participate in wilderness trips. During the school year a whole host of programs, both residential and on-site, are available for t he study of environmental issues, natural history and the coast of Maine. The camp is equipped with summer and year-round cabins and a year-round dining room and natural history center.

Child Care

We've included well-known child-care centers with good reputations as well as child-care referral services, but no matter what child-care center you are looking into, talk with staff members and the parents of the children who go there before deciding whether the center is right for you. Most the centers we've listed are licensed centers outside of the home environment because they tend to offer the most supervision of staff members. If you're looking for an in-home center, we recommend making sure it's licensed with the state, talking to parents and visiting these centers unannounced at various times of the day. Many in-home centers are advertised through the classified sections of newspapers. You might also check at churches or bulletin boards in libraries and grocery stores.

Southern Beaches Area

Carelink
55 Bowdoin St., Sanford
• **(207) 324-0735**

Carelink is a Referral Service for York County with an extensive database of approximately 260 licensed and registered day care

providers and preschool centers. People new to the area or those looking for a referral (not a recommendation) can drop in, call or fax their requirements to Carelink, which will then provide a list of providers who match the requirements. The database contains detailed information such as whether there are any animals in the home. Carelink also provides day care financial assistance to help qualified applicants pay for day-care services. In addition, they offer day-care provider training.

Child Development Center, Inc.
U.S. Hwy. 1, Wells
• **(207) 646-3987**
10 Summer St., Kennebunk
• **(207) 985-7358**

The Child Development Center has two locations and offers programs for infants, toddlers, preschoolers and kindergarteners along with before- and after-school programs. Children from 6 weeks to about age 11 are cared for in the various programs. At the Wells Center there are usually no more than 39 children being cared for at any one time by eight staff members, though many more children may be enrolled in the various programs. Eleven staff members care for a slightly larger number of children at the Kennebunk Center. There are three playground areas for children at the Child Development Centers. Infants are separate from toddlers; toddlers are separate from children older than 3. In fall, winter and spring the centers are open from 6:30 AM to 5:30 PM. In summer, they open at 7 AM.

Old Orchard Beach Area

Northern York County Family YMCA
Alfred Rd. Business Park, Biddeford
• **(207) 283-0100, (207) 283-3778**

Toddler care, nursery school, preschool, kindercare and after-school care are offered by the Northern York County Family YMCA. The day-care program operates for children 18 months to kindergarten. A nursery school program cares for children 3 through 5, and there are two kindercare facilities — one for the Kennebunk and Arundel area and one for the Biddeford-Saco-Old Orchard Beach area.

In addition, six after-school programs are held at school sites for children through 5th grade level. The six sites are in Biddeford, Kennebunk, Buxton, Old Orchard Beach and Saco, which has two sites.

St. Louis Child Care Services — Catholic Charities Maine
116 Hill St., Biddeford • (207) 282-3790
60 School St., Saco • (207) 282-3790

The St. Louis Child Care Service accepts children from 3 to 6 years old, including those who require developmental therapy. Two centers are operated through St. Louis, one in Saco and one in Biddeford. Both centers are open from 6:15 AM to 5:15 PM. The number of children in the program fluctuates from week to week but usually ranges from 60 to 70. Approximately 16 full-time staff members care for the children. A sliding-fee scale is available. In summer, the center provides a summer lunch program for low-income children in the community.

Just Like Home Child Day Care
15 Industrial Park Rd., Saco
• (207) 284-4566, (800) 660-4867
Thornton Academy, Main St., Saco
• (207) 284-4566, (800) 660-4867

Operated by the Visiting Nurse Service of Southern Maine, Inc., Just Like Home provides developmental programs for children from 6 weeks old to 6 years. They don't accept children at kindergarten age. . Just Like Home is open year round, except for major holidays like Christmas and New Year's Day. They're open from 7 AM to 5:30 PM. Expect a waiting list for enrollment.

Greater Portland Area

Toddle Inn Daycare & Nursery School
605 U.S. Hwy. 1, Dunstan Corner, Scarborough
• (207) 885-0848, (207) 883-4563

Toddle Inn provides child-care services for children 6 weeks to 10 years. The center is open from 7:30 AM to 5:30 PM and provides a before- and after-school program. Children are divided into small age group categories. Each program has its own schedule of activities with theme-based play and learning and related field trips. Children receive a hot lunch and there is a consulting doctor available if necessary. Sick child care is not provided by the center. Staff members are trained by the Red Cross in pediatric emergencies and CPR, and there is a video security system to ensure the safety of your child.

Developmental assessments, daily progress reports and newsletters are provided by Toddle Inn, and you'll also find spacious separated playgrounds, gym, dance and swimming programs and computer classes. In addition, Toddle Inn has a private elementary school serving kindergarten and 1st grade. A further program offered by the center is vacation care for children from 4 to 10 years old. A structured program of activities including field trips, skating, movies, art, music and outdoor play is offered during December, February and April school vacations. The center is open weekdays.

Lighthouse School
**525 Highland Ave.,
South Portland**
• **(207) 767-2127**

Nursery school, all-day child care and kindergarten care are offered by the Lighthouse School. The school is open from 6:30 AM to 5:30 PM and accepts children from 18 months to 6 years old. In 1998 it celebrated its 26th year in operation. The Lighthouse School operates with a standard tuition fee. There is no sliding scale, and there is usually a waiting list. Features of the school include two large playground areas and a lunch prepared in the center's kitchen. Although it's nondenominational, the Lighthouse School is sponsored by the South Portland Church of the Nazarene.

Noah's Ark Child Care Center
1520 Westbrook Rd., Portland
• **(207) 772-9691**

At this family-oriented day care, certified teachers care for infants and children through preschool in a Christian atmosphere. The program includes motor skill activities such as rolling and swinging for the babes in arms and a pre-kindergarten program for older tots. Children are served a hot breakfast, lunch and afternoon snack, and once a week the older children participate in Bible day where they sing Bible songs and have crafts centered around a nondenominational Bible lesson.

The center cares for an average of 45 children, and after-school care is available for chil-

dren through 2nd grade. In the summer the facility runs an environmental camp for preschoolers as well as vacation Bible school in the summer and at Christmas. The center is equipped with seven classrooms and three outdoor play areas, set up for different age groups.

University of Southern Maine Child Care Services
96 Falmouth St., Portland
• **(207) 780-4125**

At this child-care center geared toward children of USM students, alumni and staff, you'll find age-appropriate programs for infants, toddlers and preschool children. All teachers are first aid and CPR certified and have four-year college degrees. The facility is equipped with three sunlit classrooms, a central office and two playgrounds. It averages about 52 children. A separate center on the Gorham campus cares for about the same number of children.

The child-care service also offers a parenting center with classes, workshops, information and counseling, and the center keeps parents abreast of their children's development with daily progress reports. About 70 percent of the children who go have parents who attend the university (for more information see the "Colleges and Universities" section in this chapter), and about 20 to 25 percent are children from the surrounding communities. A small amount of financial aid is available for USM students.

Caring Place Child Care Center
27 Walnut Rd., North Yarmouth
• **(207) 829-6906**

Infants, toddlers, preschoolers and kindergartners are cared for by a professionally trained staff at this day center in a country setting. The center, started in 1987, is licensed to care for up to 75 youngsters and has on-site swimming, hot, home-cooked meals and a small farm with cows, horses, llamas, and ducks! It also has two outdoor playgrounds.

INSIDERS' TIP

If you're checking out day-care centers, drop by unannounced. You'll get a more realistic sense of how the facility is run.

Brunswick, Bath and Boothbay Harbor Area

Building Block Day Care Center
24 Park Dr., Topsham
• (207) 725-8544

This large center is bright and clean and cares for children 6 weeks old and up. It sits on a grassy lot near the town shopping center and has several outdoor play areas for children with developmentally appropriate toys. Part-time and full-time schedules are available, as is a preschool program. Before- and after-school care is also offered.

YMCA
Wiscasset Rd., Boothbay Harbor
• (207) 633-4816

Children from 6 weeks through 6 years are cared for at this licensed facility with room for up to 49 children. The play-based program seeks to expose children to developmentally appropriate equipment and involves them in short-term projects, stories, music and water and sand play. There's also an outdoor play area. Before- and after-school care is available.

If you're visiting Southern Maine or thinking of moving here, be assured that we have a wealth of fine hospitals and healthcare facilities to meet your needs.

Healthcare

No one wants to get sick while on vacation, but let's face it, illness and accidents do happen. If you're visiting Southern Maine or thinking of moving here, be assured that we have a wealth of fine hospitals and healthcare facilities to meet your needs. The largest hospital in the state is Maine Medical Center in Portland, but you'll also find medium-sized hospitals with comprehensive care in Sanford, York, Biddeford, Brunswick and Boothbay.

Each hospital has affiliated physicians and specialists. You can call the hospitals for a catalog, or check the yellow pages if you're new to the area and looking for a doctor. If it's an emergency, you'll find 24-hour emergency coverage at all area hospitals. For less urgent care, we've included a selection of healthcare centers and clinics, some of which will provide walk-in care or same day appointments, depending on volume of business.

In addition to hospitals and healthcare centers, we've listed a selection of alternative healthcare, mental healthcare and home healthcare providers in this section. Not forgetting your four-legged friends, we've also included a section on veterinarians. For emergency numbers, check out the grey box in this chapter — we hope you never have to use them.

Hospitals

Southern Beaches Area

York Hospital
15 Hospital Dr., York
• (207) 363-4321
York Hospital has served residents of Maine and New Hampshire since 1904. You'll find medical and surgical units, 24-hour emergency services and extensive inpatient and outpatient services at York Hospital. It also offers many year-round community programs and is well known for its Heart Institute and Oncology Treatment Center. The 77-bed hospital has an associated staff of approximately 55. In addition to traditional medicine, they also offer a variety of alternative treatments such as reiki and aromatherapy.

York Hospital strives to be attractive and welcoming. Some of the special "extras" offered to patients and their families and friends include same-day menu choice and room service, where dedicated volunteers deliver snacks, newspapers, games, books, videos and other amenities at no extra charge. Beverages are provided in the waiting areas, again at no charge.

For families without child car seats, York Hospital has infant safety seats for automobiles available on a loan basis. These seats are required in Maine.

If you're not feeling well and you don't know what to do, York Hospital also offers a 24-hour Tel-A-Nurse service, (800) 283-7234, where you can ask for professional medical advice.

Goodall Hospital
25 June St., Sanford
• (207) 324-4310
Since the late 1920s, Goodall Hospital has been a leader in improving the health and wellness of the communities it serves. Throughout the years it has developed programs to help people of all ages stay healthy and maintain their independence, as well as caring for them when they are ill. Today the hospital reaches beyond its walls with such programs as the Alliance for Healthy Families and Occupational Health Clinics in Sanford and Biddeford. The 49-bed hospital includes a special-care unit,

obstetrics and a 24-hour emergency room as well as all the services you would expect from an all-around facility. A medical staff of 40 is associated with the hospital.

Other programs include the Adopt a School Program, which gives elementary school students access to health and wellness information as well as the benefits of relationships with positive role models from the hospital staff. Goodall also operates Eldercare Service at four locations: two residential nursing homes, a skilled nursing center and a 22-bed residential home for Alzheimer's patients, which includes two beds for respite care for hospice patients and adult day care for those with cognitive dementia. Goodall Hospital also provides education workshops on a variety of topics including cooking, nutrition, smoking cessation and weight management. In addition, the hospital facilitates the Allied Health and Social Service Network, inviting area social service providersto monthly meetings to discuss what each is doing and network with each other.

Old Orchard Beach Area

Southern Maine Medical Center
One Medical Center Dr., Biddeford
• (207) 283-7000

Southern Maine Medical Center is the largest hospital in York County. It has 150 patient beds, state-of-the-art laboratory and radiology departments and a special-care unit for intensive care. SMMC also features a short stay surgery facility and York County's only inpatient mental-health unit. The maternity department at SMMC follows a family-centered maternity care philosophy.

In 1991 SMMC completed a $10 million renovation and construction project focused on improving the ambulatory care services offered to outpatients. Since then they have also added a pain management center, and a Phase II Cardiac Rehabilitation Program, and an occupational health and wellness program called Work Well. Most recently, SMMC began construction of a mammography center in 1997.

In addition to general hospital services, SMMC also hosts a community education program. A community information line, (207) 283-7662, provides information on current educational programming and education. A 24-hour emergency department is available.

Greater Portland Area

Maine Medical Center
22 Bramhall St.,
Portland • (207) 871-0111

The largest hospital in the state and one of the area's largest employers, Maine Medical Center is a nonprofit teaching hospital with 598 beds. People from all over the state are referred to the center for its full range of medical services. The hospital also boasts a first-class neonatal center.

Located in the heart of a Portland residential neighborhood, Maine Medical began as a general hospital in 1874 following the Great Fire of 1866, which destroyed much of the city. In 1951 it was founded under its current name. Since then it has undergone extensive renovations, the most recent of which was a $46 million expansion in 1984.

The center serves as both a community hospital and a tertiary care unit receiving patients from communities north of Boston. It also offers outpatient clinics for people who can't afford to pay for care. The emergency department is open 24 hours a day and cares for more people than any other emergency center from here to Boston. Maine Medical has the only Level I Trauma Service in the state and includes advanced burn treatment for all but the most serious cases. It also has the oldest and largest open-heart surgery program in northern New England.

Since its founding, the hospital has intermingled teaching with practice, and it offers a wide range of residency programs. In 1998 it opened the Barbara Bush Children's Hospital. In total the hospital has 675 physicians and dentists on staff as well as more than 4,500 employees. There are also hundreds of volunteers and three aux-

Photo: Maine Office of Tourism

Maine's Southern coast is a healthy and picturesque place to live.

iliaries. The hospital also runs Brighton FirstCare, a walk-in treatment center for minor injuries (see more in the Regional Health Centers and Clinics section of this chapter). In addition to other services, the Brighton Campus, 335 Brighton Avenue, (207) 879-8000, houses the 80-bed New England Rehabilitation Hospital of Portland and Brighton PainCare, an outpatient center for patients with chronic pain.

Mercy Hospital
144 State St., Portland • (207) 879-3000

Sponsored by the Sisters of Mercy, this nonprofit hospital has 200 beds and more than 550 primary-care physicians serving people in Greater Portland. and is one of the largest hospitals in the state. While providing a full range of hospital services including an emergency room, Mercy is known for its top women's health departments.

The Sisters of Mercy have always placed special emphasis on caring for the needs of women, and in 1984 Mercy Hospital was the first family-centered maternity unit in New England to offer labor, delivery and postpartum care all in the same private room. It was also one of the first hospitals in the area to offer Jacuzzis, prompting some women to drive an hour or more to have their babies here! (We know someone who did.) Certified nurse midwives are also on staff.

Mercy's Breast Health Resource Center offers comprehensive care from risk analysis to screening and education to treatment. In 1996 it opened a Women's Surgical Unit and developed two new mammography centers at 619 Brighton Avenue, Portland and on Main Street in Yarmouth.

Because of its desire to reach out to patients in need, the hospital provided more than $6.5 million in charity care, community services and uncompensated care for Medicare and Medicaid patients in 1997. The hospital has a network of five Mercy Primary Care Centers including those in Westbrook and Portland, and in 1996 helped open the new Yarmouth Family

---

INSIDERS' TIP

Maine Medical Center in Portland is often referred to as "Maine Med."

Physicians facility to provide a full range of primary care for adults and children, including obstetrics and a diagnostic facility. The hospital also provides home health care hospice services.

Brunswick, Bath and Boothbay Harbor Area

Mid Coast Hospital
58 Baribeau Dr., Brunswick • (207) 721-0181

Now in the middle of its evolution, Mid Coast Hospital was made up of a Bath and Brunswick hospital center — each with their own emergency rooms and surgical units — until July 1997, when the Bath center was closed. To make up for the closing, the Brunswick facility, which is licensed for 144 beds, added a new maternity ward. The old Bath center, now known as the Bath Health Care Center, consists of an Urgent Care Center (see our Regional Health Centers and Clinics section in this chapter) and chemical rehabilitation facilities.

By 2001 the full-service hospital plans to move into a new $35 million facility, halfway between Bath and Brunswick. Because of the trend toward shorter hospital stays and more outpatient procedures, that facility will have just 82 beds. The original Bath hospital was formed in 1909, and the Brunswick hospital opened in 1916. The hospitals coordinated their services in 1960 and finally merged in the 1980s. Mid Coast is currently the largest coastal hospital north of Portland, with 106 affiliated physicians and mental health doctors. The Brunswick center has a 24-hour emergency room, while Bath has a brand new cardiac and pulmonary rehabilitation center. The new maternity wing has a hot tub and private birthing rooms where new moms can spend recovery.

Parkview Hospital
329 Maine St., Brunswick • (207) 729-1641

With just 55 beds, Parkview Hospital provides personalized medical and surgical services for people in the Greater Brunswick community. Its maternity wing delivers more babies annually than any other hospital in the region, and it is recognized as one of the most advanced in the state. However, the birthing wing is still small enough to provide an intimate experience. Parkview has a 24-hour emergency department, a medically advanced intensive care unit, and a full range of inpatient and outpatient services.

Associated with the Seventh-Day Adventist Church, the hospital has been open since 1959 and was recently renovated — including the addition of hot tubs in its maternity wing. The hospital also offers the services of two certified nurse midwives. Parkview provides a large range of educational services such as adult and child CPR, breast-feeding classes, grief recovery, sibling classes, sign language and smoking cessation among others.

St. Andrews Hospital
3 St. Andrews Ln., Boothbay Harbor
• (207) 633-2121

This tiny hospital with 22 beds on the harbor is the only hospital in Maine with a dock to receive emergency patients by boat. It also has a 24-hour emergency room and full services including radiology, physical therapy, a cardiac rehabilitation center, long-term nursing facility, home health center and surgical center. While St. Andrews offers women's services (including obstetrics), it doesn't actually handle scheduled births. For delivery, pregnant women and their attending physicians are sent to either Parkview Hospital in Brunswick or Miles Memorial Hospital in Damariscotta. The hospital had too few births per year — it used to have about 22 — to justify a regular maternity ward.

St. Andrews is not affiliated with the Catholic church. It's named for St. Andrew, the patron saint of fishermen. The hospital has been open since 1908, and the community it serves started out as a fishing village. For information on the hospital's home-health service see our Home Health section, and for information on its Express Care Clinic for weekend walk-in treatment, see our Regional Health Centers and Clinics section.

Regional Health Centers and Clinics

Southern Beaches Area

Kennebunk Walk-In Clinic
24 Portland Rd., Kennebunk
• (207) 985-6027

Open Monday through Friday, this clinic accepts both walk-in visits and appointments. The staff includes one family practitioner, two part-time nurses and a receptionist. Laboratory and X-ray services are available for patients. Minor surgeries and sutures are done by the doctor, and patients are referred to specialists if their needs are beyond the scope of the practice. As a walk-in patient, you'll be seen between appointments.

The Medical Group
3 Shape Dr., Kennebunk • (207) 985-7174

A health center as opposed to a clinic, The Medical Group has four family practitioners and six nurses on staff. The clinic accepts new patients and offers pediatrics and obstetrics. If you need a doctor and don't have an appointment, the Center will accept walk-ins. Laboratory and X-ray services are provided for patients. The Medical Group is open Monday through Saturday. Evening appointments are also available.

Old Orchard Beach Area

Biddeford Free Clinic
189 Alfred Rd., Biddeford
• (207) 282-1138

The Biddeford Free Clinic is available to people who can't afford to buy health insurance. Founded in 1993 by Dr. Francis J. Kleeman, the clinic is staffed completely by volunteers. It's one of 200 similar free clinics across the United States and has been written up in Parade magazine (the Sunday newspaper supplement). All patients are seen on a first-come first-served basis — appointments aren't taken. The clinic is open Monday, Wednesday and Thursday from 6 to 9 PM. It is suggested that those needing care arrive early to make sure they get to see a doctor that night. On any given night you'll find around 10 volunteers helping out at the clinic. General medical care is given at the clinic as well as free, non-narcotic medication. Some laboratory work is done on-site and a dietitian is available about once a month.

University Health Care
11 Hills Beach Rd., Biddeford
• (207) 282-1516
53 Beach St., Saco • (207) 283-1407
21 Donald B. Deane Dr., South Portland
• (207) 772-7417
1250 Forest Ave., Portland
• (207) 878-9990

Operated by the University of New England, these four centers have individual specialties. Patients are seen on an appointment basis, though you can call ahead to see if they have space for a same-day visit. Most health insurance is accepted by University Health Care. The sites are open Monday through Friday (Hills Beach main center is also open on Saturday). All sites have some evening hours.

At the Biddeford site, you'll find a multi-specialty family practice residency program as well as a second site called the Alfond Center, (207) 284-1417, which specializes in osteopathic manipulative medicine. The Alfond Center hosts an Osteopathic Manipulative Medicine residency program. The main Biddeford site also

INSIDERS' TIP

If you're new to the area and looking for a doctor, call the local hospital. They will be glad to provide you with a catalog of the various physicians associated with the hospital, and their specialties.

operates an anonymous HIV testing center.

The Beach Street facility offers a specialist in family practice and internal medicine. At the Forest Avenue site, internal and gastroenterology problems are handled, and the South Portland site specializes in osteopathic manipulative medicine.

First Care
20 Heath St., Old Orchard Beach
• (207) 934-5105, (800) 760-2273

First Care is open Monday through Saturday for regular appointments and walk-in visits. On staff you'll find a family nurse practitioner, a doctor and a medical assistant. All age groups are catered to, including prenatal care. While some laboratory work is done on the premises, other lab work is sent out.

Greater Portland Area

Women's Community Health Center
92 Darling Ave., South Portland
• (207) 773-7247, (800) 666-7247

The Community Healthcare Center of Portland offers a complete range of gynecological services, including pap smears and termination of pregnancy up to 12 weeks. They also deal with sexually transmitted diseases. Two doctors and a nurse practitioner are on staff. The center is open Monday through Saturday.

Maine Medical Center — Brighton Campus
335 Brighton Ave., Portland • (207) 879-8000

This urgent-care center offers treatment for people with walk-in medical emergencies such as sprains and broken bones. It was part of another hospital until 1996 when it merged with Maine Med. The center is open from 9 AM to 9 PM daily.

Mercy Express Care Mercy Hospital
144 State St., Portland • (207) 879-3432

Open daily from 11 AM to 9 PM, Mercy Express Care offers walk-in treatment for everything from coughs and colds to cuts and sprains to chest pain and seizures. The center is a program of the Mercy Hospital Emergency Department and shares the same entrance along Spring Street. It's staffed by experienced physician assistants licensed to diagnose and treat medical problems under the supervision of the emergency department. It is also backed up by the full services of the hospital.

Brunswick, Bath and Boothbay Harbor Area

First Care Parkview Hospital
329 Maine St., Brunswick
• (207) 729-1641

This walk-in emergency department is set up to care for people with minor sicknesses and injuries and is a service of Parkview Memorial Hospital. It's open 24 hours a day.

Oasis Health Center Clinic Mid Coast Hospital
58 Baribeau Dr., Brunswick
• (207) 721-9277

Open on Tuesday nights, the Oasis Health Center Clinic is a staffed by volunteer doctors from Mid Coast Hospital who offer primary medical care to the uninsured and under-insured. Physicians offer services common to family practitioners and refer more serious cases to area surgeons who charge on a sliding scale. New patients are interviewed by the social service department. There are no specific income eligibility requirements. Patients should make appointments in advance. The center is in the ambulatory wing of the hospital.

St. Andrew's Express Care Clinic
St. Andrew's Hospital,
3 St. Andrews Ln., Boothbay Harbor
• (207) 633-2121

Open from 10 AM to midnight on Saturdays and Sundays, this walk-in center treats people with minor illnesses and injuries. It's open year round.

Mental Healthcare

Alliance for the Mentally Ill of Maine
Box 222, Augusta
• (800) 464-5767

Founded in 1984, the Alliance for the Mentally Ill of Maine (AMI-ME) is a grassroots self-help, support, education and advocacy organization of families, friends and people suffering from severe mental illnesses such as schizophrenia, bipolar disorder and ADHD. More than 3,500 individuals are members of AMI-ME through activities that include a family/caregiver respite program, family resource guide, problem solving and advocacy assistance, family education courses and a free lending and resource library.

AMI-ME also provides 28 support groups throughout the state and a religious outreach committee offering support, education and information. Networks include the child and adolescent network for families with children who have been diagnosed with mental illness; the spouse network, and the forensic network for those with relatives who are incarcerated. AMI-ME is chartered by the National Alliance for the Mentally Ill.

Southern Beaches Area

Counseling Services Inc.
453 U.S. Hwy. 1, Kittery
• (207) 439-8391

This is one of the service locations for Counseling Services Inc. (CSI). At this location they offer adult and children's counseling, alcohol and drug counseling and community support services. For more information on CSI, see Old Orchard Beach Area, below.

Spring Harbor Counseling — York
1 Bragdon Commons,
354 U.S. Hwy. 1, York • (207) 351-3140

An affiliate of Spring Harbor Hospital (see subsequent listing), Smith House offers outpatient services, medication management and dual diagnosis. Therapy is available for individuals, couples and families, and you'll also find group therapy sessions. Services are available for all age groups from children to adolescents, adults and older adults.

Old Orchard Beach Area

Crisis Response Services of Southern Maine
409 Alfred St., Park 111, Biddeford
• (207) 282-6136, (800) 660-8500

CRS provides professional counselors around the clock seven days a week for crisis and emergency services for York County residents. The Crisis Hotline is operated by a partnership between Counseling Services, Inc., Southern Maine Medical Center, Sweetser Children's Services, Visiting Nurse Service of Southern Maine, Community Partners, Inc. and the Department of Mental Health, Mental Retardation, Substance Abuse Services.

The hotline provides telephone support, crisis intervention, access to a Crisis Stabilization Unit and Mobile Intervention services. Other services accessible through the hotline include an Assertive Community Treatment Team and Psychiatric Medication Services.

Counseling Services Inc.
Kimball Health Ctr.,
333 Lincoln St., Saco • (207) 282-5188
Locke School Bldg.,
31 Beach St., Saco • (207) 286-1104
The Professional Bldg.,
1 High St., Sanford • (207) 324-1550

Counseling Services, Inc. (CSI) is a nonprofit comprehensive community mental health and substance-abuse counseling center. Since 1972 they have provided services for children, adolescents, adults, senior citizens and families at a number of sites throughout York County. Programs include family services, managed care/employee assistance and community support. Cost of services is on a sliding fee scale, based on ability to pay.

Visiting Nurse Service of Southern Maine, Inc.

15 Industrial Park Rd., Saco
• (207) 284-4566, (800) 660-4867
42 Brickyard Ct., York
• (207) 363-7632, (800) 287-7632
Deer Ridge Park, Maine Hwy. 202, Sanford
• (207) 324-3662, (800) 253-2330

Among the services offered by the VNS (see the "Home Healthcare" section of this chapter), are mental health counseling and care at home. Mental health nursing services include a mental status assessment, medication assessment, education about mental health and medication management, drawing blood for medication levels and case management. You can also receive stress-reduction training and supportive counseling and learn non-pharmacological approaches to pain control. Social services include psychosocial assessments, individual and family therapy and supportive counseling to deal with mental or physical illness. The VNS will also conduct substance abuse assessments and help with family situations that complicate medical treatment.

Greater Portland Area

Spring Harbor Hospital of Maine Medical Center

175 Running Hill Rd., South Portland
• (888) 524-0080

Spring Harbor Hospital offers Maine's most comprehensive behavioral healthcare network. They offer multi-disciplinary teams at many sites and schools and offer treatment to those with psychiatric illnesses and chemical dependencies.

At the South Portland facility, patient services include evaluation and assessment, triage and referral. You'll also find a 106-bed hospital with an intensive care unit.

Other services offered at Spring Harbor include 24-hour crisis intervention, case management and substance abuse continuing care. They also offer community and professional health forums throughout the year.

In addition to Spring Harbor's's main site in South Portland, you'll also find a branch in Scarborough and another in South Portland (see subsequent listings). Other affiliated services include Spring Harbor Counseling (see listing) and Community Care Systems of Maine, which operates specialized foster care and intensive in-home staff support services from Scarborough and Augusta.

Spring Harbor Hospital Outpatient Services

600 Roundwood Dr., Scarborough
• (207) 842-6500

Spring Harbor's Outpatient Services offers an adult, partial-hospital program with dual diagnosis and life skills tracks. Adolescent, partial-hospital psychiatric programs are also available at this satellite site of Spring Harbor.

Spring Harbor Counseling — Scarborough

153 U.S. Hwy. 1, Scarborough
• (207) 883-7455

At this Spring Harbor affiliate you'll find outpatient services for all ages from children to older adults and therapy services for individuals, couples and families as well as group sessions. Mood and anxiety disorders programs are also offered here.

Spring Harbor Counseling — Portland

66 Pearl St., Ste. 201, Portland
• (207) 874-1420

Outpatient services for adolescents, adults and older adults are offered at this

INSIDERS' TIP

Home Health Care Review is a state established agency that will assist in healthcare concerns and evaluate whether your home healthcare is being provided at a reasonable cost. You can reach HCR at (207) 945-0244 or (800) 541-9888.

facility. Individual, couple, family and group therapy are available here, as are medication management and dual diagnosis. Specialty groups such as dialectical behavior therapy and life skills are also offered.

Brunswick, Bath and Boothbay Harbor Area

Shoreline Community Mental Health Services
19 Middle St., Brunswick
• (207) 729-4171, (800) 834-4673

This community service offers comprehensive mental-health care to people in northern Cumberland County and Sagadahoc and Lincoln counties. Individual, couple, family and group services are offered at its offices in Brunswick, Bath and Damariscotta, which is just north of Wiscasset. Services are offered on a sliding scale, and the center has 24-hour crisis intervention and emergency services for children and adults.

Alternative Healthcare

Southern Beaches Area

Creative Health Balancing
169 Bragdon Rd., Wells • (207) 646-6907

Creative Health Balancing offers aura readings and energy clearing, and is operated by energy intuitives Jodie Foster and Darlene Chadbourne. Some of the issues they help people with include: physical symptoms due to energy disturbances; stress; low self esteem; releasing addictive patterns of thinking and behaving; attaining life goals; and prosperity and money issues.

Jodie and Darlene access the inner body's wisdom through intuitive aura readings. By reading the physical, emotional, mental and spiritual systems of the body, they create a comprehensive program which may include herbs, vitamins and minerals, flower essences, nutritional lifestyle changes and other supportive holistic practices to help you consciously move toward a higher level of health and vitality. Each session is individually tailored to meet your needs. Sessions are offered in person or long distance by telephone. They also offer sessions for pets, card readings, and energy clearing for home, office and business.

Northern Lights Holistic Health Center
35 Western Ave.,
Lower Village, Kennebunk • (207) 967-9850

From the moment you enter Northern Lights Holistic Health Center you feel tranquillity entering your soul. Tiny chimes tinkle a greeting as you open the door, and as you climb the stairs, the gentle sounds of meditative music drift toward you. Cheerful, multicolored glass balls hang from one of the windows, and there's a comfortable couch to sit on while you wait with a cup of complimentary herbal tea.

The center offers much more than massage. A community of independent practitioners dedicated to helping others achieve balance in their lives offer a variety of services to enhance your well being. You can take part in counseling, workshops or yoga classes, therapeutic massage, foot reflexology or reiki, or learn more about your astrological chart. The staff is more than willing to answer your questions and explain the various techniques.

Southern Maine Therapeutic Massage Clinic & Alternative Holistic Therapies
5 Bragdon Ln., Kennebunk • (207) 985-1405

Among the services offered at Southern Maine Therapeutic Massage are stress

INSIDERS' TIP

Getting hurt on vacation is not fun. Make sure to take all safety precautions when engaging in potentially dangerous activities.

management, reflexology and healing-touch therapy. Geriatric and therapeutic massage are also offered. You can also receive cranio-sacral reflexology here. Owner Kathleen A. Webb is nationally certified and a member of American Massage Therapy Association (AMTA). She has been in practice since 1992.

Your Body Works
Shore Rd., Ogunquit
• (207) 646-1322
1516 Post Rd. (U.S. Hwy. 1) Wells
• (207) 646-1322

Knotty pine and restful music are part of the peaceful, nurturing environment at Your Body Works. Founded in 1990 in Ogunquit, the company opened its Wells location in 1995. They offer Swedish massage, reflexology, neuromuscular massage, Oriental massage and sports massage. For those who really want a treat, La Stone massage therapy is available at the Wells location. If you opt for this therapy, you'll enjoy a variation of Swedish massage that involves the use of heated basalt stones on sore muscles and key tension points.

Other services offered at the Wells location of Your Body Works include body wraps and polishes and facial rejuvenation. In-season, the two centers have a combined staff of 12; in the off-season, it drops to six. Customized packages are available for clients who would like to combine services such as massages and facials. Your Body Works uses Aveda products and provides a no-sun tanning service for those who are sun-sensitive. Both locations are open from 9 AM to 9 PM daily year round.

Old Orchard Beach Area

Full Circle Wellness Center
5 Horton Ave., Saco
• (207) 283-1500, (888) 460-WELL

Some of the services you can opt for at Full Circle Wellness Center include craniosacral therapy and reiki. Integrative bodywork and therapeutic massage and alternative healing modalities are also available here, and you can also request interactive

energy work. The center is operated by AMTA member Donna L. Ridley.

Greater Portland Area

Hands On Massage
222 St. John St., Portland
• (207) 879-1710

Mary Goering, a nationally certified massage therapist, will rub your aches or injuries away in your home or at her office. Goering practices Swedish, sports, deep-tissue and on-site chair massage for business. Also practicing at the same location is Anne Knights, who can relieve stress or back pain through acupressure or shiatsu. She is also nationally certified.

Home Healthcare and Hospice Services

Southern Beaches Area

Interim Healthcare
647 U.S. Hwy. 1, York
• (207) 351-1946
62 Portland Rd., Kennebunk
• (207) 985-8585, (800) 660-4466

Interim Healthcare provides care under Medicare and Medicaid as well as through insurance companies, private out-of-pocket and HMOs. The business is accredited by the Federal Joint Commission and Accreditation of Homecare Agencies, with commendation. For more information see the subsequent Greater Portland Area section.

Visiting Nurse Service of Southern Maine
42 Brickyard Ct., York
• (207) 363-7632, (800) 287-7632

The Visiting Nurse Service of Southern Maine provides many services in York County, including home healthcare and hospice care. For more on its services, see the subsequent Old Orchard Beach Area section.

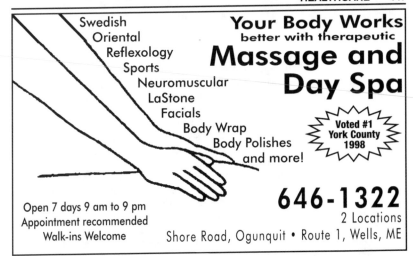

Southern Maine Health & Homecare Services

U.S. Hwy. 1, Kennebunk • (207) 985-4767

Southern Maine Health & Homecare Services (SMHHS) has been provided care for residents of the Kennebunks since 1909. In 1996 SMHHS became an affiliate of Southern Maine Medical Center in order to broaden its range of services and develop new programs. Today's services include skilled nursing services, physical therapy, occupational therapy, speech therapy, medical social work and home health aide. In addition, you'll find a nurse who is board certified in infusion therapy for high technology cases as well as a board certified psychiatric nurse on staff.

Nurses are on call and available 24 hours a day, seven days a week. SMHHS works closely with your doctor to develop a plan of care that fits your needs and budget.

Other services provided by SMHHS include adult health clinics, well-child and flu immunization clinics, community health education (including diabetic classes and nutrition counseling), and support groups for caregivers, widows and widowers. SMHHS has daily office hours for walk-in and appointment visits and maintains a medical equipment loan program to give you access to wheelchairs, walkers, commodes and more, for as long as you need them.

In addition to the above services, SMHHS operates a Hospice program for the care of those with terminal illness and short life expectancy. Care through the hospice program can include pain control and symptom management, social services for client and family, home health aide services and short-term inpatient care for respite or acute episodes.

Old Orchard Beach Area

Visiting Nurse Service of Southern Maine

15 Industrial Park Rd., Saco
• (207) 284-4566, (800) 660-4867
42 Brickyard Ct., York
• (207) 363-7632, (800) 287-7632
Deer Ridge Park, Maine Hwy. 202, Sanford
• (207) 324-3662, (800) 253-2330

The VNS of Southern Maine has its head office in Saco though it operates other centers as listed previously in this chapter. Services include mental health counseling (see previous listing) and the Just Like Home Day Care Center (see our Education chapter).

Personal Care Attendant (PCA) services include bathing, dressing, meal preparation, feeding, patient transfers and light housekeeping. They also provide respite care and companionship, run errands, and provide transportation. To find out if you qualify for PCA care, call the VNS. Some who qualify include homebound and disabled of any age, post-surgical patients not requiring skilled care and new mothers seeking postpartum help.

The VNS also provides rehabilitation at home services to help guide, teach and support patients and families of those with arthritis, cardiac disease, stroke, joint replacements, trauma, multiple sclerosis and more. A team approach involving the patient, dietitian, occupational therapy, physical therapy, physician, rehabilitation nurse and social services is used in home rehabilitation.

VNS also offers Enterostomal Therapy (ET) where ET nursing services are provided for people with selected disorders of the gastrointestinal, genitourinary and integumentary (skin) systems.

Hospice services are available to people who are no longer receiving curative treatment (like chemotherapy or radiation) and whose life expectancy is less than six months. Patients are generally referred to hospice by the primary physician, but referrals can also be made by family, friends, clergy or other health professionals. Requirements include that the patient resides in the program area, is at home at the time of admission and that a family member or friend will accept responsibility as primary caregiver.

Greater Portland Area

Critical Care Systems
24 Christopher Toppi Dr., South Portland
• (207) 775-3600

Critical Care Systems is a home infusion provider that also supplies medical equipment such as oxygen. They receive clients who call directly as well as referrals from physicians and local hospitals. All healthcare insurance is accepted by Critical Care Systems. The office is open Monday through Friday, but the phone lines are open 24 hours a day, seven days a week.

Interim Healthcare
13 Atlantic Pl., South Portland
• (207) 775-3366

Physical therapy, occupational therapy, home health aides and nurses and relief staff of all kinds are available through Interim Healthcare. In addition, they subcontract with local Visiting Nurse Services. There are 700 employees who work in the field for the company as well as 50 administrative staff in five offices. The offices are open Monday through Friday, but there's always a nurse on call, and the answering service and scheduler are also on call, 24 hours a day, seven days a week.

Visiting Nurse Association & Hospice
50 Foden Rd., South Portland
• (207) 780-6226

An in-home hospice, the Visiting Nurse Association provides support services for both the patient and the entire family. It has provided Greater Portland with at-home health services since 1921.

Community Health Services
901 Washington Ave., Portland
• (207) 775-7231, (800) 479-4331

This Medicare-certified organization has provided visiting nurses and home-health aides to people in Cumberland, southern Oxford and northern York counties since 1904. It is the official Visiting Nurses Association for the area.

Southern Maine Area Agency on Aging
307 Cumberland Ave., Portland
• (207) 775-6503, (800) 427-7411

At this agency, care managers will help you determine your need for home healthcare, develop and monitor a plan to help you live on your own, and figure out the easiest way for you to pay for at-home services. The agency is a private, nonprofit corporation for seniors in York and Cumberland counties. Services include meals on wheels, home-based care, supportive housing, volunteer opportunities and advocacy. (For more information, see our Retirement chapter.)

Brunswick, Bath and Boothbay Harbor Area

CHANS
50 Baribeau Dr., Brunswick • (207) 729-6782

Since 1947 CHANS has provided in-home care for those suffering from chronic conditions and terminal illnesses, or those who need extra support through a difficult pregnancy or with a newborn. The non-profit agency receives federal and private grants and offers registered nurses, certified home-care aides, physical therapists, occupational therapists, speech language pathologists and medical social workers. It also has a School Age Parent Program for teenage parents. Nurses and home-care aides make visits as needed, including weekends, evenings and holidays.

St. Andrews Home Health
St. Andrews Hospital, 3 St. Andrew's Ln., Boothbay Harbor • (207) 633-2121

Nurses, aides and skilled social workers affiliated with St. Andrews Hospital are available to assist people in their homes. The center's specialists are trained in rehabilitation and speech and physical therapy. It does not offer hospice service.

Veterinarians

Southern Beaches Area

Kittery Animal Hospital
195 State Rd., Kittery • (207) 439-4158

In addition to a full-service veterinary facility, Kittery Animal Hospital features animal adoption services and a boarding, grooming and retail store called Creature Comforts. Three vets and an adoption counselor are on staff at Kittery Animal Hospital. The hospital is open seven days a week, and on Tuesdays and Thursdays it is open until 8 PM. Those needing after-hours emergency service will be directed to a Portsmouth, New Hampshire facility by the answering service.

Village Veterinary
11 York St., York • (207) 351-1530

Owned and operated by Julie A. Matthews, D.V.M., Village Veterinary is a full-service veterinary facility. In addition to routine preventative exams and vaccinations, Dr. Matthews provides surgery, dentistry, laboratory and radiology services. For those wishing to try a holistic approach for their pet's care, Dr. Matthews also offers veterinary acupuncture. A 24-hour emergency service is also available. For service after hours, call (207) 759-2247.

York Animal Hospital
88 U.S. Hwy. 1, York
• (207) 363-2964

The York Animal Hospital was opened in 1977 by Dr. Ross W. Thompson and his wife, Mary, a registered animal technician. They offer medical diagnostics and therapeutics, soft tissue and orthopedic surgery, and routine preventative vaccinations. Boarding, obedience training and behavioral consultations are also available. If you have an emergency after hours, call (603) 431-3600 for York Animal Hospital's 24-hour emergency service. They are affiliated with the Seacoast Emergency Veterinary Clinic in Newington, New Hampshire, which takes care of the hospital's emergencies weekdays from 6 PM to 8 AM and 24 hours a day on weekends and holidays.

INSIDERS' TIP

Not all areas of the Southern Coast are equipped with 911 emergency service. Look in the front of the phone book to find out which towns can use this number and which towns have their own seven-digit emergency numbers. If you're not near a phone book and you have an emergency, dial '0' for the operator.

Mann Memorial Clinic for Animals
U.S. Hwy. 1 (north), Kennebunk
• (207) 985-4774

Owned by Dr. C.T. Angelos and staffed with two additional vets and two full-time technicians, Mann Memorial Clinic is respected as a friendly, caring place to bring your pets. They cater by appointment to small domestic animals such as dogs, cats, rabbits, ferrets and gerbils. After hours, 24-hour emergency coverage is provided.

Old Orchard Beach Area

Biddeford Animal Hospital
556 Elm St. (U.S. Hwy. 1),
Biddeford • (207) 282-6390

A warm environment is the key to the success of Biddeford Animal Hospital. Owned by a husband and wife veterinarian team joined by two more vets, licensed technicians and veterinary technicians, the hospital concentrates on the care of small animals. Laboratory services and surgery from routine neutering to orthopedics and endoscopies are available. Biddeford Animal Hospital is open Monday through Saturday, with evening hours Monday, Tuesday and Wednesday. After hours, emergency coverage is extended 24 hours a day with a veterinarian on call at all times.

Greater Portland Area

Scarborough Animal Hospital
29 First St., South Portland
• (207) 883-4412

Scarborough Animal Hospital has served area residents for approximately 30 years; the current staff has been on hand for about seven. Open seven days a week, the hospital cares for cats, dogs, rabbits and ferrets. There are five veterinarians and six technicians on staff.

Casco Bay Veterinarian Hospital
1041 Brighton Ave., Portland
• (207) 761-8033

You can bring your pet here Monday though Saturday by appointment. The two vets here offer a full range of services, from vaccines to checkups to surgery.

Yarmouth Veterinary Center
148 Bridge St., Yarmouth
• (207) 846-6515

This animal health center has three vets on hand to treat cats, dogs, birds and exotic pets. Medical, surgical and dental care are offered in the office or in your home by appointment. Boarding and grooming services are available. Bridge Street is just off Route 1, opposite Shop 'n' Save.

Freeport Veterinary Hospital
108 Durham Rd. (Maine Hwy. 136), Freeport
• (207) 865-3673

Complete surgical care for dogs, cats and small pets is offered at this center. House calls and emergency service are available, and the center is open Monday through Saturday.

Brunswick, Bath and Boothbay Harbor Area

Bath-Brunswick Veterinary Associates
257 Bath Rd., Brunswick • (207) 729-4164

This newly expanded and renovated animal center claims to be the largest small-animal practice in New England and has been open for 40 years. There are seven vets to care for cats, dogs and other pets, and the staff includes the state's only veterinary orthopedic surgeon. Ultrasound, endoscopy and oncology are available along with boarding. Two doctors from the office, Mark and Gail Mason, were selected as Maine's 1997 Small Business Persons of the Year by the U.S. Small Business Administration.

Bath Animal Hospital
15 Congress Ave., Bath
• (207) 443-9006

Bathing, boarding and 24-hour emergency service are available for Fido or Felix through this clinic. The center offers complete medical and surgical care to companion animals and is open Monday though Saturday.

Boothbay Animal Hospital
Maine Hwy. 27, Boothbay
• (207) 633-3447

Cats, dogs, birds and exotic pets are all welcome at this animal hospital, which also provides boarding, grooming and pet supplies. House calls are available by appointment. The five doctors who practice here also alternate between a separate practice in Wiscasset called Coastal Veterinary Care. It's off Main Street, and the phone number is (207) 882-9458.

Hotlines and 24-hour Emergency Numbers

Children's Abuse-Neglect Emergency Services, (800) 452-1999
Crisis Response Services of Southern Maine, (800) 660-8500
Family Crisis Center for Abused Women, (800) 537-6066
Maine AIDS Hotline, (800) 851-2437
Maine Poison Control Center, (800) 442-6305
Sexual Assault Response Services of Southern Maine, (800) 822-5999
Alcoholics Anonymous (Portland), (207) 774-4335
Suicide Prevention, (800) 870-9998

A growing percentage of retirees in Maine are coming from out of state. They come for the slower pace, beautiful scenery and gracious living.

Retirement

As evidenced by the many Maine seniors who pack their bags and head to Florida at the drop of the first snowflake, this isn't the first place everyone fantasizes about when they think of retirement living. So you might be surprised to find that Camden — about an hour's drive north of Bath — has been listed among the top 11 retirement communities in the nation.

The largest portion of our retirees are people who have settled, worked and raised their families here. They often continue living in their family homes, sometimes with a relative, rather than moving to retirement communities. Those who were not able to save money for retirement during their working life often settle in tax-subsidized apartments for the elderly. These tend to be nicely kept, condominium-style buildings with central meeting areas, are administered by local housing authorities.

A growing percentage of retirees in Maine, however, are coming from out of state. They come here for the slower pace, the beautiful scenery and gracious living. Those who select Maine as a retirement location tend to be people who have made plenty of money during their working years. Some buy historic homes or oceanfront cottages. Others buy into retirement communities, many of which resemble fine resorts with ocean views, wooded walkways, bike paths and plenty of activities. Buying into such a community can cost as much as $260,000, with additional monthly membership fees.

Out-of-staters who settle here are also typically younger retirees. Often they spent summers or vacations here and loved Maine so much they decided to move here permanently. In fact, quite a few seniors who can afford it choose to live in retirement communities during winter and move to their privately-owned cottages during the warmer months when it's easier to get around.

Maine seniors tend to be very independent and very active. About 35 percent of Maine residents are 45 or older. You're likely to meet them on mountain tops or open-ocean cruises, in fitness centers and at local hospitals or charity drives, where they often volunteer their time and skills. One woman we know who is in her 90s lives in her own apartment, drives herself around, swims at the YMCA every day and holds large potlucks at her cottage in Georgetown every summer.

There is plenty for older folks to do along Maine's Southern Coast — from civic organizations and activities at senior centers and clubs to fine dining, theater, dance and musical performances. Many retirement communities offer frequent outings to Portland and its many artistic and cultural events.

The state government wants to make life for seniors here even better. In 1997 Gov. Angus King appointed a commission to help attract more retirees, and the Maine State Planning Office released a report focusing on how to improve senior services and opportunities. It suggested the state promote more educational opportunities by providing free audited courses through the University of Maine and encouraging private colleges to orient more courses toward seniors. The report also suggested the state help localities expand public transportation services for retirees and help seniors save the money from their working years by reducing the overall state tax burden.

INSIDERS' TIP

Local historical societies and quilter's groups are prevalent in Maine. They offer a great way to meet other seniors.

In this chapter we will focus on some of the services, clubs, senior centers and housing options available to seniors in the Southern Coast area. Individual listings are grouped by category and are not by geographic area — our service organizations cover broad sections of the state. Service groups are arranged alphabetically, and senior clubs and centers and retirement communities are arranged in geographic order from south to north.

Services

While this category isn't meant to cover all the various senior services offered along our Southern Coast, it should give you an idea of what is available here and point out agencies that can offer more information.

Bridges
320 Water St., Augusta
• **(800) 876-9212**

Although its central office is outside our geographic coverage area, this agency provides home services in our area for seniors who don't have the time or energy to manage all their day-to-day tasks. For $12.50 to $17 an hour, seniors can get someone to shop or run errands for them, clean their house, do their laundry, drive them around, provide personal care and more. The service, offered through Senior Spectrum, is available throughout our Southern Maine coverage area from Kittery to Boothbay Harbor.

Brunswick Area Respite Program
**United Methodist Church,
320 Church Rd.,
Brunswick**
• **(207) 729-7540**

This private, nonprofit corporation provides "time-out" for families and caregivers by offering a program of socialization and exercise for the elderly in a safe and caring environment. Crafts, exercise, reading, walks, games and music are offered to participants from $3 an hour for up to a full day. The center is open every Tuesday and Thursday from 10 AM to 3 PM; call for an interview and appointment. The organization is licensed by the Bureau of Elder and Adult Services.

Senior Spectrum
320 Water St., Augusta
• **(207) 622-9212, (800) 639-1553**
**Sagadahoc County Resource Office,
54 Cumberland St., Brunswick**
• **(207) 729-1460**
**Lincoln County Coastal Rescue Center,
Upper Main St., Damariscotta**
• **(207) 563-1363**

A single phone call to this elder service organization can put you in touch with nearby social clubs, get a hot noontime meal delivered through Meals on Wheels, or have a registered nurse dispatched your way to help you make decisions about home-health services and financial planning. The nonprofit private agency offers these and other services throughout Southern Maine, including towns in our coverage area from Bath to Boothbay Harbor. Senior Spectrum is a network of community and resource centers for seniors age 55 and older. It has been serving the area since 1972 and provides services to people in their homes and communities.

Another service offered through Senior Spectrum is Senior Connections. By calling a statewide, toll-free number — (800) 876-9212 — residents can get in touch with someone who can help them find personal care services, transportation, overnight care, homemakers or people who will help out with chores, all for a competitive price. Senior Spectrum also offers financial advice regarding Home Equity Conversion Mortgages, and Care Planners at Senior Spectrum help families make decisions regarding the care of an elderly loved one. Senior Spectrum oversees an adult daycare center, the Muskie Community Center in Waterville(near Augusta), and the organization is also a good contact to find out about events, trips and classes and volunteer opportunities.

Service Corps of Retired Executives (SCORE)
66 Pearl St., Portland
• **(207) 772-1147**

This 33-year-old national nonprofit organization provides counseling and guidance at no cost to small business owners and organizations. SCORE has 400 chapters nationwide and nine chapters in Maine, the largest of which is in Portland. The 60 member-retirees

in this branch offer their services to people from Kittery to Brunswick. Their backgrounds are in everything from publishing and restaurant services to banking, industry and marketing. SCORE also presents business workshops to help people start a business, create a plan and a budget, and market it.

Southern Maine Agency on Aging (SMAA)
307 Cumberland Ave., Portland
• (207) 775-6503, (800) 427-7411

From the first call, volunteers and staff members at SMAA help area seniors determine what services they need to live as independently as possible and enjoy their golden years in Southern Maine. For more than 20 years, this agency has served seniors from Kittery to Brunswick, providing a wide range of programs — from housing assistance to delivering hot lunches to coordinating home care to providing free legal counsel. Each year SMAA receives more than 10,000 phone calls.

Through Meals On Wheels, seniors can get hot meals delivered to their homes, or they can find out about one of 19 centrally located senior centers in Southern Maine where they can dine with others. Also through SMAA, home-care coordinators will help arrange and monitor nursing services, including housework and ensuring that seniors get their proper medications. Agency advocates can answer questions about fitness, diet, finances and nutrition, either at in-home meetings or over the phone. For legal questions, the agency often refers seniors to Legal Services for the Elderly, where free legal help is offered regarding guardianship, the rights of nursing home and boarding home residents, and age discrimination.

If you don't need assistance, but you'd like to offer some, check out the many volunteer opportunities available through SMAA. The Retired Senior Volunteer Program (RSVP) connects people ages 60 and older so that they can maintain their independence. Nursing home patients can also volunteer through the program by calling elders who live alone.

Senior Centers and Clubs

There are a large number of groups for seniors along our Southern Coast, and plenty of activities ranging from exercise and educational classes to outings and luncheons to bridge, pool and poker. Because travel can be difficult in the winter, groups tend to congregate close to home.

www.insiders.com

See this and many other **Insiders' Guide** destinations online.

Visit us today!

Some of the larger centers — such as the Cummings Center in Portland and the Bath Area Senior Center — have their own facilities and are open for long periods during the week. Other senior groups get together in churches, schools and public halls on a weekly or monthly basis.

In this category we have individually listed the larger centers with their addresses, phone numbers and a sampler of activities they offer. Memberships range from $3 to $10 a year. For information on smaller clubs that meet at public facilities, contact either Senior Spectrum or the Southern Maine Agency on Aging (see listings in the Services section of this chapter).

Southern Beaches Area

York Senior Center
41A St., York Beach • (207) 363-1036

Monday through Thursday during the morning and early afternoon and on Friday in the morning only, this center is open to people ages 50 and older. You'll find a wide assortment of group trips, educational programs, social events and meal programs. Health screenings and general information for the elderly are also offered.

Senior Center at Lower Village
175 Port Rd., Kennebunk
• (207) 967-8514

The sole purpose of this privately funded community organization is to make life better for seniors in Kennebunk and Kennebunkport. Members choose from a wide selection of classes and social activities, including a book club, needlework groups, crafts, chess, tours and concerts. The center also offers assistance with government and medical forms, banking and investments. It's open 9 AM to 5 PM Monday through Friday.

Greater Portland Area

Peaks Island Senior Citizens Center
Island Ave., Peaks Island
• (207) 766-2545

All week long seniors age 55 and older get together for fellowship at this center, which is open from 9 AM to noon. On Monday and Wednesday afternoons activities such as art classes, bingo, cards and sewing are offered, and once a month the group has a membership meeting and pot luck lunch.

Portland Recreation Department Programs for Seniors
Various locations, Portland
• (207) 874-8300

Trips, events, bingo and socials are offered at various Portland locations through this arm of Portland Rec. All activities are open to seniors throughout the state, but Portland residents age 55 and older have priority on trips and events.

INSIDERS' TIP

If you were an all-state champion in one sport or another during your younger days, or if you just like to get out and exercise a little, sign up for the Maine Senior Games. They are held in Portland and sponsored by the Southern Maine Agency on Aging. Competitions are held in track and field, swimming, tennis and many other events.

Cummings Center
Munjoy Hill, Portland • (207) 874-8870

Monday through Friday from 1 to 5 PM, seniors can participate in crafts, drawing and painting, games and other social activities at this community center. Every month there are additional special events including dances, theater visits, trips and a luncheon.

Salvation Army Golden Age Multipurpose Center
297 Cumberland Ave., Portland • (207) 774-6974

You'll find plenty to get involved in at this center. Open Monday through Friday from 9 AM to 3 PM, there are arts and ceramic classes, shuffleboard, Bible classes, meals, men's club activities, swimming at the Portland YMCA and a television if you just want to watch with some company.

Falmouth Community Programs
Falmouth Town Hall, 271 Falmouth Rd., Falmouth • (207) 781-5253

Educational and instructional courses and adventure trips are offered through this community program. You'll find everything from bridge and tennis lessons to aerobics, museum outings, travelogues and cooking classes.

Brunswick, Bath and Boothbay Harbor Area

Brunswick 55-plus
6 Noble St., Brunswick • (207) 729-0757

Seniors age 55 and older gather here to participate in strength training, line dancing, oil painting, other art classes and regular trips to the Maine Mall. With a few thousand members, it is one of the largest senior groups in the state. The center is open from 8 AM to 4 PM Monday through Friday.

Bath Area Senior Center
45 Floral St., Bath • (207) 443-4937

Serving Bath and several surrounding towns with 560 members, this is one of the most active senior centers in the state. On the first Wednesday of the month members get together for a luncheon, and during the week seniors gather for bridge, cribbage, bingo, pool, poker and all kinds of exercise and art classes. On the first Tuesday of the month, the center offers free blood pressure clinics where local representatives from police departments, state and local legislators and other public servants such as bankers, pharmacists, political figures and state housing representatives are often available to answer questions and address concerns. The clinic includes free coffee and donuts. The center sponsors regular trips to area islands, dinner plays and area sites for minimal charge and holds frequent baked bean suppers. Annual membership is $10 and the center is open daily from 8 AM to 4 PM.

Housing for Seniors

In this section, we've included most private retirement communities offering independent living along the Southern Coast. However, as we mentioned before, these tend to be pricey options when compared to state-subsidized housing for the elderly. For more information on subsidized possibilities, we recommend calling the town office where you plan on living or visiting and asking for the phone number of the nearest housing authority. Housing authority officials should also be able to tell you about less-expensive facilities in the area and how to apply to live there.

Southern Beaches Area

Huntington Common
11 Ross Rd., Kennebunk • (207) 985-2810

This nonprofit community of adjoining Colonial-style houses offers an elegant atmosphere for active retirees. Located on a 36-acre wooded parcel along the banks of the Kennebunk River, the center is minutes away from sandy beaches, exquisite shops and fine restaurants. Open since 1988, Huntington Common offers independent and assisted living to 80 residents. Independent living apartments for a couple are $2,150 per month for a one-bedroom, $2,650 for a two-bedroom. A $2,500 security deposit is required. For singles, the rental fees are lower. In July 1998 the center began offering additional studios, one-bedroom and two-bedroom apartments. All residents have access to a 24-hour on-site nursing staff.

Greater Portland Area

OceanView at Falmouth
52 Falmouth Rd., Falmouth
• (207) 781-4460

On a wooded 48-acre site on a bluff overlooking Casco Bay, OceanView is an aptly-named retirement community offering both independent apartments and cottages and assisted living. The community is just minutes from Portland, and residents make frequent trips to the city to enjoy the symphony, theater, museums, fine dining and other cultural offerings. Both one- and two-bedroom cottages and apartments are available as are housekeeping and meals if desired. Cottages range from $135,000 to $250,000, and apartments begin at $112,000. The cost to secure a cottage or apartment is refunded when a new occupant moves in. There is a monthly maintenance fee as well.

Seventy-Five State Street
75 State St., Portland • (207) 772-2675

Located in Portland's inner city, this retirement center consists of brick buildings rising to meet the city skyline. The community's location offers retirees immediate access to downtown shopping, culture and dining. The majority of its residents live independently in rented studio, one- or two-bedroom apartments, although assisted care is also available. You'll find modern apartments with wall-to-wall carpeting and draperies, garden patios and access to a group gardening area, a beauty and barber shop, two libraries, in-house Sunday services, scheduled transportation throughout Portland and dining facilities. There is also a full social calendar with

beano (a New England cousin of bingo), exercise classes, creative writing, art classes, Bible studies and bowling. The cost of a one- or two-bedroom apartment is $2,560 to $2,850 per month for one person, and it includes one meal per day. A second person is an additional $300.

Bay Square at Yarmouth
27 Forest Falls Drive, Yarmouth
• (207)846-0044

This 60-apartment assisted living community opened in July 1999, making it one of the newest on the coast. It offers studio, one-bedroom and two-bedroom apartments with a 24-hour emergency alert and response system. A separate section cares for the needs of those with memory impairment. Common areas include a library, sun porch, spa/wellness center, outdoor walking gardens and a community room. Bay Square seeks to make everyone feel at home and cared for with daily meals in an elegant dining room, weekly housekeeping and many social, cultural and educational activities.

Brunswick, Bath and Boothbay Harbor Area

Thornton Oaks
25 Thornton Way, No. 100, Brunswick
• (207) 729-8033

This cooperative retirement community of private homes and apartments is set on 29 wooded acres adjoining nearby Mid Coast Hospital (see Healthcare). People who choose to live here are able to build home equity without worrying about the hassles of maintenance. Dwellings range in price from $134,000 to $218,000, and maintenance is provided by the housing cooperative. Some homes have fireplaces and hardwood floors, and the community includes walking trails, a library, lounge, dining hall, creative arts and exercise.

INSIDERS' TIP

For information on senior dining centers where you can enjoy a free noontime meal with other elderly folks, call (800) 427-7411.

The community is affiliated with Mid Coast Health Services and offers a full range of care in addition to independent living. Residents enjoy regular trips and transportation to Brunswick's restaurants and shopping areas as well as trips to some of the state's larger cities.

The Highlands
26 Elm St., Topsham
• (207) 725-2650, (888) 760-1042

Among the apartments available for rent here are those in the Benjamin Jones Porter House, once the home of William King, the first governor of Maine. Other one- and two-bedroom apartments are available in the Maine Lodge just steps away. All apartments have private balconies, and the surrounding grounds offer wooded trails for cross-country skiing and walking. If personal care is needed, assisted living is also available.

The Highlands is in Topsham's Historic District just a little more than a mile away from Brunswick's downtown shopping area. There are plenty of activities, and buses make regular trips downtown and to Portland, about 40 minutes south. Independent-living apartments range from $1,250 to $2,470 per month. Adjacent to the apartment complex are The Highlands Estates North and The Highlands Estates South, cooperative communities of cottages on a 65-acre campus. Here you'll find the same transportation and activity options, but you'll also be able to enjoy the garden, on-site hairdressing salon, an exercise center with an indoor swimming pool, and you can even bring your own pet. Cottages range in price from $189,000 to $199,000, plus a monthly fee of $500 for one occupant and $200 for a second occupant. The community is in the process of expanding.

St. Andrews Village
St. Andrews Village Information Center, P.O. Box 555, Boothbay Harbor, ME 04538
• (207) 633-0920

A bicycle path is set to run the length of this village, where cottages will dot the landscape at each end of the 60-acre campus. Once it is completed in the spring of 2000, you'll also find gardens, walking trails and plenty of trees. Drafts of the village more closely resemble a resort than a retirement community, and assisted-living and nursing care are available at the main inn. The developers are already taking priority reservations, though the village isn't yet completed. Some cottages will include garages, a terrace or porch and up to two bedrooms. Independent apartments to be rented on a month-by-month basis are also planned.

Cottages are sold on a cooperative basis, and owners pay a monthly service fee of $625 to $700 that covers grounds maintenance, 24-hour emergency response, scheduled transportation, health assessments, social events and wellness programs. Cottage prices run from $169,500 to $259,000. Apartments are offered on a rental basis, with prices ranging from $1,350 to $2,100 per month. The community is associated with nearby St. Andrews Hospital.

There is only one large, daily newspaper along Maine's Southern Coast, but there are several regional papers with a good mix of local, Maine and national news.

Media

Southern Maine has a relatively limited mix of media, but what it might lack in selection it makes up for in thoroughness.

While there are only a few local television stations here and most radio stations broadcast only general state and national news, many small towns have their own newspapers, written and published by the people who live there. These offer in-depth coverage of small-town government, usually including lists of the week's upcoming meetings.

There's only one statewide daily newspaper along Maine's Southern Coast — the *Portland Press Herald and Maine Sunday Telegram* — but there are a handful of regional papers with a good mix of local, Maine and national news. (Note that our listings also include the *Portsmouth (N.H.) Herald*, a daily that's popular in the Southern Beaches area.) Other favorites such as *The New York Times* or *The Boston Globe* are generally available at convenience stores and newsstands.

We've organized this chapter first by type of media — daily and weekly newspapers, tele-vision, cable providers and radio — and then by geographical area. That's with one exception: Our Magazines, Books and Other Publications section is not organized geographically; listings are instead in alphabetical order.

Newspapers

Dailies

Southern Beaches Area

Portsmouth Herald
111 Maplewood Ave., Portsmouth, N.H.
• (603) 436-1800
York County Office, 240 York St., York
• (207) 363-1200

This morning newspaper is published seven days a week. Though it's a New Hampshire publication, its coverage area includes the southern part of York County (i.e., Kittery, the Berwicks, Eliot and the Yorks). With a to-

Don't expect a little birdie to keep you up to date. Pick up a local newpaper.

tal circulation of 17,000, the Herald is regarded as a well-designed paper with bright color photos on the front page of each section and a good selection of hard news, lighter community articles and some national headlines. The paper also provides a local calendar of events, a sports section and a daily rundown of what's on the air. Other daily inclusions are comics, classifieds, a crossword puzzle, obituaries and an opinion page complete with a political cartoon.

Old Orchard Beach Area

Journal Tribune
Alfred Rd., Biddeford
• **(207) 282-1535, (800) 244-7601**

Published six days a week, this is one of the few surviving afternoon newspapers in the country. While most papers are out on the streets at 6 AM, the *Journal Tribune* is distributed after noon every day except Sunday. For the most part this paper's coverage area includes the Kennebunks, Arundel, Biddeford, Saco and Old Orchard Beach. Weekday circulation is 12,000; on Saturdays it's 14,000.

In addition to regular coverage of the area's municipal meetings, the paper also carries a good selection of lighter local news such as senior citizen happenings, school events and church fairs. The classified section is good, carrying a steady assortment of articles for sale, apartments for rent and automobiles for sale. Advertisements are not so copious as to overwhelm the news. Other daily inclusions are a large comics section, television listings, horoscopes and a local calendar of events.

Greater Portland Area

Portland Press Herald
Maine Sunday Telegram
390 Congress St., Portland
• **(207) 791-6650, (800) 894-0031**

This morning paper has a daily circulation of 70,000 serving communities from York to Wiscasset. The *Maine Sunday Telegram*, produced by the same company, is published every Sunday, with 130,000 copies circulated statewide.

In either publication, you'll find local news in an easy-to-read format and a wide selection of national and international news without the presence of a strong political bias. The *Portland Press Herald* was founded by the late Guy Gannett in 1921, when he consolidated the *Portland Daily Press* and the *Portland Herald*. Four years later he bought the *Maine Sunday Telegram*. Gannett sold the PPH to Blethen Newspapers of Seattle in early 1999.

The *Portland Press Herald* has five news bureaus including one in Augusta, the state capital, and one in Washington, D.C. For the last five years, the Sunday paper has won the New England Newspaper Association's top award for general excellence for a paper its size. The daily has won the same award in its division four times in that span. In 1991 it also won an international award for being one of the best-designed newspapers in the world. The voluminous classified section is the largest in the state. And you'll get a rare treat when you turn its pages — the ink won't rub off on your hands! It's made of a special water base that's better for both your skin and for the environment.

Brunswick, Bath and Boothbay Area

The Times Record
6 Industry Dr., Brunswick
• **(207) 729-3311, (800) 734-6397**
84 Front St., Bath • **(207) 443-5547**

The smallest daily in the state, this feisty afternoon paper has a reputation for holding its own against bigger budgets and larger staffs — although it is currently trying to find its feet again after a nearly complete turnover of its editorial staff in 1998. The paper traditionally offers intensive local news coverage of the communities from Freeport to Wiscasset. In the past the New England Newspaper Association has selected it as the best overall in its category.

The paper's circulation is roughly 13,000, and it has been owned by the same family since 1897. Frank Nichols bought the *Bath Daily Times* in 1897, and five years later started the *Brunswick Record*. The papers merged in 1967, and although many old-time Bath residents still hold a grudge about the merger (which moved the publishing office to

Brunswick), the paper has always maintained a Bath bureau. It also has a correspondent in Washington D.C. and selects national and international news from The Associated Press.

Now published by Douglas Niven, Nichols' great-grandson, the paper is a state leader in publishing technology. In the mid-1980s it was the first paper in Maine to print full-color photos, and it is still cutting edge in graphics and design.

Weeklies

Southern Beaches Area

The York Weekly
17 Woodbridge Rd., York
• (207) 363-4343

The York Weekly has kept the people of York in touch with what's happening in town since 1890. Published every Wednesday by James Carter Publications, the paper has four staff reporters, two staff photographers and a couple of contributing writers. In 1996 the paper won 14 awards from the Maine Press Association — several for photography and many for their news coverage.

While the major coverage area for this paper is the town of York, they do include some news from Kittery, Ogunquit and Portsmouth. In-depth articles on local issues are provided, and general community events are covered. The paper is filled with all sorts of information on what's going on in town, including a calendar of events, church schedules, letters to the editor, an opinion page, sports news, recipes, arts and entertainment.

York County Coast Star
284 York St., York • (207) 351-1010
U.S. Hwy. 1 S., Kennebunk
• (207) 985-2961

This weekly paper is jam-packed with local news, from municipal meetings and special events to the regular happenings of schools and the senior community. There are five staff reporters, each responsible for specific town coverage, and a wealth of contributing correspondents and columnists.

In addition to regular news, the paper includes a separate section, Coast Lines, that contains articles and information relating to local arts, antiques, dining, shopping and entertainment. Several pages of classified listings are printed every week, as are Town Columns (community-oriented pieces from nearby towns) and a People section that carries info on weddings, engagements, births, locals in the military and business promotions for area residents (or people from outside the area who have local relatives). The *York County Coast Star* is published by Journal Transcript Newspapers and is distributed on Wednesdays.

Old Orchard Beach Area

Biddeford Saco Courier
5 Washington St., Biddeford
• (207) 282-4337

A decade old, this free local newspaper has found its niche. Each week it's filled with local news from Saco, Biddeford and Old Orchard Beach. You'll find small articles relating to residents' promotions, wedding, military, and engagement news, plus birth announcements. The classified section includes household items for sale, giveaways, places to rent and more. There's also a weekly calendar of local events. The paper is one of four published by Mainely Newspapers and is distributed on Thursday mornings to all the households in these towns.

Old Orchard Beachcomber
5 Washington St., Biddeford
• (207) 282-4337

Co-published by Mainely Newspapers and the Old Orchard Chamber of Commerce, this publication is aimed at tourists. You won't find any serious news here, but there's plenty of fun stuff relating to vacationing on Old Orchard Beach. Television schedules and tide tables are the main inclusions for this weekly paper, which is available at hotels, motels, the chamber office on First Street, bookstores and supermarkets. It's available weekly from the last week in May to the first week in September.

Greater Portland Area

The Scarborough Leader
5 Washington St., Biddeford
· (207) 282-4337, (800) 617-3984

Another of Mainely Newspapers' offerings, the *Leader* is similar to the group's *Biddeford Saco Courier*. It covers the town of Scarborough's news and businesses and is available at supermarkets, convenience stores and bookstores. It is distributed free to households in Scarborough on Friday.

South Portland Sentinel
5 Washington St., Biddeford
· (207) 282-4337

The newest of Mainly Newspapers undertakings, The *South Portland Sentinel* was launched in 1998. It is delivered free to homes and businesses in South Portland weekly.

Cape Courier
320 Ocean House Rd., Cape Elizabeth
· (207) 767-5023

The *Cape Courier* is delivered twice a week to all households in Cape Elizabeth. The free publication contains community news and information and has been a town staple since 1987.

Maine Times
561 Congress St., Portland
· (207) 623-8955

This statewide paper with 30,000 readers tends to lean toward the left while covering a wide variety of news from across Maine. You'll find in-depth investigative news and political commentary as well as articles on the environment, arts and culture. Most readers are professionals, and about 20 percent live out-of-state. In its 30th year, the *Maine Times* split from the *Casco Bay Weekly* in May 1997. It is published on Thursdays.

The Forecaster
317 Foreside Rd.,
Falmouth · (207) 781-3661

With a circulation of 18,000, this free paper covers the local news in Falmouth, Cumberland, Yarmouth, North Yarmouth and Freeport. Crime buffs will love the weekly log of calls to the police department with everything from missing pigs to reports of large snakes.

Every Thursday, you'll find a large classified section featuring real estate, boats, antiques, music lessons, animals and even volunteer activities. The opinion page is a hotbed of local controversy. The paper is published by Forecaster Publishing and is available at convenience and grocery stores and other locations throughout the towns.

Brunswick, Bath and Boothbay Harbor Area

Coastal Journal
99 Commercial St., Bath
· (207) 443-6241, (800) 649-6241

This free, magazine-format paper is owned by Guy Gannett Communications and covers Freeport to Waldoboro, with a circulation of 21,000. Its calendar of events is a popular source for finding support groups, recreational activities and upcoming performances and activities. In each Thursday issue, you'll find a couple of local stories as well as local columnists.

INSIDERS' TIP

TV reception varies wildly in Maine. If you don't have cable or satellite TV and aren't having much luck receiving a station, try moving the television to another part of the room or to another room. We've found that we get different stations and clearer reception depending both on where the television is in the room and what room it's in.

Wiscasset Newspaper
Federal St., Wiscasset • (207) 882-6355

This paper covers Wiscasset, Westport, Alna and Dresden and includes news from the surrounding communities when it affects the people living in its coverage area. There's also a good selection of upcoming events, local sports and classifieds. The paper, which is published on Thursdays, is owned by the *Boothbay Register* and shares the same inside section (including classifieds) with that paper.

Boothbay Register
95 Townsend Ave., Boothbay Harbor
• (207) 633-4620

Roughly 75 percent of the 6,500 weekly copies of this paper are mailed to summer residents living around the country! You'll find a lot of homegrown news and sports as well as extensive advertising, which is the main reason people buy the paper. The inside section and classifieds are shared with the *Wiscasset Newspaper*, which is under the same management. In 1996 the paper won a general excellence award for being the top paper of its size in the state.

Lincoln County News
P.O. Box 36, Damariscotta, ME 04543
• (207) 563-3171

This paper covers most of Lincoln County including Wiscasset and Dresden but excluding the Boothbays. It has a total circulation of 8,700 and covers community news and town government with more than two dozen local correspondents contributing. It is independently owned and operated by the Lincoln County Publishing Company and hits the stands and stores on Wednesdays.

Lincoln County Weekly
Main St., Damariscotta
• (207) 563-5006

Two new sections focusing on family and health were recently added to this paper, which has a circulation of 4,500. It covers all of Lincoln County and includes outside information on the Maine State Music Theater and other places and events of interest. It also has strong education and business sections. The Weekly comes out on Wednesdays.

Magazines and Book Publishers

We would be remiss to list only those magazines published in Southern Maine. Instead, we've compiled a selection of magazines, books and other publications that will help you better enjoy the time you spend visiting Maine or provide you with useful information if you intend to live here. Rather than proceeding from south to north geographically, we've organized this section alphabetically by title.

Down East
P.O. Box 679, Camden, ME 04843
• (207) 594-9544

More than 84,000 people from around the country subscribe to the only monthly magazine about Maine that's published in the state. This high-quality glossy publication carries a wide variety of features on living in Maine as well as an events calendar and classifieds with real estate and rentals.

Face Magazine
500 Forest Ave., Portland
• (207) 774-9703

This music and entertainment guide comes out every other week and is distributed free across Southern Maine and seacoast New Hampshire. You'll find music and concert reviews, information on upcoming shows, and features on local bands. There's also a roundup of locally produced albums. As for styles, you'll find everything from classical to country, jazz, rock and pop. Pick it up at convenience or grocery stores.

Interface Monthly
144 Fore St., Portland
• (207) 773-4050

This business and technology magazine is distributed to 18,000 homes and businesses across northern New England. It features a wide variety of articles on issues from electronic banking to online marketing, office technology and tourism on the World Wide Web. There are also company profiles and regular stories on topics such as law technology and national business news. If you're not ready to subscribe, pick it up at newsstands throughout New England.

Lighthouse Digest
U.S. Hwy. 1, Wells • (800) 668-7737

Devoted to lighthouse news and information from across the United States, this monthly magazine includes a calendar of events. According to the editor, some people even plan their vacations around the calendar of lighthouse cruises!

Be forewarned that this publication is hard to get. It sells out quickly and is available at a limited number of places, including the Lighthouse Depot store (see our Shopping chapter) and the shop at Portland Head Light in Cape Elizabeth (see our Attractions chapter). Your best bet for landing a copy is to subscribe. For information call the above number.

The Maine Atlas and Gazetteer
2 DeLorme Dr., Yarmouth
• (207) 846-7000, (800) 452-5931

Put out by the DeLorme Mapping Company (see our Attractions chapter), this 78-page guide will get you everywhere you want to go with detailed maps of inner cities and back roads. It also lists a wide variety of Maine campgrounds, nature preserves, beaches, parks, fish hatcheries, nature trails, historic forts, lighthouses and airports.

Maine in Print
12 Pleasant St., Brunswick
• (207) 729-6333

Published by the Maine Writers & Publishers Alliance, this monthly newspaper features stories on Maine literature and literary events, including writing workshops and seminars. It also has a section focusing on where writers can get their work published. The paper comes free with a $30, one-year membership to the alliance. It is distributed to 1,500 people across the country.

People, Places & Plants
251 U.S. Hwy. 1, Falmouth
• (207) 781-7071

Focusing on gardening in the north's colder climate, this glossy magazine will get you in gear to grow a gorgeous garden in Maine's rocky soil. It includes gardener profiles, a calendar of events with plant sales, open houses and Audubon field trips, and a month-by-month maintenance and planting guide. It's published five times a year.

Phoenix Publishing
Chapman Ln., Kennebunk
• (207) 985-2661

You probably won't bump into any of their books in a regular bookstore, but you will find them in historical society libraries. Publisher of more than 200 books, this company now publishes on a contract basis only and doesn't mass market its titles. The bulk of its publications are local or state histories; the remainder are mainly regional historical volumes on specific subjects.

Portland Magazine
578 Congress St., Portland
• (207) 775-4339

This magazine is produced 10 times a year and has a circulation of 12,000. It covers a wide variety of upcoming events and issues in Portland and is often available free at area chambers of commerce. It's also sold at local supermarkets and bookstores throughout the country.

Provincial Press
98 Chestnut St., Ste. 98W, Portland
• (207) 772-8900

This press specializes in Maine's maritime history, lighthouses, shipwrecks and the Civil War. You can find their publications in many bookstores from coast to coast. A sample of Provincial titles includes Shipwrecks & Maritime Disasters of the Maine Coast, Lighthouses & Lightships of Casco Bay and Liberty Ships Eastward.

Saco Bay Reader
P.O. Box 1668, Saco 04072 • (207) 284-4119

Formerly a monthly publication, the Saco Bay Reader became a quarterly in 1997. It's a different kind of magazine, with positive and spiritual articles relating to life on the Maine coast. You'll find fiction, poetry, essays and articles as well as a nice selection of local advertisers. Complimentary copies are often available at supermarkets in the Saco area, but you may want to subscribe to make sure you receive it regularly. Call for subscription information.

Salt
19 Pine St., Portland
• (207) 761-0660

This magazine is put together by a non-profit organization that runs educational programs for students from across the country and around the world. The training revolves around producing documentary work for both photographers and writers and includes putting together this magazine, which has a circulation of 5,000. You'll find Maine topics reflecting the students' interests. Past features have included Elvis impersonators, ground fishing and development projects on the islands of Casco Bay. The artistic and literary qualities of this magazine are exceptional.

The Wise Guide
331 Cottage Rd., South Portland
• (207) 767-7314

Published weekly and distributed on Mondays, this guide features an extensive "Articles for Sale" section. If you're looking for second-hand furniture, household stuff or a car, pick up a Wise Guide from supermarkets, laundromats or bookstores.

Yankee
Yankee Publishing Inc., Dublin, N.H.
• (800) 288-4284

Your mouth will water over the great recipes in this magazine, which features articles on New England. From Connecticut to Maine you'll read about the sea, lakes, restaurants, inns, rivers and our unique New England char-

acter. The magazine is published monthly and generally available wherever magazines are sold. For subscription information call the above number.

Television

WENH Channel 11 (PBS)
268 Mast Rd., Durham, N.H.
• (603) 868-1100

Residents of York County often get better reception with New Hampshire's public broadcasting station than they do with Maine's PBS affiliate in Lewiston. Here you'll find Mystery!, British comedies like Are You Being Served?, Red Dwarf and Keeping Up Appearances as well as Masterpiece Theater.

WCSH Channel 6 (NBC)
1 Congress Sq., Portland • (207) 828-6666

In addition to the regularly televised shows you'd expect to find here, this station also produces a fair amount of its own programming and features StormCenter, a great source of weather information for newcomers to the area. Old-timers may be able to look out the window and tell how hard it's snowing, but for the more cautious, StormCenter broadcasts live from different points around the state to tell you just how intense the storm is and how long it's supposed to last. It also includes school cancellations and driving conditions. For local state news, 6-Alive comes on at 5:30 PM.

WMTW Channel 8 (ABC)
475 Congress St., Portland
• (207) 782-1800

One of the only stations in the Portland market with a local newscast at 5 PM, Channel 8 provides its viewers with news from around the state. Morning programming includes Good Morning America. The station also broadcasts local sports games including

Portland Sea Dogs baseball and Portland Pirates hockey.

WGME Channel 13 (CBS)
1335 Washington Ave., Portland
• **(207) 797-9330**

One of Southern Maine's largest television stations, WGME features all of CBS' national programming. The station offers its own news programming in the evening beginning at 5:30 PM.

WPXT Channel 15 (Fox)
2320 Congress St., Portland
• **(207) 774-0051**

You won't find much local programming on this station, but you will find Fox favorites. At 10 PM, Monday through Friday, you can catch a half-hour news segment.

WPTV Channels 10 and 11 (PBS)
65 Texas Ave., Bangor
• **(207) 941-1010**

Tune into concerts and educational programming on this Maine Public Broadcasting Station. With studios in Bangor and Lewiston, you'll find locally produced talk shows that delve into statewide issues. And for a little heady nostalgia, make sure to catch *Masterpiece Theater* and *Mystery!*. For non-cable households, the station broadcasts on Channel 10; for homes with cable, WPTV is on Channel 11.

Cable Television Providers

TCI of Southern Maine, Inc.
19 Kimball Ln., Moody Beach, Wells
• **(207) 646-4576, (800) 646-4576**

The coverage area for this cable provider includes Wells, Ogunquit, York, North Berwick, Biddeford and Cape Neddick. The general channel lineup changes from time to time as new channels are added or occasionally removed. Basic subscription to TCI will give you all the local broadcast stations listed previously as well as Boston network affiliates. An expanded service includes the Sports Channel, Animal Planet, Lifetime, Nickelodeon, ESPN, USA and the Family Channel as well as others. TCI Choice Theater package

ages include Stars, Encore and a choice of premium channels like HBO and Cinemax.

Cable Television of the Kennebunks
35 Beach St., Kennebunk
• **(207) 967-5212, (800) 585-3574**

Since 1981 this cable provider has been servicing the cable needs of the Kennebunks, Arundel, Alfred, Lyman and Dayton. Today it services more than 8,000 homes.

The standard package offers about three dozen channels where you'll find top-rated cable television networks, local broadcast networks and public broadcasting stations. If you would like to extend your service to include premium channels, there are three options. You can choose the Triple Treat package (which includes Showtime, The Disney Channel and New England Sports Network), the Double Delight package (which includes your choice of two of those three networks) or the HBO-Cinemax combo. You can also tune in local community news with Horizon Television on Channel 9, which has a community notice board and special events.

MediaOne
42 Industrial Park Rd., Saco
• **(207) 282-5916**
155 Commerce Way, Portsmouth, N.H.
• **(603) 436-6050**

Formerly Continental Cablevision, MediaOne provides cable service to Saco, Old Orchard Beach, Kittery, Eliot, Berwick and South Berwick. Programming and price vary by town. The Berwicks, Kittery and Eliot are serviced by the company's Portsmouth, New Hampshire office, while Saco and Old Orchard Beach receive service from the Saco office.

Time Warner Cable
118 Johnson Rd., Portland
• **(207) 775-3431, (800) 833-2253**

Serving communities from Scarborough to North Yarmouth and towns to the west, Time Warner Cable offers three different packages including basic service, which gets you channels 2 through 18; standard service, for channels 2 through 53; and Access, for channels 2 through 63. Access also gives you the option of buying pay-per-view movies and allows you to add HBO, Cinemax, The Disney Channel and other programming for additional costs.

Casco Cable Television
336 Bath Rd., Brunswick • (207) 729-6663

Limited service through this company will get you channels 2 through 13. Basic service provides a total of 40 channels including A&E, Discovery Channel, the Weather Channel and American Movie Classics. Premium service gives you the option of purchasing The Disney Channel, HBO, Cinemax and Showtime. Casco Cable also offers pay-per-view movies with its basic and premium services. The franchise serves Brunswick, Topsham, Bowdoin, Bowdoinham, Bath, West Bath, Phippsburg, Woolwich, Dresden, Edgecomb, Waldoboro, Freeport, Durham and Harpswell.

Radio

Adult Contemporary
WQEZ 104.7 FM, Kennebunk
WRED 96 FM, Saco
WHOM 94.9 FM, Portland (soft and easy favorites)
WCLZ 98.9 FM, Brunswick (alternative/obscure titles)

Christian
WLOB 1310 AM, Portland (Christian/talk)
WWMR 96.3 FM, Rumford (Christian/talk)
WMSJ 89.3 FM, Freeport (Christian contemporary)
WBCI 105.9 FM, Topsham (Christian/talk)

Classical
WBQQ 99.3 FM, Kennebunk
WPKM 106.3 FM, Scarborough
WMEA 90.1 FM, Portland (public radio)

College Radio
WUNH 91.3 FM, Durham, N.H. (University of New Hampshire)

Country
WOKQ 97.5 FM, Dover, N.H.
WPOR 101.9 FM/1490 AM, Portland
WTHT 107.5 FM, Portland (new country)

News/Talk
WGAN 560 AM, South Portland (news)
WZAN 970 AM, South Portland (news/talk)

Nostalgia/Oldies
WIDE 1400 AM, Saco
WYNZ 100.9 FM, South Portland
WLAM 106.7 FM/870 AM/1470 AM, Falmouth (golden oldies)

Rock
WCDQ 92.1 FM, Sanford
WBLM 102.9 FM, Portland/Biddeford (album-oriented rock)
WCYY 94.3/93.9 FM, Portland/Biddeford (modern/alternative rock)
WCYI 93.9 FM, Lewiston (alternative)
WXGL 95.5 FM, Freeport (classic rock)

Shopping
WCLZ 900 AM, Brunswick

Top 40
WMGX 93.1 FM, South Portland/Portland (classic hits)
WJBQ 97.9 FM, Portland
WKZS 96.9 FM, Falmouth/Portland

Southern Maine's houses of worship are as much a part of our heritage as they are our landscape.

Worship

Drive through just about any town along our Southern Coast, and at its center you're likely to pass a white-steepled church with a sprawling cemetery out back and perhaps a cozy parsonage or parish house next door. One of the first tasks early explorers set their hands to when they anchored ship off our rocky shore was to build churches. A 1607 map of Georges Fort, the first English colony in the New World, located in Phippsburg at the mouth of the Kennebec River (see our History chapter), depicts a chapel complete with a flag flying from the steeple. The name of one of the two ships on which this small band of seafaring colonists sailed, Gift of God, is also indicative of their faith.

Churches have long been gathering spots where communities could come together for strength and encouragement. They are as much a part of our heritage as they are our landscape. When traders began their arduous journeys through Maine's woods in the early 1600s, French Jesuits founded a mission on Mount Desert Isle (near Bar Harbor) for their salvation. The first Puritan church in the state was organized in York in 1682, and in the 1700s, when the town of Yarmouth burned to the ground three times during Indian attacks, settlers faithfully worshiped on Sunday mornings. They just grabbed their guns along with their Bibles when they headed out to church.

Worship As It Was

Our congregations don't date back quite as far as our existing church buildings, but if you're devout or just historically inclined, a tour of our distinguished houses of worship can make for a pleasant day's excursion and some spectacular pictures. Maine Forms of American Architecture, edited by Deborah Thompson, is a great reference book for anyone interested in learning more about early church and residential design in the state. We also recommend Maine's Historic Places, by Frank Beard and Bette Smith, to find out about specific historic churches and other buildings you might want to visit.

Maine's earliest churches were actually "meetinghouses" — a style of architecture found throughout New England that originated here in the 17th century. The practical difference between traditional churches and meetinghouses is that meetinghouse pews were arranged to face a rectangular preaching box centered on the side of the building instead of a pulpit at the front. Because meetinghouses were designed around Calvinist doctrine, which rejected the idea that churches were sacred, the meetinghouse was used as a public assembly hall for business as well as worship.

The oldest Maine example of this style is the Harpswell Meeting House in Harpswell Center. Constructed around 1757, the building served as a church until 1844. In keeping with its traditional usage, it remains the gathering spot for town meetings today. Though the old church pews have been removed, the rest of the building is much the way it would have appeared when first built. Meetinghouses were designed around such a common theme, you might even mistake them for houses.

A cruise down Pepperrell Road in Kittery will bring you to the First Congregational Church, which was built in 1729. The parish itself dates back to 1635. The framework of the First Parish Meeting House, on the Pool Road in Biddeford, is original and dates to 1758 when it was built as a meetinghouse for the local community. The interior was remodeled in 1840, but the hand-hewn beams and pins and the Colonial design stand out as special pieces of Maine's religious history. All town meetings were held in the structure through the Revolutionary War, and patriot James Sullivan often served as moderator.

Traditional New England churches with belfries and formal entrances emerged along the coast of Maine in the 1800s. Symbols of increasing wealth among the communities that could afford to erect them, these buildings were used purely for religious purposes. The majority of these churches were Congregationalist. An exception is St. Patrick's Church, the oldest Catholic church in New England, which is in Damariscotta Mills. It's a bit north of our coverage area but worth mentioning. On Academy Road, you'll get to the church by traveling north on U.S. Highway 1 about 15 minutes past the exit for Boothbay Harbor; simply take a left onto Maine Highway 215.

St. Patrick's was designed by Nicholas Codd, who came from Ireland to work on the chapel and to design a few prestigious homes in the county. The 11/2-foot thick walls are solid brick. The bricks were made on the shores of Lake Damariscotta, and the mortar was limestone imported from Ireland. The church was built in 1807 and it is in remarkable shape with the original altar, floors, stair railings, inner doors and two pews still standing.

Most of the churches built during the early 1800s have been torn down or extensively remodeled, but another that retains its historical dimensions and demeanor is the First Parish Church of Kennebunk. Here you'll find a domed cupola typical of Federal-style churches. Most historic Maine churches were constructed of wood, though the architectural eras following the Federal period brought increased diversity to religious architecture.

The Falmouth Congregational Church is rare because of its stone columns and brick construction, which date to 1833. The Swedenborgian Church in Bath (1843) is also a noteworthy example of Greek Revival architecture. Drive by this structure on Middle Street and you are likely to think it's an enormous mausoleum or temple, but the letter-board sign out front clearly welcomes visitors to services. The building reflects the dimensions and form of an ancient temple more accurately than any other in the state.

Another notable Greek Revival church is the Elijah Kellogg Church in Harpswell center. It is most famous for its namesake, the noted children's author who preached there during the mid-1800s. It's a rural example of a transitional Greek Revival-Gothic Revival church. As Maine communities built more churches, the styles became more ornate, leading to the construction of Gothic sanctuaries and the remodeling of others in the Gothic tradition. The Phippsburg Congregational Church of 1802 was remodeled in 1847 with Gothic accents.

St. Paul's Episcopal Church, 27 Pleasant Street, Brunswick, is notable for its early Gothic Revival design. Built in 1845 by renowned architect Richard Upjohn, it's simple in structure (there's only one story and no tower) but is marked by the board-and-batten form which Upjohn popularized throughout the United States.

One of the most famous churches in the state is the First Parish Church in Brunswick at 223 Maine Street. Also designed by Upjohn, the church was constructed at the same time as St. Paul's. The Gothic Revival church has spires pointing heavenward and intricate woodwork inside. It was here that Harriet Beecher Stowe had the vision that inspired her to write Uncle Tom's Cabin. Other notables who have attended or spoken here include Henry Wadsworth Longfellow, President William Howard Taft, John Masefield, Eleanor Roosevelt and Martin Luther King Jr.

Bath has two towering Gothic churches, though you won't be able to attend services at either of them. The Central Congregational Church of 1846 is now the Chocolate Church Performing Arts Center, and the Winter Street Church, across from Library Park, is vacant. Both are worth driving past if you head north along Washington Street. (To find out about dance, music and theater shows at the Chocolate Church, see our chapter on The Arts.) For a truly unusual example of religious architecture, seek out The Temple, off Temple

INSIDERS' TIP

Keep an eye out for public church bean suppers. They're inexpensive, the food is great, and you'll get to meet many locals.

Photo: Merry Farnum

Picturesque churches dot Maine's Southern Coast.

Avenue in Old Orchard Beach. It is one of only two octagonal buildings in the state and has been in continuous use since its construction in 1861.

The community of Ocean Park was created in the late 1800s by the Centennial Conference of Free Will Baptists as a retreat. Today, speakers from various denominations fill its pulpit. The First Baptist Church at 353 Congress Street in Portland is an inspiring Romanesque Revival structure built in 1867. Portland's Williston-West Church, 32 Thomas Street, is noteworthy for its beauty and also for being the birthplace of the American Sunday School movement. It was here that the Young People's Society of Christian Endeavor was founded in 1881.

Worship Today

Churches remain sources of strength and inspiration as solid as the Maine granite beneath them — reaching out to the poor with food banks and clothing exchanges, warming people with baked bean suppers on cold winter nights, and offering fellowship and fun at festive annual craft fairs. Worship plays a central role in the life of the community.

According to a 1989 poll by the Maine Sunday Telegram, roughly three out of five Mainers say they belong to a church or synagogue. The majority of churchgoing residents, 260,500 people (or about 22 percent of the population) were raised Roman Catholic, and Catholic churches and schools remain prevalent here. However, the actual number of active Catholics is likely less than the number of recorded members.

The three largest Protestant denominations are the Church of Christ, United Methodist and American Baptist, each with about 30,000 members statewide (or 3 percent of the population). You can find handfuls of these and other mainstream denominations generously scattered along our Southern Coast. Many individual churches have fewer than 60 or so members; while people like to come

together to worship, they often want to go to church in their own back yard. This makes for quite a few churches of the same denomination within relatively small geographic vicinities. In the Bath-Brunswick area, for example, there are nine Churches of the Nazarene within a 10-mile radius. When many of these were organized, travel on our back roads was difficult, so people stayed close to home — a necessity in the winter.

Trends across the country show that membership among the mainstream Protestant denominations is shrinking, while charismatic churches such as the Assemblies of God are growing. Maine is no different, and while such groups still have a relatively small showing here, new congregations and churches are sprouting up all the time.

Jewish synagogues claim about 9,000 members in Maine. Many Jewish synagogues (both reformed and Orthodox) are scattered throughout our Southern Coast. Several are in Portland, and there is one each in Old Orchard Beach and Bath.

The same study showed that nearly 7 percent of Mainers — 69,000 people — belong to smaller religious groups and alternative faiths. Most alternative worship groups are near our population centers, mainly Portland, as the larger numbers of residents seem to lend themselves to more diverse views and cultures. In and around our smaller towns, you're likely to find more mainstream denominations.

Portland's Feminist Spiritual Community, which isn't affiliated with any church or denomination, qualifies as an alternative faith; it aims to honor the wisdom of women. Portland is also the location of the Baha'i Center of Portland and of several Unitarian Universalist and Jehovah's Witness congregations. Both Portland and Bath have Swedenborgian churches, and Brunswick has a monthly meeting of Quakers and a Dharma (Bhuddist) Study Group. Boothbay is host to a Mormon congregation.

For a nearly complete listing of churches, assemblies and synagogues in Maine, call

INSIDERS' TIP

Former President John F. Kennedy once stopped in at Our Lady Queen of Peace church in Boothbay Harbor.

the Maine Council of Churches, (207) 772-1918, in Portland. The council can also give you the contact numbers for denominations you are interested in visiting. Because it's difficult for small congregations to maintain older (and frequently very large) church buildings, some have been converted into community centers, restaurants and retail shops. As mentioned, Bath's Chocolate Church has been made into a performing arts center! But other historic churches around the state continue to flourish.

Index of Advertisers

Index

Phippsburg Congregational Church, 472
Phippsburg (ME), 14, 27
Phippsburg Peninsula, 320
Phoenix Publishing, 466
Pickard Theatre, 295
Pie In The Sky Bakery, 166
The Pier to Camp Ellis, 318
Pine Point Beach, 351
Pine Point Fisherman's Co-op, 186
Pinederosa Camping Area, 102
Pirates Island Adventure Golf, 219, 243
Piscataqua Bridge, 6
Piscataqua River, 6
Player's Pub and Nightclub, 150
plum dandy craft gallery, 164
Plymouth Council, 28
Pockets II, 146
Popham, George, 27
Popham, John, 27
Popham Beach Bed & Breakfast, 59
Popham Beach/Hunnewell Beach, 353
Popham Beach State Park, 14, 312
Popham Colony, 27
Port Island Realty, 95
Port Lobster Co., 167
Portland Ballet Company, 12
The Portland Ballet Company, 289
Portland Coffee Roasting Co., 187
Portland Conservatory of Music, 427
Portland Farmers' Market, 188
Portland Fish Exchange, 228
Portland Head Light, 11, 225
Portland Ice Arena, 335
Portland International Jetport, 21, 250
Portland Jetport, 11
Portland Magazine, 466
Portland (ME), 5, 12, 396
Portland Museum of Art, 12, 280
Portland Performing Arts Center, 295
Portland Pirates, 12, 363
Portland Players, 293
Portland Press Herald, 462
Portland Public Library, 251
Portland Public Market, 12, 188
Portland Recreation Department Programs for
    Seniors, 456
Portland Regency Hotel, 80
Portland School of Ballet, 427
Portland Sea Dogs, 12, 359
Portland Stage Company, 294
The Portland String Quartet, 260
Portland Symphony Orchestra, 291
Portland YMCA Summer Camp, 429
Portland's Back Cove Trail, 319
Portland's Downtown District, 6
Portside Antiques, 200
Portsmouth Herald, 461
Portsmouth (NH), 375
Portsmouth Naval Shipyard, 6
Portsmouth Naval Shipyard Museum, 214
Powder Horn Family Camping, 104
The Powder House Gallery, 282
The Pride Motel and Cottages, 77
Prince of Fundy Cruises, 223

Prince of Fundy Cruises - The Scotia Prince,
    370
Pring, Martin, 27
Properties By The Sea, 405
Provincial Press, 466
Prudential Prime Properties, 404

Q

Quaker Tavern Farm B&B, 49
Queen Anne's War, 29
Queen Elizabeth II, 12

R

R. Jorgensen Antiques, 161
Rachel Carson National Wildlife Refuge, 307
Rachel Carson Nature Preserve, 8
Radisson Eastland Hotel Portland, 80
Radley's Market, 174
Railroad Co. & Museum, 250
Ram Island Dance Company, 289
Ram Island Light, 236
RE/MAX By The Bay, 408
RE/MAX Coastal, 405
Real Estate Agencies, 403
Recompense Shore Campsites, 107
Red Paint People, 26
Red's Eats, 138
Reid State Park, 14, 312, 355
Reilly's Bakery, 173
The Rental Guide, 95
Resort at Wells Beach, 73
Respite Program, 454
Restaurants, 111
Retirement, 453
Ricetta's Brickoven Pizzeria, 126
Richard's Restaurant, 136
River Place, 162
River Tree Arts, 289
River Tree Arts Gallery, 284
River Tree Arts/WBQQ, 290
Riverside Municipal Golf Course, 332
Roberts, Kenneth, 8
Roberts, Kenneth (1885-1957), 286
Robinhood Free Meeting House, 138
The Rockaway Hotel, 69
Rockin Horse Stables, 338
Rockmere Lodge, 44
Rocks Beach, 317
Rocktide Inn, 87
Rocky Mountain Quilts, 160
Roebuck-Boynton Real Estate, 410
Roma Cafe, 129
Romano's Macaroni Grill, 126
Roosevelt, Eleanor, 472
Rotary Park Beach, 348
Royal River, 12
Royal River Canoe Route, 325
Royal River Natural Foods, 187
The Royal River Cannery, 131
Rumford Falls Paper Company, 34
Rundlett Cottage Rentals, 90
Russell Acres Farm & Produce/Orchard Dell
    Deer Farm, 167